KV-637-749

MULTILINGUAL MATTERS 45
Series Editor: Derrick Sharp

Language and Ethnicity in Minority Sociolinguistic Perspective

Joshua A. Fishman

MULTILINGUAL MATTERS LTD
Clevedon · Philadelphia

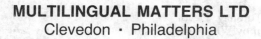

Library of Congress Cataloging-in-Publication Data

Fishman, Joshua A.
 Language and ethnicity in minority sociolinguistic
perspective.
  1. Anthropological linguistics. 2. Linguistic
minorities. 3. Sociolinguistics. I. Title.
P35.F5 1988   408.9   88-10030

British Library Cataloguing in Publication Data

Fishman, Joshua A.
  Language and ethnicity in minority sociolinguistic
  perspective — (Multilingual matters).
  1. Ethnic groups.   Social interactions.   Role
of language
I. Title II. Series
305.8

ISBN 1-85359-006-1
ISBN 1-85359-005-3 Pbk

Multilingual Matters Ltd
Bank House, 8a Hill Road   &   242 Cherry Street
Clevedon, Avon BS21 7HH   Philadelphia, Pa 19106–1906
England   U.S.A.

Index compiled by Meg Davies
Typeset by Editorial Enterprises, Torquay, Devon
Printed and bound in Great Britain by WBC Print, Bristol

שמואליקן אַ מתּנה:

ווען די צוווײגן, בלעטער, זינגען

אויף מײַן לשון, ברומען, שאַלן,

וועל איך אויך, אַלץ איינס מײַן עלטער

קוויקן זיך פֿון יונגע קוואַלן.

Contents

CONTENTS

Acknowledgements

The majority of the chapters in this book have appeared in one form or another in a variety of previous publications, and I would like to thank all of the publishers concerned for granting permission to reproduce the material in this present work. Full bibliographic references of the sources appear at the foot of the title page for each chapter, and include the names of the publishers where previous publication has been in book form. For journal papers, the publishers concerned are: Uppsala University (*Uppsala Studies in Cultural Anthropology*), Multilingual Matters Ltd (*Journal of Multicultural and Multilingual Development*), Thomas Spira (*Canadian Review of Studies in Nationalism*), University of Illinois Urbana-Champaign (*Studies in Language Learning*), Linguistic Society of the Philippines (*Philippine Journal of Linguistics*), Didier Érudition (*Études de Linguistique Appliquée*), Center for Migration Studies of New York (*International Migration Review*), Canadian Psychological Association (*Canadian Journal of Behavioral Sciences*), Cambridge University Press (*Language in Society* and *Annual Review of Applied Linguistics*), and Monash University Centre for Migration Studies (*Journal of Intercultural Studies*).

Introduction

'Language and ethnicity' has been an underlying theme in my work for most of my professional life. I have been encouraged many times to organize a selection of my papers on that theme, sometimes by colleagues, sometimes by students and sometimes by publishers, but it was not until the summer of 1987, at the Summer Linguistic Institute of the Linguistic Society of America, when I once more taught a graduate course on this topic, that the stimulus, the opportunity and the encouragement to do so all came together at the same time. The present selection comprises those of my papers from 1972 and thereafter that I still find theoretically productive and heuristically useful for current work on language and ethnicity. I have eschewed earlier papers because the best among them (e.g. my 1965 paper on 'Varieties of Ethnicity and Varieties of Language Consciousness') have been anthologized several times and I have, therefore, preferred to give some consideration to accessibility too, rather than remain with the major criteria of interest and value, as a basis of selection. Whether I have succeeded, at least to some degree, in balancing these three balls is something the reader will have to decide.

In recent years, a few sociolinguistics have 'discovered' the principle of 'self-serving interest' in commenting on minority efforts to foster their language and ethnicity goals. This 'discovery', tantamount to the rediscovery of the wheel, is disturbing not only because it reveals how weak an impression the sociology of knowledge has made on some scholars, but because it starkly reveals the projective tendency in operation. Self-serving interest is not recognized in one's self, in one's own views and writings, or in the establishments with which one identifies, but with others, with outgroups, at times with groups who are merely seeking for themselves an approximation to the same ability to control their sociocultural boundaries and to safeguard or fashion the nature of their intergenerational sociocultural reality that stronger establishments have already attained and, therefore, take for granted. Such relative self-determination, when engaged in by the ingroup, is viewed as 'only natural', as democratic, as creative, as healthy and as insightful. When similar goals are pursued by outgroups these goals and the means utilized to attain them are decried as 'self-serving', as 'disturbing of civility', as 'reflecting the atypical interests of atypical élites rather than the un-manipulated interests of the rank and file', etc., etc. When views such as these enter into the annals of scholarship on language and ethnicity, the degree to which scholarship imitates life becomes apparent. Scholars who empathize with outgroups and with the furtherance of cultural democracy are found to be wanting in the very ways that the groups whose goals they facilitate have been found to be wanting.

I cannot and do not claim that my views on language and ethnicity are unbiased. I have also pursued and taught the history of knowledge and the sociology of ideas for much too long to take such a claim on anyone else's part seriously, particularly in the social sciences or in any other area of endeavor that has social ramifications. The best I can hope for is (a) to state my biases, (b) to seek as much contact with empirical evidence as is possible, since such contact may lead me to revise my views, and (c) where no such contact is really possible, as is the case with many of our most central convictions, to accept the fact that social scientists (including myself) are only human, i.e. that they have values and that these values do show, must show, whether they are on my side of the fence or on the other. In the latter connection it is my hope that discussion can continue, with as little acrimony as possible and as much realization as possible that 'truth' is an elusive handmaiden and is rarely to be found completely in one camp or another. This is particularly apropos in the area of language and ethnicity, when the 'data' frequently consists of reflections upon and interpretations of historical cases and texts which leave much to be desired in terms of certainty as to what actually did happen or was meant, not to mention the sampling issues that inevitably plague such data.

My values in the area of language and ethnicity predate my professional career; indeed, I suspect that these values are responsible for my gravitating toward sociology of language as a whole and toward the study of language and ethnicity in particular. I was socialized by parents and by an organized, first-generation American immigrant sociocultural environment that pointed me toward minority ethnolinguistic goals, problems, and efforts from a very tender age. My parents dedicated their lives to this arena of endeavor, within their own ethnolinguistic frame of reference, and I, although never leaving that frame of reference outside of my perspective on the issues of language and ethnicity, have tried to tackle these issues both on a broader, more inclusive front, as well as in theoretically more generalizable ways. I have spent a good bit of my intellectual life studying, testing, revising and theorizing or generalizing in connection with language and ethnicity. In the process, intellectual issues have added to, tempered and, to a degree, inevitably peripheralized my childhood and adolescent convictions, but I know that they are still there, below the surface, if only to urge me on to take another look, to be more definitive, to tap another faucet, to leave the field in less disarray than I found it, at least to bring its applied and its theoretical aspects into closer contact with one another.

Most sociolinguists (although, regrettably and inevitably, not all) favor, and seek to foster, a culturally and linguistically heterogeneous world. Consciously or unconsciously, they are the disciples of Herder and Whorf, although perhaps not as much in their daily work as in their underlying, sublimated motivations. Although I too am a Herderian and a Whorfian, I also realize, because I am a sociologist, that there is no arbitrary lower limit to the number of submerged minorities seeking some form of recognition and protection so that their intergenerational self-guided ethnolinguistic continuity can be more successfully attained, retained and fostered. If all such entities were to seek and receive political self-rule, that would lead to an immensely fractionated world insofar as the free flow of ideas, goods, and populations is concerned. I, therefore, differentiate between ethnicity, nationalism and nationism, hoping for maximal encouragement to foster the first on as micro-unit a basis as is able to muster support for its claims, while hoping, simultaneously, for maximal encouragement to foster as many democratic macro-unit arrangements as possible in connection with the third. The European Community may yet be a step in that direction, a direction that recognizes that a compromise aiming to attain both micro-level guarantees and assistance at the ethnocultural level and macro-level goals and economies of scale at the econo-technical level is a difficult goal, precisely because of the intervention of nationalism, but 'a consummation devoutly to be wished', nevertheless. I do not argue directly for such arrangements in the papers that follow, but mention them here, at the very outset, in order to make it clear where my values lie and to make some claim for the rationality as well as for the moral decency of world order based upon them and upon their building-blocks: ethnoculturally pluralistic polities.

For years, I have served on the faculty of a graduate school of psychology, being directly affiliated with its doctoral programs in clinical, developmental and health psychology. As a result of this affiliation, I have been able to relate language and ethnicity to psychological dimensions that remain outside of the boundaries of this collection, as well as to relate psychological process to language and ethnicity in ways that I hope inform this collection without being too intrusive therein. I have always intended my language and ethnicity efforts to be primarily sociolinguistic and to be formulated in such a way as to bring sociolinguists to sociology and sociologists to the study of language in society. Nowhere is the predominant sociolinguistic ignorance of sociology and the equally great sociological ignorance of sociology of language (which subsumes sociolinguistics) than in connection with language and ethnicity. Having now mentioned the four underlying constituents of this collection and of my approach to the topic area (my pluralistic values, my familiarity with sociology, my familiarity with the sociology of language, and my ongoing background involvement in psychology), the time has come to plunge into the collection itself, with the fervent hope that it will find favor in the minds of those who grapple with it.

SECTION 1:
What is ethnicity and how is it linked to language?: Phenomenological and socio-historical considerations

I do not believe in worrying endlessly about definitions, but some preliminary demarcation of the field of discourse is, obviously, both necessary and desirable. Ethnicity is a self-and-other aggregative definitional dimension of culture. It is a dimension that deals with 'us' vs. 'them' and with 'them' vs. 'them'. It is not necessarily a conscious, highlighted or salient dimension of daily life (these characterizations all pertain to *ethno-nationalism*, at a later stage in ethnic socio-historical development and one that we must certainly examine), but it is close to consciousness and contrastive experiences easily call it into consciousness.

Ethnicity is not usefully definable in terms of units of size or scale. It may be a property of aggregative units as small as bands, clans or settlements, or it may characterize aggregative units occupying specific regions in particular countries, entire countries or even several neighboring countries, i.e. ethnic affiliation and political affiliation need not be identical. Ethnicity strains toward a self-contained, self-sufficient, culturally autonomous basis of aggregation, i.e. it strains toward and is experienced as being societally complete, inter-generationally continuous and historically deep.

Neither occupational groups (tailors), nor single-sex groups (women), nor limited-age groups (adolescents), nor social classes (workers) are normally ethnic groups, because they usually constitute parts of cultures rather than cultures in their own right, although in particular circumstances they may all develop ethnoid attributes and self-concepts and, given sufficient polarization, some of them may attain the status of full and distinct ethnicity.

Above all, ethnicity is phenomenological, i.e. it is self-perceived or attributed, it exists only as human aggregates utilize it as a basis of aggregation and of socio-cultural organization, it exists as it is recognized, interpreted, and experienced. It is commonly recognized bodily, implemented behaviorally and evaluated emotionally. It is viewed as having both inner and outer characteristics and consequences, causes and effects. It is not a tidy natural science construct, but, rather, a subjective cultural construct that fills and directs the hearts and minds and daily rounds of human beings and aggregative systems. It is cosmological: it provides an apparently distinctive way of understanding life, history, the world, the universe.

Ethnicity is not synonymous with all of culture, being merely the aggregative definitional dimension thereof, the overlap between the two being a function of societal modernization. At earlier stages of societal development, ethnicity tends to a greater overlap with culture as a whole and there are ethnic ways of dressing and building, plowing and curing, worshipping and fighting, engaging in commerce and engaging in art, sports or study. Ethnicity may be less conscious but more pervasive. In more modern life, ethnicity retreats into a corner of social experience under the impact of international influences (influences whose ethnic origins are unknown or overlooked, and widely accepted across national boundaries), but, perhaps precisely therefore, it is often rendered more conscious and is more manipulated as a boundary mobilization mechanism.

Ethnicity is also not distinctively related to inter-group conflict. This is not to say that ethnicity may not become the basis of such conflict, but similar bases can develop from any and all other aggregative principles, be they religious, economic, occupational, residential, political, ideological, etc., etc. We must all bemoan ethnic conflict and the hideous cruelties that it has fostered, but there is no other basis of aggregative identity, bar none, that has not engendered similar cruelty. The cruelty quotient of ethnicity is not distinctive and does not help us to differentiate it from other grouping dimensions. The fact that this is still not widely believed or known is an indication that ethnicity in Western social theory is vastly more sinned against than sinning.

Finally, ethnicity is in no way synonymous with minority status. The pan-Western tendency to equate the two is merely the result of the disadvantages of minority ethnic groups, indigenous or immigrant, on the one hand, and a carry over of the older pejorative equation between ethnicity and lack of 'Christian civility', on the other hand. If such usage were to be taken seriously, it would run into the assumption that 'all those ethnics' had no ethnicity 'back where they came from', where they were in the majority, and only acquired that feature, ethnicity, upon arriving, physically or phenomenologically, in modern societies dominated by others. This usage confuses the phenomenon with a particular context in which it is observed. 'Ethclasses', the co-occurrences of class and ethnicity, doubtlessly exist, but they do so for minorities and majorities, for lower classes and upper classes. 'Ethclassicity' is a particular circumstance for ethnicity to be in and it must not be confused with the phenomenon of ethnicity more generally.

At every stage, ethnicity is linked to language, whether indexically, implementationally or symbolically. There is no escaping the primary symbol-system of our species, certainly not where the phenomenology of aggregational definition and boundary maintenance is involved, when ethnic being, doing and knowing are involved. Initially however, language is but one of a myriad of minimally conscious discriminanda. Ultimately, it is not only a conscious factor but may become a primary cause, a rallying cry, a prime concern and a perceived first line of defense. The ever-present link between language and religion (what would religion be without language?) not only sanctifies 'our language' but helps raise language into the pale of sanctity even in secular culture. Under secular-nationalist auspices, language becomes part of secular religion, binding society together and mobilizing it to face whatever its challenges are taken to be.

Whoever approaches this entire configuration only from the point of view of empirical considerations will miss the point. The point is not whether ethnic boundaries and their link to language are real or specious, genuine or created, valid or exaggerated, self-serving or altruistic, ethnocentric or objective, dividing or unifying. The point is that ethnicity is an inevitable dimension of aggregative definition and action as well as occasionally a deeply felt, a deeply moving and a deeply meaningful one. It is intertwined with loyalty and sanctity and, therefore not to be laughed out of court or trivialized, reduced and translated into something else. It constitutes a complex of changing forces and considerations, not easily appreciated by the academic empiricist who does not share its values and who (whether he recognizes it or not) usually has his own ax — and his favorite aggregative ax — to grind. Ethnicity is there, for all of mankind some of the time and for some of mankind all of the time. It behoves us, at the very least, to try to understand why this is so, as well as its link to language.

In this section, I bring four papers in order to examine the issues adumbrated above, to distinguish between ethnicity and racism, and to provide a case study to illustrate that the link that is often viewed and defended as an initial cause, can have very human, very tenuous and very conflicted origins in the efforts of sociocultural élites. Once élites succeed in gaining a mass following and institutional bases for their ethnolinguistic reconstructions further linkage-changes become both more difficult and more dislocative.

1 Language, ethnicity and racism*

'In Irish, not merely does our mind react to the same beauty, the same delicacy of inflection and suggestion that delighted our fathers, but we can still share through it the desires and hopes, the failures and successes, the nobility and even, in a healing manner, the human weakness of practically the whole of our recorded history' (Brennan, 1969: 71).

Language and ethnicity: Overlooked variables in social theory and social history

Many discussions of ethnicity begin with the struggle to define 'it'. While I am certainly interested in defining (or delimiting) ethnicity, I am even more interested in what the definitional struggle in this day and age reveals, namely, that the social sciences as a whole still lack an intellectual tradition in connection with this topic. Social scientists and social theorists have neither reconstructed nor developed with respect to ethnicity (nor, indeed, with respect to language and ethnicity) either a sociology of the phenomenon *per se* or a sociology of knowledge concerning it, much less a synchronic view of the link between the two, in any major part of the world of social life and social thought. Thus, here we are, in the late twentieth century, with God only knows how few or how many seconds remaining to the entire human tragi-comedy on this planet, still fumbling along in the domain of ethnicity, as if it had just recently appeared and as if three millenia of pan-Mediterranean and European thought and experience in connection with it (to take only that corner of mankind with which most of us are most familiar) could be overlooked. Obviously that is not our attitude toward other societal forms and processes such as the family, urbanization, religion, technology, etc. For all of these we manifestly delight in the intellectual traditions surrounding them. I must

*Originally published in *Roundtable on Languages and Linguistics*, 1977, pp. 297–309.

conclude that our intellectual discomfort and superficiality with respect to ethnicity and our selective ignorance in this connection are themselves ethnicity-related phenomena, at least in part, phenomena which merit consideration if we are ultimately to understand several of the dimensions of this topic that we are still waiting to be revealed.

This is not the place to undertake so grand an expedition, nor have I the ability to take you everywhere that this topic (the sociology of language and ethnicity and the sociology of knowledge with respect to it) must lead us. Suffice it to say that we must try to carry both the reconstruction and the analysis of social history and social theory from classical Hebrew and Greek times through to the twentieth century, up to and include the 'rebirth of ethnicity' in many Western locales during the past decade. In the process we must attend to the Roman Empire, both in the West and in the East; to the early Church and the Church Fathers; to Islam as a Euro-Mediterranean presence, to medieval and renaissance life and thought throughout Europe; to the reformation and counter-reformation; to the commercial and industrial revolutions viewed both as social change/continuity and as stimulants to social thought and social theory; and finally, to the rise of modern intellectual schools and social movements. In this last we must particularly examine the capitalist-Marxist clash, and the Marxist–Herderian–Weberian differences in sociological and anthropological thought and in political and economic action, both in the ominous nineteenth and in the cataclysmic twentieth centuries. At this time I can only try to select a few themes here and there that may provide some clues to language and ethnicity viewed in such a perspective.

What is ethnicity?

Since one of my objectives (in what might very well be a life-time task in and of itself) is to disclose what social theorists have said about ethnicity, including how they have defined it, my initial definitional passions can be satisfied at a general oriental level which gives me as much latitude as possible to attend to all forms and definitions of ethnicity (see Isajiw, 1974, for detailed attention to the definitional issue). What I am interested in is both the sense and the expression of 'collective, intergenerational cultural continuity,' i.e. the sensing and expressing of links to 'one's own kind (one's own people),' to collectivities that not only purportedly have historical depth but, more crucially, share putative ancestral origins and, therefore, the gifts and responsibilities, rights and obligations deriving therefrom. Thus, what I am interested in may or may not be identical with all of society and culture, depending on the extent to which ethnicity does pervade and dictate all social sensings, doings and knowings, or alternatively (and as is increasingly the case as society modernizes) only some of these[1], particularly those that relate to the questions: Who are we? From where do we come? What is special about us? I assume (together with Le Page & Tabouret-Keller, 1982) that these questions can be answered differently at different times by the same respondents (and, all the more so, by different respondents). It is in this context that I also want to monitor whatever link there may be to language as an aspect of presumed ethnic authenticity.

The theme of fundamental 'essence'

Both ancient Israel and ancient Greece conceived of the world as made up of a finite number of ethnicities with characteristic and fundamental biological 'essences' and, therefore, histories or missions of their own. This theme, with its undercurrent of bodily continuity and triumph over death, has its counterpart in modern Herderian and nationalist thought and has been continually present in the pan-Mediterranean and European world, as well as in much of the African, Asian, and Native American worlds. This essence is transcendental and ultimately of superhuman origin, and language is naturally a co-occurring part of the essential blood, bones, or tears. Thus, the view that the deity (or deities) necessarily speak(s) to each ethnicity in its own language and could not conceivably do otherwise, is also a recurring view (albeit one that is not always accepted and, therefore, one that is also contradicted). It is a view related to a cosmology in which language-and-ethnicity collectivities are seen as the basic building blocks of all human society. In more modern thought, the superhuman origin of this co-occurrence and its dependence on biological essences are questioned. However, many theoreticians and philosophers still hold that ethnicity and ethnogenesis (i.e. the coming into being of ethnicities and of language–and–ethnicity linkages) is a natural and necessary fact of human social life (for a recent Soviet view along these very lines, see Bromley, 1974). Eastern European and Eastern Mediterranean thought is particularly noteworthy along these latter lines (Jakobson, 1945) and it is here in the Euro-Mediterranean complex that we find today most generally and insistently the view that language authenticity is a natural and necessary part of a mystically inescapable physical/cultural collective continuity.

The theme of metamorphosis

Seemingly at odds with the above view, but at times syncretistically subscribed to in addition to it, is the view that ethnicities can be transcended and that new or 'higher' levels of ethnic integration can be arrived at, including the level of terminal de-ethnicization, i.e. of no ethnicity at all. The argument between those who view ethnicity as fixed and god-given and those who view it as endlessly mutable begins with Plato and Aristotle, the former proposing that a group of de-ethnicized Guardians of the City be created so that uncorrupted and uncorruptable, altruistic and evenhanded management of the polity could be attained. There would be no husband-wife relationships among them since all women would belong to all men and vice versa. Similarly their offspring would have no fathers and no mothers since all male adults would be fathers to all children, all female adults would be their mothers, all children would belong equally to all adults and vice versa. Only a group such as this — a group whose members had no differentiating inter-generational biological continuities — could devote itself to the public weal, since, having neither property nor family, it could view the general need without bias, without favoritism, without greed, without conflict of interest, all of which Plato considered necessary accompaniments of ethnicity. Aristotle hotly contested this view and stressed that, whatever the dangers of ethnicity might be, those who do not initially love and feel uniquely bound to specific 'others' could not then love mankind nor have the benefit of generalized 'others' firmly in mind. A child who belongs equally to one and all belongs to no one. The challenge of ethnicity, as Aristotle saw it, was one of augmenting familial love, expanding the natural links to one's own 'kind,' so that these links also include others who are more distantly related, rather than doing away with the initial links and bonds as such.

This theme too is developed consistently — the expansion and transmutation of language and ethnicity to a higher, more inclusive level of both being repeatedly expressed by early Christian thought, e.g. St. Augustine, Roman thought, medieval thought (including much of moral philosophy) and by capitalist statism. Going even further, de-ethnicization and linguistic fusion are expressed as ultimate, millenial goals by some modern Christian social theorists, by classical Marxists as well as classical capitalists, and as inevitable if regrettable outcomes of modern industrial society by Weber and the entire 'grand tradition' of modern social theory from Saint-Simon to Parsons.

Ethnicity as disruptive, irrational, and peripheral

The darker side of ethnicity is commented on by almost all ancient and medieval thinkers, but usually as only one side of the coin, i.e. as only half of the entire phenomenon which has both positive and negative features. However, the more completely negative view begins with Plato, as already mentioned, in relation to matters of state. In this connection it receives its quintessential formulation by Lord Acton, John Stuart Mill, and other establishment-oriented defenders of Western capitalist democracy. For them, state-forming ethnicity was nothing but the disrupter of civility, a base passion, a nightmare, a wild evil that still lurked in the backward parts of Europe but that had, thank God, already been tamed and superseded in Great Britain, France, Spain, Holland, and in the other early and enlightened beneficiaries of political consolidation and econo-technical growth.

This view coincided with a developmental theory defining 'legitimate' language-and-ethnicity, namely, that the link between them and the currency that they both enjoyed *in the West* were by-products of political and economic stability. That is, they were the legitimate creations of centuries of continuous governmental, commercial, military, and religious stability. This view, that the benign, wise and stable state creates its corresponding and legitimate nationality, was long the dominant view in the West. The thought that the nationality might undertake to create a state for itself was anathema, viewed as unnatural, unjust, unwise, and simply a wild and wanton disruption of peace and civility. The thought of a Breton or Rumanian ethnicity was as roundly abhorred by 'proper' society *then* as the thought of a Quebecois ethnicity is in some circles *today*. Indeed, the evil, instinctual penchant of 'illegitimate' language-and-ethnicity movements to undertake disruptive state-formation was thought to be the basic negative dynamic of minority ethnicity, and so it is for some to this very day. Thus, the confusion of ethnicity with politically troublesome collectivities, with rambunctious minorities, with 'difficult' peripheral and vestigial populations, began long ago.

However, classical Marxism was not very different from capitalist establishment statism in this respect. Mill had held that the language and ethnicity movements, particularly in their nationality-into-state phase, were despicable 'irrationalities' that had to be contained at all costs, evils to be compromised with only grudgingly if the established political order was to be maintained (note, for example, the compromise escape clause of 'once defeated but historical nations' as an interstitial category between Mill's and Acton's two major categories: 'goodies': 'peoples with histories', and 'baddies': 'peoples without histories'). Initially, Marx and Engels were equally vituperative with respect to nation-into-state language and ethnicity movements (and, ultimately, made equally grudging and opportunistic exceptions in connection with them), due to their obviously disruptive impact on the class struggle and on proletarian unity. However, if language-and-ethnicity movements for Mill were merely vile passions, they were for Marx and many of his followers also vile figments, lies, and chimeras, objectively no more than mere by-products of more basic economic causes, phantoms manipulated by leading capitalist circles in order to fragment and weaken the international proletariat.

Needless to say, both Mill and Marx have their followers today, who ascribe to language and ethnicity linkages all manner of evil and evil alone, including genocide. Furthermore, this purportedly objectivist view is still very much alive among these social scientists who deny any subjective validity or functional need for ethnicity, and who see it only as an essentially manipulated (and therefore, basically inauthentic), manufac-tured by-product of élitist efforts to gain mass support for political and economic goals (Gellner, 1964). They basically sympathize with Engels' lament of a century ago (1866):

'There is no country in Europe where there are not different nationalities under the same government. The Highland Gaels and the Welsh are undoubtedly of different nationalities to what the English are, although nobody will give to these remnants of people long gone by the title of nations, any more than to the Celtic inhabitants of Brittany in France . . . . The European importance, the vitality of a people, is as nothing in the eyes of the principle of nationalities; before it the Roumans [sic] of Wallachia, who never had a history, nor the energy required to have one, are of equal importance to the Italians who have a history of 2,000 years, and an unimpaired national vitality; the Welsh and Manxmen, if they desired it, would have an equal right to independent political existence, absurd though it be, with the English! The whole thing is absurdity. The principle of nationalities, indeed, could be invented in Eastern Europe alone, where the tide of Asiatic invasion, for a thousand years, recurred again and again, and left on the shore those heaps of intermingled ruins of nations which even now the ethnologist can scarcely disentangle, and where the Turk, the Finnic Magyar, the Rouman, the Jew and about a dozen slavonic tribes live intermixed in interminable confusion.'

To this very day ethnicity strikes many Westerners as being peculiarly

related to 'all those crazy little people and languages ou
unwashed (and unwanted) of the world, to phenomena tha
fully civilized and that are more trouble than they are wo

Ethnicity as creative and healing

Autochthonous ethnicity theories commonly refer to the responsibilities incumbent upon the carriers of the intergenerational essence, i.e. to the duties that those of 'one's own kind' have, duties to be and to do in particular authentic ways; and of course, these theories also refer to the individual and collective rewards of such faithfulness. However, various more generalized ethnicity theories have taken this kind of thinking a step higher. Classical Hebrew thought contains a recurring emphasis on the perfectability of ethnicity, i.e. an emphasis on its highest realization via sanctification. It was not only Jewish ethnicity which could be so elevated and attuned with the Creator's designs and expectations (Fishman, Mayerfeld & Fishman, 1985), although Hebrew thought is, understandably, repeatedly more concerned with the theoretical perfectability of Hebrew ethnicity (just as it is with the actual shortcomings of Hebrew ethnicity). Hebrew thought is an early source for the recurring message that sanctified ethnicity is ennobling, strengthening, healing, satisfying. Its thought proclaims the message of the joy, the wholeness, the holiness of embodying and expressing language-and-ethnicity in accord with the commandments of the Master of the Universe: 'for they are our life and the length of our days.' Whosoever lives in the midst of his own kind, speaking his own language and enacting his own most divinely regulated traditions in accord with these imperatives, has all that one could hope for out of life (also see Fishman, 1978).

The joys of one's own language and ethnicity are subsequently expressed over and over again, from every corner of Europe and in every period. In modern times this feeling has been raised to a general principle, a general esthetic, a celebration of ethnic and linguistic diversity *per se*, as part of the very multisplendored glory of God, a value, beauty, and source of creative inspiration and inspiring creativity — indeed, as the basic human good. It is claimed that it is ethnic and linguistic diversity that makes life worth living. It is creativity and beauty based upon ethnic and linguistic diversity that make man human. Absence of this diversity would lead to the dehumanization, mechanization, and utter impoverishment of man. The weakening of this diversity is a cause for alarm, a tendency to be resisted and combatted. In Herder and in Mazzini, in the Slavophiles in Kallen — indeed, in much of modern anthropology and anthropological linguistics — the theme of ethnic diversity and the sheer beauty of cultural pluralism provide an unending rhapsody. This view both tantalizingly merges with and also separates from general democratic principles, with the rights of man, and the inalienable privilege to be one's self, *not only to be free but to be free to be bound together with 'one's own kind'* (Talmon, 1965). On the one hand, democracy also subsumes an alternative right, namely, to be free from ethnicity, i.e. the right and opportunity to be a citizen of the world rather than a member of one or another traditioned ethnic collectivity. On the other hand, democracy guarantees the right to retain one's own ethnicity, to safeguard collective ethnic continuity, to enable one's children to join the ranks of 'one's own kind', to develop creatively, and to reach their full potential without becoming ethnically inauthentic, colorless, lifeless, worse than lifeless: nothingness.

Dimensions of language-and-ethnicity

The foregoing themes provide us with many insights into language and ethnicity, and into how language and ethnicity have been viewed in a particularly influential part of the world as well. The themes themselves are not independent of each other. Many of them relate to a putative ethnic essence that is intergenerationally continuous among 'one's own kind' and is absorbed via the mother's milk. Thus, there is commonly a 'being' component to ethnicity, a bodily mystery, a triumph over death in the past as well as a promise of immortality in the future, as the putative essence is handed on generation after generation. There are a few escape hatches in, and a few escape hatches out, and a terrifying state of liminality in between, but the physical continuity of a *corpus mysticum* continues. And language is part of that corpus. It issues authentically from the body, it is produced by the body, it has body itself (and, therefore, does not permit much basic modification).

Just as commonly, language is part of the authentic 'doing' constellation and the authentic 'knowing' constellation that are recurringly assumed to be dimensions of ethnicity. Ethnic doing and knowing are more mutable and, therefore, in danger of inauthenticity. Ethnic doing is a responsibility that can be shirked. Ethnic knowing is a gift that can be withheld. The basic desideratum, ethnic being, is necessary but not sufficient. There is everything to be gained and everything to be lost, and language is recurringly part and parcel of this web (Fishman, 1977). In premobilization ethnicity it is naturally, unconsciously so (Fishman, 1965), whereas in mobilized ethnicity it is a rallying call, both metaphorically and explicitly (Fishman, 1972).

Autochthonous theories gravitate toward the metaphorical and metaphysical views of the language and ethnicity link. External objectivists reduce the mystery to the needs of the military and the economy, with the school system merely exploiting language and ethnicity in preparing recruits for both. Autochthonists see language and ethnicity as initial essences, or causes. External objectivists see them as manipulable by-products. However, both agree that they are generally there together. Hovering over them both is the problem of how to interpret the 'we-they' differences that are, unconsciously or consciously, part of the experience of ethnicity, which brings me to racism.

Ethnicity and racism

Racism is one of many words that have been so broadened in modern, popular usage as to have lost their utility. Democracy and socialism are two other such terms, but whereas the latter have become all-purpose terms of approbation (viz., people's democracy, guided democracy, National Socialism, etc.), the former has become an all-purpose put-down. I would like to rescue *racism* from that dubious distinction, to limit its semantic range, in order more clearly to distinguish between ethnicity and racism as social phenomena and as social theories, and thereby, to focus pejorative usage more tellingly.

Relative to ethnicity, racism is not only more focused on the 'being' component (therefore having even fewer escape hatches from it than does ethnicity), but it also involves an evaluative ranking with respect to the discontinuity between ethnic collectivities. Ethnicity is an enactment (often unconscious) and a celebration of authenticity. Racism inevitably involves more heightened consciousness than does ethnicity, not only because it is an 'ism', but because its focus is not merely on authenticity and the celebration of difference or collective individuality, but on the evaluation of difference in terms of inherent better or worse, higher or lower, entirely acceptable and utterly objectionable. Ethnicity is less grandiose than racism. It has no built-in power dimension while racism, being essentially hierarchical, must have the concept of dominance in its cosmology and requires the constructs of superior races, dominant stocks, master peoples. By their words and deeds, ethnicity and racism are importantly different.

Herder, though anti-French to the hilt (like many German intellectuals struggling against French cultural hegemony within the disunited German princedoms at the beginning of the nineteenth century), is rarely, if ever, racist. He proclaims:

> 'No individual, no country, no people, no history of a people, no state is like any other. Therefore, the true, the beautiful and the good are not the same for them. Everything is suffocated if one's own way is not sought and if another nation is blindly taken as a model' (Herder, *Sammtliche Werke*, v.4, p.472).

Is not this still a dominant ethic and motivating dynamic in cultural anthropology to this very day? Herderian views must be understood as a plea and a rhapsody for an ethnically pluralistic world in which each ethnicity can tend its own vineyard as a right, a trust, and a point of departure for new beauty and creativity yet undreamed of. Such pluralism is, however, strange to racism, since the dynamics of racism represents a call and rationale for domination rather than for coexistence. While ethnicity can proclaim live and let live, racism can proclaim only bondage or death to the inferior.

Of course, every ethnicity runs the risk of developing an ethnocentrism, i.e. the view that one's own way of life is superior to all others. It may even be true that some degree of ethnocentrism is to be found in all societies and cultures (Bidney, 1968), including the culture of secular science itself, to the degree that they are all-encompassing in defining experience and perspective. The antidote to ethnocentrism (including acquired anti-ethnic ethnocentrism, which may be just as supercilious and uncritically biased as is ethnic conditioning) is thus comparative cross-ethnic knowledge and experience, transcending the limits of one's own usual exposure to life and values (a theme which has long appeared in the literature on ethnicity). Characteristic of postmodern ethnicity is the stance of simultaneously transcending ethnicity as a complete, self-contained system, but of retaining it as a selectively preferred, evolving, participatory system. This leads to a kind of self-correction from within and from without, which extreme nationalism and racism do not permit.

The modern heroes of racism are Gobineau in France (see, for example, Biddess, 1966, 1970a, b), Houston Stewart Chamberlain (1899) in England, and a chorus of German philosophers, scientists, and politicians (see, for example, Barzun, 1937; Gasman, 1971; Mosse, 1966; Weinreich, 1946). From their works it becomes clear that the language link to racism is as invidious as racism *per se*. Hermann Gauch, a Nazi 'scientist', was able to claim:

> 'The Nordic race alone can emit sounds of untroubled clearness, whereas among non-Nordics the pronunciation is . . . like noises made by animals, such as barking, sniffing, snoring, squeaking . . . That birds can learn to talk better than other animals is explained by the fact that their mouths are Nordic in structure' (quoted in Mosse 1966:225).

Here we have the ultimate route of racist thought: the demotion of the 'others' to a subhuman level. They are animals, vermin, and are to be subjected to whatever final solution is most effective and efficient.

Concluding sentiments

These remarks must not be taken simply as a defense of ethnicity. Ethnicity has been recognized since ancient times as capable of excess, corruption, and irrationality, this capacity being one of the basic themes accompanying its peregrination across the centuries. The very term *ethnicity*, derived from the Greek *ethnos* (used consistently in the Septuagint to render the Hebrew *goy*, the more negative term for nationality, as distinct from *'am*, the more positive term), has a decided negative connotation in earliest English usage (see OED: *ethnic* 1470, *ethnist* 1550 and 1563, *ethnicize* 1663, *ethnicity* 1772, *ethnize* 1847). These connotations — heathenness, superstition, bizarreness — have not fully vanished even from modern popular usage, e.g. ethnic dress, ethnic hairdos, ethnic soul. Thus, we need not fear that the excesses of ethnicity will be overlooked.

Racism itself is one of the excesses into which ethnicity can develop, although racism has often developed on pan-ethnic and perhaps even on nonethnic foundations as well.[2] However, the distinction between ethnicity and racism is well worth maintaining, particularly for those in the language-related disciplines and professions. It clarifies our goals, our problems, and our challenges as we engage in bilingual education, in language planning, in language maintenance efforts, and in a host of sociolinguistic and anthropological enterprises. The distinctions between religion and bigotry, sexuality and sexism, socialism and communism, democracy and anarchy, are all worth maintaining. No less worthwhile is the distinction between ethnicity and racism. Unfortunately, we know more about racism than about ethnicity, and more about the conflictual aspects of ethnicity than about its integrative functions. This is a pity, particularly for American intellectuals, since we too (regardless of our pretense to the contrary) live in a world in which the ethnic factor in art, music, literature, fashions, diets, childrearing, education and politics is still strong, and needs to be understood and even appreciated. Not to know more about ethnicity, about the ethnic repertoires of modern life, the endless mutability of ethnicity since the days of ancient Israel, the variety of prior thought concerning ethnicity (e.g. the various and changing views as to its power or centrality as a factor in societal functioning and social behavior) is also to limit our understanding of society and of the role of language in society. Language and ethnicity have been viewed as naturally linked in almost every age of premodern pan-Mediterranean and European thought. When ethnicity disappeared from modern social theory in the nineteenth century, language, too, disappeared therefrom. We may now be at the point of reappearance of both in modern social theory and we must prepare ourselves, accordingly, to benefit from and to contribute to the sensitivities and perspectives that a knowledge of language and ethnicity can provide, without overdoing them. Only in this way can the 'ethnic revival' in the United States be fully understood.

Notes to Chapter 1

1. For an account of racism's more complete domination of modern culture, see Banton's paper in Zubaida (1970). For a preliminary differentiation between ethnicity and racism, see the penultimate section of this paper.
2. The terminology of ethnicity often included the word *race* (e.g. *raza*) in the sense of ethnicity as employed in this paper. This is but one of the semantic alternatives that a sociology and a sociology of knowledge pertaining to ethnicity must be aware of and must try to illuminate.

Bibliography

BARZUN, J. 1937, *Race: A Study in Superstition*. New York: Harper.
BIDDESS, M. D. 1966, Gobineau and the origin of European racism, *Race: Journal of the Institute of Race Relations*. 7, 225–70.
— (ed.) 1970a, *Gobineau: Selected Political Writings*. London: Cape.
— 1970b, *Father of Racist Ideology: The Social and Political Thought of Count Gobineau*. London: Weindenfeld and Nicholson.

BIDNEY, D. 1968, Cultural relativism, *International Encyclopedia of the Social Sciences*, 3, 543–47.

BRENNAN, REV. M. 1969, Language, personality and the nation. In BRIAN O. CUIV (ed.), *A View of the Irish Language*. Dublin, Stationery Office.

BROMLEY, Yu V. 1974, Soviet ethnology and anthropology, *Studies in Anthropology I*. The Hague: Mouton.

CHAMBERLAIN, H. S. 1899, *The Foundations of the Nineteenth Century*. New York: Fertig.

ENGELS, F. 1866, What have the working class to do with Poland? *Commonwealth*. March 24, March 31 and May 5.

FISHMAN, D. E., MAYERFIELD R. & FISHMAN, J. A. 1985, *'Am* and *goy* as designations for ethnicity in selected books of the Old Testament. In J. A. FISHMAN, *et al. The Rise and Fall of the Ethnic Revival*. Berlin: Mouton de Gruyter, 15–38.

FISHMAN, J. A. 1965, Varieties of ethnicity and varieties of language consciousness. *Georgetown University Roundtable on Languages and Linguistics, 1965*. Edited by Charles W. Kreidler, 69–79.

— 1972, *Language and Nationalism*. Rowley: Newbury House. Also in *This Volume*, parts I and III.

— 1977, Language and ethnicity. In H. GILES (ed.), *Language and Ethnicity in Intergroup Relations*. New York: Academic Press, 15–57.

— 1978, Positive bilingualism: some overlooked rationales and forefathers. *Georgetown University Roundtable on Languages and Linguistics, 1978*. JAMES E. ALATIS (ed.), 42–52.

GASMAN, D. 1971, The scientific origins of National Socialism, *Social Darwinism in Ernest Haeckel and the German Monist League*. London: Macdonald.

GELLNER, E. 1964, *Thought and Change*. Chicago: University of Chicago Press.

HERDER, J. G. *Sammtliche Werke*. 33 vols. B. SUPHAN, E. REDLICH et al., (eds.) Berlin, 1877–1913.

ISAJIW, W. W. 1974, Definitions of ethnicity, *Ethnicity*. 1, 111–24.

JAKOBSON, R. 1945, The beginnings of national self-determination in Europe. Review of Politics. 1945, 2, 29–42. Reprinted in J. A. FISHMAN, (ed.), *Readings in the Sociology of Language*. The Hague: Mouton, 1968.

LEPAGE, R. B. & TABOURET-KELLER, A. 1982, Models and stereotypes of ethnicity and language, *Journal of Multilingual and Multicultural Development*, 3, 161–92.

MACRAE, D. 1960, Race and sociology in history and in theory. In P. MASON, (ed.), *Man, Race and Darwin*. London: Oxford University

Press, 76–86.

MOSSE, G.L. 1966, *Nazi Culture: Intellectual, Cultural and Social Life in the Third Reich*. London: W.H. Allen.

RJASANOFF, N., MARX K. & ENGELS F. über die Polenfrage 1916, *Archiv für die Geschichte des Socialismus und der Arbeiterbewegung* (Leipzig). 6, 175–221.

TALMON, J. L. 1965, *The Unique and the Universal*. London: Secker and Warburg.

WEINREICH, M. 1946, *Hitler's Professors: The Part of Scholarship in Germany's Crimes Against the Jewish People*. New York: Yiddish Scientific Institute-YIVO.

ZUBAIDA, S., (ed.) 1970, *Race and Racism*. London: Tavistock.

2 Language and ethnicity*

The recent increase in societal attention to ethnicity has fostered a rebirth of interest in ethnicity among social scientists as well. The latter interest has, in part, focused upon the former increase in societal attention, addressing itself to the question of why apparently larger numbers of individuals, in Western as well as in non-Western societies, have recently recognized and even stressed their ethnicity more than was the case just a few years ago. Since this development was contraindicated by so much of modern social theory, it raises the serious question of why social theory was so unprepared for its occurrence,[1] as well as the even more basic related question of why the 'rebirth of ethnicity' ('the ethnic revolution') occurred at all. A future, full-dressed attempt to explore the relationship between language and ethnicity cannot ignore questions such as the foregoing, if only because that 'relationship' cannot possibly be well understood if ethnicity itself is not treated more seriously — both in theory and in practice — in connection with language. The recent study of ethnicity has already produced a voluminous literature. What follows here, is no more than a sampling and a tentative integration of that literature along lines that may shed some new light on a relationship which also has too long been taken for granted.

What is ethnicity?

There is no logical reason why ethnicity cannot be rigorously understood. However, as with many other 'social concepts' (MacIntyre, 1973; Care, 1973) our problems in understanding ethnicity are not basically logical ones. Much more central to the difficulties that are encountered with this concept are (a) the large number of (b) interrelated factors that the concept subsumes. As a result, there are also many different conceptions of ethnicity (Isajiw, 1974) — contrasting, conflicting

*Originally published in H. GILES (ed.) 1977, *Language and Ethnicity in Intergroup Relations*. New York: Academic Press, 83–98.

and contradictory — to such an extent that the disagreements between them are themselves significant objects of study. The significance of these definitional disagreements lies not only in that they reveal biases as to the worth or role of ethnicity in social life, and that they do, but that they reveal the extent to which ethnicity is a historical (i.e. a changing) phenomenon which accommodates different weightings or emphases in connection with the large number of interrelated factors that it subsumes. No wonder then that there have been many and recurring road blocks in an attempt to define and understand ethnicity.[2]

Ethnicity is rightly understood as an aspect of a collectivity's self-recognition[3] as well as an aspect of its recognition in the eyes of outsiders. Ethnic recognition differs from other kinds of group-embedded recognition in that it operates basically in terms of paternity rather than in terms of patrimony and exegesis thereupon. However, like other types of group-embedded recognition, it is an avenue whereby individuals are linked to society, i.e. to social norms and to social values. Like them, ethnicity represents an avenue whereby understandings of 'the world at large' are arrived at, that is to say, through ethnicity ordinary individuals are not only linked to collectivities — and social integration is attained thereby — but to notions of 'life', 'society' and 'the world' as well. Touching, as it may, both the deeper as well as the more superficial layers of awareness and of commitment, ethnicity thus tends to be componentally and experientially multifacetted, combining both 'inherited' and 'acquired' aspects, both 'stable' and 'changing' ones, both 'existential' and 'contrastive' characteristics, both 'rational' and 'extra-rational' views. All in all, ethnicity is certainly a complex phenomenon but a fathomable one and, seemingly, a far more hardy and important one, even in modern life, than many scholars had assumed. Its relationship to language behavior is but another important reason for taking a fresh look at it. The approach adopted here is initially one 'from within', i.e. the ethnicity experience as reported, 'witnessed', explicated by those participating in it and who believe 'it to have a nature because they feel it . . . as an immediate thing' (McWilliams, 1973). Subsequently, several perspectives 'from without' will be added to fill out the total picture, particularly insofar as social theorists have commented upon ethnicity.

Paternity

The notion of ethnicity requires a central concept or chord around which all others can be clustered. This central experience is here termed paternity, and deals with the recognition of putative biological origins and, therefore, with the hereditary or descent-related 'blood', 'bones', 'essence', 'mentality', 'genius', 'sensitivity', 'proclivity' derived from the original putative ancestors of a collectivity and passed on from generation to generation in a bio-kinship sense. 'Outside' observers may quibble as to whether the assumed bio-kinship of ethnicity is real, mythical (i.e. mixture of history and elaborate legend) or fictive, but 'inside' participants often react to this dimension as a mystery of transcendental proportions. It may be forgotten; it may be overlooked; it may be played down; it may be denied to escape charges of racism. It is this constellation that has come to be referred to as 'primordial', after Shils (1957) and Geertz (1963). Primordiality denotes both primacy, in the sense of a presumably original essence, as well as primitivism or irreducibility, in the sense of a presumptive discontinuity between 'those who have it' and 'those who do not'. Ethnicity is, in part, but at its core, experienced as an inherited constellation acquired from one's parents as they acquired it from theirs, and so on back further and further, *ad infinitum*.[4]

There may be escape hatches, of course, permitting both the acquisition of a given ethnicity by those who do not have it (or who have it only in part as a result of 'mixed' parentage), as well as the loss of it by those who do. But these escape hatches are considered as involving unusual circumstances often ritually and affectively heightened, precisely because they require tampering with the natural order, and with very deeply felt differences. Ethnicity is experienced as coming 'with the blood if not through it' (Gambino, 1975). When we deal with ethnicity, we may be dealing with some of the strongest assumptions and some of the most powerful investments in which social man is involved.

A kinship metaphor (ancestors: grandparents, parents, brothers, sisters, etc.) is not an accidental aspect of the notion of ethnicity. 'Kinship' is the basis of the felt bond to one's own kind. It is the basis of one's solidarity with them in times of stress. It is the basis of one's right to presume upon them in times of need. It is the basis of one's dependency, sociability and intimacy with them 'as a matter of course'. Indeed, just as the immediate kinship group may be the limiting case of ethnicity (Tobias, 1973), so ethnicity may be the maximal case of societally-organized intimacy and kinship experience (even though, as we will see, heightened ethnicity may severely alter these experiences of quiet ethnicity). Little wonder then that the lexicon of ethnicity reflects the grammar of 'kinship'[5], with its stress on putative ancestry, parents, children and siblings. This lexicon not only heightens the interdependence of the ethnic bond but it infuses it with the overtones of a deeply moral obligation. Little wonder then that ethnicity experiences, characteristics and ethnicity differences are charged with emotion and that the symbols of the paternity dimension of ethnicity are often so |powerful| (i.e. so mobilizing with respect to collective behavior) and so experientially special with respect to individual behavior. Indeed, it is impossible to grasp the intensity of the ethnicity experience — an intensity which leads to the heights of altruism and to the depths of cruelty — without grasping the corporeal and kinship 'certainties' from which that experience is derived.

A vast number of traits and behaviors have been taken to reflect the paternity aspect of ethnicity: obviously physical traits, temperamental qualities including intelligence ('mind'), and, quite commonly, language, i.e. those features of social behavior that either are biological givens or that are commonly assumed to be such by virtue of their apparent relationship to physical development and decline.

The paternity parameter of ethnicity and the genealogical myth or ideology that surrounds it and elaborates it, is a reflection of the need for and the search for felt historical depth ('roots') which both individuals and ethnic collectivities often reveal (Levenson, 1971). Through common, distant ancestry, ethnicity experiencing individuals and collectivities gain a feeling of continuity, a sense of permanence across time, across death, from eternity to eternity. Through ethnic collectivities, individuals feel augmented and come to experience immortality as an immediate physical reality. To be without ethnicity is, for some, 'to be faced with one's death' (de Vos & Romanucci-Ross, 1975a).

It is precisely because language is so often taken as a biological inheritance that its association with ethnic paternity is both frequent and powerful. It is 'acquired with the mother's milk'. It is not only shaped by the inherited organism of speech but it, in turn, shapes the mind and the mental processes (Fishman, 1960; Fishman & Spolsky, 1976). It is saturated with the tears and joys of the ancestors. It is loved with all one's being. How could it be otherwise, particularly if the Ultimate Power used (this) language in creating the ancestors and, indeed, in creating the world itself? The language often carries(d) within itself the power of ultimate creation and of ultimate destruction. Indeed, it may be unconsciously perceived as a corporeal reality in and of itself and, simultaneously, as part and parcel of the ethnic corporeal reality, which in turn, may be an expression of the Everlasting Presence in space and time. Unmobilized ethnicity often includes such assumptions in a passive, matter-of-fact-way. Mobilized ethnicity often makes language into a dynamic *corpus mysticum*. It is not only the conveyor of other ethnic symbols. It is not even merely an ethnic symbol in and of itself. It is 'flesh of the flesh and blood of the blood' and, therefore, all the more powerful as a conveyor, as a symbol, and as a *summum bonum*, well worth living and dying for.

The paternity aspect of the language-ethnicity link is frequently remarked upon in conjunction with inter-ethnic communication. Although such communication may be a simple and effortless matter under conditions of quiescent ethnicity it may be experienced as a palpable, physical difficulty, as an effort and as a burden, when ethnicity is mobilized and manipulated. Inter-ethnic communication under the latter circumstances is often reported to be painful, to be revolting, to be physically obnoxious or unnatural, rather than merely to be difficult. Bridging the unbridgeable and crossing putatively natural discontinuities is obviously more difficult than one would imagine on the basis of 'linguistic distance'. The paternity dimension in the ethnicity experience (and, therefore, in the language-ethnicity link) helps account for much of the unanticipated surplus difficulty.

Patrimony

Paternity and patrimony are constantly interacting in ethnicity; they may reinforce each other, fuse into each other, but may yet be recognized as distinct (Hicks & Kertzer, 1972). As constructs they are poles along a continuum, as realities they are shifting and interpenetrating. The paternity dimension of ethnicity is viewed as less negotiable, patrimony as more so (more interpretable, more changeable), even though it is somehow ultimately also legitimized by an appeal to origins. However, the ethnic patrimony is learned and has about it the aura of human fallibility, whereas paternity is inherited and has upon it the stamp of ancestral perfection. Therefore, the border between the two is an uncertain one, as it must be between co-ordinate systems that are in tension, and the same feature will at times be viewed as inherited and at other times as learned, as essential or as dispensable, as unalterable or as conditioned. Like status and process, paternity and patrimony always coexist, even though the one is more ontological and the other more behavioral.

'Ethnic patrimony' and 'culture' are highly interrelated but not necessarily one and the same. Phenomenologically not all of culture need be viewed as descent-related. Not all of culture is experienced as own- and other-descent-group defining. Nevertheless, there is obviously a cultural component to ethnicity (Deshen, 1974, 1975)[6]. Ethnicity is not just a state of being (as paternity implies), but it also a behavioral or implementational or enactment system (as patrimony implies). The paternity dimension of ethnicity is related to questions of how ethnicity collectivities come into being and to how individuals get to be members of these collectivities. The patrimony dimension of ethnicity is related to questions of how ethnic collectivities behave and to what their members do in order to express their membership. The former maintains that one must either be or not be of a given ethnicity ('escape hatches' and mixed-parentage notwithstanding). The latter recognizes that one either may or may not fulfil the obligations of ethnicity. As a result, the patrimony dimension is suffused with moral implications, with judgements of good and bad, with specifications (stereotyped 'markedness') in terms of which one is evaluated and in terms of which one evaluates others *vis-à-vis* the fulfilment of own-group membership requirements. Paternity defines those who inherit a heritage. Patrimony is the bulk of that heritage (of collectivity-defining behaviors) *per se*, which some may put to good use and others may squander and still others may ignore entirely. Paternity is evaluative primarily *vis-à-vis* those who are outside the fold.[7] Patrimony, on the other hand, is evaluative both on an external *and* on an internal dimension. Conceptual systems and cosmologies that emphasize the paternity to the exclusion of patrimony (or vice versa) break out of the fold of ethnicity *per se* and become either racial/caste systems, on the one hand, or achieved status systems, on the other hand. It is a defining distinction of the ethnicity experience that it requires both paternity and patrimony emphases, regardless of the tension and the movement that may go on between them.[8]

Language behaviors (particularly mother tongue attitudes), although importantly patrimonial, often reveal the 'pull' of unalterable paternity, in the face of organized attempts to plan, change, improve, or modernize the language. However, far before that stage is reached language is recognized as a guide to 'kinship'-interpreted group membership, as a desideratum and demonstration of such membership. Language is commonly among the conscious 'do' and 'don'ts' as well as among the unconscious ones: that is, it is among the evaluated dimensions of ethnicity membership (whether consciously or not). It is particularly touched by the sanctity of verbal rituals, and by the specialness of written ones, and, quite naturally, comes to be classed with the sanctities of which they are part and which depend upon them. Language is not only code but Code. For the ethnicity experience language is much more than 'merely communication' just as ethnicity is much more than 'mere life'. Thus, just as language is likely to be associated with the mysteries of paternity so it is more than likely to be related to the sanctity of patrimony as well. 'Even though one may not be conversant with the language ... [this] can be excused as part of a 'lost' or 'stolen' cultural tradition' (Beer, 1976) which reborn ethnicity must rescue, together with and even through the language itself.

The paternity-linked problems that can complicate inter-ethnic communication when ethnicity is heightened can also have their counterparts with respect to the patrimonial dimension of the ethnicity experience. Inter-ethnic communication often raises questions of propriety, decency, of loyalty, of 'crossing-over'. Faithfulness to patrimony is often viewed as being opposed to frequent inter-ethnic communication, and, indeed, to genuine paternity, since 'true sons and daughters' do not 'cross-over'. Similarly, intra-group communications that reveal linguistic traces of inter-ethnic communication, are similarly liable to criticism for lack of purity, for inauthenticity, for the moral and ethical lapses that such traces are taken to betray. Non-reciprocity of inter-ethnic communication is often natively attributed to linguistic unintelligibility. As Hans Wolff revealed (1959), members of group A may claim to understand members of group B, at the same time that the latter claim not to understand the former. Such attitudinally based non-reciprocity in intelligibility may well be accompanied by widely different levels of linguistic influence of language A on B and of B on A. Finally, the implications of interlinguistic influences may well be interpreted very differently in the two societies. Such implications (as to person propriety and membership-in-good standing) will vary with ethnic saliency (i.e. with degree of heightened manipulation or mobilization of ethnicity), but, all in all, are an aspect of ethnicity phenomenology, to which we now turn.

Phenomenology

We must be interested in ethnicity phenomenology for two reasons: most basically, because we must be concerned to understand how the members of ethnicity collectivities view ethnicity (their own, that of 'others', as well as how the 'others' view 'them'), how and when these views change (in content and in saliency), and the relationship between the foregoing views and views as to other types of collective identity that are considered to be available. Actors' views of their ethnicity are a part of their ethnicity; certainly they are a part of their ethnic identity (yet to be discussed). However, we must also be concerned with phenomenology of yet another order, namely, our own, as scientific observers, commentators and systematizers. There must be a relationship between these two views of ethnicity and, if so, we must be aware of what this relationship is.

   If we merely report the ethnicity views of actors we are descriptivists, reporters, cameras. On the other hand, if we merely design our own definitions and theories of ethnicity, these may have little to do with the actors' perceived reality and, if so, what have we explained? Obviously, we must go back and forth between description and explanation, between observation and interpretation, between the actor's view and the analyst's view (Mitchell, 1974). We must be alert to counter-evidence, or our discussion will continue without due regard to the data of description. We must define to some extent before we engage in wide-scaled observation, otherwise it will not be clear what it is that we wish to observe. However, as we observe more and more, we must change our initial definitions to fit the actual data, as needed. Our ultimate goal is to derive (to demonstrate, to construct) an analyst's phenomenological system that is descriptive and explanatory of the actors' phenomenological system. Understanding ethnicity is a process of the same kind that Geertz outlines for understanding cultural systems in general: it is a matter of explicating the explications (Drummond, 1975; Geertz, 1973).

   Ethnicity is concerned not only with an actor's descent-related being (paternity) and behaving (patrimony) but with the meanings that he attaches to his descent-related being and behaving (phenomenology).[9] Ethnicity notions are, for actors (and for analysts too, for that matter), part of the total structure and organization of meaning as it relates to the nature of life, the nature of mankind, the nature of nature, the nature of the supernatural. All these meanings may be implicit, rather more subconscious than conscious, yet they are real nonetheless, since they are utilized in noting, ordering and acting upon a particular subset of experiences out of the infinite variety that floods in upon the senses. Actors have a certain understanding of reality and that understanding (implicit and unarticulated though it may be) both feeds into as well as comes out of their ethnicity understandings. Ethnicity understandings may be part of a larger system of moral understandings and intuitions, part of a far more inclusive cosmology than that related to recognition of 'one's own kind'. However, if we fully understand how actors understand ethnicity we simultaneously understand at least part (and often more than just a small part) of how they understand the world at large and their relation to it.

   Actors' ethnicity views inform their views of history, of the future, of the purpose of life, of the fabric of human relationships. Since ethnicity often deals with very powerful, presumably irreducible, beliefs, feelings and bonds, it is all the more likely to be importantly related to all-embracing ways of viewing, to Weltanschauungen, to cosmologies. Since ethnicity is often part of a collectivity's highest (or deepest) cultural symbolism, a symbolism that is wholistic and that serves profound integrative functions, it is vital that we grasp these meanings, for in doing so we are likely to grasp something truly vital not only about ethnicity, but about a society or culture as a whole. Indeed, it is for this very reason that a reconsideration of the role of ethnicity is so vital for the improvement of social theory. Finally, it is only at the level of phenomenology that we can discover the particular resolution of the paternity-patrimony tension system that has been arrived at at any given time, as well as the interpretation (or meaning) that has been assigned to that resolution. Ethnicity is 'the "cup of custom" (patrimony) passed on by one's parents (paternity), from which one drinks the meaning of existence . . . through which one envisions life (phenomenology) . . . It is both a means and an end' (de Vos & Romanucci-Ross, 1975a).

The phenomenology of the assumed link between language and ethnicity is an absolute desideratum if we are to fathom any collectivity's reactions to the use or non-use of its language in ritual, in official/governmental domains, in education, or its reactions to language planning or to the admission of languages of wider communication (such as English) into various domains of social behavior (Fishman, 1977) Does an ethnic collectivity perceive links between its language and the mysteries of paternity and the morality of patrimony, and, if so, how are these links interpreted? The language of own-ethnicity is often assumed to be indicative of homegrown honesty and decency and wit and subtlety (such that even dishonesty may be viewed as being crafty in a familiar and almost pardonable way), not to mention partnership in the here-and-now and co-destination in the hereafter. The phenomenology of language and ethnicity may reveal how the language is characterized as well as why it has come to be the way it is (e.g. holy, rich, refined, musical, soft, exact, practical, pure, etc.); which of its current features are particularly significant (e.g, difficulty for 'others', dissimilarity from other languages, 'goodness of fit' with respect to ethnic sanctity, etc.); what communication tactics are to be employed across boundaries (should 'we' use their language or should 'they' use ours?), what potential and latitude exist with respect to mutability of the language, what is its mission (its transcendental purpose)? Views such as the foregoing are not inevitable — but where the link exists there is a phenomenology, an exegesis, with respect to which it is imperative for us to know, if we are to understand how that link is understood.

The recurring symbolic role of language in the ethnicity experience

All that has been said, above, implies the degree to which language can be vastly more than a means of communication. Obviously, language can also be a very powerful symbol (in this discussion, a symbol of ethnicity) as well as a verity (a deity) in its own right.

By its very nature language is the quintessential symbol, the symbol par excellence. Symbols stand in a part-whole relation to their referents. Their preliminary function is to evoke the whole. All language stands in this very relation to the rest of reality: it refers to, it expresses, it evokes 'something' in addition to itself. However, in the process of symbolizing it tends also to become valued in itself. Speaking well, commanding the language, versatility in language, these often become specifically valued in their own right, above and beyond what is spoken about or the purposes of speakers. Symbols which stand for valued wholes are particularly likely to become functionally independent and, therefore, to become valued in their own right (Turner, 1969, 1975) rather than merely as symbols alone.

In view of the foregoing, it becomes clearer why language is more likely than most symbols of ethnicity to become the symbol of ethnicity. Language is the recorder of paternity, the expresser of patrimony and the carrier of phenomenology. Any vehicle carrying such precious freight must come to be viewed as equally precious, as part of the freight, indeed, as precious in and of itself. The link between language and ethnicity is thus one of sanctity-by-association. This link is more likely to arise and to be singled out, although neither is more inevitable than that obtaining between other parts of the ethnicity complex and the entire constellation. Anything can become symbolic of ethnicity (whether food, dress, shelter, land tenure, artifacts, work, patterns of worship), but since language is the prime symbol system to begin with and since it is commonly relied upon so heavily (even if not exclusively) to enact, celebrate and 'call forth' all ethnic activity, the likelihood that it will be recognized and singled out as symbolic of ethnicity is great indeed. This likelihood is both increased and exploited when ethnicity is manipulated into ethnic consciousness since language is crucial for relaying the good word, the message, the call, and, as such — even without any linguistic features that make it unintelligible to others — it easily becomes 'more than' a means of communication, even more than symbolic of the ethnic message; indeed, it becomes a prime ethnic value in and of itself.

Indisputably, many ethnic groups do not have a distinctive language or lose it along the way. Although the strength of their bonds may suffer as a result, their certainty that their language is essential to them may also remain undiminished. It is even possible that language may be dispensed with entirely as a crucial ethnic symbol. Nevertheless, it is always highly likely to be and to become such because of its peerless symbolic role in paternity, patrimony and phenomenology alike.

The role of boundaries in ethnicity

It is often claimed that the boundary between an ethnicity collectivity and those that surround it is at least part of the meaning of ethnicity experience per se, that is to say, self-recognition contains within itself a recognition that there are other collectivities whose ethnicity is different (Barth, 1969; Tobias, 1973). There are others, however, who sense a stage and variety of ethnicity in which even own-group recognition, i.e. the recognition of one's own ethnicity collectivity, is minimal and, therefore, a stage and variety in which consciousness of boundaries and of other ethnicity collectivities across these boundaries is also minimal (Nahirny & Fishman, 1965; Fishman, 1965). Certainly, if the notion of ethnic identity requires heightened ethnic consciousness, then it may very well be that ethnic identity logically requires not only boundaries (contrast) but opposition across boundaries for such identity to be most fully articulated. Certainly, all would agree that ethnicity is most consciously and forcefully enacted when both contrast and opposition, boundaries and conflict, are consciously recognized.

Such consciousness is greatest and most constant among ethnicity collectivities that are small enough and weak enough to require constant alertness (mobilization) on behalf of and via their ethnicity, namely minority groups. The concentration upon minority groups and inter-group conflict in the study of ethnicity (e.g. Glazer & Moynihan, 1975; Cohen, 1974a, b; de Vos & Romanucci-Ross, 1975b; Bell & Freeman, 1974), and particularly in the American sociological study of ethnicity, has tended to highlight such boundary phenomena as inter-group relations (Morris, 1968; Gittler, 1974),[10] boundary crossing (assimilation: Gordon, 1975) and boundary changing (incorporation, secession: Horowitz, 1975; Singer, 1962). It would, perhaps, be well to recognize these as special topics within the far more inclusive pale of ethnicity, rather than to view them as the sum total of ethnicity, or as the heart of the matter. If there can be no heartland without boundaries, however distant they may be, there can also be no boundaries unless there is a heartland. The two may well be interdependent, as may also be consciousness with respect to them.

The study of ethnic boundaries, and of conflict or transactions across them, has also promoted a possibly exaggerated stress on unity or harmony within the ethnicity collectivity. Indeed, it has been claimed that unity within rests upon opposition without (Gluckman, 1956) and, conversely, that unity within elicits opposition without (Tobias, 1973). Granted the pertinence of both of the above views, it should also be recognized that neither unity nor opposition are constants, that there is considerable disunity within any ethnicity collectivity, and that such disunity exists precisely in connection with the enactment and interpretation of ethnicity, just as there is far from constant opposition without. Indeed, Barth himself, one of the most stimulating researchers and theoreticians of boundary phenomena (1969), stresses transactional complementarity rather than conflict across ethnicity boundaries in plural societies. (Concerning the latter and the 'consociational ethnicity' that they support, also see Smith, 1969b.) This stress also leads Barth to greater sensitivity to the preservation of separateness, rather than merely to assimilation, as a possible consequence of intergroup relations. For Barth (as well as for Smith), ethnic boundaries are the loci for exchange of goods, exchange of services and exchange of information, rather than merely the loci for 'exchange' of power pressure (as they are for Cohen, 1969. 1974a, b). Ethnicity collectivities are symbiotically relatable to each other, rather than merely conflictually relatable, and as such, they do not take on the form of minority hostages within some amorphous all-encompassing 'larger society' or 'society at large.' True though the latter model may sometimes be in political terms, it does not always capture even the political truth, let alone the phenomenological truth available to ordinary actors.

Finally, it is appropriate to recognize that boundaries may also exist within the ethnicity collectivity, rather than merely between such collectivities. The ethnicity collectivity is not simply one, large, un-differentiated mass. It subsumes regions, networks, families, occupations, classes and various other cultural and social boundaries which may become ethnicized or which may be the uneasy remains of subjugated independent ethnicities. All in all boundaries, whether between or within ethnicity collectivities, are no more objective realities than are the ethnicity paternities, patrimonies or phenomenologies that they separate. Bound-aries must be noticed by actors, interpreted by actors and implemented by actors. The functions of boundaries within and between ethnicity collectivities may well flow from such prior considerations just as much as they subsequently help determine them. However, once boundaries have been heavily invested with interpretations and enactments, they acquire a logic and a dynamic of their own, and can become, as do all other ethnicity phenomena, 'reasons sufficient unto themselves' and, therefore, exceedingly difficult to alter.

There is considerable similarity between the nature and functions of ethnicity boundaries and the nature and functions of language boundaries. This is a natural consequence of the easy involvement of the latter in the implementation and symbolization of the former, as well as a function of the inherent arbitrariness and manipulability which both types of boundaries manifest.

The symbolic boundary-function of language is certainly significant above and beyond any natural boundary-function that languages may have on the basis of their mutual intelligibility *per se*. Judgements and evaluations as to the intelligibility, meaning, intent and purpose of utterances often follow upon and flow from pre-established judgements as to the ethnicity (or sub-ethnicity) of their speaker, and therefore, judgements as to their acceptability, character, 'proclivity', intent and purpose as interlocutors and as (group) 'representatives'. The recognition of language boundaries, the interpretation of language boundaries and the manipulation of language boundaries are all ethnically encumbered behaviors, as are either the acceptance or the rejection of whatever language boundaries that may 'exist' at any particular time. To the extent that ethnicity functions are normatively allocated or felt to pervade all (rather than only some) varieties of a language, to that extent all varieties (rather than only some) will also function as inter-ethnic boundary maintaining devices as well.

Mutability of ethnicity

Notwithstanding their self-perceived link to eternity, ethnicity experiences do change, every bit as much as do cultural and societal phenomena more generally. The bulk of our recently rekindled interest in ethnicity may itself be a byproduct of widespread change in the saliency of ethnicity in Western life. Indeed, we may be over-reacting to this recent greater saliency, just as we did to its earlier submergence. Beginning with the eighteenth century, Western social theory had assumed that the submergibility of ethnicity implied its transitory quality and that its assumed transitoriness, furthermore, doubly implied its significance. Today, as well, the assumed saliency of ethnicity (or, more exactly, the post-submergence saliency) is often viewed as merely transitory and, therefore, as equally indicative of the insignificance of ethnicity. Obviously, the mutability of ethnicity requires careful consideration since it is both an aspect of the experience as well as a subtle projective device for the study of investigator bias.

Mutability of content

Our earlier discussion of paternity, patrimony and phenomenology prepares us to realize that these dimensions of the ethnicity experience are themselves differentially alterable. Paternity notions, dealing as they do with the transcendental, mystical 'essence' of ethnicity, are normally least alterable. This link to ethnicity via its mediating 'kinship' metaphors, is the relatively unnegotiable and untouchable core of ethnicity. At most, this core would seem to be mutable in saliency rather than in content *per se*. Patrimony, on the other hand, presents a significantly different picture. Not only does change occur with respect to patrimony but it is seen to occur, and, therefore, may be feared, espoused, resisted, supported (Arens, 1975). Because of its link to paternity, planned change in patrimony is often rationalized as a return to essentials, i.e. as authenticity directed, or, at least, as authenticity-concordant rather than discordant. However, this is phenomenology rather than patrimony *per se*. Enactment differences, that is, interpersonal or inter-familial or inter-network differences in ethnicity-marked behaviors, are commonly 'understood' as being the result of change (across time, across space, across experiential subgroups) or as change *en flagrante*. Nevertheless, change in content does not necessarily denote change in wholistic meaning and change in meaning does not necessarily denote change in ethnic identity. Identity itself, in the furthest inner recesses of the soul (a formulation that should not elicit discomfort in conjunction with ethnicity, since that is how ethnicity is reported to be experienced in its more conscious phases), may be complexly multifaceted, and has the capacity to shelter, and, therefore, to reaffirm layers or sections that have been submerged, forgotten or even denied. Identity seems to be closer to paternity than to patrimony, to substance than to action, to feeling than to believing or understanding, and, as a result, changes more slowly, more partially and less consistently than do either behavior or ideology. Nevertheless, it too does change, both overtly and covertly, and such change may involve a heightened, marked, decomposition-recomposition, liminality experience (Turner, 1975b), with a sweetness or bitter-sweetness all its own. Certainly, in a world marked by change (and often wrecked by change), changes in ethnicity content should not appear as strange or as odd or as amusing as their detractors make them out to be. The resulting constellation is not necessarily experienced any less as a phenomenological whole than is that constellation available to those presumably liberated from ethnicity, on the one hand, or to those who have remained close to the primordial core, on the other hand. Ultimately, mutability of content has almost no limit, as the research on language planning has independently demonstrated (Fishman, 1977) but, nonetheless, authenticity is commonly experienced (and espoused) as not only being undamaged but even as being enhanced. 'The more it changes the more it remains the same' is certainly a phenomenological truism as far as ethnicity content and language corpus are concerned.

Mutability of membership

Recent research and theory have paid considerable attention to 'cross-over', that is, to leaving one ethnicity for another, to re-ethnification or assimilation into a new ethnicity (Patterson, 1975; Smith, 1975; Tobias, 1973). In contrast with earlier assimilation research and theory, in which it was often unconsciously assumed that de-ethnification was an end in itself, one that resulted in a free and rational man with no ethnic fetters whatsoever, most newer inquiries recognize that some other form of ethnicity is by far the more usual outcome of the process. Although unblemished by over-attachment to the view that 'ethnic identity, like other statuses, is negotiable' (thus playing down the deeply mystic and transcendental qualities of the paternity component), the newer concern with cross-over has introduced many worthwhile sensitivities into this area of consideration. It not only recognizes that 'modern' man considers all of his social, cultural and even physical attributes as 'options', to be put to use as judiciously as possible in pursuit of self-selected, achieved status goals (being 'as capable as the mythological Greek, Proteus, of changing social behavior with context', de Vos & Romanucci-Ross, 1975a), but that he often initially does so in accord with the very patrimonic behaviors that are being demythologized and abandoned in the process. 'Modern' man is not only viewed (perhaps exaggeratedly) as a shrewd calculator of membership benefits, but as a sensitive recognizer of alternative value systems and of the built-in (de)limitations in any ethnicity system. The internal view that 'ethnicity has nothing to do with x', implies recognition of, or at least attribution of, a gap within the fine fabric of a particular paternity-patrimony-phenomenology ethnicity experience. It implies that there are alternative guides to behavior and to identity than ethnicity, an implication that ethnicity systems themselves may not recognize. However, curiously enough, finding and exploiting the weak spots in any ethnicity system requires a very refined sensitivity to and utilization of the system. Thus, just as the meaning of cross-over is predetermined by a delimited meaning of ethnicity, so the means of cross-over are often predetermined by delimited means of ethnicity. As a result, cross-over 'opportunity' will be better used by those . . . (accustomed) to understand and exploit ethnically biased opportunities to maximal advantages (de Vos & Romanucci-Ross, 1975a).

Cross-over is rarely a single brutal act of betrayal. It is normally the resultant of countless instances of inter-ethnic behavior and of other behavior interpretation acceptable within the ethnicity system (Kuper, 1969). Its gradualness and its piecemeal acceptability within the tradition leave much of the process of cross-over as far from consciousness as most of ethnicity *per se* often is. Finally, cross-over is a two-way street. It is rarely a 'once and for all affair', particularly if engaged in without dramatic discontinuity, and the deepest kernel of original paternity-identity may exist (or co-exist) with newer notions long after behavioral cross-over is assumed and seen to have occurred (Salamone, 1975). Indeed, the boundary between social change and cross-over is a long and subtle one and this too makes recrossing both easier and more common, both behaviorally and phenomenologically. Finally, even a conscious disavowal of former ethnicity, rare though it be, does not always erase deeper layers of feeling and sensitivity toward it, as the research on ethnic proto-élites amply demonstrates (Beer, 1975, 1976b; Brass, 1976; Fishman, 1972; Fox, 1974). Language cross-over, both in the sense of usage and usage claiming, is similarly subtle and reversible, particularly in connection with mother tongue usage and usage-claiming (Fishman, 1966).

Mutability of saliency

Ethnicity is not only variable as to its content and as to its constituency but as to its saliency as well. The latter variability has been built into sociological theory insofar as it touches upon the socio-historical developmental progression from ethnicity to nationality (Fishman, 1965, 1972). But our recent experience has also sensitized us to the possibility of a rise in the saliency of ethnicity without the degree of purposive focus that is normally associated with nationality/nationalism being reached thereby. Certainly, little of the past decade's 'rebirth of ethnicity' has involved nationism (i.e. the aspiration for an independent state apparatus), one of the common goals of Western nationalisms in the pre and post World War I eras.

Previous to the most recent period in which a 'rebirth of ethnicity' is said to have occurred in many settings, many Western social theorists had foreseen the 'death of ethnicity'.[11] It is relative to their premature and widely published obituaries that the 'rebirth' appears to be particularly startling, if not disconcerting. Certainly that which is already dead (or inevitably destined to die) is not likely to be considered a worthy object of inquiry and analysis. Both of the paternity-derived metaphors — death and rebirth — reflect the strange passion with which matters relating to ethnicity are pursued. Clearly, ethnicity did not die in the West (and hence did not require a miraculous rebirth), but it had increasingly been lost sight of in view of the rise of other, more mobilized, sub-state and statewide collectivities which increasingly cut across ethnicity boundaries and elicited loyalties of their own (see Berger (1975) for an indication of these very circumstances in Western Europe). The very consolidation of the state-apparatus *per se* was not unrelated symbolically to ethnicity, but this consolidation also implied for many not only the disappearance of sub-state ethnicities but the disappearance of ethnicity *per se* at the policy level in advanced ('modern') political entities. Obviously, ethnicity has a quiet life, which is very 'congenial to its nature,' and which we must come to recognize if we are also to understand its periods of salience.[12]

Fundamentally, however, if we have recognized that ethnicity is variable in content and in constituency, then we have also come quite a way toward recognizing that it need not be mutually exclusive *vis-à-vis* other identities which may, at times, be more salient without thereby totally or irrevocably replacing ethnicity. Man's (and particularly modern man's) peculiar capacity for multiple loyalties, multiple identities and multiple memberships, apparently permits ethnicity to exist and coexist without being noticed either by actors, observers or analysts. It also permits both the rapid and the slow ethnification of collectivities initially formed on other bases and therefore underlies ethnogenesis, as Soviet, Chinese and American theoreticians have realized (Gellner, 1975; Bromley, 1974; Singer, 1962) and as both Plato and Aristotle anticipated in their dispute concerning the Guardians of the City, some 2500 years ago.

Recent speculation pertaining to ethnicity has become increasingly cognizant of the foregoing (see particularly Fox, 1974 and Brass, 1976). It has recognized that ethnicity in the West has generally ceased being a part of social structure (i.e. of persisting and normatively valid social relations) and has increasingly become part of social organization (i.e. of collective — often *ad hoc* — navigation or negotiation of the alternatives available within social structure). As a result, ethnicity has increasingly been utilized to cope with the breakdowns of Gesellschaft, to exploit the limitations in society's ability to cope with its problems on a rational, formalized, bureaucratized basis alone.

While the above pertains to the manipulability of ethnicity (our next topic), rather than merely to its presumed resurgence, it is worth pointing out that a small but persistent group of social theoreticians had always realized that 'Gemeinschaft has survived and is doing nicely' (Greeley, 1974), and that it was there precisely because Gesellschaft alone could not fill the very social vacuum that it tended to create.[13] Thus, there is an approach to recently renewed ethnic saliency which would attribute it to the very insensitivity to (or neglect of) ethnicity which is fostered by modern social organization with its stress on recruitment into the rational industrial system. The model of society implicit in such a view is a hydraulic one. Just as an ethnicity-stressing-society is viewed as possibly malfunctional because of its stress on the supra-rational (on mystic bonds based upon ultimate paternity and the obligations that these present for daily behavior), so a rationality-stressing-society is viewed as possibly malfunctional because of its neglect of the collective belongingness and intimacy needs of 'man in general' and of dislocated, dispossessed and exploited 'modern' man in particular (Berlin, 1972). Perhaps a less reductionistic formulation would be that history is not merely a record of 'the decline of community' but also a record of the recurring 'quest for community' (Nisbet, 1953) and in the course of both decline and quest ethnicity too will wax and wane (in saliency as well as change in content and in constituency).

The mutability of language is a truism in the language sciences and need hardly be stressed here. Mutability of membership in the speech (or speech and writing) community is also well-documented (Fishman, 1966, 1972). Mutability of language-salience particularly in conjunction with the shifting salience of ethnicity *per se,* has received less empirical attention, but that too is now beginning to be reversed (see e.g. Fishman & Hasbacher, 1965; Fishman, 1965, 1969). Perhaps the point that needs to be stressed is not only that the saliencies of language and ethnicity often co-vary but that they may also vary independently. We are examining a frequently occurring link rather than an inevitable one. The new stress on Black ethnicity brought forth some stress on Black English, but proportionately far less than did the stress on Macedonian ethnicity with respect to the Macedonian language (hitherto a rural variety of Bulgarian).

Obviously, the saliency of language in ethnicity is often related to perceived autonomy and historicity (Stewart, 1972) and to componential consciousness (Weinreich, 1980). Pidginization-creolization may long prolong such consciousness and, therefore, counteract language saliency (Fishman, 1973), but even this is manipulable and can be overcome. Heightened language consciousness not only mobilizes and solidifies the ethnicity collectivity but convinces its constituency that the language it honors is its true ancestral mother tongue, and, as such, is not only an embodiment of the ancestral genius but one worthy of further manipulation in order to make it even more authentically ancestral. Thus, mutability and manipulability are intimately and necessarily related to each other, in ethnicity, in language, and in the link between them.

The manipulation of ethnicity

Another shortcoming of hydraulic theories of ethnic saliency is that they do not adequately recognize the role of conscious purposiveness *vis-à-vis* ethnicity. Ultimately, hydraulic theories remain as mystic as the 'ethnic needs' for which they seek to account. Manipulation theories account for variation in the saliency of ethnicity on a much more testable and rational basis: ethnicity becomes salient when its activating suprarational power is recognized, organized and exploited. Such recognition, organization and exploitation are viewed as particularly modern developments fostered by a combination of modern circumstances.[14]

Premodern ethnicity is, so far as the ordinary actor is concerned, minimally self-conscious. At best, it recognizes ethnic categories; ethnic blocs for the purposive, instrumental exploitation of ethnicity are unknown. The phenomenology of premodern ethnicity is primarily a self-evident, inward-oriented theodicy. Ethnicity, as a highly conscious, instrumental, outward-oriented ideology, is abundantly in evidence in the Western world since the sixteenth century and in other parts of the world since the nineteenth century (Fishman, 1972) and is certainly characteristic of much of the 'rebirth of ethnicity' during the past decade or decade and a half. Indeed, for some students, the manipulation of ethnicity and its symbols towards political (i.e. power (re) distributing, resource (re) allocating) ends is the heart of the phenomenon of ethnicity *per se*, at least in its modern setting (Cohen, 1969, 1974a, b). The study of 'ethnic strategies' has been termed 'the sociological thrust' in the investigation of ethnicity (Cohen, 1969, 1974a, b; Tobias, 1973). Whether or not a full-fledged review of the literature would tend to confirm this characterization, it remains evident that ethnicity is not inherently a backward-looking ('past-oriented') appendage (as claimed by de Vos, 1975) but that it can be as activatable, purposive and dynamic as any other 'modern' collectivity rationale.

Economists, as well as sociologists and political scientists oriented toward economic realities as basic factors of modern life, have pointed to inter-regional economic discrepancies as generating and as preserving ethnicity differences (Deutsch, 1953, 1966; Hirschman, 1958; Hechter, 1971, 1973, 1974). Recent advances in communication opportunity and expectation have purportedly facilitated the mobilization of populations that are objectively or subjectively disadvantaged. Proto-élites whose change-over aspirations may have been stymied recognize and capitalize upon the potentialities for power as leaders of the bearers of a distinguished paternity and patrimony such as is 'really' theirs. When the class struggle and political action along class-related lines have proved themselves incapable of rectifying the inequities experienced by regio-ethnic collectivities, then ethnicity becomes an even more logical basis of instrumental organization (Van den Berghe, 1967; Glazer & Moynihan, 1975). Indeed, it is exactly when modern developments and processes — whether under capitalist or socialist auspices — have generally moved the bulk of the population ahead for many years under a given state apparatus, while no similar progress (economic, cultural, political) has been experienced by 'peripheral' collectivities, that the latter are particularly attracted to — and stand to benefit from — intensified and instrumentalized ethnicity (D. Bell, 1975). Thus, modern industrial economy, far from fostering meritocracy and a purely rationally and functionally organized society, merely initially depresses and finally changes (and accentuates) the function of ethnicity from inner-directed social intergration to outer-directed competition.[15]

The persistence of ethnicity cleavages in competitive modern societies is now coming to be viewed as a result of certain essential features of such societies themselves, features that were not at all foreseen by Parsons and his predecessors in the grand tradition of 'modern' Western social theory. Indeed, the advantages of ethnicity may grow (or at least grow at particular junctures), rather than shrink, under 'modern' urban conditions: advantages vis-à-vis getting ahead by wrestling from 'the system' more than would otherwise be derived in income, education, recognition and decision making (co)responsibility. The more 'modern' society is open to strangers (resident foreigners, migrants, immigrants, seasonal laborers), the more ethnicity must become one of the operational bases for the negotiations of these strangers with 'society at large', particularly if their social and economic assimilation is blocked and other forms of social action are controlled.[16] As a result, not only is it true, that ethnicity becomes more salient because it becomes more useful (or useful in a new way), but that there are particularly 'modern' conditions that lead to ethnicity becoming more salient and useful, perhaps alternatively to the utility of other bases of instrumental organization.

A few words of caution may be in order before leaving this topic. Instrumental manipulation theory represents an attempt to explain the variable saliency of ethnicity rather than to illumine ethnicity *per se*. It views ethnicity as exploitative, counter-exploitative or counter-reactive (Young, 1970). Its underlying model is not based upon hydraulics or cyclicality as much as upon reinfection and contagion. It is as if ethnicity were an old, infected wound which is often about to heal completely as a result of the plentiful introduction of rational antibiotics, only to have it become reinfected by contagion from outside sources or from the premature cessation of treatment. Essentially, the theory suffers from the fact that it is not ethnicity *per se* that is of concern to it but the recrudescence of less statusful, narrower, 'peripheral' identities. Thus, it is the disadvantaged, boundary threatened ethnicities that it particularly has in mind, rather than those of securer collectivities.[17]

On the other hand, instrumental manipulation theory identifies a major gap that existed in modern Western social theory as a whole, a major miscalculation of the possible usefulness of market-unrelated characteristics with respect to mobility in market-dominated societies. It is particularly the continuous utility for political leverage *vis-à-vis* changing social problems, of proportedly eternal and transcendental ethnicity experiences and symbols, that was not well understood. It was their capacity for organizing and heightening unconscious cosmologies, thereby raising them to the level of ideologies (that is, the conversion of quiescent ethnic phenomenology collectivities into dynamic ethnic ideology collectivities), that modern social theory did not anticipate — because of weaknesses within that theory that reach far beyond its handling of ethnicity — and that manipulation theories of ethnicity make clear. Finally, just as studies of the mutability of ethnicity indicate that there is generally an ethnic way of crossing-over, so studies of the in-strumentalization of ethnicity indicate that there are many acceptable *non*-ethnic means of heightening ethnicity. The mass media, political parties, economic associations, educational agencies and cultural agencies utilized by modern ethnicity movements, are derived neither from original paternity, patrimony nor phenomenology experiences. They are borrowed and adapted from across-the-boundary. In this sense, at least, 'modernization' not only feeds or exploits primordiality, but it also updates it. It leads it into the world of secular means and makes ethnicity a powerful contender in that arena. If, as a result, ethnicity is more 'alive' under 'modern' circumstances, it may also be more easily abandoned (as a result of its demystification) when and if its utility is no longer as great as other alternatives with which any and all instrumentalities are always compared. The bulk of modern social theory arose when such alternative instrumentalities (particularly those of class, market and state) were more productive of social mobility. The result was the well nigh complete misunderstanding and neglect of ethnicity. An exclusive focus on its instrumental nature today would be similarly one-sided and un-enlightening.

Just as the organized manipulation of ethnicity produces heightened ethnic consciousness and, therefore, nationality identity, so it can produce heightened language consciousness and language loyalty. Both processes can produce something far different from 'the original' paternity-dominated and patrimony-based point-of-departure. Nevertheless, phenomenologically the manipulated product is not only continuous with 'the original', but its bulwark, and resurrection, the preservation and intensification of its very heart and soul, inspired by its spirit and, in the eyes of the faithful, an inspiration for countless generations to come. The authenticity of these claims is of much more minor interest than their existence within a self-authenticating system. The ethnicity system is a self-confirming hypothesis. It fashions the powerful truths in which it believes and by their power is all the more able to make them come true.

Civility, rationality and individuality

The ethnicity literature abounds with the equation of ethnicity with irrationality, pre-rationality, emotionality and group-determined or collectivity-referenced bias. A good bit of the fear, opposition and rejection of ethnicity, both in the writings of the social theory masters as well as in the love–hate fascination for ethnicity of the past decade, can be explained on this basis. On strictly professional grounds scholars are not only intellectualizers and rationalizers themselves, but also champions of all that is intellectual and rational in society. For many, ethnicity shows clear signs of being 'counter-indicated' on this basis and therefore, is considered inimical to the perfection of society that many sociologists have consciously or unconsciously pursued.[18]

There are, of course, some protests to the contrary. Barth certainly implies that the complementarity of genuinely plural societies is a highly sensible and productive arrangement, far more so than the constant intergroup competitiveness of many begrudgingly pluralistic societies. Similarly, many of the discussions of the political or more generally instrumental capacities of modern ethnicity collectivities contain an embarrassed acknowledgement of their rationality in so far as attaining greater group mobility (or other desired goals) is concerned. Certainly both the organizational structures and the practical goals of 'neo-ethnicity' are very far from being 'breakdowns in modernization', as Fox (1975) has clearly indicated. Since ethnicity collectivities are rationally effective bases of organized action, since the relationship between such collectivities need be no more conflicted than are inter-group or intra-group relationships more generally (most of these also not being known for their lack of conflict, incivility or irrationality — see Merton, Coser and other theorists who recognize that conflict is endemic in social life), then we must conclude that much of the opposition to ethnicity is explainable on grounds other than, or in addition to, the 'irrationality' claim that is so often verbalized.[19]

One of the major dimensions underlying the rejection of ethnicity is the implicit model adapted by non-Marxist social science of the evolving and desired relationship between the individual and society. Parsons' equation of 'modernity' with the liberation or generalization of values from their earlier focus on fixed social positions is noteworthy in this connection. It is the individual who is (implicitly and explicitly) the locus of reality in American and many other 'modern' systems of values. The 'modern' experience, in:ellectually and socially, has been one of separating personal efficacy — the ultimate 'modern' value? — from descent and from other extra-individual characteristics. Strange as it may seem, Western sociology has generally not fostered a greater and more sympathetic understanding of the utility of collectivities, but, rather, has usually contributed instead to the widespread cult of the individual which has had such deep roots in Western life and in Western thought from the time of Wycliffe and particularly since the consolidation of capitalism and Protestantism. The individual's attributes, his mutability, his equality, his independence, his work effectiveness, his individuality as an ultimate good, these have occupied a more and more central and often unconscious role in Western thought. The origin of moral direction is from God to the individual directly — rather than from God to some collectivity (or representative of a collectivity) and thence to the individual — and 'each is endowed by his creator with certain inalienable rights, among these life, liberty and the pursuit of (individual!) happiness'. Individual virtue is individually rewarded. Group problem-solving comes up with no better solutions than that which would have been attained by the best individual working by himself (Lorge & Solomon, 1960). The evolution of man seems to move inexorably toward the freeing of man not only from community but even from society.

Actually, the rhetoric of recent advocates of ethnicity has turned much of the above rhetoric of ethnicity detractors on its head. Those who were wont to follow the French enlightenment in calling for the abolition of ethnicity as being representative of 'the power of the dead over the living' are now informed that it is the establishment that is dead and ethnicity that is alive, spontaneous, unfettered, spirited and beautiful (Graña, 1962). Those who disdain ethnicity as a form of 'group-think' are now informed that relative to the bureaucratic, meritricious, impersonalized nature of 'central society' ethnicity represents an enlightened form of participatory tours-meeting democracy, a breath of fresh air, the logos of the free spirit. Seemingly, there are many who sense that the differentiation of man has led to a society so rationalized as to bring about every bit as much a loss of autonomy via the operation of efficiency oriented institutions (whether under capitalist, communist, democratic or authoritarian auspices) as had been or would be brought about via real or mythical Gemeinschaften.

The contrast between deeply imbedded philosophical, intellectual and religious views such as the foregoing defenses of and opposition to ethnicity is not hard to see. Nevertheless, both opposition and defense often exaggerate the degree of dependency of the individual upon his collectivity which most ethnicity experiences require or presuppose, just as they exaggerate the actuality (rather than the myth) of individualism in non-ethnic society. Indeed, ethnicities do not so much glorify collectivities as a whole, in toto, as they point to exemplary individuals whom the community should emulate. Ethnic history is commonly the linking of generations via biologically linked individual models viewed as generational representatives. Thus, ethnicity links members to exemplary individuals fully as much as it links them to exemplary behaviors and exemplary thoughts.[20] Ethnicity certainly recognizes individual merit and demerit, rather than merely collective merit and demerit. Thus, while it is undoubtedly true that ethnicity involves a social contextualization and valorization of the individual (in terms of descent-related self-definitions, worldviews and values) this contextualization need not be collectivity-focused in any lemming-like, instinctual sense any more than any other socioculturally informed behavior. Indeed, the ethnicity experience itself may involve unavoidable strains between group solidarity and individual independence and the resolution of this strain should be a variable in the study of ethnicity rather than a foregone conclusion within that realm of discourse. The Hindu notion of the caste united by common paternity and invariant patrimony, and inextricably bound to a larger hierarchically articulated whole, and the Western vision of free-floating self-actualization may be equally extreme positions along a continuum.[21] There is no reason to think that ethnicity itself does not function comfortably across quite a range along this continuum, nor that the social personality and the social integration that it engenders when present in the same moderation as one would specify for sexual, religious, social class or political membership — are anything but positive essentials of society. Certainly, 'modernized' ethnicity seems to be just as able to accommodate to and to gratify the individuality strivings of its actors as it has recently demonstrated itself able to accommodate to and to gratify outward oriented strivings with which it had not previously been associated in Western social theory.

Just as the organized manipulation of language (language planning) does not imprison the tongue nor enslave the human verbosity (much writing and most speaking going on outside of its envisaged or attainable control), so organized manipulation of ethnicity does not begin to exhaust ethnicity *per se*. Within the pale of the normal, daily, routine ethnicity of the usual life cycle, there can exist not only the gratifying sense of meaningful community for which it is justly famous, but, largely unnoticed, civility, rationality and individuality, both in word and in deed, as well.

Conclusions

It is the thesis of this presentation that the recurring link between language and ethnicity cannot be fathomed without greater systematic familiarity with the nature, the mutability and the manipulability of ethnicity *per se*. Although the link is not an inevitable one it is clearly a highly likely one, both as a result of the general symbolic function of language as well as because of its specific implication in the paternity, patrimony and phenomenology dimensions of ethnicity experiences. These experiences deserve to be better understood, because to slight them and to jump immediately into the language-ethnicity link exposes us to all of the problems so unknowingly faced by much recent research and theory on the 'rebirth' of ethnicity. Neither the purported 'rebirth' nor the recurring 'link' can be well understood without explicating ethnicity as a seemingly valid explication of reality (as this chapter has attempted to do), on the one hand, and as a serious topic in the history of ideas, in the sociology of knowledge, and in the development of Western social theory (which still very much remains to be accomplished).

Ethnic collectivities will exist as long as human societies exist, and, indeed, new ethnic collectivities are constantly coming into being and old ones are continuously being rediscovered and refurbished. As long as this is so, languages will continue to be both symbolic of these collectivities and instrumental for them, with respect to their self-concepts, their antagonisms and their co-operative potentials. For most of humanity most of the time, the 'social condition' calls for both language and ethnicity, and social science, not to mention mankind in general, will just have to learn to live with both. A first step in that direction would be to understand them both better, separately as well as in combination. Hopefully this chapter is a modest contribution in that connection.

Acknowledgements

Prepared for an ACLS-sponsored conference on 'Ethnicity in Eastern Europe', University of Washington, Seattle, Washington, June 11–13, 1976. All rights reserved. I am indebted to the Institute for Advanced Study, Princeton, New Jersey, for typing and bibliographical assistance in the preparation of this paper during the 1975–76 academic year at which time I was a Member of its School of Social Science.

Notes to Chapter 2

1. The pained surprise of the professional sociologist, when faced by the recent apparent 'resurgence of ethnicity' in the USA, in various parts of Western Europe, and even more widely, is reminiscent of the profession's failure to either anticipate or account for the civil rights movement a decade and a half earlier. The earlier failure was poignantly and tellingly described as 'a failure of sociological imagination' by the then-president of the American Sociological Association (Hughes, 1963). The current failure to appreciate the continued role of ethnicity may be shared with anthropology and political science as well, both of which have had a greater ongoing awareness of crucial ethnic dimensions in social behavior, but neither of which anticipated (any more than did sociology) that these dimensions might still be so applicable to so much of 'modern' Western life. The term 'ethnicity' itself is traceable via the *OED* to 1772 (Nugent tr. *Hist. friar Gerund* I 332. 'From the curling spume of the celebrated Egean waves (,) fabulous ethnicity feigned Venus (,) their idolatress (,) conceived'). Einar Haugen (1975) has reported its earlier use in the professional social science literature to be 'as a synonym for the census term

"national origin", in two articles that appeared in 1950 (McGuire, 1950 and Hollingshead, 1950) this being three years earlier than the 1953 usage by D. Riesman mentioned by Glazer & Moynihan (1975). Haugen interprets the greater utility of the term, relative to 'national origin', as due to the fact that the latter 'could not be applied to Negroes or Jews, and even less to American Indians'. Thus, in modern American usage the term seems to avoid much of the sense of paganism or heathenism implicit in its etymology (*ethnos* being the Greek term most frequently used in the *Septuagint* to render the Hebrew 'goy': nation, people, particularly non-Jewish nations or peoples) and to 'cover' all those not included in the apparent ethnic unmarkedness of mainstream Anglo-American ('WASP') society (Nahirny & Fishman, 1975). For a similar contrast ('tribal brotherhood' *v.* 'universal otherhood'), in a much more restricted context, see Nelson (1949).

2.   Three major roadblocks that seem to have consistently plagued considerations of ethnicity in modern social theory are as follows (after Nahirny & Fishman, 1975):

(a) The roadblock in modern political theory is encountered in almost all basic works from Acton (mid-nineteenth century) to Kedourie (contemporary). This view relegates ethnicity to the role of despoiler of civility and modernity, thereby purportedly leading to non-rational extremism in political life. The W. Bell & Freeman (1974) and Cohen (1974) volumes have particularly large concentrations of studies reflecting this view. Although there is no denying that ethnicity has been manipulated for disruptive and conflictual purposes (as has religion, social class and every conceivable political view), it is, nevertheless, unfortunate to confuse the exploitation of ethnicity with the phenomenon of ethnicity *per se*. However, this confusion (tantamount to confusing sexuality with sexism) has deep roots in Western social theory and it is, therefore, necessary to ask when and why it arises, what other views and social developments accompany it, and what are the alternative views of ethnicity which this particular roadblock has sought to counteract, even as it has passed over what ethnicity indicates 'about the organization and integration of complex societies' (Fox, 1974).

(b) The roadblock in ideological outlook is probably most fully encountered in classical Marxian theory in which ethnicity is viewed, at best, as a mere byproduct of other, more basic factors, and as a 'survival of barbarism' at worst. The greatest scorn appears to be heaped upon the ethnicity of the powerless, i.e. upon those who have no state-apparatus of their own. Their collectivities are referred to as 'non-historical' and they are consigned to the Lumpengesindel (low rabble, tagrag), deemed to be without saving grace or future, and vilified for any possible deleterious effect they may have on the prophesied unification of the proletariat. The modern, less dogmatic expression of this roadblock is particularly noticeable in Glazer & Moynihan's (1975) volume, both in terms of the many authors who attempt to translate ethnicity into social class-differences, and in terms of the number that are deeply puzzled either as to why such translation cannot be negotiated theoretically or as to why events of the past decade did not permit this translation to occur in real life. The ideological rejection of ethnicity as a 'real' dimension of modern life not only does a disservice to the exploration of the topic (see, e.g. Hacker, 1976), but also completely overlooks theorists of various historical periods, most of whom have been almost entirely eclipsed in modern social theory (however, note Cuddihy, 1975), who have emphasized ethnicity to the virtual exclusion of all other factors. Somewhere between these two ideologically determined extremes — and practically unknown to Western social science — are the recent grapplings of Soviet and Chinese 'ethnographers' who simultaneously seek to study the endless mutability of ethnicity and to render its infinite adaptability commensurable with the demands of avowedly immutable ideology. Certainly, the need to reduce ethnicity to 'something else' requires and deserves careful analysis, as does the need to reduce everything else to ethnicity, because *any* juxtaposition of ethnicity and other factors facilitates hypotheses concerning the relative weight or power of both ethnicity and other factors under varying social and intellectual circumstances.

(c) Finally, the roadblock in conceptual level fosters the view that ethnicity is pertinent to minority groups alone, and, therefore, leads to consideration of it in connection with issues of discrimination and intergroup relations, rather than as an aspect of all traditional, large-scale self-identifying behavior. This roadblock, particulraly apparent in the de Vos & Romanucci-Ross (1975), Greeley (1974), Hunt & Walker (1974) and Dinnerstein & Reimers (1975) volumes, is the most unconscious and pervasive of all and requires particular historical treatment in order to render it both conscious as well as correctable. It shares with the political roadblock a focus on social disorganization and group manipulation. It shares with the economic determinism roadblock a conviction that ethnicity is but a reflection of 'something else' (in this case: discrimination or disadvantage). But, in addition to the foregoing, it has a focus of its own, namely on boundary phenomena and on contrastivity such that the 'heart of the matter' (ethnicity as realized when unthreatened by boundary-maintenance issues) remains unnoticed. By studying ethnicity only in groups struggling to overcome rejection this struggle and ethnicity *per se* have been spuriously confused.

The interrelatedness of all three of the above roadblocks, across modern political, ideological and conceptual approaches to social theory, deserves much patient exploration. Although additional types of roadblocks may well be discernible, and although combinations of those now discernible may yet be identifiable, the fact remains that for nearly two centuries the bulk of Western social theory has taken an implicitly anti-ethnicity stance. This stance has even denied to Western social theory — as applied to the West itself — the insights of the anthropological traditional gained from the study of ethnicity in pre-modern and small-scale collectivities, thus leaving modern society and modern social thought alike ill-prepared to fully understand the phenomenon of ethnicity or its seeming resurgence in Western society in recent years. The need for a thorough reconceptualization of the entire topic has come to be realized and indeed, has recently been called for by a few investigators (W. Bell, 1974; Berger *et al.*, 1975; Greeley, 1974; Hechter, 1973; Metzger, 1971).

In attempting to both trace and bypass the above roadblocks, Nahirny and I have embarked on a study of the role of ethnicity in Western social theory and in social behavior. The extent to which we view ethnicity as requiring socio-historical contextualization in order to be understood can be gauged from the following abbreviated outline of our current work:

I. 'Pre-modern' Views of Ethnicity in their Historical and Social Contexts
  1. Ancient Israel
    (a) Intra-ethnic subdivisions: tribes and their symbolic and functional replacements;
    (b) the distinction between Jewish and non-Jewish ethnicity (*'am* and *goy*) and the changing views of both, as society develops from pastoral to agricultural to urban stages;
    (c) the impact on Israelite ethnicity views of the diaspora: Babylon, Greece, Egypt;
    (d) the impact on Israelite ethnicity views of the confrontation with Christianity;
    (e) the 'ethnicity-as-extended kinship' view.
  2. Greece and Rome
    (a) Herodotus and the recognition of intra-Greek as well as Greek-Barbarian ethnic differences;
    (b) Plato and Aristotle, particularly the problem of whether the Guardians (of City government) should have ethnic loyalties;
    (c) Tacitus: Romans *v.* Barbarians;
    (d) Cicero;
    (e) the problem of social and physical distance (the Greek Diaspora and the Roman Empire): mother tongue? fatherland?;
    (f) continuation of 'kinship' symbolism.
  3. From the Church Fathers to the sixteenth Century
    (a) Early Christianity as a de-ethnicizing movement;
    (b) Christians as 'The Third People';
    (c) Eastern Christianity and the retention of ethnicity;
    (d) St. Augustine: ethnicity in the City of God;
    (e) Medieval Catholicism: The Christian Unity of Civilization (theory and practice);
    (f) Thomism and ethnicity;
    (g) problems of diversity: urban growth, Jews and other strangers, territoriality and personality principles in law;
    (h) ethnicity in Renaissance thought. Machiavelli, More, Erasmus;
    (i) Protestantism and ethnicity;
    (j) Lutheranist, Calvinist and Sectist/Mysticist social theory with respect to ethnicity;
    (k) 'kinship' — symbolism and its continuity.
II. The Role of Ethnicity in Modern Models of Society: Changes in Society and in Theory
    (a) Political and economic 'modernization' and its impact on daily life in Western Europe (particularly in England, France, Germany and the Low Countries) and on scholarship;
    (b) the social-evolutionary schemes of the French School: Rousseau, Comte, Durkheim;
    (c) the integrative role ascribed to the state, the economy and to religion and the corresponding abandonment of ethnicity in social theory. The Herderian protest;
    (d) Spencer, Toennies and Pareto;
    (e) Marx and proletarian solidarity as the real ethnicity;
    (f) Weber and the 'regretable but inevitable loss of Gemeinschaft';

(g) Gobineau, Gumplowitz and racism: ethnicity reduced to one dimension;

(h) Slavophile social thought: ethnicity as diffuse and enduring solidarity;

(i) Austro-Hungarian social democracy: The modernization of theories of ethnicity and the implementation of modern ethnic policies;

(j) Nationalism: The elephant that Western social theory overlooked;

(k) Linguistics and biology: academic bias and objectivity;

(l) Wundt, Freud, Jung and the social-psychology of ethnicity;

(m) Frazer, Levi-Strauss and the avoidance of ethnicity as Western anthropology looks at the West;

(n) Parsons and the rejection of ethnicity in American social science.

III. Attempts at New Societal Models: Dissatisfaction with Society and with Social Theory

(a) Ethnicity theory in modern Soviet and Chinese ethnografia: change and stability;

(b) mini-theory prompted by the recent 'rebirth of Ethnicity' in the USA and Western Europe.

IV. Concluding Integrative Formulations:

All in all, we can but echo W. Bell's observation that 'ethnicity is a research topic of central interest which has still unfulfilled potential for development into systematic and unified theory' (1974).

The evolving, recurring and differing views and theories of ethnicity that have come before should tell us much about social change and social integration, as well as about ethnicity per se, and, therefore, in the final analysis, they should provide us with insight into ethnicity as an avenue of social orientation and social organization. On the basis of all of the foregoing, it should be possible to build a more systematic model of ethnicity-in-society, perhaps one that recognizes it as simultaneously but varyingly operative in the familial-personal bonds of which the ancients spoke most (i.e. in the Gemeinschaft or primitive collectively, but not only in such), in the functional bonds of which the moderns speak so much (i.e. in the Gesellschaft or civil collectively, but not only in such), and in the ideological-symbolic bonds which have generally been rather overlooked by Western social theory (i.e. in the ideological collectively, but not only in such). Perhaps all of these bonds are constantly and everywhere operative, albeit in differing degrees and with greater or lesser salience under particular societal circumstances which a social-historical review will particularly enable us to recognize.

3.   Use of the term self-recognition is deliberate here, so as not to imply a high level of (ethnic) consciousness as an invariant aspect of ethnicity. Indeed, consciousness of ethnicity is itself a crucial *variant* in any theory of ethnicity and, as such, it should not be posited as *invariant*. Specifically, self-recognition is used here to avoid the implication of the heightened state of awareness which the terms 'identity' or 'consciousness' imply.

Furthermore, 'ethnic identity' requires extensive psychological exploration (see, e.g. de Vos & Romanucci-Ross, 1975), whereas it is particularly the socio-cultural analysis of ethnicity to which this chapter is directed. In addition, much of the psychological work on identity has been focused on childhood and adolescence (however, note Erikson's study of Gandhi (1969) in comparison to his earlier work on Luther (1958) and on identity, youth and crisis more generally (1968), rather than on adulthood). This fact also tends to make 'identity' less useful for our purposes here since adults are also likely to be active in re-interpreting ethnic membership, content and saliency.

4. Because of its biological basis ethnicity must be conceptually related to, as well as differentiated from, both 'race' and 'caste'. Many of the characteristics of ethnicity that follow in this discussion help us to do just that. To anticipate: both 'race' and 'caste' are even more biologically polarized than is ethnicity and, therefore, lack most of the escape hatches and the patrimony stress (with all of its transitional possibilities) available to ethnicity. In short, ethnicity is more *behavioral* than race and less *hierarchical* than caste, and, therefore, it is ultimately less frozen than either the one or the other, notwithstanding its biological foundations. Both race and ethnicity are interpreted in terms of local history to such an extent that W. Bell rightly observes that neither 'can be fully understood within the boundaries of a single society' (1974). The relationship of *ethnicity* to *race* currently seems more distant in English, particularly in American English, than it is felt to be in French, Spanish, Italian or various other European languages in which an expression such as 'the French race' is quite possible and acceptable (Petersen, 1975). Some 50 years ago such an expression was also not unusual in American English usage. (Even today, English usage such as the following is encountered: 'Already at the dawn of history the (Irish) language had welded us into a people apart . . . and . . . made possible our unexampled resistance in later times . . . (and) the intellectual, moral, social and aesthetic endeavours of our race . . . through . . . long, fruitful ages of mutual interaction . . . the Irish mind and the Irish language grew . . . into one another with the exquisite delicacy of adjustment characteristic of organic things' (Brennan, 1969). Note the use of 'race' to denote the Irish, as well as the 'organic' reference pertaining not only to their 'mind' but to their language.) The Negro-White race issue and Nazi racial policy have both served in recent years to surround the term 'race' with far more opprobrium than is connected with the term ethnicity, although the conceptual proximity of the latter to the former is, at times, polemically exploited (Zolberg, 1973). For a reminder of how racial theories and language theories came together in nineteenth century Europe, see Said (1976).

5. Following Schneider (1969, 1972) it is probably desirable to place kinship in parentheses ('kinship') in order to stress that it is the view rather than the reality with which we are concerned. For a variety of 'kinship' quotations spanning centuries of Western social theory pertaining to ethnicity, see Nahirny & Fishman (1975). For the role of the paternity-kinship notion in medieval Western political/statist history — in which the state itself, based on ethnic origins, becomes a corpus mysticum — see Kantorowicz (1950-51). Smith, who focusses primarily on Caribbean and African plural societies stresses the restriction of 'connubium' as the ultimate basis of ethnic differentiation (1969a,b). For the interpretation of 'kinship' and neighbourhood notions, see Stea & Soja (1975). For the political/power significance of 'kinship', see Sweet (1975) and, particularly McWilliams (1973) who points out that 'the terms of kinship are written on the gates which guard the mysteries of politics . . . Our strongest descriptions of relations between men are analogies to kinship'.

6. The possible isomorphism of culture and ethnicity is also a matter of degree,

being greater for small-scale, pre-modern collectivities. The separations between religion and knowledge, nationality and citizenship, morality and science, purpose and authority which increasingly mark 'modern' life have their counterpart in the increasing separation between ethnicity and the rest of culture as society becomes increasingly 'rationalized' in terms of efficiency and power considerations (Cuddihy, 1975). This separation contributed to the illusion (so prevalent among nineteenth century theorists) that ethnicity had died or been dispensed with entirely in the West. Similarly, the early greater identity between ethnicity and culture led (and leads) to the opposite view among many anthropologists studying small, pre-modern societies, many of whom conclude(d) that culture and ethnicity are necessarily isomorphic.

7.   This is not to say that ethnicity does not permit sub-ethnicities, for it does. However, each of these, in turn, includes both a paternity dimension experience and a patrimony dimension experience. Thus, the above discussion must be understood as pertaining to a particular level of ethnicity. For a discussion of how ethnic sub-identities fractionate or combine into new superordinate ethnicities, see Horowitz (1975). The ethnicity-sub-ethnicity distinction is not necessarily a mutually accepted one, and, furthermore, the 'part' may be viewed as *more* (rather than necessarily as *less*) statusful than the whole, either in general or in particular situations. Some examples of part-whole and greater-lesser status ambiguity are: Italian-Sicilian, Indonesian-Japanese, French-Occitan, Southerner-Texan, etc. Sub-ethnicity utilizes the metaphor of 'distant-kin' and, therefore, may involve a felt contradiction (can one be both distant and proximate?) as well as rivalry with respect to 'real'/spurious paternity and patrimony. If sub-ethnicity weakens the 'larger', ethnicity may either weaken as well or may be strengthened thereby, depending on the casual factors involved and on the drift of re-identification. Both the Hispanic and the Arab worlds contain numerous widely differing interpretations of whether a simple ethnicity-plus-sub-ethnicities or multiple separate ethnicities are felt to obtain. The ethnicity-sub-ethnicity distinction is often 'objectively' ambiguous for reasons of uncertain level of analysis, not unlike those which are worrisome in social research more generally.

       Note, for example, the differing interpretations of Baron (1952) and deVaux (1961) as to the impact of settlement in agricultural Canaan upon the ancient Israelite tribal sub-ethnicities. Baron concludes that tribalism, which he believes to have been *muted* in favor of a single collective ethnicity by confrontation with common enemies in the Arabian desert, regained the upperhand as a result of the regionalism prompted by sedentary agriculture in the absence of external threat. deVaux, on the other hand, concludes that tribal organization, which he believes to have been *strengthened* by desert warfare and by the conquest of Canaan, became superfluous in the early post-conquest agricultural setting and that clans and families then came to the fore. Thus, both agree on the direction of change in ethnic organization, from larger scale toward smaller scale, but disagree as to which level of scale was dominant in early post-conquest days.

8.   Among the components of experienced ethnicity that best reveal the frequent tension between its paternity and its patrimony dimensions, are language and territory. Both are widely interpretable as inherited *and* God-given (Kantorowicz, 1950-51.). Both are widely recognized as learned *and* earned and, therefore, as necessarily relearnable *and* re-earnable generation after

generation (Weber, 1964; Deutsch, 1975). The traditional Jewish view of the detachability of both language and territory from ethnicity, even though both are viewed as highly important attributes, deserves to be traced through the Western legal and social science tradition, because of its possible influence in connection with State implementation of the territoriality *vs.* the personality principle in ancient and medieval law and religion. For a recent publication that assumes ethnicity and territory to be two quite separate (rather than merely separable) entities, see Suttles (1970). For an unexpectedly close relationship between land and language among three Iroquoi nations, see Oliviero (1976): '. . . their land . . . is part of their culture and language. All ceremonies revolve around Mother Earth (Informant 1:5)'.

9. This treatment of the phenomenology of ethnicity as a meaning system is highly indebted to Tobias (1973). I am also grateful to Tobias for several stimulating discussions of ethnicity during the 1975-76 academic year during which we were both at IAS. Others to whom I am indebted for their helpful questions and comments are Keith Basso, Vladimir Nahirny and Judith Guskin.

10. A typical view, somewhat more muted than others, is that of Morris (1968). 'Ruth Benedict said . . . it is not *race* that we need to understand, but *conflict*; so, for an understanding of ethnic groups in a social system, it is not on racial or cultural differences that we need to focus our attention, but on group relations'. The implied congruence between *conflict* and *group relations* should be noted, as well as the assumption that it is obviously more productive to study *ethnic groups* than *ethnicity*, and ethnic groups with *in a single social system* rather than the separate cultural, historical, comparative, economic or other aspects of such groups. Neither the paternity, patrimony, nor phenomenology dimensions of ethnicity experience is recognized. Boundary issues are immediately defined as *the* basic issues, thus implying that highly bounded groups are either the only ethnicity collectivities or the only ones worthy of study. Each of these assumptions involves a very marked narrowing of the field and, together, they go far toward explaining (a) the self-imposed conceptual and theoretical impoverishment of much ethnicity research, and (b) the well nigh complete disappearance of ethnicity considerations from the formulation of general social theory. For a recent de-emphasis of boundaries, particularly in connection with the study of a large and secure ethnic collectivity in quiet times, see Gorer (1975). Schwartz (1975), on the contrary, is among the most recent emphasizers of boundaries, asking 'why is all this (ethnicity) necessary? What is the problem? Perhaps all we need . . . (for ethnicity to appear) is the existence of more than one individual, and, beyond this, more than one . . . group of people'. In this respect, he was anticipated by Horwitz (1971) who well expressed the view that boundaries intensify all ethnicity experiences. A generalization of the 'boundary' issue in the study of ethnicity is the 'comparative' issue in social research more generally. The assumption that any referent (group, culture, class, etc.) can best be 'understood' by comparison with a contrastive referent merits more reflection than it has commonly received.

11. At the time that he made it (1966), few American sociologists would have disagreed with Parsons' analysis that '. . . the universalistic norms of society have applied more and more widely. This has been true of all the main bases of particularistic solidarity, ethnicity, religion, regionalism, state's rights and class . . . Today, more than ever before, we are witnessing an acceleration in

the emancipation of individuals of all categories from these diffuse particularistic solidarities (p. 739)'. Parsons' embarrassment re the above prediction is evident in his 1975 attempt to explain (or rather explain away) the 'rebirth' of ethnicity which Lawrence Stone has recently (1976) included among the phenomena which he has recognized as part of 'a new cycle of the sacred.'

12. I would like to note Clifford Geertz's observation (personal conversation) that until very recently North African Moslem villagers had no notion of their ethnicity, whereas their 'Moslemness' was very apparent to them. Geertz claims that villagers referred to themselves and to one another simply as clan members or as village members and that any notion of being Arabs (not to say Moroccans) was quite foreign to them. He is careful to stress that the latter notions were (more) common (and dynamically so) among urban and educated populations for whom Moslemness was usually (not always) also a prime marker. I would like to add in this connection, that the separation between ethnicity and religion in Islam (as in Orthodox Judaism) is a quite recent and only partially realized one, and that the self-evident, unnamed and unnamable ethnicity of Geertz's North African Moslem villagers agrees fully with my own observations and assumptions concerning unmobilized and unthreatened ethnicity more generally. Finally, in view of the variability that inevitably characterizes ethnicity experiences/behaviors (every bit as much as it characterizes all experience/behavior), mutability of content, membership and saliency may be expected to be particularly great for populations at lower levels of mobilization, thus explaining the discrepancies that often arise between 'the labeled' and 'the labelers' (Moerman, 1965, 1968; Arens, 1975), particularly if they are operating at different levels of abstraction and with different biases (including ethnicity awareness and its accompanying terminological and conceptual fields).

Although experiencing and labeling are not one and the same, at least three levels of 'naming' come into play in connection with the latter: the self-label of members' ethnicity of any collectivity, the label that members of a given ethnicity collectivity utilize for members of another given ethnicity collectivity, and, finally, the label that the purportedly objective, outside ('scientific'?) observer utilizes (particularly when he is building a general theory). The labels used may not be in agreement either when compared at any one point in time, or when compared across time. Such disagreements are most obvious if they result in the *same* collectivities being assigned *different* aspects of paternity, patrimony and/or phenomenology. Indeed, discrepancies such as these are, in part, a result of the mutability of the dimensions of the ethnicity experience *per se*, rather than merely a result of the different perspectives ('levels') from which these may be regarded or as a result of the different weightings that may be assigned to them singly or in combination. However, the problem of 'all too ready' labels in search of convenient referents is one that is by no means unique to the study of ethnicity and, indeed, is a problem which is recognizable in every aspect of our everyday lives. Nevertheless, consensuses are reached (albeit sometimes erroneously) in interpreting most of the ambiguities of phenomena of everyday life, and they are equally reached in interpreting the phenomena of ethnicity. At the state of heightened ethnicity, disagreements in labeling are far fewer than they may have been previously, this in itself representing temptation for the student of ethnicity to study it only in its more salient circumstances.

13. On the whole, sociology's morbid fascination with the 'death of Gemeinschaft' is rivaled only by urban anthropology's strident assertion that it is still 'alive and well' in Paris, London and New York (not to mention Nairobi, New Delhi and Lima). Greeley has most recently formulated a balanced view in this connection: 'Because whole new areas of relationships have been created it does not follow that old forms have been eliminated. It merely means that they no longer exhaust the totality of life. When it comes to . . . role relationships where either intimacy or trust are involved, there is still a strong tendency to choose people to whom we can say in effect 'Your mother knew my mother' . . . Informal and primary relationships survive in an industrial, contractual society . . . They provide the very stuff out of which the society is created and the cement that keeps it from coming apart . . . Because they provide self-definition and also a substructure within the larger society, ethnic groups are a strong positive asset' (1974). Note that while Greeley is still thinking of ethnicity in terms of minority groups, his basic notions can be transferred to ethnicity in the mono-ethnic or boundary-distant context as well.

14. In between the hydraulic and purposive models of ethnic saliency there are also more complex cyclical theories. One of these is Wallace's (1968) which is particularly concerned with nativism and revivalism. Although Wallace recognizes change in the saliency of a heritage, and recognizes organized or manipulated efforts as being the primary forces in connection with such changed saliency, his work is primarily concerned with small, non-Western societies that have been extremely dislocated by Western influences. More basically, however, his theory pertains to religio-cultural change more generally (even more generally than in cases of nativism and revivalism) rather than the changes in the salience of ethnicity *per se*. Hansen's law of the 'return' of the third generation is another cyclical theory, but one that is closer to the ethnicity experience *per se* (see Nahirny & Fishman, 1965; Bender & Kagiwada, 1968).

15. This competitive-combative feature of manipulated ethnicity has strengthened both the status quo-('civility')-protecting rejection of ethnicity as well as the Marxist revolutionary rejection of ethnicity (except, transitionally, when it is in the integrative service of the proletariat). Plax (1972) reveals the possibility that investigators may prefer to study heightened/salient ethnicity because it is easier for them to do so than to study its more quiescent manifestations. Thus, investigator ease and investigator bias may both reinforce each other and at the same time further the 'negative image' of ethnicity in intellectual circles.

16. In this very context, ethnicity collectivities are viewed as engendered by and useful for the conflicted nature of all society and of modern plural society in particular (Rex, 1959). Solidarity becomes a prerequisite for combating prior or 'other' solidarity, and ethnicity is viewed as solidarity ready-made and waiting to be activated. In connection with this activization (manipulation) process, Brass (1976) correctly points out that 'boundaries are made sharper, . . . old symbols acquire new subjective significance, and . . . attempts are made to bring a multiplicity of symbols and attributes in to congruence with each other'. This observation is applicable to language as well. Finally, in connection with the purposive manipulation of ethnicity, the alternating selection between broader and narrower options should be mentioned. The situational factors in choosing between Monhegan and American Indian ethnicity have been studies by Hicks & Kertzer (1972) and those involved in

choosing between Cape Verdean, Portugese and Black ethnicity have been studied by Baxter (1971).

17. The manipulation of such ethnicities has also been studied by experimental social psychologists whose concern has been to influence (foster, improve, strengthen) the self-concepts of minority group members via translating their lower 'statuses' into more effective competitive 'processes'. The work of Banks (1978) may be seen as an effort to translate Black patrimony into situational-contextual-interactional factors which tend to enable Blacks to perform as well or better than Whites. In actuality, all memberships, ethnic or otherwise, are simultaneously status and processes. As a result, process characteristics are potentially always available to attain change in status characteristics.

18. Mead (1975) states this in characteristically straightforward fashion: 'The right to a distinctive culture and language, to a distinctive adaptation to the environment . . . has conflicted and conflicts today with the egalitarian individualistic doctrines of the Protestant founders of the United States'. Her paper pertains primarily to ethnic minorities within the USA, but also to small cultures everywhere now arriving at the brink of modernity. For both of these, membership in the dominant (world) culture is defined on the basis of material success on the one hand and 'abstention from foreign ways, foreign food, foreign ideas, foreign accents, foreign vices' (p. 189), oñ the other hand. Mead is uncertain whether the 'melting pot' or 'pluralism' will or should triumph. Devereux (1975) is far less ambivalent. His attack on any and all ethnicity, whether of minorities or majorities, is the most blistering of any to appear in recent years. His rejection of ethnicity is fully conceptualized along the dimension of individuality (which is but a transmutation of the civility roadblock referred to in note 3): for he views it as 'prima facie evidence of the impending collapse of the only valid sense of identity: one's differentness, which is replaced by the most archaic pseudo-identity imaginable' (1975). It is obviously Devereux whom de Vos, in the same volume, has in mind, when he takes to task those who 'mistakenly assume that individuation or autonomy means a lack of allegiance to any group. They fail to see that modern man is also searching for meaning and ultimate units of social belonging and (for) a sense of survival through such belonging' (1975).

19. I intend neither to 'psychoanalyse' social scientists in general or social theorists in particular, nor to enquire whether their own life experiences (often including an escape from ethnicity or a cross-over experience) may not have led them to their prevalent negativeness toward ethnicity. Efforts along such lines would not be unproductive, but would not be particularly innovative, since there are many prior indications that social science (including this very discussion) is inevitably biased by the forces upon its practitioners (Ravetz, 1971).

20. Tobias (1973) points out the greater stress of certain ethnicity cosmologies toward principles (phenomenologies) (e.g. The Buddhist-Thai) and the greater orientation of others toward paternity and patrimony (Confucian-Chinese). These differences should be examined in terms of the historical and sociocultural factors from which they may have resulted.

21. See Zijderveld (1970) for a critique of 'emotional agnosticism', described as a definitely anti-ethnic and yet irrational departure from 'ascetic intellectualism'. The value of his paper resides in its reminder that free-floating impulse release can be every bit as irrational as ethnic group-relatedness (and may even be more so, from the point of view of social effectiveness).

References

ARENS, W. 1975, The social history of an ethnic group, *Africa* 45, 426–37.

BANKS, W. C. 1978, Toward a reconceptualization of the social-cognitive bases of Black achievement orientations, *Review of Educational Research.* 48, 381–97.

BARON, S. W. 1952, *A Social and Religious History of the Jews.* Vol. I., New York: Columbia University Press.

BARTH, F. 1969, Introduction. In F. BARTH (ed.), *Ethnic Groups and Boundaries.* pp. 9–38. Boston: Little, Brown and Co.

BAXTER, D. 1971, *Ethnic Identity and Social Organization among the Portugese of New Bedford, Massachusetts.* Ms., Department of Anthropology, Brandeis University.

BEER, Wm. R. 1975, The social class of ethnic activists in contemporary France. Paper presented at the Conference on Ethnic Pluralism and Conflict in Contemporary Western Europe and Canada, Cornell University, May. (Department of Sociology, Brooklyn College — CUNY.)

— 1976a, Ethnicity and the linguistic factor in France. Paper prepared for the Annual Meeting of the American Sociological Association, August. (Department of Sociology, Brooklyn College — CUNY.)

— 1976b, *Ethnic Activists in Contemporary France: Social Class and Social Mobility.* (Ms., Department of Sociology, Brooklyn College — CUNY.)

BELL, D. 1975, Ethnicity and social change. In N. GLAZER & D. P. MOYNIHAN (eds), *Ethnicity: Theory and Experience.* pp. 141–74. Cambridge, Massachusetts: Harvard University Press.

BELL, W. 1974, Comparative research on ethnicity: a conference report, *SSRC Items* 28, 4, 61–64.

BELL, W. & FREEMAN, W. E. (eds) 1974, *Ethnicity and Nation-Building.* Beverly Hills: Sage.

BENDER, E. I. & KAGIWADA, G. 1968, Hansen's Law of 'Third generation return' and the study of American religio-ethnic groups, *Phylon* 39, 360–70.

BERGER, S. E. *et al.* 1975, New perspectives for the study of Western Europe, *SSRC Items* 29, 34–37.

BERLIN, I. 1972, The bent twig: a note on nationalism, *Foreign Affairs* 51. 11–30.

BRASS, P. R. 1976, Ethnic groups and nationalities: The formation, persistence and transformation of ethnic identities over time. Paper prepared for the Conference on Ethnicity in Eastern Europe, University of Washington, Seattle. June 1976.

BROMELY, Y. V. 1974, *Soviet Ethnology and Anthropology (Studies in Anthropology* I). The Hague: Mouton.

CARE, N. S. 1973. On fixing social concepts, *Ethics* 84, 10–21.

COHEN, A. 1969, Political anthropology: The analysis of the symbolism of power relations. *Man* 4, 217–35.

— 1974a, *Two-Dimensional Man: An Essay on the Anthropology of Power and Symbolism in Complex Society*. London: Routledge and Kegan Paul.

— 1974b, The lesson of ethnicity. In A. COHEN (ed.), *Urban Ethnicity*. pp. 9–24. London: Tavistock Publications.

CUDDIHY, J. M. 1975, *The Ordeal of Civility*. New York: Basic Books.

DESHEN, S. 1974, Political ethnicity and cultural ethnicity in Israel during the 1960's. In A. COHEN (ed.), *Urban Ethnicity*. pp. 281–309. London: Tavistock Publications.

— 1975, *Ethnic Boundaries and Cultural Paradigms: The Case of Southern Tunisian Immigrants in Israel*. (Ms., Department of Anthropology, Bar Ilan University.)

DEUTSCH, A. W. 1975, Reflections on the complexity of the concept 'ethnicity'. In S. POLL & E. KRAUSZ (eds), *On Ethnic and Religious Diversity in Israel*. Ramat Gan, Bar Ilan University.

DEUTSCH, K. W. 1953, (1966). *Nationalism and Social Communication: An Inquiry into the Foundations of Nationality*. Cambridge: MIT Press.

DE VAUX, R. 1961, *Ancient Israel: Its Life and Institutions*. (Translated from French by JOHN MCHUGH.) New York: McGraw-Hill.

DEVEREUX, G. 1975, Ethnic identity: Its logical foundations and its dysfunctions. In G. DE VOS & L. ROMANUCCI-ROSS (eds), *Ethnic Identity: Cultural Continuities and Change*. pp. 42–70. Palo Alto: Mayfield.

DE VOS, G. 1975, Ethnic pluralism: conflict and accommodation. In G. DE VOS & L. ROMANUCCI-ROSS (eds), *Ethnic Identity: Cultural Continuities and Change*. pp. 5–41. Palo Alto: Mayfield.

DE VOS, G. & ROMANUCCI-ROSS, L. 1975a, Ethnicity: Vessel of meaning and emblem of contrast. In G. DE VOS & L. ROMANUCCI-ROSS (eds), *Ethnic Identity: Cultural Continuities and Change*. pp. 363–90. Palo Alto: Mayfield.

— 1975, Preface. In G. DE VOS & L. ROMANUCCI-ROSS (eds), *Ethnic Identity: Cultural Continuities and Change*. pp. 5–6. Palo Alto: Mayfield.

DINNERSTEIN, L. & REIMERS, D. M. 1975, *Ethnic Americans: A History of Immigration and Assimilation*. New York: Dodd-Mead.

DRUMMOND, L. 1975, Making a difference: a symbolic analysis of intergroup relations in Guyana. Paper presented at the meeting of the American Anthropological Association, San Francisco, December (Department of Anthropology, University of Montana).

ERIKSON, E. H. 1958, *Young Man Luther*. New York: Norton.

— 1968, *Identity: Youth and Crisis*. New York: Norton.

— 1969, *Gandhi's Truth*. New York: Norton.

FISHMAN, D. E. 1976, 'Am and goy as Designations for Ethnicity in the Pentateuch. (Ms., Erna Michael College of Jewish Studies, Yeshiva

University.); revised and expanded J. A. FISHMAN *et al.* (1985) *The Rise and Fall of the Ethnic Revival*. Berlin: Mouton de Gruyter, pp. 15–38 (with RENA MAYERFELD and J. A. FISHMAN).

FISHMAN, J. A. 1960, A systematization of the Whorfian hypothesis, *Behavioral Science*, 5, 323–39.

— 1965, Varieties of ethnicity and language consciousness, *Monograph Series on Languages and Linguistics* (Georgetown University), 18, 69–79.

— 1966, (ed.) *Language Loyalty in the United States*. The Hague: Mouton.

— 1969, Puerto Rican intellectuals in New York: some intragroup and intergroup contrasts, *Canadian Journal of Behavioral Science*, 1, 215–26. Also this volume, part V.

— 1972, *Language and Nationalism: Two Integrative Essays*. Rowley, Massachusetts: Newbury House. Also this volume, parts I and III.

— 1973, The phenomenological and linguistic pilgrimage of Yiddish: (Some examples of functional and structural pidginization and de-pidginization). *Kansas Journal of Sociology*, 9, 127–36.

— 1977, The sociology of language: Yesterday, today and tomorrow. In R. COLE (ed.), *Current Issues in Linguistic Theory: Invited Lectures at the 1975 Summer Linguistic Institute*. pp. 51–75. Indiana University Press.

FISHMAN, J. A. & HESBACHER, P. 1965, Language loyalty: Its functions and concomitants in two bilingual communities, *Lingua* 13, 145–65.

FISHMAN, J. A. & SPOLSKY, B. 1976, unpublished.

FOX, R. G. 1974, *Ethnic Nationalism and the City*. Application for NSF Grant. Mimeo., Department of Anthropology, Duke University.

— 1975, *Industrial Urbanism and the Development of Ethnicity*. Application for renewal of NSF Grant. Mimeo., Department of Anthropology, Duke University.

GAMBINO, R. 1975, *Blood of My Blood: The Dilemma of the Italian-Americans*. New York: Doubleday.

GEERTZ, C. 1963, The integrative revolution: primordial sentiments and civil politics in the new states. In C. GEERTZ (ed.), *Old Societies and New States: The Quest for Modernity in Asia and Africa*. pp. 105–57. New York: Free Press.

— 1973, *The Interpretation of Cultures*. New York: Basic Books.

GELLNER, E. 1975, The Soviet and the savage, *Current Anthropology* 16, 595–601.

GITTLER, J. B. 1974, Cultural pluralism in contemporary American society: An analysis and a proposal, *International Journal of Group Tensions* 4, 322–45.

GLAZER, N. & MOYNIHAN, D. P. 1975, Introduction. In N. GLAZER & D. P. MOYNIHAN (eds), *Ethnicity: Theory and Experience*. pp. 1–26. Cambridge, Massachusetts: Harvard University Press.

GLUCKMAN, M. 1965, *Custom and Conflict in Africa*. Oxford: Blackwell.

GORDON, M. M. 1975, Toward a general theory of racial and ethnic group relations. In N. GLAZER & D. P. MOYNIHAN (eds), *Ethnicity: Theory and Experience*. pp. 84–110. Cambridge, Massachusetts: Harvard University Press:

GORER, G. 1975, English identity over time and empire. In G. DE VOS & L. ROMANUCCI-ROSS (eds), *Ethnic Identity: Cultural Continuities and Change*. pp. 156–72, Palo Alto: Mayfield.

GRAÑA, C. 1962, Cultural nationalism: the idea of historical destiny in Spanish America, *Social Research* 29, 395–418.

GREELEY, A. 1974, *Ethnicity in the United States: A Preliminary Reconnaissance*. New York: Wiley.

HACKER, A. 1976, Cutting classes, *New York Review* 4, 15–17.

HAUGEN, E. 1975, Language and ethnicity. Paper presented at the Canada-Iceland Centennial Conference, Winnipeg, October 1975. (Programme in Scandinavian Languages and Literatures, Harvard University, 1975).

HECHTER, M. 1971, Towards a theory of ethnic change, *Politics and Society*, 2, 21–45.

— 1973, The persistence of regionalism in the British Isles, 1885–1966, *American Journal of Sociology* 79, 319–42.

— 1974, The political economy of ethnic change, *American Journal of Sociology* 79, 1151–78.

HICKS, G. L. & KERTZER, D. 1972, Making a middle way: problems of Monhegan Identity, *Southwestern Journal of Anthropology* 28, 1–24.

HIRSCHMAN, A. O. 1958, *The Strategy of Economic Development*. New Haven: Yale University Press.

HOLLINGSHEAD, A. N. 1950, Cultural factors in the selection of marriage mates, *American Sociological Review* 15, 619–27.

HOROWITZ, D. L. 1971, Three dimensions of ethnic politics, *World Politics* 23, 232–44.

— 1975, Ethnic Identity. In N. GLAZER & D. P. MOYNIHAN (eds), *Ethnicity: Theory and Experience*. pp. 111–40. Cambridge, Massachusetts: Harvard University Press.

HUGHES, E. 1963, Race relations and the sociological imagination, *American Sociological Review* 28, 879–90.

HUNT, C. L. & WALKER, L. 1974, *Ethnic Dynamics: Patterns of Intergroup Relations in Various Societies*. Homewood, Ill: Dorsey.

ISAJIW, W. W. 1974, Definitions of ethnicity, *Ethnicity* 1, 111–24.

KANTOROWICZ, E. H. 1950-51, *Pro Patria Mari* in medieval political thought, *American Historical Review* 56, 472–92.

KNUTSSON, K. E. 1969, Dichotomization and integration. In F. BARTH (ed.), *Ethnic Groups and Boundaries: The Social Organization of Cultural Differences*. pp. 86–100. Boston: Little, Brown and Co.

KUPER, L. 1969, Ethnic and racial pluralism: some aspects of polarization and depluralization. In L. KUPER & M. G. SMITH (eds), *Pluralism in Africa*. pp. 459–87. Berkeley and Los Angeles: University of

California Press.

LEVENSON, J. R. 1971, *Revolution and Cosmopolitanism: The Western Stage and the Chinese Stages*. Berkeley, CA.: University of California Press.

LORGE, I. & SOLOMON, H. 1960, Group and individual performance in problem solving related to previous exposure to problem, level of aspiration, and group size, *Behavioral Science* 5, 28–38.

MACINTYRE, A. 1973, The essential contestability of some social concepts, *Ethics* 84, 1–9.

MCGUIRE, C. 1950, Social stratification and mobility patterns, *American Sociological Review* 15, 195–204.

MCWILLIAMS, W. C. 1973, *The Idea of Fraternity in America*. Berkeley, Ca.: The University of California Press.

MEAD, M. 1975, Ethnicity and anthropology in America, In G. DE VOS & L. ROMANUCCI-ROSS (eds), *Ethnic Identity: Cultural Continuities and Change*. pp. 173–97. Palo Alto: Mayfield.

METZGER, L. P. 1971, American sociology and black assimilation, *American Journal of Sociology* 76, 627–47.

MITCHELL, J. C. 1974, Perceptions of ethnicity and ethnic behavior: an empirical exploration. In A. COHEN (ed.), *Urban Ethnicity*. pp. 1–35. London: Tavistock Publications.

MOERMAN, M. 1965, Ethnic identification in a complex civilization: Who are the Lue? *American Anthropologist* 67, 1215–30.

— 1968, Being Lue: uses and abuses of ethnic identification. In J. HELM (ed.), *Essays on the Problem of Tribe*. Seattle: University of Washington Press.

MORRIS, H. S. 1968, Ethnic groups, *International Encyclopedia of the Social Sciences* 5, 167–72.

NAHIRNY, V. C. & FISHMAN, J. A. 1965, American immigrant groups: ethnic identification and the problem of generations, *Sociological Review* 13, 311–26.

— 1975, *The Role of Ethnicity in Social Theory*. (Ms., IAS Seminar, Department of Sociology, Hunter College—CUNY and Department of Psychology, Yeshiva University.)

NELSON, B. 1949, *The Law of Usery: from Tribal Brotherhood to Universal Otherhood*. Princeton: Princeton University Press.

NISBET, R. A. 1953, *The Quest for Community*. New York: Oxford University Press.

OLIVIERO, M. B. 1976, Report of Field Research on Native American Indian Language Use: A Sociolinguistic Inquiry.(Ms., Department of Sociology, Kirkland College.)

PARSONS, T. 1966, Full citizenship for the Negro? In T. PARSONS & K. B. CLARK (eds), *The Negro American*. pp. 739ff. Boston: Houghton Mifflin.

— 1975, Some theoretical considerations on the nature and trends of change of ethnicity. In N. GLAZER & D. P. MOYNIHAN (eds), *Ethnicity:*

Theory and Experience. pp. 53–83. Cambridge, Massachusetts: Harvard University Press.

PATTERSON, O. 1975, Context and choice in ethnic allegiance: A theoretical framework and Caribbean case study. In N. GLAZER & D. P. MOYNIHAN (eds), *Ethnicity: Theory and Experience*. pp. 305–49. Cambridge, Massachusetts: Harvard University Press.

PETERSEN, W. 1975, On the subnations of Western Europe. In N. GLAZER & D. P. MOYNIHAN (eds), *Ethnicity: Theory and Experience*. pp. 177–208. Cambridge, Massachusetts: Harvard University Press.

PLAX, M. 1972, On studying ethnicity, *Public Opinion Quarterly* 36, 653–74.

RAVETZ, J. R. 1971, *Scientific Knowledge and Its Social Problems*. Oxford: Clarendon Press.

REX, J. A. 1959, The plural society in sociological theory, *British Journal of Sociology* 10, 114–24.

SAID, E. W. 1976, Raymond Schwab and the romance of ideas, *Daedalus* 105, 151–67.

SALAMONE, F. A. 1975, Become Hausa: Ethnic identity change and its implications for the study of ethnic pluralism and stratification, *Africa* 45, 410–25.

SCHNEIDER, D. M. 1969, Kinship, nationality and religion in American culture: toward a definition of kinship. In R. F. SPENCER (ed.), *Forms of Symbolic Action*. pp. 116–25. Seattle: University of Washington Press.

— 1972, What is kinship all about? In P. REINING (ed.), *Kinship Studies in the Morgan Centennial Year*. pp. 32–64. Anthropological Society of Washington, Washington, D.C.

SCHWARTZ, T. 1975, Cultural totemism: ethnic identity, primitive and modern. In G. DE VOS & L. ROMANUCCI-ROSS (eds), *Ethnic Identity: Cultural Continuities and Change*. pp. 106–32. Palo Alto: Mayfield.

SHILS, E. 1957, Primordial, personal, sacred and civil ties, *British Journal of Sociology* 8, 130–45.

SINGER, L. 1962, Ethnogenesis and Negro Americans today, *Social Research* 29, 419–32.

SMITH, M. G. 1969a, Pluralism in precolonial African societies. In L. KUPER & M. G. SMITH (eds), *Pluralism in Africa*. pp. 91–152. Berkeley and Los Angeles: University of California Press.

— 1969b, Some developments in the analytic framework of pluralism. In L. KUYPER & M. G. SMITH (eds), *Pluralism in Africa*. pp. 415–58. Berkeley and Los Angeles: University of California Press.

SMITH, W. R. 1975, Beyond the plural society: economics and ethnicity in middle American towns, *Ethnology* 14, 225–44.

STEA, D. & SOJA, E. 1975, Environmental and spatial cognition in African societies, *SSRC Items* 29, 3, 37–40.

STONE, L. 1976, *The Family, Marriage and Sex in England, 1500–1800*. (Ms., IAS Seminar, Department of History, Princeton University.)

SUTTLES, G. D. 1970, *The Social Order of the Slum: Ethnicity and Territory in the Inner City*. Chicago: University of Chicago Press.

SWEET, L. E. 1975, Discussion and criticism: On racism and terminology, *Current Anthropology* 16, 670.

TOBIAS, S. F. 1973, Chinese Religion in a Thai Market Town. Unpublished doctoral dissertation. University of Chicago.

TURNER, V. W. 1969, Forms of symbolic action: introduction. In R. F. SPENCER (ed.), *Forms of Symbolic Action*. pp. 3–25. Seattle: University of Washington Press.

—— 1975a, Symbolic studies, *Annual Review of Anthropology* 4, 145–61.

—— 1975b, *Variations on a Theme of Liminality*. (Ms., IAS Seminar, Committee on Social Thought, University of Chicago.)

VAN DEN BERGHE, P. L. 1967, *Race and Racism: A Comparative Perspective*. New York: Wiley.

WALLACE, A. F. C. 1968, Nativism and revivalism, *International Encyclopedia of the Social Sciences* 11, 75–80.

WEBER, M. 1964, Enstehung ethnischen Gemeinsamkeitsglaubens, Sprach und Kulturgemeinschaft. In M. WEBER (ed.) *Wirtschaft und Gesellschaft, Grundriss der Verstehenden Soziologie*. pp. 365–71. Koln-Berlin: Winckelmann, Kiepenhauer u. Witsch, Studienausgabe.

WEINREICH, M. 1980, [*Geshikhte fun der yidisher shprahk*. Four volumes. Yivo Institute for Jewish Research, New York. English translation (by S. NOBEL & J. A. FISHMAN)] *History of the Yiddish Language*. University of Chicago Press.

WOLFF, H. 1959, Intelligibility and interethnic attitudes, *Anthropological Linguistics* 1, 34–41.

YOUNG, F. 1970, Reactive subsystems, *American Sociological Review* 35, 297–307.

ZIJDERVELD, A. C. 1970, Rationality and irrationality in pluralistic society, *Social Research* 37, 23–47.

ZOLBERG, A. R. 1973, Tribalism through corrective lenses, *Foreign Affairs* 5, 728–39.

3 'Nothing new under the sun': A case study of alternatives in language and ethnocultural identity*

Today, in almost all of the Western world (and in the ethnopolitically consolidated and econotechnically modernized world more generally), nothing seems more 'natural' than the current linkage between a particular ethnocultural identity and its associated language. For Frenchmen, that language is French and for Spaniards it is Spanish. What could be more 'natural'? However, by their very nature, cultures are primarily *conventional* rather than truly *natural* arrangements and, therefore, even these links, apparently natural though they seem, need to be examined more carefully, perhaps even more naively, and such fundamental questions as 'Was it always so?' and 'Why, when or how did it become so?' need to be raised. Such questions commonly reveal that what is considered 'natural' today was not always considered to be so, not only because of lack of awareness (even today there may be Frenchmen who are not conscious of French as a reflection of, a symbol of and a contributor to their identity), but because even those few who *were* originally aware of the functions of language in the above ways were themselves of different minds and purposes.

That such alternative programs (and, therefore, alternative language-and-ethnicity linkages) exist is frequently recognized among specialists who have studied pre-modern ethnocultural configurations. 'Who are the Lue?' Moerman asks (1965) and provides a host of different views both by outsiders (neighbors of those whom some call Lue) and by insiders (those who sometimes call themselves Lue), in which the ethnocultural designation, the language designation and the link between the two all

*Originally published in ANITA JACOBSON-WIDDING (ed.) 1983, *Identity: Personal and Socio-Cultural*. Uppsala: Uppsala Studies in Cultural Anthropology. Vol. 5, 263–287.

show variation. Similar cases are more difficult to find in contemporary Europe, but they are not completely unknown even there, particularly among some of its Eastern and Southern Slavic groups (see, e.g. Magocsi, 1978 on the Subcarpathian Rus). In less-developed and/or less-consolidated settings (and the U.S.A. may well be one of the latter), instances such as these are much more common. All such cases, wherever they occur, lead us to be more sensitive to the possibility of earlier, less consolidated periods (or regions) in the development of ethnolinguistic identity even among those populations for whom current linkages have lasted for centuries, and, even more decidedly, to sensitize us to changes in ethnicity and in language and ethnicity linkages that are ongoing today (see, e.g. LePage & Tabouret-Keller, 1982).

Still rarer, however, is a case such as the one to be examined here, in which *ethnocultural identity per se is well established*, both by internal and by external definitions, but *its 'natural' vernacular language counterpart is still symbolically unfinalized* and, therefore, subject to widely differing programmatic formulations. The case itself pertains to early nineteenth century Eastern European Jewish society, but its problems are generalizable to the late modernization of other societies with intact sacro-classical traditions. In such societies (other major examples of which are the Greek case in Europe, the Islamic Arabic case in the Near East and North Africa, the Tamil case in South Asia and the Mandarin Chinese case in East Asia), diglossia between what are consensually viewed as 'separate languages' has persisted long after its disappearance in Western Europe. In Western Europe, the typical diglossic pattern H/L began to be resolved in favor of the vernaculars even before the Reformation ended in the full triumph of the latter as symbols of national identity. This process began first in the Atlantic seacoast countries with massification of participation in commerce, industry and armed service. In Central and Eastern Europe, however, the domination of former or current sacroclassical languages for serious writing continued much longer so that German, Russian and finally Italian achieved full general recognition as vernaculars symbolic of national identity and worthy of governmental, literary and educated usage only by the eighteenth century. Thereafter in Europe, the pattern L_H/L_L (instead of former H/L) in which varieties of the former L are used for both formal/written and informal/spoken functions was denied only to minorities that lacked state apparatuses under their own control, a denial which implicitly recognized the dynamic as well as the symbolic nature of the language and ethnicity link (Fishman, 1972). For Jews and Greeks, however, no such resolution was possible for yet other reasons. Sacroclassical languages continued to reign supreme for them, both functionally and symbolically, and their vernaculars remained in the shadows on both accounts.

The traditional Jewish vernacular roles

H/L is not an adequate formulaic representation of the role of Jewish vernaculars in traditional Jewish society. Jewish vernaculars (Yavanic in Greece, Judezmo in Spain and then in the Balkans, Chuadit in Provense,[1] Tsarfatic in France, Italkic in Italy, Yiddish in Germany and then in Eastern Europe, Yahudic in most Moslem lands) always had more than spoken vernacular functions. Indeed, they were regularly used for such sanctity-proximate functions as the oral, written (later printed) translation of prayers, oral (later printed) translation of Bible and of Talmud[2] and as the discourse language for the study of Talmud (Fishman, 1981a). Note, however, that although these vernaculars were admitted into the pale of sanctity, they never functioned independently or exclusively in that pale. They were always merely co-present in the realm of sanctity as assisting, attending, serving vehicles rather than as primary or exclusive ones. Thus, even though the true societal allocation of languages to social function in traditional Jewish communities was a complex one,[3] the vernacular alone was never in full sway in any H function. At the point at which our case begins, toward the end of the eighteenth century, several earlier attempts at promoting Yiddish, the then 900-year-old Central and Eastern European Jewish vernacular, to serious H functions had already failed.[4] However, the spread of modern ideas and processes into Eastern Europe guaranteed that additional attempts would be made, resisted and defended. Not since the times of Aramaic had a Jewish vernacular been a major bone of inter-rabbinic Jewish contention.[5] With the coming of modernization in Eastern Europe, a century and a half of 'vernacular debate' was launched in which the modernizers themselves were far from united as to the solution that they advocated. Not only were various vernaculars advocated (Jewish as well as non-Jewish) but even Loshn-koydesh — the holy tongue itself — was advocated for modern purposes, oral as well as written.

The Haskole comes to Eastern Europe

Like modernization more generally, vernacular awareness came to

Jewish Eastern Europe from Germany in particular and from 'Western Europe' more generally. Modernization as a diffuse whole was the goal of a movement known as *haskole* ('enlightenment'). Since it was an intellectual current more than a political one, it was variously interpreted and had no real organizational apparatus. Its ideological/philosophical counterpart had already strongly impacted German Jewry by the time it began to influence Jewish intellectuals in the eastern Austro-Hungarian Empire (particularly in Galicia[6]) and in the western Czarist Empire. Its spokesman and fountainhead in Germany had been Moses Mendelssohn (1729–80), and many of its earliest protagonists in Eastern Europe had been his students during their younger years. However much they may have differed amongst themselves, they all tended to share three views: (a) modern knowledge and modern behavior was bringing about major changes in the co-territorial societies that surrounded Jewish Eastern Europe, (b) as a result, it was urgent for Jewish society also to change in many ways, both internally as well as *vis-à-vis* the co-territorial societies, and (c) it was the responsibility of Jewish intellectuals to formulate, interpret and guide this change process for the maximum benefit of the Jewish people as a whole. These three views were so broad and nebulous that they did not differentiate between the parent *haskole* in Germany and its child, the *haskole* in Eastern Europe. In reality, however, both with respect to their programs and their consequences, the two *haskoles* differed markedly. Whereas the former aimed at sociocultural and political *integration* of Jews (redefined only as a religious group: 'Germans of Moses's persuasion') into 'society at large' and, therefore, rejected the notion of separate Jewish *kehiles* (community councils) or a separate Jewish vernacular (given that a separate Catholic vernacular or a Protestant vernacular would have seemed equally superfluous), the latter generally viewed Jews as a *separate* ethnocultural entity in need of political rights, on the one hand, and of economic, educational and cultural modernization, on the other hand. However, the latter goals were not unambiguous *vis-à-vis* the need for separate governing community councils or for a separate vernacular (or, even if there *were* to be such, maintenance of their unique functions) and, accordingly, these and other related issues remained 'on the agenda' and the Eastern haskole debated them bitterly and at seemingly interminable length. Insofar as the 'language issue' was concerned, three major views arose: (i) that Yiddish could serve as the medium of early modernization but that it might very well be replaced later by Polish or another co-territorial vernacular, (ii) that Hebrew itself should optimally serve as the vehicle of modernization but that German might initially need to be used since it was the only 'enlightened' language to which Jews had ready access and (iii) that Yiddish alone was capable of

integrating modernity and tradition in such a way that the new would fit
harmoniously with the old. These three views received their earliest
extensive formulation in Galicia in the first quarter of the nineteenth
century by three bearers of enlightenment (=maskilim), M. Mendl
Lefin-Satanover, Tuvye Feder and Yankev Shmuel Bik. The clash
between these three left echoes which reverberated clearly in the
vernacular/cultural programs of Zionism, Bundism and Folkism, more-
focused social, cultural and political *movements* that came into being
before the century ended or soon thereafter.

Menakhem Mendl Lefin[7]-Satanover (1749–1826)[8]

Lefin-Satanover was rightly called 'the father of the Galician haskole'
since he encouraged many other Jewish intellectuals ('proto-élites,' I have
called them elsewhere, 1972) to cultivate and to spread enlightenment
among Eastern European Jews. Although he was an ordained rabbi and
an acknowledged Talmudic master, he also studied mathematics and
natural sciences, both in German and in French, and visited Berlin often
so that he could converse with Mendelssohn (who considered Lefin-
Satanover his most important 'Polish' pupil) and with *maskilim* from the
east as well as from the west. He was among the very first Galician Jewish
intellectuals to express the view that it was not only permissible but
incumbent upon Jews to study modern subjects if they were not only to
become citizens of their respective countries but defenders and adapters
of Jewish society in modern contexts. Indeed, Lefin-Satanover formulated
a rather complete program for the intellectual and cultural improvement
of Jewry. He submitted this plan — written in impeccable French — to
the Polish Sejm. A further indication of Lefin-Satanover's own substantial
interaction with non-Jewish society is certainly the fact that it was his
friend and patron, Count Adam Czprtoryski (whose wife and children he
tutored in various subjects and who had granted him a life-long stipend
so that he could devote himself to scholarship and enlightenment) — a
member of the Polish royal family — who had asked him to prepare such
a plan for the Sejm's *Committee on the Jewish Question*. Lefin-Satanover's
plan (1791/1792) called for the establishment of Polish public schools for
Jewish youngsters. After their traditional 'coming of age' (as 13 year-olds),
Jewish boys were to be required to attend these schools so that they could
take courses in mathematics, natural sciences, modern agricultural
methods, Polish history and customs as well as 'rational Jewish subjects'
(e.g. Maimonides), *all to be taught in Polish*. The avowed purpose of these

schools was to prepare graduates who would become modern communal leaders and leaders in the struggle against *khasidism*.[9] Although Lefin-Satanover's plan did not elicit any great support in the Sejm — Poland itself underwent its second partition in 1793 and its third in 1795 and the Polish nobility that served in the Sejm was presumably preoccupied with more pressing matters — his plan is adequately indicative of his goal: to combat mysticism, to foster rationalism and to bring Jews into touch with the modern world in general and with its Jewish counterpart in particular.

Lefin-Satanover was not overly disturbed by the failure of his sweeping plan to elicit support. He embarked on less ambitious and more piecemeal 'educational efforts.' He translated into exceptionally clear and simple Hebrew the French volume by S.A. Tissot, *Avis au peuple sur sa santé* (1761), calling it *Refues ho-om (Cures of the People)*.[10] He did the same for parts of Benjamin Franklin's *Poor Richard's Almanac (Kheshbn hanefesh*, 1809). In both cases, he attracted a larger than usual readership for secular writings in Hebrew, not only because of interest in the material *per se*, but because he insisted on simple Hebrew, without flourishes, without biblical metaphors, endless asides, literary allusions, puns or any of the other stilted conventions that had long dominated Hebrew writing, whether secular or religious. He obviously wanted his books to be read by ordinary folk.[11] Nevertheless, no matter how hard Lefin-Satanover tried to write in a 'simple, understandable and interesting' way — in order to meet his self-imposed obligation (as a maskil) to spread modern learning among the people, he finally realized that there was no way in which this goal could be attained as long as Hebrew was his vehicle of communication. Only through Yiddish, his mother tongue and that of all his readers, could he really reach *everyone* (men and women, old and young, rich and poor). Finally, he decided to do exactly that — to publish a serious book in Yiddish — regardless of the break with convention that such a step represented.

Lefin-Satanover's Bible translations into Yiddish

The idea to render selected parts of the Old Testament in Yiddish had come to Lefin-Satanover much earlier, during his visits to the famous German-Jewish philosopher and modernizer, Moses Mendelssohn, in Berlin, in the late 1770s and early 1780s. Mendelssohn himself had translated the Pentateuch and provided his own commentaries thereto (in 1783), both in High German, 'in order that everyone might be able to

understand it easily and quickly.' Up until then, only Yiddish translations
were available. These were entirely unacceptable to Mendelssohn for
three reasons: (i) they were in Yiddish, (ii) they were in archaic Yiddish
and (iii) they were inaccurate. For Mendelssohn, Yiddish was not only a
hideous corruption of German (a view that he adopted from gentile
contemporaries such as Goethe [Low, 1979] and that he helped spread
among Jews and gentiles alike), but an utterly objectionable barrier
between German Jews and 'other Germans,' generally (Mendelssohn,
1782). The fact that some of the contemporary Yiddish translations were
poorly done (certainly so by Mendelssohn's sophisticated and critical
standards) and that they were in an archaic calque variety that was almost
as distant from the everyday Yiddish that German Jews spoke as it was
from the standard German that Mendelssohn *wished* them to speak, only
made *his* translation (published in Hebrew characters since the majority
of Jews who could understand German could not read the adapted Latin
characters [these being termed galkhes, i.e. 'tontured script']), all the
more acceptable to those who did not share his reformist philosophy.
However, if it was possible to translate the Bible into German so that
German Jews could understand it easily and quickly, that was distinctly
not a viable solution for the Galician and other Eastern European Jews
whom Lefin-Satanover sought to reach. Over the centuries of residence
in Slavic environments, their Yiddish had lost many of its earlier German
features until it was, by Lefin-Satanover's time, far less mutually
intercomprehensible with standard German than was the far more German
Yiddish of Mendelssohn's 'public'. Clearly, it was only via Yiddish that
Lefin-Satanover could reach his widest public, whether for the purpose of
making the Bible understandable to everyone or for the purposes of
spreading knowledge, rationality and enlightenment more generally.
Lefin-Satanover was always the rationalist in his approach to Yiddish. He
referred to it as a vital instrument if he were to 'bring culture and
enlightenment to the Jewish population of Poland' (in a letter to his
subsequently famous student Yoysef Perl, 1808).

As it happened, Lefin-Satanover's translations were clear breaks
with long established tradition — not so much quantitatively (there *had*
been many and much more extensive translations before his) as
qualitatively and visually. He concentrated on five books of philosophy
(Proverbs, Psalms, Job, Ecclesiastes and Lamentations), since he
believed them to be particularly likely to move readers to think for
themselves, to reflect and to ponder on their own. However, only one
of these five saw the light of day during his lifetime (Proverbs, 1813,
published in Tarnapol), and it created such a storm that he abandoned

his plans to publish any of the others. What exactly was it that was so revolutionary about them?

The revolutionary nature of Lefin-Satanover's translations

Lefin's translations departed from the norm of Yiddish-in-print[12] in three dramatically striking ways, all of which have to be considered programmatic rather than merely idiosyncratic or accidental. To begin with, his translation was printed in square Hebrew letters (*oysiyes merebues*) i.e. in a typeface that had until then almost always been reserved for printing sanctified texts such as the prayer book, the Old Testament or Talmud. Although there *had* already been some minor precedent for setting aside the centuries-old distinctive typeface for Yiddish (*vaybertaytsh*, it was called, i.e. the typeface used in Yiddish translations or popularizations ostensibly for women[13]), the typeface that Lefin chose was definitely a break with a deeply ingrained and culturally consensual visual norm. To set aside that norm was to call attention to an implicit new status for Yiddish, an implicit independence of Yiddish from subservience to Loshn-koydesh; it was a rejection of the cultural assumption that only Loshn-koydesh could utilize *oysiyes merebues*. It was a visual declaration of equality or even of accentuation. Such a declaration had been made a century or more earlier by another rebel and had ended rather sadly in full capitulation (Stein, 1970).[14] After Lefin, however, the ice was broken and Yiddish-in-print never again returned to its previous 'segregated' typeface.

However, Lefin's translation of Proverbs caused a storm at the *textual* level which greatly surpassed (and outlasted) any hackles that it raised at the *visual* level. Basically, this was due to the fact that Lefin also rejected the centuries-old linguistic-stylistic-substantive tradition with respect to Yiddish translations of hallowed texts. In accord with that tradition, Yiddish-in-print followed conventions established in Germany literally centuries earlier. As a result, it was twice removed from the spoken vernacular of Eastern Europe. All written (printed) language follows a convention of its own and is by no means a faithful reflection of the language as popularly spoken. However, in the Yiddish case, perhaps because its serious written/printed functions were always rather tenuous and restricted, this distance was further magnified by the preservation of an archaic written norm. Furthermore, in accordance with that norm, the Yiddish employed was not only heavily impacted by German, both

lexically and grammatically, but Hebraisms that were completely assimilated into Yiddish were never employed in translation of words of
Loshn-koydesh origin. This convention, of course, further accentuated
(artificially so) the Germanic nature of the translation and further
distanced it from spoken Yiddish. Finally, at a more purely stylistic level,
Yiddish translations of holy or sanctified writ were more than translations;
they were also abbreviated commentaries. Since it was assumed that those
who needed the translations were incapable of following the many learned
rabbinic commentaries that had been written in Loshn-koydesh about
every nuance of the original texts, the Yiddish translations constantly
departed from the texts themselves in order to provide snatches of those
commentaries. As a result, those Yiddish readers who really could not
follow the Loshn-koydesh original at all could, at times, be quite unsure
as to what in the translation was text and what was commentary, since the
latter was often unidentified as such while being interwoven with the
former.

In one fell (but very deft, very sophisticated, very delicately orchestrated) literary swoop, Lefin abandoned all three of the above conventions.[15] His translation of Proverbs approximated popularly spoken
Yiddish to such an extent that even today, 170 years later, it strikes the
reader as somewhat overly 'familiar,' 'informal' or 'folksy,' much more so,
e.g. than does the superb modern Yiddish translation of the complete Old
Testament by Yehoyesh (completed some 120 years after Lefin's work).
However, not only did Lefin utilize slavisms and contractions galore
(indeed, he may have purposely over-used them), all of them implying
popular speech and all of them reinforcing the distance that modern
Eastern European Yiddish had traveled over centuries from its Germanic
origins, but he did not hesitate to translate Loshn-koydesh terms in the
originals with their corresponding Loshn-koydesh equivalents in Yiddish
as long as the latter were fully indigenized and widely employed. This, too,
of course, accentuated the autonomy of Yiddish from its German (and
non-Jewish) origins and stressed its distinctly Jewish nature.[16]

Finally, Lefin's translation was precisely that and no more. There
were no commentaries, no asides to help the reader, no paraphrasing of
diverse rabbinic insights over the centuries. There was only the translated
text, beautifully, movingly, sensitively rendered. Whoever wanted more
than that would have to study further, just as did those who had access
to the original. Like any really competent translation, therefore, Lefin's
work led the really serious reader back to the original rather than replacing
it; it encouraged further independent study rather than implying that the
reader could go no further.

Although Lefin's motives are still subject to interpretation (some Yiddish scholars still refuse to attribute to him a truly positive attitude toward Yiddish),[17] his conscientious approach to the task he had undertaken is beyond doubt. In one of his letters, he put it this way: '. . . to exert myself to approximate it [the Yiddish of his translation] to our language and to distance it from German . . . exactly as it is spoken nowadays among us . . . the language of our eastern Podolye.'[18]

It seems to me that such conscientiousness, such awareness of Ausbau,[19] such sensitivity to the flavor of slavisms and hebraisms, implies not only stylistic artistry but the furthering of a program of action in which Yiddish would exercise new symbolic functions. In his translations, Lefin was carrying forward his original plan submitted to the tottering Polish Sejm in 1791–92: a plan to fashion Jews into a more modern people, a people fully in touch with its own tradition but yet capable of adapting it, adding to it selectively by controlled contact with surrounding cultures, evaluating it (thinking it through) by means of more massive participation in these processes rather than merely by means of blind reliance on rabbinic authorities, on the one hand, or on foreign models — even highly regarded German models — on the other hand. Indeed, not only would we miss the significance of Lefin were we to interpret his translation as a mere stylistic achievement *today*, but we would be unable to explain the controversy that immediately arose in connection with it *then*, when it appeared. It was viewed programmatically both by those who reviled it as well as by those who defended it. To do any less today would be tantamount to seeing things less clearly today, with the passage of time, than they were seen by the maskilim of that very day and age.

Tuvye Feder and the attack upon Lefin's translation

Not only was Lefin's translation brutally criticized *qua* translation but its clearly-sensed promotion of Yiddish was rejected precisely on those grounds. The self-proclaimed 'leader of the opposition' faction of maskilim was Tuvye Gutman Feder (1760–1817), a well-known grammarian, Old Testament scholar and, like most maskilim of that time, a dedicated follower of Mendelssohn. Although similar in background to Lefin, in many ways (Feder, too, was a Galitsianer, i.e. born and educated in *Galitsiye*, and was widely read in Western languages, particularly German), Feder was far less fortunate with respect to earning the wherewithal to feed, clothe and house his family and himself. Disinclined, as were also most maskilim, to earn his livelihood by means of serving as a rabbi of a particular community, and unable to receive support, as did Lefin, from any major benefactor so that he might be able to spend his life in quiet and productive scholarship, Feder and his family were constantly on the move in search of funds. Not only did he frequently have to stoop to such time-consuming but traditionally low-paying pursuits as scribe, reader (of the weekly lection), cantor and preacher, but he was forced, on occasion, to write flattering doggerel about wealthy Jewish as well as non-Jewish 'personages' in the hope of some monetary reward. Accordingly, he acclaimed Czar Alexander I for his victory over Napoleon in a lengthy poem, *Hatslokhes aleksander* (= The Triumph of Alexander), and was constantly on the look-out for an opportunity to come to greater attention in some potentially rewarding connection. Although Lefin's translation of *Proverbs* provided him with a seemingly perfect chance to do just that, it also enabled him to express views that both he and other maskilim believed deeply and had subscribed to previously, albeit in less-focused fashion.

Indeed, Lefin's translation seems to have struck Feder as virtually a personal afront. Not only was he irked by its apparent advocacy of 'common/vulgar Yiddish', but he was exasperated that a fellow maskil could so falsely interpret and so foully mishandle the mission of the *haskole* and the goals of its great leader, Moses Mendelssohn. In order to publicize his defense of the true haskole, as he interpreted it, Feder authored a lengthy and bitter attack on Lefin and on his work. Since he lacked the funds necessary to publish his work, he circulated it in manuscript form among other maskilim, in order both to publicize it as well as to raise the funds that would enable him to have it printed. The literary form of his attack, entitled *Kol mekhatsetsim: sikhe beoylem haneshomes (Voice of the Archers: A Discussion in the World of the Spirits)*, was that of a heavenly trial in which maskilim of various earlier periods gathered to indict Lefin. They charged — in Feder's characteristically intemperate prose — that Lefin's translation was full of filth and that it literally stank to high heaven. 'Whoever sees it runs away. It should be hacked to pieces. It should be burned in fire. Its name should never be recalled. The foul scroll, which the prematurely senile Lefin has penned . . . seeks only to find grace in eyes of concubines and maidens/old maids and even they flee from it saying: "Are there not enough madmen without him?"' The maskil Isaac Eichel, who had translated *Proverbs* into High German only some few decades before, charged Lefin with committing treason against Mendelssohn. 'He spits in the face of refined speakers; only the language of the coarse finds grace in his eyes.' This 'vulgar language' is variously referred to as a mixture of all tongues, a gibberish, a monstrosity. No wonder, then, that the heavenly court finally rules that Lefin's work must be burned and its ashes discarded in a cesspool!

Feder's hyperbole both confuses and lays bare quite a variety of purported shortcomings insofar as Lefin's translation is concerned. One of the themes that almost all of Lefin's heavenly prosecutors stress is the purportedly unaesthetic nature of Yiddish relative to either Loshn-koydesh, on the one hand, or High German, on the other. This view went considerably beyond Mendelssohn's own dictum as to the so-called dwarfed and disfigured nature of Yiddish (interestingly enough, Mendelssohn himself was a hunchback) and referred to Lefin's well-known rejection of the florid phraseology and the high-flown rhetoric that typified the Hebrew style of most other maskilim. Lefin had ridiculed that very style (known as *melitse*) as 'impenetrable without prior oral explanation by the author'. He had consistently sought to avoid the *melitse* style from his very earliest writings in Hebrew and had only embarked on his Yiddish translations when he was clearly convinced that even a simple and direct Hebrew was a barrier to comprehension that most Jews could not cross. Thus, Lefin was a twofold enemy, since he was an opponent to elegant, sophisticated usage even when he wrote Loshn-koydesh. Feder's stress on elegance (in Loshn-koydesh if possible, but in High German at the very least) was not merely an aesthetic whim. It reflected the conviction that only those who controlled and practised the florid and platitudinous *melitse* style were worthy of intellectual leadership among Jews. It was not only Loshn-koydesh, therefore, that had to remain the symbolic language of Jewish modernization (yes, Feder, too, was a champion of modernization; all of his grammatical and biblical analyses clearly identifying him as breaking with rabbinic scholarship and its traditional legalistic focus), but it had to be that variety of Loshn-koydesh that was furthest from what the ordinary Jew could possibly fathom. Lefin, on the other hand, had not only opted for as much transparency and non-élitism as possible in his Loshn-koydesh but had taken the next step, to ultimate transparency and non-élitism in print, namely, to contemporary spoken Yiddish *per se*. From Feder's point of view, Lefin and he stood poles apart even were they both to write in Loshn-koydesh; given, however, that Lefin had chosen to bring enlightenment in Yiddish, 'a language of darkness,' he was clearly a renegade beyond the pale.

In Feder's view, modernization would transform Jewish life without reaching the stage that Lefin had striven for from the outset: the stage in which each Jew had access to basic Jewish and modern sources and was capable of thinking these through himself without recourse to khasidic or other mystic obfuscation. Accordingly, Feder firmly believed that traditional Jewish diglossia required hardly any adjustment at all for the purposes of modernization. Loshn-koydesh would remain in its H position but would be used for both traditional and modern purposes. If its symbolic status as representing, embodying the fostering the highest Jewish intellectual order required any supplementation at all, then obviously this should come only from High German, the unchallenged language of modernization par excellence in all of Eastern and Central Europe. For Feder, Yiddish played no role at all in the symbolic order of Jewry. For Lefin Yiddish at least had an effective mission to perform, a utilitarian service to discharge. If Lefin came to Yiddish without any illusions as to its beauty, its dignity, or its traditional validity as a Jewish medium, nevertheless, as a pragmatist he wanted it to be used effectively, movingly, tellingly, *as the major carrier (at least initially) of Jewish modernization*.

Yankev Shmuel Bik (1772–1831) and the defense of Yiddish

Both Lefin and Feder had their followers and the dispute between them quickly engulfed the still rather small world of Eastern European maskilim, even though Feder's manuscript was no more than just that and literally had to be passed around from hand to hand. However, it was quite clear that Lefin was by far the more highly regarded and better connected of the two, if only because of his longer and more distinguished record of intellectual contributions to *haskole*, the many students whom he had added to the ranks of the maskilim and his many wealthy patrons, Jewish as well as Polish (the latter making him a figure to be respected if not admired). As a result, many arose to defend him more out of rejection of Feder's untempered and irresponsible diatribe than out of any basic agreement with Lefin's program or the implicit role of Yiddish therein. However, his main defender, Yankev Shmuel Bik, a former student and longtime admirer of Lefin's, not only agreed with what Lefin had done but outdid him, particularly in his advocacy of Yiddish as a symbol of the very best in the Eastern Europe tradition. Bik, too, like most other maskilim of the time and, most particularly, like Lefin, translated a considerable number of works from German, French and even English into Loshn-koydesh. Like Lefin, he was also greatly preoccupied with the need for 'productivization' of the small town Jewish poor. Being independently wealthy (even more so than Lefin), he devoted a good bit of his time and money to encouraging Jews to enter agriculture and the artisan trades. He also supported many scholars and writers (as well as 'would be' scholars and writers) — including Lefin himself during certain years — thereby enabling *them* to devote themselves uninterruptedly to their studies and writings and enabling *him* to become more fully aware of the gaps and contradictions in their thinking. This thorough familiarity ultimately contributed to his unique view among *maskilim* that *haskole* lacked involvement, lacked follow-through, indeed that it was 'cerebral' to such a degree that it lacked warmth, feeling and 'love for Jews as concrete people' as contrasted with 'concern for Jews as an abstract problem'. This stress on concrete and all-embracing love for Jews led Bik ultimately to demand greater toleration and even admiration for *khasidism*. It was to *khasidism* that he bade the *haskole* look if it were ever to learn to do more than educate, criticize or scold Jews. A khasidic rabbi cared for his flock, helped them in time of need, comforted them in time of sorrow. Bik saw no need to surrender these admirable traditional virtues in the process of modernization; least of all did he want to displace Jewish *Gemeinschaft* by a maskilic *Gesellschaft* (Tonnies, 1957 [1887]).

In 1815, some two years after Feder's manuscript had initially become known, Bik's reply, in the form of a lengthy letter, made the same rounds, from hand to hand, among Eastern European *maskilim*. Bik's defense of Yiddish constitutes the very heart and core of his letter, clearly indicating once again that much, much more than personal animosities and stylistic preferences lay at the very foundation of the disagreement between Lefin and Feder. Indeed, Bik's defense of Yiddish became the classic defense of that language, repeated by all its ideological champions (as distinct from its various pragmatic implementers) ever since. Bik's letter made the following three major points:

1. *Yiddish has been the language of Jewish traditional life for centuries*

Bik lists the names of the greatest and more revered sages of Central and Eastern European Jewry during the past many centuries and reminds Feder (and all opponents of Yiddish) that they all spoke Yiddish, taught their students in Yiddish and discussed and defended their Talmudic interpretations with other scholars in Yiddish. This being the case, Bik argues, it is incumbent upon Feder (and others) to respect this vernacular and even to honor it.[20] Furthermore, Bik adds, other Old Testament translations in Yiddish have existed in appreciable numbers before, going back to the *Mirkeves hamishne* of 1534 and the ever popular, revised and reprinted Pentateuch for women, *Tsene-urene* (1628). These were all rightly admired and highly valued for spreading familiarity with the Old Testament among ordinary, less educated men and women. There is no reason, Bik concludes, for Lefin's translation to be viewed any differently. Here, of course, Bik sidesteps the issue of modernization and the possible role of Yiddish as symbolic of Jewish mastery of modern subjects, modern roles and modern responsibilities. Modern challenges and modern solutions are questionable verities. Bik, therefore, relates Yiddish to the unquestioned great names and books of the past. In this way, he assures its positive historicity against Feder's charges of corruption and bastardization.

2. *Other modernizing nationalities do not hesitate to utilize their vernaculars to improve the lot of the everyday man*

By arguing via analogy with the peoples of Central and Western Europe — and thereby avoiding comparisons with many Eastern European nationalities whose vernaculars were still generally unrecognized for serious purposes, symbolic or pragmatic — Bik turns the tables on Feder. To deny Jews the use of Yiddish in the course of their modernization is to deny them a major avenue to knowledge which all modern nationalities of Europe were clearly delighted to have. Via their vernaculars even peasants have become literate and able to read and understand by themselves. Is this not something that Jews too should be encouraged to do, Bik asks rhetorically. Therefore, Bik concludes, instead of being exposed to criticism and ridicule, Lefin should really be congratulated and encouraged because works such as his (and more are needed!) spread knowledge and ethnic pride among the people at large. By discussing Lefin in a comparative framework *vis-à-vis* the great vernacular educators of the gentiles, Bik utilizes a favorite debating tactic and intellectual stance of the *haskole* ('Oh, if we could only learn a lesson from the successful experience of the already modernized nationalities') against Feder and for Lefin and Yiddish.

3. *Yiddish is no more linguistically inadequate than other vernaculars were at a comparable stage of modernization involvement*

Here Bik specifically refers to other 'mixed languages' (primarily to English) and other languages previously used primarily by 'uneducated classes' (primarily German) and indicates that both of these languages succeeded fully in becoming 'cultivated languages'. Cultivated languages need not be made in heaven, Bik says. Such languages are the by-products of generations of assiduous effort on the part of sages and writers who use them in order to communicate with each other and with the masses about new and important topics. As a result of such use by intellectuals, these languages, no matter how rough they may initially have been, become elegant, sensitive and refined instruments. The same can certainly occur to Yiddish. It is clear from the immediately above that Bik envisioned what we now call language planning, both in its *corpus* planning and in its *status* planning aspects (Rubin & Jernudd, 1971; Fishman, 1974; Rubin et al., 1977). He recognized that all languages are initially rather ill-suited for societal functions that they have not hitherto discharged. He also recognized that intellectuals change and adapt languages by putting them to new functions. With respect to Yiddish, he points to an area of responsibility that maskilim should assume rather than shirk.

Bik's three point agenda *vis-à-vis* Yiddish — traditional co-sanctity, modern utility, intellectual responsibility — clearly indicates that he surpassed his teacher Lefin in this respect. Lefin, unsurpassed stylist that he was and linguistic innovator that he was, rarely goes beyond pragmatic claims and practical plans in his view of Yiddish. Bik raises Yiddish to the level of a symbolic verity: it is symbolic of the Jewish traditional past and present and, given responsible intellectual devotion, it can become symbolic of the modern Jewish future as well.

Dénouement: personal and linguistic

None of our heroes (or antiheroes) came to a particularly 'happy ending'. Feder, always in dire need of funds, permitted himself to be 'bought off' by the money that Bik and other friends of Lefin offered. Ostensibly this money was to make up for the deposit that Feder had already given to the printer in Berditshev for publishing *Kol mekhatsetsim*. However, it seems doubtful that Feder had ever paid any printer anything, and the fact that he also never published his letter replying to Bik (see Verses 1983 for the text of this letter, hitherto lost and recently discovered) and further attacking Lefin would seem to substantiate the interpretation that his personal need for money had a higher priority than his need to publicize his views. He died in 1820, barely five years later, a bitter and defeated man. Thirty-three years later, when Feder, Lefin and Bik had all long since gone on to their eternal rewards, *Kol mekhatsetsim* was finally published, more as a curiosity than for any intrinsic interest in it. Lefin fared somewhat better, but he never recovered from the anguish and embarrassment that he experienced due to Feder's attack. He never published any of his other Old Testament translations, although in 1873, almost 50 years after Lefin's death in 1825, his translation of Ecclesiastes *was* published.[21] Fragments of his translations of Psalms and Job, as well as the complete translation of his Lamentations, can be found in an archive in Jerusalem.

It was not until the beginning of the 20th century that Yiddish achieved either the full *practical* recognition that Lefin advocated or the full *symbolic* recognition that Bik had recommended.[22] By then, modern secular Yiddish literature had begun to flower. On the other hand, Hebraism and Zionism had become well established as, in part, profound anti-Yiddish movements. While it cannot be said with any certainty that they were directly influenced by Feder's thinking, their rejection of Yiddish and enthronement of Hebrew often utilized many of his arguments. Indeed, echoes of the great debate of 1813–1815 linger on to this very day. Ultimately, external forces (Nazism, Communism and democratic assimilation) became the greatest enemies of Yiddish. However, internally, within the Jewish fold, the symbolic value of Yiddish often continues to be argued pro and con. It has remained an internally conflicted language and those who value it most are once again (since post-holocaust days) engaged primarily in an *internal* argument with others with whom they share a common ethnocultural identity. The parties to this argument share a common ethnoreligious identity and yet differ as to the language(s) which symbolize(s) that identity for them.

Conclusions

Substantive

The dissolution of a diglossia situation that has endured for centuries under the impact of modern massification processes has most usually involved the elevation of L. The variety hitherto employed primarily for everyday verbal rounds, informality and intimacy is functionally elevated and symbolically promoted to more dignified and status-related pursuits and identities. So it was with the demotion of Latin and the promotion of the vernaculars in the long process of Western European modernization. In this process, vernaculars triumphed as a result of changed power relationships, not only on a social class basis ('the masses and bourgeoisie' vs. the 'traditional élites' involving church, throne and gentry) but also on a regional/ethnocultural basis. Had Cataluña, Friesland, Wales and

Provence been the integrative centers for consolidating and modernizing Spain, The Netherlands, Great Britain and France, Catalán, Frisian, Welsh and Occitan might have become the vernaculars symbolic ('naturally so') of those new econotechnical and ethnocultural *national* (as distinct from regional or subnational) constellations.

However, the fact that vernaculars have so generally triumphed — both functionally and symbolically — upon the dissolution of diglossia, does not mean that it was or is inevitably so. Indeed, generally speaking, pro-vernacular ideologies were rather late in *establishing* themselves. The process of doing so was doubly, perhaps even excruciatingly, difficult where the H and its sanctified traditions were fully indigenized and where econotechnical consolidation and modernization were long delayed. In Greece, in Ashkenazi Jewry, in Italy, in Russia — and later in the Islamic sphere — serious efforts were undertaken to combine modernization with vernacularization of the H. Only in Russia were these efforts discontinued in a decisive way at a sufficiently early point so that modernization and the state apparatus became substantially identified with the vernacular in early modern times. In the other locales, vernaculars have either triumphed in much delayed or vacillating fashion (Greece, Italy), or they have never fully triumphed at all (Ashkenazi Jewry and the Arabo-Islamic sphere). Indeed, by the time controlled and attenuated modernization was attained in most of the latter instances, the adherents of the traditionally symbolic Hs were frequently able to adapt them sufficiently for new functions so that it was the sanctified Hs rather than the plebian Ls that became symbolic of both modern identity and continuity with the past.

The case under discussion reveals the typically labile nature of the language and ethnicity identity link in early modern circumstances. Each of our three 'heroes' possessed the same mother tongue and yet had markedly different views as to its symbolic significance for the purposes of modernization and its attendant social identity formation. Similarly, each of our three 'heroes' was fully and identically 'identified' ethnoculturally. Furthermore, each was a modernizer, in his own eyes, in the eyes of colleagues, in the eyes of their everyday coethnics and in the eyes of co-territorial non-Jews. Indeed, in many ways, they were highly similar and, nevertheless, their views of their shared traditional H, of their shared folk vernacular, of their shared co-territorial vernacular and of their shared language of wider communication differed widely. Thus, although it may well be inevitable for *language in general* to become symbolic of modern ethnocultural identity — after all, what better symbol system than language do we possess to convey and foster such identity — it is far from inevitable that any *particular language* (or variety) will become symbolic for any particular ethnocultural identity.

Ethnocultural identities are composites of continuity and fortuitous historical fortune. Germanic populations have been romanized, Celtic populations have been de-Celticized, Amerindian populations have been hispanicized and the resulting ethnocultural identities have, in time, 'felt good,' natural and authentic. Similarly, any one of the three options represented by our heroes could have triumphed and have fostered its own authentic identity. They each represented a fine-tuning of the ethnocultural identity (a modernization thereof) in a context in which basic ethnocultural identity had long been established and was by no means in doubt. However, even fine-tunings can be difficult and disputatious, can lead in different language and identity directions. The fact that one or another triumphs only means that the others are less *fortunate*. The winner was not necessarily more *authentic ab initio*. The loser was not necessarily less so. Any stable language and ethnocultural identity link ultimately comes to seem natural, 'worked out.' Another, quite unlike it, would also have ultimately felt just as natural and just as authentic, had it emerged victorious.

The cases of extremely delayed (or nonexistent) vernacular symbolic promotion — delayed in all instances well beyond entry into significant modern identity and often beyond politically independent econotechnical control — may well have certain features in common. One of these would seem to be *unsubordinated indigenous classicals* (and their accompanying élites) with overriding religious significance. Where *religion has not only NOT been separated from the rest of culture* but, indeed, still serves to integrate the whole, to provide it with its élites/caretakers and to provide one and all with the major status rewards that society proffers, *external H languages often come to be initial channels of secular modernization*. In the ensuing struggles between the indigenous classicals and the external Hs (each with their respective élites) the vernaculars become 'poor thirds,' particularly when *the classicals themselves undergo modernization for econotechnical purposes*. Under such circumstances (e.g. in the Arabic world, in Greece, in China, in Somalia) the *vernaculars cannot even claim sole pride of indigenousness*, which they could do if the external Hs were to appear to emerge victorious. In each of these cases *ethnic identity may not be at all in doubt* (or in dispute) but its accompanying written *vernacular may be long (or permanently) submerged*. While the case of Yiddish *vs.* Hebrew (Loshn-koydesh, later: Ivrit) *vs.* German/Polish (later: other coterritorial vernaculars) also definitely has its own particularistic characteristics, it would seem to share (and to suggest) many general sociolinguistic circumstances of far broader interest, particularly the *difficulty of displacing an entrenched indigenous élite that ultimately adapts its classical for modernization purposes.*

Another substantive point that this study raises pertains to modernization *per se* as both a problem for and an aspect of contemporary ethnocultural identity. Such identity comes about not only as a clarification or consolidation *vis-à-vis external alternatives* but, importantly, also as a clarification and consolidation *vis-à-vis various internal alternatives* (alternatives within the same ethnocultural constellation) as well. Both types of alternatives are frequently differentiated in terms of the degree or content of their modernization, i.e. of their *combination* of authenticity (*unmarked 'own' aspects*) and modernization (*initially 'foreign' aspects*), a combination which is quintessential for all nationalist movements. For some insiders and during some periods of time such a combination is viewed as impossible, as incommensurable, as tantamount to being both Protestant and Catholic simultaneously. However, not only is even the latter possible (as some recent research on language and ethnic identity among adolescents in Northern Ireland reveals), but syncretism is a far greater principle of nonideological daily life than either intellectuals or élites care to recognize. Ultimately, the issue becomes not *whether* but *what or how much* of the outside to admit into the inside, how much of the new (and once-foreign) to indigenize, synthesize, to incorporate into the preexisting and phenomenologically 'authentic' tradition. Modern ethnic identity includes many hitherto foreign/modern ingredients that may once have appeared disjointed and contentious but that have now been digested and authenticized nevertheless. The 'purification' movements that arise before this process is completed should remind us that the outcome is neither easy nor preordained with respect to any *particular* modern import.

The foregoing point would seem to flow into the next (and last): 'objectively small differences' may yet have subjectively huge consequences and, indeed, be experienced by insiders as objectively huge. Fully shared highest order preferences do *not* foreclose significantly different lower order preferences. Indeed, once highest order preferences are shared (as they were among the three protagonists on which this paper is focused) there would seem to be no other outlet for human creativity (or is it combativity) than in connection with lower order preferences and, accordingly, the latter too easily become rallying cries for ethnocultural/philosophical value-differences pertaining to 'the future of the people,' the ideal society and, therefore, the ideal identity as well. No matter how inconsequentially small the differences may seem to be to 'objective outsiders,' there is always (in language or in culture more generally) further differentiation between social networks (not to mention individual differences), both between and within higher order groups, and, therefore, further opportunity to ideologize, to mobilize and to exacerbate on the basis of such differentiation. 'Objective similarity' is obviously of more minor significance than the subjective interpretation of social differentiation and of the power possibilities or rivalries with which such differentiation is readily associated. Once differentiations become ideologized, and have their own élites to interpret, defend and cultivate them, they can continue virtually interminably (or until one party or another emerges as the definite victor in very physical and material terms). At the earliest stages, when few 'members' are as yet conscious of the differences and of the interpretations later given to them, a large number of final solutions may be possible and are certainly available. However, such flexibility is counteracted by the very élites that exploit the differences that always exist, lower order differences though they may (seem to) be. After the internal struggle is over — and it may last for generations if not for centuries — the authenticity for which men, women and children live and die is at hand (at least temporarily). 'Authenticity' is the winning alternative; what was once one among many alternative differentiation-constellations is finally popularly understood (and elitisti-cally defined) as 'the only way' (i.e. as no alternative at all), as God-given, as authentic, as really and truly the only possible ethnocultural identity for the group in question.

Methodological

I do not really mean to separate substance from method but do so here so that the latter can more easily be given the attention that is its due. The study of language and culture relationships is, in large part, a struggle against parochialism and ethnocentrism masquerading as universalism. However, as a topic area long productively dominated by anthropologists, there is some danger that fieldwork and ethnography by Westerners working in non-Western settings may, consciously or unconsciously, take on the aura of a universal super-method. Perhaps one of the contributions of this paper may be that it calls into question such methodological parochialism and ethnocentrisms. If so, it attempts to do so in several respects.

It stresses the study of *historical* cases, utilizing standard historical primary data (manuscripts, letters, diaries of a bygone age), neither accessible to ethnographic study nor to survey research nor experimentation. While it is no longer *generally* necessary to do, it may bear repeating in an area where little research has heretofore used this method, that 'actors' or 'members' who can no longer be observed can still be cautiously studied — and hypotheses concerning them advanced and tested — on the basis of extant historical materials. Like *every other method of social research*, this one has its very definite limitations (the *individual researcher's interpretation of fortuitously preserved* — and therefore *incomplete* — records), but, again like *every* other method, it has produced a small number of clearly first-rate works. We would certainly all be poorer without the *historical* studies of Weber, Freud and Erikson, among many others. Methodological imperialism is not only ethnocentric (and, therefore, *unbecoming* for the study of language and culture) but it would make us all *poorer* in the process.

This paper also raises (or at least heightens) the issue of whether the researcher (the observer) must always be of a different ethnoreligious identity than that which pertains to the subject population (the observed). Much social research following a variety of methodological preferences (rather than historical research alone) calls this shibboleth into question and even the study of language and culture, in its most recent urban and applied ramifications, has also begun to do so. There are, of course, great risks when observer and observed share ethnoreligious or any other important aspects of identity: lack of detachment, lack of perspective, lack of broadly contrastive framework. We are certainly well aware of the fact that ethnic movements (as well as social class movements, religious movements, political movements and intellectual movements) can lead (and have led) to seriously biased and purposively invidious research. While such caricatures and miscarriages of social research must clearly be unmasked, disowned and discredited, the risks they pose must not blind us to the *assets* of much research that is conducted by observers who share many central aspects of social identity with their subjects. Such shared identity may carry with it huge amounts of detailed knowledge that can never be equalled or acquired by outsiders. If such knowledge can be objectified and if the research utilizing it is accompanied by high levels of motivation as well, then the resulting combination may be extremely worthwhile in highly generalizable respects. While it may be true that only Freud was able to psychoanalyze himself, countless extremely worthwhile historical, sociological, literary and psychological studies have been done by researchers who have grown up and been trained in the very contexts that they have then undertaken to study.

Finally, although *this* methodological point shows the indivisibility between 'methodology' and 'substance' even more than do the others, this paper seeks to remind us that élites (spokesmen, leaders, intellectuals) and proto-élites are worthy of study. It seems to me that this is particularly so in connection with research on modern ethnic identity. Modern society is characterized by the massification of participation in industrial, educational, political and military operations. This massification is orchestrated and rationalized by élites who not only act as conduits of innovation but as the planners, managers and polarizers of sociocultural identity for the masses. In modern society, even more than in earlier periods of social development, élites are the major actors in the ongoing drama of sociocultural change and of identity consolidation and change. Élites speak to/write to the masses and reach them via modern identity–forming media, often on a fairly continual basis. Thus, rather than study only the nameless, most impersonal actors and most pervasive institutions that are involved in the identity formation and reformation process, we must also study élites *per se* if we are to understand why and how modern sociocultural identity takes a certain turn or polarizes on a certain issue. It is idle, I think, to pursue the question of which is more important, the mass or the leaders, the nameless or the named, the widespread ways and values or the goals, purposes, consciousness and conflictedness of élites. The two are in constant interaction, all the more so in modern society, and *both* must be studied if a complete picture of modern sociocultural identity, including ethnic identity, is to appear. To fail to do so because the study of élites lies outside the purview of a certain disciplinary or methodological camp is to become a captive rather than a master of disciplines and methods alike, thereby delaying rather than advancing the shedding of light on ethnic identity processes in the modern world.

Notes to Chapter 3

1. *Provense* (three syllables) is an area similar to but not identical with Provence. *Provense*, like all Jewish culture areas, is defined by the boundaries of its distinctive regional adaptation of Jewish rites and traditions. Similar references to Jewish languages of Greece, Spain, France, Italy, Germany, etc. are merely convenient shorthand expressions for Jewish culture areas that predate any of the foregoing political designations. In each case, a Jewish vernacular was coterminous with a particular rite and set of customs, as validated by its local/regional rabbinic authorities. Although the latter also strove to function within the fold of supra-regional Jewish conventions, local/regional rites and customs were, nevertheless, always considered ultimately binding whenever the two (the local/regional and the supra-regional) were in disagreement. For

LANGUAGE AND ETHNOCULTURAL IDENTITY

a review of all circum-Mediterranean Jewish vernaculars (since the decline of vernacular Hebrew) in the framework of their own rites and customs, see Weinreich, 1980 [1973].

2. Talmud — A vast compilation of what was originally the unwritten Oral Law, the Talmud is the accepted final arbiter and legal code for Orthodox Jews. Its two divisions are the Mishne or text of the Oral Law (in Hebrew) and the Gemore (in Aramaic), which supplements and comments upon it. Separate compilations were produced in Palestine (5th century C.E.) and in Babylonia (6th century C.E.), with the latter coming to be authoritative in view of its greater length and completeness.

3. $\mathrm{RR:LK/jvc} + \mathrm{RW:LK} + \mathrm{RS:jvh}$

$$\overline{\mathrm{SR:jv_1} + \mathrm{SW:LK/jv_2} + \mathrm{DS:jv_3}}$$

(RR = religious reading (study) and prayer
LK = Loshn-koydesh (Biblical/Talmudic/Medieval Hebrew/Aramaic)
jvc = Jewish vernacular calque for word-by-word translation of RR in such a fashion as to remain as close as possible to the grammar of the LK original
RW = religious writing (e.g. rabbinic responsa)
RS = religious spoken interaction (e.g. Talmudic discourse pertaining to LK texts)
jvh = Jewish vernacular 'high,' i.e. as spoken in learned discourse
SR = secular reading (entertainment or practical reading)
jv1 = written Jewish vernacular in secular literature
SW = secular writing
jv2 = written Jewish vernacular in letters, diaries
DS = daily speech
jv3 = the variety of minimally sanctified verbal interaction)

Note the meager presence of Jewish vernaculars in H-related functions and the meager presence of Loshn-koydesh in L-related functions.

4. The most noteworthy earlier failure along these lines was that of Arn b'r Shmuel of Hergershausen, approximately a century earlier than the point at which our first 'hero's' temerity became widely known in 'enlightened circles'. Arn b'r Shmuel composed and had a unique prayerbook (*Liblekhe tfile* 1709) printed, which consisted both of his Yiddish translations of parts of the traditional prayerbook and certain chapters of Psalms, as well as of Yiddish prayers or supplications that he himself had composed for specific recurring occasions (e.g. 'a beautiful prayer to ask that man and wife live together affectionately'). Although his intentions were to enable simple folk understand more fully and feel their prayers (rather than to only semiunderstand and semifeel them as was — he believed — necessarily the case when they were in Loshn-koydesh), his 'heretical prayerbook' was banned by local rabbinic authorities. 'Several generations later, in 1830, in the attic in the house of study of Arn b'r Shmuel's native town, hundreds of copies of this confiscated book

were found' (Tsinberg, 1943 [1975], v.6, 256–259 [v.7, 225–227]). See note 12, below. *Note*: the Ashkenazi (Yiddish) pronunciation of Loshn-koydesh terms and titles is the basis of the transliteration employed in this paper.

5. Aramaic (technically Judeo-Aramaic, since various varieties of Aramaic were employed throughout the Near East and, subsequently, further east up to and including Tibet) was not always accepted as on a par with Hebrew, notwithstanding the fact that major portions of the books of Daniel and Ezra are written in this language. It is clear that the majority of all Jews spoke Aramaic from the earliest days of the Second Temple and that countless sanctified traditional writings and prayers were composed in this language or in a mixture of Aramaic and Hebrew. Nevertheless, the Talmud Yerushalmi reveals (Sotah 49) that many sages were opposed to Aramaic and demanded that Hebrew be spoken, whereas others defended its use (Sotah 7). However, ultimately the genetic similarity between the two languages, the fact that Aramaic persisted as a Jewish vernacular for some 1400 years (from the fifth century B.C.E. to the ninth century C.E.), and the final fact that so much of rabbinic authority continued to be recorded in that language (even down to modern times) won out and the two together (Hebrew and Judeo-Aramaic) were dubbed Loshn-koydesh, the holy tongue, and became fused in popular thought, even as they were in function and in structure.

6. Today a region in southeastern Poland and in the northwestern Ukraine, Galicia was part of Poland during the latter Middle Ages. During the first partition of Poland (1772), most of it was transferred to Hapsburg rule and on subsequent partitions the area under Hapsburg (Austro-Hungarian) rule was extended. (Between the two World Wars, it was again primarily under Polish rule but since the end of World War II, it is once more divided between Poland and the Ukrainian S.S.R.). Because of its exposure to more Western, modern and liberal Austro-Hungarian policies, Galicia became a gateway for the diffusion of modern studies and ideologies into Jewish Eastern Europe. Thus, 'the Galician enlightenment' is considered the dawn of modern Western ideologies among Eastern European Jews and, more generally, *galitsianer* came to be viewed as a culture type (sophisticated, wily, capable of flattering and hoodwinking more traditional folk in order to get their way) by Eastern European Jews from other regions. For abundant further details see Magocsi 1983.

7. In accord with traditional usage, the name should properly be transliterated Levin. However, Lefin himself wrote it with the equivalent of an f in Hebrew letters, probably because he associated the Hebrew/Yiddish grapheme for *v* with its German equivalent. Since the German *v* was pronounced as an *f*, he therefore wrote his name with a *fey* in Hebrew and Yiddish. In more recent articles, the tendency to refer to him as *Levin* seems to be gaining the upper hand. I have retained Lefin's own usage here in order to indicate how far-reaching was the influence of German-sponsored modernization.

8. My account of Lefin, Feder and Bik depends heavily on the major Yiddish, English and Hebrew sources, e.g. Tsinberg, 1943 [1975]; Levine, 1974; and Shmeruk, 1964, 1971. I have also used Vaynlez, 1931; Cooper, 1978; Verses,

1938; Haberman, 1932 and various other sources secondarily, e.g. the English materials in the 10-volume *Encyclopedia Judaica* (1970).

9. *Khasidism* (also transliterated Hasidism): movement founded in Poland in the eighteenth century in reaction to the academic formalism of rabbinic Judaism. By stressing the mercy of God, encouraging joyous religious expression through song and dance and de-emphasizing the centrality of traditional study, it spread rapidly among the poor and uneducated. Although pronounced a heresy in 1781, it became and remains a notable force in Orthodoxy.

10. Lefin's translation (*Refues ho'om* 1794) was actually the second translation of Tiddot's volume for Jewish readers. It had already been translated/paraphrased into Yiddish by Moyshe Markuze, a contemporary of Lefin, in 1790. Although Markuze's rendition (*Oyzer yisroel*) may be considered the first book to approximate spoken Eastern Yiddish, it was, nevertheless, heavily colored by stylistic remnants and influences derived from German and from Western Yiddish, on the one hand, and by anti-khasidic asides and implications, on the other hand. In many respects, Lefin's translation was an improvement over Markuze's: it was certainly closer to the original and contained no interpolations or editorializing by the translator. On the other hand, it was in *Loshn-koydesh*, rather than in Yiddish, so that popular as it became, it could not penetrate deeply into the lay public. Later, Lefin combined the advantages of both translations when he too switched to Yiddish but remained true to the originals that he translated without inserting into them opinions of his own.

11. Women generally received no formal Hebrew education and could not be expected to understand even a simple Hebrew text on their own. Boys were taught (in schools under communal auspices) to recite prayers and ritual benedictions in Hebrew and, if their parents could afford to keep them in school beyond that point (ages 5–6), also to read the (Hebrew) Pentateuch and translate it into Yiddish and, ultimately, to study the Judeo-Aramaic Talmud and its classical commentaries and to argue their fine points in Yiddish. None of these texts, however, prepared them to read secular material on relatively modern matters, and, in addition, the latter type of reading matter was often prohibited or at least discouraged by rabbinic authorities.

12. So widespread is the popular assumption that Yiddish was traditionally utilized only for oral functions (oral translation of text, oral argumentation of text and face-to-face intimacy or daily routine) that a minor aside here concerning the ancient lineage of Yiddish-in-print may be in order. Yiddish-in-print traces back to early sixteenth century northern Italy, that is, to very close to the invention of movable type (circa 1437) and possibly, therefore, to before the convention of Loshn-koydesh-in-print. Prior to the appearance of Yiddish-in-print, utilization of Yiddish-in-manuscript was well established with extant manuscripts now being traceable back to the thirteenth century (Weinreich, 1980). By and large, Yiddish-in-print consisted either of secular writings (poems, stories, novels) of an entertainment nature, on the one hand, or of translations (often word by word) of prayerbook and Old Testament text on the other hand, through to the nineteenth century, at which point a much more

diversified repertoire of secular Yiddish-in-print comes into being, including an extensive practical, educational and ideological literature. By the late nineteenth century, scientific scholarship publication in Yiddish also becomes common.

13. I write 'ostensibly for women' in order to indicate that many of the Yiddish publications in vaybertaytsh were not only also *read* by men but some of them were primarily *intended* for men. The fly-leaf rationale 'written in simple Yiddish so as to be understandable to women and girls' was often no more than camouflage in order to avoid the wrath of rabbinic authorities who zealously protected (and directly benefited from) the diglossic tradition in accord with which Yiddish was not used in other than an auxiliary (translating, popularizing) function insofar as serious publications, particularly those related to the sanctified topics or pursuits for which rabbinic ordination was considered necessary, were concerned.

14. Arn b'r Shmuel of Hergershausen's *Liblekhe tfile* (1709) had also been set in *oysiyes merebues*, a fact which might well have contributed to its being banned and confiscated by the rabbinic authorities of the time. See note 3, above.

15. For a close comparison of Lefin's translation with those published before him and with those then in vogue, as well as with the modern translation by Yehoyesh (1941), see Shmeruk 1964 (Yiddish) and 1981 (Hebrew).

16. For a thorough-going review of the various literary 'dialects' of nineteenth century Yiddish, from those most distant from the spoken language of Eastern Europe to those most faithful to spoken speech, see Roskies, 1974. For a modern restatement and implementation of the view that Yiddish should be consciously de-Germanized and moved 'away from German,' see Weinreich, 1938 [1975].

17. Shmeruk, in particular, is dubious as to Lefin's motives and tends to attribute the latter's style to literary virtuosity rather than to ideological or programmatic goals. Others (e.g. Mark, 1956) interpret Lefin in more consciously pro-Yiddish terms. Shmeruk is undoubtedly correct in reminding us of several anti-Yiddish comments in Lefin's earlier writings. Lefin may well have gone through several phases in his attitude toward Yiddish, but it seems clear to me that while working on his translations, his views are overwhelmingly positive, particularly for a maskil of his day and age. Other maskilim, too, had to swallow their initial pride and to use Yiddish to get their ideas across to the average Jew, but Lefin was one of the first to do so and to display unusual satisfaction and warmth (rather than just virtuosity) in the process. For continued maskilic reluctance in this connection down to the end of the century, see Miron, 1973.

18. Lefin's reference to 'our eastern Podoyle' is interesting both linguistically and geographically. His choice of words here, 'mizrekh podoyle shelonu,' is made up of two hebraisms and one slavism. Although the first hebraism (mizrekh = east) and the slavism (podoyle = Podolia, a somewhat more easterly Galician region largely under Czarist rule after 1793) are unsubstitutable in Yiddish today, the last hebraism (shelonu = our) is not normally employed. Its use, instead of the more normal *undzer* (of Germanic stock) gives the entire

phrase a very striking and decidedly non-Germanic flavor. The region referred to in this fashion can be interpreted either as the area in which Lefin himself resided, at the easternmost point of the Austro-Hungarian/Polish border, where both states met with the lands occupied in 1793 by Czarist Russia, or as referring to the region father east in Czarist Russia *per se*, where the impact of German on Yiddish was even less than in Galicia.

19. *Ausbau*, literally 'building out' or 'building away,' applies to the process of consciously distancing a weaker language from another that is functionally stronger, competitive with the weaker and genetically close to it. Via *Ausbau*, the weaker is rendered progressively more dissimilar from the stronger so that it cannot readily be viewed as a dialect of the latter but will appear fully independent of it. *Ausbau* is contrasted with *Abstand*, wherein two languages are naturally so dissimilar that neither can be taken as a dialect of the other (Kloss, 1967). While the interdialectal diversity of Yiddish (no greater than that of Dutch or Swedish) added some urgency to the codification of its modern written standard (as was also the case for Dutch, Swedish, etc) its genetic similarity to German remained an 'issue' — both among adherents and opponents — even after this standardization had been achieved.

20. Bik is the first in what subsequently became quite a long list of very prestigious Orthodox spokesmen to praise Yiddish and to point out its merits as a vehicle and shield, or defender, of tradition. For such statements by the Khsam Soyfer of Pressburg (1762–1839), see Weinreich 1980 283. For such statements by Nosn Birnboym in the 1930s and by Rabbi Joseph B. Soloveitchik in very recent days, see Fishman, 1981b, vii–viii and 160.

21. Lefin spent the rest of his life working on a new translation/edition of the *Guide for the Perplexed*, originally written in Judeo-Arabic by Maimonides (1135–1204), the greatest Jewish philosopher of all times, and never again entered the arena of public debate or of pro-Yiddish activism. The fact that he spent his last decade entirely engrossed in a volume seeking to synthesize religion and rational philosophy certainly implies some loss of certainty that enlightenment programs of action alone could solve 'the Jewish problem'. Lefin's champion, Bik, died at the age of 59 in a cholera epidemic in Brod, having become infected while tending to the needs of the sick and hungry. He, at least, remained an involved activist to the end, giving his life in daily exertion for his fellows rather than in labor over one manuscript or another. In 1833, two years after Bik's demise (he was the last of the three to die, although he was also the youngest at the time of his death), his letter to Feder, and Feder's hitherto-unpublished reply were finally published in the maskilic journal *Keren hemed*. The only importance that can be ascribed to this otherwise esoteric posthumous publication is that it made Bik's strong and clear views available to pro-Yiddish maskilim of the latter part of the century. The major figure among them, Y.M. Lifshits, quoted it in its entirety in 1863 in connection with his effort to convince maskilim in the Czarist Empire that Yiddish was the only language via which they could reach, educate and dignify the mass of Russian-Polish Jewry.

22. Modern symbolic and practical dignification came with the adoption of a

pro-Yiddish (and pro-Jewish secular cultural) resolution by the Jewish Workers Bund of Russia, Poland and Lithuania and with the First World Conference for the Yiddish Language in Tshernovits, both in the first decade of the twentieth century. The former is analysed in Hertz 1969 and the latter in a paper of mine (1980b). Assigning any symbolic priority to Yiddish, but particularly the extreme view that Yiddish *alone* was of modern ethnocultural significance, came to be termed Yiddishism. While Yiddishism never became a mass movement in and of itself, it heavily influenced all left-wing Jewish ideologies (including left-wing Labor Zionism, not to mention Jewish anarchism, socialism and communism). These sought a complete change of authority systems within the Jewish fold. Yiddishism influenced modern Jewish secularism as a whole, reconceptualizing Jews as a 'nationality' rather than as a 'religion' (Gutman, 1976). For a Yiddish-secular rejection of the purely linguistic stress of extreme Yiddishism, see Lerer, 1940. For a review of the architects of Yiddishism (not all of whom were Yiddishists in the extreme sense of the word), see Goldsmith, 1976.

Bibliography

COOPER, E. 1978, Yaakov Shmuel Bik leor teudot hadashot [Jacob Samuel Bick in the light of new evidence] *Gil'ad* IV–V, pp.535–47.

FERGUSON, C. A. 1959, Diglossia, *Word* 325–40.

FISHMAN, J. A. 1967, Bilingualism with and without diglossia; diglossia with and without bilingualism, *Journal of Social Issues*, 29–38.

— 1972, *Language and Nationalism: Two Integrative Essays*. Rowley, MA: Newbury House.

— (ed.) 1974, *Advances in Language Planning*. The Hague: Mouton.

— 1980a, Bilingualism and biculturism as individual and as societal phenomena, *Journal of Multilingual and Multicultural Development*, 1, 3–16. Revised, This Volume, part II.

— 1980b, Attracting a following to high-culture functions for a language of everyday life: The role of the Tshernovits Language Conference in the 'rise of Yiddish', *International Journal of the Sociology of Language* 24, 43–74. Also This Volume, part V.

— 1981a, The sociology of Jewish languages from the perspective of the general sociology of language: A preliminary formulation, *International Journal of the Sociology of Language* 30, 5–18.

— (ed.) 1971b, *Never Say Die! A Thousand Years of Yiddish in Jewish Life and Letters*. The Hague: Mouton.

GOLDSMITH, E. S. 1976, *Architects of Yiddishism at the Beginning of the Twentieth Century*. Rutherford NJ: Fairleigh Dickinson University Press.

GUTMAN, S. 1976, *The Faith of Secular Jews*. New York: Ktav.

HABERMAN, A. 1932, Tuvye Feders kol mekhatsetsim (Tuvye Feder's 'Voice of the Archers'), *YIVO Bleter* 3, 4–5, 472–75.

HERTZ, J. S. 1969, The Bund's nationality program and its critics in the Russian, Polish and Austrian Socialist movements, *YIVO Annual of Jewish Social Science* 14, 53–67.

KLOSS, H. 1967, 'Abstand' languages and 'Ausbau' languages, *Anthropological Linguistics* 9, 7, 29–41.

LEFIN, M. M. 1791–92, *Essai d'un plan de réforme ayant pour objet d'éclairer la nation juive en Pologne et de redresser par là ses moeurs*.

LE PAGE, R. B. & TABOURET-KELLER, A. 1982, Models and stereotypes of ethnicity and language, *Journal of Multilingual and Multicultural Development* 3, 161–92.

LERER, L. 1940, Der blik az yidish is der tamtsis fun yidishkayt — di sakone fun der formule 'lingvistish-sekularistish' (The view that Yiddish is the quintessence of Jewishness — The danger of the formulation: 'linguistic-secularistic'), in his *Yidishkayt un andere problemen* (Jewishness and Other Problems). New York: Matones, 68–94. (Reprinted in J. A. FISHMAN (ed.), *Never Say Die! A Thousand Years of Yiddish in Jewish Life and Letters*. The Hague: Mouton, 1981, 313–42.)

LEVINE, H. 1974, *Menahem Mendl Lefin: A Case Study of Judaism and Modernization*. Harvard University, Ph.D. Dissertation.

LIFSHITS, Y. M. 1863, Di fir klasn [The four categories] *Kol mevaser* 2, 323–28, 364–66, 375–80, 392–93. (Includes Y.S. Bik's letter to Tuvye Feder [1815].) (Reprinted in J. A. FISHMAN (ed.), *Never Say Die! A Thousand Years of Yiddish in Jewish Life and Letters*, The Hague: Mouton, 1981, 259–66.)

LOW, A. D. 1979, *Jews in the Eyes of the Germans: From the Enlightenment to Imperial Germany*. Philadelphia: ISHI.

MAGOCSI, P. R. 1978, *The Shaping of a National Identity: Sub-Carpathian Rus', 1848–1948*. Cambridge MA: Harvard University Press.

MAGOCSI, P. R. 1983, *Galicia: A Historical Survey and Bibliographic Guide*. Toronto: University of Toronto Press.

MARK, Y. 1956, Di hoypt-eygnshaftn fun mendl satanovers mishle-iberzetsung (The major characteristics of Mendl Satanover's translation of Proverbs), *Yidishe shprakh* 16, no.4, 108–14.

MENDELSSOHN, M. 1782, Against bastardization of languages. In E. JOSPE (ed.), *Mose Mendelssohn: Selections from His Writings*. New York: Viking, 106 (also see p.78).

MIRON, D. 1973, The commitment to Yiddish, in his *A Traveler Disguised*. New York: Shocken, 1–33.

MOERMAN, M. 1965, Ethnic identification in a complex civilization: Who are the Lue? *American Anthropologist* 67, 1215–30.

ROSKIES, D.-H. 1974, Yidishe shraybshprakhn in 19tn yorhundert (Yiddish literary dialects in the 19th century), *Yidishe shprakh* 1–3, 1–10.

RUBIN, J. & JERNUDD, B. (eds) 1971, *Can Language be Planned?* Honolulu: University Press of Hawaii.

RUBIN, J., JERNUDD, B. H., DAS GUPTA, J., FISHMAN, J. A. & FERGUSON, C. A. 1977, *Language Planning Processes*. The Hague: Mouton.

SHMERUK, K. 1964, Vegn etlekhe printsipn fun mendl lefins mishle iberzetsung (Concerning a few principles of Mendl Lefin's translation of Proverbs), *Yidishe shprakh* 24, no.2, 33–51.

— 1971, *Sifrut yidish bepolin* (Yiddish Literature in Poland). Jerusalem: Magnes.

STEIN, S. 1970, Liebliche Teffiloh — a Judeo-German prayer book printed in 1709, *Leo Baeck Institute Yearbook* 15, 41–72.

TISSOT, S. A. 1761, *Avis au peuple sur sa santé*.

TONNIES, F. 1957, *Community and Society (Gemeinschaft und Gesellschaft)*. Translated and edited by C. P. LOOMIS. East Lansing: Michigan State University Press [1887].

TSINBERG, Y. 1943, *Di geshikhte fun der literatur bay yidn*. New York: Shklarsky (In English: Zingberg, Israel. *A History of Jewish Literature*. New York, Ktav, 1975.)

VAYNLEZ, Y. 1931, Mendl lefin-satanover, *YIVO-bleter* 2, 4–5, 334–57.

VERSES, Sh. 1938, Yankev-shmuel bik, der blondzhendiker maskil. (Yankev Shmuel Bik, the groping maskil). *YIVO-bleter* 13, 505–36.

— 1983, Hanusaḥ hamakori habilti yadua shel igerat shmuel yaakov bik el tuvye feder (The unknown original version of Shmuel Yaakov Bik's letter to Tuvye Feder), *Kiryat Sefer*, 58 no.1, 170–87.

WEINREICH, M. 1938, Daytshmerish toyg nit (Germanisms are not acceptable), *Yidish far ale*, 97–106. (Reprinted in *Yidishe shprakh*, 1975, 34, 1–3, 23–32.)

— 1980, *History of the Yiddish Language*. Chicago: University of Chicago Press. (Translated by Sh. NOBLE & J. A. FISHMAN from the four-volume Yiddish original. *Geshikhte fun der yidisher shprakh*. New York, YIVO, 1973.)

YEHOYESH, 1941, *Toyre, neviyem, ksuvim* (Pentateuch, Prophets, Scriptures). New York: Yehoash.

4 Language and nationalism: Two integrative essays[1]*

'It is easy for speakers of English, secure in the imperialism or even colonialism of their language — conquering and settling, as it were, whole vocabularies of German, French, Latin and Arabic — to scorn what appears to be puerile or at least pedantic defensive linguistics. Secure in the farflung domain of our language, we cannot really understand the desperate defensiveness of those who stand against us. Is not language, after all, merely a means of communication, and, as such, to be judged merely in pragmatic terms? If a better means is available, should it not be adopted? Can there be any real virtue in maintaining inefficient, obsolescent, or even obsolete languages? Surely serious men of affairs have more important tasks than to worry about the origins of words, their esoteric meanings, their linguistic "purity." To the defenders of other languages, the case appears quite differently ... (They) have found in those languages not merely a means of communication but the genius of their nationhood. And not alone among the non-European languages has this been the case.'

(Polk, 1970)

דאָס בוך ניב איך איבער
מײַן מאַמען און מײַן מאַמע־לשון

Language and nationalism foreword by Herbert C. Kelman

That nationalism is a powerful force in the modern world is by now a well-worn cliché. What we need are some powerful analytic models to give a degree of order and coherence to the numerous and varied

*Originally published in *Language and Nationalism*, 1972, Rowley, Mass.: Newbury House.

phenomena that are often subsumed under this label. There is the nationalism underlying anti-colonial struggles, such as those in Algeria, Vietnam, or Angola; the nationalism of separatist movements, whether in Biafra, Bangladesh, or French Canada; the nationalism of the Afrikaners that demands apartheid in South Africa; the clashing nationalisms in the Middle East that block resolution of the Arab-Israeli conflict; the competing nationalisms that create continuing tensions in such multi-ethnic states as Belgium, Yugoslavia, or Cyprus; the emerging nationalism that helps to unify such multi-ethnic states as India; the revolutionary nationalism of China or Cuba; the counter-revolutionary nationalism of Greece; the nationalism of smaller states that has helped to break down the image of a monolithic world communism; the nationalism of the great powers that has limited the effectiveness of the United Nations as a peacekeeping force. Perhaps most fascinating, at least for the American observer, is the nationalism of Black Americans — an almost classical case of the emergence of national consciousness in a group that, only a few short years ago, very few scholars would have described as a nationality.

The Black American movement is one of three nationalist movements (the others being the Yiddish secularist and the Hebrew Zionist) that Dr. Fishman cites in his Preface to Language and Nationalism as ones that he has witnessed at first hand and that he has wanted to understand more deeply. Chapters 4 and 9 of this volume do indeed provide considerable insight into these movements and new perspectives on them, placing them in relationship to other nationalist movements that have arisen over a wide range of times and places. Dr. Fishman's analytic model, which offers a coherent framework for the varied examples of nationalism cited in the last paragraph (and which, incidentally, would exclude some of these examples from the definition of nationalism), seems to fit these three movements very well. Yet, by a remarkable *tour de force*, these cases — which clearly provided the emotional impetus for his work and which the work, in turn, illuminates — are barely mentioned in the text and only rarely in the footnotes. His broad overview draws, with an impressive display of scholarship, on numerous historical examples, but not on those personally closest to him. Thus, on the one hand, Dr. Fishman is emotionally involved in the issues he discusses — an involvement that both feeds his interest in nationalism and enhances his insight into it; on the other hand, by a conscious decision, he distances himself from the problem as he proceeds to derive and apply generalizations.

Closeness and distance is one of several interrelated polarities that characterize this book and make it a unique contribution to the study of nationalism. Another pair of often polar approaches that Dr. Fishman's analysis bridges and combines is that of the historian and that of the social scientist. The book is primarily a social-scientific contribution: it is highly analytical and aims toward deriving general propositions. At the same time, it is heavily historical, both in its attempt to trace the historical development of nationalism and its various manifestations, and in its use of historical cases to illustrate general propositions and the specific forms they have taken.

The value of combining social-scientific and historical approaches is readily apparent, for example, in Dr. Fishman's discussion of the role of social change in promoting nationalism. He analyses nationalism as a response to both the problems and the opportunities created by social change — to the heightened need for re-establishing group identity in the face of rapid change and to the heightened awareness that group membership can serve as a basis for exclusion from or inclusion in the benefits accompanying such change. In doing so, he gives historical content to various analytical dimensions, such as the two sources of attachment — sentimental and instrumental — to a political system or nationalist movement which I have distinguished in my own work on nationalism (Kelman, 1969). At the same time, he provides an analytical handle for understanding the contradictions inherent in nationalism: that it makes extensive use of the institutions and techniques of mass society while seeking to counteract the alienating conditions fostered by that society; that it flourishes in urban centers while searching for the rural roots of the national culture and often espousing an anti-urban ideology; and that it promotes modernization while locating ethno-cultural authenticity in continuity with the distant past. These built-in-tensions of nationalistic ideology may account for its enormous power, as a potentially constructive as well as destructive force.

Overlapping the two polarities I have described so far — distance vs. closeness of the focal object and social science vs. history as the disciplinary approach — is that of the perspectives from which the phenomena of nationalism are examined. Again, Dr. Fishman combines two perspectives that are often antagonistic: that of the critical analyst and that of the sympathetic observer. In keeping with his stance as a social scientist, he applies his analytic tools to revealing, for example, the myth-making efforts by which nationalist movements create a noble and authentic past around which a population can be mobilized, the often arbitrary processes of integration and differentiation — minimizing some differences and maximizing others — by which the boundaries between in-group and out-groups are defined, and the self-fulfilling prophecies by which national unity and resistance to transnational integration are promoted. Both the first part of the chapter, which deals with the nature of nationalism in general, and the second, which focuses on language, demonstrate that the supposedly natural bases for defining a national group or selecting a national language are usually the end-points of social processes that are functional for the advancement of a nationalist movement or political state, that are deliberately fostered by the relevant élites, and that are heavily buttressed by rationalizations.

Yet at the same time it is clear that, in his critical analysis, Dr. Fishman is not merely exposing the myths and rationalizations that underlie nationalist movements and their roles in language planning. He is sympathetic to the efforts of various groups to achieve ethno-cultural integration, to define and authenticate their group identity, and to utilize language as a vehicle for unity and authenticity. Though these efforts — inevitably — involve some convenient myths and arbitrary boundaries, they are grounded not only in basic human needs, but also in genuine ethno-cultural values and bonds. Dr. Fishman clearly sees the emergence of national consciousness as a process combining deliberate creation and genuine discovery. He brings to his analysis of this process a warm understanding of individual and group needs for finding roots and a deep appreciation of the emotional, esthetic, and practical significance of a group's unique cultural products — and particularly of its language — in confirming its sense of rootedness.

There is, finally, one other polarity that this book bridges: that between political and cultural definitions of nationalism. Unlike many current writers, Dr. Fishman does not define nationalism as a primary political ideology, linked to the establishment or enhancement of a nation-state. Rather, he presents it as an ideology designed to unify a group and to promote its interests by organizing that group around a more inclusive ethno-cultural identity and elaborating its unique beliefs, values, and behaviors. The push toward an independent political state is a possible and in fact rather frequent outcome of nationalist ideology but it is not, in Dr. Fishman's usage, a defining characteristic of that ideology. This definition does justice to those efforts at ethno-cultural mobilization — historical and contemporary — that are not directed toward an inde-pendent state, while at the same time illuminating the role of ethno-cultural mobilization as a powerful political force. Although my own work has proceeded in the opposite direction — starting out with nationalism as a political ideology with major ethno-cultural inputs (rather than as an ethno-cultural ideology with major political outcomes) — I see a great deal of virtue in Dr. Fishman's approach. It does seem to cut through much of the confusion and ambiguity that characterize the literature on nationalism. It provides a far better handle than most analyses, for example, in accounting for the recent development of a nationalist movement among Black Americans.

Dr. Fishman's approach is, of course, ideally suited to highlighting the relationship between nationalism and language, since language is both a major focus and tool of ethno-cultural integration. The analysis illuminates the relationship in both directions. Its major purpose is to clarify the role of language and language planning by exploring nationalist influences on these processes. No less important, however, is its contribution to our understanding of nationalism itself by exploring the ways in which language and language planning give shape and expression to it. Even our understanding of a nationalist movement like that of Black Americans, in which language does not play an obviously central part (as it does, for example, among French Canadians), can be enhanced by an analysis of the sentimental and instrumental implications of the group's linguistic patterns. I feel personally indebted to Dr. Fishman for introducing me to his analysis of language as an aid to understanding nationalism and for encouraging me, despite my lack of background in the field of sociolinguistics, to explore the relationship between the two (see Kelman, 1971). Perhaps the best way I can express my gratitude is by passing the word to other students of nationalism and urging them to begin their exploration of language and nationalism with the two integrative essays.

Language and Nationalism: Preface

A very few concerns have been at the forefront of my awareness in preparing the two essays that constitute this monograph. The first of these has been to gain sociohistorical and cross-national perspective with respect to language planning, a process which several colleagues and I are currently investigating via a variety of empirical and quantitative social science methods (Fishman, 1973). I have previously tried to locate my sociological inquiries within their broader human contexts (Fishman *et al.*, 1966; Fishman *et al.*, 1968a,b; Fishman *et al.*, 1971b). As one initially trained in historical research and much engrossed in the lessons of history to this very day, I frankly tend to see the best problems of the sociology of language as those that are closely linked to historical developments of lasting social significance (Fishman, 1971c, 1972a,b).

Language planning, like all planning, usually entails both a *direction* toward which movement is desired as well as an overall *justification* for movement in the specified direction. The planners and planning agencies, the detailed and daily processes of planning, and the cross-pressures, bargaining and compromises to which they are commonly subjected, all of these interact in movement toward overarching goals which may well involve not only language but other areas of nationality functioning as well. A common link between the direction of language planning and the direction of other planning efforts in many countries may be the nationalist ideological underpinnings that they may all share.

Nationalist ideologies are often so broadly formulated that there remains room for wide differences of opinion as to how they should be implemented. In addition, nationalist goals are frequently amended or supplemented by more timely and more precise goals. Nevertheless, nationalist theories and philosophies are often sufficiently pervasive and persistent that they provide important constraints, tendencies, and rationales for future planning, even after their own initial and most marked goals are attained or replaced. The past is frequently an influential modifier of present and future ingenuity and nationalism has been one of the most common and lasting interpretive links between the past, present, and future of nationalities. As a result I have kept before me the hypothesis that nationalist builders and planners (who may differ in ever so many ways) tend to turn to and return to nationalist philosophies in the pursuit of their strivings, in the language arena as in others.

In the pages that follow, I would like to examine the extent to which the language planning that has been pursued in many localities and in many periods has been guided by nationalism, i.e. by 'the social movements, attitude and ideologies which characterize the behavior of nationalities engaged in the struggle to achieve, maintain or enhance their position in the world' (Wirth, 1936). In order to do so, however, it seemed desirable, first of all, to become familiar with the formations and the transformations of nationalism itself, and second, to examine how and why language so commonly comes to be one of the ingredients in nationalist goals and programs. If these first two topical clusters can profitably be viewed as revealing sufficient regularity across-time and across-nations, then our consideration of the impact of nationalism on language planning *per se* would be all the more revealing.

However, if I have hoped, not just on this occasion but also again and again, that history could inform my social science ('The contribution of history is *perspective*. This is no small matter.' Landes & Tilly, 1971: 2), I have hoped equally much that social science would inform my history.

One of the truly esthetic experiences afforded by modern quantitative social science is encountered in its striving for parsimony in all explanatory efforts. I have, accordingly, asked myself whether nationalism, early and late, East and West, could not advantageously be viewed as a recurring constellation along a small number of parameters. As in all factor analytic explorations the dimensions themselves might be more or less orthogonally related to each other. Furthermore, as in all such efforts to gain conceptual parsimony, different instances of the phenomenon under study (here the flowering of nationalism and language planning) could receive widely different loadings on the dimensions derived. As a result, neither a Procrustean bed nor an endless array of unique cases has appealed to me, and I have wondered whether I, an outsider to the normal pursuit of social history, could steer an enlightening course between the two and yet arrive at a goal rather more characterized by the canon of parsimony than by its absence.

In all frankness, yet another goal has been in my awareness, at least from time to time, and the fact that it has not always been visible to me has not blinded me to the possibility that, after all, it might have been the most important of all, if only because it combined emotional and intellectual tension. I have witnessed three nationalist movements myself, at first hand so to speak (the Yiddish secularist, the Hebrew Zionist, and the Black American), and I have dearly wanted to understand them better and, above all, to understand why I respond to them as I do. Nevertheless, I have decided to do so by engaging in a once removed, twice removed, thrice removed mode of analysis, the hope that the wider canvas would illumine the narrower, while the narrower passion would drive me on to examine one hidden corner after another in the broader picture.

I have not been unaware of the fact that my topic, the nationalist impact on language planning, is (both emotionally and intellectually) not a popular one, particularly among American scholars. Nationalism is often viewed as a perversion, language planning as either impossible or undesirable. The rich, the white, and the safe have always been more than a little suspicious of problems particularly prevalent among the poor, the colored, and the endangered — even when they have deigned to help them, to guide them, or even to serve them. If even a historian of recent Black nationalism could conclude from his labors that other people have gladly left their ethnic ties behind them but 'only the Negro has had to invent a spurious nationalism to cope with his extraordinary position,' then what seems to be lacking is not so much sympathy as empathy, not so much knowledge as perspective, not so much information as understanding. If we listen only to each other we hear constant references to the 'excesses' of nationalism. However, without at all condoning them, we must grant that excesses occur in connection with every cause in which men believe strongly. Are we then to condemn dedications and convictions, or merely to pray for their greater mutual toleration? If we also listen to the third world we hear:

> 'This I know: we of Indonesia and the citizens of many countries of Asia and Africa have seen our dearest and best suffer and die, struggle and fail, and rise again to struggle and fail again — and again be resurrected from the very earth, and finally achieve their goal. Something burned in them; something inspired them. They called it nationalism. We who have followed and have seen what they built, but what they destroyed themselves in building — we, too, call their inspiration and our inspiration, nationalism. For us there is nothing ignoble in that word. On the contrary, it contains for us all that is best in mankind and all that is noblest' (Sukarno, cited in Snyder, 1964: 337).

Hearing this, it has seemed to me, we must not ask if the passion is 'good,' if it is 'justified,' if it is based on 'valid arguments.' Rather we must ask 'why does it occur, and when, and how can its obvious power be most productively channelled?'

The literature on nationalism — both that produced by nationalists *per se*, as well as that of those commenting upon the phenomenon from the sidelines — is voluminous. If one also attempts to follow this literature, as I have, in several languages and over a span of half a century or more, the task is literally endless as well as thankless. In order to remain afloat on this ocean of words — an ocean in which I, as a normal quantifier, first had to learn to swim — I have emphasized those writings dealing with language and only sampled those more generally or specifically (directionally) oriented. The major amount of time and freedom required for an undertaking of this kind was made available to me by the International Division of the Ford Foundation and by the East-West Center. To them, and most particularly to the colleagues with whom I have worked on language planning research under Ford Foundation auspices since 1968 (Das Gupta, Jernudd, Ferguson, and Rubin), and to all of the participants in the May 1969 Consultative Meeting on Language Planning Processes (see Rubin & Jernudd, 1971) who so helpfully and encouragingly commented on an earlier version of this monograph, go my sincere thanks for their assistance and their stimulation. Their patience and their support will be repaid, at least in part, and my own hopes for this monograph will be realized, if now, on the basis of some of the dimensions that it suggests, the *empirical* measurement and description of nationality beliefs, actions, attitudes and emotions can be more fully related to corresponding differentials with respect to language behavior and behavior toward language (of which language planning is but one example).

Part I: The nature of nationalism

'For, whosoever is of such mean reason that he thinks his birthplace the most delightful under the sun, will also prefer his own vulgar tongue, that means his mother tongue, to all others . . . . But we, whose Fatherland is the world, as for the fish the sea . . . we have found out that there are many places and cities, and we believe more noble and more delightful ones, than Tuscany and Florence from which I derive and of which I am a citizen; and that many nations and peoples use a more delightful and useful language than the Italians.'

Dante Alighieri, in his *De Vulgari Eloquentia*, Book I, section 6.

'As you speak the French language by nature, it is reasonable that you should be the subject of the King of France. I quite agree that the Spanish language should belong to the Spaniard and the German to the German. But the whole region of the French language must be mine.'

Henry IV, to deputies of newly acquired provinces, according to Pierre Nathieu in his *Histoire de Henri IV*, 1631.

'Has a nationality anything dearer than the speech of its fathers? In its speech resides its whole thought domain, its tradition, history, religion and basis of life, all its heart and soul. To deprive a people of its speech is to deprive it of its one eternal good . . . With language is created the heart of a people.'

Johann G. Herder, in his *Briefe zu Beförderung der Humanität*, 1783.

'Indeed, we can hardly conceive a more glorious object, a more sublime spectacle, than a nation . . . who could form and highly refine a language, write elaborate works on its grammars and compose hymns and prayers while their brethren in other parts of the world could hardly think it possible to represent the elementary sounds in their speech by visible characters.'

A Hindu, *Bengal Magazine*, 1875-76, 4, 367.

'Up, ye Slovaks, still is living our true Slovak language while our loyal hearts are beating for our nation. Living, living, yes and deathless is the Slovak spirit. Hell and lightning, hell and lightning rage in vain against us.'

Slovak National Anthem

'To have a state composed of peoples who speak the same language, or to make only those peoples who speak the same language an independent state seems more natural and most desirable.'

Ziya Gökalp in *Turk Yurdu*, 1914.

Preliminary definitions

The basic concepts in any discussion of nationalism deals primarily with transformations in sociocultural integration on the one hand, and, secondarily, with transformations in political-operational integration, on the other hand. In view of the long and varied history of interest in both of these phenomena in scientific as well as in lay circles (sociocultural collectivities and their supposedly distinctive characteristics having been commented upon by Herodotus and other ancient scholars, commentators, and leaders) it is not at all surprising that usage varies considerably, both from language to language as well as from period to period. The definitions that follow are not motivated by any conviction as to their purported terminological superiority, but rather, in order to indicate the usage that will be followed in the present discussion.[2]

Nationality

The designation *nationality* will be employed to indicate sociocultural units that have developed beyond primarily local self-concepts, concerns, and integrative bonds. The term stands in contrastive juxtaposition to others such that it presupposes at least a level of sociocultural integration more elementary (i.e. simpler, smaller, more particularistic, more localistic) than the one it designates, namely *ethnic group*,[3] if not also a level of sociocultural integration that is more advanced (i.e. larger, more inclusive, more complex, although still characterized to some extent by ethnicity). Although the term 'nationality' can be traced back over a century in its present usage (see, e.g. Acton, 1907; originally published 1862) it first came to be 'widely applied during the first quarter of this

LANGUAGE AND NATIONALISM: TWO INTEGRATIVE ESSAYS   107

century in connection with the well-known political problem of reconciling the sovereignty of states with the autonomy of ethnic groups' (Znaniecki, 1952: xiv).

In connection with the prevalent use just referred to, the term 'nationality' is neutral with respect to the existence or nonexistence of a corresponding political unit or polity. Indeed, it is precisely because the human populations encompassed by the designations *nationality* and *polity* need *not* be isomorphic that it becomes possible to more clearly pursue the issue of the circumstances under which sociocultural groups (i.e. groups distinguished by customs and values pertaining to their daily and all-encompassing goals and behaviors) do or do not have or seek polities of their own.

If the term is *not* intended to denote absence or presence of control over a polity (although it is not meant to rule out political activity toward that or other ends, viz. Akzin, 1964), it *is* intended to denote a more advanced degree and inclusive scope or scale of effective organization and of elaborated beliefs, values, and behaviors than those that obtain in the case of ethnic groups *per se*. The organization–behavior–ideology inter-actions referred to focus *directly* upon the preservation, strengthening, and guided development of the presumably distinctive customs and values of nationality, and, only *indirectly* (in order to safeguard the above) upon whatever political, economic, religious, or other social systems may be considered necessary for that purpose.

Nationalism

The more inclusive organization and the more elaborated beliefs, values, and behaviors which nationalities develop on behalf of their avowed ethnocultural self-interest constitute the referents of the term nationalism.[4]

Some few writers, among them Wuorinen (1950), prefer the terms national consciousness or nationality consciousness, particularly when referring to less militant manifestations of conscious ethnicity than those for which they reserve the term nationalism. However, it seems to me that the further introduction of strength or saliency considerations into a notion which already, in part, depends on such considerations for its differentia-tion from ethnicity *per se* may be more troublesome than helpful for the purposes of initial nonquantitative discussion. In addition, of course, nationality consciousness would seem to refer, at best, only to the cognitive aspects of nationalism rather than to their more complex cognitive, conative (valuational and affective), and overt realizations.

Far more prevalent are those who tie the term nationalism either to the pursuit of political independence, or thereafter, to the maximization of interpolity economic (or other) advantage. In this connection I believe Baron's approach (1947) to be more productive, in that it considers nationalism to be essentially conscious or organized ethnocultural solidarity which may or may not then be directed outside of its initial sphere toward political, economic, and religious goals. In Parsonian terms one might say that while nationalism derives from the pattern maintenance and integrative subsystems of general social systems, the interdependence of subsystems is such that it also commonly interacts with the adaptation and goal attainment subsystems as well. Since political independent territoriality *is* so common a goal in the modern era, I have proposed that the cluster of behaviors-beliefs-values pertaining specifically to *its* acquisition, maintenance, and development be separately designated as *nationism* (Fishman, 1968a).

Nation

In our discussions that follow, the term *nation* will primarily refer to any independent political-territorial unit which is largely or increasingly under the control of a particular nationality.[5] In order not to anticipate the subsequent discussion in detail, I will only suggest at this juncture that the term may be usefully contrasted with such terms as *state*, *polity*, or *country* which do not necessarily denote either independence *vis-à-vis* external control or the predominance of a single nationality *vis-à-vis* internal control. The past two hundred years have undeniably witnessed the eclipse of several multinationality states and the appearance of larger numbers of polities whose leaders have aspired to reach the goal of single-nationality nations. As Znaniecki observes, 'the conception of "national land" . . . is rooted first in the old idea of "patria" or "fatherland" and is obviously connected with the myth of common origin' (1952: 96). This means whereby nationalism and nationism both strive to confirm this myth (i.e. their efforts to produce a better fit between the theory of common ancient origin and the reality of common current interdependence) and the role of language in these efforts, constitute the story I wish to tell.

Recurrent components of nationalism

Having decided to define *nationalism* as the organizationally heightened and elaborated beliefs, attitudes, and behaviors of societies acting on behalf of their avowed ethnocultural self-interest, it is clear that for such societally organized goal activity to occur it is first necessary for populations to become convinced that they possess in common certain unique ethnocultural characteristics, and that these similarities, over and above obvious local variations and subgroup differences, are of *importance* to them. Neither of these traits (*recognition* of common ethnocultural characteristics and *conviction* with respect to their overriding importance) is part of the biologically given nature of mankind. Neither of them has existed in all ethnically different groups at all times. Indeed, such organized and heightened affiliative beliefs, attitudes and behaviors among larger populations that are not exposed to messages or contacts from outside their immediate environments are seemingly quite uncommon. Most non-industrial, non-urban, non-literate populations have primarily exhibited very local or 'primordial' attachments to near kin and to the immediately experienced customs and social structures related to them. Broader ties or allegiances among such populations are normally restricted to their immediate political, religious, or cultural élites (local nobility, clergy, and scribes) who *have* had nonlocal experiences which *have* exposed them to the ideas and the structures of ethnocultural unity and the organization of authenticity.[6]

Lest we assume that such localism is limited to dark and distant backwaters it should be pointed out that all European histories are replete with accounts of the separatism and particularism of their rural populations until comparatively recent days. It is, of course, true that the last extensive manifestations of such views and behaviors in Europe are restricted to its least modernized Central, Eastern, and Southeastern areas. These began to seem anomalous in the middle of the last century when Brauner [a participant in the first All Slav Congress, Vienna, 1848] told an anecdote of how peasants in the district of Sacz in West Galicia, when asked whether they were Poles, replied: 'We are quiet folk.' 'Then are you Germans?' 'We are decent folk' (Namier, 1944: 107). However, the continuation of such narrower or smaller scale affiliative beliefs, values, and behaviors even in modern days in somewhat the same area is indicated by Znaniecki's report that a 1934-35 ' . . . investigation of the inhabitants of the marshy Pripet area (which between the two World Wars was included within Poland) showed that nearly half of those peasants who were ethnically White Ruthenians did not know that such a nationality existed

and considered themselves as merely belonging to local communities'
(1952: 82). It is out of just such ethnocultural fragmentation that
nationalism creates a broader and more conscious unity.

Broader unity

A basic component, then (at least of early nationalism), is an
insistence on the expansion of the scope of perceived commonality of
ethnocultural characteristics to a point far beyond their original, directly
experienced, primordial bounds. Nationalism, at least for hitherto traditional or transitional populations, represents an expansion of affiliative
beliefs, attitudes and behaviors so as to include far more distant (indeed,
purely figurative) kin, far more distant authorities, and far more inclusive
commitments than those that are immediately available to or directly
impinge on their daily experiences. This is not to say that premodern
societies have been entirely removed from central value systems, for this
would be overstating the case (Shils, 1961), particularly in light of the
ability of larger religious systems to penetrate into even the most backward
and isolated areas and to maintain personal 'spokesmen' there. However,
in premodern periods the articulation between peripheral and central areas
was, at best, fragmentary, because of both functional and structural
difficulties. Communication difficulties and differences in beliefs, values,
and behaviors reinforced each other[7] to the point that only clearly
overwhelming social forces could overcome the overriding cognitive and
affirmative isolation of traditional populations for more than brief
interludes.

Not infrequently the unifying social forces involved were (and are) not
merely multidirectional social and economic changes but the direct force
of arms as well. Looking back, scarcely half a century after the Revolution,
upon the royal as well as the republican contributions to the unification
of France, Michelet had no doubt but that its broader unity, purchased at
the cost of countless lives, was a supreme good: 'This sacrifice of the
diverse interior nationalities to the great nationality which comprises them
undoubtedly strengthened the latter ... . It was at the moment when
France suppressed within herself the divergent French countries that she
proclaimed her high and original revelations' (1846: 286). Thus, even later
nationalisms, those which combined smaller regional nationalities into
greater nationalities — rather than merely those that transform
particularistic ethnic groups into initial nationalities — often include
broader unity among their basic drives.

It is via the experience of broader unity that the common man comes to recognize his relationship and his interdependence with a human population most of whose members he has never met and to believe that this relationship and interdependence are and always have been quite naturally rooted in various ethnocultural similarities between him and his far-flung 'kin'. However, two exaggerations need to be guarded against in this connection. The first is of a *post hoc ergo propter hoc* nature, namely to conclude that perceived broader unity *necessarily* stems from perceived *ethnocultural* similarity (rather than from other integrative bonds along more purely economic, political, religious, or special purpose grounds). Broader ethnocultural similarity is not a 'natural' basis of human grouping; certainly it is not the prime basis for *political* integration throughout human history.[8] It is also not a necessary outcome of perceived broader unity of purpose or values. Thus, where it *is* attained and stressed it deserves attention in its own right, rather than as a natural consequence of increased flow of communication or other possible expressions and implementations of broader unity *per se*.

Secondly, it would be wrong to imply that either broader unity or any of its possible consequences and concomitants are either fully replacive or neatly stagewise phenomena. Rather, it represents awareness and ex- periences that wax and wane differentially in various population segments and, therefore, it must be understood as always coexisting with narrower and sometimes more primary awarenesses and experiences.

Stressed authenticity

'When seen as a movement, nationalism represents a series of stages in the struggle of a given solidarity group to achieve its basic aims of unity and self-direction' (Symmons-Symonolewicz, 1965: 1,965). A second basic component of nationalism is its stress on ethnocultural characterization and on the authenticity, purity, and nobility of the beliefs, values, and behaviors that typify the community of reference. In its most generalized and theoretical form, as expounded by those who could rise above the problems of their own local nationalities in order to seek out more encompassing rationales, nationalism became an ode to the beauty, the morality, and the value of diversity *per se*. It was claimed that 'no individual, no country, no people, no history of a people, no state is like any other. Therefore, the true, the beautiful, and the good are not the same for them. Everything is suffocated if one's own way is not sought and if another nation is blindly taken as a model. Civilization consists primarily in the potentialities of a nation and in making use of them' (Herder, *Sämtliche Werke*, v.4, p.472; cited by Kohn, 1944: 433).[9]

It is part of the specific nature of the nationalist (rather than any more generally reformist) stress on authenticity to find it in the lower classes and in the distant past. 'The lower orders are seen as being not simply primitive peasants, but as the source of national creativity . . . . Salvation must come from below' (Minogue, 1967: 60-61), if only because the peasantry has hitherto been more isolated from the foreign fads and influences to which others (particularly cosmopolitan intellectuals, estranged upper-class strata and urbanites more generally) are so likely to be exposed or to seek exposure.[10] The peasantry, and, at times, the lower classes more generally, have more fully and faithfully preserved the ethnocultural distinctiveness of the past and it is the past, in all its authenticity and glory, that constitutes the main storehouse from which nationalism derives its dynamism for changing the present and creating the future.

Whereas traditionalisms of various kinds seek a return to or a preservation of the genuine past,[11] nationalism seeks to 'render the present a rational continuation of the past' (Bromage, 1956: 29), indeed, it seeks and creates a usable past. 'The very idea that they [specified populations] should be united is founded upon the doctrine that, however much their folk cultures may differ, they are essentially similar as compared with those of other collectivities and that this similarity is essentially due to a common historical background' (Znaniecki, 1952: 30).[12]

While it is true that nationalism both seeks out and cultivates the Little Tradition of an ostensible past — with its folksongs, folktales, proverbs, folk dances, costumes, pastimes, and expressions — it finds not only purity and authenticity in the past but also (and particularly) greatness. It is this greatness, rooted in authenticity, that can (it is hoped) inspire current masses to make new efforts, to overcome new dangers, and to achieve new (and even greater) greatness. Thus, in seeking the collaboration of the Hungarians in his quarrels with the Habsburg Emperor in 1809, Napoleon issued a proclamation saying

'You have national customs and a national language; you boast of a distant and illustrious origin; take up then once again your existence as a nation. Have a king of your choice, who will rule only for you, who will live in the midst of you, whom only your citizens and your soldiers will serve . . . . Meet therefore in a National Diet, in the manner of your ancestors' (cited by Kedourie, 1961: 94).[13]

Similar reconstructions of the past were made by other nationalist spokesmen. Rumanian leaders proclaimed all the contentious polyglot areas that lay before them to be elements of the ancient Roman colony of Dacia (held by Rome from A.D.107 to 270) and the Rumanians to be the heirs of the Romans in bringing Christianity and civilization to the Balkans (Kolarz, 1946: 173). At roughly the same time, Irish leaders called upon their fellowmen to recognize that they constituted a

> '. . . race which at one time held possession of more than half Europe, which established itself in Greece and burned infant Rome . . . after overthrowing and trampling on the primitive peoples of half Europe . . . We alone . . . escaped the claws of . . . the victorious eagles of Rome; we alone developed ourselves naturally upon our own lines outside of and free from all Roman influence; we alone were thus able to produce an early art and literature and — we are our father's sons' (Hyde, 1894: 117-31).

All this being true 'it behooves us to know the nature and source of that former greatness, that we may be encouraged to restore as far as possible all that was great and beautiful in the past and so make our country — as we fervently hope — a "Nation once again!"' (Flannery, 1896: 13). As we read these and similar words today we cannot but recognize their energizing, mobilizing purpose and effect. The past is being mined, ideologized, and symbolically elaborated in order to provide determination, even more than direction, with respect to current and future challenges.

Nationalism is not so much backward-oriented — particularly where, as in most of Europe, it has been free to be eclectic with respect to the past and with respect to a very distant past at that — as much as it seeks to derive unifying and energizing power from widely held images of the past in order to overcome a quite modern kind of fragmentation and loss of identity. In this sense, nationalism may be seen as quite reality-oriented, both in its intuitive recognition of the power of past images of greatness, as well as in its intuitive response to the anonymity and insecurity that are common concomitants of actual or impending change to post-traditional life-styles. Nationalist movements stress authenticity in order to legitimize their demand for goal-oriented unity, a unity that is purportedly also authentic, in that it too existed at an earlier time when small communities and emotionally satisfying interactions between community members were still the rule. The division of labor and the differentiation of experience are not only interrelated with the emergence of unnatural and impersonal societies but also with the loss of broader unity and authenticity. Thus, nationalism claims to reverse the modern affective imbalance between mechanical and organic solidarity,[14] between Gemeinschaft and Gesellschaft, between the sacred and the secular, in order thereby to release for current purposes the ancient but still available (although too often dormant) unity and genius of populations who would otherwise be fractionated and de-ethnicized by modern adversaries, both human and technological.

Nationalism's stress on authenticity-oriented belief, attitude, and behavior may well be crucial in modern and modernizing mass-societies in order to reach, influence, and activate large numbers of individuals who actually lead quite different and separate daily lives and who only interact with a very small proportion of the total community of broader unity throughout their entire lifetimes. Small communities can transmit and implement their narrower unity and authenticity directly through the social structure, i.e. through the face-to-face interactions that are permissible according to local cultural norms. Larger societies must transmit and implement fidelity to large-scale unity by means of the institutions of mass culture: formal organizations, communication media, schools, and government *per se*.[15] Thus, nationalism is likely to utilize the institutions and techniques of massification at the very same time that it seeks to provide an ethnocultural solution for the rootlessness and meaninglessness that technologically based massification itself engenders.[16]

Basic forces: Social change

Economic development

Nationalism provides a redefinition and mobilization of personal and group identity, purpose, and possibilities. Such redefinition and mobilization become attractive when their prior, more traditional counterparts, are rendered inoperative or nonproductive as a result of social change. Throughout human history populations have become more conscious of and more concerned with their ethnicity when it has been impressed upon them that they could expect certain benefits — or that they were denied certain benefits — as a result of it. In more or less modern days such impressions have most frequently spread together with the spread of basic and far-reaching social change. Thus, nationalism in Europe spread most rapidly at a time when, on the one hand, Napoleon was disrupting its political concepts and conventions, and, on the other, when '. . . the industrial revolution, accompanied by a prodigious increase in population, was gradually penetrating everywhere, transforming methods of production, disturbing traditional social relations and creating vast urban conglomerations. New wealth was being created and new social classes were coming to the top who would, sooner or later, claim and obtain their share of political power' (Kedourie, 1961: 95).

A constantly recurring theme in analyses of modern nationalism is to point to industrialization in particular (or to economic change somewhat more broadly) as its most basic or important cause.[17] This view is justified on the grounds of the undeniable disruptive impact of industrial and other economic transformations on prior affiliative and integrative bonds and rationales. It is further justified on the basis of the use to which nationalism has more recently been put in connection with planned economic development efforts and in the mobilization of successively poorer strata of the world's population.[18] This argument has then been traced back to historical parallels which imply that it is particularly compelling at a 'transitional' stage in economic development, when 'the masses are mobilized but not yet assimilated' (Ingelhart & Woodward, 1967: 40, paralleling similar statements in Deutsch, 1953), and when a new awareness dawns with respect to the attainability of personal achievement and the real social mobility consequences of such achievement (McClelland, 1961). Some students of nationalism have carefully attended to both the disruptive and the facilitative or motivating aspects of economic change. Thus, Friedland comments perceptively that

'the social structures generating prenationalist movements are already transitional in that . . . inroads have been made into the subsistence economy and the society is increasingly involved in the cash nexus; stratification of the indigenous population is beginning, particularly as some autochthones are educated along Western lines' (Friedland, 1968: 17–18).

Several students of nationalism have pointed to the fact that its economic preconditions have successively come into being in different parts of the world. As a result, when its early disintegrative and reintegrative consequences had already spent their force in one part of the world (to be followed by subsequent stages that we will examine below), its impact then began to be felt in yet other, initially neighboring and ultimately quite distant areas, into which industrialization or other basic economic change had subsequently penetrated.

'If the whole world could have been industrialized simultaneously and uniformly, national differences might not have been emphasized. As it was, however, no two countries were at any given time in exactly the same stage of industrialization and each sought . . . to insure its own industrial development' (Hayes, 1931: 236).

If we add to the above temporal variation the fact that most countries undergoing industrialization or other profound economic changes were by and large multinationality states, and that economic changes generally tended to favor one region of such states over others, then we obtain a picture not only of *inter*state nationalistic tensions but, even more basically, of *intra*state cleavages as well.

'The integration of the plural society is based primarily on a system of relationships between culturally differentiated groups of unequal status and power. This system of relationships not only reflects the power structure of the political order under which it is subsumed, but it also serves to express the maintenance or change of that political order. More precisely, any change capable of altering the structure of intersectional relations will have consequences for the political order of the society' (Depres, 1968: 7).

Around each newly developing center of major economic ascendency, systems of ethnocultural, social, and political integration were developed which tended to favor those populations that controlled newly necessary human and natural resources and that tended to exploit, submerge, or displace those about them that did not. It became increasingly difficult for the latter 'to improve their life chances without changing their sectional membership or, alternatively [if that was felt to be impossible], without seeking to improve the status and power of their respective cultural sections' (Depres, 1968: 7). Thus, as a concomitant and consequence of widespread and fundamental economic changes influencing both inter-polity as well as intrapolity relations, and the impact of which was both disruptive (for masses of common folk) and facilitative (for the favored few), nationalist movements initially spread as newly favored populations (from the point of view of whatever economically based changes were then uppermost) sought to protect themselves from the claims and controls of concurrently less preferred (but previously or co-established) sociopolitical units (e.g. England *vis-à-vis* France). Subsequently, nationalist movements spread as hitherto backward groups, formerly under the sway or shadow of regions that had already experienced social change and social advantage, began to savor or even only to anticipate their own day in the sun, i.e. their own growing correspondence between newly valuable and localized natural and human resources (e.g. Ireland *vs*. England). Finally, nationalist movements spread even further as counterreactions against the policies of once submerged populations that, having come to possess newfound power based on economic development, wielded it most pointedly against former partners in poverty (e.g. Hungarians *vis-à-vis* Slovaks in the Habsburg Empire). Economically advantaged groups are always relatively more conscious of and protective of their groupness. Disadvantaged groups become similarly conscious only as a result of partial changes in their circumstances which, more than anything else, merely serve to heighten their sense of relative deprivation and the fact that it is enforced on the basis of group membership. There is thus a strong contrastive element in nationalism, which, like broader unity and stressed authenticity, is likely to have language planning consequences as well.

The sequential economic development argument, predominant though it is among students of nationalism, is frequently felt to lack a final clincher. That is, sequential economic development and all of its ensuing disorganization, reorganization, rivalry and opportunity may well be facilitative of various kinds of reintegrative and reformist movements. What evidence is there of a *necessary* link between such developments and the massive appeal of broader ethnocultural unity as well as of stressed ethnocultural authenticity? In large part, the argument for such a direct link is based on a presumed need to restore ethnocultural bonds, but of a kind appropriate to the new level of economic massification, once the old primordial bonds have been rendered inoperative. Nationalism thus appears as a natural cure for a natural ailment: the restoration of more meaningful and appropriate ethnocultural loyalties subsequent to the disruption of older ones that are no longer functional, in the light of widespread economic change. The view that distinctive ethnocultural integration is a basic human need, that modern technology is disruptive of this need, and that nationalism represents a natural attempt to *restore* ethnocultural balance (or to *create* it at a higher level) is well over a century old in writings on this matter.[19]

Nationalism: One of many co-occurring responses to a variety of co-occurring changes

In contrast to those many scholars who have viewed nationalism as following inevitably or, at least primarily, from the dislocations occasioned by rapid and large-scale economic transitions (and from the increased integrative capacities, opportunities and needs which these have fostered) are those who have emphasized the equal or great importance of noneconomic causation. Some, like Hayes, have pointed to the fact that in earlier eras economic change led to multination states or empires rather than to the crystallization of single-nationality states.[20] Others, like Akzin, have pointed to the importance of long-drawn-out armed conflicts as formative of political centralization and, subsequently of nationality consciousness, as a result of state-sponsored efforts to resist external threat via unified and stressed action.[21] Still others have pointed particularly to the modern decline of religious affiliation as a primary integrative bond of broader sorts and have considered nationalism as nothing more than the 'religion of modern man.'[22] Others, finally, have stressed the contagious power of the ideals of nationality as such. Presumably, these ideals were always waiting for recognition and finally, when first recognized and propagated, due to whatever circumstances in whatever part of the globe, they inevitably spread to others by infection, by example, and by the inexorable workings of the *Zeitgeist*.[23] The latter view is sufficiently vague, that it does not so much propose a particular rival to economic change as it suggests that such change must itself be viewed in a broader framework of ongoing change as well as continuing stability. This last position, then, leads us conveniently to more complex (multifactor) interpretations of the links between nationalism and social change.

Although no other single 'basic cause' has received as much attention as the economic, most modern scholarship has shifted to an emphasis on economic change as one of several concurrent kinds of large-scale social change and nationalism as one of several interrelated responses to the problems and opportunities concurrent with or resulting from such change.[24] The most common cited trio of interacting and co-occurring causes and effects is that cited by Talmon in connection with the question 'Why did nationalism appear and triumph precisely at the time it did?' In his reply he pointed to 'the decline of religious sanctions and the weakening of the religious framework; the doctrine of the rights of man and the democratic sovereignty of the people; and economic and social processes at the onset of the Industrial Revolution' (1965: 17). Essentially, Talmon is pointing to the functional demise of a former principle of broader unity, to the rise of an ideology of mass participation and free competition in political processes, and to the dislocation of small-scale ethnicity such that ethnocultural bonds on a wider scale became both necessary and possible.[25]

Since the political consequences of nationalism have been of greatest interest to American social scientists, it is the relationship between nationalism and mass participation in politics that has received the greatest amount of attention.[26] Deutsch has stressed the fact that in the multi-nationality states it was usually not really desired nor immediately feasible to economically and politically absorb all of those who were dislocated (mobilized) by economic and technological change. On the other hand, even those who were absorbed normally met 'serious disappointments and frustrations of many of the new hopes, claims and expectations.' As a result, the first steps toward economic and political modernization were normally 'followed by the rise of more extremely nationalistic leaders, platforms or parties within each ethnic group, and by a more exclusive stress on ethnic in-group values and interests' (1957: 62). These leaders, in turn, courted popular support by stressing the need for greater popular participation in the political processes of the multinationality state and greater popular gain from ultimate political separation from the state. Thus,

> 'nationalism is historically tied to the growth of democracy. Indeed, it has been asserted that nationalism was the essential condition for the democratizing of the modern state. Against such a view, it seems sounder to see democracy and nationalism in a "dialectic" relation . . . . They were in their origin contemporary movements and therefore many of the conditions for one also served to condition the other' (Friedrich, 1963: 560).

While nationalism remained primarily concerned with the ethnocultural basis of organized activity and democracy with the processes of free participation and competition, both borrowed adherents and platform planks from the other. Both were strengthened by masses of dislocated humanity that clamored for activization and organization on the basis of wider bonds and behaviors. 'Where the disease is various, no particular definite remedy can meet the wants of all. Only the attraction of an abstract idea, or of an ideal state, can unite in common action multitudes who seek a universal cure for many special evils and a common restorative applicable to many different conditions' (Acton [1862] 1907: 222). Nationalism was (and is) one of a small number of such 'abstract ideas' dealing with an 'ideal state', all of which have competed with each other and increasingly intermingled with each other during the past 200 years of worldwide efforts to cope with the pains and pleasures of basic and rapid social change.

Basic forces: Élites

Widespread, basic, and long-continuing social dislocation capable of fundamentally changing the opportunity and power relations between groups within multiethnic states must be *perceived* as such, *exploited* as such, and, to some extent, *made* into such. The crucial catalysts in this connection are proto-élites who are (or feel) excluded from the power and influence they covet and who possess the personal gifts or material resources to move symbols and masses toward desired sociopolitical regroupings. In the development of nationalism the above general formulation can be further refined by considering the élites who recognized, moved, and represented the broader collectivity before the advent of nationalism and its concurrent social and economic changes. In country after country, we find that only the nobility and those clerics and other intellectuals united with them were conscious of their broader unity and of their national roles. Thus, 'the French nobility [in the eighteenth century] had long regarded themselves as racially and morally distinct from the rest of the French population. They alone were the nation[ality]' (Minogue, 1967: 10). Slowly, at first, those social classes included within and recognizing themselves as part of the nation[ality] began to expand, particularly with the growth of the higher bourgeoisie, which was generally the first class, outside the nobility and the intellectuals, to be incorporated into the ruling or political class. This expansion of power and of national identity occurred first in Western Europe. Thus, notwithstanding Rousseau's identification of the 'nation' with the 'people,' it remained true there, as elsewhere, that by the mid-nineteenth century only the upper classes consistently 'identified themselves with the nation and the national interest . . . . The lower classes . . . [were] excluded from both a real stake in the national economy and an active partnership in the determination of the policy of "their" nation' (Kohn, 1968: 64). Indeed, when nationalist doctrines and aspirations were first communicated to localistic populations they were often initially rejected, precisely because they were interpreted as self-serving upper-class, intellectual, or urban fabrications,[27] if they were understood at all. The spread of nationalism is, therefore, marked not by its existence in the upper reaches of society, but by its successful communication to and activation of the urban (and ultimately also the rural) lower middle and lower classes. Such spread frequently involved a new intellectual and economic proto-élite just as much as it involved a new class of respondents.

Successful nationalist proto-élites 'form an increasingly coherent intellectual community activated by the ideal of a culturally united and socially solidary national society, which should include all the people whose folk cultures are presumed to be essentially alike, and who are supposed to share the same historical background . . . [and] who should be equally separated from peoples with different cultures' (Znaniecki,

1952: 25, 81). These proto-élites, then, are the essential synthesizers, separators, popularizers, and organizers on whom the spread of nationalism depends. They not only create or further the broader unity and heightened authenticity that they seek, but they plant an awareness of both of these desiderata in a population that is becoming increasingly receptive to unifying and activating solutions of many kinds;[28] they point to the success of nationalist struggles in distant cultures and in other times with which the ordinary man would hardly be familiar,[29] they spread the views of spokesmen that might otherwise remain unnoticed,[30] and, in general, they heighten awarenesses that are only latent, so that not only will masses come to feel that they constitute a nationality but that they will also be willing to act upon the basis of that feeling.[31]

The role of élites in creating both the awareness and substance of broader unity and authenticity is of particular interest to us in view of the parallels that exist between these efforts and directions and those that pertain to language planning *per se*. Obviously, intellectuals and other élites begin not only with their own goals and biases but also with some preexisting raw materials which these biases can shape. 'A leader is almost bound to utilize those elements in the underlying population and its culture which lend themselves to . . . manipulation and exploitation' (Friedrich, 1963: 557). History and ethnography are the reservoirs of symbols and myths, heroes and missions which nationalist élites first mine and then refine in their quest for ethnically unifying and energizing themes. Every group has 'some heroic forefather who called for national unity or national reassertion in the past' (Deutsch, 1964b: 51), some gallery of great poets or sayers and some archive of moving poetry and sayings, some aspirations that have remained with it as echoes and memories in folktales and folk songs. These are the building blocks of unity and authenticity that nationalist élites discover, augment, and combine. 'We find everywhere a curious searching for historical ancestors . . . to reconstruct . . . [the] past as the most glorious, like a lost paradise . . . in search after what a Magyar poet called "ancestors, ancestors, you glorious ancestors . . . you tempests shaking the whole world"' (Jaszi, 1929: 259-60).

The crucial role of scholarship in this entire enterprise is clear, but it is also clear that many nationalist scholars 'acted in the dual role of scholars and men of politics, their scholarly work was directly influenced by political demands. Their efforts in either field were inseparable' (Kohn, 1955: 158). The origins of broader unity were pushed back further and further.[32] Literatures were discovered and, if necessary, created wherever 'what was admirable did not exist and what existed was not admirable.'[33] At the same time, boundaries also had to be established. If unity and authenticity within the pale were intensified, then the differences separating insiders from outsiders were magnified. Here, too, the élites worked with pre-existing building blocks, as well as with their concepts of the feasible and the desirable, in order to define 'who should stand with whom against whom' (Sulzbach, 1943: 134). By serving in each of these capacities, as unifiers, as cleansers, and as differentiators, nationalist leaders revived and created affiliative symbols, beliefs, attitudes, and behaviors which could, in time, lead toward the objective integration that 'had always existed.' Just as folklore itself is merely the accumulation in the public domain of items that had their definite individual innovators, so the creation of nationalist unity and authenticity represent an élitist acceleration and organization of the normal and constant interaction between *gehobenes Primitivgut* and *gesunkenes Kulturgut*.

The success of élitist efforts was not always startling. It often came haltingly, in little things, and among the petit bourgeois rather than among the masses.[34] In part, this was due to quite understandable and predictable counterforces existing fully outside of the élite ranks, but in part it was also due to the nature of the early nationalist élites themselves. Large proportions of them stemmed from other backgrounds than the people whom they sought to organize.[35] Others had long lived or been educated abroad, or in exile, and were only marginally ethnic in their personal lives.[36] In one way or in another, they had become so different from those whom they were trying to unify and to energize that part of the emotional and intellectual intensity of their work is interpretable as a search for personal identity and for a usable personal past.[37] In truth, the intellectuals of whom mention has been made are in large part more accurately designated as an 'intelligentsia,' i.e. as a 'phenomenon essentially connected with the transition. An intelligentsia is a class which is alienated from its own society' (Gellner, 1964: 169).[38] It was this fact of alienation which enabled these élites (whose own life-styles, self-understandings, and power potentials had changed) to envision broader unities and deeper authenticities than those that really existed, and, at the same time, to experience additional hardships and rebuffs in initially communicating their vision to others. Nationalist élites frequently went through an agonizing process of remaking themselves before they succeeded in remaking 'their' peoples. Such individuals could also envision the remaking of language itself![39]

Basic forces: The urban condition

If widespread and basic social disorganization and reorganization constituted the major need- and opportunity-systems to which nationalism was a possible response, and if élites were the major formulators, synthesizers, and emphasizers of this response, then urban centers were the primary arenas in which these needs, opportunities and responses encountered and magnified each other. The city has long been pointed to as the vortex of social change in general and of the kinds of change related to the entire gamut of modernization-and-development processes in particular.[40] Dislocation from the social structure of the traditional countryside was there maximized, as were the cumulative impact of occupation and educational change, the growth of voluntary organizations and associations, the influence of mass media, and the constant interaction of insecurity, competition, and conflict. The eighteenth and nineteenth century fathers of modern sociology, Durkheim, Mannheim, Simmel, and Weber, all reflected at length upon the impact of the city on social life, upon its uprooting tendencies, as well as upon its consequences in terms of the expansion and reformation of linkages between individual, group, community, and national functioning. Twentieth-century sociology has been filling out this picture on an increasingly empirical, quantitative, and international scale ever since.

While most investigators have been at work detailing the contribution of urbanization and urban centers to the appeal of (and need for) new and massive solutions for the ills of mankind, students of nationalism have been similarly attentive to the links between urbanization and urban centers on the one hand, and broader ethnocultural unity and authenticity on the other. These links include the re-establishment of collective or supraindividual identification and the creation of broader kinship ties,[41] which nationalist movements have provided and stressed for those who have not only lost their former individual statuses and group identifications, but who, additionally, have often found themselves blocked from attaining new status and security subsequent to urban relocation, precisely on ethnocultural grounds.

From the point of view of social history, it is convincingly evident that the city not only grew as a result of the very same changes that disrupted primordial localism, but that it also (a) attracted those whom it had uprooted and (b) put them in touch with the élites who had congregated in urban areas even earlier, and (c) as a result, finally put the uprooted in touch with each other and converted them into a new force in social, political, and cultural affairs.[42] The city was thus a factor not only in creating and fostering nationalism, but also in providing nationalism with the power that it attained, i.e. nationalism captured urban élites and proletarians at the very time that urban centers definitively displaced the countryside as the loci of national power, national culture, and, therefore, national identity.

The growth of nationalism is, to a large extent, marked by the *occupation* (*or reoccupation*) of the city by hitherto largely rural ethnocultural groups and by their *utilization of the city* as a device for their own greater ethnocultural unity, authenticity, and modernity. The city has everywhere been a gathering point for foreign residents.[43] However, in multiethnic states before the growth of nationalism, the foregoing was further complicated by the fact that the cities were dominated by economically more advanced, culturally 'foreign' groups who blocked the economic and cultural advancement of the few indigenous rural folk who were attracted to it.

> 'In the early 19th century Bucharest was still a Greek town, in 1848 Prague, Plzeň [Pilsen] and Ljubljana had German majorities, and as late as the second half of the nineteenth century, the most important towns in Finland were mainly Swedish, Riga and Tartu (Worpat) were German, the towns of Bulgaria mostly Greek and those of the Dalmatian coast, Italian' (Kolarz, 1946: 14).

As long as these 'foreign' islands were largely commercial in nature they neither absorbed nor attracted major numbers from their respective rural hinterlands. Whenever such movement did occur on a minor scale, it resulted in a change from rural-peasant to urban-commercial nationality and language. 'Thus, the Ukrainian migrating to town became Russian, the Slovak leaving his village became Magyarised, the Czech moving to the German town enclaves of inner Bohemia and Moravia became Germanized' (Kolarz, 1946: 15). Even if some of them were of the populist persuasion and halfheartedly glorified the 'pastoral harmony of the countryside, they tended to view this same culture as an integral part of the peasant way of life, and, as such, as unbecoming for men of refinement and education' (Nahirny & Fishman, 1965: 322). From the point of view of the peasant 'the contrast between the city and the village was ... regarded in a painful way. For them the city was not Ukrainian and the city was not peasant. The city was alien and hostile' (Skoreventanski, 1919, cited by Sullivant, 1967: 47). However, growing industrialization of the towns and other attendant and concurrent social changes[44] finally made it impossible for these centers to remain 'foreign,' either numerically or culturally. 'Great masses of population, which the feudal agricultural system could not employ, gathered in the manufacturing towns and often altered . . . their former ethnic composition' (Jaszi, 1929: 256). The conflict that ensued on behalf of social amelioration, political participation, and cultural recognition was, therefore, an urban conflict. The growth of nationalism is the spread of this conflict, from the intellectuals to the middle classes to the proletariat *within* the towns, from the primary industrial centers to those of secondary importance, and from a purely conflictual or reactive to an increasingly creative and more encompassing level.[45] Thus it was with considerable justification that Michelet referred to the towns as the points 'in which the nationalities [he meant, of course, the sub-French nationalities] have condensed their self-expression (ont résumé leur génie)' [1846] (1946: 27), while Kolarz, writing 100 years later about a very different part of Europe, observed that nationalism 'centers on the town and regards it as the very symbol of national existence' (1946: 16).[46] This was the case notwithstanding the fact that some cities, like Vienna, served several nationalist causes at one and the same time (see Trevor-Roper, 1962: 15).

The importance of the city in enabling élites to 'interact with each other and to concentrate upon the tasks of communicating' (Doob, 1964: 245) has been stressed by several investigators.[47] Indeed, Deutsch makes the complex co-occurrence of élites-masses-communication channels-economic|interaction- and- city| part of|his basic definition of nationality in the modern age. Far fewer are those who have pointed out that the national cultures created by nationalist élites were essentially urban cultures even when they included strongly anti-urban ideological components. It was from Geneva that Rousseau pointed out that the distant provinces were the ones most closely related to 'the genius and customs of a nation,'[48] but it was the Genevans themselves and other urbanites that he hoped to influence. Similarly, the German nationalists who believed that 'urban growth was something positively evil — an alienation from the countryside and from the rural virtue which was specifically German' (Minogue, 1967: 75) were all members of the urban élite who wanted nothing more strongly than to influence other city folk and to shape the content of their urban lives. The ideology of nationalism is anti-urban only in that it locates the origin of broader unity and authenticity in the pre-urban past. However, having identified the source of all that is good (whether in language or in other respects) it then seeks to make the values, beliefs, and behaviors stemming from this source available to, acceptable to, and incumbent upon those living in modern urban settings. The first 'urban revolution,' that of the Ancient Near East, 'produced one invention, the invention of writing, which changed the whole structure of the cultural tradition' (Goody & Watt, 1963: 344). The urban revolution during the growth of nationalism produced another invention (or innovation) of similarly great significance: urban national culture. Both of these urban by-products have had very different consequences for language change and language planning.

Dialectic

It is quite apparent, from the foregoing, that there is a built-in dialectic within nationalism, a quite inevitable tension between its major components. Most obvious is the tension between the requirements of modernization and those of authentification. The one emphasizes the instrumental uniformities required by modern politico-operational integration and is constantly straining toward newer, more rational, more efficient solutions to the problems of today and tomorrow. The other emphasizes the sentimental uniformities required by continuity-based sociocultural integration and is constantly straining toward purer, more genuine expressions of the heritage of yesterday and of long ago.

A potential conflict also exists between the goal of authentification and that of unification since, in reality, prenationalist authenticity is highly localized. As a result, the supralocal authenticity sought by nationalism must, to a large extent, be elaborated and interpreted, rather than merely returned to or discovered ready-made. The more stress on real authenticity, therefore, the more danger of regionalism and ultimate secessionism. The more stress on unification/uniformation, the less genuine authentification.

Even unification/uniformation and modernization are frequently at odds with each other. Some modern goals might well be more fully or easily attained via the encouragement of diversity (e.g. relations with important neighboring sources of supply might well be improved if ethnic minorities speaking the same languages as those used in the sources of supply were encouraged to maintain their distinctiveness), while some pre-existing uniformities are actually weakened rather than strengthened by industrialization, urbanization, and other modernity tendencies (e.g. the weakening of religious bonds).

It is part and parcel of the essence of nationalism to incorporate these potentially conflicting themes in its basic ideology. Similarly, it is part and parcel of the essence of nationalism to engage the dialectic that is caused by the tension between these themes and to derive from this dialectic a constant procession of solutions to the problems engendered by its own ideological commitments. It is this dialectic between potentially conflicting elements which constantly recharges the dynamism of nationalist causes. Their business is always unfinished because none of the goals of nationalist ideology is ever fully attained or even substantially assured, not only because of possible outside opposition, but also because of the internal instability of any resolution between its own contending components. 'Nationalism is a device for reconciling the universal with the particular. The adaptation of a universal theory or ism to a special circumstance is the creation of an ideology in the truest sense of the term' (Binder, 1966: 197–98). Universal gods have always had their special people; universal ideals, their special champions. Social intellect and social emotion seem to require both.

Nationalist integration and differentiation: Reality and limits

There has been considerable difference of opinion during the past century as to whether the basic ideological premises of nationalism were (or are), in fact, true or false. The brunt of recent writings on this topic particularly those that emanate from Western centers of scholarship, tend to stress the mythical nature of the unity and authenticity that nationalist movements need to create and then seek to implement.[49] It is obviously true that folk custom and ethnicity frequently shade off into one another via endless minor variations and that the inclusive and exclusive lines that have been drawn in relatively modern times are frequently marked by arbitrariness, opportunism, and irrelevant appeals to long vanished and dubious geographic, cultural, or political entities. However, it would seem equally irrational, if not more so, to refuse to see that the *validity* of these appeals has been of lesser significance, by far, than their efficacy.[50] Their efficacy is indicative of far more (and more pervasive) flexibility and malleability of self-definition in relatively recent times than most scholars seem to have thought possible. Indeed, if it is also true that even the seemingly homogeneous populations of the distant past were themselves products of integration processes operating upon diverse ethnic components (see below), then we are faced by a remarkable as well as reoccurring human capacity to bring about and to accept changes in ethnocultural group membership.

However, an understanding of the rise of nationalism does more than indicate that unmobilized populations can be ethnoculturally integrated via recourse to a large number of different but equally dim and artificially colored or manipulated 'memories.' It does more than indicate that the outer limits of the 'includible' are often flexible and can be stretched to the most distant reaches manageable in terms of the available means of influencing, co-ordinating, and controlling mass behavior. Indeed, it shows that populations frequently cannot tolerate such integrative attempts and that there are integrative 'times and tides' which set limits that seem to be every bit as real as the technological and economic factors on which the control of human behavior is based.

Thus, if broader ethnocultural integration often appears to be far more acceptable than anticipated, so does ethnocultural differentiation. Indeed, once the limits of further integration have been contested, ideologized, and implemented in certain ways and to certain degrees, it seems very difficult for those affected thereby to surrender one set of elaborated ethnocultural self-definitions on behalf of others (see, e.g. Clark, 1938).

Several investigators have pointed to conflict or confrontation with other groups that are *already* at the nationality level of awareness as a limiting factor upon the further integration of two indigenous or contiguous populations. Thus, whereas isolated 'foreign' islands may undergo repeated re-ethnization if their hosts are economically and culturally receptive, it is posited that neighboring indigenous groups cannot continue to do so once intergroup conflict has contributed to mutual nationality consciousness and to Great Traditions incorporating the experience of intergroup conflict.[51] At this point further integration seems to be possible only as a result of the realization of long-term superordinate threat[52] or the defeat and systematic denationalization of one of the two parties. Even these latter circumstances seem to leave traces that last for centuries, even at a purely oral and secretive level, and that protect the seeds of differentiation until some subsequent opportune time arrives.

Thus, exactly because the 'natural distributions' of ethnocultural integration and differentiation are either too gradual, too inconsistent, or too nonsalient for the purposes of effective mass organization of human and physical resources, nationalism intensifies and restructures both. In this respect nationalism, like much other goal-directed behavior, con-stitutes a self-fulfilling prophecy. However, in addition, while so doing, it also sets into motion self-perpetuating and self-intensifying processes (processes that are aided and abetted by other concurrent social change) that render the centers of nationality-conscious societies extremely resistant to either other-integrative or disintegrative efforts.

The transformations of ethnocultural integration

Most of our observations thus far have concentrated upon the early stirrings or the *appearance* of nationalism among hitherto traditional populations within multiethnic states. It is well known, however, that nationalism often continues to function well beyond the period of initial mobilization, although there would seem to be nothing inevitable about its subsequent stages or their sequencing. One of the most common features of nationalist development is that which focuses nationalism upon the attainment of the political-operational integration attainable via the machinery of the state. The possible relationships between these two types of integration, ethnocultural and politico-operational, have been frequently (and varyingly) commented upon. These relationships between nationality and polity present us with further useful perspective on the transformations of ethnocultural integration,[53] particularly since it is the machinery of the state that is so frequently paramount in language planning.

The relationship between nationalism and the mono-ethnic state has appeared to be so natural and so inevitable wherever it *has* come into being, that it is not surprising that the particular relationships and sequences obtaining in given parts of the world at given times in history have seemed to contemporary commentators to be the only (or the only 'natural' and 'normal') relationships that could (or should) obtain.[54] Thus, while it seems clear that the Fichtean-Herderian ideal of the mono-ethnic state is, today, quite closely approximated in several Western European (as well as other) nations, it is also clear that in each of these, if one looks back far enough and deep enough, one finds the process of successively broader unification of once ethnically different groups. ' . . . Like the worlds of which the astronomers tell us that some are in the nebulous stage, some supporting life, and others growing cold, [so] all Nationalities not simple are combinations of Simple Nationality and into a Secondary Simple Nationality, fused from all the primary, they all tend to pass' (Zangwill, 1917: 43). Where the consolidation of the state preceded the age of mass nationalism, 'where the framework of the state was strong enough and persistent enough, it . . . *created a common nationality* out of very different linguistic and cultural groups. *Languedoc* was very like

Catalonia and very unlike north France, yet it finally became thoroughly French' (Strayer, 1966: 23).

The wonder of what had happened is apparent in the sensitive observations of contemporaries:

'Today all the inhabitants of France who were born within the Kingdom are reputed to be of the same nation ... They are all Frenchmen ... Now birth rules nationality: In those times [during the great wars with England] it was filiation through the male line ... "People" and "nation" then meant very different things. A nation consisted of persons living according to the same laws or customs. A people was a collection of nations. Now these two words have the same signification' (Dubos, 1735: 260-62; cited by Barzun, 1932).[55]

Obviously, the stable, centralized state had not only brought those under its rule 'into closer and closer association with each other' while cutting them off from those outside of its control, but it had, in the selfsame process and over centuries, forced them 'to work together and to adapt to each other, to gain a clear sense of identity, to smooth out some of their regional differences, and to become attached to their ruler and the institutions through which he ruled' (Strayer, 1966: 23).[56]

The state-nation[ality]

Because of the firm establishment of the state in Western Europe before the appearance of modern mass nationalism,[57] and because of the substantial ethnocultural integration ensuing from the long stability of the politico-operational institutions there, a very definite view of the *nature of nationality* had developed in the West and a very definite impression of the primacy of *polity over nationality* had come to be widely accepted by the time mass nationalism appeared as a predominantly Central, Eastern, and Southern European 'aberration.' As for the nature of nationality, it was in the West primarily a territorial attribute. ' ... A child of whatever parentage, if born under the British flag, can claim British nationality. Indeed, the [popular] English language lacks a word to describe 'nationality' distinct from or contrasted with the citizenship derived from territory and State' (Namier, 1952: 21). As for the sequential relationship between the formation of nationality (in the ethnocultural sense in which we have been using the term in this essay) and the attainment of statehood, it was obvious that 'it is the state which has come first and created nationality and not vice versa.' This was as obvious to dignified churchmen and bourgeois political leaders who sought to *preserve the state* against the onslaught of foreign concepts of nationalism, as it was to Western socialists, anarchists, and communists who were committed to the *demise of the state* and, thereby, to the demise of nationality as a force which fragmented the proletariat.[58] It is this view of the nationality-polity relationship and this stage of ethnocultural and politico-operational integration which Pflanze and others have recently designated as the 'State-Nation' and which may be contrasted with the 'Nation-State,' the latter being a view and a stage of more recent and noticeably turbulent origin.

Because nationalism in Western Europe was already a creature of well-established states by the opening of the nineteenth century it was subjected to the controlling influences which nineteenth century Western European political doctrines imposed upon the state itself. As a result, Western nationalism — a nationalism that flowed from common institutions and their evolved safeguards — seemed to Western observers to be respectful of and based upon individual liberties, a loyal opposition, the balance of powers, etc. Even today, there are those whose view of European nationalism is so strongly colored by the Western experience alone that they claim that 'in Europe the strong independent state with a fairly effective government and a common pattern of law enforcement and observance preceded nationalism and both preceded democracy' (Myrdal, 1968: 119). However, the majority of Western intellectuals around the middle of the nineteenth century clearly recognized the difference between their presumably open and rational nationalism and the closed, tribal, vindictive, disruptive, and altogether wicked nationalisms then brewing among the Central, Southern, and Eastern Europeans upon which they heaped scorn and invective.

'The State may in course of time produce a nationality,' they claimed, 'but that a nationality should constitute a State is contrary to the nature of modern civilization . . . . [Such a creature] is an ideal unit, founded on the race, in defiance of the modifying action of external causes, of tradition and of existing rights. It overrules the rights and wishes of the inhabitants, absorbing their divergent interests in a fictitious unity, sacrifices their several inclinations and duties to the higher claim of nationality and crushes all natural rights and all established liberties for the purpose of vindicating itself' (Acton [1862] 1907: 288).[59]

Two and three generations later enlightened Westerners were still convinced that theirs was the only legitimate link between state and nationality.

'The facts of the situation are that the nation born of the emancipation of the peasantry effected, for reasons which were primarily
military, the unity of the language, then of the culture, and thus left
the impression of a common race. But by a singular inversion of
perspective, education has contrived to spread exactly the opposite
view to be the initial factor which, by means of the mother tongue has
imposed upon all its sons traditions, aptitudes and a genius which is
their own and made them brothers united into one nation' (Delaise,
1927: 219).

This inclination to deride ethnocultural nationalism has, by and large,
been continued in the West for over a century, with little scholarly and
even less general recognition that such derision itself reflects a stage in the
evolution of ethnocultural and politico-operational integration. While
others were just beginning to dig into and reconstruct their ethnic pasts,
Western intellectuals were already beginning to extol nonethnic and
supraethnic rationality. Instead of still seeking unsullied rural models of
broader unity and authenticity they could already extol the classically
evolved, regionally neutralized and centrally reinforced or validated
nature of their institutions, processes, and symbols.

The nation[ality]-state

The Western European model of state-nationality could, with some
little effort, be slightly amended to apply beyond the primary confines and
experiences of England, France, Spain, Portugal, Holland, and
Scandinavia from which it was derived. As nationalist pressures built up
in other parts of Europe it became impossible to deny them *all* any
legitimacy whatsoever. A distinction came to be drawn, therefore,
between the somewhat legitimate claims of Italian, German, Hungarian,
Polish, and Greek nationalists, and the patently illegitimate ones of the
primarily Eastern and Southern smaller Slavic nationalities. The former
at least represented the aspirations of 'historic peoples,' that is, of peoples
who had once been formed by states of their own and who had, due to
the misfortunes of history, lost their political independence. Their
agitation for political unification, recognition, or liberation could, at least,
be understood, particularly since it left the major premise of the primacy
of the state untouched. The same could certainly *not* be said for the
atomized nonhistoric peoples that also clamored and intrigued for
attention. Friedrich Engels' views in this connection coincided exactly with
those of bourgeois commentators and demonstrated how terrified the left

and the right *both* were of the 'chimera' of nationality which obsessed the ethnic rabble of South-East Europe and which could 'never be satisfied or exhausted and always continued to assert itself' (Acton [1862] 1907: 298). Engels, like Acton, felt that it was absolutely necessary to distinguish between 'the right of the great European nations to separate and independent national existence . . . and those of numerous small relics of peoples which, after having figured for longer or shorter periods on the stage of history were finally absorbed as integral portions into one or another of these more powerful nations' (cited by Namier, 1944: 51; for the full original see Engels, 1866 or Rjasanoff, 1916).[60]

It is not possible to reconstruct here the complete interaction between the Western view that the Eastern and Southern European nationalities were 'peoples without history' and the feverish efforts of the latter, intensified as the nineteenth century progressed, to discover, formulate, and create their respective (as well as their joint) histories. It should be clear, however, that the so-called peoples without history also initially lacked two of the major forces which are essential for the creation of history in modern days: their own upper classes[61] and their own centers of ethnic culture and communication.[62] As these came into being (with the increased penetration of industrialization into their areas) so did their nationalisms and their histories; the process of *nationalities seeking to create their corresponding monoethnic states* — a process that had already vanished from the memory of Western European historiography — was fully launched. So intense were their efforts and so widely shared were their ideals in the universe with which they were concerned that the nationality-state and the objective primacy of ethnocultural nationality became as self-evident in the intellectuals and mass movements of suppressed Eastern and Southern European nationalities as were the state-nation and the primacy of political nationality in the intellectual and mass movements of Western Europe. 'Nationality in the West (west of Germany) means your passport. In Central and Eastern Europe, with their mixed population, it means ultimately your race' (Talmon, 1965: 21).

The model of nationality accepted by the 'peoples without history' was both a reaction *against* Western European views as well as a wholehearted *adoption* of Western European attainments. The ideal model was that of 'a single people, traditionally fixed on a well-defined territory, possessing a distinctive culture and shaped to a common mould by many generations of shared historical experiences' (Emerson, 1962: 103). The philosophical and ideological underpinnings of this model were primarily Herderian in the most immediate sense, both in its deprecation of the multiethnic polity as well as in its deification of the unique and pure nationality.[63] However, whereas Herder was concerned only with safeguarding the beauty and originality of each and every culture — and particularly with cleansing German culture of its fascination and inferiority in the face of all things French — his ideas quickly had political consequences as well.[64] The nation came to be defined and pursued as a cultural rather than as a political entity, as a unit that could remain healthy only if it grew 'within the chrysalis of the individual [i.e. of the autochthonous] culture' (Snyder, 1968: 58) and only if it served the unity and authenticity of the culture that had given birth to it.[65] More so even than the historic nations, the so-called ahistoric nations required governmental protection and encouragement of their cultural uniqueness. It was not enough to 'discover their ancient history, find the continuity of their ancient traditions, recreate their half-forgotten languages, remember their old literatures, and, with the aid of ingenious statistics retrace on the map the generous ... frontiers of the past' (Trevor-Roper, 1962: 18-19). It was also necessary to shield and to further these desiderata, via the machinery of the state, so that they would never again become or be viewed as peoples without history.[66]

Historical perspective reveals that questioning the legitimacy of an opponent's nationality is undoubtedly an ancient ploy. Similarly old is the tack of seeking recognition for one's self by joining in the nonrecognition of less fortunate claimants.

'At the Council of Constance (1414) ... the English being the least numerous, posed as champions of the right of each nation[ality] to be counted as the equal of every other. Yet, to "appease" the Germans, they joined with them in ignoring the rights of Hungarians, Czechs, Poles and Scandinavians to separate identity and separate vote' (Hayes, 1942: 8; also see Loomis, 1939).

Even within the ranks of the nineteenth century latecomers themselves, invidious distinctions of this kind were common.

'Croat leaders demonstrated little interest in the project (a Congress of Nationalities planned for 1895) ... reluctant to place themselves on the same level as the so-called "non-nations" — the Rumanians, the Slovaks and particularly the Serbs — for fear that they would jeopardise the constitutional status of Croatia' (Hitchens, 1970: 394).

Similarly, those nationalities recently (re)admitted to the ranks of the politically recognized, quickly championed the primacy of state-nationality over nationality-state processes to their own advantage. Thus, quite obviously, both processes have long been in operation, have frequently been purposefully misconstrued, and have often been cyclically related to each other.

Other transformations

While state-nation and nation-state processes may thus fruitfully be viewed as contrasted transformations of each other (without at all being viewed as necessary or exhaustive processes re the accommodation of their components in the annals of history), they have both revealed instances of further expansions as a possible subsequent stage of their development. Even broader cultural unities and more abstract authenticities are recognizable, which indirectly confirm the arbitrariness of the boundaries set at previous stages of nationalism. These broader aspirations may claim *irridentas* not previously liberated or united during earlier integrative efforts, or they may point to *similarities* with neighbors that come to be viewed as more basic and as stemming from a still earlier and even more authentic cultural era than that responsible for dissimilarities formerly noted. Such broader nationalisms are frequently referred to as 'pan movements.'[67] However, even with respect to their pan movements, the state-nations and the nation-states show differences which are consistent with their developmental stages and their resulting needs and aspirations. The pan movements of state-nations smack of thinly disguised imperialism (economic, territorial, or cultural) since they involve expansion beyond well-defined and traditionally established cultural borders and political controls.[68] The pan movements of nationalities-seeking-states involve an exploration of delimitation and integration possibilities, a search for reliable strength, for the power of numbers as a substitute for weaknesses of various kinds.[69]

Finally, unsuccessful nationalism too must be recognized as a possible outcome of attempts at sociopolitical mobilization and integration. This outcome obtains where potential changes in the allocation of roles and resources do not materialize or are reversed, when proto-élites do not succeed in mobilizing populations toward a certain definition of unity and authenticity, or when a competing élite (and the particular underlying socioeconomic changes and overarching symbolism with which it is associated) succeeds in attracting support or marshaling forces to a greater extent than do its rivals. Various examples of nationalisms that vanished but 'might have succeeded' will be mentioned in the following sections and notes. Suffice it to say at this point that nationalism exists as an 'alternative instrumentality which is exploitable on behalf of culturally differentiated groups in any plural society' (Depres, 1967, 1968) as well as on behalf of any segment of the social pluralism that remains strong long after ethnic pluralism *per se* has weakened (Mazrui, 1969b). Nationalism is a phoenix that is repeatedly capable of arising not only out of its own ashes but out of whatever other injustices modern societies perpetrate.

Nationalism in the 'new' or 'developing' nations

The appearance of several score 'new' polities since the conclusion of World War II has stimulated a somewhat strengthened interest in nationalism among American social scientists, much as did the redrawn map of post-Versailles Central, Eastern, and Southern Europe. Much of this interest is contrastive, i.e. it is sensitive to differences and similarities between developments in parts of Africa-Asia, on the one hand, and parts of Europe-America, on the other. However, far more attention has been lavished upon such comparisons in the sphere of political-operational integration than upon sociocultural integration, and the concepts of modernization and development which dominate recent inquiries into the 'new' polities have relatively seldom been focused upon the transformations of nationalism *per se*. Thus, our concluding effort in this essay will be to review the literature on the 'new' polities from this very point of view, particularly since it is in the same 'new' polities that the lion's share of language-planning ventures are currently underway and will continue in the forseeable future.

Broader ethnic unity and greater authenticity

We may conveniently begin with Friedrich's reminder that ethnic diversity is far from sufficient 'cause' for the development of nationalism or the growth of nations. With very few exceptions, nationality-states and state-nationalities 'did not happen in [pre-World War II] China, India or Africa, though in all of these continent-wide human societies, various kinds of political orders — states — were erected' (1966: 22). Nevertheless, the rumblings of modern nationalism in these areas can be traced back quite far and seem, in many respects, to be quite similar in emphases to those that we have already reviewed in connection with various stages and regions in European social history. Certainly, purposive emphases on the broader ethnocultural unity of traditional and particularistically oriented populations living in isolation from each other are much in evidence 50 and even 100 years ago, particularly in areas throughout which indigenous Great Traditions had been long established. Thus it was claimed that

> 'the Hindus of every part of India resembled each other in all essential matters, in their traits of character, in their modes of thinking, in their social institutions and even in their dress and amusements ... Socially, religiously and ethnologically they all belonged to the same race. All showed descent from common ancestors, worshiped the same gods and goddesses, employed the same scriptural language (Sanskrit), and, in ordinary intercourse used one of the dialects derived from the same mother tongue' (McCully, 1940: 244; paraphrasing an editorial in the Calcutta *Tribune* of September 19, 1885).[70]

As in Europe in an earlier period, age-old struggles are remembered, indeed heightened, as indicators of ancient nationality. For the Vietnamese their Great Tradition includes 'the winning of independence from China in the tenth century and their own later expansion into Chan and Khmer territories' (Kennedy, 1968: 80). Similarly, Htin Aung 'has cited evidence from Burmese nationalism from the eleventh century and has claimed that throughout their long history the Burmese have always been conscious of their nationality, bordered as they have been by great neighbors in China and India' (Kennedy, 1968: 81-82).

Whether of early vintage or not, there is also a widespread and recurring emphasis on indigenous authenticity as the basis of internal sociocultural integration and simultaneous divergence from foreign (normally European) ways.[71] Observers mention not only such mundane matters as the readoption (or invention) of indigenous dress,[72] footwear, or hair styles,[73] and not only protests against European models in connection with each of these and other aspects of everyday life,[74] but also the rapid ideologization of authenticity. Authenticity was proclaimed to be valuable because it was an autochthonous creation,[75] handed down from periods of past greatness,[76] and incorporated within itself the promise of future glories yet to come.[77] Indeed, the very names adopted by several new nations upon their (re-)birth were such as to recall the glories of a culturally indigenous broader unity which had existed in the past (e.g. Ghana, Mali) and which could serve as guiding (or, at least, as motivating and stimulating) examples with respect to the future. Nevertheless fuller authenticity and broader unity were, in and of themselves, not enough.

From Indonesia we hear that what is wanted is 'both Western science and Eastern philosophy, the Eastern "spirit" in the culture' (Sjahrir, 1947: 67-68; written 1935, while a political prisoner). From Japan: 'What is merely modern — as science and methods of organization — can be transplanted, but what is vitally human has fibres so delicate and roots so numerous and far-reaching that it dies when moved from its soil. Japan . . . cannot be turned into a mere borrowed machine. She has her own soul which must assert itself overall' (Tiedemann, 1955: 55 and 81). From the Arab world: 'The Arab wants modernization, but has no desire to lose his own identity in the process. To be an evolué is too heavy a price to pay. In brief, the problem for the Arab is to westernize without becoming westernized' (Pfaff, 1970: 165). Is this possible? Is it possible most particularly, where it is firmly believed that

> 'Our Imperial Ancestors have founded our Empire on a basis broad and everlasting, and have deeply and firmly implanted virtue. Our subjects, ever united in loyalty and filial piety, have from generation to generation illustrated the beauty thereof. This is the glory of the fundamental character of our Empire . . . guard and maintain the prosperity of our Imperial throne, coeval with heaven and earth. So shall ye not only be our good and faithful subjects, but render illustrious the best traditions of your forefathers. The way here set forth is indeed the teaching bequeathed by Our Imperial Ancestors, to be observed alike by their Descendants and Subjects, infallible for all ages and true in all places' (from the Japanese Imperial Rescript on Education, 1890; cited by Tiedemann, 1955: 113-14).

Almost miraculously, a reconciliation of the old and the new *is* possible, indeed all the more possible, if 'the new regime, so alien to all the traditions of the past, is [viewed as] only a return to [even more] ancient institutions. The new era is called Maiji, which means *restoration* [of enlightened rule]' (Delaise, 1927: 231). All in all, however, 'periods of extensive Westernization' are likely to be followed by 'periods of retreat during which "excesses" and "incongruities" are violently attacked and the quest for "the true Japanese way" undertaken. One can discern at least four great swings of the pendulum in the hundred years that followed 1860' (Scalapino, 1964: 126).

Indeed, if there is any difference between earlier European and later Asian-African nationalisms, it would seem to be not so much in the nature of the sentimental and instrumental components utilized, or in the compromises between them, as in the earlier primacy of state-formation over sociocultural integration in the new polities of Africa and Asia. Perhaps this is because continuity with the real and immediate past is too great to permit the sheer *amount* of purposive selection and reformulation practiced in Europe. Perhaps it is because state-formation came everywhere before major industrialization and dislocation had destroyed the ethnic identity of major population segments. For whatever reasons, it seems that African and Asian nationalisms have thus far experienced little that parallels the fragmentation of the Austro-Hungarian, Czarist, and Turkish Empires as a result of the awakening reunification and self-authentification of submerged nationalities. In most cases the colonial administrative boundaries have been maintained and (almost everywhere but in post-independence India) the thrust of mass-mobilization has clearly focused much more upon political-operational integration within those boundaries than upon their abandonment on behalf of the self-actualization of submerged nationalities. The retention, by and large, of ethnically irrelevant international boundaries has probably resulted in greater prominence being given more quickly to supra-ethnic ideologies and programs[78] than was the case in Central, Eastern, and Southern Europe where the nationality and its own mononation state was so commonly the initial rationale for mass mobilization. It may be, therefore, that language planning too, in these nations, is likely to be proportionately less influenced by ideologies of ethnocultural unity and authenticity and, to the extent that it is centrally sponsored, that it will be under relatively greater pressure to further supra-ethnic political-operational integration than was the case in early stages of language planning among awakening and newly awakened European nationalities. This is, at least, a reasonable hypothesis for investigation, although it requires basically historical reconstruction, on the one hand, and that plus the empirical evaluation of still current efforts, on the other.

Pervasive social and economic change

Several investigators and commentators, indigenous, European, and American, have observed that nationalism in Africa and Asia is a concomitant of the severe dislocation and fargoing disruption of traditional life that both colonialism and anticolonialism bring into being (see e.g. Ranger, 1968a,b). Some have pointed to nationalism as appealing to those whose lives have become dislocated by the introduction of modern cash economy. Others have pointed to the annihilation of tribal, ethnic, and linguistic barriers which the rapid modernization of either commerce or industry of necessity brings to pass.[79] Several have also pointed to the improvements which the new economy permits, to the problems that follow in their wake, to the opportunities available to a selected few,[80] and how these few subsequently utilize the rhetoric of nationalism in order to distribute and exploit these opportunities more fully.[81] Nationalism is, therefore, not merely a by-product or a response to the evils or the disorganization of unplanned change. It is also an instrument on behalf of further directed changes.[82] Even the agony of military defeat by Western powers has such consequences in that it helps bring to the fore new indigenous élites that are more selective with respect to the uses of the past in directing the future.[83]

To some extent the eclectic and imaginative use of the past that we reviewed in conjunction with more recent European nationalisms seems to be more evident in many parts of Negro Africa than in most parts of Asia (Abu-Lughod, 1967). The great indigenous ethno-religious traditions of Buddhism, Confucianism, Shintoism, and Islam seem, thus far, to have been too omnipotent and omnipresent to be innovatively reformulated for new nationalist purposes. Rather they seem to have been put to most active use by early nationalists primarily for the sake of their large-scale integrative potentials.

'By means of this [Hinduism], all Hindus would be bound by the tie of brotherhood. By means of it, the Bengali, the Hindustani, the Rajput, the Maratha, the Madrasi, in short, all Hindus, would be of one heart. The aspirations of all would be the same . . . for the Hindu nation, by retaining its ancient religious and moral civilization . . . would stand as the best and foremost of all nations on the face of the earth' (McCully, 1940: 262; paraphrasing an article by Raj Narain Bose, 1881-82).

Only at much later stages, after the preindependence boundaries of new states have been successfully maintained, are there also movements to break or decrease the traditional influences of the ethno-religions by means of state regulation, much as there had been, earlier, in Europe.[84] Nevertheless, since language planning is also quite often engaged in, from the very outset, as a *means* of first attaining or approximating much needed stability, it may be reasonable to expect that it too will initially be greatly influenced by religious considerations in those new nations that correspond to indigenized ethno-religious Great Traditions. In all of these cases this might be viewed not merely as religious intrusion but as the necessarily greater influence of the old (including religion) on the emergence of a new view of nationality, where the old is still part and parcel of daily ethnicity itself, even among élites, and is, therefore, an integral part of nationalism throughout its formative years. In the West, religion and nationalism were institutionally separable forces that utilized each other (or opposed each other), whenever they could for their own purposes. In the East, no such alternation is possible as long as these forces are still to such a large extent intertwined and viewed as being one and the same.

Élites

Nationalism in Asia and Africa began, as an ideological and organized movement, much as it had in Europe, i.e. as an élitist-intellectual phenomenon (if we can include students, young officers, and bureaucrats among the élites).

'An outstanding common feature of Asian nationalism has been the remarkable role of its student communities. Both in Burma and in Indonesia the major strength of the nationalist forces was provided by their student populations. In Burma even the principal leadership came straight from the University' (Singhal, 1967: 281).

However, the same picture is reported from Africa as well.

'It is generally true that students while abroad were emphatic and radical in their nationalism. Complete physical separation from Nigeria . . . aroused a desire, particularly among the more sensitive and impressionable, to glorify their traditional culture, usually by suppressing its unattractive features and exaggerating the qualities that they believed superior or unique . . . Most of the efforts to awaken respect for and appreciation of African culture started among African students abroad' (Coleman, 1963: 63).

It is no accident, therefore, that so many of the nationalist and indigenized socialist movements of the Third World were, as they had been earlier in Eastern Europe, movements of the educated young. They were truly young in more than name. But these movements frequently continue to be primarily an élitist concern, largely because of the absence of a substantial bourgeoisie and the seeming failure of most national economies to materially and irrevocably alter the daily lives of the bulk of their populations. In Asia and Africa alike nationalism is not yet a self-priming mass phenomenon. Rather, it is primarily 'an attempt of intellectuals to arouse the masses,' first for the attainment of independence, and then for attaining modernization goals.

'Nationalism . . . is commonly seen as a force for good by all those in the intellectual élite who are bent on planning policies aimed at development. To them fostering nationalism will provide the means of breaking down inhibitions and obstacles' (Myrdal, 1968: 111 and 118).

At a less consciously utilitarian level, nationalism in both Africa and Asia is an attempt on the part of intellectuals to identify with the masses. However, as was the case previously in Europe, many Asian and African intellectuals are also alienated from the masses.

'Am I perhaps estranged from my people? Why am I vexed by the things that fill their lives and to which they are so attached? Why are the things that contain beauty for them and arouse their gentler emotions only senseless and displeasing for me?' (Sjahrir, 1947: 66).

Consequently,

'. . . conscious of the wide gap between their modes and levels of living . . . and those of the villagers and urban slum dwellers, the intellectual élite compensate for their alienation by romanticizing the masses . . . The peasants are [viewed as being] rational, intelligent, hard-working and zealous' (Myrdal, 1968: 62).

Similar also to earlier European nationalisms is the built-in dilemma between modernization goals for the future and the glorification of the virtues of the traditional past. Throughout much of Africa this is resolved at a very abstract level since 'the African nationalist still has before him almost the entire task of creating the nation[alities] in whose name he professes to speak' (Emerson, 1962: 94). Thus, 'in arguing the basis of *ujamaa* or African socialism, Julius Nyerere of Tanganyika contended that its roots lay in the traditional communitarianism of the indigenous society that had broken down with contact with the West' (Friedland, 1968: 22).[85]

However, no such total breakdown occurred in Turkey, Egypt, India, Pakistan, Burma, Japan, or pre-Communist China. Thus, when many of their intellectuals rejected the West as a model for national regeneration, they were not merely following in the footsteps of earlier English, German, and Italian rejections of French culture, or of Slavophilic rejection of mechanistic Western European enlightenment. On the one hand, their romanticized indigenous Great Traditions were much more alive and pervasive than the eclectic and frequently mythological reconstructions referred to in Europe. On the other hand, both the help and the ways of the West were far more necessary for immediate modernization purposes than were either French culture (to Germany) or Western enlightenment (to Russia) a century or a century and a half ago. Thus, while both African and Asian nationalism must quickly aim at modernization (rather than go through a prolonged emphasis on ethnic authenticity)[86] and, therefore, cannot afford to really bite the Western hands that feed them, much Asian modernization, in particular, is also encumbered by the proximity and vitality of the wider ethnoreligious traditional unity on which it leans in its efforts to attain mass mobilization and reintegration.

The urban condition

If, as is likely, the city had earlier contributed to, intensified, and finally exploited the '. . . pervasive uncertainty arising from the breakdown of immemorial rural routines' throughout Europe, and, therefore, 'lent special emotional intensity to late 19th century nationalism' (McNeill, 1963: 819, it seems to play a similarly crucial role in forming whatever mass base there is for African and Asian nationalism. Once again we find the city (and its economic opportunities) mentioned as a prime factor in bringing together dislocated and ethnically divergent populations,[87] in intensifying their miseries by highlighting both relative and actual deprivation,[88] and in providing the organizational structures whereby these dissatisfactions could be channeled into nationalist movements.[89] As a result, nationalist movements throughout Africa and Asia were able to develop substantial degrees of urban support,[90] particularly for short-term and concrete goals, even though the towns have long remained primarily commercial rather than industrial in nature.[91]

> 'Often, the major urban centres provided the setting for "middle class nationalism," while the surrounding countryside was virtually untouched by the movement. In the story of Arab nationalism, Damascus, Baghdad, Cairo and Ankara all loom large, and this pattern is paralleled elsewhere, from Bombay to Rangoon and from Bangkok to Tokyo . . . Large urban communities tended to develop a character of their own and to concentrate some of the tensions which were elsewhere dispersed . . . The towns provided the natural centers for political demonstrations, attacks on the property of alien governments or groups and internal revolutionary plotting and activity' (Kennedy, 1968: 91).

However, it is Asian nationalism, particularly, which has also made the more concerted effort to reach into the rural areas, in part as a result of its specific ability to rely upon a large number of local religious functionaries to carry its message, and in part because of its greater utilization of the ethnoreligious tradition in general. The impact of radio on bringing nationalist views into rural areas and, generally, to nonliterate populations, has, thus far, been little discussed (but note Kennedy, 1968: 93, and several indexed references in Fishman *et al.*, 1968a) and even less studied in any systematic fashion. It is undoubtedly of major importance, both for language planning as well as for modern nationalism as a whole.

Integration and differentiation

To some extent traditional intra-Asian and intra-African divergences have been utilized for the purposes of modern national differentiation. Long-standing anti-Japanese memories have played just such a role in China and in Korea, the record of ancient anti-Chinese struggles are part of Vietnamese national awareness, anti-Islamic consciousness is a common aspect of popular Hinduism,[92] etc. However, more prevalent by far, and more differentiating, is the anti-Western sentiment that is reported in the literature dealing with country after country, particularly so in the cases of countries with ancient and indigenous ethnoreligious traditions. The West as such has been attacked not only for colonialism but for 'mental colonialism,'[93] not only for debasing indigenous cultures with foreign values but for having no values to offer at all other than material gain and technical mastery. This alone would not be too different from earlier intra-European rejections (most of which contrasted indigenous moral and cultural beauty with shameless and exploitative foreign avarice), were it not that an early functional compromise with the avowed enemy is required in order to attain the very goals that are most immediate for all post-independence Asian and African nationalisms.

'The nationalist movement, especially in those underdeveloped countries which have older traditions, must willy-nilly make a new synthesis. The real problem is that of finding the terms on which they can coexist honourably with the technology and civilization of the West . . . [since] it is not possible for these societies to accept the West completely' (Gadgil, 1955: 150).

Thus, nationalist movement after nationalist movement in Asia that has started out as primarily anti-Western in nature has been forced by the course of events to pursue Westernization,[94] in a way that Germans never had to turn to France, nor Czechs to Germans, nor Slovaks to Hungarians, nor Ukrainians to Poles, nor even Russians to the West.

The process of differentiation in Africa (and in those countries of Asia that do not correspond to indigenous Great Traditions) is only partially the same as that just sketched. The discovered fragments of lost civilizations permit the more unambiguous retention or adoption of Western ways and their easier combination with those indigenous fragments that have been interpreted as nationally unifying and authentic. Subsequently, a 'new generation bursts forth with a "discovery" of their national essence, amazed that its novelty has never been recognized before' (Hartz, 1964: 12). Between this national essence and modernization no great dilemma exists and no painful compromise is required, since both are essentially new and unencumbered by established or ideologized large scale animosities. It may, therefore, be that westernisms or internationalisms will be less fully barred from Tanzanian or Indonesian language planning, at least in its early stages, than from that in India or in Egypt.

The transformation of ethnocultural integration

While it is true that 'the term "nationalism" [has been] . . . applied indiscriminately throughout the vast [African and Asian] continents to every show of resistance against the old colonial rule' (Snyder, 1968: 66), as it has to most anti-Western or even anti-White reactions since the termination of colonial rule, it nevertheless seems true that ethnocultural nationalism is very much a growing part of the Afro-Asian scenes. 'Nation building in the contemporary world . . . is a matter of building group cohesion and group loyalty for purposes of international representation and domestic planning' (Friedrich, 1966: 32) and this is the very purpose to which nationalism is most frequently put in the new nations. Precisely because it is so necessary to 'divert Afro-Asian peoples away from parochial concerns toward the larger issues of modernization' (Minogue, 1967: 89), it is revealing to find country after country utilizing (and struggling with) the most unifying and authenticating contours of the indigenous pasts available to them for this very purpose. 'Not the least interesting aspect of the modernization of [these] profoundly diverse societies is the recurrent theme of nationalism. The nation-state remains both fulcrum and goal: increasing modernization stays within the framework of nationalism rather than . . . internationalism' (Snyder, 1968: 10).

Superficially, the nationalisms of most 'new nations' show similarities to those of the recent nation-states of Europe as well as to those of that continent's old state-nations: Like the 'unhistoric' submerged nationalities many of the peoples of sub-Saharan Africa had lost contact with their past unity or greatness. They needed new élites (even if they had never lost their old ones) in order to attain statehood. However, here the similarity ends, since statehood did not come as a result of nationality (re)formation and intensification, nor did it follow nationality lines. The peoples of several Asian countries, on the other hand, had not lost contact with either their immediate or their larger ethnoreligious histories and élites. Nevertheless, once again differential ethnicity was not usually the basis of their political-organizational independence. Thus, among all the new polities, the number of nationality-states (i.e. states whose borders correspond reasonably closely to the territory inhabited by a single newly self-conscious nationality) are rather few.[95] 'The exceptions apart, it is striking that existing boundaries have remained intact as colony after colony has become independent . . . Countries including many languages and culture groups, like most African and Asian ones, have not split up, and those taking in only part of a single language group . . . have [usually] . . . not united' (Kautsky, 1962: 35). By and large, therefore, we are dealing primarily with the development of state-nationalities,[96] whether or not substantial great traditions are available to them. If no such integrating traditions corresponding roughly to the national frontiers are available, then obviously they must be created by the state for the purposes of its own preservation and modernization. If such *are* already available, then their *supra-ethnic* realizations are utilized by the state in order to avoid the fragmentation-potential inherent in their more local or regional deviations. However, in almost all cases we are dealing with state-nationalities that lack the centuries of previous consolidations around supraregional symbols and institutions of statehood which marked nineteenth-century England, France, Scandinavia, Iberia, or even Russia and the Austro-Hungarian Empire.[97] We are dealing with state-nations whose lack of experience in statehood is like that of the more recent European nation-states some 40 years ago, but who generally lacked the internal cohesiveness that those had and who are infinitely less developed *vis-à-vis* their former masters than was true either in Eastern Europe or in the Americas. Finally, we are dealing with state-nations who utilize nationalism in order more quickly to become like nation-states, on the assumption that greater group cohesion and group loyalty will bring the attainment of modernization more quickly into reach.

There can be little doubt that the relative absence of ethnic correspondence in connection with the political borders of most new polities is related to the interest in pan-movements revealed by some of their élites. In Africa, pan-Negro movements or, at least, pan ideologies and philosophies, began prior to independence, just as they had in the Balkans and among the Tartars prior to World War I[98] and in the Near

East and other parts of Asia prior to World War II.[99] The more remarkable thing about pan-Islamism and pan-Africanism, however, is their continuation as ideologies even after the creation of separate states. In some pan-movements, this may be ascribed primarily to personal vision or ambitions,[100] in some it may be due to the apparent danger of superordinate threat,[101] but in all cases their success or failure would also seem to be related to the absence or presence of overriding ethnocultural differentiation between the populations or regions involved.[102] Certainly, however, the attainments of pan-movements have thus far been too limited (even if the European Common Market and the Scandinavian efforts at co-operation are added to pan-Arabism and pan-Africanism) to lend much support to Hans Kohn's prediction that the twentieth century might yet become known as 'the age of pan-nationalism' (1968: 64).

Notes to Chapter 4

1. See Chapter 9 of this volume for Part II of Language and Nationalism. The bibliography to Part I is found together with the bibliography to Part II on pp. 338–67.
2. The best sources for reviewing the terminological variation in this general field of inquiry are Carr (1939), Snyder (1954), and Zernatto (1944). I have found the greatest conceptual clarification with respect to *terminology* in the work of Akzin (1964), Wirth (1936), and Znaniecki (1952) and my own usage, in terms of the distinctions that it draws and the processes to which it refers, is most directly similar to theirs. Readers seeking other useful introductions to the study of nationalism should certainly consult such justifiably well-known general works as those by Deutsch (1953, rev. ed. 1966), Doob (1964), Emerson (1962), Kedourie (1961), Kohn (1944 and 1955), Shafer (1955), and Snyder (1964). All of the above have highly useful bibliographies, as do Pinson (1935) and Deutsch (1956). The new *International Encyclopedia of the Social Sciences* has informative articles on nationalism and related topics by Kohn (1968), Kazemzadeh (1968), Rustow (1968), and Levine (1968).
3. As here employed ethnic group subsumes such prenational societies as are commonly designated by the terms clan, band, tribe, etc. It is to this more general sense of the term that Akzin refers (1964: 29) when he states that '. . . the point at which the ethnic group has both exceeded purely local dimensions and become of significance in the political sphere . . . is the point at which the appellation . . . nationality can be applied to it,' or 'the ethnic group at the point when it begins to loom . . . as an active factor . . . is referred to as a . . . nationality'.
4. A few examples of recent and relatively nonjudgmental definitions of this term may be of help in pointing out certain differences in emphases between authors. Znaniecki (1952: 21) comes closest to my own use in stating 'we shall define the term nationalism as the active solidarity of "national culture" society'. Kedourie (1961: 81) draws upon older discussions of 'national will' when he states '[Since] national self-determination is, in the final analysis, a

determination of the will . . . nationalism is, in the first place, a method of teaching the right determination of the will'. There is a touch (and sometimes more than just a touch) of mocking rejection in Kedourie's treatment of nationalism which is evident in the above definition. Rosenblatt (1964) is representative of those who are concerned with differentiating between nationalism and either less formalized or more rabid ethnic behaviors, viz: 'Nationalism, more often than ethnocentrism, involves loyalty to a politically distinct entity, membership in an elaborately organized and relatively populous social grouping, adherence to a formalized ideology, and performance of relatively stereotyped allegiance-expressing behavior' (p. 31). I consider Rosenblatt's reference to 'membership in a politically distinct entity' to be an unproductive restriction, since it unjustifiably singles out one of several possible goals of nationalism as a necessary attribute. In addition, like the historian Kedourie, the psychologist Rosenblatt does not stress the ethnocultural mainsprings which serve as points of departure for all other nationalist behaviors. Finally, while the furtherance of ethnic self-interest is recognized by Wirth (1936) in his definition of nationalism, he tends to specify the latter quite narrowly as 'the ideology of nationality' rather than as a rather broadly organized system of interrelated and elaborated ethnic beliefs, values, and behaviors. Lieberson's recent sociological definition (and confrontation between ethnic and class differences as well as similarities) nevertheless mistakenly limits nationalism to state-forming ethnic groups.

5. Rustow (1968b) provides a conveniently brief indication of the varying meanings of the term *nation*. The treatment of this topic is more extensive in Carr (1939), where varying usage in English, French, German, and Russian is reviewed. The most extensive review of the different connotations of the term, from ancient times through to the modern era, is that of Zernatto (1944). It is partly because of the excessively many connotations of the term (sometimes referring to the polity, as in the American pledge of allegiance to 'one nation, under God, indivisible,' sometimes to all of the inhabitants of a polity, and sometimes to any relatively large and solidary cultural group), that many writers have so clearly come to prefer *nationality* (rather than *nation*) for the more specific designations for which I have reserved it in this paper. Znaniecki noted (1952) that from the middle 1930s and throughout the 1940s 'in view of this terminological confusion, the editors of several encyclopedias have omitted the term "nation" altogether' (International Encyclopedia, Encyclopedia of the Social Sciences, Encyclopaedia Britannica, Handwörterbuch der Staatswissenschaften). In more recent years the term has again come to be much used with at least some tendency to favor the kind of usage to *nationality* that I prefer.

6. The contrast between *traditional*, *transitional*, and modern populations, not only in terms of beliefs, attitudes, and behaviors related to broader and more authentic ethnicity but in terms of identification with nonlocals, media participation, literacy, and political participation more generally, is convincingly presented in Daniel Lerner, *The Passing of Traditional Society* (Glencoe, Ill.: Free Press, 1958). Contrasts of this kind are inherent in much of the recent and extensive social-psychological and sociological literature on the development and modernization of the 'new' nations. The political historian Akzin (1964: 49–50) depicts the prenationalist era as one in which ' . . . the relative immobility of the large masses of mankind, coupled with their lack of literacy,

kept their outlook geared to the immediate social group with which they experienced close personal contact (village, clan, tribe), thus making them regard as strangers all those who ... lived beyond these narrow confines'. Akzin's reference to the role of illiteracy in maintaining the particularism that he describes anticipates our subsequent discussion of the contribution of literacy in the vernacular to the formation of broader affiliative bonds between separated clusters of vernacular speakers.

In like manner, Lerner's description of traditional society (particularly in the Moslem Near East) anticipates several points that will figure again in our discussion below: 'Traditional society is non-participant — it deploys people by kinship into communities isolated from each other and from the center, ... it develops few needs requiring economic interdependencies, ... people's horizons are limited by locale and their decisions involve only other *known* people in *known* situations. Hence there is no need for a trans-personal common doctrine formulated in terms of shared secondary symbols — a national "ideology" which enables persons unknown to each other to engage in political controversy or achieve "consensus" by comparing their opinions' (1958: 50).

Perhaps the most perceptive discussion of the interaction between tradition and modernity and of the *resilience* of the former even in current social life is that of Shils (1971).

7. The importance of communicational discontinuities in curtailing broader unity may be great even where local societies are rather highly developed in many other ways. Thus Aristotle believed that communities suffered if they consisted of fewer than 10 or more than 10,000 inhabitants (*Ethics*, IX, 10, 3) and the considerably larger barbarian communities were, for him, not real communities at all (*Politics*, VII, 4). Obviously, both technological and ideological change are required to enable small and discontinuous social units such as those known to Aristotle, which normally 'identified only with themselves,' to begin ' ... to identify with other social units ... In the protonationalist phase social cohesion begins to expand. Groups formerly in conflict with each other begin to see common elements with respect to a more esoteric and differentially defined social unit. While a traditional response would define all outside groups as threatening, a protonationalist response differentiates the external social force and distinct social units act together ... against a mutual external threat' (Friedland, 1968: 16–17).

8. 'The essence of the integrative relationship is seen as *collective action to promote mutual interests* ... It is both the *range* of functions in which they engage corporately, as well as the particular *kind* of functions that is important' (Jacob & Toscano, 1964: 5), and, we might add, that differs widely.

9. I have *not* consulted the original German version in order to determine the term that Herder used which Kohn translated as 'nation.' Echoes of the view expressed by Herder are still commonly heard in nonnationalist (or even antinationalist) anthropological and linguistic circles as providing the rationale for the collection of ethnographic, folkloric, and linguistic data on small and vanishing cultures before their individuality is lost forever. For an enlightening discussion of the anti-French and anti-rationalist origins of Herder's views and of their roots in earlier and contemporary philosophical and literary thought, see Kedourie's chapters 2, 3, and 4 (Self-determination, State, and Individual, and The Excellence of Diversity; 1961: 20–61).

10. 'Among the long-forgotten masses of Anatolia the "real Turk" was happily discovered, unaware that his language and customs . . . were about to become a political asset. The intelligentsia was urged to learn the history, folklore and traditions of the Turkish masses' (Karpat, 1964: 269–70).

11. The distinction between seekers of a genuine and total past and seekers of a usable and eclectic past has been made by many students of protest movements in differentiating between nativist and revivalist movements, on the one hand, and cargo cults and nationalisms, on the other (see, e.g. Depres, 1967, 1968 for summaries of such distinctions). In connection with nationalism Gellner (1964: 171) claims that 'ultimately the movements invariably contain both elements, a genuine modernism and a more or less spurious concern for local culture, or rather the re-employment of what had been a traditional culture for the enrichment and the trappings of a new education-rooted way of life'.

12. Znaniecki concludes the cited passage with the unwarranted observation that 'This doctrine is a joint product of ethnographers and of historians', thereby slighting the large variety of possible interactions between 'gehobenes Primitivgut' and 'gesunkenes Kulturgut' in the formation of doctrines of this kind.

13. Such nationalistic pleas to prospective allies were a favorite device of Napoleon in attracting popular support and give evidence of the widespread existence of latent nationalist sentiments in Central and Eastern Europe even in the early years of the nineteenth century. Thus, in setting up the Grand Duchy of Warsaw in order to enlist Polish support for his invasion of Russia, he urged a Polish delegation to 'show yourselves worthy of your forefathers. They ruled the house of Brandenburg; they were the masters of Moscow; they took the fortress of Widden; they freed Christianity from the yoke of the Turks' (cited by Kedourie, 1961: 94).

14. While popular evolutionary thought may underlie or strengthen some of the search for ancient origins that typifies modern nationalism, it is also strikingly true that Western social and political theory had come to be concerned with interpreting the losses and gains attributable to modernization long before Darwinism came to the fore. While Durkheim was by no means the first to suggest that the difference between the old and the new was *a difference in the basis of solidarity* (which difference, in turn, was derived from the division of labor), his impact on his own contemporaries and subsequent élites in Central and Eastern Europe and in Africa and Asia was quite striking. Similarly noticeable was the impact upon Durkheim himself of the social philosophy of several French writers (in particular Rousseau, Descartes, Comte, and Saint-Simon) whose views had contributed to earlier formulations of the impact of modernity on European society.

Durkheim recognized 'only two kinds of positive solidarity which are distinguishable by the following qualities:

   a. The first binds the individual directly to society without any intermediary.
   b. Society is not seen in the same aspect in the two cases. In the first, what we call society is a more or less organized totality of beliefs and sentiments common to all the members of the group: this is the collective type. On the other hand, the society . . . is a system of different, special functions which definite relations unite (p.129) . . .

It is the division of labor which, more and more, fills the role that was formerly filled by the common conscience. It is the principal bond of social aggregates of higher types' ([1893] 1933: 173).
In the second he depends upon society, because he depends upon the parts of which it is comprised.

Clearly Durkheim believed that both types of solidarity were found in all societies but that there was a secular trend from the first to the second as societal complexity increased.

15. Gellner (1964: 155) observes that 'in simple societies culture is important, but its importance resides in the fact that it reinforces structure. In modern societies culture does not so much underline structure; rather, it replaces it'. It is the latter condition which Gellner (1969: 173) believes to be the peculiar characteristic of affiliative behavior of modern nationalism which is 'marked by features such as the non-intimate, mass nature of the loyalty-evoking group, the definition of membership by (in effect) culture, and the fact that membership is direct and not mediated by intervening subgroups'.

16. Depres (1967) has stressed that one of the outcomes of technologically based social similarity in plural societies is that 'interdependent units tend to comprise culturally differentiated rather than socially differentiated' clusters of persons. This observation gives us a glimpse of how uniformation and diversification may not only be concomitant aspects of the very same social changes, but how an increase in the one (social uniformation) may lead to greater stress on the other (ethnocultural uniqueness) as a principle or device of mobilization. As we will subsequently see, those language planning efforts that are guided, even in a general way, by nationalist authenticity strivings must also balance these two simultaneous trends. On the one hand, indigenous national languages must be quickly developed to render them usable for modern governmental, industrial and scientific functions that are highly similar (i.e. supra-ethnic or non-ethnic) throughout the world. On the other hand, the languages so developed must also follow (and, at times, even devise) patterns that are thoroughly authentic and unique. In a way, these strictures are evocative of those imposed by Stalin's dictum that Soviet minority cultures might be national in form provided they were socialist in content (J. Stalin, 'O politicheskikh zadachakh universiteta narodov vostoka,' *Sochineniia*, 7 [18 May 1925]).

17. As examples, note ' . . . the national movements [in Eastern and Central Europe] would not have arisen . . . if it had not been for the growth of the capitalist system and the industrial revolution' (Carr, 1939: 112), and ' . . . the great transoceanic expansion of European commerce and economy at the close of the Middle Ages was closely related to the rise of national states along the Atlantic seaboard . . . The economic differentiation of nationalities . . . has been striking' (Hayes, 1960: 34).

18. As examples, note 'The repeated association between deliberate economic development and extreme nationalism is surely not accidental. Nationalism presents an essentially nonrational unifying force that may ease and rationalize the hardship of personal change [during economic development]' (Moore, 1965: 36–37), and 'Since the Industrial Revolution nationalism has drawn much of its strength from successively lower levels of material civilization . . . That the difference in poverty is so great and that the world's poorest peoples are so numerous . . . are perhaps the fundamental facts behind much of today's

nationalistic insistence on national separateness and economic and political barriers' (Deutsch [1953] 1966: 191), and 'And why does this situation [nationalism] obtain? . . . The erosion of the given, intimate structure of traditional society, an erosion inherent in the size, mobility and general ecology and organization of industrial society, or even of a society moving in this direction' (Gellner, 1964: 157).

19. Two examples that span 120 years are the following: 'Nationalism . . . would redeem modern man from his fearful loneliness and from the malaise of living in the impersonal mechanized world of industrial society' (Michelet, [1846] 1946: 44) and 'The vision of progress towards a common industrial society that the 18th century foresaw, and that people like Mill and Tocqueville in the 19th century came to fear, is plainly being realized in the 20th century. But it also seems plain that this thesis has its antithesis in the rise of modern nationalism . . . a tendency to emphasize differences in the midst of a common movement toward similar institutions and modes of existence . . . [and a] need for a sense of identity in a world where ancient bonds of kinship and community are weakening and the correlative demand for some principle of integration among large numbers of people' (Sutton, 1968: 1–2).

The relatively more psychological emphases of the first statement, above, and the more sociological emphases of the second, still represent the poles toward which most comments relating nationalism to modern economic development tend to gravitate. For additional psychological formulations (linking the appeal of nationalism with feelings of anxiety and alienation, fear of failure and incompetence, bewilderment at loss of traditional ways as well as compensatory identification stemming from early and continuing frustrations), see such valuable summaries as Doob, 1964; Katz, 1965, and Rosenblatt, 1964. Those who are particularly interested in this level of analysis may also find many stimulating formulations in older studies, such as those by Pillsbury, 1919 and Katz, 1940.

20. 'Exponents of the economic interpretation of nationalism would do well to take a long-range view of history and especially to ponder an interesting contrast between "results" of economic development at the beginning of the Christian era and "results" of economic development in our age. At the earlier time a remarkable expansion of commerce, acceleration of industry and development of capitalism were attended by the swift expansion of tribal states and city-states of diverse nationalities into a multilingual cosmopolitan state known as the Roman Empire; localism was transformed into imperialism; nationalism, if it existed at all, was weak. The contrast certainly suggests that economic development of itself does not create nationalism or cosmopolitanism but that it merely speeds up a political tendency which for other reasons is under way' (Hayes, 1931: 297–98). Without questioning Hayes' conclusion it should be pointed out that several students of Roman history have, indeed, pointed to a mass Roman nationalism as a major force during the early period of Roman expansion and to an élitist Roman nationalism during the subsequent periods of Empire. 'The Roman who was a Spaniard or African or an Italian was also a "Roman"' (Barrow, 1949: 116). That such Roman nationalism did not commonly go far beyond élitist ranks is viewed as a weakness of the regime attributable, basically, to the absence of economic, industrial, and technological change sufficiently massive and continuing to penetrate, mobilize, and Romanize the countryside.

21. 'Certain long-drawn-out armed conflicts, such as the series of wars between Christians and Moslems in Spain, between Russians and their neighbors, the Hundred Years War across France, did much to arouse national consciousness among those concerned' (Akzin, 1964: 45). The difference between 'national(ity) consciousness' and nationalism, particularly in terms of massive and organized activity has already been mentioned. In the absence of sufficient economic-technological development, even long-drawn-out wars did not truly long involve the entire populace (as do the citizen armies of today), nor long disrupt them from returning to their particularistic and localistic forms of economic, social, and cultural integration (as do modern wartime controls). As a result, nationality consciousness due to protracted hostilities had no post-emergency operative base and, therefore, unlike modern nationalism, it tended to evaporate outside of the area of localized conflict, as well as soon after the cessation of hostilities, and to remain merely as raw material for future nationalist exploitation (Braunthal, 1946). As a result, e.g. several regional Spains, rather than a single united Spain, emerged from the 'reconquista' and these have not fully united to this very day owing to the uninterrupted force of regional life and the general lack of major scale instrumental integration (Menéndez-Pidal, 1945; Linz, 1970).

22. The relationship between nationalism and religion and the purported rise of nationalism as a result of the decline of religion are both very involved topics that cannot be adequately treated in an essay of this kind. Nevertheless, because the ties between nationalism and religion are of significance for an understanding of nationalism in a number of developing countries, as well as for an understanding of some of the language planning problems there encountered, a few observations concerning these matters are justified at this point.

   Recently, Myrdal has stated that the extensive interpenetration of nationalism with religion in South and Southeast Asia represents a major contrast with the predominantly secular and even anticlerical nature of nationalism in Europe (1968: 119, 2112, etc., although contradicted elsewhere). This view of the purported secularism (and the, presumably, greater rationalism) of European nationalism essentially follows in the path of Durkheim's dictum: 'If there is one truth that history teaches us beyond doubt it is that religion tends to embrace a smaller and smaller portion of social life' ([1893] 1933: 169); and is in agreement with Kohn's 'universal sociological law' ('religious groups lose power when confronted with the consciousness of a common nationality and speech' [1932: 229]). Similar general formulations can be found in Emerson (1962: 158); Kedourie (1961: 101); Minogue (1967: 147) and others. Znaniecki includes the development of a secular culture and a secular literature among the defining characteristics of societies that have attained nationality status (1952: 21). A more cautious formulation is that by Inglehart & Woodward (1967: 32), who merely claim that language and nationality 'seems' more important than religion as a basis of political cleavage in modern societies; but this is true only insofar as it becomes linked with differences in social mobility'. Baron, the only scholar who has attempted a truly intensive and comparative analysis of modern nationalism and religion, is even more cautious (1947). His position seems to be that there has rarely been a major establishment of the one without the other (actually, that their concepts are fully intertwined) and that whichever has been the weaker of the two has always attempted to draw strength from the other, without being controlled by it. The fact that European polities have increasingly become religiously neutral in their international dealings should not blind us to the fact that 'all major Continental nationalities, except the long-divided Germans and Hungarians, overwhelmingly belong to a single denomination' (p.17). As a result, religion, polity, and nationality have become for the most part complementary terms covering the same human groups when viewed from an intrapolity perspective.

The examples of religious *preservation*, *cultivation*, and *dependence upon* ethnic and nationality differences are legion, including all European religious groups during all periods of European history. For early examples of predominantly national forms of Christianity note the patriarchate of Alexandria (Hardy, 1946) and the Armenian Church, which first 'adopted Monophysitism out of opposition to Persian [i.e. Nestorian] Christianity. They used it finally as a barrier to defend their nationality' (Woodward, 1916: 48). Furthermore, 'among Eastern Christian Churches, some (e.g. Armenian, Coptic, Syrian) retained an ethnic character, making of religion a strong supporting element both of the fact of nationality and of sentiment-laden national consciousness. Others — the Russian, Bulgarian, Rumanian, Serbian — developed ... an increasingly autocephalous structure because the mother Greek Orthodox Church was not regarded by worshippers and clergy as sufficiently close from an ethnic viewpoint' (Akzin, 1964: 47–48). 'Roger Bacon and Bartholomew, known as Anglicus, were among the first [13th century] to call attention to the nation[ality] as a factor in state and society' (Akzin, 1964: 14). 'Catholic clerics, being the main intelligentsia in medieval society, were also the main promoters of national literature and recorders of national history' (Baron, 1947: 13). 'At the Council of Constance the spirit of nationalism was not only present, but received concrete expression in its most menacing form in the method of voting by nations' (Powers, 1927: viii). The nationality-promoting role of Hus, Wycliffe, and Luther among Protestant leaders has frequently been pointed out and is too widely known to require citation here. The Greek hierarchy played a similar role from the eighteenth century on regarding itself 'as the guardian of the Greek nation from both the Latins and the Turks, and considering this nation distinguished not only by its Orthodox religion but also by the Greek language' (Sherrard, 1959: 178). Judaism, of course, 'must be considered an ethnic religious system because its institutions and practices are closely tied to the land of its origin ... and so preserve the distinctive identity of the community' (Sopher, 1967:5–6).

Corresponding references pertaining to nationalist exploitation of religion are literally too numerous (and perhaps too self-evident) to merit citation. From the Gothic ruler's choice of Arianism rather than Catholicism (Woodward, 1917) to the Croatian, Slovenian, Slovak, Polish, and Irish uses of Catholicism to establish their separateness and pursue their independence, there has been a constant reliance by European secular leaders on their particular religious traditions, institutions, and hierarchies to serve nationalist purposes in general and the causes of the newly developing national languages in particular (Grentrup, 1932). Above and beyond the foregoing there is the more general reliance of European nationalism on such fundamental Judeo-Christian religious concepts as 'chosen people,' 'promised land,' and 'sacred language.' These enabled nationalists to immediately draw upon a bountiful source of established images and associations implying divine sanction, to the end that it rang true to say that 'The day when France, remembering that she was, and must be, the salvation of mankind, will place her children around her, and teach them France, as faith and as religion, she will find herself living and firm as the globe' (Michelet [1846] 1946: 241).

Hayes (1942), more than most students of this particular problem, has documented the constant interdependence of religion and nationalism in Europe from earliest times. 'A mere history of doctrinal aspects of schism and heresy will hardly make clear why, for example, the Monophysite heresy of the fifth century found embodiment in schismatic national churches for Egyptians, Armenians and Syrians' (p.4). However, just as religion made use of national sentiments in the prenationalist past, so has nationalism made use of religious sentiments, in more modern days. Hayes indicates Napoleon's awareness of the power of religious sentiments (for eliciting national feeling on his behalf) to such an extent that it 'made a Catholic of me when I had finished the war of Vendée, made a Muslim of me when I had established myself in Egypt . . . If I governed a Jewish people I would re-establish the Temple of Solomon' (p.10). Chateaubriand, believing that 'the most appropriate instinct in man, the most beautiful, the most moral *c'est l'amour de la patrie*' concluded, as a result, that 'the Church is to be cherished because it is the best teacher of nationalism' (pp.9-10). Finally, in the view of 'such atheistic or agnostic ultra-nationalists as Maurice Barrès, Charles Maurras and Gabriele d'Annunzio, the Catholic Church . . . should be preserved because it represents the national tradition' (p.10). Lest it be assumed that only religion can thus be exploited to serve nationalist ends today, note Lipset's remarks concerning a similar use to which socialism has been put (1968: 102–07).

The upshot of the foregoing, it seems to me, is that European religions were long the carriers of ethnicity and nationalism at the same time that they pursued their respective universalistic truths. While the last 200 years of European history have been marked by the greater prominence of nationalism as a unifying and organizing force, particularly in political affairs, the relationship between the two has merely been reversed (nationalism now being an important carrier of religious imagery and religious distinction) rather than weakened. By the time of the industrial revolution the European multinationality state had already made an ally of religion and had learned to control it rather than be controlled by it. 'For each melting pot is not merely fusing religion into the state church, it is also fusing the church itself into the world of the state' (Zangwill, 1917: 66). Submerged nationalities, therefore, struggled primarily against secular forces and rarely against fundamentally religious ones. If a long-term change has occurred between religious and secular predominance in political affairs, it came with the Reformation and Counter-Reformation in the sixteenth and seventeenth centuries (see, e.g. Powers, 1927: 202, theses 21 and 25), rather than with the rise of nationalism in the eighteenth and nineteenth. Thus, the distinction between Europe and Asia is not so much the relative absence of secular nationalism in the latter as much as the relative absence of secularism *per se*, either among those against whom nationalism must struggle, or among those it seeks to influence. In addition, of course, Western states (and in the East, especially China and

Japan, have developed *civil* religions that interlock with the more traditional religions, in very substantial ways (see, e.g. Bellah, 1967; Yang, 1961).

23. '[Nations] are connected more with the concepts of honor than with the idea of wealth. The nation is not an economic group' (Sulzbach, 1943: viii). The last Minister for Nationalities of the Austro-Hungarian Empire, having witnessed himself the seemingly endless sequential progression of nationality movements concluded, more evenhandedly, that 'if we study the intellectual and moral struggles of the heroic period of nationalism, we distinctly recognize that we face not only the introduction of a new method of economic production but, at the same time, the establishment of a new scale of moral values' (Jaszi, 1929: 258). In this same vein another observer has noted that 'the materialistic explanation does not hold good for a nationalist movement like, for example, the Polish whose moving spirits were the gentry and whose source of inspiration was the historic past and memories of an aristocratic freedom, and hardly an economic grievance against the foreign rulers or the rapid pace of social change' (Talmon, 1965: 18). Talmon, like Jaszi, does not deny 'the great influence of economic forces on the forms of national consciousness and the patterns of nationalist strategy', but concludes that 'economic factors alone cannot be considered to have been the matrix of nationalism' (p.17).

24. The notion of locating nationalism within a nexus of interrelated causes and effects occurred to Acton over a century ago when he considered the revolutionary theories of his age. 'There are three principal theories of this kind,' he wrote, 'impugning the present distribution of power, of property and of territory, and attacking respectively the aristocracy, the middle class, and the sovereignty. They are the theories of equality, communism and nationality. Though sprung from a common origin, opposing cognate evils and connected by many links, they did not appear simultaneously. Rousseau proclaimed the first, Babeuf the second, Mazzini the third' ([1864] 1907: 273).

25. A very similar linkage is posited by Kohn when he concludes that 'As a phenomenon of modern European history the rise of nationalism is closely linked with the origins of popular sovereignty, the theory of government by the active "consent of the governed," the growth of secularism, the lessening of the older religious, tribal, clannist, or feudal loyalties, and the spread of organization, industrialization and improved communication' (1968: 64).

26. In an equally (though opposite) one-sided approach, most communist social theoreticians have tended to concentrate on only two aspects of the interactions of nationalism with other processes: (a) the 'positive' contribution of nationalism to the breakdown of feudalism and, therefore, to the emergence of both the bourgeoisie and the working class, and (b) the 'negative' contribution of nationalism, under bourgeois dominance, to the inevitable international unification of the working class. In practice there has been a trend toward increasingly nationalist brands of communism since the end of World War II (Snyder, 1968: 304–19). An Asian observer comments as follows: 'As long as communism worked in cooperation with nationalism it continued to flourish, but once the clash occurred its fate was more or less sealed, for nationalism is still the most powerful force' (Singhal, 1967: 283).

At the level of theory, no post-World War II revisionist integrative statement of the relationship between nationalism and communism (see, e.g. Glezerman, 1970; Potekhin, 1958; Rodinson, 1968) has yet attained widespread recognition rivaling in any way that formerly accorded the writings of Marx, Engels, Lenin, and Stalin on this topic. Marx and Engels were largely guided by considerations of parsimony that led them to prefer the nationalism of a few superstates over that of an endless procession of microstates (in each of which the proletariat would be smaller, weaker, and more easily influenced by fabricated, pseudonationalist diversionary antagonisms). This view is summarized in Engels 1866 and in Rjasanoff 1916. Subsequent theory was more sophisticated, providing for an evolutionary-transformation approach to the development of a nationality. Thus in 1913 (in *Prosvescheniye* nos. 3–5; subsequently included in the collection entitled *Marxism and the National Question* [1942]) Stalin outlined a stagewise progression from the clan, through the tribal community (still based largely on kinship), the ethnic group, and the narodnost (a not yet fully unified or precisely defined linguistic-territorial-economic co-occurrence) to the nation/ality. However, the basic task of such theory was neither descriptive nor predictive, but, rather, manipulative. Just as Lenin had admonished his disciples to 'consider each national demand, national separation, from the vantage point of the class struggle of the workers' in order not 'to confuse the right of self-determination with the actual usefulness of it' (Dadrian, 1968: 35), so Stalin frankly observed that '. . . the interests of the proletariat and the rights of a nation . . . are two different things' (*Works*, v. 2: 322). For orthodox international communism, nationalism is obviously no more than an exploitable distraction, at best, particularly in view of the contratheoretical fact that in modern times 'vertical cleavages have been more important than horizontal ones' (Binder, 1964: 152). For the language policy consequences of such ambivalence see Desheriev *et al.*, 1965 (for a defense) and Weinreich, 1953b (for an indictment). A studied attempt to present a balanced view is that of Lewis, 1972.

27. Several examples of such early total or partial rejections are given by Kohn (1968: 64). This problem of élite formations and reformations has been particularly emphasized by Kedourie (1961), Minogue (1967), and other historians and philosophers, schooled as they are in the textual analysis of the writings of great men, even though they have been aware that societal circumstances favorable to the élites under study were as necessary as the felicity of their formulations. For a more judicious recognition of the role of élites, one that relates them to social and economic changes affecting the masses, see Friedrich (1963).

28. The mid-nineteenth century German nationalist spokesman and activist Friedrich Ludwig Jahn stressed his contributions along these very lines in the concluding passage of his *Selbstverteidigung* (written in the third person): ' . . . [he] served his Fatherland throughout his life . . . to turn away all things un-German and foreign (*Undeutschheit und Ausländerei*) and led the confused back to the path of virtue and honor.' Jahn composed his own epitaph: 'I held fast to the idea of German unity, as if it were an unhappy love' (Snyder, 1952: 41).

29. 'Karel Havlicek, a popular leader of the Czech national movement had a daily column in his paper under the heading "The Irish Repeal Movement", in which he described from day to day the situation of the unhappy island and the growing force of the nationalist movement [there] . . . at a time when censorship made all political action impossible [in the Austro-Hungarian

Empire]' (Jaszi, 1929: 260).

30. 'The philippic of Björnstjerne Björnson, the great Norwegian poet, against the policy of Magyarization of Count Albert Opponyi [was widely distributed and] aroused more indignation in the hearts of the oppressed nationalities than the policy of assimilation itself' (Jaszi, 1929: 267).

31. The intended contrast is between Zangwill's oft quoted (but never authenticated) phrase that 'a nation is a body of people who feel they are a nation' and Buber's more differentiated view [1933]: 'A people is a phenomenon of life, nationality (which cannot exist without national feeling) is one of consciousness, nationalism is one of superconsciousness' (cited by Baron, 1947: 3). Actually, Zangwill's usage is well aware of the action potential of nationalism, viz: 'Nationality degenerates into nationalism. Fire is a good servant but a bad master, and the same flame that vivified sub-nationality turns nationality into a belligerent fireship' (1917: 49).

32. Thus, French unity was traced back to Ancient Gaul in Théophile Lavalée's *Histoire des Français depuis le temps des Gaulois* (Paris, 1830), and German unity to the struggle against Rome in the second century B.C. in Johann Sporschil's *Geschichte der Deutschen von den ältesten Zeiten* (5 vols. Regensburg, 1859–60). One of the first such historical creations of greater unity was Francesco Guicciarcini's *La Historia di Italia* published in Florence in 1561, three full centuries before the attainment of Italian unity.

33. The allusion here is to Minogue's apt characterization of Rousseau's view of society around that time (1967: 41–42). Minogue concludes 'He was, in fact, dominated by an overpowering nostalgia for the past.' It is this nostalgia that nationalism modernizes and activates.

34. Thus, after the unsuccessful revolution of 1848, Prague Germans, nevertheless, commented on the fact that 'the Czech national colors and dress were much in view, talking Czech in public was becoming *bon ton* . . . The Students' League broke up, and a "Slavia" ranged itself (as yet fraternally) by the side of a "Teutonia"; the Czechs left the literary society "Concordia" and formed the "Svornost." Innocuous intellectual activities of a "folk-character," hitherto countenanced by the Germans, were assuming a political complexion' (Namier, 1944: 100). A similar straw in the wind appeared 'at the occasion of a splendid ball in Zagreb [1840], at which Croatian ladies pinned to their bosoms a star on whose points the names . . . Dalmatians, Croatians, Montenegrins, Slavenians [*sic*], Bulgarians and Serbs were engraved. In the center of the star the following words were to be read: "God help us to union!"' (Jaszi, 1929: 262).

35. Kolarz presents a long list of nationalist leaders who were themselves born outside of the group or area to which they subsequently devoted their efforts, or whose parents were 'foreigners' who had socialized their children into their own (i.e. the parental) cultural tradition, rather than into the tradition of the people in whose midst they resided. For an account of the ethnic self-redefinition of such 'foreign' élites (as well as the refusal of others to do so) see Lindman (1963) or Wuorinen (1931).

36. The peculiar perspective and sensitivity coming from years of life in exile is revealed by Michael Collin's statement: 'I stand for an Irish civilization based on the people and embodying and maintaining the things — their habits, ways of thought, customs — that make them different — the sort of life I was brought up in . . . Just the sort of donkey and just the sort of cart that they

have at home . . . Nobody who has not been an exile will understand me, but I stand for that' (cited by Minogue, 1967: 22–23).

37. It is probably an exaggeration to claim as does Trevor-Roper, that 'all great nationalist leaders have been only half-national themselves. Their followers may be — generally are — true nationals: authentic, autochthonous, monoglot, aborigines of the tribe, bigoted fundamentalists of the faith. But the leaders, it is well known, tend to be marginal in their nationality, perhaps inspired by secret doubts of their nationality' (1962: 20–21). The above seems to stand at the opposite extreme of the reality of incipient nationalism from Pye's claim that 'before the nation can develop, leaders must emerge who have found integrity in their own quests for identity and who can hence speak in terms that will bring meaning to other people's search for identity' (1961: 219).

38. For a basic discussion of the difference between 'intelligentsia' and 'intellectuals' in a content pertinent to incipient nationalism see Vladimir Nahirny (1962).

39. There is little available in the way of analysis of the nonintellectual élites upon which all nationalist movements were and are also dependent. The political, military, financial, commercial, and industrial risk takers who are among the first to foresee the possible gains of a reorganization of society and its institutions of power on the basis of nationality, have been characterized by Deutsch (1957: 88) as including 'some of the least secure among the powerful with some of the most powerful among those who . . . [are] just ceasing to be powerless'. As for the kinds of individuals most likely to follow the lead of such risk takers and innovators, Moore (1965: 42) suggests those who 'are marginal to the traditional order . . . young wives in traditional Chinese households . . . the Indian caste untouchables, the younger sons in a system of male primogeniture, merchants "unclassifiable" in feudal Japan, dispossessed landlords subsequent to land reform, the indigenous . . . landless poor'. Moore's comments return us to the basic discontent upon which nationalism operates and which the élites attempt to channel. The aptness of élitist formulations may well be a minor factor in explaining the variance in nationalist success when contrasted with the real pressures for mass participation in organized ameliorative efforts along ethnically advantageous lines.

40. 'The process of urbanization has usually been very closely related to the breakdown of at least some of the more traditional ascriptive criteria of status, whether tribal, estate or regional ones, and to the development of somewhat more flexible and variegated social strata; to the upsurge of social mobility through occupational, educational and political channels, and to the development of a great variety of forms of social organization, ranging from various functionally specific enterprises to various civic and voluntary associations and professional groups . . . All these processes have created a status system of great fluidity and ambiguity. The assurance of a fixed given position which spilled over into most of an individual's institutional roles was being continually undermined . . . by the very nature of the system of social organization . . . [and by] continual changes and structural differentiation. Hence, although these developments usually opened up new perspectives of advancement and change of status, status necessarily became also a focus of insecurity, awareness and political conflict' (Eisenstadt, 1966: 11). 'We have identified education, urban experience and occupation (especially industrial experience) as three of the most powerful influences determining individual

modernity' (Smith & Inkeles, 1966: 369). Several investigators, among them Lerner (1958) and Deutsch (1953), have effectively used indices of urbanization in lieu of indices of industrialization, mobilization, or modernization that are so much more difficult to obtain.

41. The appeal of social-psychological variables, such as these in connection with the urban locus of nationalist movements, is apparent in the writings of a large group of scholars, classical and modern, such as Hertz ('. . . The personality and prestige that the individual cannot attain in his own name may be accessible to him in the form of collective personality in which he has a share' [1944: 274]), Rosenblatt ('Needs to be related to something supra-individual, to have goals or to "belong", are greater among deracinated or marginal individuals' [1964: 134]), Simmel (' . . . Indivduals [previously] liberated from historical bonds now wished to distinguish themselves from one another . . . It is the function of the metropolis to provide the arena for this struggle and its reconciliation. For the metropolis presents peculiar conditions . . . the opportunities for the development of both these ways of allocating roles to men' [in Hatt & Reiss, 1957: 645]), and Wirth ('In view of the ineffectiveness of actual kinship ties [in the city] we create fictional kinship groups' [1938: 62]).

    Whether all of the above reactions to urbanization always occurred 'naturally' or were also, at least in part, derivative, is open to question in view of the concurrent intellectual condemnation of the city. 'Nothing promotes an appreciation of nature more than urban growth' (Minogue, 1967: 75).

42. 'The centre, or the central zone, is a phenomenon of the realm of values and beliefs. It is the centre of the order of symbols, of values and beliefs which govern society . . . As long as societies were loosely coordinated, as long as much of the economic life of the society was carried on outside any market or almost exclusively in local markets, the central value system invariably became attenuated in the outlying reaches . . . The emergence of nationalism, not just the fanatical nationalism of politicians, intellectuals and zealots, but as a sense of nationality and an affirmative feeling for one's own . . . is a very important aspect of this process of the incorporation of the mass of the population into the central institutional and value systems' (Shils, 1961: 117, 124 and 128).

43. Just prior to World War II, Wirth (1938: 59) was still able to observe that 'the foreign born and their children constitute nearly two-thirds of all the inhabitants of cities of one million and over. Their proportion of the urban population declines as the size of the city decreases, until in the rural areas they comprise only about one-sixth of the total population'. While Wirth is pointing primarily to the results of modern immigrations involving largely rural and recently urban populations, the underlying factors involved are not too different from those that brought previously urbanized populations to foreign cities in multiethnic states before the rise of nationalism.

44. 'Not until the emancipation of the serfs in Austria in 1848 and in Russia in 1861, were the silent people able to . . . enter other social classes or, above all, take work in the towns' (Kolarz, 1946: 16).

45. That several cities underwent this process not once but several times is evident from the fact that 'The Slovaks can prove that in 1920 only 16% of the population [of Bratislava=Pozsony=Pressburg] was Magyar, whilst the Hungarians, basing their claims on the census of 1910, can show that 40% was

then Hungarian and only 18% Slovak . . . The Germans refer to the census of 1880 wherein 65% of the population is shown to have been German' (Kolarz, 1946: 16). In the interim 'some of the town dwellers who had [originally come from the land and had] gone over into the camp of the ruling strata changed their language and nationality' not once but twice or even oftener (p. 15).

46. 'It is the decisive nature of the metropolis that its inner life overflows by waves into a far flung national arena . . . The most significant characteristic of the metropolis is this functional extension beyond physical boundaries' (Simmel, in Hatt & Reiss, 1955: 643).

47. See, e.g. Deutsch (1953: 101), Hayes (1960: 81), Lerner (1958: 71), and Wirth (1938: 62), all of whom stress that the city facilitates communication from élites to masses in view of its higher density of interaction networks, communication channels and media, and communication occasions.

48. 'It is in the distant provinces . . . where the inhabitants move about less and experience fewer changes of fortune and status that the genius and customs of a nation should be studied' (Rousseau, cited by Namier, 1952: 26).

49. As sensitive a commentator as Gellner considers it fruitful to observe that there is substantial error in each of the 'three principle components' of the doctrine of nationalism. 'One is a piece of philosophical anthropology: men have 'nationality' as they have a nose and two eyes and this is a central part of their being. The second is a psychological contention: they wish to live with those of the same nationality and above all resent being ruled by those of another one. The third is an evaluative contention, and adds that this is rightly so' (1964: 150). Gellner concludes that 'nationalism is not the awakening of nations to self-consciousness: it invents nations where they do not exist' (p. 168). Deutsch, on the other hand, views the process of nationality formation as being entirely rational: 'When there is a significant high level of important transactions, many of which bring joint rewards, the people who have experienced these mutual transactions will like them. When these transactions are highly visible, easy to identify and differentiate, people . . . form images of the community or of the group involved in the transaction' (1964b: 54).

50. In this connection, Sorel observes: 'The myth must be judged as a means of acting on the present; any attempt to discuss how far it can be taken literally . . . is devoid of sense' (1961: 125).

51. The point I wish to stress is that differences are not naturally 'divisive' (nor are similarities unifying) until highlighted as such. It is not the experience of difference that is divisive but the interpretation given to the experience. Thus, the 'highly' differentiated and clustered world of settlements, nodes of transport, centers of culture, areas and centers of language, divisions of castes and class, barriers between markets, sharp regional differences in wealth and interdependence' (Deutsch, 1953: 187) are only *potentially* divisive in the sense that they do not further integration. These must first interact with conflict or competition in order to be experienced as justifications for differentiation (Katz, 1965: 566). The nationality level of society facilitates such interpretive experiences between groups since 'sociologically a nationality is a conflict group. The self- and group-consciousness generated by nationalistic movements corresponds to the nature of the inter-group relationship that exists between one nationality and another' (Wirth, 1936: 224–25).

The insufficiency of 'consciousness of differences' for the purposes of maintaining differentiation is well documented by Hugelman (1931), who traces German national feeling as far back as the reign of Charlemagne, and by Heinz Zatcheck (1936), who extensively catalogs the many expressions of antipathy between natives and 'foreigners' during the period of the late middle ages. Yet, because these cases had no ideology of nationalism behind (or immediately ahead of) them, most of them proved to be inferior in strength and influence to the integrative experiences that subsequently followed. They did not feed into larger secondary systems that could maintain themselves once the initial irritations had receded into the past (Hayes, 1960: 29). On the other hand, some of these irritations came to be cumulatively interpreted by members of those groups whose self-interests and self-concepts had come to be *organized*, at least in part, in mutually contrastive terms. It then seemed far more significant than it had previously that 'at the start of the Second Crusade in 1147, the French army of Louis VII and the German army of Conrad III were kept separate lest they battle each other instead of the Muslems' (Hayes, 1960: 28). Indeed this seemed particularly significant over 600 years later to Thomasius when he proclaimed (about 1687) ' . . . If our German forefathers were to rise from the dead and come amongst us they might think they were in a foreign land. Everything French seems to be in fashion — French food, French clothes, French speech and even French diseases' (Blackall, 1959: 13). Over a century and a half later, Herder elaborated nearly 800 years of Franco-German conflict into a philosophy with immense and almost immediate political ramifications (although 'his own interest was predominantly spiritual-aesthetic: he was fighting the cultural and literary predominance of France and politics hardly entered' into his awareness (Talmon, 1965: 106). Thus, while Fichte was exaggerating somewhat when he claimed (1807) that ' . . . Men cannot *fit* themselves into a new nation once a communal existence [*das Volkseyn*] has entered their natural existence and consciousness' (cited by Namier, 1952: 22), he was, by and large, not far from what might be a currently acceptable formulation concerning indigenous populations that have undergone long-term and pervasive nationalist ideologization. For a veritable catalog of selective remembering and forgetting of past animosities see Braunthal, 1946.

52. Apropos the relevance of superordinate threat, note, e.g., Wuorinen's observation that after the mid-century intensification of Russification efforts in Finland 'Finn and Swede-Finn stood shoulder to shoulder. They thus proved beyond challenge that much of the 'language fight' had involved grievances and prejudices of no lasting import and . . . had not destroyed the higher loyalty toward nation[ality] and country as a whole' (1950: 474). (For further details concerning the threat of Russification as a moderating influence in Finn vs Swede-Finn differentiation see Lindman, 1963 and, particularly, Wuorinen, 1931). Note, however, that superordinate threat was important in *two* ways. It brought the Finns and Swede-Finns of Finland *closer together* (which is not, of course, to say that they have ever been fully integrated ethnoculturally), on the one hand, and increased their differentiation from the Russians, on the other hand. Common enemies have played a similar role in unifying the Spanish kingdoms (the Moors), the Flemish lowlands (the Spanish), the Scottish districts (the English), the German principalities (the French), etc.

53. An examination of the varying relationships between nationality and polity

will also enable us to avoid the dangers foreseen by Wirth: 'As long . . . as we continue to confine ourselves to a particularistic analysis of the nationalism of different countries and epochs, on the one hand, and treating nationalism as a single undifferentiated phenomenon, on the other hand, there is little prospect of scientific advance on this subject' (1936: 724). A further danger that is worth guarding against, however, is that of establishing purely classificatory 'types of nationalism' which do not provide for transitions, transformations, or links from one to the other. To the lengthy list of older classificatory typologies (many of which have been mentioned in passing above), the more recent additions by Snyder (1964), Haas (1964), and Chilcote (1969) should be noted.

54. This shortsighted view of 'naturalness' even applies to the very link between nationality and polity itself. Thus, while Kedourie (1961: 116–17) is certain that 'nationalists consider that political and cultural matters are inseparable and that no culture can live if it is not endowed with a sovereign state exclusively its own', he overlooks thereby the counter-arguments of a large number of nationalist leaders on all continents and the stable counterpolicies of several more-enlightened multiethnic states. Tagore's (1920: 9) view of the relationship between polity and community is encountered among spokesmen for other nonpolitical nationalist movements: 'a nation, in the sense of the political and economic union of a people, is that aspect which a whole population assumes when organized for mechanical purposes. Society as such has no ulterior purpose. It is an end in itself. It is a spontaneous self-expression of man as a social being . . . The political side . . . is only for a special purpose. It is for self-preservation. It is merely the side of power, not of human ideals'. Depres (1967: 10) comments on the difference between cultural and political goals as follows: ' . . . a nationalist movement has as one of its distinguishing characteristics a professed ideology which makes a chauvinistic appeal to a shared tradition of one type or another. Theoretically, an independence movement may or may not share this goal', to which I would merely add, 'nor vice versa.'

55. That these varying meanings and the words themselves continued to be troublesome for many is evident from the comment that 'never have the names *Nation* and *State* been so repeated as today. These two words were never pronounced under Louis XIV and the idea [nation] itself did not even exist . . . This comes from the Parlement [*sic*] and the English' (René Louis de Voyer [d'Argenson], *Journal*, June 26, 1754, p. 262; cited by Barzun, 1932).

56. Snyder too refers to the fact that 'a common sovereignty provides common institutions' as a result of which 'the nation developed within the chrysalis of the state . . . in the Western Atlantic world' (1964: 58). Katz discusses 'institutional nationalism' at length and contrasts it, as transitional, between statism per se and cultural nationalism. 'Institutional nationalism centers around certain societal purposes and national goals. Thus, American nationalism may consist in part of belief systems about the political institution of democracy, and the economic institution of free enterprise, and the related institution of technology as the expression of American national purpose. Value systems centering around these institutions can exist independently of values about the national state itself, but they are often linked to one another or even fused. Thus, nationalism has an input from the dominant institutions

of the society. Advancing national interests means extending these institutions' (Katz, 1965: 360). It should not be supposed that *all* long established multinationality states necessarily foster the development of institutionally based state-nationality. This outcome is a result not only of common institutions but of internal processes of change, centralization, and in common mobilization or ideologization of the populations involved.

57. The primacy of state (or, in our terms, nation) over nationality obviously influenced and shaped the nature of other integrative forces in Western Europe in addition to the force of nationalism. Thus, Barker observes (in his review of the Reformation and nationality): 'There is what I should call Etatism, as well as nationalism, in our English Reformation, and in the beginning there is more etatism than nationalism, although there was always some nationalism there. In other words, the English Church began as a State Church, rather than a national church, but in the course of time the position was gradually changed and inverted' (Barker, 1932: 340).

58. Engels was the first collectivist spokesman to interpret nationality and nationalism as a malevolent by-product of the bourgeois state. Since that time socialist, communist, and other collectivist movements have been disrupted on several occasions, both by the nationalism of state-nationalities (where long stabilized states have formed broader nationalities) and by the nationalism of nationality-states (when recently integrated nationalities have sought or gained states of their own). Nevertheless, we still find Rocker (1937: 200, 536) claiming that 'the nation is not the cause, but the result of the State. It is the State which creates the nation, not the nation the state . . . And with the State will disappear also the nation — which is only the state-folk — in order that the concept of humanity may take on a new meaning'. Even capitalists ridiculed state-nations that were of recent vintage and had not yet fully digested the groups upon which they had fed. Zangwill quotes The (*London*) Times as referring to 'That maze of cross-bred Celts, Sumarians, Hellenes, Iranians, Semites and Caucasians shot through with Turanians, which we call the Turkish people' (1917: 49). The tone is much the same as that employed in current popular references to African state-nations. Thus, even the state-nation is legitimate only if it is old.

59. Countless others wrote in a similar vein, particularly in England, throughout the nineteenth century. At the time the Irish, Scottish, and Welsh seemed to be fairly well incorporated into the lower rungs of British society and 'an underemphasis on nationality became intellectually fashionable in England' (Akzin, 1964: 18) until well into the twentieth century. Among leading intellectuals, only Byron, John Stuart Mill, and Disraeli seem to have spoken up on behalf of the claims of the newer nationalities during the nineteenth century and even they were less than completely evenhanded about the principle of nationality to which these nationalities referred. Thus, J.S. Mill strongly criticized the nationality principle as 'tending to make men indifferent to the rights and interests of any portion of the human species, save that which is called by the same name and speaks the same language as themselves. These feelings are characteristic of barbarians . . . In the backward parts of Europe and even (where better things might have been expected) in Germany, the sentiment of nationality so far outweighs the love of liberty that the people are willing to abet their rulers in crushing the liberty and independence of any people not of their race and language' (in 'The French Revolution and its

Assailants,' *Westminster Review* (April 1849), cited by Namier, 1952: 32). All in all, however, Mill was more inclined than were most of his contemporaries to recognize that the nationality-forming potential of common political antecedents depended on their historical priority in comparison to other integrating sentiments. 'When nations, thus divided, are under a despotic government which is a stranger to all of them . . . and chooses its instruments indifferently from all, in the course of a few generations identity of situation often produces harmony of feeling and the different races come to feel toward each other as fellow countrymen. But if the era of aspiration to free government arrives before this fusion has been effected, the opportunity has gone by for effecting it' (reprinted 1910: 366).

60. The vehemence of Engels' remarks is perhaps understandable if we recognise, as he did, that the fractionated nationalist movements presented a grave danger to the ideal of a parsimonious victory of the proletariat. 'There is no country in Europe where there are not different nationalities under the same government. The Highland Gaels and the Welsh are undoubtedly of different nationalities to what the English are, although nobody will give to these remnants of peoples long gone by the title of nations any more than to the Celtic inhabitants of Brittany in France . . . The European *importance*, the *vitality* of a people is as nothing in the eyes of the principle of nationalities; before it, the Roumans [*sic*] of Wallachia who never had a history, nor the energy required to have one, are of equal importance to the Italians who have a history of 2000 years, and an unimpaired national vitality; the Welsh and Manxmen, if they desired it, would have an equal right to independent political existence, absurd though it be, with the English! The whole thing is absurdity. The principle of nationalities, indeed, could be invented in Eastern Europe alone, where the tide of Asiatic invasion, for a thousand years, recurred again and again, and left on the shore those heaps of intermingled ruins of nations which even now the ethnologist can scarcely disentangle, and where the Turk, the Finnic Magyar, the Rouman, the Jew, and about a dozen Slavonic tribes live intermixed in interminable confusion' (Engels, 1866; also reprinted in the Appendix to N. Rjasanoff, 1916). For continuing evidence of the struggle of small Slavic groups against such views see Glaskow, 1971.

61. 'The upper classes of the more backward peoples adopted the culture and language of the higher civilization, thus changing their nationality . . . Poland, where Lithuanian, White Russian, and Ukrainian nobles changed over to Polish nationality, provides here a no less striking example than Hungary where Slovak, Rumanian and other nobles merged into the Magyar nobility' (Kolarz, 1946: 13). In a sense, the upper classes underwent re-ethnization. As a result of favorable social and economic changes they were incorporated into a new and broader unity. Nationalism performed a similar function for the masses, with an accompanying stress not only on broader unity but on authenticity as well. The second-time-around de-ethnization and re-ethnization of estranged intellectuals, returning them to the fold, undoubtedly contributed additional intensity to nationalism in Southern and Eastern Europe.

62. ' . . . The peoples without history were peoples without town life . . . The towns without their habitat did not bear the imprint of their national language and customs . . . The cultural centers of the inarticulate peoples were necessarily located outside their proper sphere' (Kolarz, 1946: 44). This last

comment pertains to the fact that when the first nationalist élites of the submerged Central, Eastern, and Southern European nationalities began to organize, they were forbidden to engage in the educational, cultural, and political activities which they considered essential for the purposes of mass mobilization. As a result, many of the most outstanding among them were forced to leave (or flee) to foreign centers of intellectual activity, many of which (e.g. Vienna, Budapest, Odessa, Constantinople, Lvov, and even Paris, London, and Geneva) long had very sizable colonies of expatriate intellectuals who created, studied, and intrigued *there* while maintaining clandestine contacts with their homelands. The experience of prolonged foreign residence and intergroup contact undoubtedly contributed to the 'theoretical ethnicity' evolved by many exiled or self-exiled intellectual spokesmen for the peoples without history.

63. Herder contended that 'the empire of the Ottomans and the Grand Mogul are corrupt states which comprise a multitude of nations; while the States of China, of the Brahmins, and of the Jews are wholesome states which, even if they perish, leave the nation intact, because it has been able to withstand intermixture with other nations' (Kedourie, 1961: 59). The Jewish tradition, of course, accepts the distinction-between-peoples as God-given-without-invidiousness, in that each nation has its own mission: 'When the Most High divided to the nations their inheritance, when he separated the sons of Adam, he set the bounds of the people' (Deuteronomy 32:8).

64. The intensity of anti-French and anti-foreign feelings in Germany and Italy was so great (particularly as a result of the long frustrated political unification of both of these nations whose historicity was acknowledged even in the West) that in both of them the nation-state philosophy was clearly dominant by the eighteenth century, if not earlier, even though their contacts with Western intellectual circles were infinitely greater than those obtaining for Hungary, Poland, or Greece. Thus, German philosophers and literati ridiculed the rationality of French and British social and political thought and declared it to be a mechanistic outcome of the ethnic and cultural mongrelization of their underlying populations. However, when a unified Germany finally appeared, it was not at all the nation-state that had been prophesied and so long ideologized. It not only included many non-Germans (Alsatians, Lorrainers, Danes, Poles, etc.), but it failed to include all of the Germans (particularly those that remained under Habsburg rule). A large proportion of the population it coveted in order to become a true nation-state was scattered throughout predominantly Slavic and increasingly nationalistic 'peoples without a history' to the east of them. The resulting tensions between German reality and German theory produced well-known catastrophic consequences for Germany and her neighbors.

The Italian case is also an interesting hybrid, but in this instance the outcome was in accord with Central European thought, whereas the view propounded was in accord with Mazzini's basic dedication to Western notions of popular sovereignty. However, the 'mission of Rome' was such an entrenched element in Italian thought and the plebian fractionization of Italian daily life so shocking a reality to Italian intellectuals, that the conflict between the nation-state and the state-nation remained as constant themes in post-unification Italy, even as they had been before. Thus, the libertarian Mazzini could exclaim that since the world had twice before been united by

Rome, Imperial and Papal, '. . . why should not a new Rome, the Rome of the Italian people . . . arise to create a third and still vaster unity?' (cited by Namier, 1952: 30) while the authoritarian Massimo d'Azeglio could proclaim 'We have made Italy; now we must make Italians' (cited in Sturzo, 1927: 13). For further analyses of German and Italian nationalism as hybrid expressions of state-nation and nation-state cross-pressures see Pflanze, 1966.

65. The Habsburg Empire itself presents many particularly interesting similarities relative to some of the current 'new nations' in that, on the one hand, it was still very far from fostering a state-nationality and, on the other hand, its ruling classes normally resisted any efforts to fractionate it into a number of nationality-states. Akzin comments that in the latter decades of the Empire nation-state views were quite predictably held 'by writers belonging to non-dominant nationalities who sought the dissolution of the Empire, whereas many of those belonging to dominant nationalities (German-Austrian, Hungarian) tended to value the state mainly because of its role as an instrument in service of the[ir particular] nation' (Akzin, 1964: 17 and 44), thus leaving no very articulate body of opinion to function on behalf of the state as a whole, i.e., as a supranational object of patriotism or nationism.

66. The extent to which American scholars have largely had the nation-state context in mind when criticizing nationalism is evident from comments by Pillsbury ('The nation is cause, the state effect,' 1919: 773) and Gellner ('It is not the aspirations of nations which create nationalism; it is nationalism which creates nations,' 1964: 174). Kohn rejects this '. . . "closed" nationalism [which] stresses the nation's autochthonous character, the common origins (race, blood), the rootedness in the ancestral soil' as being 'romantic, anti-Western and anti-Enlightenment . . . Their ideal society was to be found in the tribal or premodern past, in emphasis on *Eigenart* or *samobytnost*' (Kohn 1968: 66). Among the scholars who have been most aware of the social and historical contextualization of both processes, one must mention Lemberg 1964 and Symmons-Symonolewicz 1965, 1968 and 1971, neither of whom has attained the recognition he deserves. Like Passerin d'Entrèves they stress that 'in those parts where amalgamation of state and nation had long been achieved, patriotism could find expression in the proud assertion of the liberty won and sanctioned by means of free institutions which were held out for the admiration of the world . . . But where nations were still broken up into a multiplicity of political units, patriotism could not but take the shape primarily of a demand for unity and independence' (1967: 179). Generally speaking, the transition from one process into the other is little recognized.

67. There have been few major treatments of pan-movements as a general phenomenon in the years since World War II. Among the more helpful brief reviews, the ones by Kazemzadeh (1968), Kohn (1962, see chapter on 'The Global Awakening of Peoples') and Snyder (1964, see chapter on 'Nationalism and Supranationalism') should be mentioned because of their bibliographic usefulness particularly with respect to Pan-Slavism and Pan-Germanism in Europe and Pan-Turkism and Pan-Arabism in parts of the Moslem world. Pan-Africanism in particular still lacks sufficient integrative empirical investigation but will probably receive more attention if the notion itself obtains broader social and political support. (See Decraene, 1961; Mazrui, 1963; Legum, 1965; Geiss, 1967; Hazelwood, 1967; Markakis, 1967; Langley, 1969; Walshe, 1970; and Waters, 1970.)

68. 'Pre-Soviet Pan-Slavism had two distinct stages: the non-political, cultural, democratic one, in which Czech and Slovak intellectuals played the dominant part; and the conservative nationalist, political one, led by an unusual combination of [largely Russian] intellectuals, bureaucrats and the military' (Kazemzadeh, 1968: 367). Recent French and Portuguese efforts to declare their colonial possessions as being essentially extensions of their respective 'metropolitan' cultures are other recent examples of state-nation pan-movements.

69. ' . . . [Initially] pan-Slavism stimulated scholarly interest in Slavic antiquity, spurred linguistic and archeological studies, encouraged the collection of folklore, and gave the Czechs, Slovaks, Serbs, Croats and Bulgars a sense of worth and importance through membership in a vast and glorious community' (Kazemzadeh, 1968: 367). Jan Kollar, the Slovak nationalist poet, wrote that ' . . . if the various branches of the Slav race were of metal, he would make a unique statue of them. From Russia the head, from Poland the breast, from Bohemia the arms and from Serbia the legs. Before such a colossus Europe would kneel down' (Jaszi, 1929: 256). In an earlier period, very similarly, 'The Catalans tended to look upon their Aragonese and Valencian neighbors as closely akin to themselves. The Valencians talked a variety of the same language, and both Aragon and Valencia had been their associates in the great medieval federation and formed part of the Crown of Aragon to which Catalonia belonged' (Elliot, 1963: 43).

70. Vivid personal experiences of broader ethnocultural unity are described by many writers in recollections of their childhood. Thus, Chaudhuri recounts how nationalist agitation came to his attention in 1905, when he was still a child, after Lord Curzon had proposed the administrative partitioning of Bengal, as follows: ' . . . my father asked us to bathe in the river first and then in a state of cleanness tie the thread round our wrists as a token of the brotherhood of all Bengalis. We were to observe that day as a day of national mourning and fasting.' This recollection is immediately joined to one which stresses authenticity. 'We also put away all our clothes manufactured in England and put on dhotis made in the Indian mills' (Chaudhuri, 1951: 219).

71. 'Most significantly, however, appeals are made to the unity and identity of the indigenous populations, particularly with respect to external social units resident in the country' (Friedland, 1968: 19).

72. Speaking primarily of interwar East and West Africa, one investigator comments: 'There was a resuscitation in some countries of traditional clothing and where (as in Tanganyika) genuine traditional clothing was inappropriate a neotraditional costume was invented or borrowed' (Friedland, 1968: 21).

73. With respect to the period of the late 1860's in Bengal, Roy (1962: 243) reports: 'Many again not only learnt to speak Hindi but vaunted *Nagrai* shoes (of the kind used only recently by the village people in U[pper] P[radesh] and Bihar) and *Sikha* (a tuft of hair at the back of the head)'.

74. One aspect of growing nationalist sympathies in late nineteenth century Burma ' . . . was a protest against the use of footwear in the precincts of pagodas and monasteries; this protest gained such general support that Europeans had to comply with it' (Furnivall, 1956: 143).

75. 'The unique superiority of the Aryan culture lay in the fact that it had developed entirely independent of any other existing civilization and unaided by the precepts or examples of any earlier or contemporary culture' (McCully,

1940: 249, paraphrasing an anonymous article in *Bengal Magazine*, 1875–76, 4, pp. 367–68).

76. 'Is it not now a well established fact that at all events we were among the first civilized nations and that our forefathers were poets and philosophers when those from whom are descended the great nations of Europe had hardly risen above the hunting or nomad state, or had even acquired a distinctive national name?' (McCully, 1940: 248, paraphrasing an unsigned article in the *National Magazine*, 1875–76, 1, p. 338).

77. ' . . . While every other ancient nation which had created a great civilization — the Egyptians, Chaldeans, the ancient Greeks, the Romans — had disappeared, we, the Hindus had survived; this could only mean that we were a chosen people who were destined, or rather ordained, to have a future more glorious than even their past' (Chaudhuri, 1951: 221).

78. 'The 20th century has added another revolutionary dimension to nationalism. Nationalism has also become a socially revolutionary movement, demanding equal economic and educational opportunities for all . . . and the active promotion of the welfare of the socially underprivileged . . . By the middle of the 20th century all "young" nationalist movements had also become socialist movements' (Kohn, 1968: 64).

79. ' . . . a new vigorous industrial pattern, a new social and industrial consciousness, and a new way of organizing and doing things . . . have created a new climate . . . have annihilated many tribal, linguistic, ethnic barriers and divisions . . . [and are] largely responsible for the unification of African tribes' (Sithole, 1959: 74). Also see Eastman, 1971.

80. 'Typically, the introduction of Western techniques of medicine cuts the death-rate and population begins to increase rapidly. This creates difficulties which a traditional system of agriculture cannot deal with, and men are therefore driven away from their villages into cities, mines and plantations which grow up in the wake of Western economic enterprise . . . Their situation is transformed in a way difficult for Europeans to understand, for in Europe this transformation has been spread over several centuries' (Minogue, 1967: 84).

81. 'Some natives are recruited into a local police force; others are trained as clerks in local government or industry, and, therefore, become literate . . . A few lucky or pertinacious young men [ultimately] set out for universities of the imperial country . . . Often it may happen that for several generations the European educated are content to operate within a European framework. But the time always comes when this educated élite makes a bid for power and when it does so it commonly uses the rhetoric of nationalism' (Minogue, 1967: 85–85). Kautsky notes that colonialism 'produces the [native] intellectuals and yet, by its very existence, it frustrates them and hence arouses their opposition' (1962: 49). The Angolan case is particularly instructive in this connection (Wheeler, 1969) because of the role of the *assimilados*.

82. 'When the transition to independence is also accompanied by extensive efforts at economic revolution, various intermediate social structures that shared or captured loyalties in the pre-industrial system are undermined. Nationalism . . . is offered as a source of identity to subsititute for the tribe or village . . . *Nationalist ideology provides a rationale for the mulititude of changes in way of life*' (Moore, 1965: 34).

83. After the failure of the Boxer Rebellion the classical Chinese tradition came

to be viewed by young radicals 'as something in which one might rummage for things of current value; it had never been anything like that in previous times.' Even the name of the country was changed, in order to foster a new and greater unity, from ' . . . *T'ien hsia*, a cultural realm [below heaven] in which everything of value was cultivated by the mandarin class . . . to *Chung-Kuo*, the all-inclusive [middle Kingdom] state, the nation' (Minogue, 1967: 90–91). Conversely, the Japanese victory over Russia (1905) had a strongly positive impact on élites throughout Asia in their efforts to arrive at more modern but yet indigenous self-concepts. Tagore's evaluation of the Japanese victory was that it 'broke the spell under which we [Asians] lay in torpor for ages' (1920: 50). Another Indian observer commented 'What? an Eastern Nation facing a Western Nation on a field of battle? What? The white people were not then resistless? They had been met and overthrown by a coloured race, by men like themselves? A thrill of hope ran through Asia. Asia invaded, Asia troubled by white "spheres of influence," with settlements of white people, insolent and dominant, rebelling against Eastern laws, rejecting Eastern customs with contempt, humiliating coloured nations in their own lands, and arrogating powers to which they had no right. Despair changed into hope. Asia awoke, and with Asia, India' (Besant, 1926: 159–60).

Blond's reconstructed account of the Japanese reaction to the Russian fleet's request to negotiate conveys the deep emotion of the moment as well as the deep emotion that such tales are intended to elicit at every successive recitation: ' . . . an international code signal was run up [the mainmast of the *Nicholas I*]: XGH. The signals officer of the watch immediately translated: We ask to negotiate.

'Togo made no move. He seemed to turn to stone. The officers surrounding him were equally motionless, equally silent. They looked at the Russian ships, still under heavy Japanese fire. But more than one mouth was opened in amazement or to utter an exclamation at what came next.

'The other Russian ships, acting almost together, were striking their colors. And when the Russian flags had disappeared below their bridges, another flag was run up on every ship: the Rising Sun, national emblem of Japan. The Russians had struck their colors and run up their enemy's flag to make it quite clear that they were surrendering. It was a heartbreaking spectacle. Even on Togo's bridge there were officers whose hearts were thumping uncomfortably, officers with lumps in their throats and tears in their eyes. "Admiral, they are surrendering," said his chief of staff in a voice that was unsteady, almost shrill. "Does not the spirit of Bushido require us to cease fire?"

'Togo took one more look at the signal flying from the mast of the *Nicholas I* and at the Japanese flags on the other ships. "Cease fire," he said.

'And he ordered all the ships to form a wide circle around the enemy. This scene was played out on May 28, 1905, at a quarter to eleven in the morning, in waters situated approximately eighteen miles southwest of Liancourt rocks' (Blond, 1960: 221-33).

Even the Japanese victories over the Allies at the beginning of World War II were regarded as providing a valuable lesson for indigenous populations by nationalists seeking to unify and activate them (see Singhal, 1967: 278).

84. The interdependence of nationalism and religion is even more evident throughout Asia than it was in Europe. Not only were religious leaders and

functionaries at the very forefront of most nationalist movements (see Furnivall, 1956: 142–44 and 201 in connection with Burma; McCully, 1940: 260–67 and infra in connection with India; Heyd 1950, infra, in connection with Turkey; Nuseibeh, 1956, infra, in connection with Arab nationalism in general and Egypt in particular), but the very notion of nationalism other than in an ethno-religious context was commonly rejected as a Western aberration that was either abhorrent or impossible under local conditions. Zurayq, the great Egyptian-Arab nationalist of the nineteenth century, proclaimed that '. . . true nationalism can in no sense be incompatible with true religion, because in its essence it is naught but a spiritual movement, which aims at the regeneration of the inner forces of a nation and the realization of its mental and spiritual potentialities. Nationalism, being a spiritual movement, must go hand in hand with religion and derive from it strength and life . . . True religion . . . emanates with nationalism from the same spring' (Nuseibeh, 1956: 92). The very conception of India as the 'motherland,' symbolized by the figures of the goddesses Durga, Vani, and Lakshimi, represented an effort to develop a religious basis for nationalism, or the assumption that the religious sentiment of the Hindus was far easier to arouse than any national feeling. Tagore, e.g., held that India was 'a plant which would never thrive but in the soul watered by the hand of Faith — a nationality of religious union' (McCully, 1940: 267, paraphrasing an article published by Tagore in 1895). Finally, Muhammad Iqbal, one of the principal forerunners of the drive for an independent Pakistan, 'explicitly repudiated the Western concept of the nation as . . . territorially defined . . ., holding the latter incompatible with both Islam in general and the special position of Islam in India' (Emerson, 1902: 107).

All in all India must be viewed as a mixed case, making for less explicit use of religion in pursuit of national sociocultural integration than do the nations of Islam or Theravada Buddhism. Thus Jinna fully supported Iqbal's view (see above) noting (in 1940) that 'the British people, being Christians, sometimes forget the religious wars of their own history and today consider religion as a private and personal matter between man and God. This can never be the case in Hinduism and Islam, for both of these religions are definite social codes which govern not so much man's relations with his God, as man's relations with his neighbor. They govern not only his law and culture but every aspect of his social life' (cited by Bolitho, 1954: 126–27).

Along similar lines Smith points out that 'Islamic history is calculated to begin not the year Muhammad was born . . ., nor when he began to receive divine revelations, but when the Muslim community came to power in a state of its own. The year 1 A.H. marks the establishment of Islam as a religio-political sovereignty in al-Madinah' (1954: 22–23). Cady makes a related point with respect to Buddism in Burma. 'The most important positive basis on which popular allegiance to the King was acknowledged by the leading ethnic peoples of Burma (the Burmans, Mons, Shans and Arakanese) was that royalty functioned as the promoter and defender of the Buddhist faith . . . a function which was regarded by Burmans as the very *raison d'être* of the State' (1958: 8). Mehden cites numerous details concerning the usefulness of religion in the Burmese and Indonesian nationalist movements (1968) as does Hajime (1967) with respect to Japan and Kumar (1969) with respect to India.

From the foregoing it seems clear that religion and nationalism have not only served each other in Asia (as they had in Europe), but that they are commonly presented as one and the same to the masses as a means of pursuing and maintaining the political independence and stability of multi-ethnic states whose boundaries have been, in part, inherited from colonial days and, in part, from precolonial multi-ethnic empires. Certainly, one cannot speak about nationalism in Asia as an ideological replacement either for localistic tradition as a whole or for religion more specifically, it is being so widely felt that ' . . . reformation, in order to be true and abiding, must mean not only the introduction of new civilization, but a revival of the old culture as well. It must not be a mere introduction of Western customs, but also a resuscitation into new life of the lingering vitality still to be found [in the larger ethnoreligious community]' (McCully, 1940: 254; paraphrasing an article by Keshub Chundra Sen published in 1871).

85. For similar claims in other parts of Africa as well, see Friedland & Rosenberg (1964) *African Socialism*. Also note Myrdal's reference to India's 'rich mythology about the ancient village as a perfect democracy with a rational cooperative organization of production and community life, where caste observance was less rigid and degrading, and women enjoyed a higher status' (1968: 77). For more recent integrative summaries re the indigenous and roots of economic modernization ideologies see Jumba-Masagazi (1970), Gregor (1967), Hanna & Gardner (1969), and Auma-Osolo & Osolo-Nasubo (1971).

86. Although Herder, Mazzini, and even the great Slavic nationalists influenced them, African and Asian nationalists were obviously more taken with Western European liberal nationalism (with its emphasis on the state as the provider of unity of institutions, universal civil rights, and universal social services) than by Eastern European ethnic cultural nationalism (with its emphasis on the mononationality state as a protector of monocultural authenticity). They, however, did provide additional rationale for the rejection of 'foreign influences.' (For many interesting details and formulations, see Mazrui's 'Some Sociopolitical Functions of English Literature in Africa' (1968: 183-98).) Kolarz remarked about the Germans, Russians, Poles, Italians, and Magyars (*vis-à-vis* the new nationalities) that they 'always play . . . the roles of both Jekyll and Hyde. They are both oppressors and liberators, bringers of darkness and bearers of light' (1946: 50). The same observation holds true *vis-à-vis* the West as a whole and much Asian or African nationalism.

87. 'With the coming of mines, towns and cities, the different tribes of Africa found themselves thrown together. Tribesmen who had never had anything to do with one another found themselves living together in one area, working side by side with one another . . . With the coming together of these tribes the horizons of many Africans have been greatly extended' (Sithole, 1959: 68–69).

88. 'This general pattern — of an African town separate from and economically and politically subordinate to a European town, the two towns being closely linked in regard to their economies and administrative systems but un-believably remote in respect to their human relationships — has an obvious bearing on the genesis of African nationalism' (Hodgkin, 1956: 73). For extensive treatments of the economic nexus of modern African and Asian nationalisms see Wildenman & Parkalla, 1966 and Johnson, 1968.

89. 'The exuberant growth of associations in African towns is a point which has often been noticed. There are three ways in which these Tribal Associations contribute to the development of African nationalism. They provide a network

of communications entirely under African control . . ., they tend to foster or keep alive an interest in tribal songs and dances, history, language and moral belief . . ., they play an active part in [financing] the education of an African elite' (Hodgkin, 1956: 87).

90. 'The membership [of TANU, the nationalist party, in post-World War II Tanganyika] was vast but concentrated in the towns and in rural centers of population where, most often, the influence of the modern economy was felt most strongly. Among nomadic tribes TANU influence was much less significant' (Friedland, 1968: 16).

91. ' . . . in one essential respect at least mid-twentieth century Dakar and Lagos differ from mid-nineteenth century Leeds and Manchester: the cause of their existence, the basis of their economic life, is not factory industry but commerce' (Hodgkin, 1956:64).

92. 'Nothing was more natural for us than to feel about Muslims in the way we did. Even before we could read we had been told that the Muslims had once ruled and oppressed us; that they had spread their religion in India with the Koran in one hand and the sword in the other; that the Muslim rulers had abducted our women, destroyed our temples, polluted our sacred places' (Chaudhuri, 1951: 226).

93. 'Characteristically, the nationalist leaders stress the moral, religious, or spiritual superiority of their culture to the materialism, utilitarianism and technocracy of the West . . . They hail the distinctive contributions of native music, literature, art and poetry, and warn against the 'mental colonialism' that has separated the intellectuals from their cultural heritage and subjected them to the alien values of the dominant European civilization' (Sigmund, 1963: 32).

94. For examples of several such reluctant acceptances of Westernization due to the urgency of modernization, see Rustow 1957, Kumar 1969, and Nandy 1970. Elsbree reviews the attempts of the Japanese occupation force to exploit anti-Western sentiments on behalf of its Greater Asia Co-Prosperity Sphere, the subsequent switch to gratifying local nationalist aspirations (such as encouragement of publication and broadcasting in Bahasa Indonesia throughout the occupied Dutch East Indies), and, finally, the ' . . . awakening . . . to the fact that nationalism was a stronger and more demanding force than they had imagined and demanded greater concessions than they had anticipated' (1953: 165). Japanese experience in attempting to direct submerged nationalisms against an enemy external to the supranational state (in order to deflect them from being directed against the supranational state itself which kept them submerged) was as unsuccessful as that of the Habsburg Empire mentioned above (see footnote 65).

95. The few nationality-states among post-World War II additions to the family nations are (clearly) Somalia, Korea, (less clearly) Burma, Vietnam, Cambodia, Laos, (and least clearly) Malaysia, Israel, and the Moslem state of the Maghreb and the Near East. The Moslem states mentioned have such substantial pan-Arab ties that their ethnic individuality at the national level is still in the process of formation. Israel is faced by the problem of fusing two large streams of immigrants, those from Western and those from non-Western countries of origin. Malaysia, Burma, and new states carved out of former French Indochina all contain substantial numbers of Chinese and other minority peoples.

96. Curtin (1966) sees the dominant force in recent African politics as the desire to build nations of the state-nation type. He views the first two decades of the African revolution as a clean sweep of the state-nation type. The state is to create the nationality, not the reverse. As noted earlier, this is also Kautsky's view (1962). See Mushkat 1971, Rotberg 1962 and 1966 for the opposing view that African nationalism is essentially nonethnic in origin and in purpose.

97. This may be what Silvert means when he concludes that 'nationalism in contemporary underdeveloped areas develops in manners organically different from the classical British and American patterns' (1963: 442). My own view is that it is not so much in its early stirrings that the most striking differences are found between the two as in their respective relationships to subsequent state formation. The British and American states both started with ethnically rather homogenous groups (i.e. they were originally nation-states) and have evolved into state-nations as they expanded to include successive other-ethnic populations under slowly modified symbols and institutions. This is *not* the case with respect to most of the states to which Silvert refers.

98. 'In the latter half of the 19th century and after, Macedonian, Great Bulgarian and Pan-Slav sentiments and political movements, coexisted in South-Eastern Europe (Hodgkin, 1956: 21). 'Pan-Turkism was born in the last quarter of the nineteenth century among the Tartars of the Crimea and the Volga . . . [as] a reaction against the encroachment of . . . Russian nationalism . . . Although theoretically [Ismail Bey Gasprinski, its formulator] . . . envisaged the union of all Muslim peoples, his activity was directed at Russia's Turkic masses . . . [and] Pan-Slavism [was his] . . . intellectual model' (Kazemzadeh, 1968: 369). Also see Zarevand, 1971 (Armenian original 1926; French translation 1930).

99. 'During the period of Arab nationalist opposition, first to Turkish and later to British and French rule, one could find layers of Druse, Lebanese, Greater Syrian and Pan-Arab nationalism imposed one above the other' (Hodgkin, 1956: 21–22). The modern Indian case is a better example than Pan-Arabism of a relatively successful pan-movement since, except for the fringe areas which became Pakistan, Burma, and Ceylon, the efforts of Gandhi and the Indian Union Party to convince millions that 'the past of India, with all its cultural variety and greatness, was a common heritage of all the Indian people, Hindu, Moslem, Christian and others, and their ancestors had helped to build it' (Nehru, 1953: 6–7) have thus far succeeded tolerably well, at least at the political-operational level. That this outcome was based, in part, upon the reality as well as upon the ideal of Hindu sociocultural integration is evident from such observation as 'Ambala in Upper India was over 1100 miles from Calcutta . . . But nothing struck the Bengali as strange and made him feel that he was in a new country. Instead he saw the same plains, the same people working in the fields, the same well-irrigation, the same village congeries, the same naked peasantry, and the same women with veiled heads and armlets to the elbows. Such uniformity proved that India was designed by nature to form a grand national unity' (McCully, 1940: 245; paraphrasing an article of Bholonath Chandra published in 1881). That broader and narrower loyalties cannot only coexist but be repeatedly accommodated to each other at successively higher levels of integration is a point neatly stressed by Mazrui 1969a, Ranger 1968b, and Ronen 1968; Skinner's paper (1959), and the entire symposium which it introduces, is particularly informative in this connection.

100. 'Dr. Sukarno, in his days of power, promoted a state called Maphilindo . . ., a pan-Malay creation . . . [with] a certain cultural and political plausibility which might give it a future' (Minogue, 1967: 13–14). Note, however, that Dr. Sukarno's dream of uniting *Ma*laysia, the *Phil*ippines, and *Indo*nesia (=Maphilindo) was itself merely an extension of the earlier Indonesian nationalist reference to the 'medieval empire of Majapahit, which from a Javanese capital had claimed control over a large part of the Indies and of the Malay peninsula. That many of these claims lacked solid historical evidence to support them does not detract from the importance of Majapahit to modern Indonesian nationalism, and not least in the years after independence'(Kennedy, 1968: 82–83).

101. 'The failing fortunes of Muslim states, and their inability to withstand the pressure of European imperialism, gave rise to the pan-Islamic movement that called for the union of Muslim peoples and states against Western aggression and domination . . . It . . . preached a supranational doctrine at the same moment that Western nationalism was beginning to stir up the peoples of the Middle East . . . Jamal al Din [its founder and principal ideologist, 1838-1897] failed to sense the growth of nationalism among the Persians, the Turks and the Arabs' (Kazemzadeh, 1968: 369). For a confirming interpretation of pan-Islamism as an early stage (rather than as a subsequent further elaboration) of Arab nationalism, see Keddie (1969).

102. 'Whenever we try to talk in terms of larger units on the African continent, we are told that it can't be done. We are told that the units we would so create would be 'artificial.' As if they could be any more artificial than the 'national' units on which we are now building' (Nyerere, 1961, reprinted in Sigmund, 1963: 209). Subsequently Nyerere makes even clearer his conviction that no essential ethnic differences divide Negro Africa: 'I believe that . . . the role of African nationalism is different — or should be different — from the nationalism of the past; that the African national state is an instrument for the unification of Africa and not for dividing Africa; that African nationalism is meaningless, is dangerous, is anachronistic, if it is not at the same time pan-Africanism' (p. 211). Senghor's philosophy of 'Negritude' is similarly supraethnic and supralocal in design, extolling as it does 'the whole complex of civilized values — cultural, economic, social and political — which characterize the black peoples, or, more precisely, the Negro-African world . . . The sense of communion, the gift of myth-making, the gift of rhythm, such are the essential elements of Negritude which you will find indelibly stamped on all the works and activities of the black man' (*West Africa*, Nov. 4, 1961; reprinted in Sigmund, 1963: 249). See also Irele (1969).

SECTION 2:
Language maintenance and language shift in ethnocultural perspective

The pursuit of continuity, conceived of as authenticity, is a natural component of ethnicity (and a conscious responsibility of nationalism), and reveals itself in connection with any and all of the rounds of daily life, including language and all of the cultural expressions that are dependent upon language. Cross-cultural contact, therefore, is often viewed as a potential source of unmanageable, or at least undesirable, culture change and of language shift, given that power differentials are to be expected between ethnic groups in interaction. In actuality, culture change is as natural, as ongoing and as common as the quest for cultural continuity, the latter often being no more than the *post-hoc* legitimization of the former. The two constantly interpenetrate and serve to contextualize each other. However, the reaction to them from an intra-ethnic perspective is understandably different.

Language maintenance, the process and pursuit of inter-generational linguistic continuity, is a reflection of sufficient indigenous control over and delimitation of ongoing inter-group interaction processes so that they do not overpower the indigenous ethnocultural system. This system remains essentially intact if the outside influences acting upon it are few, distant or inherently weak, or, if otherwise, provided they can be channelled so as to impact only certain pursuits, restricted sub-populations, specific regions, etc. The indigenous system's ability to channel outside influences establishes the ethnocultural equivalent of political boundaries, import restrictions and media regulation at the polity level. Ethnic channelling of outside influences functions via the normal mechanism of imposing cultural sanctions, i.e. dispensing cultural rewards and cultural punishments. Accordingly, ethnocultural systems whose indigenous rewards and punishments are weak in comparison with those of the external groups with which they interact, cannot control the influences that stream in upon them and, therefore, they undergo more wide-ranging and more rapid cultural change than do ethnocultural systems whose rewards and punishments are still relatively strong. Inter-ethnic relations may deteriorate and ethnicity may become more conscious as the internal debate concerning the long and short-term implications of culture change and language shift intensifies. Those who too readily decide to swim in the sea of greater material opportunity may be accused of disloyalty; those who reject any and all opportunities related to other-ethnic inspired social change may be viewed as backward, biased and self-ghettoizing.

The concern for ethnocultural (including ethnolinguistic) continuity need not be an all-or-none affair and it need not be limited to minorities. Languages that originally enter from the 'outside' need not sweep the field and displace their predecessors in each and every pursuit. The indigenous ethnocultural system of rewards and punishments may be more successful at home than in the factory, in church than in the school, in the residential neighborhood than in the marketplace, precisely because some pursuits are more quickly or more fully inter-group interactive or influenced than others. A *modus vivendi* may come into being such that partial language shift occurs, that is: the indigenous language is displaced in some pursuits but not in others, and a new pattern (a holding pattern) of inter-generational continuity is then stabilized. If such a complementary allocation of languages to functions remains intact for generations (three generations as a minimum), both languages may come to be looked upon as indigenous, i.e. as ethnically legitimized and harmonious, each in its own 'place'. Such an arrangement, of controlled, widespread and stable intra-group bilingualism, is much rarer and more difficult to attain than meets the eye and needs to be thoroughly analyzed. The initial compromise and the evaluation of future opportunities to alter the compromise (whether in favor of the original vernacular or in favor of the objectively more recent intruder) can become additional consciousness-raising junctures that both draw upon and contribute to ethnic ideology and ethnic practice.

All ethnocultural pursuits are not equally suitable safeguards insofar as language maintenance is concerned. If a home-and-neighborhood vernacular is to be assured inter-generational stability, then the indigenous system of rewards and punishments must protect the home-and-neighborhood from dislocations that emanate from cross-ethnic marriages, from inter-ethnic residential patterns, from inter-ethnic print and non-print media particularly likely to influence the young, etc. If a school or church language is to be assured inter-generational continuity then these institutions, the bulwarks of the written and formal spoken language in most modern societies, must be sufficiently societally protected, societally rewarded and societally rewarding to withstand outside influences on an inter-generational basis. Reversing or containing language shift involves reversing or containing culture change, a difficult feat, given the inevitable disparities in power between one ethnoculture and another and, particularly, given that language use is dependent upon and reflective of so many large scale cultural processes, demographic, residential, economic, religious, etc., outside of those that are of immediate interest to, or under the immediate influence of, ethnocultural authorities. Few things are more evocative of intra-ethnic debate and ethnic consciousness than interpreting the prospects and planning the possibilities of reversing language change.

On their own turf, even small but intact ethnocultural systems can successfully withstand and control or channel much larger and stronger ones in most pursuits, even though an outside language may come to be well understood and even widely admired or mastered. Thus, in The Netherlands, Dutch is not threatened by English, except for the most advanced econo-technical pursuits, even though children early learn enough English to follow and to mimic the endless deluge of radio and television programs (as well as cinema and pop-songs) from Great Britain or the U.S.A. However, Dutch cultural authorities and models are still substantially in control of most ethnocultural core-processes (home, neighborhood, church, elementary school and lower-to-middle work-sphere), and the rewards and punishments related to these systems are still sufficiently strong, so that parents and siblings, neighbors, co-parishioners and pastors, co-students and teachers, and co-workers and employers generally speak Dutch to the young and to each other, even though they could easily do so in English as well. The same is not as true for the reward system pertaining to Frisian (*vis à vis* Dutch), an indigenous minority regional language in The Netherlands, and it is generally even less true for immigrant languages in The Netherlands insofar as controlling and rewarding the ethnolinguistic boundaries upon which the inter-generational continuity of their vernaculars is concerned. The latter have very little cultural space that is fully under their own control and their internal debate as to whether and how to cope with their ethnocultural dislocation is usually much more highlighted than it is among Netherlanders in general.

The language and ethnicity web is often experienced as a seamless and completely interdependent one. When the two-in-one come apart, it is quite common for one component to outlive the other. In many instances, the language is lost but the sense of ethnic continuity remains. The Irish are a good example of this, as are the Jews (if we consider their post-exilic Jewish vernaculars, e.g. Yiddish, Judesmo, Yahudic, Mugrabi, Chuadit, etc., and even vernacular Hebrew, insofar as Israelis who have resettled abroad are concerned). On the other hand, the opposite phenomenon also obtains. Englishmen who have resettled in the U.S.A. maintain their language but become 'Americans', many native Tagalog speakers in the Philippines maintain their language but become Filipinos, many native Serbian speakers in Yugoslavia now consider themselves 'Yugoslavs', etc. However, the empirical truth, that the knot *can* be untied, does not change the phenomenological truth that the link is indissoluble, nor the objective truth that even the continuous component in the new compound is not really identical with what it was in the old compound. The phenomenology of continuity and change has its own life, a different life than that which external theories and evaluations can fathom, a life very much like that of other belief and faith systems. The phenomenological reality is just as real as that of externally confirmable reality and it is the former that leads to language restoration and revival efforts, long after the outside observer would swear that none of the original sparks were still glowing. Ethnic theory motivates a return to more authentic ethnicity, foretells it and rewards it, holding out hope and providing direction to the outnumbered and submerged, and doing so far longer than meets the outside eye or seems reasonable to the outside mind. Similarly supra-rational, if not more so, are the often groundless fears of majorities that constantly see 'separationists' and 'seditionists' under their beds and in their closets, without appreciating the contribution to pluralism that is dependent upon them, and upon them more than upon 'others'.

5 Bilingualism and biculturism as individual and as societal phenomena*

Bilingualism and diglossia

The relationship between *individual* bilingualism and *societal* diglossia is far from being a necessary or causal one, i.e. either phenomenon can occur with or without the other (Fishman, 1967). As such it is but one more example of the possibility of weak relationships between various *individual* behaviors and their corresponding *societal* counterparts. Wealthy individuals can be found in both rich and poor societies. Traditional individuals are recognizable within both modern and traditional societies. Diglossia differs from bilingualism in that it represents *an enduring societal arrangement*, extending at least beyond a three-generation period, such that two 'languages' each have their secure, phenomenologically legitimate and widely implemented functions. This chapter raises for consideration the corresponding problem of arrangements at the individual and societal levels in conjunction with the phenomenon of biculturism, particularly as these pertain to ethnic identity.

Kinds of diglossia: Linguistic relationships

Following usage that has become widely accepted ever since Ferguson's seminal article of 1959, H will be used to designate the *superposed* variety in a diglossic society, i.e. the variety that is learned *later*

*Originally published in *Journal of Multilingual and Multicultural Development*, 1980, vol.1, 3–15.

in socialization (and, therefore, is *no one's mother tongue*) under the *influence of one or another formal institution outside of the home* (and, therefore, is *differentially accessible* to the extent that entry to formal institutions of language/literacy learning [typically: school, church, government] is available). However, departing from Ferguson's initial formulations and restrictions, several different kinds of linguistic relationships between Hs and Ls (the latter being the universally available and spoken [mother]tongues and varieties of everyday life) may be recognized:

(a) *H as classical, L as vernacular, the two being genetically related*, e.g. classical and vernacular Arabic (Kaye, 1970; Zughoul, 1980), Kntharevusa and Demotiki (Toynbee, 1981, Warburton, 1980), Latin and French among francophone clergy and francophone scholars in earlier centuries, classical and vernacular Tamil, Sinhalese, Sanskrit and Hindi, classical Mandarin and modern Pekingese, etc. The Hebrew-modern Hebrew case is only marginally of this kind (Even-Zohar, 1970) because modern Hebrew has only had less than a century in which to function as a vernacular.

(b) *H as classical, L as vernacular, the two* not *being genetically related*, e.g. Loshn-koydesh (textual Hebrew/Aramaic) and Yiddish (Fishman, 1976) (or any one of the several dozen other non-Semitic Jewish Ls, as long as the latter operate primarily in vernacular functions rather than in traditional literacy-related ones (Weinreich, 1980).

(c) *H as written/formal-spoken and L as vernacular, the two being genetically unrelated to each other*, e.g. Spanish and Guarani in Paraguay (Rubin, 1968), English (or French) and various vernaculars in post-colonial areas throughout the world (Fishman, Cooper & Conrad, 1977; Parasher, 1980, etc.).

(d) *H as written/formal-spoken and L as vernacular, the two being genetically related to each other*. Here only significantly discrepant written/formal-spoken and informal-spoken varieties will be admitted (rather than any and all written-spoken variety distinctions), i.e. discrepancies such that without schooling the written/formal-spoken cannot even be understood (otherwise every dialect/standard situation in the world would qualify within this rubric), e.g. High German and Swiss German, standard spoken Pekingese (Putonghua) and Cantonese, Standard English and Caribbean Creole, Occitan and French (Gardy & Lafont, 1981), etc.

There are, of course, various more complex cases within each of the above major clusters. Thus there are several instances of dual Hs in conjunction with a single L, one H commonly being utilized for ethnically encumbered or traditional H pursuits and the other for ethnically unencumbered or modern pursuits. For example, in conjunction with type (a), above, we find various stable Arabic speech communities that have both Classical Arabic and English or French as H and a vernacular Arabic as L. The Old Order Amish also reveal a complex form of type (a) involving High (Luther Bible) German and English as H and Pennsylvanian German as L. On the other hand, Hasidim in America reveal a complex form of type (b) involving Loshn-koydesh and English as H and Yiddish as L (and in Israel: Loshn-koydesh and Ivrit as H and Yiddish as L [Fishman, 1982, also this volume, Chapter 19; Poll, 1980]). Many developing nations hope to establish a type (c) pattern involving both a Western Language of Wider Communication and one or more favored standardized vernacular(s) as Hs and the same (or even more) local vernaculars as Ls. Thus, in the Philippines, we find a national policy fostering English and Pilipino/Filipino as Hs and, e.g. Tagalog as L. Note, however, that in all these 'more complex' cases a long-standing indigenous variety/language is available at the H and the L level, even if modern H functions are also shared with a language (or languages) more recently imported or imposed from without.

Stability via compartmentalization of the societal allocation of functions

The above rapid review of a dozen or more instances of relatively stable and widespread societal bilingualism (i.e. diglossia) was intended to discount the view that only in connection with classicals can such stability be maintained. Classicals are a good example of diglossia situation, of course, but sociologically speaking, what they are an example of is not classicism *per se* (nor even of traditional religion, with which classicals are usually linked) but of a stress on *social compartmentalization*, i.e. on the maintenance of strict boundaries between the societal functions associated with H and L respectively (Fishman, 1972). Sanctity/secularity, ascribed social stratification such as in caste distinctions/achieved social status, indigenousness/foreignness, traditionalism/modernism, these and others are all *possible* bases of rather rigid and stable compartmentalization in societal arrangements and, therefore, in the allocation of languages (or language varieties) to such arrangements.

There is much in modern life that militates against such compartmentalization. Among the hallmarks of modernization, as expounded by the great sociologists of the past two centuries, is the increase in open networks, in fluid role relationships, in superficial 'public familiarity' between strangers or semistrangers, in nonstatus-stressing interactions (even where status differences remain), and, above all, in the rationalization of the work sphere (the sphere that has, presumably, become the dominant arena of human affairs). All of these factors — and the constantly increasing urbanization, massification and mobility of which they are a part — tend to diminish compartmentalization, whether in the language repertoire or in the social behavior repertoire surrounding language *per se*. However, they do not make it impossible, as the many instances of stable diglossia in the modern world reveal.

The presence or absence of social compartmentalization in language-use in bilingual settings leads to very different *societal* arrangements with respect to bilingualism, which, after all, is an *individual* behavioral manifestation. Similarly, the presence or absence of social compartmentalization in ethnocultural behavior in bicultural settings leads to very different *societal* arrangements with respect to biculturism, which, after all, is also an *individual* behavioral manifestation. Thus, ultimately, if we are concerned with the various possible relationships between bilingualism and biculturism, we must be concerned with the co-occurrence patterns differentiating between *societally* compartmentalized and uncompartmentalized biculturism. However, relatively little has been written, so far, about the possible relationships between societal ethnocultural compartmentalization and individual biculturism; certainly little in comparison to the literature on the possible relationships between societal diglossia and individual bilingualism. Let us, therefore, first re-examine the latter literature and then apply its concepts and contexts to the former topic.

TABLE 5.1 *The relationships between bilingualism and diglossia*

Bilingualism	Diglossia	
	+	−
+	1. Both Diglossia and Bilingualism	2. Bilingualism without Diglossia
−	3. Diglossia without Bilingualism	4. Neither Diglossia nor Bilingualism

Types of diglossia-bilingualism relationships

Both diglossia and bilingualism are continuous variables, matters of degree rather than all-or-none phenomena, even when compartmentalization obtains. Nevertheless, for purposes of initial conceptual clarity, it is simpler to treat them both as if they were dichotomous variables. Treated in this fashion there are four possible combinations between individual bilingualism and societal diglossia as Table 5.1 indicates, and we will proceed to consider them one at a time.

Bilingualism and diglossia (cell 1)

The occurrence of bilingualism and diglossia has already been discussed, above. Let us, therefore, merely summarize our observations in this connection at this time. This is a *societal arrangement* in which individual bilingualism is not only widespread but institutionally buttressed. (Obviously we are using *bi/di* as generics and intend that our comments with respect to them also apply to more complex cases as well, i.e. to cases of tri/ter, quadri/tetra, etc.) 'Membership' in the culture requires that the various languages that are recognized as pertaining to such membership be implemented in culturally 'correct' contexts, i.e. that the H (or Hs) be utilized in (the normatively appropriate) H contexts and the L (or Ls) be utilized in (the normatively appropriate) L contexts. The separate locations in which L and H are acquired immediately provide them with separate institutional supports. L is acquired at home, as a mother tongue, and continues to be employed there throughout life while its use is extended also to other familial and familiar (intimate, affect-dominated, emotion and spontaneity-related) interactions. H, on the other hand, is never learned at home and is never utilized to signal such interactions. H is related to and supported by other-than-home institutions: education, religion, government, higher/specialized work sphere, etc. The authority and the reward systems associated with these separate institutions are sufficient for both L and H to be required at least referentially (if not — due to possible access restrictions in the case of H — overtly) for membership in the culture, and the compartmentalization between them is sufficient for this arrangement not to suffer from excessive 'leakage' and from the resulting potential for language spread and shift.

The above picture is, of course, at least somewhat idealized. Diglossic societies are marked not only by compartmentalization conventions but by varying degrees of *access restriction*. Similarly, in addition, Hness (whether in lexical, phonological or grammatical respects) does creep into L interactions (particularly among the more educated strata of society), viz., the case of 'Middle Arabic' and 'Learned Yiddish', and, contrariwise, Lness does creep into H interactions (particularly where access restrictions are minimal; note, for example, the completely Yiddish phonology of Ashkenazi Loshn-koydesh). Nevertheless, the perceived ethnocultural *legitimacy* of two languages as 'our own' (i.e. neither of them being considered foreign, even though one or the other might, in point of historical reality, be such), and the *normative functional complementarity* of both languages, each in accord with its own institutionally congruent behaviors and values, remains relatively undisturbed.

Diglossia without bilingualism (cell 3)

Since diglossia applies to societal arrangements, *political* arrangements may certainly be included under this rubric. Given this fact, we must recognize political or governmental diglossia whereby two or more differently monolingual entities are brought together under one political roof. Not only were various empires of old characterized by diglossia without bilingualism (except for small commercial, military and civil service élites) but various modern states may be so classified: Switzerland, Belgium, Canada, and, at least in terms of early Leninist idealism, the U.S.S.R. This is diglossia in accord with the territoriality principle (McRae, 1975). It requires that we set aside our earlier *intra*societal notion of widespread bilingualism and extend it to the political recognition and institutional protection thereof on an *inter*societal-politywide basis. There is full freedom of press in Switzerland, but, nevertheless, one cannot publish a German newspaper in Geneva or an Italian one in Bern, regardless of whether this might be desirable in terms of short-term population movements. Similarly, King Ahasuerus of old, who 'reigned from India even unto Ethiopia . . . sent letters into all the King's provinces, into every province according to the writing thereof, and to every people after their language' (Esther 1: 1 and 22). Thus, we note that in this great multilingual empire of old, there was not only territorial diglossia at the governmental level (as between the various written languages for governmental use) but also societal diglossia between the (one) written and the (several) spoken languages of each province.

Wherever an absent nobility controls a peasantry from afar by means of a small military, governmental and commercial presence which mediates between the absent masters and the local indigenous populations, diglossia without bilingualism is in effect. Most forms of colonialism throughout the world (whether under capitalist or communist auspices) are, therefore, also instances of political/territorial diglossia without widespread demographic-indigenous bilingualism. When substantial numbers of colonizers have settled in the erstwhile colonies and access to H is not restricted in so far as indigenous populations are concerned, a transformation may ultimately take place to that of diglossia *with* bilingualism (i.e. cell 1, above).

Bilingualism without diglossia (cell 2)

Both diglossia *with* bilingualism and diglossia *without* bilingualism are relatively stable, long-term arrangements. However, since these are highly interpretable and judgemental dimensions (*how* stable does a sociopolitical arrangement have to be before we consider it long term?), let us once more agree to use a three-generational rule of thumb in connection with them. There are obviously innumerable bilingual situations around the world that do not last up to or beyond three generations. These are characterized not only by language spread but also by language shift. In some instances indigenous languages are swamped out by intrusive ones (B → A = B) as in the case of many native American, aboriginal Australian and not a few non-Russian Soviet populations as well (Silver, 1974; Kriendler, 1982). In other instances, immigrant languages have disappeared as their speakers have adopted the languages of their hosts (B → A = A), doing so particularly given the long-term absence of newly arriving monolingual mother-tongue speakers from the homeland. What both of these otherwise quite different contexts reveal in common is an absence of social compartmentalization such that the languages of hearth and home (of indigenous peoples, on the one hand, and of immigrants, on the other) can protect themselves from the greater reward and sanction system associated with the language of new institutions to which they are exposed and in which they are involved (see Fishman 1980 for further discussion of differences between these two subtypes of bilingualism without diglossia).

As a result of the lack of successful compartmentalization, both A and B compete for realization in the same domains, situations and role-relations. Since, with the exception of fleeting metaphorical usage (humor, sarcasm, etc.), linguistic functional redundancy cannot be maintained intergenerationally and gives way to the stronger functional system, the language with stronger rewards and sanctions associated with it wins out. In the American and Soviet contexts, three generations or less have generally been sufficient for this process to run its course where sufficiently small, impacted and dislocated groups have been involved. A relatively few larger groups, groups strong enough to maintain or to fashion a reward system under their own control (whether in the home, the community, the church, or elsewhere), may succeed in establishing and maintaining the compartmentalization needed for diglossia or to do so at least at the areal level, even in the absence of newly arriving monolingual recruits. However, none of these can really opt for a completely territorial solution (implementing compartmentalization via secession or isolation). Without compartmentalization of one kind or another — at times attained by ideological/philosophical and even by a degree of physical withdrawal from establishment society — the flow process from language spread to language shift is an inexorable one. Although it may, at times, require more than three generations for its inroads to be clearly discerned, the functionally unbalanced nature of the bilingualism that obtains (both in terms of *who* becomes bilingual and who remains monolingual, to begin with, and the power-differentials/reward- and sanction-differentials of the remaining monolingual A and monolingual B domains) always leads displacively and replacively only in one direction.

Neither bilingualism nor diglossia (cell 4)

The outcome of uninterrupted (i.e. uncompartmentalized) bilingualism-without-diglossia is neither bilingualism nor diglossia. Some settings, however, are characterizable in this latter fashion without ever having gone through the former stage. Korea, Yemen, Cuba, Portugal and Norway have all experienced relatively little immigration within the past three generations and have few if any indigenous minorities. However, many settings that *have* initially had numerous immigrants or linguistic minorities or both have translinguified (or exterminated) them to a very large degree. New Zealand, in so far as its indigenous Maoris are concerned, and Ireland, in so far as Irish speakers are concerned, are examples of the 'successful' implementation of policies of this kind, as are several indigenous and immigrant groups in the U.S.S.R., U.S.A., Spanish America, the Arab Moslem world, Israel and others.

Strictly speaking, of course, no socially complex speech community is fully homogeneous linguistically. Different social experiences (in work, education, religion) lead to different socially patterned varieties of talking (and even of writing) and different regional dialects may maintain themselves in a stable fashion even after former communications and interactional barriers are gone. Nevertheless, if we hold to a definition of bilingualism as involving consensually separate 'languages', there are of course numerous speech networks, speech communities and even polities that may be characterized in this fashion. Normal foreign language instruction and tourism clearly lead neither to stable bilingualism nor to diglossia.

What is the ethnocultural counterpart to diglossia?

We are now ready to broaden our discussion from a treatment of sociolinguistic parameters alone (bilingualism and diglossia) to one involving ethnocultural dimensions as well. In the latter connection, however, we are faced with the lack of a terminological and conceptual distinction such as exists between bilingualism and diglossia. If we employ biculturism to designate the *individual* pattern in the ethnocultural realm, paralleling our usage of bilingualism in the sociolinguistic realm, what can we use to designate the *societal* pattern in the ethnocultural realm, paralleling our usage of diglossia in the sociolinguistic realm? Most investigators use 'bicultural' in both instances (i.e. for both individual and societal phenomena) with considerable confusion and circumlocution as a result. Saville-Troike (1978) has suggested the term *dinomia* (two sets of norms, i.e. two cultures) for societially widespread biculturism. This is certainly a worthwhile suggestion, but, in a sense, it is a bit too broad for our purposes. Culture is a much broader designation than ethnicity, particularly in connection with modern complex societies. It deals with norms pertaining to all of human behavior, belief, and valuation. Ethnicity is a narrower concept, particularly in modern times. It focuses on 'peopleness relatedness', that is: on those cultural behaviors, values and beliefs that are related to 'peopleness authenticity', i.e. to membership in a particular people and its defining tradition (Fishman, 1977a; also this volume, Chapter 1). At earlier stages of social development, all of culture is ethnically defined and defining. How one dresses, what one eats, the kind of work one does, how one's house or furniture is built — these are distinctively peopleness-related behaviors. At later stages of social development, many of the above behaviors (and many values and beliefs as well) have become ethnically neutralized because of their widespread ('international') currency. Even though cultures continue to coincide with broad ethnic designations, ethnicity recedes into a smaller corner, indeed, at times, into a residual corner of culture, so that only a much smaller set of behaviors, values and beliefs are considered (by 'insiders' or by 'outsiders', be they scholars or not) as ethnicity-related, implying, defining, because they are viewed as 'authentic' and associated with discontinuity across ethnic boundaries and/or self-definitions. Language behavior (particularly mother-tongue use) is very frequently considered to be ethnicity-related, implying, defining.

If what is of concern to us is the co-occurrence between bilingualism/diglossia and the enactments of single versus multiple norms and identities in the realm of ethnocultural behavior, beliefs and values, then we may find it useful to utilize bicultural for the *individual* manifestations in this realm, but what are we to use for the societal counterpart thereto? It is in this connection that I would like tentatively to suggest the term *di-ethnia*. Like bilingualism, biculturism is an individual asset or debit that corresponds to no particular societal institutions or concerns. Without such it is not intergenerationally maintained. However, like diglossia, di-ethnia is a sociocultural pattern that is maintained by means of specific institutional arrangements. The arrangements, as we will see, require (as they do in the case of diglossia) repertoire compartmentalization. However, ethnic compartmentalization and linguistic compartmentalization are only weakly related to each other in any causal sense. Thus, not only can we find bilingualism with and without diglossia (cells 1 and 2), as well as diglossia with and without bilingualism (cells 1 and 3), *all without di-ethnia*, but we can also find

(a) multiculturism with and without di-ethnia, as well as
(b) di-ethnia with and without either bilingualism or diglossia.

As we will note, multiculturism and di-ethnia do not form a fourfold table (a counterbalanced 2 x 2 table) as do bilingualism and diglossia. The reason for this is that di-ethnia is a rarer phenomenon than diglossia and a far, far rarer one than biculturism as well.

Biculturism and di-ethnia in various bilingualism-diglossia contexts

When bilingualism and diglossia obtain (cell 1 above) di-ethnia may yet be absent. Thus, Paraguayans do not view Spanish and Guarani as pertaining to two different ethnocultural memberships. The two languages are in complementary distribution, of course, in so far as their macro-societal functions are concerned, but they are both accepted as indicative of the same ethnocultural membership: Paraguayan. Both languages are required for full membership in the Paraguayan people and for the implementation of complete Paraguayanness. The same is true with respect to Geez and Amharic among Ethiopian Copts. Only one people-ness is involved, albeit different functions are fulfilled by each language and the two together constitute the whole, as they do for speakers of a vernacular Arabic who read/write Koranic Classical (and/or classical) Arabic. Certainly, neither di-ethnia (societal biculturism) nor individual biculturism are involved in cases such as these.

When diglossia is absent but bilingualism is present (cell 2), multi-culturism may well be present but di-ethnia not. This is the context of transitional bilingualism and transitional biculturism on the one hand, and of ordinary cross-cultural contacts on the other hand. Neither passes the three generation test and the bilingualism they prompt is either ultimately lost, integrated or transitioned into translinguification, just as the biculturism they prompt is ultimately either lost, integrated or transitioned into transethnification. Note, however, that language shift and ethnocultural shift need not proceed apace; indeed, language shift for American immigrants has commonly proceeded more rapidly than has their re-ethnification (Fishman *et al.*, 1966, 1980). Nevertheless, ethnicity maintenance (particularly at any long-term creative level or in any central domain) requires strong institutional support, as does language maintenance, rendering the other ethnicity inoperative (consensually unacceptable) in certain functions — or even rejecting the functions *per se* — if two ethnocultural systems are to operate side by side on a stable and widespread basis. Two sets of ethnic behaviors and identities must be in complementary distribution and strongly compartmentalized, as must be their language usage counterparts, if they are to constitute something more than transitional arrangements. It is just such complementarity and compartmentalization that this cell (cell 2) lacks, and, as a result, acculturation (and, in cell 4, assimilation) finally result.

Cell 3 also is inhospitable to di-ethnia. Since the diglossia encountered there is that based upon the territoriality principle it is, once again, only a small class of middlemen (civil servants, commercial representatives, professional translators) who have any need for being bilingual, and even most of them have no need for either biculturism or di-ethnia. At any rate, they hardly constitute a complete society or ethnocultural aggregate unto themselves.

819282192888

Stable societal biculturism: Some U.S.A. examples

We have made the rounds of our 2 × 2 table and have not encountered di-ethnia in any of its four cells. Actually, stable, societal biculturism *does* exist in *part* of cell 1, but the purpose of our initial 'go-round' has been attained if it has clarified the *rarity* of the phenomenon we are pursuing. *Most of modern life is inhospitable — whether ideologically or pragmatically — to compartmentalization between a people's total repertoire of behaviours and values.* Fluidity across role and network boundaries and, indeed, the weakening and overcoming of boundaries, is both a goal and result of most modern behavior and its emphasis on efficiency and reciprocity/solidarity in social behavior. Little wonder then that our examples of di-ethnia will derive primarily from nonmodern contexts.

The Old Order Amish and the Hasidim represent two patterns of di-ethnia on American shores. Both groups maintain a pattern of bilingualism and diglossia (cell 1) for their own *internal* needs involving Luther German and Pennsylvania Dutch on the one hand, and Loshn-koydesh and Yiddish, on the other hand. In addition, both groups control their own schools wherein their children are taught to become proficient in English (speaking, reading, writing) so that they *can* engage in 'the other culture' within carefully prescribed limits of kind and degree. The 'other culture' is viewed as necessary and the 'own culture' is, therefore, in necessary complementary distribution with it. In both cases actualization of the 'other culture' is restricted to economic pursuits and relationships and even in this domain, limits are carefully observed. Electricity may be used for pasteurization (the latter being required by state law) among the Pennsylvania Dutch, but not for refrigeration of their own food or to power modern farm machinery (Hostetler, 1968, 1974). The 'outside world' must be engaged to some unavoidable degree — and for such purposes the outside language must be learned — but this degree must be a limited one and, ultimately, even it is rationalized as necessary for the maintenance and well being of the 'inside world'.

It is probably not accidental that the rural Old Order Amish and the urban Hasidim both accept another culture only in the econotechnical domain, this being the most universalized and, therefore, the least ethnically encumbered domain of modern society. Nevertheless, the primary point of generalizable interest in connection with them is not so much the specific area in which their stable societal biculturism is expressed as the fact that it is stabilized by:

(a) *not* integrating the two cultures involved but by *keeping them separate*, in a state of tension *vis-à-vis* each other, i.e. compartmentalization is recognized as necessary so that the outside world will not intrude upon (*spread* into: Cooper, 1982; displace/replace: Fishman, 1977b) the 'inner world': and

(b) not accepting or implementing 'the other culture' in its entirety but, rather, implementing it selectively and in a particular domain so as to keep it in complementary distribution with their 'own' H-governed and L-governed domains. English is specifically excluded from home use (where it would threaten their own L mother tongues) and from religious use (where it would threaten their own sacred Hs). Thus, just as no speech community can maintain two languages on a stable basis (past three generations) if they are both used in the same social functions and, therefore, stable societal bilingualism (diglossia) depends on institutionally protected functional sociolinguistic compartmentalization, so no ethnocultural collectivity can maintain two cultures on a stable basis past three generations if they are both implemented in the same social functions (family, friendship, work, education, religion, etc.), and therefore, stable societal multiculturism (di-ethnia) depends on institutionally protected ethnocultural compartmentalization.

Does di-ethnia exist elsewhere as well?

Di-ethnia is a relatively rare phenomenon — much rarer than its individual counterpart, biculturism. It is found beyond the three-generation cut-off in the Moslem world where traditional behaviors, dress, diet and values dominate most of life but where modern econotechnical roles require different dress, diet and languages and do so not only for *inter*-group interactions but for *intra*-group interactions within this arena as well. Similar compartmentalization is encountered beyond the three-generation cut-off among various segments of Japanese, Chinese (Hong Kong, Singapore), Native American and non-Russophone Soviet society. Di-ethnia of a more marginal or peripheral kind is sometimes also found among stable populations living at long-established political borders and sharing market days and other limited collective experiences (e.g. sports contests). Finally, and even more exceptionally, di-ethnia is still encountered at times even after language shift has eroded bilingualism and diglossia to the vanishing point. Thus, even with the transethnification of Blacks and aborigines, a deep-seated and often conflicted di-ethnia at times reveals itself.

The bicultural 'thrust' of bilingual/bicultural education

The term 'bicultural' is often introduced quite innocently in connection with Title VII bilingual education in the U.S.A. Neither the
institutional stability nor the functional compartmentalization of this
phenomenon, if it is to be pursued seriously and societally, is recognized.
Indeed, unknowingly, the arrangements entered into usually foster
biculturism in the most dislocative sense, i.e., they are transitional and
transethnifying. They are commonly condescending, trivializing and
peripheralizing in connection with the marked culture ('thingification' I
have called it elsewhere) and Anglo-Americanizing even when they least
suspect. The basic compartmentalization of societal functions and the vital
institutional protection of *marked* sociolinguistic and ethnocultural behaviors, beliefs and values upon which stable societal biculturism (di-
ethnia) crucially depends are not only unrecognized but would probably
be anathema if they were recognized. In distinction to the destructive Title
VII empty-headedness in this connection is the conscious and conscientious societal multiculturism often pursued by ethnic-community-
sponsored 'parochial' schools in the U.S.A. Unfortunately, while the
former (Title VII) programs are numerous and tragically destructive, the
latter (ethnic-community 'parochial') programs are too few and, tragically,
too weak to attain their goals. America is the poorer in each case, but for
quite opposite reasons.

Conclusions

Just as diglossia is the stable, societal counterpart to individual
bilingualism, so di-ethnia is the stable, societal counterpart to individual
biculturism. Di-ethnia requires societal compartmentalization as well as
institutionally protected functional specificity. These desiderata are hard
to attain and to retain — both ideologically and structurally — under
'modern', interactive, mobile and individualistic urban industrial conditions. However, some groups have, intuitively or consciously, displayed
a capacity and an inclination for exactly such arrangements. Minorities
that do not control econotechnical and political boundaries of their own
are particularly dependent on ethnocultural and ethnolinguistic
boundary-maintenance arrangements in order to secure their intergenerational continuity within a larger context of ongoing change.

On critiquing diglossia: A postscript

The bedrock on which the di-ethnia construct rests is the diglossia construct. The former is an extension into the realm of ethnocultural identity of the basic sociolinguistic notions of the latter. Accordingly, it would be well to attend to the occasional criticisms of the diglossia construct in order to determine their implications for a program of empirical research and theoretical elaborations of the total diglossia-di-ethnia nexus.

Ideological interference

It is always important to attempt to differentiate between ideological and intellectual criticism, however much the two are, of necessity, intertwined. I take as ideological criticism the rather uninformed but symptomatic view that diglossia patterns *necessarily* coincide with high rates of illiteracy in H. The Swiss German/High German case is sufficient to disprove that assertion, as well as to call into question the allied but somewhat more sophisticated assertion that diglossia obtains only under rather primitive, highly traditional and rigidly stratified sociocultural conditions. Modern Western cultures too, not to mention modernizing Third World settings such as those encountered in many parts of the Moslem world and the Hindu world, have maintained quite classical diglossia arrangements in parts of their sociolinguistic repertoires while modernizing and de-compartmentalizing other areas of national life. On the other hand, most high illiteracy areas in the world today are not diglossia-impacted at all (certainly not in the sense of consensually 'separate' languages or huge discrepancies between the spoken and written varieties of the 'same' language). Thus, while it is true that traditional society is more compatible with diglossia (just as it is more compatible with boundary 'status quos' of all kinds), it is *not* true that diglossia arrangements are not possible under (or are in any way causally related to) political, econotechnical or ideological/religious/philosophical arrangements of whatever kind. Indeed, it is part of the intrigue that the modernization/continuity dialectic presents to all serious investigators who approach it without prior overriding polemic intentions (see, e.g. Streng, 1979), that 'easy solutions,' such as those that appeal to those whose reformist socioeconomic passions leave them no patience for tradition at all, are often simply not viable from their more experienced, accepting and concerned internal perspective. The twentieth century has proved without a doubt that Jacobinian solutions are *not* universally attractive, nor are they universally effective even where they are considered attractive. The price that society may need to pay for diglossia arrangements (a price such as well-defined territoriality principles or intimacy/local vs. formality/supra-local distinction conventions) may be worth every penny, relative to the price of 'simplified' equalization solutions that would destroy such arrangements but bring with them a host of attendant problems tantamount to cultural disruption as well.

The accompanying criticisms that accuse diglossia arrangements (or diglossia-focused scholars) of being unsympathetic to the economic mobility aspirations of 'the masses of urban poor,' or to economic factors in social change and in social control, are simply further evidence of a regrettable tendency to confuse one's own political-ideological rejection of a particular sociocultural convention with the responsibility for objective and parsimonious description of that convention. Economic factors and socioeconomic 'advancement' may or may not be the crucial factors at any particular time or in any particular sociocultural context in which the language and ethnicity nexus is being investigated (Reitz, 1980). To assign unquestioned priority to such factors is a type of vulgarization that social scientists should eschew, every bit as much as they eschew vulgarization of their pet political principles. It is even stranger, however, to find economic determinists opposing diglossia, as if its abandonment *per se* could be an effective means of altering class-related economic facts, processes and potentials. That would certainly seem to be a case of replacing economic determinism with linguistic determinism (hardly an improvement). It is the breathless penchant for simplistic determinism as a whole, and for ideological determinism in particular, that mars the academic judgement in such instances. However, there may and need be no prior agreement on the *desirability* of diglossia *in any* particular instance in order for researchers to proceed with the intellectual task at hand. To my mind, indeed, there is no good reason always to *favor* diglossia or to consider it to be a wise or desirable social arrangement for the solution of each and every ethnocultural problem, any more than there is any good reason to oppose it always. Nevertheless, there must be a common quest to determine when and to what extent it does obtain, how it came into being, what its consequences are relative to a particular focus of interest, which factors tend to strengthen or weaken it, etc. Such a quest can be pursued only if the ideological passions can be sublimated, at least temporarily, and the intellectual permitted to roam relatively undisturbed. Even the difficulties that remain will be substantial.

Intellectual issues

The intellectual critique of diglossia is, of course, the more important of the two lines of criticism occasionally encountered. Unfortunately, whereas the ideological criticism has simply disregarded the scientific issues, the intellectual has simply not gone far enough with them. It has gotten bogged down in elementary methodological issues which pertain to social science research in general or to sociolinguistic research more pervasively and whose extensive literature the critics are blithely unaware of. As a result, it does not bring the field any closer to more powerful research on diglossia *per se* nor even to a more knowledgeable view of methodological issues in general. One criticism often addressed to the diglossia construct is that it is too removed from the data of everyday speech and behavior. But why should one restrict sociolinguistic and ethnocultural research and theory to that particular level of data and data analysis? The tendency to reductionism, to accept as real only that which is elementary, palpable, directly sensed and quotable, is certainly an unaccepted scientific limitation in all but the most provincial backwaters of the social science enterprise today. Certainly society and culture are 'real' at levels higher than those that ethnography alone can reveal (which is merely to question the 'exclusive truth' of ethnography, rather than its truth value for problems at its own level of analysis and conceptualization). Certainly this is the hoary issue of levels of analysis, that some are only now discovering due to their own provinciality, being sublimely unaware of its several-centuries-old intellectual past. Methodological monism will get us nowhere with respect to epistemological or substantive issues in the future, just as it has gotten us nowhere in the past. There are various levels of analyses, various types of data, various approaches to proof and they must each be appreciated for their contributions (for, indeed, they have all made contributions), as they must each be criticized for their limitations and blind spots (for they all have them) and, above all, they must be used together, in tandem, to reinforce and clarify each other, for the sake of the common enterprise.

To have to argue such points now is to take time out to 'rediscover the wheel' when the real issue is to use all kinds and sizes of wheels more effectively and more interactively. All the wheels are real. All the social sciences and social science methods correspond to a fruitful vision of reality. That *should* not be at issue in this day and age, although, unfortunately, it is.

Constructs are, of course, still constructs and they must not be reified and confused with 'things'. But the scientific enterprise is, at its most advanced, precisely a quest for more parsimonious and more powerfully explanation- and prediction-linked constructs. All levels of analysis wind up with constructs which are derived from intellectual operations (interpretation, categorization, comparison, judgement as to likeness or unlikeness) performed upon data. Diglossia (as well as some of its subsidiary constituents such as 'domains' which have been well critiqued in Breitborde, 1983) is just such a construct and is in no way different in this respect from constructs such as 'language X,' society, culture, social class, ethnic group, etc. None of these constructs is self-evident, self-explanatory, nor given in direct experience. The construct 'culture' does not itself explain *when* a particular culture came into being, *why* it changed and *why* it ultimately may have merged or been destroyed. These all remain to be researched, and, in any particular instance, documented at various levels of analysis, long after the utility of the construct 'culture' is no longer in doubt (although its detailed formulation may well continue to undergo revision and improvement, as nearly all constructs do, forever and a day). However, the law of parsimony also applies to all of these latter efforts at documentation, clarification, specification and explanation, both of particular cases relative to certain constructs as well as of constructs *per se*. It is not enough to have a laundry list of variables ('economic, social, historical, linguistic, demographic, institutional, etc.') and to present the empirical relationships obtaining between them, however exactly and exhaustively. The quest for generalizable findings, for theory that bridges or distinguishes, systematically and parsimoniously, between cases and cases, that recognizes recurring types of outcomes, leads again and again to the formulation of more underlying notions, factors or constructs, as well as to statements of probabilities of if-then relationships (whether quantitatively formulated or not) between them. The process is a fairly endless one, but ultimately no serious social science effort can or should avoid constructs or a parsimonious factorial approach to their elucidation in terms of empirical variables as well as in terms of yet other constructs.

What then remains to be done in the realm of diglossia research and theory? Less fear of social boundaries *per se* would help, as various European social scientists have fully recognized (e.g. Strassoldo, 1982; Luhmann, 1971, Raffestin, 1980 and Schwartz, 1979). Less ideological sniping at 'irrelevant pluralism' would clear the field of partisan polemics. However, more data on a variety of cases illustrating diglossia in various degrees, more intermethodological/interdisciplinary/intertheoretical research, more concern for various 'types' of diglossia, more attention to degrees of diglossia in various 'types' of social and cultural change/continuity contexts, more theory building on empirical bases and with a striving toward parsimony: these are truly crucial. They are the true scholarly agenda. 'Diglossia,' i.e. the basic construct *per se*, is too deeply and fruitfully imbedded in the basic sociolinguistic notion of 'societal allocation of function' (e.g. Charpentier, 1982; Martinet, 1982; Tabouret-Keller, 1982), i.e. in the very implementation of language varieties on consensually recognized and different occasions, to be either disregarded or neglected at one's own peril. In addition to its socio-sociolinguistic centrality, it has also been a fruitful focus for those concerned with more linguistic-sociolinguistic issues (Wexler, 1971). It requires, as does the rest of the sociolinguistic enterprise, a dispassionate passion for inquiry, well-formulated and well-informed, above and beyond ideological and political sympathy or antipathy.

References

BREITBORDE, L. B. 1983, Levels of Analysis in Sociolinguistic Explanation. *International Journal of the Sociology of Language*, 39 (entire issue).

CHARPENTIER, J. M. 1982, Quand et où parler de bilinguisme et de diglossie? *La Linguistique* 18, 65–84.

COOPER, R. L. 1982, Toward a general theory of language spread. In R.L. COOPER (ed.), *Language Spread: Studies in Diffusion and Social Change*. Arlington (VA): Center for Applied Linguistics (provisional titles).

EVEN-ZOHAR, I. 1970, L'birur mahuta v'tatfkida shel leshon hasifrut hayata badiglosiya [Toward clarifying the scope and function of the language of literature under diglossia]. *Hasifrut* 2, 286–302. English abstract: 443–46.

FISHMAN, J. A. 1963, Bilingualism with and without diglossia; diglossia with and without bilingualism, *Journal of Social Issues*, 23(2), 29–38.

— 1972, *The Sociology of Language: An Interdisciplinary Social Science Approach to the Study of Language in Society*. Rowley: Newbury House.

— 1976, Yiddish and Loshn-koydesh in traditional Ashkenaz: The problem of societal allocation of macro-functions. In A. VERDOODT & R. KJOLSETH (eds), *Language in Sociology*. Louvain: Peeters, 39–42.

— 1977a, Language, ethnicity and racism, *Georgetown University Roundtable on Languages and Linguistics*, 297–309. Also, this Volume, part 1.

— 1977b, The spread of English as a new perspective for the study of language maintenance and language shift. In J. A. FISHMAN, R. L. COOPER, A. W. CONRAD *et al.* (eds), *The Spread of English*. Rowley: Newbury House, 108–36.

— 1980, Language maintenance and ethnicity, *Harvard Encyclopedia of American Ethnic Groups*. Cambridge: Harvard University Press, 629–38.

— 1982, Attracting a following to high culture functions for a language of everyday life. In R. L. COOPER (ed.), *Language Spread: Studies in Diffusion and Social Change*. Bloomington (IN) and Arlington (VA): Indiana University Press and Center for Applied Linguistics, 291–320. Also *This Volume*, part V.

FISHMAN, J. A. *et al.* 1966, *Language Loyalty in the United States*. The Hague: Mouton. (Reprinted New York, Arno Press, 1978.)

FISHMAN, J. A., R. L. COOPER, A. W. CONRAD, *et al.* 1977, *The Spread of English*. Rowley: Newbury House, 1977.

GARDY, P. & LAFONT, R. 1981, La diglossie comme conflit: L'exemple occitan. *Langages* 15(61), 75–91.

HOSTETLER, J. 1968, *Amish Society*. Baltimore: Johns Hopkins (revised edition; 3rd edition 1980).

— 1974, *Hutterite Society*. Baltimore: Johns Hopkins.

KAVE, A. S. 1976, Modern standard Arabic and the colloquials. *Lingua* 24, 374–91.

KREINDLER, I. 1982, The changing status of Russian in the Soviet Union, *International Journal of the Sociology of Language* 30, entire issue.

LUHMANN, N. 1971, *Soziologische Auflkärung I*. Opladen: Westdeutscher.

MCRAE, K. 1975, The principle of territoriality and the principle of personality in multilingual states. *International Journal of the Sociology of Language* 4, 33–54.

MARTINET, A. 1982, Bilinguisme et diglossie, *La Linguistique* 18, 5–16.

PARASHER, S. V. 1980, Mother tongue–English diglossia: A case study of educated Indian bilinguals' language use, *Anthropological Linguistics* 22, 151–62.

POLL, S. 1980, Loshn koydesh, Yiddish and Ivrit among ultra-Orthodox Jews in Israel, *International Journal of the Sociology of Language* 24.

RAFFESTIN, C. 1980, *Pour une Geographie du Pouvoir*. Paris: Librairies Techniques.

REITZ, J. G. 1980, Effects of economic position on ethnic group cohesion. In J. G. REITZ (ed.), *The Survival of Ethnic Groups*. Toronto: McGraw-Hill, Tyerson.

RUBIN, J. 1968, *National Bilingualism in Paraguay*. The Hague: Mouton.

SAVILLE-TROIKE, M. 1978, *A Guide to Culture in the Classroom*. Rosslyn: National Clearinghouse for Bilingual Education.

SCHWARTZ, T. 1979, The size and shape of a culture. In F. BARTH (ed.), *Scale and Social Organization*. Oslo, Universitetsvorlaget, 215–52.

SILVER, B. 1974, The impact of urbanization and geographical dispersion on the linguistic Russification of Soviet nationalities. *Demography* 11, 89–103.

STRASSOLDO, R. 1982. Boundaries in sociological theory: A reassessment. In R. STRASSOLDO & G. DELLI ZOTTI (eds), *Cooperation and Conflict in Border Areas*. Milan: Franco Angeli, 245–71.

STRENG, F. J. 1979, 'Sacred' and 'secular' as terms for interpreting modernization in India, *Religious Traditions* 2(1), 21–29.

TABOURET-KELLER, A. 1982, Entre bilinguisme et diglossie; du malaise des cloisonnements universitaires au malaise social, *La Linguistique* 18, 17–43.

TOYNBEE, A. 1981. The Greek languages' vicissitudes in the modern age. In A. TOYNBEE, *The Greeks and Their Heritages*. Oxford: Oxford University Press.

WARBURTON, P. 1980. Greek diglossia and some aspects of the phonology of common modern Greek. *Journal of Linguistics* 16, 45–54.

WEINREICH, M. 1980, *History of the Yiddish Language* (translated from the Yiddish original [*Geshikhte fun der yidisher shprakh*, New York, YIVO, 1973, 4 vols.] by S. NOBLE & J. A. FISHMAN). Chicago: University of Chicago Press.

WEXLER, P. 1971, Diglossia, language standardization and purism, *Lingua* 27, 330–54.

ZUGHOUL, M.R. 1980, Diglossia in Arabic: Investigating solutions, *Anthropological Linguistics* 27, 201–17.

6 Language maintenance and ethnicity*

After two decades of modern sociolinguistic inquiry *into language maintenance and language shift* in the U.S.A. and after one decade of renewed academic interest in the *transformations of ethnicity* in the U.S.A., the time is probably ripe to attempt to bring these two normally separate areas of inquiry into more focused interaction with each other. In addition, it may also be possible, due to the substantial amount of work that has recently gone into each of these topics in settings outside of the United States, to seek more general (i.e. more widely applicable) theoretical formulations with respect to these topics, and to do so without in any way decreasing local (U.S.A.) validity. Indeed, it is my goal in this paper to attempt to enhance local validity by means of increased comparative perspective.

Interactions between ethnolinguistic collectivities: A typology of resolutions

There appear to be three major and recurring resolutions to inter-action between two separate monolingual ethnolinguistic collectivities when such interactions are viewed from a perspective of more than three generations of time depth. If we take A to be indigenous and B to be intrusive in a particular setting then:

Resolution 1: $B \rightarrow A = A$
Resolution 2: $B \rightarrow A = B$
Resolution 3: $B \rightarrow A = B + A$

*Originally published in *Canadian Review of Studies in Nationalism*, 1980, 229-48.

In Resolution 1 the intrusive language is lost.[1] In Resolution 2 the indigenous language is lost. In Resolution 3 both languages are maintained. Obviously, these are three very different resolutions and the social circumstances leading to them are likely to be very different as well. Nevertheless, if possible, we must find a single conceptual framework within which to pursue our inquiry so as to make comparisons between one setting and another (or between one resolution and another) possible. Our goal in this connection is to come to some conclusion as to *when* (i.e. the circumstances under which) each resolution obtains and what the *involvement of ethnicity* might be in each of them.

Resolution 1: The intrusive language is lost

The first observation to offer in connection with Resolution 1 is that it is only one of three possible patterns, rather than the only one. Although this is the pattern that corresponds to the predominant American immigrant experience, it is not a universal, not a moral imperative, and not even the only resolution *vis-à-vis* that (or other immigrant) experience *per se*. Nevertheless, it *is* a common resolution and one which enables us to investigate several factors that have been hypothesized or confirmed with respect to language shift.

Legal requirements re A or prohibitions re B

A recurring obstacle faced by intrusive languages are '*prohibitions*' *vis-à-vis* their use in public/official/written functions or alternatively, '*requirements*' that previously established languages be so used. What is crucial in this connection is not so much *primum mobile* alone (the fact that social systems that are established *first* acquire an inertia and an establishment that continues their predominance *vis-à-vis* later arrivals on the social scene) but the role of laws (= formal and authoritative sanctions and prohibitions) in maintaining *primum mobile*. There are certainly many polities at present in which there *are* language laws that declare specific languages to be 'official', 'national' or permissible/optional for specific functions. What is, therefore, most interesting insofar as U.S.A. sociolinguistic reality is concerned, is the *paucity* of language legislation and legalistic formulations *vis-à-vis* language (Fishman, 1980). Indeed, the U.S.A. is in the company of a relatively few countries in the world that have no *de jure* national or official language (Falch, 1972; Touret, 1972).

That the foregoing is so is not for want of trying (viz. the Hayakawa Amendment, proposed in 1982, to make English the official language of federal government services). At the very beginning of the nineteenth century the patriot-lexicographer Noah Webster inquired of Chief Justice John Marshall whether there could be either a law or a constitutional amendment declaring 'The American language' to be our sole national and official language. It was the Chief Justice's opinion then — and our highest courts have consistently agreed with him ever since — that any such legal provisions on behalf of English would be counter to the freedom of speech and freedom of religion provisions of the American constitution. Accordingly, local legislation requiring English or prohibiting other languages has consistently been struck down by the courts (Heath, 1977). Out of nearly two centuries of such precedents there has developed a purely *de facto* legal posture relative to language in the U.S.A. On the one hand, no languages may be prohibited and no languages may be favored on a *de jure* basis, and, on the other hand, government services (and monies) must be available *de facto* in whatever languages are required in order to achieve equity (fairness, justice) for all segments of the population.

Given this history of language law in the U.S.A., the Lau decision (1974) and the Mendoza and Black English rulings (both in 1979) appear as quite recognizable and consistent 'affirmative action' steps that seek no more than parsimonious equity. It is not cultural pluralism nor language maintenance that they pursue but the pragmatic view that (particularly in the absence of any official or national language) government must equitably serve everyone and if a ('sufficiently' large) segment of the population cannot be so served in English, other languages must be employed. However, since *both* parsimony *and* equity are involved, many government-sponsored programs (bilingual education among them) 'legitimately' aim at fostering English. Thus, other languages are both to be used *as needed* in connection with government-sponsored, conducted or supported programs in the health, education, welfare and justice areas, but, presumably no longer than necessary, i.e. not beyond the point where any population's English is good enough for it to be equitably served in the language that can be used to serve 'everyone else.' Cultural pluralism and parsimonious equity are very far from being one and the same thing.

Our brief excursion into U.S.A. language-related law and legislation reveals more than the interesting fact that there is relatively little such law and legislation in the U.S.A. and that what there is, is neither mandatory with respect to English nor prohibitory with respect to other languages. What is suggested, in addition to the foregoing, is the relatively noncrucial nature of law and legislation in the entire language maintenance-language shift process. The historically effective U.S.A. experience with relinguification and re-ethnification of millions upon millions of immigrants has transpired in a context relatively innocent of laws requiring such relinguification or re-ethnification to take place. Thus, it must be clear that other processes, not necessarily ones explicitly formulated and formalized via laws, are the fundamental causes or influences in connection with language maintenance and language shift. Furthermore, just as language shift may be exceedingly common — when viewed across a period beyond three generations after the arrival of intrusive Bs in the territory of A — even in the absence of language laws, so language maintenance may be equally common even when there are laws to the contrary. *Leges sine moribus vanae*: laws without underlying social support processes are in vain for they cannot accomplish their goals. On the other hand, these same goals that some seek to attain via laws might be accomplished even without explicit laws on their behalf if conducive social circumstances obtained.

Other sociolegal traditions make much greater use of language laws than does the U.S.A. (Savara & Vigneault, 1975; Colloque, 1978). Post-revolutionary France immediately adopted a law 'abolishing' the regional languages (Provencal [= Occitan], Alsatian, Breton, Catalán, Basque, all of which were disparagingly referred to as 'dialects'). These languages exist to this very day — indeed there are organized movements on behalf of each of them (Tabouret-Keller, 1981) — but reliance on legal coercion seems to be part of the French sociocultural tradition. This tradition also seems to be alive and well in French Canada, where a whole spate of pro-French (and, therefore, explicitly or implicitly anti-English) laws have been passed in Quebec since the 'separatists' gained power (Mallea, 1977). There can be no doubt about it. Language laws — like all laws — doubtlessly engender and reinforce social attitudes and behaviors related to their goals and purposes. However, they are not in themselves sufficient 'causes' with respect to these attitudes and behaviors. Laws require authoritative implementation (rewards, punishments) but not even authoritarian governments can endlessly continue to implement laws that do not gain general acceptance and that are not reinforced by and congruent with basic societal processes, rewards and values. Therefore, it is to such that we now turn.

Intergroup social dependency

Even in the absence of specific laws on behalf of A, the A establishment may be sufficiently entrenched and organized as to make rewards to Bs contingent on interactions *with As and in A*. The result is that a host of social dependency relationships are developed such that material, econotechni al, professional, governmental and educatioaal rewards are available to Bs not only to the extent to which they master A but also to the extent that they interact with As. In the absence of strong and compartmentalized reward traditions to the contrary, this channelling of rewards to Bs in such a way as to foster *inter*group social dependency relationships via language A finally also impacts B *intra*group status relationships as well. Within B speech communities and speech networks *per se*, status recognition is channelled to Bs that are A speakers. Mastery of A among Bs thus no longer serves merely as an indicator of social dependency upon and interactive frequency with As, but it also becomes a *desideratum and, finally, a hallmark of leadership status within the B community itself.* At this point, language spread becomes language shift. Ultimately this transition reaches the B family unit *per se*. Bs learn A not *outside* of the family context (in school, at work, 'outside') but precisely *within* the family context, from parents, older siblings and other adult relatives whose *status within the family* is enhanced by the fact that they have mastered A (Fishman *et al.*, 1966). Finally, Bs learn A as a mother tongue from B-mother-tongue parents who have become A speakers. In the absence of a rather rigid and fargoing compartmentalization which is difficult to maintain (and, therefore, rare) in modern interactive life (Fishman, 1980), separating the home and the immediate ethnic community from A-interactions and A-language and A-related statuses, such as is available, e.g. to Amish, Hasidic or traditional Islamic families (or other communities sheltered by distance, rurality or major philosophical-religious-ideological ramparts), what begins as the language of social and economic mobility ends, within three generations or so, as the language of the crib as well, even in democratic and pluralism-permitting contexts.

The ubiquity of social dependency relationships in fostering language shift is truly amazing. In the U.S.A., in the U.S.S.R, among southern European 'guest workers' in northern Europe, among immigrants to Australia, among urbanizing Indians in North, Central and South America, among urbanizing populations in West and East Africa, among overseas Chinese and overseas Indians-from-India, the story repeats itself again and again. It is related to social mobility but it is not social mobility *per se*, since relinguification and re-ethnification also occur in nonmobile middle and even in lower social classes to the extent that they too become dependent on direct interaction with A speakers and the rewards that the latter control. Bartenders become relinguified to the same extent as clerks; salesmen to the same extent as dentists; auctioneers to the same extent as nurses and other sub-professionals; even though the social status of bartenders, salesmen and auctioneers is lower than that of clerks, dentists and subprofessionals (Lieberson & Curry, 1971). Indeed, education and social mobility are merely higher order abstractions that may mask the lower order reality involved: the decompartmentalization of sociolinguistic interaction, such that the ethnically encumbered domains (from the point of view of intrusive Bs: home, community, church) respond to the same hierarchy of rewards and statuses as do the ethnically unencumbered domains (school, work sphere, government). The dependency-based reward system pertaining to B functioning and status in the latter is finally also triumphant in connection with B functioning and status in the former. Thus, it is the weakening and, finally, the destruction, of *B-requiring-role-relationships among Bs* (in addition to the adoption of A-requiring-role-relationships between Bs and As), and the concomitant *weakening of B as a requirement sine-qua-non for B-ness* (rather than merely as a metaphorical, dispensible, negligible, quaint, humorous outdated indicator of B-ness) that is at the heart of the language shift issue. A weaker reward system crumbles not only as a result of frontal attacks from stronger systems, but also as a result of becoming dependent upon the stronger systems and, therefore, rewarding those of its own members (including those who are most highly rewarded by the stronger system directly and who can mediate between the two) to help channel the rewards of the stronger system into the networks of the weaker. When the weaker system begins to reward Bs for their A-ness, insiders for their 'outsideness', then its dependency is sealed and language shift with respect to its mother tongue is certain. (For research on several U.S. Hispanic examples of this type see references in Hudson-Edwards & Bills, 1982; López, 1976 and 1982; Skrabanek, 1970 and Veltman, 1983.)

Relinguification as a marker of membership; re-ethnification as a marker of modernization

Even with relinguification, the sense of B-ness can continue among Bs. Since relinguification generally precedes re-ethnification (Fishman *et al.*, 1966) new patterns of B-ness arise out of the social dependency relationship discussed above. These new patterns of B-ness (-via-A) are not only implemented in socializing the younger generations born 'in the new country' (or in the new context) but they are also implemented in socializing new immigrants coming from the old country (or from the old context). In the context of advanced social dependency relationships where B-ness-via-A is the new norm, new immigrants translinguify even more rapidly than the 'old timers' did (Nahirny & Fishman, 1965). Newly arriving Bs are translinguified by their 'own kind', rather than by dint of painful interaction with As. They are translinguified in the context of B-ness and Bs. A is ultimately needed by them not only for interaction with the 'outside world' and its greater reward systems, but for interaction with the 'inside world' and its spontaneous warmth, affection, solicitude and proximity to authenticity. Newly-arriving Bs find B churches operating in A, B periodicals in A, B educational and cultural agencies and societies in A, B leaders and spokesmen who speak only A, etc. Indeed, ultimately, a new language-and-ethnicity pattern has been established, one in which A is the language of living B-ness whereas B is associated with foreign, old-fashioned and/or scholarly-specialist associations with B-ness. At this stage the only way to be a mainstream B, a B who is neither schismatic nor parochial, a B capable of combining and profiting from the 'best of both worlds', is to be a B-via-A.

The above message is not lost upon more recently arriving Bs. In addition, however, the 'old country' too has frequently changed relative to the 'good old days' when Bs first began arriving in major numbers upon the shores of A-land. B-land too has become relatively modernized and urbanized, although its average standard of living may not have fully caught up with that of A-land or with that of the early immigrants from B-land who resettled in A-land. Thus, Bs keep coming to A-land in search of 'greater opportunity' (and other rewards as well), but they are now importantly different Bs than were their predecessors, the 'old-timers'. The differences between B 'old-timers' and their A hosts was not primarily a difference in language alone, but, rather a difference in all the ethnically encumbered rounds of life: in food patterns, dress patterns, family patterns, socialization pattern, worship patterns, amusement patterns, courtship patterns, educational levels and *Weltanschauung* more generally. Most of these differences no longer obtain, or have been significantly lessened with respect to newcomers arriving when the stage of B-ness-via-A is already well articulated. They are, indeed, as close to As in most extra-linguistic respects (and, sometimes, they are even closer to them) than are the grandchildren of the original B oldtimers. Thus, the newest-arriving Bs have less of a transition to make from B-ness to A-ness than did the oldtimers. They, therefore, adapt to their new surroundings more rapidly, more in the stance of equals among equals, with primarily a 'mere' language bridge to cross. And in crossing this language bridge they obtain help not only from As but from Bs as well. Indeed, although a pattern of B-ness-via-A is ready-made and available for them, it is often not even needed or not wanted. The newcomer Bs are close enough to the world of the As, in terms of shared outlooks, values, norms, goals and experiences, to find the pattern of B-ness-via-A to be 'quaint,' inauthentic at best and, commonly, simply unnecessary and superfluous. They are more predisposed to the next step: A-ness *per se*. The emotional investment in B-ness that the 'old-timers' had and, in part, passed on to their children and grandchildren, is not there for thoroughly secularized, modernized and urbanized newcomers (Nahirny & Fishman, 1965). The drama of confrontation, the agony of rejection and accommodation, the intergenerational contest to attain mobility but not to lose one's soul — all these are lacking for the newcomers. Had they wanted to remain Bs, they would have remained in B-land. Having come to A-land as co-moderns, the offers of *landslayt* to help them acquire 'A for B-ness-via-A' strike them as funny. They increasingly help themselves to A for A-ness *per se*.

At this advanced stage of language shift, B may well continue a vestigial existence. It will, of course, continue to be used by the 'parochials', i.e. by non-mainstream Bs. It is also still found on some letterheads and on some office doors and even on some store windows evocative of mainstream B-ness. However, its major function among the latter is clearly metaphorical. It is used (by those who still know it) primarily in exceptional circumstances: to designate humor, irony, satire, affect, or to put it even more broadly — to indicate symbolic contrastivity to normal functioning. However, the predominance of *such* usage is itself an indication of shift. Metaphorical usage is basically a normatively consensual departure from the usual situational/functional allocation. In order to engage in appropriate and acceptable metaphorical usage it is necessary first to be a master of normal situational usage. For a story or punch line in B to 'sound funny' it is necessary not only to know B but also to know and agree that one usually speaks A when humor is not intended. Metaphorical usage is not intergenerationally continuous but, rather, fleeting, changeable, marginal and nonreciprocal. Its association with B may not be the last straw but it is definitely the last act. Language maintenance is clearly impossible on a metaphorical basis alone.

The potential for rebirth: the roots live on

All three of the processes discussed above (use of legal sanctions, fostering social dependency relationships via channelling rewards to Bs in terms of their use of A, co-opting Bs to become agents of A and of A-ness) are subject to the limitations of the real world. This is particularly true for the second process since the A reward system itself goes through periodic as well as long-term change, that is to say, it may not always *wish* to be equally rewarding to Bs, *nor can it always be as rewarding to Bs as it (or as they) might wish to be*. Thus, the likelihood of a residue of unrewarded, ungratified and unco-opted Bs is, realistically speaking, quite appreciable. There are Bs who have bet on A and A-ness but who have lost their bets or received a much smaller payoff than anticipated. Their social-mobility hopes and aspirations have been thwarted. The wrench of relinguification (and even re-ethnification) did not result in the *qui-pro-quo* that might have made it all worthwhile (not only in the 'outer world' but in the 'inner world' as well). A disappointed proto-élite, disappointed even after making difficult and conflicted compromises and overtures, is again ripe for relinguification and re-ethnification, i.e. for the journey 'back home.' As the perfidy of the 'outer world' becomes manifest the comforts of the 'inner world', including its genuineness, its transcendental (rather than opportunistic) truth value, its altruistic authenticity and its consoling acceptingness, above all, its humaneness above and beyond instrumental goals, become increasingly clear, compelling, and deserving, not only of loyalty but of organized recognition, focused concern, and devoted leadership. A disappointed ethnic proto-élite rediscovers its roots, all the more so in order to atone for having abandoned or neglected them. A disappointed ethnic proto-élite redirects its energies and redefines its goals: its members become the defenders of the defenseless, the mobilizers of the unmobilized, the unifiers of the disunited and the authenticators of the tradition that was being lost, has been lost or might be lost. A disappointed proto-élite turns inward and in finding its own roots it revives them. In so doing, it may revive B as a language, B-ness as an authentic experience, and the B-and-B-ness link as sacred responsibility, drive, motivation and commitment. Thus, just when some are proclaiming the death of B, others may be heralding its revival and, indeed, its eternity. More usually, however, the above goals may be unattainable and only symbolic snippets of them are implemented.

A disappointed ethnic proto-élite is more likely to be urban than rural, because it is in urban areas that the promise and the potential rewards for relinguification are greatest. As a result, the counter-mobilization that disappointed proto-élites engage in is also likely to be urban. Urban areas, therefore, are centers of conflicted ethnicity and of ethnic conflict, both at the between-group and at the within-group levels. Urban areas represent the greatest dangers for relinguification but also the greatest early successes of revival movements, given their promise to comfort the alienated and the twice-alienated.

Resolution 2: The indigenous language is lost

North Americans are likely to think that immigrant languages (Bs in our shorthand) always go by the board by the time three generations have elapsed and, therefore, that A always emerges not only victorious but even stronger than it was before, having co-opted the immigrants into its greater reward system. However, this view reveals a paucity of sociohistorical perspective, since there are equally many and equally noteworthy cases of the opposite kind, i.e. cases in which the resolution $B \rightarrow A = B$ obtains. Indeed, even the 'American case' itself was initially of this latter type, since there were indigenous languages throughout North, Central, and South America before the Anglo-Franco-Hispano-conquerors and settlers arrived. Several other contexts usually viewed today as examples of the $B \rightarrow A = A$ sequence were actually originally examples of the opposite kind. Australia and New Zealand, although more recently (post-World War II) hospitable to non-English-speaking immigrants, also originally represent instances of the second resolution $B \rightarrow A = B$, because there too there were indigenous populations prior to the arrival of the Anglo-Europeans (Benton, 1978). Indeed, the major instances of language shift in world history are probably of this kind, including in its ranks the Romanization of most of Gaul and Iberia, the Arabization of most of the Middle East and North Africa, the Sanscritization of most of the Indian peninsula, the Swahilization of large parts of East Africa, the Sinoization (particularly in script) of much of East Asia, and, currently, the relentless and continued Russification of the Soviet Union (Lewis, 1972; Kreindler, 1982; Silver, 1974).

In many respects the underlying dynamics in Resolution 2 are similar to those reviewed in conjunction with Resolution 1, above, but this time the shoe is on the other foot. Intrusive B is by far the stronger of the two ethnolinguistic entities and it, therefore, ultimately swamps out the indigenous language and ethnicity constellation. It is the intruders who establish the predominant system of legal sanctions. It is the intruders whose econo-technical, educational and cultural superiority (and, at times, whose sheer numbers) results in a reward system that fosters social dependency relationships on 'aborigines' and 'autochthons' who want to get ahead. It is the original population that forms a transmission system for the relinguification and re-ethnification of its own outlying and, therefore, late-urbanizing and modernizing brethren. Nevertheless, given all of the above similarities between Resolution 1 and Resolution 2, there is still at least one major difference between them (and several minor ones as well).

Language shift of any kind (in the context of either resolution) is an indicator of dislocation. It implies the breakdown of a previously established societal allocation of functions; the alteration of previously recognized role-relationships, situations and domains, so that these no longer imply or call for the language with which they were previously associated. Such dislocation is to be expected among intruders, be they immigrants or occupants. After all, they have left their old homes, their familiar places, and, often, their cultural self-sufficiency. As a result, one is not surprised to observe their subsequent alienation. Their old pattern does not quite work any longer but, at least initially, no new integration has become sufficiently established to provide the certainty, the bases of clear understandings, identities and expectations, formerly provided by the old. An immigrant father's authority at home is questioned, directly or indirectly, by a young whippersnapper who speaks A better than he does, who quotes A-ideology better than he does, and who even earns more than he does. The intricate web of family statuses and values is questioned, is found wanting, is increasingly inoperative. All this we expect among immigrants and other intruders and, indeed, all this underlies the B → A = A picture delineated earlier. What then must we conclude if we find this same picture among indigenous populations, populations who have *not* left their old homes, nor their familiar places, nor the territorial bases of their cultural integrity and continuity?

What we must conclude from B → A = B is *extremely great dislocation*: the dislocation of conquest, of genocide, of massive population resettlement such that locals are swamped out, engulfed, deracinated and decimated by intruders, be they conquerors or settlers. The Anglo-American uprooting and destruction of Native Americans and the Russo-Soviet decimation of White Russians, Ukrainians, Jews, Germans, Poles and many, many of the smaller Central and Far Eastern Asian peoples is sugar coated as 'frontier democracy' and 'the greatest good to the greatest number' on the one hand and as 'creation of the new Soviet people', on the other hand, but it is, in both cases, the *excruciatingly painful and disruptive dislocation and annihilation of local peoples*. Other B → A = B contexts may lie further back in history but they were doubtlessly equally ruthless, regardless of the religious, ideological or philosophical rationales that accompanied and 'legitimized' them. The metric of terror is inverse to time and distance. Wherever neither three generations of time nor the shelter of distance is/was available to temper and mute the dislocative ('internal colonization') process (Hechter, 1971, 1974) instances of B → A = B are likely to be especially sad examples of man's inhumanity to man.

And yet the roots revive at times, even after the tree has been burnt seemingly beyond recognition or recovery (Eastman, 1979). There are limits to the power of B to either annihilate or incorporate A and the usual history of establishment vacillation between the one and the other is peculiarly likely finally to produce the very proto-élites who come to be the initiators and leaders of rebirth and revival language-and-ethnicity movements. Just as such proto-élites were once (and, in some cases still are) legion among disappointed Anglicized Irishmen, Francofied Provençals, Hispanicized Cataláns, Danicized Norwegians, Germanized Czechs, Hungarianized Slovaks, Serbianized Croatians and assimilated Jews throughout the West, so their ranks are currently swelling among Chicanos, Puerto Ricans and Amerindians in the U.S.A., among Ukrainian and other non-Russian-nationality spokesmen among Soviet resistors, and among Africans and Asians of a large number of local ethnic origins. The phenomenal increase in languages of education and government since the end of World War II is a result of such recoveries from external and internal colonization. The end of this process is not yet in sight. Significantly, such revival and rebirth movements, in attempting to overcome and undo the punitive dislocations to which their constituencies were exposed, turn to ethnicity and to the presumed language-and-ethnicity link, rather than to either social-class ideologies or religious philosophies alone for this purpose. In so doing, they seem to tap a well of emotion, or commitment, of longing, related to the 'dynamo of history' (that both Herder and Whorf recognized), hibernating in their ancestral language and identity. The more dislocated a segment of mankind becomes, the greater seems to be its penchant for putative roots, for its origins, for 'authenticity.' The scholar's determination that these identities are composed of great slices of fabrication and imagination are beside the point, in the same way that all rational empiricism is beside the point when emotional needs are uppermost. It is the *need for a sense of historically deep, glorious and intact authenticity* that so typifies the disappointed ethnic proto-élites and their followers, rather than for any *need that the authenticity* responses that they employ be rationally verifiable and validated. The recurring role of language in such movements is eloquent testimony to the ability of this sublime symbol system to symbolize the fondest and most fervent dreams, hopes and wishes of which mankind is capable.

Resolution 3: Both the intrusive and the original language are retained and indigenized

Given our earlier analysis of diglossia (Fishman, 1980), there is no need, at this point, to review in detail the societal and the political arrangements that undergird a resolution of this third kind. Still uncovered, however, by our previous treatments, are some of the internal differences within this particular resolution and the strains to which it is exposed.

The territorial counterpart to B → A = A + B is A/B, i.e. A and B are utilized in separate sections or functions of a common polity. The seeming stability of this arrangement (in the Swiss case, e.g. regardless of demographic realities such as the resettlement of many, many thousands of Italian speakers in the German and French cantons) nevertheless does not itself completely halt the social processes of language shift (McRae, 1964 and 1983). The regions are not economically equal and, therefore, the richer one(s) beckon(s) to the inhabitants of the poorer one(s) and the latter, as migrants to greener pastures, become examples of resolution 1, B → A = A. In addition, even though they remain in their own valleys, the numerically and economically weak Romansch become examples of resolution 2 *vis-à-vis* their vastly more numerous and prosperous German speaking neighbors (Billigmeier, 1979). Thus, not even the territorial principle is immune to change and to strain and to the irredentist cry of troubled true-believers that they be enabled to return to their mother tongue and motherland of old (McRae, 1975).

The stresses and strains of shift can be all the more obvious when it is *social* rather than *territorial/political* diglossia that obtains. Basically two different sub-patterns can constitute the societal counterpart to resolution three. Although both are equally instances of B → A = A + B, one realizes the right-hand side of the equation as A/B, and the other, as B/A. In the first instance the intrusive language remains as the common vernacular whereas the indigenous language is retained for H functions alone. This is, in part, the anomolous position of Irish today, particularly outside of the *Gaeltacht* (Western coastal) region, such that Irish has been 'kicked upstairs', so to speak, and is used only for various ceremonial purposes, whereas istrusive English (Hiberno-English to be sure) has become the vernacular of Irishmen and Irishness.[2] A similar situation pertained with respect to Judeo-Aramaic (= Aramic or Targumic) in ancient days when it increasingly displaced Hebrew as the Jewish vernacular until the latter was retained only in hallowed functions (Weinreich, 1979). Judeo-Aramaic itself was subsequently displaced as a vernacular by other Jewish languages and was vestigially retained as a co-hallowed variety, alongside and intermixed with Hebrew, as the co-language of two millenia of sacred and hallowed Loshn-koydesh texts.

Far more common is the second sub-pattern of resolution 3, namely, that in which the intrusive language B is retained for H functions, displacing the indigenous or otherwise prior H, whereas indigenous A is maintained in its prior vernacular functions. This pattern is illustrated by the various central administrative languages of empire in classical Eastern Mediterranean antiquity (Lewis, 1976). They replaced each other rather completely as administrative Hs (Sumerian, Akkadian, Aramaic, Greek, Latin, etc.), leaving the local vernaculars relatively untouched (except in the cases of more powerfully impacted populations and places, where these Hs ultimately became vernacularized or fused with local vernaculars). These classical situations are rather similar to current H uses of English, French and other languages inherited from periods of colonization (e.g. Chinese in Tibet and Russian in Outer Mongolia). Their H statuses are obvious in presumably post-colonial areas that are still highly dependent on their former colonizers for economic, political and educational guidance and assistance (Fishman, Cooper & Conrad, 1977).

The strain in both of the above-mentioned sub-patterns of societal diglossia is the strain toward equalization or symmetry. Movements arise for the re-vernacularization of asymmetric Hs, i.e. of Hs that were once also Ls but that lost all vernacular functions. Of these movements, the vernacularization of Hebrew has succeeded (and, as a result, has endangered the longevity of all other Jewish vernaculars [Fishman, 1978]) whereas those on behalf of Irish, Sanskrit, Classical and Classicized Greek, Latin and Classical Arabic have not. Similarly, movements arise for the elevation of asymmetric Ls (i.e. of Ls that were once also Hs but that lost all H-culture functions). The movements on behalf of Catalán, Galician and Occitan today and on behalf of Flemish prior to World War II were of this type. Even where Ls never had H varieties and H functions of their own (e.g. in the case of Pilipino or, generally speaking, Yiddish) there is a strain to develop and to devise such, almost as a moral imperative and as a strain toward closure, toward completion, toward local self-dignity and self-respect, particularly if there is a proto-élite whose power position would benefit from such elevation. Thus, these latter strains are easily ethnically encumbered and expressed and they contribute to movements of ethnic cultural autonomy and political self-determination.

Ethnicity as stabilizer, destabilizer and restabilizer

In each of the resolutions that we have reviewed above, we have encountered ethnicity (in the form or ethnic revivals, returns to ethnic roots, ethnic memories and loyalties) as a potential source of destabilization. Although it is true that ethnicity can be appealed to and can function in this fashion (Fishman, 1972), it is, however, by no means true that *destabilization* of past patterns (be these of societal allocations of language functions or of any other culture patterns) is any more part and parcel of the basic phenomenon of ethnicity than is the opposite tendency: the *stabilization* of societal patterns. Indeed, each and every one of the above resolutions can (and, if undisturbed, ultimately does) develop its own sense of ethnic normalcy, naturalness and legitimacy, i.e. it is subject to being stabilized in terms of ethnic authenticity rather than merely to being destabilized on such grounds. It is all the more crucial, therefore, that we have a clear understanding of ethnicity *per se* and of its seemingly inevitable link to language in general and to language maintenance in particular.

Generically, 'ethnicity' pertains to 'peopleness', i.e. to actions, values, views or attributions pertaining to belonging to a people. As with many other social behaviors, actors and attributors may not agree with respect to 'people-ness' behaviors and attributions. We (outsiders) may call people 'communists' who do not think they (insiders) are communists or even know what communism is. Similarly, outsiders may call others (insiders) Irish, or Puerto Ricans or Ruthenians who do not themselves call themselves such and who do not even think they are such. Whenever 'outsiders' (particularly a class of outsiders known as social scientists) and 'insiders' do not agree on social designations, that itself is worthy of study, but it does not invalidate the outsider's designation any more than when certain outsiders designate 'phonemes' or refer to 'prose' in other people's speech, even though the others have never been aware of either phonemes or prose. Certainly, a *societal phenomenon* and *awareness of that phenomenon* are *not* one and the same thing. Thus, ethnicity (like most other societally patterned phenomena) can exist either with awareness or without awareness on the part of members of social aggregates. Note, however, that ethnicity with awareness is likely to be something quite a bit different from ethnicity without it (just as prose differs when speakers are aware of it and when they are not).

Ethnicity is 'peopleness', i.e. belonging or pertaining to a phenomenologically complete, separate, historically deep cultural collectivity, a collectivity polarized on perceived authenticity. This 'belonging' is experienced and interpreted physically (biologically), behaviorally (culturally) and phenomenologically (intuitively). Where it is experienced or attributed on only one or another of these three dimensions it might easily be reduced to other constructs, but characterized as it is on all three it is a very mystic, moving and powerful link with the past and an energizer with respect to the present and future. It is fraught with moral imperatives, with obligations to 'one's own kind', and with wisdoms, rewards and proprieties that are both tangible and intangible. Above all, in its quiescent state, it is part of the warp-and-woof of daily life, part of all the customs, traditions, ceremonies and interpretations related to the collectivity that is defined by them, distinguished by them and responsible for them. As such, it is language-related to a very high and natural degree, both overtly (imbedded as it is in verbal culture and implying as it does structurally dependent intuitions) and covertly (the supreme symbol system quintessentially symbolizes its users and distinguishes between them and others). Indeed this is so to such a degree that language and ethnic authenticity may come to be viewed as highly interdependent. Thus it is that ethnicity is focused on authenticity (continuity of being, of doing and of knowing) while it is as modifiable (both in content and in saliency) and as manipulable (that is: consciously used as a basis of mobilization) as are other bases of human aggregation (economic, religious, ideological, political) focused on other assumptions and other dimensions.

Ethnicity then, in its unconscious, everyday routines of 'we-ness', phenomenologically normalizes and indigenizes any particular sociolinguistic allocation of functions. Spanish is thereby rendered authentic in Latin America, and Arabic in the Near East and North Africa, and Yiddish among Ashkenazim. Although in each case these languages initially came 'from the outside' they have been adapted and internalized, at least by most (if not by all) speech networks in the ethnicity collectivities to which they pertain, and are viewed now as indigenous, authentic, genuinely their own, part of their daily ethnic identity. Thus it is that unconscious, unthinking, unmobilized ethnicity comes to be a great stabilizer of each and any resolution of the B → A intrusion. But the very unconsciousness of the unmobilized ethnicity of ordinary social life also makes it a potential and a flexible source of untapped energy for élites who are concerned with changing the status quo to a presumable *status quo ante*.

Nationalism (= conscious, mobilized ethnicity) and its opponents

The quiet cocoon of routine ethnicity (that protects and provides an implicit eternity of past authenticity to each of the resolutions we have reviewed) can be energized, organized and manipulated by proto-élites to counteract or to foster any particular language-and-ethnicity link and any particular B → A resolution that ordinary folk have taken for granted. Thus, guided, exploited, mobilized (and, therefore, conscious) ethnicity has, particularly in modern times, been one of the great destabilizers of the *status quos* so precious to all establishments, including the pet non-ethnic, supra-ethnic or anti-ethnic establishments that are preferred by advocates of other-than-ethnic bases of human aggregation. Given the repeated though unconscious link of language to unconscious ethnicity, its link to conscious, activated ethnicity (= nationalism) has been equally recurring and ever so much more dynamic. Conscious ethnicity movements are more than likely to become or incorporate conscious language movements as well. Together they seek to *foster* specific B → A resolutions and to undo others. Language loyalty movements are, therefore, normally part of larger movements to *activate* and *use* unconscious language-and-ethnicity linkages in order to attain or reallocate econotechnical, political and cultural/educational power. Such movements are normally part of much larger, more encompassing social change movements. They stress ethnic identity consciousness (and even ethnic identity change) in order to attain the ends defined by their proto-élites and, understandably, they have been much attacked and maligned by the counter-élites or proto-élites that are threatened by them. Capitalist theoreticians have attacked language loyalty movements as barbarous and uncivilized for breaking up capitalist empires (e.g. the former Anglo-empire in Quebec that was headed in the direction of B → A = B, and the former Dutch empire in Friesland that was headed in a similar direction), and for delivering whole sections of them into the clutches (and coffers) of counter-establishments. Communist theoreticians have attacked language loyalty movements as false and fractionating for breaking up a larger proletariat (that might be led by a single supra-ethnic establishment) into smaller proletarian establishments each with its own leadership (Engels, 1866). Capitalist élites have rejected minority language loyalty movements (such as those in regions of Spain or France or Great Britain) as communist conspiracies. Entrenched Communist élites have rejected minority language loyalty movements (such as those in Croatia and the Ukraine) as capitalist conspiracies. 'Neutralist' sociologists have attacked language loyalty movements as chauvinistic ativisms (Patterson,

1977), as backward-looking incivility, as romanticist *Gemeinschaft* longings in an age of *Gesellschaft* efficiency and market-place ethos. No one, it seems, likes language loyalty movements, unless *they* or their favorite causes can profit or gain from them. And yet such movements abound and their end is not in sight!

Language loyalty movements are most commonly associated with attempts to foster and focus modernization via channelling and exploiting authenticity longings. Beginning with the various disappointments of failed or flawed B → A resolutions, these movements utilize language as a *medium* for reaching the largest possible target population and as a *symbol* of the purported 'authenticity,' 'unity' and 'mission' of that population. Thus, it is through language loyalty movements that ethnicity becomes a conscious, organized, and dynamic factor in language shift, since every language maintenance movement, from the point of view of what is the 'marked' language at any particular time and in any particular place (e.g. on behalf of French in Quebec in 1970), is also a factor in language shift from the point of view of the 'unmarked language' (e.g. with respect to English in Quebec as of 1970). Clearly, language loyalty movements are consciously mobilized and manipulated attempts to utilize ethnicity bonds and ethnicity affect and action potentials for the purposes of establishing or disestablishing a particular societal allocation of language functions. Whereas everyday, unconscious ethnicity is quietly involved in the myriad of daily actions that go into language maintenance and language shift, heightened and politicized ethnicity movements, including language loyalty movements as part and parcel of the entire nationalism thrust, are involved in conscious and often rowdy publicity-seeking actions on behalf of language maintenance or language shift. Such movements typically seek to alter the laws, to prohibit the social dependency relationships, and to dislocate populations from those traditional socialization and related practices that resulted in or fostered undesirable B → A resolutions, regardless of whether those were consciously or unconsciously implemented.

Resolutions and counterresolutions: An endless progression

We live in a world of tensions and countertensions, of movements and countermovements, of revolutions and counterrevolutions. Accordingly many modern-language loyalty movements are attempts to effect counterresolutions to the B → A resolutions that preceded them. However, even when they succeed as such, they too may no more be final resolutions than were the ones that they came to overturn. Successful counterestablishments become establishments in their own right and subsequent counterestablishments may ultimately arise to contest or reform them. After some two centuries of such language-related resolutions and counterresolutions, in pursuit of solutions to the dilemmas of modernization, two seemingly contradictory trends seem to have been strengthened:

(a) More languages than ever before have been recognized for governmental and governmentally protected functions, their number having risen from 30 to approximately 200 in the present century alone (Deutsch, 1942; Fishman, 1976).
(b) A single *lingua franca* — English — has spread further than ever before for supra-local econotechnical, political, diplomatic, educational and touristic purposes (Fishman, Cooper & Conrad, 1977).

The above two processes seem to be sufficiently counterbalanced — socio-functionally and in terms of the power and stability of the rewards associated with each of them — that the likelihood of either one swamping the other in the near future seems rather negligible on any but a very local scale or brief period. Furthermore, neither process seems yet to have run its course so as to reach its outer limits. While (or, perhaps, also because) additions to the ranks of 'standard,' 'national' and 'official' languages can still be expected, particularly in the Third World, international reliance on English is also increasing, with Mainland China, the Arab world and even the U.S.S.R. constantly increasing their utilization of this 'latter-day Aramaic.' Finally, these two processes are guided by equally modernized and language conscious élites and, therefore, neither is likely to be found ideologically wanting in terms of long term or short term rationales.

As a result of the 'stand off' illustrated by the two above-mentioned international processes, a bilingual compromise may come to be resorted to more and more frequently, at least outside of the English mother-tongue world. Such a compromise will not only recognize English and local standard languages as being in complementary distribution, but it will also set the stage for the recognition of even more hitherto-unrecognized languages, the latter two seeking a complementary distribution of functions between themselves and locally super-posed languages. All of these processes, in turn, underlie the truly amazing international growth in enrichment bilingual education since the end of World War II. While B → A tensions continue throughout the world, more and more authorities are experimenting with language planning — of which bilingual education is one example — in order to find a way out of the endless chain of resolutions and counterresolutions that has typified sociolinguistic policy heretofore. Instead of co-opting proto-élites by translinguifying and transethnifying them, they are now more and more frequently given a well controlled and delimited 'share of the action' among their 'own kind' while, at the same time, they obtain access to the language of wider communication and some of its results as well. Will it work? Only time will tell.

Notes to Chapter 6

1. I do not intend to pause here to examine the methodological and conceptual issues of *when* a language is 'lost', i.e. of *how we can recognize that language shift has occurred* with respect to particular societal functions and with respect to mother-tongue functions in particular. There is a justifiably extensive technical literature on this topic, much of which has been reviewed most recently in Fishman, 1977. A somewhat related literature is that dealing with language spread. Language spread does not necessarily imply language shift, since languages can spread into new (culturally unprecedented) functions and, thereby, not engender language shift with respect to previously existing functions of the speech community. The literature on language spread has been reviewed by Cooper, 1982. The present paper may be considered as picking up the language spread trail at a more advanced point than that which is of concern to Cooper, i.e. at the point when language spread *has* impinged upon *previously existing language functions* and, therefore, when it has changed from being merely language spread to being language shift as well. For the very final stages of language shift see Dorian (1977) and Dressler & Wodak-Leodolter (1977) on language death.

2. Actually the complete formula for most parts of Ireland would probably require $B \rightarrow A = (A + B)/B$ since English is encountered both in H and in L pursuits. At any rate, Irish is now generally devoid of vernacular functions (particularly outside of the *Gaeltacht*) and is in danger of being 'respected to death' in its honorific H functions.

References

BENTON, R. A. 1978, Problems and prospects for indigenous languages and bilingual education in New Zealand and Oceania. In B. SPOLSKY & R. L. COOPER (eds), *Case Studies in Bilingual Education*. Rowley: Newbury House, 126–66.

BILLIGMEIER, R. H. 1979, *Crisis in Swiss Pluralism*. The Hague: Mouton.

COLLOQUE/COLLOQUIUM. 1978, *Linguistic Minorities and Interventions: Towards a Typology*. Quebec: Laval University Press.

COOPER, R. L. 1982, A framework for the study of language spread. In R. L. COOPER (ed.), *Language Spread: Studies in Diffusion and Social Change*. Bloomington and Washington, D.C.: Indiana University Press and Center for Applied Linguistics, 5–36.

DEUTSCH, K. 1942, The trend of European nationalism — the language aspect. *American Political Science Review* 36, 533–41; also in J. A. FISHMAN (ed.), *Readings in the Sociology of Language*. The Hague:

Mouton, 1968, 598–606.

DORIAN, N. 1977, The problem of the semi-speaker in language-death. *International Journal of the Sociology of Language* 12, 23–32.

DRESSLER, W. & WODAK-LEODOLTER, R. 1977, Language preservation and language death in Brittany. *International Journal of the Sociology of Language* 12, 33–44.

EASTMAN, C. M. 1979, Language reintroduction: activity and outcome of language planning, *General Linguistics* 19, 99–111.

ENGELS, F. 1866, What have the working classes to do with Poland? *Commonwealth*, March 24, March 31, May 5.

FALCH, J. 1972, *Contributions à l'étude du statut des langues en Europe*. Quebec: Laval Univ. Press.

FISHMAN, J. A. 1972, *Language and Nationalism: Two Integrative Essays*. Rowley: Newbury House.

— 1976, *Bilingual Education: An International Sociological Perspective*. Rowley: Newbury House.

— 1977, The spread of English as a new perspective for the study of language maintenance and language shift. In J. A. FISHMAN *et al.*, *The Spread of English*. Rowley: Newbury House, 108–36.

— 1978, The sociolinguistic 'normalization' of the Jewish people. In E. POLOME (ed.), *Archibald Hill Festschrift IV*. The Hague: Mouton, 223–31.

— 1980, Bilingualism and biculturism as individual and as societal phenomena. *Journal of Multilingual and Multicultural Development* 1, 3–15. Revised, This Volume, part II.

FISHMAN, J. A. *et al.* 1966, *Language Loyalty in the United States*. The Hague: Mouton.

FISHMAN, J. A., COOPER, R. L. & A. W. CONRAD *et al.* 1977, *The Spread of English*. Rowley: Newbury House.

HEATH, S. B. 1977, A national language academy? Debate in the new nation, *International Journal of the Sociology of Language* 11, 9–44.

HECHTER, M. 1971, Towards a theory of ethnic change. *Politics in Society* 2, 29–45.

— 1974, *Internal Colonialism: The Celtic Fringe in British National Development, 1536–1966*. London: Routledge and Kegan Paul.

HUDSON-EDWARDS, A. & BILLS, G. D. 1982, Intergenerational language shift in an Albuquerque barrio. In J. AMASTAE & L. E. OLIVARES (eds), *Spanish in the United States: Sociolinguistic Aspects*. Cambridge: Cambridge University Press, 135–53.

KREINDLER, I. 1982, The Changing Status of Russian in the Soviet Union, *International Journal of the Sociology of Language* 33 (entire issue).

LEWIS, E. G. 1972, *Multilingualism in the Soviet Union*. The Hague,

Mouton.
— 1976, Bilingualism and bilingual education: The ancient world to the Renaissance. In J. A. FISHMAN, *Bilingual Education: An International Sociological Perspective*. Rowley: Newbury House, 150–200.
LIEBERSON, S. & CURRY, T. J. 1971, Language shift in the United States: some demographic clues, *International Migration Review* 5, 125–37.
LÓPEZ, D. E. 1976, Chicano language loyalty in an urban setting. *Sociology and Social Research* 62, 167–75.
— 1982, *The Maintenance of Spanish over Three Generations in the United States*. Los Alamitos: National Center for Bilingual Research.
MALLEA, J. R. (ed.) 1977, *Quebec's Language Policies: Background and Response*. Quebec: Laval Univ. Press.
MCRAE, K. D. 1964, *Switzerland: Example of Cultural Co-existence*. Toronto: Institute of International Affairs.
— 1975, The principle of territoriality and the principle of personality in multilingual states, *International Journal of the Sociology of Language* 4, 33–54.
— 1985, *Conflict and Compromise in Multilingual Societies: Switzerland*. Waterloo: Wilfrid Laurier University Press.
NAHIRNY, V. & FISHMAN, J. A. 1965, American immigrant groups: ethnic identification and the problem of generations, *(British) Sociological Review* 13, 311–26.
— 1966, Ukrainian language maintenance efforts in the United States. In J. A. FISHMAN *et al.*, *Language Loyalty in the United States*. The Hague: Mouton, 318–57.
PATTERSON, O. 1977, *Ethnic Chauvinism: The Reactionary Impulse*. New York: Stein and Day.
SAVARA, J. G. & VIGNEAULT, R. (eds) 1975, *Multilingual Political Systems: Problems and Solutions*. Quebec: Laval Univ. Press.
SILVER, B. 1974, The impact of urbanization and geographical dispersion on the linguistic Russification of Soviet nationalities. *Demography* 11, 89–103.
SKRABANEK, R. L. 1970, Language maintenance among Mexican-Americans, *International Journal of Comparative Sociology* 11, 272–82.
TABOURET-KELLER, A. (ed.) 1961, Regional Languages in France, *International Journal of the Sociology of Language* no. 29 (entire issue).
TOURET, B. 1972, *L'Aménagement constitutionnel des Etats de peuplement composite*. Quebec: Laval Univ. Press.
VELTMAN, C. 1983, *Language Shift in the United States*. Berlin: Mouton.
WEINREICH, M. 1979, *History of the Yiddish Language*. Chicago: Chicago University Press, (= vols. 1 and 2 of the original four-volume Yiddish edition, 1973; translated into English by S. NOBLE & J. A. FISHMAN.)

7   The societal basis of the intergenerational continuity of additional languages*

Intergenerational mother tongue continuity

In stable, indigenous societies, mother tongues reveal intergenerational continuity. Although a degree of language change is constantly ongoing, nevertheless parents and children can be said to speak 'the same language', i.e. the mother tongue of the parents is handed on to their children. Indeed, intergenerational cultural continuity so largely depends upon intergenerational mother tongue continuity, and vice versa, that we have come to expect the one when the other obtains and have largely lost the sense of 'the wonder of it all' which is at the base of all scientific inquiry. Once we begin to ask questions about this seemingly natural and effortless 'expected' process, the many things that *could* go wrong begin to become more obvious. Even if we set aside the many still problematic aspects of language acquisition *per se* and focus only on the topic of continuity, many questions come to mind. Many parents have learned additional languages after (or even during) their own childhood. Why aren't those subsequent languages, which must have been learned because of the advantages with which they were associated, handed on as mother tongues to the children of these parents? At any given time, at least half of the non-English mother tongue world seems to be learning English. Why isn't this language then handed on to the next generation as its mother tongue, thereby saving it much time, effort and expense and max-

*Originally published in K. R. JANKOWSKY (ed.) 1985, *Scientific and Humanistic Dimensions of Language. Festschrift for Robert Lado*, Amsterdam: John Benjamins, 551–58.

imizing for it the benefits to be derived from English? Indeed, given all the trials and tribulations of 'small national languages' (Fishman, 1984), it is really quite surprising that these normally do continue to experience intergenerational continuity and are not voluntarily replaced by languages of wider communication that their mother tongue speakers have mastered on an interregional or international basis.

Intergenerational continuity of minority mother tongues

The greatest light on the above questions has been shed by empirical research and theoretical formulations pertaining to minority (or sub-national) languages. Here intergenerational mother tongue continuity is very frequently not only endangered but actually not attained. The basic issue is now understood to be one of boundary maintenance, both *between cultures* as well as between domains *within cultures*. National languages are protected by national boundaries. Where minority cultures are strong enough to protect their cultural boundaries (and, of course, interested in doing so), they produce the same defenses for their ethnocultural mother tongues. They separate populations into insiders and outsiders and they define the cultural desiderata — including language — which are required for inside membership. Under such circumstances, even small minorities can attain intergenerational mother tongue continuity (viz. Old Order Amish); lacking them, even large ones cannot (viz. Spanish-Americans, German-Americans, Polish-Americans, Franco-Americans, etc.; Fishman *et al.*, 1984).

Boundaries imply separation, the control of boundary crossing, the regulation of imports, the definition of desirable and undesirable international relations. Minority cultures, whether indigenous or immigrant, are often prohibited from exercising such controls. They are required/compelled to utilize outside products, institutions and personnel for sensitive inside functions in family, religious, educational and economic pursuits. Democratic governments may not utilize compulsion but accomplish the same destruction of minority boundary maintenance via fostering interactive dependency and open access in industry, education and government. As a result, insiders not only learn the outside language but use it with one another, inside, for advantages within the minority community itself. This becomes 'the beginning of the end' of minority mother tongue intergenerational continuity. The outside language not only has maintained its unrestricted outside advantages but has attained unrestricted inside advantages as well (Fishman, 1981).

Note that the ultimate problem of intergenerational minority mother tongue continuity is not that of maintaining cultural boundaries *vis-à-vis* the *outside*. The Old Order Amish and the Hasidim have all learned English (indeed, Amish schools typically devote only a morning once a week to Luther German, their religious 'classical' language, and no time at all to instruction in Pennsylvania German, their vernacular). The ultimate problem is regulating *the extent to which outside desiderata* (in our case: language) *can be utilized for internal pursuits*. If the outside language is utilized basically for carefully controlled interactions with outsiders, then it cannot become the mother tongue of the next generation. In any intact culture, one's children are, by definition, insiders, not outsiders, and are communicated with via the language for insiders, the mother tongue. The cultural arrangement whereby one language is reserved for one set of ethnoculturally approved and regulated functions (e.g. outside relations) and another language is reserved for another set of ethnoculturally approved and regulated functions (e.g. inside relations) is an example of *diglossia* (Fishman, 1980a). In its most general terms, diglossia both represents and requires the maintenance of *intercultural* and *intracultural* boundaries. Whereas the latter may not be possible without some degree of the former, the former alone is not sufficient for intergenerational mother tongue continuity.

If it is the latter, *the maintenance of intracultural boundaries*, that is crucial for intergenerational minority group mother tongue maintenance, then we can more easily understand why it is that small national languages so commonly achieve intergenerational mother-tongue maintenance even though (as in Holland, for example) almost all adults below the age of 40 have acquired English fluency. Small national languages, beset with problems though they may be, not only benefit from sufficient intercultural (inter-national) boundaries to protect their own sociocultural establishments, but they also preserve sufficient intra-cultural boundaries to make sure that cultural imports get only so far and no further. Even when 100% of all Dutch adults will know English, each new generation of Dutch offspring will have to learn that language anew and away from home. Each new generation of Dutch children will start off as Dutch monolinguals and will initially speak only Dutch at home, with their parents, siblings, relatives, friends and neighbors. As they subsequently acquire English in school and via mass media exposure, the above pattern will remain substantially unaltered. They may subsequently discuss a very few topics with some of the above individuals in English, but these will either be fleeting or defined in terms of a different set of role relationships (e.g. advanced technology co-experts rather than siblings).

Intergenerational additional language continuity in national societies

The Dutch case also brings us to the question of intergenerational continuity of additional languages. Such continuity is not hard to conceptualize in the case of societies in control of their own polities. Such societies control their own educational and media systems and, therefore, can assure that generation after generation of students will be taught the same additional language as long as it seems advantageous to do so. Controlling, as they do (which, of course, does not mean freezing), their inter-cultural boundaries for their own advantage, they can discontinue fostering one language of wider communication (e.g. German), or relegate it to briefer study during the later elementary school years (e.g. French), while introducing another (e.g. English) and giving it earlier as well as more curricular exposure. Controlling, as well, their intra-cultural boundaries, they need not be concerned that such stress will threaten the mother tongue (the national language), particularly since Dutch language requirements for participation in the economy, government, church, mass media and education can also be kept at high levels. The result of such boundary maintenance is that English never becomes a requirement for *membership* in the Dutch ethnoculture, although it does become a widespread skill advantageously associated with such membership.

No one will ever say to a youngster whose English is poor 'You are not a good Dutchman; you have neglected a mainstay of Dutchness. You can only lead an impoverished Dutch life and, were you to be taken as a model, Dutch culture itself would be impoverished by the example you are setting.' The intergenerational continuity of 'English as the favorite additional language', stable though this may be, is not confused with Dutchness, any more than is the stability of algebra in the school. *Vis-à-vis* Dutchness, both English and algebra are viewed as highly desired aspects of a well educated and advantageously educated person. However, English is always *outside*-oriented in terms of its basic rationale and curricular orientation. It is definitely not intended to be, nor will it become, an *inside* language of Dutch society *at large*.[1]

Intergenerational additional language continuity of religious classicals

In addition to the school and media systems, there is yet another avenue of intergenerational continuity for additional languages. Latin,

Koranic Arabic, Prayerbook and Biblical Hebrew, Talmudic Aramaic, Luther Bible German, Old Church Slavonic, Ecclesiastic Greek, Ecclesiastic Armenian and Geez are just a few examples of religious classicals that have long been maintained on an intergenerational basis. In some cases, these languages are target (i.e. textual) languages to which ample school time is devoted over the course of many years. In other cases, they are 'merely' learned by virtue of repeated use in services and other rituals. In some cases, the power of state (polity) authority is added to that of religious authority in order to require learning of these languages. In other cases, the separation of church and state is clear and sharp, and it is 'the church itself' that must accomplish the intergenerational transmission. 'Church itself', of course, is a simplification of ethnocultural reality which the Western European tradition of separation of church and state tends to foster. Churches are very commonly (indeed, nearly always) not only ethnoculturally encumbered but ethnoculturally specific. Religion is not only part and parcel of ethnocultural life but indigenous religions are usually quite specific in ethnocultural terms as well. Even the universal religions have all developed quite specific ethnocultural variants, and the overwhelming majority of ethnocultures are religiously quite homogeneous. Thus, even when we say that a given religious language achieves intergenerational continuity due to church efforts (church schools, church attendance, church influence on home ritual, etc.), we must keep in mind that the church is an aspect of the ethnoculture and a reflection of the ethnoculture's boundary maintenance capacity.

To some extent, religious classicals are similar to the position of English in Holland. No matter how highly regarded, how well taught and how fluently learned, they remain additional languages for specific functions and do *not* become the mother tongue of subsequent generations. In other respects, however, religious classicals are like ethnocultural mother tongues. They define the 'inside', they are ethnocultural membership requirements until and unless church authorities decide otherwise. Discontinuities are possible. Latin is no longer the common ritual language of the Catholic Church. Hebrew has been minimized in Reform Jewish worship and seriously compromised in Conservative Jewish worship. Armenian has been de-emphasized in Armenian Prelacy churches in the U.S.A. and Greek is no longer exclusively used in Greek Orthodox Patriarchate churches in the U.S.A. The Missouri Synod Lutheran Church has been practically de-Germanized during the past quarter century. Except for the Latin example, above, however, all of these are examples of minority groups unprotected by strong boundary maintenance mechanisms *vis-à-vis* their surrounding 'outside' contexts. In general, among indigenized churches serving indigenous/indigenized populations, religious classicals remain robust features of ethnocultural membership throughout the world. They do so by successfully controlling who may become and remain a member, i.e. by controlling boundaries with the 'outside', and by adequately regulating the differences between ethnocultural religious behavior of one kind (e.g. the sermon) and ethnocultural religious behaviors of other kinds (e.g. the service), i.e. by controlling boundaries within the 'inside'.

Intergenerational additional language continuity of religious classicals among minorities

Ethnocultural minorities with religious classicals are engaged in a two-front struggle. Not only must they seek to maintain control of their intergroup and intragroup boundaries insofar as their vernaculars are concerned (e.g. Pennsylvania German, Yiddish, demotic Greek, Palestinian Arabic), but they must also seek to do the same insofar as their religious classicals are concerned (e.g. Luther Bible German, Classical Hebrew/Aramaic, Ecclesiastic Greek, Koranic Arabic). Generally, the two fronts are closely related to each other, and success or failure on the one is related to success or failure on the other. Nevertheless, when differentials develop, it is recurringly the religious classical that is retained longer than the vernacular. The religious domain has more authoritative (and, therefore, more resistant) boundaries than does the minority ethnocultural system as a whole, it is less exposed to majority society, its language use is more ritualized and more sanctified, and its whole posture is more tradition-and-stability oriented (rather than progress-and-change oriented). As a result, American Jews are much more protective of Prayerbook/Biblical Hebrew and Talmudic Aramaic than they are of their Yiddish/Judezmo vernaculars. English-speaking Greek-Americans preserve at least some Ecclesiastic Greek in their church services, and Palestinian Arab-Americans and Chinese-Americans continue to prepare their children in Koranic Arabic and classicized Cantonese/Mandarin even after they are fully English-speaking 'third generation ethnics' (Fishman, 1980b). Because religion is concerned with eternals rather than externals, it is more conservative, less compromising and more compelling insofar as boundary maintenance is concerned.

Intergenerational continuity of heritage mother tongues as additional languages among minorities

Minorities that have already undergone the process of language shift, as a result of insufficient boundary maintenance of the two kinds that we have discussed above, nevertheless frequently attempt to assure the intergenerational continuity of their erstwhile mother tongues as additional languages. This effort results in the establishment of schools to teach *de novo* the language that was formerly acquired at home and then merely reinforced or polished at school. Since such school-based heritage mother tongues correspond to neither an outside nor an inside societal reality, they are somewhat akin to foreign languages and, generally, are only meagerly or marginally mastered. Nevertheless, parental (and grandparental) sentiment may continue to be substantial, and this sentimental or symbolic basis can, when buttressed by societal rewards, school devotion and pedagogic expertise, result in appreciable language learning for specific functions (recitations, festive rituals, literary appreciation, etc.). However, notwithstanding the generally high level of ethnocultural community sentiment for teaching the erstwhile mother tongue as a school subject, and notwithstanding the successes experienced along these lines in the lower grades when students are still largely oriented toward home and school rewards, nevertheless the level of mastery attained usually reaches a plateau and then declines in adolescence as larger societal experiences, rewards and orientations become predominant. Be this as it may, the erstwhile mother tongue may continue to be taught as an additional language on an intergenerational basis. It becomes a *rite de passage* for the young, but, unlike religious classicals, it has no safe institutional base of its own outside of school. Without widespread societal change, mother tongue revival on a school basis alone is extremely unlikely (Macnamara, 1971). The school may persist in teaching the language, but in societal terms it will be little more than a relic of bygone days because, like several other recondite subjects, it has no corresponding out-of-school validity.

Summary

Just as it is by no means certain that mother tongues will enjoy intergenerational continuity, so it is not impossible for other (additional) languages to enjoy such continuity. Languages of wider communication (such as English), religious classicals (such as Koranic Arabic) and heritage languages that have ceased to be mother tongues can all be recurringly transmitted to new generations. For this to be accomplished, these languages must have their clear and assured societal functions. Their intergroup boundaries as well as intragroup boundaries must be effectively regulated so that these functions will not be captured by other languages. Languages that have only within-school functions may nevertheless experience intergenerational continuity, particularly where the school is treated as a central social institution and safeguarded against unwanted outside influences. This is difficult to accomplish, particularly for minority ethnocultures that have failed to protect their inter- and intragroup boundaries before.

Notes to Chapter 7

1. During 1982–83, I was fortunate enough to be a Fellow of the Netherlands Institute for Advanced Study (Wassenaar). Since half of the fellows were Dutch and half drawn from various parts of the world, the working language of the Institute was English. As a result, it was usual for Dutch fellows to converse in English if non-Dutch fellows were present. Similar conventions have developed at various Dutch institutions of advanced research and education even when only Dutch nationals are involved. Notwithstanding these minor apparent exceptions to the above rule, the ultimate reference in such discussions remains the outer, non-Dutch scientific community.

References

FISHMAN, J. A. 1980a, Bilingualism and biculturism as individual and as societal phenomena. *Journal of Multilingual and Multicultural Development* 1, 3–15. Also, *This Volume*, part II.
— 1980b, Minority language maintenance and the ethnic mother tongue school. *Modern Language Journal* 64, 167–72.
— 1981, Language maintenance and ethnicity. *Canadian Review of Studies in Nationalism* 8, 229–48. Also, *This Volume*, part II.
— 1984, The particular trials and tribulations of small national languages. In A. GONZALES (ed.), *Sibayan Festschrift*. Manila: Linguistic society of the Philippines. Also, *This Volume*, part III.
FISHMAN, J. A. *et al.* 1984, *The Rise and Fall of the Ethnic Revival: Sociolinguistic Perspective on Language and Ethnicity*. Berlin:

Mouton.

MACNAMARA, J. 1971, Successes and failures in the movement for the restoration of Irish. In J. RUBIN & B. H. JERNUDD (eds), *Can Language be Planned?* Honolulu: University Press of Hawaii. 65–94.

8 The spread of English as a new perspective for the study of 'language maintenance and language shift'*

In the 1960s I first advanced the notion of 'language maintenance and language shift' (LMLS) as a pivotal topic for the sociolinguistic enterprise (Fishman, 1964).[1] Since that time the sociology of language has become a reality and the study of language maintenance and language shift has become one of its recognized topics, with very definite links to all of the theoretical as well as all of the applied ramifications of the parent field. Nevertheless, in all of this time, the perspective on language maintenance and language shift has remained the one from which I originally approached it: the minority language or the small national language faced by pressures related to a much bigger national or international language. Although considerable progress has been made from that vantage point, a different approach to LMLS, namely, one whose perspective is that of the more powerful (the waxing, the spreading) language — the spread of English, for example, might now provide further stimulus to this topic. Conversely, the sociology of English and other languages of wider communication (LWCs), a relatively new area of concentration within the sociology of language, might also now benefit by being examined within the context of such more general concerns as language maintenance and language shift.[2]

*Originally published in *Studies in Language Learning*, 1976, No.2, 59–104.

Habitual language use (at more than one point in time)

The volume in which this chapter was originally included brought together as much evidence as possible concerning the substantial, and apparently still growing, use made of English throughout the non-English mother-tongue world. Obviously, neither *where* nor *why* can be studied unless the issue of *whether* is fully explored. This issue, then, is the first and basic topic of the study of language maintenance and language shift, and it is itself divisible into considerations of *degree of bilingualism* (i.e. *how much* each language is employed) and *location of bilingualism* (i.e. in *what social contexts* each language is employed). At this juncture the second subdivision is more intriguing than the first, precisely because more sociolinguistic progress was needed, and had been made, in connection with it during the late 1960s and early 1970s.

Degree and location of bilingualism

In the mid-1960s the concept of 'bilingual balance' was at its zenith. It conceived of bilingualism in overall, global terms and proceeded, via various measures, to determine whether individual bilinguals were X dominant, Y dominant, or balanced. The measures employed were generally reflections of speed or automaticity of response and, presumably, context free. That language that was 'globally' stronger would, it was believed, issue forth more quickly, more effortlessly, more flawlessly.

The following decade witnessed the well-nigh complete abandonment of the global approach. Almost all measurement of degree of bilingualism today is sociofunctionally contextualized, i.e. measures of degree are still employed but with as much societal embeddedness as possible. Thus, were we to study any population today with respect to use of English, or were we to compare any two populations in this respect, our inquiry would immediately be in terms of how much English is spoken, heard, read, or written *in one context or another* (at home, in school, at work, in connection with government, etc.), rather than merely in terms of how much English is spoken, heard, read, or written. This certainly represents a sociolinguistic victory over earlier societally detached approaches.

Our concern for English as an additional language must particularly sensitize us to certain degree and location intersections. Additional languages are often more characterized by contextual specificity than are first languages; they may be more widely heard and read than spoken or written, i.e. they may be more frequently utilized on the level of comprehension than on that of production. Thus, more refined measures may be needed — measures that can not only make the above media and overtness *distinctions* but also focus upon particular combinations of degree and location of bilingualism with considerable precision.

Domains of language behavior

Not only is the principle of societal contextualization rather well established now insofar as the measurement of bilingualism is concerned, but the particular type of contextualization referred to as 'domain analysis' is also quite widely accepted. It has travelled the often rocky road from theoretical construct (Fishman, 1964) to operational and theoretical validation (Fishman, Cooper & Ma, 1971) and has been found useful in a great variety of discussions and research on bilingualism, far and beyond language maintenance and language shift alone (e.g. most recently, Clyne, 1976; Solé, 1975; Zirkel, 1974). Certainly the notion of institutional domain (and all of the lower level social interaction notions upon which it depends, particularly role relationship, topic, and situation) should be utilized in the study of English as an additional language. The phenomenological reality of major social institutions (family, education, government, work, religion, etc.) is a guide to the normative allocation of languages in within-group bilingual settings and probably in between-group bilingualism as well (since this is the locus of initial LWC spread).[3] Consciously or not (depending on more general factors related to level of awareness and sophistication relative to sociocultural norms), members of speech (-and-writing) communities utilize such major social institutions, and the situations most commonly pertaining to them, as guides for navigating through the unpredictable currents of interpersonal communication in bilingual settings. Certainly the researcher too must discover and then utilize these as well, whether in their macrolevel or in their microlevel realizations.

The same greater specificity that marks additional languages with respect to media and overtness variance undoubtedly also marks them with respect to domain variance. Whether they are disproportionately *absent* (other than *metaphorically*) in the family and religion domains (an *atypical* situation insofar as social phenomenology is concerned) and whether they are disproportionately *present* in the (higher) education, (technological) work, (imported) mass media and intergovernmental domains, our measures must be able to make these distinctions and then to reflect usage in the more crucial domains with sufficient precision to be able to capture changes in degree of usage over time. These would, of course, be desirable features for LMLS measures under *any* circumstances, but the sociofunctional imbalance of LWCs is often so great that the relevance of these desiderata becomes much clearer. Indeed, the typical domain distribution of additional languages may be so skewed that it may be instructive to compare LWCs in non-mother-tongue settings, not only in terms of the domains or patterns in which they predominate (e.g. technological higher education: reading), but also in terms of a measure of domain dispersion/concentration *per se*.[4]

Domain dispersion measures must be related to a particular population, of course, whether it be that of a network, a neighborhood, a city, or a nation. The sociolinguistic question that comes to the fore — once any socially contextualized measurement of language use is obtained — is whether it implies the absence or the presence of a speech (-and-writing) community in the technical sociolinguistic sense of situational variance predominating over demographic variance (Fishman, 1972b: 81–83). The full answer to this question is obviously not determinable from an analysis of language use data *per se*, but *without* rather sensitive language-use data the answer cannot be pursued at all.[5]

The dominance configuration

Our quest for a configurational recognition of bilingualism is part and parcel of our dissatisfaction with global designations or dominance, whether these be psychological (stronger/weaker), sociological (upper/lower) or otherwise. Configurational thinking has led us as far as dummy tables (whether with qualitative or quantitative entries) implying data on language use by media, overtness, domains, role-relations, etc. (Fishman, 1972b). For whatever reason, we have not passed beyond the dummy-table stage to the actual-table stage for anything resembling a complete configuration (see Tables 8.1 and 8.2, reproduced from Fishman, 1972b), although there have been a few approximations thereto in early research (e.g. Greenfield & Fishman, 1970). It may be that this is as it should be, or must be, since dummy tables are merely ambitious theoretical exercises and as such, they lack the substantive focus of all empirical research. On the other hand, it may be that something not only simpler but also more revealing, more intercomparable (across studies) is what is called for. Certainly, if pattern analysis were more advanced than it is as a data-analysis approach, some might prefer to develop LMLS configurational thinking in that direction. At the moment that does not appear to be very promising and has largely been abandoned, even in the area of personality/preference measurement from which it was derived. Perhaps it is better that we struggle with the demands of overambitious theory (to which we have now added the domain dispersion concept) than that we settle for premature and artificial mathematical parsimony.

Continuing issues in domain analysis

The limits of domain analysis must also be recognized. They come to the fore more evidently when dealing with actual samples of speech or when restricting one's self to a particular domain. Both of these foci of the study of interlingual variation are quite common and share an emphasis on the analysis of *social dynamics*, rather than on the analysis of *social location*, for which domain analysis was initially advanced. While it is not necessarily true that institutional domains are static constructs (since domain boundaries are neither obvious nor set), they are, nevertheless, normative, cognitive-affective orientations. As such, they must always be distinguished from interactional behavior *per se* and their precise relationship to such behavior must be studied as a separate issue.

TABLE 8.1 *Intra-group Yiddish-English maintenance and shift in the United States: 1940–70; summary comparisons for immigrant generation 'secularists' arriving prior to World War I (dummy table for dominance configuration, Table 8.2)*

Sources of Variance					
		Family role-rels.	*Neighb. role-rels.*	*Work role-rels.*	*Jew Rel./Cult. role-rels.*
Media	*Overtness*	*1 2 3*	*1 2*	*1 2 3*	*1 2*
Speaking	*Production*				
	Comprehension				
	Inner				
Reading	Production				
	Comprehension				
Writing	Production				
	Comprehension				

Source: Fishman, 1972b.

TABLE 8.2 *Part of 'dummy table' (Table 8.1) in greater detail*

Media	Overtness	Domains	Role-Relations	Summary Ratings 1940	Summary Ratings 1970
Speaking	Production	Family	Husband-Wife	Y	Y
			Parent-Child	Y	E
			Grandparent-Grandchild	—	E
			Other: same generation	Y	Y
			Other: younger generation	E	E
		Neighborhood	Friends	Y	E
			Acquaintances	Y	E
		Work	Employer-Employer	E	E
			Employer-Employee	E	E
			Employee-Employee	E	E
		Jewish Rel./Cult.	Supporter-Writer, Teacher, etc.	Y	Y
			Supporter-Supporter	Y	Y

Source: Fishman 1972b.

However, cognitive-affective norms along macroinstitutional lines are phenomenological guides to verbal behavior in bilingual settings. As such, they have a certain validity *vis-à-vis* behavior; as such, they can be differentially self-reported by members of speech communities; and, as such, they can be investigated and revealed by skillful investigators. However, as mentioned, often the investigator's interest is in subdomain dynamics rather than in domains *per se*. In that case, and that is very frequently the case when we are dealing with a corpus of texts derived from interactions in a particular domain, domain analysis *per se* is no longer at issue and no longer of particular interest (e.g. Scotton ms., Basso 1979).

Whether or not there is a Heisenberg indeterminacy phenomenon at play here, such that one cannot *simultaneously* study institutionalized domain location and subdomain interactional dynamics, it is still true that the two types of analyses must be interrelated if an exhaustive understanding is to be arrived at of the 'sociolinguistic economy' of any total speech community or speech network. Only such an exhaustive effort can reveal whether the dynamic factors that are documented for a particular domain, or for a given set of social relationships, also obtain for *all* domains. If they do, then domains *per se* are of clearly secondary importance (note Fishman, 1964[1966]: 438; Fishman, 1972b: 93). If they do *not* (i.e. if there are *domain-specific* role-relationships, situational places, situational times, network types, interaction types, etc.), then domains must be retained, precisely so that the societal location of different social dynamics can be indicated. Certainly, domains must also be defined if self-report data *does* reveal domain distinctions even if the sociodynamic analysis of texts does not. Finally, since many anthropologists, linguists, and ethnomethodologists are more inclined to study texts and their concomitant interactional behaviors whereas many sociologists and political scientists are more likely to study more macroscopic self-report data, the latter are far more likely than the former to find domain analysis necessary and useful. However, whether or not domain analysis is undertaken should not be the result of disciplinary considerations as much as it should flow from 'level of abstraction' considerations, 'kind of data' considerations, and ultimately from 'purpose of study' considerations.[6] It seems particularly likely that many studies of the spread of English as an additional language *will* find domain analysis useful, precisely because the presumed skewedness in locational use, skewedness in medium, and skewedness in overtness of use still remain to be documented.

Sociocultural processes relatable to LMLS

The first dozen years of work on LMLS recorded the bulk of progress, theoretical, methodological, and empirical, in connection with the first subsection of the field as a whole, namely, that concerned with measurement of habitual language use. If the next dozen years were to record similar progress in conjunction with the field's second major subsection, sociocultural processes leading to or inhibiting LMLS, then we would really have come a long way toward our basic goal. Unfortunately, this second step is far more difficult to take than the first, if only because it requires detailed understanding of social organization, social change, and social indicators, topics which are rather new and difficult for sociology as a whole. In the absence of such understanding, descriptive studies that proceed via ad hoc lists of social categories (generation, social class) and social agencies (press, church, radio, schools) will continue to be reported without adding at all to our systematic knowledge of LMLS in general or of LWC spread in particular.

Our two basic societal questions relative to the spread of English (or any LWC) can be put very easily: (a) Why is it that some non-English mother-tongue countries (or other political units of analysis) have witnessed greater utilization or acceptance of English over the past decade or two (e.g. China: Lehmann, 1975; Senegal: Senghor, 1975) than have others (e.g. Philippines, Tanzania)?, and (b) Why is it that the spread of English, wherever it *has* occurred abroad, has *not* resulted in the kind of massive mother-tongue replacement with which we are so familiar in immigrant settings in the U.S.A., Anglo-Canada and Australia? Although the first question is more basic for our purposes, both questions confront us with the need to find parameters that can clarify settings varying all the way from no language shift at all through to complete language shift, so that we can explain the relative absence of the former *vis-à-vis* English, as well as the well-nigh complete absence of the latter. Interestingly enough, there are very few indications of ideologized and organized opposition to English abroad for particular societal functions. Nevertheless, we do *not* have the impression that it is therefore 'merely a question of time, resources, and priorities' such that 'sooner or later, the entire world will have some control of English as an additional language.' In other words, it is not simply that all LWCs reach their functional limits — in part, because of competing spheres of interest with other LWCs — but that there may, in addition, be something about the particular auspices and processes through which English and other LWCs have been diffused during the past quarter century or so that sets these limits at a lower level than those formerly set for Latin, Arabic, and Spanish and even for French, Chinese, and Russian.

Generally speaking, social change theory is the weakest link of modern sociology, but there are, nevertheless, a few promising points at which to start in seeking to push closer to answering the questions posed. Some of these are discussed next.

Language, power, and resources

Spreading languages that are not being imposed by force[7] must provide (or promise to provide) entrée to scarce power and resources or there would be little reason for indigenous populations to adopt them for intergroup use, or, by extension, for certain subsequent intragroup use as well. Thus we must begin tracing the spread of a LWC to the power differentials with which its possession is associated. Obviously these differentials have their cognitive, affective, and overt behavioral counterparts (about which see the later section, 'Behavior Toward Language' pp. 249–52), but it is their objective distributional documentation that is being referred to here. Entrée to better positions, to useful specialized knowledge, to more effective tools, to more influential contacts (and thereby to control over human and material resources), to more desirable consumable goods, to more satisfying high-culture behaviors (and to their low-culture counterparts), or merely to the new and different in whatever domain, as long as that too is considered desirable — these are among the basic desiderata of intergroup contact and, therefore, of LWC spread as well.

We must begin with actual or assumed need for resources and power at any point of intergroup contact and with language as a possible key to a desired (re)distribution of such resources and power on an intragroup basis as well. In those settings in which either the myth or the reality of social mobility is widespread, bilingualism is repeatedly skewed in favor of the more powerful, with the language of greater power being acquired and used much more frequently than that of lesser power.[8] When the *same* language is the language of greater power (or power-sharing trends) in setting after setting, then we are dealing with a LWC and with a spreading LWC as well. In the case of English it is clear that two centuries of British and American colonial, commercial, industrial, scientific, and fiscal power have left a substantial legacy in higher education, government, trade, and technology. It is this legacy, in its domain and social-dynamic realizations, that needs to be investigated in all non-English mother-tongue settings that may be of interest in connection with the actual or possible spread of English.

The underlying concept is simple enough but it has rarely been fully documented. What is needed, in any setting, are hypotheses concerning the resources, privileges, and powers differentially related to knowledge and use of English (or any other LWC) and the cross-tabulation of such with degree and location of bilingualism involving English (or any other LWC). Such cross-tabulations should reveal stronger and weaker correlations, some that are more class or age dependent and some that are less so, and, all in all, provide excellent clues to the processes that are fostering the spread of English as well as to the mechanisms upon which these are dependent and the domains in which these are concentrated. Settings which hold no interest for mother-tongue speakers of English or for other (i.e. foreign) speakers of English as an additional language, and settings where the indigenous population has (or sees) little of rather tangible worth to gain by acquiring English, are likely to be settings that will lag behind others with respect to the spread of English. Languages are rarely acquired for their own sake. They are acquired as keys to other things that are desired. We must first identify and document what these are,[9] if only because such documentation will help us explain why, how, and among whom English as an additional language is or is not spreading.

The diffusion process

To have identified the sources or forces upon which the spread of English is dependent is one thing; to identify the processes via which the spread proceeds is another. Where English itself is an import (i.e. it is *not* accompanied by the massive presence of at least semifluent speakers of English from abroad, as often occurs in settings of tourism, student concentration, resource exploitation, military bases, etc.), then its spread is, of necessity, from the top down, i.e. from governmental, commercial, industrial, cultural, or other élites to the populace. This type of spread will often follow established patterns and channels of élite to mass influence, although, on occasion, special methods have been attempted in connection with language spread (e.g. 'going to the people' in pre-revolutionary literacy efforts of Russian *narodniki*, or resettlement and mixture of populations in Zionist Hebraization efforts). Cities have long been the focal points of organized propagation efforts (and, it must be noted, of organized resistance efforts as well). For language spread, schools have long been the major formal (organized) mechanisms involved, particularly for those considered to be of school age and school-worthy. Those who are beyond school age or who are not considered school-worthy[10] are sometimes also reached via special mechanisms (such as mass media, after-work educational programs, and vacation programs). Serious élitist efforts on behalf of an additional language often take on ideological overtones and involve an interlocking network of reward and communication options (e.g. those utilized in Canada in the mid-1960s to 'encourage' Anglos to learn French, those utilized until recently in Ireland on behalf of Irish, those used to encourage Spanish immersion for Anglos in the American Southwest). The efficacy of all these efforts, formal and informal, seems to vary considerably.

A number of possibly important considerations that have been mentioned so far should be reviewed before proceeding:

1. Diffusion as the ultimate or long-term context, even when an initial imposition stage obtains
2. Spread from the top (*gesunkenes Kulturgut*) rather than from the bottom (*gehobenes Primitivgut*): the determining role of élites
3. Urban focal points of spread (and of organized resistance thereto)
4. Normal propagation channels as well as special ones
5. Schools as major formal vehicle of additional language acquisition; post-school populations require special handling
6. Ongoing reward efforts, including access to power and resources
7. Efficacy determination (evaluation) and reformulation of program.

Of course, all of the preceding considerations must be viewed in the context of general resource availability, priorities in national development, countermovements from indigenous and external counter- (proto-) élites, reinforcement from other ongoing developments (e.g. transfer of populations, tourism, and political alignments), and general effectiveness of education and other large scale governmental operations. We still have no study encompassing all of these factors and viewing the acquisition of English as an additional language as a process which interacts with the major social, cultural, economic, and political processes of the national (let alone the international) context — not the least of which is the common need to foster *internal ethnic consolidation* via a national language which, in many cases, is also no more than an *additional* language. When viewed in the above light, the *relative* impotence of the school — certainly when it is denied vigorous societal support — becomes more obvious. Indeed, English is learned best when there are extraschool social forces abetting and rewarding its acquisition (Fishman, 1976b). Little wonder then that LWCs are not widely replacive of indigenous mother tongues (MTs), particularly if the stage of vigorous imposition is brief and relatively nondislocating of populations and their more normal social processes. The usual problem is learning them at all and maintaining, rather than containing, them.

Concomitant processes

Some of the processes accompanying efforts on behalf of English or other LWCs deserve a few words of separate attention.

The LWC setting versus the immigrant setting

For our purposes it is particularly instructive to note that the LWC setting (in which a powerful language enters into the social space of an established population) and the immigrant language setting (in which a normally powerless population enters into the social space of an established language) may well reveal appreciably different patterns in this connection. Whereas immigrant settings have been hypothesized regularly to go through the cycle of domain overlap (MT dominant), domain separateness, and domain overlap (OT dominant), the LWC spreading by diffusion among indigenous populations may commonly stabilize at the second stage. Certainly the history of language spread among indigenous populations (see, e.g. Tabouret-Keller, 1968, 1972; Lewis, 1971, 1972, 1976; Kahane, ms.) is far *less* marked by mother-tongue replacement and far *more* marked by the sociofunctional separation of languages than is the typical history of (im)migrant language settings (Hofman & Fisherman, 1971; Lewis; 1975). The lesser dislocation of indigenous populations attendant upon the spread of unimposed (or post-imposition) LWCs — (leaving intact a great deal of the indigenous family, community, government, religious, and cultural structures with their established authorities and mutually established responsibilities) — is certainly the decisive difference between the two settings. Indigenous populations have a firm base to hold on to while seeking the rewards that are (said to be) contingent upon the acquisition of an additional language; immigrant populations do not characteristically have any such base. (For an interesting exception, see Pryce, 1975.)

The reverse phenomena obtain but are rare. Immigrant 'language islands' *have* maintained themselves for centuries (usually on the basis of *primum mobile*: massive numbers and control of resources sufficient to firmly establish authoritative institutional structures of their own and, therefore, to regulate intergroup contacts). In such cases (e.g. German in parts of the U.S.A., French in Quebec, Chinese in Malaysia, and Tamil in Sri Lanka) their acquisition of the 'other tongue' (the national or bridging language) may well follow the LWC model rather than the typical immigrant language model. Similarly, a few nonimpositional LWC settings *have* resulted not only in mother-tongue *displacement* (from one domain or another) but in mother-tongue *replacement* as a whole (e.g. the very slow but steady Aramization, Hellenization, or Romanization of various populations in the classical world, as well as the Anglification and Francofication of indigenous European, African and Asian élites in the modern world). In such cases the reward system related to the initially additional language was sufficiently open, strong, and dislocative (often involving intermarriage, resettlement, and sociocultural change to an unusual degree, at least for certain select networks) that the resultant constellation may have been more similar to the usual immigrant case than to the usual unimposed LWC case.

Thus, the typical 'immigrant case' and the typical unimposed 'LWC case' are merely abbreviated labels for the extreme poles of sociocultural processes accompanying language maintenance and language shift. Mother-tongue replacement is an indication of a dislocated society undergoing other massive changes and unable to establish or maintain institutional protection for its MT (mother tongue). Such dislocation is less common under circumstances of the diffusion-based spread of LWCs. As a result, it is possible for the host society to control the propagation of LWCs in accord with its own designs, and these are frequently quite specific and restrictive. They may involve mother-tongue displacement from a few domains (even this may not be the case where the domains themselves and the LWC 'arrive together,' so to speak, as part and parcel of the same broader forces and tendencies), but certainly not its replacement in the most ethnically encumbered domains of family, religion, and other cultural preserves and value systems.

Ethnic and ideological encumberedness

Ethnicity — whether ideologized or not — is a strong bastion of immigrant languages, although rarely strong enough to withstand the onslaught of change. A diffusion-based LWC must also come to grips with the ethnicity values, sentiments, and overt behaviors of an indigenous population. These expressions of ethnicity are likely to be far better protected among indigenous populations than they are in the typical immigrant case and, in modern times in particular, they are likely to be explicitly related to the indigenous language(s). A spreading LWC can be viewed as a threat to indigenous ethnicity and to its symbolically elaborated structures. If the LWC itself is also ethnically or ideologically encumbered, it is more likely to be viewed as a threat (or actually to be so) than if the LWC is relatively unencumbered in the ethnic or ideological sphere (Fishman, 1976, see chap. 9). It is part of the relative good fortune of English as an additional language that neither its British nor its American fountainheads have been widely or deeply viewed in an ethnic or ideological context *for the past quarter century or so*.

To some extent this de-ethnicized (or minimally ethnicized) posture was also part of the earlier spread of Latin and Greek, and, to an even greater extent, of the even earlier spread of Akkadian and Aramaic. The obvious more recent contrasts are with Arabic, Russian, and Spanish, each of which were (and often still are) strongly associated with a particular nationality, religion, or ideology. English is, of course, identified by some with capitalism, colonialism, and bourgeois values, but it not as *uniquely* identified with any of them, nor as *strongly* identified with any of them (because of its competing association with democracy, individual liberty, civil rights, religious tolerance, for example) as is Arabic with Islam, Russian with Marxist communism, Chinese with Maoist communism, or as was Spanish with conquistador Catholicism. Indeed, in much of the Third World, and elsewhere as well, the image of English may well be ethnically and ideologically quite neutral, so that it may be related much more to appreciably generalized, de-ethnicized, and de-ideologized *process variables* (modernization, urbanization, technological know-how, consumerism, and a higher standard of living in general) than to any ethnicity or ideology viewed as particularly English or American. Furthermore, English as as additional language abroad often has a momentum that is hardly related to Anglo-Americandom (through the auspices of Dutch, Arab, Japanese, and various other non-Anglo-American English publications and broadcasting abroad). It would be interesting to determine whether this is recognized or not (see next section, 'Behavior toward Language') and whether views concerning ethnic and ideological encumberment do or do not effect the actual knowing, using, and liking of English as an additional language. At the level of élitist planning for (or against) LWC spread, the presence or absence of overt ethnic or ideological entanglement of the target language is obviously of importance and should also be examined in conjunction with the next section. At this point, however, it is germane to inquire whether there may not be certain stages in the sociocultural development of a host society when ethnic or ideological encumberedness is more of a handicap for the spread of a LWC than such encumberedness would be at other stages. Current theory points to host factors and contact factors as being just as important as are pre-contact factors in determining the outcome of any diffusion process (Schermerhorn, 1970). In line with these and other considerations it would seem reasonable to posit pre-ideologization and post-ideologization periods of easiest penetration for LWCs. Thus, either before or a good while after any host population has experienced its own intense and conscious ethnicization or ideologization (often coinciding with the early period of more focused urbanization, industrialization, modernization, and political integration efforts), it would be most likely to be more permeable by LWCs related to foreign ethnicity or ideology. During the white-heat period of indigenously organized ethnicity even ethnically and ideologically unencumbered LWCs may face difficulties. In line with these considerations English would probably be viewed most negatively today in Latin America, where its negative referents — imperialism, capitalism, exploitation, '*el coloso del norte*' — are highlighted not only by nationalisms but by the increasing pace of local economic growth (Solé, personal communication).

All in all, it would seem to be highly desirable to be alert to the current plethora of research on ethnicity (and the few attempts to conceptually integrate that research, e.g. Cohen, 1974; Glazer & Moynihan, 1975; Fishman, ms.) in our efforts to understand the variable acceptance and rejection of English and other LWCs.

Cross-polity and social indicators

Another approach to social change that merits our attention — and a relatively rigorous and quantitative approach to that — is the entire social indicator 'movement' that has come to the fore in the past decade (Sheldon & Moore, 1968; Fox, 1974; Sheldon & Parke, 1975). For the field of LWC study, the selective utilization of social indicators would make it unnecessary to construct and conceptualize *de novo* the large number of societal measures that have already been suggested and, indeed, operationalized by others. Measures (and accompanying theories) have been developed dealing with the allocation of time, quality of life in metropolitan areas, resource allocation in education, dimensionality of national goals at the small community level, interstate and international measures of social, political, and economic circumstances, and so forth.

In addition, the various cross-polity compendia (e.g. Banks & Textor, 1963; Russett *et al.*, 1964; Ernst, 1967; Kloss & McConnell, 1974; and others) are also good sources of operational and theoretical leads. All in all, I would urge careful consideration of 'piggy-back' possibilities such as these in conjunction with future LMLS research in general and research on the spread of English and other LWCs in particular. Since social change theory and research are among the fundamental bodies of societal knowledge and speculation with which LMLS and LWC research must be in contact, the cross-polity and social indicators fields currently strike me as being two potentially useful areas with which to stay in close touch.[11] Both of these approaches are 'good bets' for picking up early macro-sociological indicators pertaining to the socioeconomic and sociocultural processes that are most pertinent predictors of the spread of English (or any other LWC). Among the dimensions well worth monitoring in this respect are Anglo-American investments (though even Dutch, Japanese, and Arab investments are probably English-related in many countries with the exception of their own homelands), in view of the fact that English instruction (and perhaps other types of English use) is noticeably high in many countries in which such investments are also noticeably high (e.g. Mexico, Brazil, Peru) — notwithstanding the reversibility of these relationships in the course of growing cultural nationalism and related tendencies to impose indigenous controls on foreign investors.

The selection of indicators that complement each other across a range of sociocultural, socioeconomic, and related sociopsychological dimensions promises to be particularly rewarding (Land & Spilerman, 1975). The fact that development is not linear, and that its relationship to LM and LS is often reversed does not mean that properly executed studies (repeated at sufficient and appropriate intervals) cannot pick up changes that occur — in whatever direction.

Summary

In the early and mid 1960s, when I first attempted to organize the field of LMLS study, the idea of organizing an international LMLS file did not seem as impossible as it does today. Not only has the whole notion of culture and area files elicited far less interest in recent years than it did in the 1950s and before, but there are obviously too few workers in the LMLS and LWCs fields to handle the volume of data collection and processing that would be necessary in order to render such a file operative. Nevertheless, when viewed in connection with a particular LWC (English, French), the matter is far less discouraging. The materials accumulated in conjunction with this very project (see Conrad & Fishman, 1976) move us a little distance along the way toward providing what is needed. With a little continuous effort and support such a file could be kept current, could be transformed into more quantitative and accessible shape, and could be subjected to periodic analyses and interpretations.[12]

In review, before proceeding to the third and final broad topic area within the field of LMLS, the following concerns and sensitivities have come to the fore more clearly by virtue of considering concomitant sociocultural change processes from the vantage point of the spread of English and other LWCs.

1. The diffusion-based spread of LWCs to relatively undislocated indigenous populations is likely to be controlled by the élites of these populations rather than being entirely under the aegis of outside propagators. Such control (ideological and institutional) normally results in the stabilization of LWCs at a domain

separation stage (diglossia). Mother-tongue *displacement* among élites and other relatively favored population segments, rather than mother-tongue *replacement*, is thus the rule (in contrast with the typical pattern in the immigrant setting).

2. Ethnic and ideological encumberedness can pose problems for the spread of diffusion-based LWCs, particularly during those periods of sociocultural development when host societies are experiencing heightened ethno-ideological concerns of their own.

3. Social indicator theory/research and cross-polity files are two promising approaches to documenting the spread of LWCs in general and of English in particular.

During the late 1960s and early 1970s there had been only slight progress in systematizing knowledge of the social processes that facilitate or inhibit LMLS. LWC perspective on this topic is valuable, providing, as it does, sensitivies and hypotheses that cannot be derived as readily from work on immigrant and minority settings alone. Nevertheless, much still remains to be done, not only in conjunction with LMLS but also in conjunction with the basic fields in sociology upon which LMLS study must depend.

Behavior toward language

This entire area of concern not only appears to be much more important to current researchers, but also strikes them as more understandable and systematizable than I would have predicted (but not more than I would have hoped for) in the mid-1960s. I suspect that the turning point for many American students was the burgeoning of scholarship on (and scholarly involvement in) *language planning*, particularly with respect to its policy formulation, linguistic codification, linguistic elaboration, and overall evaluation stages. The undeniable evidence and experience gained with languages that were being fostered (or curbed) and consciously altered (rather than merely liked or disliked) made the entire area of behavior toward language come alive far more than could my own attempts to portray it and my urgings that it be given attention in the 1960s. I hope that this momentum can now be transferred to the consideration of behavior toward language in contexts of LMLS in general and of LWC spread in particular. There is some evidence that this is being done (e.g. Cooper, 1975a).

Affective behaviors: A component of the attitudinal constellation

The late 1960s and early 1970s witnessed considerable progress in the entire language-attitude area (e.g. Agheyisi & Fishman, 1970; Fishman, 1969; Fasold & Shuy, 1973; Cooper, 1974, 1975b; Lewis, 1975) — much of it in the context of LMLS and LWC study. Since the state of general theory and methodology relative to language attitudes is so much more advanced than it was then, the time has come to focus the systematic views and methods that have been developed more squarely upon the substantive issues of concern to us here.

Several investigators have recognized the need to distinguish between (and then to try to relate) affect toward particular *languages* and affect toward the *speakers* of these languages. This can only be done if study designs are adopted that do not confound these two dimensions (as sociolinguistically uninformed researchers in the 1960s confounded them). This distinction would seem to be particularly apropos to English, in view of the growing body of simultaneous impressions that 'everyone is trying to learn it,' that 'no one particularly likes it,' and at the very same time, that 'Americans are less popular than they were a quarter century ago.' Actually, we have little enough data on the first component of this trio and practically none at all on the remaining two in relation to the first.

If it were to prove true that there is little affect toward English (of the kind lavished upon MTs but upon few LWCs, French being a noteworthy modern exception) it would still be desirable to find out which features of the language 'are considered attractive or unattractive, proper or improper, distinctive or commonplace' by various populations, including judgements of 'beautiful' or 'ugly,' 'musical' or harsh' relative to other languages, be they MTs or LWCs (Fishman, 1964). However, given the generally low affective profile that is assumed to obtain for English, it may well be necessary for all of our affective measures that pertain to it to be even more sensitive and subtle than would otherwise have to be the case. It is obviously more difficult to differentiate between sub-areas of low (or no) affective intensity than between sub-areas of high intensity.

The general relationship between learning, using, and *liking* English has been found to be low (Fishman, 1976a; Cooper & Fishman, 1976 as well as in other studies, for example, Riley, 1975). This compounds the dilemma that we reported in the 1960s *vis-à-vis* vicarious immigrant languages in the U.S.A. and in Australia, many of which were *liked* (by their former users and their children and grandchildren) but *not used*. In the case of English, we may be witnessing the complementary occurrence:

a language being *used* but *not* much *liked*. Certainly this needs to be much better documented than it is at the moment, as do the interrelationships between affect toward English and attitudes (including affects, cognitions, and overt behaviors) toward modernization, language consciousness, national consciousness, and other aspects of sociocultural tension and change. Obviously, languages are not liked or disliked in a vacuum, but rather liked or disliked as symbolic of values, of peoples, of ideologies, of behaviors. It is the symbolic nature of English and affect with respect to its associations that we must seek to explore more widely. A beginning in this direction has been made by Spina (1974).

Cognitive behaviors: Knowledge and beliefs

We have accomplished far less with respect to what people *know* and *believe* about English than we have with how they *feel* about it. Not only has the ethnic and ideological encumberedness (or lack thereof) of English not been studied, but even the dimensions of language feeling, belief, and action posited 20 years ago by Stewart (1968) have remained largely unstudied. (These dimensions are vitality, historicity, autonomy, and standardization.) Less systematically interrelated parameters of knowledge and belief have also been ignored — utility of the language in social advance (i.e. the necessity for learning English in order to qualify for particular positions or privileges), perceived difficulty of the language 'globally' as well as in terms of related-unrelatedness to the first language, growth or decline in number of local speakers, specific features of recognized similarity/dissimilarity of the language relative to own MT, national language or other LWC among others. The entire cognitive response to language has gone largely unrecognized with respect to English (see, however, parts of Riley, 1975). Perhaps highlighting the distinction between the affective and the cognitive components of language attitude will result in as much attention being devoted to the latter as to the former. The current imbalance between the two — or, alternatively, the current tendency to make no distinction between them and, therefore, constantly to study the one confounded with the other — is much to be regretted.[13]

Overt behavior toward language

The final component of the attitudinal constellation is overt behavior, the obvious heartland of the entire topic of 'behavior toward language.' It represents an area waiting for explorers, all the more so since many of its dimensions have now been anticipated. The area of status planning with respect to English remains unexplored in most settings in which English *is* already a widely available additional language (e.g. Scandinavia, the Near East, West Africa, India, Southeast Asia, Oceania). It is even all the more unexplored in settings in which no such availability is possible or desirable. The same is true with respect to corpus planning *vis-à-vis* similarity/dissimilarity between the national integrating language and English.[14] We are certainly ignorant with respect to commitment-readiness on behalf of English (Fishman, 1969), although some populations have gone to considerable pains to enable their children to have access to it (e.g. 'New Canadians' in Quebec) and although the impression remains that there is 'no love lost' on behalf of English. Certainly English is put to considerable use by many of the major foes of American and British capitalism in order to spread their own counter philosophies among nonnative users (readers, understanders) of English (see particularly, Lehmann, 1975 for evidence of Chinese preparation to use English abroad in order to spread the doctrine of Mao).

Notwithstanding the relatively neutralized ethnic and ideological image of English it still seems to be true (both from IRPLPP data [Fishman, 1974] as well as from our own) that English is considered to be more acceptable for technology and natural science use than for political and social science use, and that it is least acceptable of all for local humanistic and religious purposes. The same progression might also obtain for any foreign language — LWC or not — but the differences in acceptability for these various uses might be less in the case of English than for ethnically or ideologically more encumbered LWCs. Similarly, younger populations (indigenous 'nationals' *not* minority group members) seem less resistant to English (whether affectively or overtly) than were their parents and teachers during their own adolescent years (Fishman, 1974, 1976a). This may be an aspect of their lesser general ideological involvement relative to that of their elders, as well as a reflection of the generally lower level of nationalism throughout the world today in comparison to the 1875–1950 period. If all of the foregoing could be documented — and a small international documentation center could do so over a period of years — the topic of overt behavior toward English would come into its own and, simultaneously, so would the study of the spread of English relative to other LWCs.

Summary and conclusions

A new look at LMLS reveals several promising developments and changes in this field, not only since 1964 but even since 1972. Certainly, a new look at LMLS from the point of view of spreading LWCs in general, and from the point of view of the spread of English as an additional language in particular, prompts a number of hypotheses or emphases that might not otherwise come to the fore.

All in all, it appears that most progress has been made in conjunction with the measurement of habitual language use, and the least in conjunction with sociocultural change processes. Intermediate between these two is the progress made in conjunction with behavior toward language. Apparently, the more societally embedded a topic has been, the less progress there has been in connection with it; conversely, the more language-focused the topic, the more progress there has been. In part, this relationship reflects the greater precision of scholarly work with language as a result of the more highly systematic nature of language and language behavior. The social sciences in general and sociology in particular simply have not reached the same level of precise and systematic analysis, in part because they are focused upon behavior which is simultaneously more complex and less systematic than language or language use *per se*. The discrepancy between these two parent fields, from which LMLS (and all of the sociology of language) must derive its basic theories and methods, is reflected in the discrepancies between one subtopic and the other within the area of LMLS itself.

As far as the spread of English and other LWCs is concerned the following points have come to the fore.

With respect to habitual use

1. Since additional languages, including LWCs are often marked by great contextual specificity, more refined measures are required — measures than can focus upon particular combinations of *degree* and *location* of bilingualism with considerable precision.
2. In view of the greater contextual specificity that seems to mark LWC use, future dominance configurations might well benefit from a measure of skewedness or of domain dispersion/concentration. Such a measure would be useful in comparing configurations across networks within the same or similar communities.
3. Domain location, social dynamics, and conversational interaction each represent worthwhile and interrelatable levels of analysis for the study of LMLS.

With respect to sociocultural change relatable to LMLS

4. The distinction between the military imposition of LWCs or their
   diffusion, on the one hand, and the distinction between their
   spread from the top downward or from the bottom upward, on the
   other hand, are crucially related to the rate and degree of LWC
   spread, as well as to the mechanisms of spread most likely to be
   involved.
5. During the past quarter century or so, the spread of English has
   usually been via diffusion. Its spread has most commonly
   proceeded from the top downward and has depended upon real
   or hoped for entrée to governmental, technological and industrial,
   commercial, or modern cultural rewards. Its spread has depended
   not only upon schooling but also upon special channels pertaining
   to the above institutional domain-related substantive fields and
   their associated social behaviors.
6. The indigenously controlled spread of LWCs among relatively
   undislocated populations commonly stabilizes in the pattern of
   domain separation (diglossia) and mother-tongue displacement
   (rather than replacement) among élitist and relatively favored
   population segments. The continued spread of English as an
   additional language, outside of initially élitist networks, is dependent on the more widespread availability of the rewards (real
   or imaginary) with which *it* is associated as compared to the
   availability of rewards associated with its national or international
   competitors.

With respect to behavior toward language

7. The spread of English is currently apparently accompanied by
   relatively little affect — whether negative or positive — and by
   correspondingly meager American and British ethnic or ideological connotations. The staying power of LWCs may derive from
   ethnic neutrality every bit as much as the staying power of minority
   languages may derive from ethnic relatedness.
8. On the whole, English as an additional language is more learned
   than used and more used than liked. The three (learning, using,
   and liking) are little related to each other.
9. Consistent exploration of this area, in conjunction with the
   sociolinguistic parameters of institutional domains, social behaviors, and conversational interactions, may help to clarify it
   further as well as relate it more fully to the other topics of LWC
   study.

   In attempting to conceptualize the spread of English from the point
of view of LMLS more generally, as well as in relation to the spread of
other LWCs in particular, it also becomes clear that the possibilities for
inter-LWC language planning at an international level have been all too
ignored both in research and in policy. Intrastate LWC planning has
proven possible both in Canada and in India. More such planning at an
international level, involving both trade-offs and co-operation, may yet
prove to be feasible and advantageous to all concerned.

Acknowledgements

   The author is grateful to Andrew Cohen, Andrew Conrad, Robert L.
Cooper, Vladimir Nahirny, Jonathan Pool, and Carol Scotton for their
helpful comments on an earlier draft of this paper.

Notes to Chapter 8

1. This paper assumes that the reader is familiar with at least one of the three
   versions of my original paper (Fishman, 1964[1966], 1972b [in Spanish: 1974]),
   although its major points can be followed without such familiarity by those
   familiar with the language maintenance and language shift field *per se*.
2. Our basic concern in this chapter is with *the sociology of English as an
   additional language* in all countries, but particularly in countries where English
   is the mother tongue of a minority of the population. Most of our comments
   will be focused directly upon this concern. Nevertheless, other languages such
   as Russian, French, Arabic, Chinese, and Swahili, that are also widely used
   today as second languages, as well as Akkadian, Aramaic, Greek, and Latin,
   that were once so used, will also be referred to for purposes of greater
   cross-national and diachronic perspective. Although further specification is
   possible, an LWC will be defined simply, to begin with, as any language widely
   used as a second or additional language, thus subsuming, for the time being,
   international languages, lingua francas, vehicular languages, contact
   languages, and other intergroup communication varieties (such as Hausa,
   Lingala, Pidgin English).
3. When LMLS is pursued from the point of view of the
   threatened/minority/smaller language in an intergroup context, it is necessarily
   its *intragroup* maintenance that is the focus of attention and the spread of the
   intrusive language is also monitored relative to the same intragroup base.
   However, when LMLS is pursued from the point of view of the more powerful
   language, *intergroup bilingualism* must be studied first and only then can the
   question of new intragroup functions for the spreading LWC be examined.
   Thus, the study of LWCs represents a two-way broadening of concern, from
   a primarily intragroup orientation to a more balanced concern for both
   intergroup and intragroup bilingualism, and from a primarily maintenance

orientation to a more balanced concern for both maintenance and shift. Finally, note that the domains of intergroup use of LWCs may well be indicative of the first domains of intragroup use of a spreading LWC (at least nonmetaphorically).

4. This suggestion is not to be interpreted as implying that a universal set of domains be sought or utilized. Such a universal set would doubtlessly render more commensurable the dispersion measures obtained from various settings in which English (or another LWC) is an additional language, but spurious commensurability is worthless elegance. The domains utilized must have local validity from within. They must be tentatively derived and then confirmed or revised on the basis of internal evidence of various kinds. In any speech-and-writing community of interest to us there will be not only language use variance due to the within-group use of English but also variance due to such use of (varieties of) the mother tongue and, possibly, of other languages as well. Such variances in language use must be carefully examined in initially positing and ultimately validating domains and in computing dispersion indices for the various languages and varieties (including English) that are employed by particular networks.

5. At this point in my original treatment(s) of LMLS I discussed the compound/co-ordinate distinction which has fallen somewhat into disuse and it is to be doubted whether better language-use data can revive it. While it is still a heuristically appealing distinction, its neuropsychological base has not been nearly as certain as was originally thought to be the case. At this very writing, psychoneurological interest in bilingualism is again growing and new evidence has again been adduced to the effect that the languages utilized by bilinguals are differently processed (Kaplan & Tenhoutten, 1975). This new evidence is not yet unambiguous with respect to the compound/co-ordinate distinction but, rather, merely implies such evidence might be forthcoming. At any rate, the attitudinal-phenomenological and the sociofunctional validity of the distinction may be quite substantial, regardless of its neurological status.

    The above-mentioned appeal of the distinction is based upon its commensurabililty with the *extremes* of social contextualization and its absence. It is not a distinction that can assist us directly in measuring degree or location of bilingualism, but, rather, one that may help further enrich the location consideration, in view of the different stages of English use that may obtain in any setting in which it is an additional language. As such, we will return to it in the next section ('Sociocultural Processes Relatable to LMLS').

6. There is, of course, a finer-grained level of analysis that may well be related to sociodynamic analysis, just as the latter is to domain analysis. I have in mind the explication of a *particular* interaction, an exercise to which ethnomethodologists and symbolic anthropologists are so inclined. I do not rule the latter type of analysis out of the total sociolinguistic enterprise. Indeed, I believe that such analyses provide many worthwhile clues for more generalized social dynamics analyses, just as the latter, in turn, provide vital clues insofar as domain location and verification are concerned. In this light, Table 8.2 could also have a sub-table contributing to it, detailing the social behavioral dimensions of, e.g. family or work interaction alone. Furthermore, there could be still finer-grained tables contributing to that sub-table, and so forth.

    Finally, it is in conjunction with a dynamic model of the use of English as an additional language — one that is concerned with the recurring situational and interactional implementation of normative expectations — that the metaphorical or meta-communicational use of English would be reported. A bit of English — and sometimes more than a bit — creeps into mother-tongue conversations, both among those who know more than a bit of English and those who do not know any more than that — for purposes of emphasis, humor, sarcasm, status-stressing, leg-pulling, rank-pulling, etc. Such use of English is not always due to circumstances similar to those that govern the use of English terminology when the mother tongue still lacks a handy term for referents in the world of technology or other 'Western wisdom.' Metaphorical phrases are typically motivationally contrastive or connotative rather than referentially denotative. They point to the speaker, to his/her relationship to the interlocutor, to their temporary withdrawal from the 'conventions of speaking' that normally obtain between co-members of a speech community. Under such circumstances English is often employed, just as French or German were in a former generation, to imply rather than to specify, even though perfectly good mother-tongue phraseology is available to all concerned and would be handled with facility. Nevertheless, English is used precisely because it is *not* what is normatively expected and because doing so *does* italicize a snatch of conversation and more clearly mark it as special in the speaker's intent and, it is hoped, in the hearer's interpretation as well.

7. 'The question of whether a given language is imposed by force is an objective, as well as a subjective, one. Even if a language is not believed by its promoters or by its targets to be imposed, it may in fact be imposed. But the whole voluntarism-coercion debate tends to be metaphorical, if not metaphysical . . . There are substantial forces pushing for English across state boundaries, and these are accompanied by laws within many countries that make English a compulsory subject of instruction in compulsory schools, and by professional recruitment patterns that make a knowledge of English a prerequisite to many kinds of advancement. If this be voluntarism . . .' (Jonathan Pool, personal communication).

   All of the dimensions mentioned by Pool deserve to be retained for study, viz. the objective/subjective distinction *vis-à-vis* imposition, the advocate's phenomenology versus the target's phenomenology with respect to imposition, and finally, the distinction between armed intervention or enforcement and the more ordinary compulsion of social life with its legal and normative pressures. However, it is my view that this very complexity (i.e. the multiplicity of forces within any notion of force) makes the topic of imposition a multidimensional continuum worth retaining rather than dispensing with. In this chapter, wherever gradations are not explicitly mentioned, the term 'imposition' implies the use of obvious military force and not the reliance upon nonmilitary means of compulsion (the laws and conventions to which Pool perceptively refers). (Note my use of the term 'diffusion' which is here employed to refer to a *type* of spread rather than to spreading *per se*.)

   The military, the police, and the secret service are ubiquitously in the background, as we have all come to realize in the past decade, often as part of the conventions of everyday social life. However, their background rather than foreground presence, their invisibility rather than visibility in social processes, may be a useful primitive indicator of whether imposition is in effect. Of course imposition may fade into 'diffusion via regular channels,' and of course participants, observers, and analysts may differ about when or whether direct imposition has ended. Considerations such as these, as mentioned earlier, are eminently worthy of study.

As for voluntarism, I do not see how it can be utilized as a variable in social research. Its societally patterned manifestations must be studied in relation to societal structures, societal functions, societal values, and societal symbols. (Also see Ravetz, 1971.)

8. 'The direction of language-acquisition is not always in favor of the language of higher socioeconomic status when a lingua franca is needed. Note use of Swahili in East Africa and Pidgin in West Africa. The 'big' man learns the low status language; the 'little' man doesn't have to learn English . . . Explanation exists on a more abstract level than demographic variables' (Carol Scotton, personal communication). (Also see Scotton, 1972, 1975, 1976.)

The above observation is doubtlessly of value, in that it serves to correct an unconscious view as to the availability of social mobility, both as a motive and as a reality, which is quite widespread among American and other Western investigators. Nevertheless, it must also be realized that it pertains to a very small proportion of the contact conditions involving English or other LWCs today. With decolonization and modernization, the 'big man' has not disappeared (nor even been replaced by a local counterpart) as much as acquired a rather large corps of active associates at various levels of government, economy, and education. This associative role, often accompanied by all of the accoutrements of political, economic, and cultural independence, does foster the widespread myth (see 'tunnel effect' discussion in note 9) — even if not the equally widespread reality — of social mobility opportunity. Western largesse is increasingly funneled through nationals rather than through outsiders. These nationals, as co-gatekeepers, are the initial locus and constant wellspring of LWC spread, as long as power-sharing and resource-sharing processes, pretenses, and aspirations continue. For internal counterprocesses, see the next section, 'The Diffusion Process.'

9. Again, the foregoing is not to say that all those among whom English may be spreading will actually gain access to the power or resources with which English is associated. Indeed, there may be considerable discrepancy between aspiration and achievement in this respect. However, the fact that the relationship between English and resources does hold for some (or even for most) may long have a strong motivating effect even upon those for whom it does not (yet) hold. For a discussion of this possibility, in terms of general economic development, see Hirschman (1973). Hirschman calls this phenomenon of delayable and indefinite gratification 'the tunnel effect' and points to its greater applicability in societies marked by still traditional extended-family responsibilities, relative ethnic homogeneity and avowedly earned status. He points out, however, that the tunnel effect (i.e. imagining that one is about to see the light at the end of the tunnel) cannot last indefinitely. To the extent that the acquisition of an additional language is dependent upon institutionalized (rather than function-oriented) instruction, it may well become stabilized for far longer periods than the economic behaviors to which the tunnel effect initially applies.

There are, of course, contexts in which indigenous élites seek to limit both the spread of their own ethnic mother tongues as well as the spread of outside LWCs associated with Western power and resources development and, instead, foster the spread of a third option associated with neither (e.g. Swahili). Note, however, that these élites themselves do increasingly acquire English (or another international and interregional LWC), that their position is often motivated or rationalized in terms of supra-ethnic authenticity integration, and, finally, that their ability to sustain their initial position will depend on political factors ultimately linked to power sharing and to social mobility for wider segments of their national societies. Both ideological and resource links to the outside world need to be considered in this connection.

10. The economic development literature contains many cost-benefit studies comparing, among other things, the costs of educating students (short term), the benefit of their increased productivity (long term), and their decreased productivity during the very time that they are in the classroom or literacy program (short term). It is to such considerations, as well as to others mentioned by Thorburn (1971) and Jernudd (1971), rather than to more obviously ideological or academic ones, that I am referring with the term 'school-worthy.'

11. When writing on LMLS in the 1960s I was fortunate enough to relate this topic to Schermerhorn's theoretical model of intergroup relations which was then at a very early stage (1963[1964]) of its development. Subsequently it struck the fancy of Verdoodt (1968) and later, after it was developed into book-length dimensions, it also proved to be of interest to Paulston (1975). On the whole however, Schermerhorn's model has proved to be too complex, too qualitative, and too immigrant/host related (and, perhaps, too focused upon minority groups in the American sense) to be of widespread interest to sociolinguistic researchers in general or to LMLS students in particular.

12. It is regrettable that the International Center for Bilingualism Research has not been able to keep such files for monitoring the fortunes of French as a LWC and that the Center for Applied Linguistics has not been able to do so for English. Both Centers have been able to keep exhaustive country files, but these need to be combed and integrated at fixed intervals — across countries as well as for international agencies and for such functions as trade and diplomacy — if LWC information is to be derived from them.

13. A good example of cognitive (and affective) response to English is cited by Levenson (1971) in his discussion of Chinese 'bourgeois cosmopolitanism' in the 1920s: 'And what was more cosmopolitan, anyway, than to be a French, not an English translator? The relative eclipse of France in the twentieth century, except in culture, made French the language of the purest cultural sophisticate; English speakers were more likely and more than likely, to be just gross utilitarian lackeys, serving imperialist business and politics, not Shakespeare' (p.25). Various national (and international, e.g. Esperantist) literatures would yield a rich harvest of quotations that could not only be treated as data but also help generate hypotheses and empirical-data-gathering instruments.

14. It is likely that English is recognized as lexically richer than most other LWCs today in connection with high status roles pertaining to technology, industry, commerce, finance, weaponry, etc. This makes English a useful model in corpus planning, whether this is consciously recognized as such or is masked under the label of internationalisms and translation loans. However it also gives English lexical items a power that is greater than the ability of corpus planners to control (Fainbert, 1974). Indeed, these may diffuse via *gehobenes*

primitivgut routes, from below, rather than being at all dependent on élitist populations, institutions, or mechanisms. As a result, the foreign-markedness of Englishisms may be appreciably briefer than that of other foreignisms that are more dependent on trickling down from above.

References

AGHEYISI, R. & FISHMAN, J. A. 1970, Language attitude studies. *Anthropological Linguistics* 12:137–57.

BANKS, A. S. & TEXTOR, R. B. 1963, *A Cross-Policy Survey*. Cambridge, Mass.: MIT Press.

BASSO, K. H. 1979, *Portraits of 'The Whiteman': Linguistic Play and Cultural Symbols amongst Western Apache*. Cambridge: Cambridge University Press.

CLYNE, M. 1977, Nieuw-Hollands or Double-Dutch. *Dutch Studies* 3, 1–20.

COHEN, A. (ed.) 1974, *Urban Ethnicity*. London: Tavistock.

CONRAD, A. & FISHMAN, J. A. 1976, (Chap 11) *Studies in Language Learning* No. 2.

COOPER, R. L. 1974, Language attitudes I. *International Journal of the Sociology of Language* 3: entire issue.

— 1975a, Sociolinguistic surveys: The state of the art. *Conference Proceedings: International Conference on the Methodology of Sociolinguistic Surveys*. Arlington, Virginia: Center for Applied Linguistics.

— 1975b, Language attitudes II. *International Journal of the Sociology of Language* 6: entire issue.

ERNST, M. L. 1967. *The Comparative International Almanac*. New York: Macmillan.

FAINBERG, Y. A. 1974, Official Hebrew terms for parts of the car. *International Journal of the Sociology of Language* 1:67–94.

FASOLD, R. W. & SHUY, R. 1973, *Language Attitudes: Current Trends and Prospects*. Washington, D.C.: Georgetown University Press.

FISHMAN, J. A. Recent research and theory concerning ethnicity: concepts and findings. Ms.

— 1964, Language maintenance and language shift as a field of inquiry. *Linguistics* 9:32–70. Revised in *Language Loyalty in the United States*. The Hague: Mouton, 1966.

— 1969, Bilingual attitudes and behaviors. *Language Sciences* 5:5–11.

— 1972a, *The Sociology of Language: An Interdisciplinary Social Science Approach to Language in Society*. Rowley, Mass.: Newbury House.

— 1972b, Language maintenance and language shift as a field of inquiry: revisited. In his *Language in Sociocultural Change*. Stanford: Stanford

University Press. 76–134. In Spanish, in *Estudios de Etnolingüística y Sociolingüística*, edited by P. GARVIN & Y. LASTRA, Mexico City: Universidat Nacional, 1974.

— 1974, The comparative dimensionality and predictability of attitudinal and usage responses to selected centralized language planning activities. *Proceedings* (of the Association Internationale de Linguistique Appliquee, Third Congress, 1972), edited by Albert Verdoodt. Vol. 2. Heidelberg: Julius Gross. Pp. 71–80.

— 1976a, (Chap 13) *Studies in Language Learning* No. 2.

— 1976b, *Bilingual Education: An International Sociological Perspective*. Rowley, Mass.: Newbury House.

FISHMAN, J. A., COOPER, R. L., MA, R. *et al.* 1971, *Bilingualism in the Barrio*. Language Sciences Monograph No. 7. Bloomington: Indiana University.

FOX, K. A. 1974, *Social Indicators and Social Theory: Elements of an Operational System*. New York: Wiley.

GLAZER, N. & MOYNIHAN, D. P. (eds) 1975, *Ethnicity: Theory and Experience*. Cambridge: Harvard University Press.

GREENFIELD, L. & FISHMAN, J. A. 1970, Situational measures of normative views in relation to person, place and topic among Puerto Rican bilinguals. *Anthropos* 65: 602–18.

HIRSCHMAN, A. O. 1973, The changing tolerance for income inequality in the course of economic development. *Quarterly Journal of Economics* 87: 544–66.

HOFMAN, J. E. & FISHERMAN, H. 1971, Language shift and maintenance in Israel. *International Migration Review* 5:204–26.

JERNUDD, B. H. 1971, Notes on economic analysis for solving language problems. In J. RUBIN & B. H. JERNUDD (eds), *Can Language be Planned*? Honolulu: University Press of Hawaii. Pp. 263–76.

KAPLAN, C. D. & TENHOUTTEN, W. D. 1975, Neurolinguistic sociology. *Sociolinguistics Newsletter* 6(2): 4–9.

KAHANE, H. 1975, The rise and spread of the Lingua Franca in the medieval Mediterranean world. *Proceedings of a Conference on Bilingualism and Applied Linguistics*. Champaign-Urbana, University of Illinois. Ms.

KLOSS, H. & MCCONNELL, G. D. 1974, *Linguistic Composition of the Nations of World: I. Central and Western South Asia*. Quebec City: Laval University Press.

LAND, K. C. & SPILERMAN, S. (eds) 1975, *Social Indicator Models*, New York: Russell Sage.

LEHMANN, W. P. (ed.) 1975, *Language and Linguistics in the People's Republic of China*. Austin: University of Texas Press.

LEVENSON, J. R. 1971, *Revolution and Cosmopolitanism*. Berkeley: University of California Press.

LEWIS, E. G. 1971, Migration and language in the USSR. *International Migration Review* 5:147–79.

— 1972, *Multilingualism in the Soviet Union*. The Hague: Mouton.

— 1975, Attitude to language among bilingual children and adults in Wales. *International Journal of the Sociology of Language* 4:103–26.

— 1976, Bilingualism and bilingual education: The ancient world to the Renaissance. In J. A. FISHMAN, *Bilingual Education*. Rowley, Mass.: Newbury House.

LIEBERSON, S. 1970, *Language and Ethnic Relations in Canada*. New York: Wiley.

PAULSTON, C. B. 1975, Questions concerning bilingual education. (Note: Provisional title.) In *Proceedings of the 1974 InterAmerican Conference on Bilingual Education*. Arlington, Virginia: Center for Applied Linguistics.

PRYCE, W. T. R. 1975, Industrialism, urbanization and the maintenance of cultural areas: North East Wales in the mid-nineteenth century. *The Welsh History Review* 7 (3):307–40.

RAVETZ, J. R. 1971, *Scientific Knowledge and its Social Problems*. Oxford: Clarendon.

RILEY, G. A. 1975, Language loyalty and ethnocentrism in the Guamanian speech community. *Anthropological Linguistics* 17:286–92.

RUSSETT, B. M. *et al.* 1964, *World Handbook of Political and Social Indicators*. New Haven: Yale University Press.

SCHERMERHORN, R. A. 1964, Toward a general theory of minority groups. Paper presented at the annual meeting of the American Anthropological Association, November 21, 1963, San Francisco, California. Published: *Phylon* 25: (1964).

— 1970, *Comparative Ethnic Relations: A Framework for Theory and Research*. New York: Random House.

SCOTTON, C. M. A proposal to study language choices. Ms.

— 1972, *Choosing a Lingua Franca in an African Capital*. Edmonton, Alberta: Linguistic Research.

— 1975, Multilingualism in Lagos — what it means to the social scientist. *Sixth Annual African Linguistics Conference, Ohio State Working Papers in Linguistics* No. 19, 78–90.

— 1976, Language in East Africa: Linguistic patterns and political ideologies. In J. A. FISHMAN (ed.), *Advances in the Study of Societal Multilingualism*. The Hague: Mouton.

SENGHOR, L. S. 1975, The essence of language: English and French. *Cultures* 2(2):75–98.

SHELDON, E. B. & MOORE, W. E. (eds) 1968, *Indicators of Social Change: Concepts and Measurements*. New York: Russell Sage.

SHELDON, E. B. & PARKE, R. 1975, Social indicators. *Science* 188 (no. 4189, May 16, 1975):693–99.

SOLÉ, Y. R. 1975, Language maintenance and language shift among Mexican American college students, *Journal of the Linguistic Association of the Southwest* 1:22–48.

SPINA, J. M. 1974, Adolescent attachment to Canada and commitment to a national community. Ms.

STEWART, W. A. 1968, A sociolinguistic typology for describing national multilingualism. In J. A. FISHMAN (ed.), *Readings in the Sociology of Language*. The Hague: Mouton. Pp. 531–45.

TABOURET-KELLER, A. 1968, Sociological factors of language maintenance and language shift: A methodological approach based on European and African examples. In J. A. FISHMAN et al. (eds), *Language Problems of Developing Nations*. New York: Wiley. Pp. 107–18.

— 1972, A contribution to the sociological study of language maintenance and language shift. In J. A. FISHMAN (ed.), *Advances in the Sociology of Language* Vol. 2. The Hague: Mouton. Pp. 365–76.

THORBURN, T. 1971, Cost-benefit analysis in language planning. In J. RUBIN & B. H. JERNUDD (eds), *Can Language be Planned?* Honolulu: University Press of Hawaii. Pp. 253–62.

VERDOODT, A. 1968, *Zweisprachige Nachbarn*. Vienna: Braunmüller.

— 1971, The differential impact of immigrant French speakers on indigenous German speakers: A case study in the light of two theories. *International Migration Review* 5:138–46.

ZIRKEL, P. A. 1974, A method for determining and depicting language dominance. *TESOL Quarterly* 8:7–16.

SECTION 3:
The ethnic dimension in language planning

Some sort of language planning, i.e. consciously organized, authoritative efforts to allocate resources (rewards and sanctions) in connection with language, has probably always gone on. This seems a reasonable assumption, since collectives have always engaged in language choices *vis-à-vis* themselves or language policies *vis-à-vis* their neighbors or the minority populations in their own midst. Every ancient society of which we have any knowledge reveals a repertoire of functionally differentiated languages or language varieties, and as a result, children had to be socialized (and adults, guided, reminded or 'assisted') to acquire and to utilize the varieties and languages that authorities considered appropriate for specific functions. Sociolinguists often take the repertoire of any speech community as a 'given' and do not pause to inquire how it was arrived at. If we are to judge by any aggregates of which we have knowledge today, it must be concluded that the allocation of varieties/languages to functions was rarely arrived at without dissent, on the one hand, and without the imposition of authoritative reinforcement, on the other, and it is in the 'working out' of dissent and in the imposition of reinforcements that language consciousness and true language planning come into being.

It is particularly in connection with the 'status planning' of written functions, and, therefore, of languages that are to be most closely related to and preferred for such statusful domains as government, religion and education, that language planning is first and most obviously apparent from the historical or semi-historical record. It is in this light that we must view Ahasuerus' announcement of his decision to depose Vashti and to seek a new Queen by sending letters 'into every province according to the writing thereof and to every people after their language' (Book of Esther, 1:22). More recent status planning, unfortunately, has been far less pluralistic and has called into play considerations of relative ethnic

advantage and disadvantage. Access to government, religion and education are valuable societal commodities and, as such, it should come as no
surprise if they are not really made universally available, even under
regimes that claim such universality as a purported value.

Even where all languages are considered equal before the law, 'some
languages are more equal than others', perhaps inevitably so, in the
'determining text' of the law and in its interpretation and enforcement. It
is equally inevitable, therefore, as modernization and language consciousness both increase in a multilingual/multicultural world and in
multilingual/multicultural nations, that the link between language status
planning and ethnicity will increase rather than decrease. Language status
planning becomes a means of assuring social control and social ascendency
for those ethnically related interests that are already in power, just as it
becomes a desideratum for those ethnically related interests that seek to
increase their power or at least to gain sufficient control over their own
lives to assure their intergenerational ethnocultural continuity. This
process of contested status planning is recognizable at the level of major
world powers, such as the United States or the U.S.S.R., at the level of
more minor powers such as Spain or the Philippines, and at the level of
non-state-forming minorities, such as Frisians or Maoris, as long as they
are still capable of engaging in concerted language status planning.

Recent efforts in the U.S.A. to provide English with the status of
'official' governmental language, both at the federal and state levels, are
clearly status-planning attempts that are related to fears, probably
unfounded, that the ethnic composition of the country is changing in ways
that would endanger the power position of the Anglo and Anglified
mainstream. The charges of divisiveness, aimed at minority language
groups in general and at Hispanics in particular, only thinly mask the
middle-class insecurities that have fueled the increasingly conservative
tenor of American public life during the past decade. The fact that there is
no hint of functional danger to the unifying (even though unofficial) and
mobility-providing role of English in American life is of relatively little
consequence in the face of irrational fear, weakly disguised prejudice and
uninformed hostility, all of which lead to the wrong solution to (and to the
exacerbation of) the real economic and social problems which characterize
inter-ethnic reality in the U.S.A. The 'English official' efforts merely come
as the capstone to more long-term tendencies to downgrade foreign
language learning, to emasculate bilingual education and to consider
minority language maintenance as beyond the pale of the national interest
in human resources protection and cultivation. Mainstreams, whether in the
U.S.A. or in the U.S.S.R. and whether in the capitalist or in the Communist

worlds more generally, exhibit every bit as much of the ethnic irrationality *vis-à-vis* language and language planning as these very same mainstreams are wont to ascribe to the minorities in their own midst and elsewhere in the world.

The process of regional (as distinct from central, polity-wide) language status planning in Spain and in the Philippines is also an ethnically involved one, just as it frequently is in Canada, France, Belgium, India, Malaysia, China and elsewhere. This is not to say that language *per se* is really an independent factor in either civil strife or in the processes effecting gross national product, for, as we will see in Section 4, below, such is not the case, but that language everywhere becomes symbolically intertwined with ethnic interests and differentials, whether at the polity or at the regional levels. Indeed, smaller national languages are doubly threatened, once by their relative insignificance on the world scene (evidenced by the small and often decreasing number of foreign diplomats and businessmen that 'bother' to learn these languages, favoring, instead, one or another 'world language' even when pursuing goals that obviously require the co-operation and agreement of authorities in the middle-range countries *per se*) and, secondly, by the regional languages within their own realms whose advocates continue to campaign for recognition and cultivation at the sub-national level of their particular languages and, in doing so, seek for themselves various functions that have heretofore been solely discharged by the national language. As long as minority claims are still weak, the goals of their advocates are often for 'freedom of choice' and 'cultural democracy'; however, the urge for local supremacy, at least in one or another domain that is symbolic of statusful modernity, cannot be long denied, particularly as economic and political grievances seek their cultural and symbolic counterparts.

Another step downward in the ethno-symbolic scale is reached when we consider the status planning needs of demographically dispersed and numerically small minorities, whether immigrant or indigenous (but particularly so if immigrant). If and when the stage of ethnic consciousness is reached, due to the efforts of current or past intelligentsias, the thrust toward status planning is inescapable, even if governmental recognition is not seriously at issue. Local school use and local mass-media (print and non-print) use, often on a voluntary basis, where and when a sufficient 'demand' is evident, is all that is advocated. Nevertheless, even such goals are problematic. On the one hand, such functions have hitherto been discharged by the national/official language and the powers that stand behind such languages are disinclined toward time-sharing and power-sharing, particularly when claimed by the few and the weak. On the other hand, there is a serious question as to whether rushing into the secondary societal domains, particularly above and beyond the elementary school and the lower work-sphere, is really more constructive than dislocative. Before the primary domains of the home, neighborhood/friendship and religious functions are 'nailed down', is there any conceivable benefit from focusing on the more exposed secondary domains (higher education, mass-media, higher work-sphere) in which different ethnic establishments compete with one another and in which the reward potential of the most powerful is particularly likely to triumph, thereby re-ethnifying and re-linguifying those whose mobility strivings it encompasses?

Thus, at every stage and at every level of language planning, we find an involvement with ethnicity, and in language corpus planning no less than in language status planning. Modern language consciousness requires modern corpus planning in order to cope with the expression of modernity itself, at least at the level of everyday life, and to do so from one's own (rather than only from an outside) ethnocultural point of departure. However, corpus planning requires an image, a model of 'the good language', and such an image itself is likely to be ethnically suffused. Indigenousness, authenticity, purity, autonomy — these are all ethnically marked directions in corpus planning, seeking to distance the linguistic expression of modernization from ideologically proscribed 'contamination', similarity or dependency *vis-à-vis* historically counter-indicated languages and their ethno-national support-systems. Orthography and lexicon, writing system and grammar, number system and phonology, all contribute to the image of 'the good language' and all are susceptible (differentially susceptible, to be sure) to ethnocultural considerations and to ethnocultural strictures in conjunction with corpus planning.

Both ethnicity and language pervade most of social life and it is inevitable, therefore, that ethnicity will also influence the direction of modern language planning, the latter being merely one aspect of modern culture planning and identity planning. It is precisely because modernity is such a magnet, such a danger to the overt-behavioral, emotional, intellectual and identificational indigenousness of current social integration, that the ethnic component of language planning has become, if anything, greater and less permissive than it was in centuries past. The weak and the late want to catch up with the strong and the early, but, like the strong and the early, they also want to be themselves and to determine what that means, in language as well as in as many other ethnocultural arenas as they consider crucial. The claims of the strong and the early that such efforts are destructive of civility, rationality and progress might appear more tenable if they were less obviously self-serving.

9 Language and nationalism: Two integrative essays*

Part II: The impact of nationalism on language and language planning[1]

'. . . when the minde is fraught with matter to deliuer, it is still in pain vntill it haue deliuered, and therefor to haue the deliuerie such, as maie discharge the thing well, and content all parties, both by whom and to whom the matter is deliuered, it seketh both home helps, where theie be sufficient, and significant, and where the own home yeildeth nothing at all, or not pithie enough, it craueth help of that tung, from whence it receiued the matter of deliuerie. Hence commeth it that we haue our tung commonlie both stored and enlarged with our neighbours speches, and the old learned tungs.'

Richard Mulcaster, *The First Part of the Elementarie*, 1582.

'. . . Charlemagne enriched his native tongue, which was Teutonic, by reducing it to rules, composing its grammar, and naming all the months and winds in that language.'

François Eudes de Mézeray, in his *Abrégé chronologique, ou Extraits de l'Histoire de France*, 1676.

'. . . As literature and politeness gain ground in a nation, and according to the duration of their reign, they extend their influence in the language, the commonality in such times acquiring the knowledge of several expressions invented by the learned . . .'

Johann David Michaelis, in his *Commentationes*, 1774.

'. . . By what Hands, and what way Improvements in Language are capable of being effected or promoted: Individual and simple Practice, individual Instruction, free Association, governmental Authority.'

Jeremy Bentham, in his 'Essay on Language' 1820.

*Originally published in ¦Language and ¦Nationalism,¦ 1972, Rowley, Mass.: Newbury House.

'. . . If Welsh had been developed as German had been developed during the past 100 years by some of the greatest men who had ever lived . . . Welsh today would have been looked upon as one of the most perfect languages on the face of the earth.'

Father Hayde of Cardiff, 1837.

'. . . The want of modern scientific words in Irish is undeniable . . . [but] once Irish were recognized as a language to be learned as much as French or Italian our dictionaries would fill up and our vocabularies ramify, to suit all the wants of life and conversation.'

Thomas Davies, 1845.

The vernacular as the medium of nationalism

The lingering hostility of American social science scholarship (as well as of much of Western social science scholarship more generally) toward nationalism has also been transferred to the role of the vernacular in nationalist movements. Although this scholarship has produced numerous observations to the effect that a common vernacular is, in itself, insufficient *cause* for sociocultural or political-operational integration, and, although there are similarly many observations that both kinds of integration *have* come to pass without the presence of a common vernacular, both of these observations tend to miss a major point that needs to be examined. Such observations are more concerned with proving or disproving the validity of nationalist ideology (or of a particular nationalist ideology) concerning the crucial role and the superior quality of the vernacular (or of a particular vernacular) than they are with clarifying *why such views have so frequently come to be held and to be held so fiercely and by so many.*

It is not at all necessary to take a position with respect to the absolute necessity of a common vernacular for the formation of broader integrative or affiliative bonds to recognize that nationalist movements have very commonly utilized and championed vernaculars in order to attain their particular broader integrating and authenticating goals. Indeed, it is not even necessary to claim that nationalism was particularly unique among modernization movements in this respect. Humanism, the Renaissance, and the Reformation — all of them being European intellectual movements whose populist and nonuniversalist facets became apparent far before the advent of mass nationalism — all utilized and prized the vernaculars for reasons somewhat similar to one large cluster of reasons that also obtained in the subsequent case of nationalism itself.[2] Thus, vernacular emphases, purely as a *functional* matter, began in the West 'with the decline of supranational and theoretically universal cultural elements such as the founding of all Western education on a thorough and often exclusive training in the classical languages, the role of French as the language of diplomacy and international relations,' and, in the East, with the decline of 'erudition [solely] in [classical] Arabic in all Islamic countries, [and] the exclusive use of classical Chinese as the literary language until Hu Shih's language revolution in 1917' (Kohn, 1968: 65). Even the classical Western European empires recognized and utilized the local vernaculars for communication and control on a mass basis. Thus Barrow indicates that 'native languages flourished in the Roman Empire' and that 'St. Augustine, as Bishop of Hippo, found it necessary to engage priests who knew Punic, and this though Africa had been a province for centuries' (Barrow, 1949: 115–16). Therefore, as in many other respects, nationalism's *utilization* of the vernacular is not so much a clear break or departure relative to earlier periods as much as is the intensity with which it pursued this utilization and, in particular, its rationalization thereof.

The functional dependence of new proto-élites on the vernaculars was a reflection of the need of these élites to communicate with, organize, and activate recently urbanized but still predominantly illiterate populations. Less obvious is the fact that these populations often had neither a single vernacular (but, rather, a socially, regionally, and experientially differentiated *continuum of vernaculars*), nor a vernacular that could readily be put to the modern ideologizing and organizing purposes that new proto-élites had in mind. Even less obvious is the fact that many would-be élites themselves did not know the vernacular that had to be utilized if their goals were to be attained. The sociocultural alienation of the aristocratic and bourgeois leadership of the prenationalist period had produced an imposing array of discontinuities between the masses and those normally expected (and expecting) to be their leaders. The early and mid-seventeenth century Irish chronicler Conell MaGeoghagan laments that 'because they cannot enjoy that respect and gaine by their said profession as heretofore they and their ancestors receaved, they set naught by said knowledge ... and choose rather to put their children to learne English than their native language' (cited by Ó Cuív, 1969: 2). Two hundred years later we encounter the same lament not only in nationalist writing of awakened proto-élites of Western European minorities (e.g. 'We have no royal, princely nor aristocratic families among us to influence our customs. The few rich ones who live in the country are strangers to the people as regards language, and foreigners in respect to religion'

[Southall, 1893: 250]) but in similar writings throughout Central, Eastern and Southern Europe as well. By the end of that century the linguistic re-ethnification of new proto-élites was far advanced throughout formerly 'nonhistoric' Europe.[3] A rather similar process has more recently been evident in African and Asian nationalist movements (e.g. 'Just how powerful this feeling is may be seen in the number of English-educated Chinese [in South East Asia] who are now furtively and hurriedly learning the Chinese language' [Purcell, 1953: 243]), although South Asian élites in particular had commonly combined their earlier personal modernization with continual allegiance to intact or restructured regional great traditions. The proto-élitist conversion comes prior to mass nationalist mobilization. The former also has more than a tinge of *mea culpa* to it.

The re-ethnification of proto-élites is no less an authentification experience for the fact that it served personal and class interests.

'Had the mineral wealth of the principality been discovered by the natives, and could it have been properly put to use before they were subdued to English rule, they might have preserved their language and been the foremost among British subjects in wealth, manufacture and arts' (H.L. Spring, *Lady Cambria,* 1867; cited by D.G. Jones, 1950: 113–14).

How much more appropriate then that this wealth be returned to the nationality to which it rightfully belonged by self-proclaimed guardians who not only appreciated this wealth but the language as well. The control of the one legitimized the control of the other. Indigenization of the language, at the very least, was 'a great stirring up [that] portended no one knew exactly what; meanwhile it was a useful lever for doing many desirable things' (a paraphrase of the views of the Irish nationalist leader Moran; McCartney, 1967: 48), including, of course, 'excluding from their jobs the old bourgeoisie and substituting for them new men' (Meillet, 1928: 52), men who identified with the people, who were increasingly of the people, and, therefore, genuinely deserving of their stewardship. For all of these reasons nationalist proto-élites have been much more than 'theoretically' interested in the vernacular, as well as in language learning *per se.* For prospective proto-élites the vernacular was (and is) very much an instrument of power — for themselves and for the people.[4]

Whereas vernacular literacy and vernacular education had begun to gain ground slowly in Europe prior to the appearance of mass nationalism, the latter was crucially dependent on both, particularly in an age when the mass media included neither radio nor television but only the popular lecture or the printed word in one form or another. The coming of vernacular education (often by means of illegal schools[5]) and the introduction of vernacular literacy often brought very dramatic consequences in their wake.[6] As one who lived through such a period recounted: '. . . the older peasants called themselves Masurians and their speech Masurian. They lived their own life forming a wholly separate group and caring nothing for the nation. I myself did not know that I was a Pole till I began to read books and papers, and I fancy that other villagers came to be aware of their national attachment in much the same way' (Slomka, 1941, cited by Kedourie, 1961: 120). Obviously, the reading of books and papers referred to was possible on a mass basis only in the vernacular. Such reading among the previously illiterate not only forged a new bond with language, an awareness of language as part of a rebirth of self and of assertive self consciousness, but it also put proto-élites into touch with masses whom they would otherwise hardly have reached and never have influenced. The crucial functional role of vernacular education for the arousal and maintenance of nationalism leads Gellner to conclude that 'modern loyalties are centered on political units whose boundaries are defined by the language . . . of an educational system' (1964: 163).[7]

The vernaculars were functionally favored not merely by élites seeking to unify and to activate the masses, but by the very processes of urbanization and modernization of which nationalism in developing nations is so often a part and which new élites sought and seek to harness for specific substantive purposes. Industrial urban life is dependent upon widespread literacy (which normally means vernacular literacy) and/or on vernacular mass media in order to train and co-ordinate its skilled labor force. However, modernization involves not only literacy-dependent economic changes and the co-ordination of intricate literacy-dependent economic roles, but also secure political-operational consolidation which, as several recent observers have pointed out, is based upon the attainment and maintenance of mass consensus.[8] Even those nations following the state-nation pattern toward nationality formation are often dependent upon vernacular literacy, if not upon vernacular education, in order to secure the modern political-operational stability and participation without which ultimate socio-cultural integration cannot come to pass. Thus, nationalist theoreticians need not be suspected of either conscious or unconscious self-aggrandizement when they stressed the need to recognize, utilize, standardize, and modernize the vernaculars. Some saw it simply as a military necessity ('How were recruits to be instructed if they did not understand the language of their leaders? How were orders to be rapidly transmitted to these immense moving bodies of men? Above all, how was moral cohesion between them to be attained?' [Delaise, 1927:

172]). Others saw it as an invaluable tool for the spread of nationalist ideologies in the light of which nationalism itself was merely a first stage (Dadrian, 1967: 32). Most recognized that it not only had 'identitive integrating power' (Etzioni, 1965), but that such power was *useful*, all the more so because its broad boundaries were vague and manipulable.

The instrumental dependence of unificatory nationalism on the vernacular is, therefore, not greatly different from that of other modern mass movements, whatever their political or economic coloration. Thus, it is particularly in connection with the authenticity emphases of nationalism that its more unique interrelationship with the vernacular becomes manifest. Modern mass nationalism goes beyond the objective, instrumental identification of community with language (i.e. with communication)[9] to the identification of authenticity with a *particular* language which is experientially unique and, therefore, functional in a way that other languages cannot match, namely, in safeguarding the sentimental and behavioral links between the speech community of today and its (real or imaginary) counterparts yesterday and in antiquity. *This* function of language tends to be overlooked by other mass modernization movements and *its* utility tends to be ignored by them. Nationalism stresses this function, a deeply subjective function, as a *summum bonum*, and demonstrates decisively that 'the rational and the romantic are not wholly alternative or antagonistic but are at least in some measure, complementary ... The romantic form is essential to the solution of the problem of identity, for *its* content can only be categorical' (Binder, 1964: 136).

Language as [part of] the message of nationalism

Although there are pitifully few studies that focus on a vernacular as a substantive (rather than as a functional) hub of nationalism, the view that a people's individuality resides in its language is very old. One ingredient of the holy trinity (holy people, holy land, holy language), language has been regarded as a defining characteristic of a nationality, within the sphere of the Judeo-Christian tradition, since Biblical days. It is this context of *potential* sanctity that so long preserved vernaculars in the West (as well as in the East) as *potential* symbols, until more recent times when they actually became overwhelmingly powerful symbols and causes[10] (e.g. 'An Arab is a person whose mother tongue is Arabic, who has lived or who looks forward to living on Arab soil, and who believes in being a member of the Arab nation.' Article 10 of the Constitution of the Socialist Arab Resurrection Party [Ba'th] cited by Sharabi, 1966: 96).

For our purposes it is necessary to differentiate between the question of whether language is *indeed* a necessary and sufficient criterion of nationality and the question of whether such has been the view of modern nationalist movements. While both questions have received very little social science attention (notwithstanding Snyder's claim that 'All major works on nationalism stress in detail the significance of language' [1954: 20]), the first has generally been answered in the negative and the latter in the affirmative.[11] It is to the latter question alone that we will direct our attention in the hope that an attempt to illuminate it will also help us understand *why* 'the criterion of nationality' has so frequently been found 'in the shibboleth of language' (Toynbee, *A Study of History*, VII, p. 536) and *why* nationalism so often 'generates a new kind of political community occupied with a common cultural heritage, especially in terms of language' (Friedrich, 1963: 559).

Language as the link with the glorious past

One of the major motivational emphases of modern nationalism has been that the ethnic past must not be lost for within it could be found both the link to greatness as well as the substance of greatness itself. It was on both of these accounts that 'the mother tongue became almost sacred, the mysterious vehicle of all the national endeavors' (Jaszi, 1929: 262), particularly for those whose current greatness was far from obvious. For the 'peoples without history,' history and language were two sides of the same coin. The vernacular was not merely the highroad *to* history, it was *itself* 'the voice of years that are gone; they roll before me with all their deeds' (from Macpherson, 1760, cited by Hayes, 1937: 16). It was felt that 'in its mother tongue every people honors itself; in the treasury of its speech is contained the charter of its cultural history' (Ludwig Jahn, cited by Rocker 1937: 295). As a result 'a language [and] a history' were viewed as twins since together they constituted 'the two first needs of a people . . . There is not a new nation in Europe which has not been preceded by from fifty to eighty years of philology and archeological studies' (Etienne Fournol, *Les Nations Romantiques*, Paris, 1931: 206; cited by Sulzbach, 1943: 24). Little wonder then that linguists were, on occasion, 'compared to surgeons who restore to its natural function a limb which had been almost paralyzed but not severed from the national body' (Kahn, 1950: 157).

Lest it seem that only the 'upstart' nationalities of Central, Eastern, and Southern Europe viewed their vernaculars as direct bonds with historical glory (and, therefore, with either the reality or the potentiality for current glory), it should be pointed out that the historic nations too were not averse to such views. Michelet, in mid-nineteenth century, held that 'in this [French] is continued the grand human movement [so clearly marked out by the languages] from India to Greece and to Rome, and from Rome to us' [1864] 1946: 240 while the first stirrings of Pan-Indian nationalism produced claims that 'Sanscrit was the most enduring monument of the past greatness of the country and was destined to act as one of the most powerful agents in India's future regeneration' (McCully, 1940: 255). As for Arab thinkers in the latter part of the nineteenth century, 'the "great days of their past" were not just, as in the West, the flowering of a vaguely related culture — the way that Greece and Rome were vaguely related to Britain and France — but were directly related to the men of this period linguisticaly, religiously, and, as the Arabs loved to emphasize, by ties of kinship' (Polk, 1970: xiii). The heirs of past greatness deserve to be great again. The heirs of triumphant unity in the past must themselves be united in the present and future. The heirs of past independence cannot but be independent again. The purported continuity of the language was the authenticating device for finding, claiming and utilizing one's inheritance.

Language as the link with authenticity

Directly, via the language per se

History consists of names and dates and places but the essence of a nationality is something which is merely implied or adumbrated by such details. This essence exists over and above dynasties and centuries and boundaries; this essence is that which constitutes the *heart* of the nationality and which leads to its greatness; the essence of a nationality is its spirit, its individuality, its soul. This soul is not only reflected and protected by the mother tongue but, in a sense, *the mother tongue is itself an aspect of the soul*, a part of the soul, if not the soul made manifest.[12] The major figure in placing language squarely at the emotional and intellectual center of modern nationalism's concern for authenticity was doubtlessly Johann Gottfried Herder (1744–1803). Although he was himself influenced by others (particularly by the works of Vico, e.g. *The New Science*, 1725) in developing his views, as well as associated with others in propagating them (e.g. Fichte), the phrases, concepts and emphases that have cropped up again and again during the past two centuries, throughout the world, wherever vernaculars are defended or admired, tend to be his. His writing was seminal in developing the complementary views that the mother tongue expressed a nationality's soul or spirit, that since it was a collective achievement *par excellence*, language was also the surest way for individuals to safeguard (or recover) the authenticity they had inherited from their ancestors as well as to hand it on to generations yet unborn, and, finally, that worldwide diversity in language and in culture was a good and beautiful thing in and of itself, whereas imitation led to corruption and stagnation.[13] The Slavs openly recognized him as the fountainhead of Slavic nationalist thought. Consciously or unconsciously his words have been repeated by those who claimed that 'without Finnish we are not Finns' (Wuorinen, 1931: 62) or that 'the role of Arabic in the life history of the Arabs . . . is [to be] the register of their creativeness, a symbol of their unity, and an expression of their mental and artistic aptitudes' (Nuseibeh, 1956: 69) or that 'Our language, the expression of our people, which can never be given up . . . is the spiritual foundation of our existence' (Catalonian Cultural Committee, 1924: 13).[14]

The contrastive position of 'Germany' *vis-à-vis* its insultingly proud Romance neighbors to the west and its hopelessly crude Slavic neighbors to the east may have contributed to the Herderian view that languages were huge natural divides. Perhaps personal preoccupation with the literary, standard language was also contributory to the view that the boundaries between languages were more fundamental, lasting, clear, and implicational than political boundaries, religious boundaries, or other behavioral systems. Politically, religiously, and behaviorally Germany was even more fractionated than the Slavic east! Only language implied an ideal genotypic unity that could counteract the phenotypic horrors of the day. From the very first a distinction of the langue-parole type permitted Herder and other language nationalists both to have their cake and to eat it too: to champion an ideal norm and to create it at the same time.

Both the exact nature of the nationality-and-language link, and the strength of this link, have been argued by seemingly dispassionate social commentators and social scientists on the one hand and by proudly passionate nationalist writers and activists on the other. The views of these two types of participant observers are typically and predictably different. In the first case we find doubt if not derision. The 'requiredness' of the link, i.e. the view that it is unquestionable and given-in-nature, is obviously questioned by those who consider that social conventions have social rather than supernatural or species-wide bases. Thus, Pfaff states that 'considerations of language, history or geography are valuable, to justify what one already believes, but they do not necessarily lead to that belief' (1970: 159). Sapir is more charitable. He admits that 'a particular language tends to become the fitting expression of a self-conscious nationality' but adds that 'such a group will construct for itself ... a race to which is to be attributed the mystic power of creating a language and a culture as twin expressions of its psychic peculiarities' (1942 [1933]: 660), i.e. the link is ultimately man-made but ascribed to supernatural forces in order to hallow it. Such a thorough student of nationalism as Lemberg is more critical however. He considers the imputed link to have been put to uses which reverse the natural order of things. In discussing the early fifteenth-century Hussite revolt he observes 'Hier war das Umgekehrte dessen eingetreten ... Nicht ein Staat hatte seine Bewohner zur Nation gebildet, sondern ein durch Sprache abgegrenztes Volk hatte sich an einer sozialen und *religiosen* Revolution die es als seine Sendung auffasste, zur Nation geformt und hatte den über seiner Grenzen hinausreichenden Staat erobert' (Lemberg, 1964, vol.I: 108–09).

Between the foregoing views (essentially that nationalisms tend to find or inflate the symbols that they require in language as in other respects) and those of most involved nationalists there is a huge chasm. Between the two major positions only few adopt the view that language has *become* symbolic and as such *should* be preserved, cultivated, protected, and advanced. Such moderate views were more common in premodern settings (e.g. 'Methinks the nations should make their language triumphant also, and all the more because there are Laws against it. For why should a free people retain any marks of slavery?' Robert Huntington, Provost of Trinity College [Dublin], 1686; cited by Ó Cuśv, 1969: 2), but are still sometimes encountered (e.g. 'Are we not able to rise above our sectional interest and local patriotism and adopt as our national language the mother tongue of Dr. José Rizal, our greatest hero and martyr, who ardently wished that some day we should speak one language,' Rojo, 1937: 60; or 'Remember, you have a national language of your own. Use it [Malay] when you are together,' Abdul Rahman cited by Miller, 1959: 47). What is striking about such views is, on the one hand, their awareness of language as a prime and fitting group symbol, and, on the other hand, of the need for organized human intercessation on its behalf.

The view that language and nationality are inextricably and naturally linked also begins in a low key. When St. Stephen's crown was offered to Ferdinand of Austria (1527), in order to strengthen Hungary's resistance against the Turks, the new ruler pledged 'Nationem et linguam vestrum servare non perdere intendimus' (cited by Dominian, 1917: 154). Spenser, in his *View of Ireland*, indicates the naturalness of the link by a single phrase: 'So that the speech being Irish the heart must needs be Irish' (cited by Flannery, 1896, title page), as does a Welsh writer of the same period ('Our tongue cannot be learned by a stranger; its fire burns only in a native breast,' cited by Southall, 1893: 212).

With the coming of modern mass nationalism the entire relationship is not only more urgent but more demanding as well. What was hitherto often enough viewed as a natural link is now also a cause, a goal, and obligation. 'Without its own language,' Herder wrote, 'a Volk is an absurdity (*Unding*), a contradiction in terms' (vol. I, p.147; cited by Barnard, 1965: 57). As a result 'Die Sprache ist nicht des Menschen wegen da, sondern dieser hat die Pflicht die als nationales Idol zu ehren . . . Die Sprache hat Rechte; der Mensch hat keine' (Koppelman, 1956: 93). From modern Germany this emphasis spreads its way throughout Europe. In Ireland, Davies writes (in English) precisely what Herder might have written:

'To impose another language on . . . a people is to send their history adrift . . . to tear their identity from all places . . . To lose your native tongue, and learn that of an alien, is the worst badge of conquest — it is the chain on the soul. To have lost entirely the national language is death; the fetter has worn through . . . Nothing can make us believe that it is natural . . . for the Irish to speak the speech of the alien, the invader, the Sasanoch tyrant, and to abandon the language of our kings and Heroes . . . No! oh, no! the 'brighter day shall surely come' and the green flag shall wave on our towers and the sweet old language be heard once more in college, mart and senate' (Davies, 1945 [1845]: 73).

How natural then that the slogan of the times became 'Ireland, not free only but Gaelic as well; not Gaelic only but free as well!' (Beckett, 1966: 417).

Language equals nationality and nationality equals language; the slogan finally reverberates far beyond its initially European boundaries. 'A land qualifies as part of the Arab patrimony if the daily speech of its inhabitants is the Arabic language' (Izzeddin, 1953: 1) is essentially a modern European view of the matter (indeed Chejne claims that 'It was at the insistence of Christians and Westernized Muslims that the language took on a new dimension and became a secular symbol of a national creed as embodied in the concept of 'urūbah (Arabism);' 1969: 172), as is the view that 'it is because of our language that the Senhalese race has existed for 2400 years' (from a debate in the Ceylonese State Council 1944, cited by Kearney, 1967: 748).

However, the inseparability for the God-given link between language and nationality is not the most that can be claimed. Such a claim might well be advanced for other desiderata as well. The ideological pinnacle of language nationalism is not reached until language is clearly pictured as *more* crucial than the other symbols and expressions of nationality. This pinnacle too has been scaled time and again in the annals of modern nationalism and in very characteristic contrastive contexts at that. In pre-nationalist days the primacy of the language-nationality link, on the rare occasions that such primacy was claimed, was in terms of its greater collective significance than the symbols with which élites alone (or primarily) were involved. 'A language is mightier far than any number of books which may have been written in it, for such productions, great though they be, at best embody what was in the hearts and minds of individual men; but language, on the other hand, is the impress and life of a nation' (cited by Southall, 1893: 236). When viewed from the perspective of nationalist ideology, however, language primacy is claimed precisely in comparison with other collective symbols, in comparison with other referents of mass participation, mass involvement, and mass sanctification. Language is worthier than territory. 'A people without a language of its own is only half a nation. A nation should guard its language more than its territories —'tis a surer barrier, a more important frontier than fortress or river' (Davies, 1945 [1845]: 71). Language is worthier than the institutions of government. 'Even if a Volk's state perishes the nation remains intact, provided it maintains its distinctive linguistic traditions' (Herder 1877/1913, vol. XIV, p.87; cited by Barnard, 1965: 58) and, therefore, 'Although the Arabs find themselves politically divided, their language betrays a unity more basic than any single institution' (Chejne, 1969: 174-75). 'Language is not an art form, it is *the* art form of the Arabs' (Polk, 1970: xvii). Indeed, language is even worthier than religion, for 'There is no doubt that the unity of language is more durable for survival and permanence in this world than the unity of religion' (Rendessi, 1958: 125). Little wonder then that 'the theorists of Arab nationalism have assigned to the language the first place as a factor constituting the Arab nation' (Nuseibeh 1956: 77). The same conclusion has been reached by the theorists of other modern nationalisms as well. Political fortunes wax and wane. Religions are often shared with other peoples and, at any rate, have a too firmly established élite of their own, tradition of their own, and task orientation of their own to be easily captured and manipulated by newly aspiring proto-élites. Religion is often viewed as an embarrassment by modern man. In language, on the other hand, one has a secular symbol (if such is desired) that can simultaneously draw upon and lean upon all of the sanctity that religion has given to texts, to writing systems, and to word imagery *per se* (see below), at the same time that it is manipulated by, and that it serves, a basically new élite and a new set of problems, goals and methods. Modern societies have an endless need to define themselves as eternally unique and language is one of the few remaining mass symbols that answers this need without automatically implying one or another short-lived and non-distinctive institutional base. Institutions may come or go, but none of them get to the heart of that which is eternally unique. Institutions must routinize in order to maximise and therein lies their failure, emotionally, and ultimately, practically as well. Language, on the other hand, is viewed as contraroutine. It is for its readers a universe which is simultaneously constantly expanding and, yet, very much their own. 'Y se extiende como si no tuviera término ni orillas el mar immense del castellano. Y no pone el sol' (Capdevila 1940: 164).

Indirectly, via widespread oral and written imagery

Nationalism glorifies the vernacular not only directly but indirectly as well, by honoring and experiencing as symbols of collective greatness and authenticity the most pervasive products of verbal versatility. 'The sagas of the Norsemen, the vedas of the Hindus, the Pentateuch ... of the Hebrews, the Homeric poems, the Virgilian hexameters, all the famed deeds of the brave men before Agamemnon ... have served to inspire linguistic groups with corporate consciousness and to render them true nationalities' (Hayes, 1937: 17). The mother tongue was the vehicle whereby history reached the lower mass and whereby folklore reached the upper class. Poetry, songs, proverbs, mottos, and tales — these all involve basically language behaviors and language products and both history and authenticity are manifestly made and safeguarded by their recitation. Over and over again one finds that both the context and the form of vernacular oral and written literature are pointed to, by élites and laymen alike, as inspiring, unifying, and activating nationalist stimuli. It was even so in the case of Latin literature. 'Rome is the heroine inspiring Romans to heroic deeds to fulfill her destiny' (Barrow, 1949: 117). In the case of nationalist literature, however, the target population was no longer élitist but, rather, the largest audience attainable.

The interaction between the mother tongue and experiences of beauty, devotion, altruism, and righteousness — in short, the tie between the mother tongue and collective 'peak' experiences — does not depend on abstract ideologies concerning the 'ethnic soul' or the 'national spirit.' Such experiences are more directly and formatively provided via the oral and written literatures in the vernacular that both anticipate and accompany mass nationalism. Herder's view that national character was an impossibility in the absence of a folk-song tradition has since been echoed by others, both laymen and literati, in the East as in the West. 'Literature has always consolidated the nation-forming power of language . . . For men of feeling, destiny will ever be hailed in the word that stirs. The harvest reaped by Cavour was of Dante's sowing' (Dominian, 1917: 318-19). Whereas Macpherson merely claimed that his forged fragments had been collected 'among a people so strongly attached to the memory of their ancestors . . . as to have preserved . . . in a great measure uncorrupted to this day' the poetry of their ancestors, nationalist spokesmen also recognized a crucial causal nexus in the opposite direction, i.e. the literature (oral or written) preserves the nationality, rather than vice versa. Thus '[Grimms' fairy tales] have enabled us to understand that we, the German people, bear the power and the conditions in ourselves to take up and carry on the civilization of old times, that we are a folk with a high historical mission' (Franke, 1918: 176) and 'In his [Runeberg's] poems we recognized ourselves and felt that we were one people, that we had a fatherland and were Finns' (cited by Wuorinen, 1931: 79). Similarly, the *Marseillaise* is sung 'so solemnly, so ceremoniously' that it and the language of which it is a part must be viewed as 'outpourings of an eternal French soul' (Hayes, 1930: 235). The Kalevala (self-styled as 'Songs of ancient wit and wisdom/Legends they that once were taken/from the pastures of the Northland/from the meads of Kalevala') is hailed as a 'Homeric poem which the people had brought forth in times immemorial . . . handed down from generation to generation in the course of centuries . . . A mighty monument to the genius of the Finnish people . . . no foreign influences had ever marred it' (Wuorinen, 1931: 75). Similarly, 'the guzlar's ballad is the symbol of national solidarity. His tunes live within the hearts and upon the lips of every Serbian. The pjesme may, therefore, be fittingly considered the measure and index of the nationality whose fibre it has stirred' (Dominian, 1917: 322). We find the link between language, language product and nation expressed even more directly in Arndt's patriotic hymn:

> Was ist das deutsche Vaterland?
> So nenne endlich mir das Land!
> So weit die deutsche Zunge klingt
> Und Gott im Himmel Lieder singt.

Das soll es sein, das soll es sein
Das ganze Deutschland soll es sein.[15]

However, even Tagore's more gentle and lyrical images often served a
definite nationalist purpose. 'Thus lyricism was the second note in the
emotion we felt at the coming of nationalist agitation and its poignancy
lay in the continuous evocation of the beauties of nature: the waters, the
green grass, the golden cornfields of Bengal, the fragrance of mango
blossoms in the Spring' (Chaudhuri, 1951: 221). Similarly, religious verse
helped many to find 'a new definition of Maharashtra: The land whose
people go to Pandharpur for pilgrimage ... Marathi speaking people,
coming from different castes but singing the same songs, the same verses
of the Varkari cult' (Karve, 1962: 22). The use of established genres for
collective peak experiences ('Men shouted, women wept, youths went into
near-hypnotic trances. The effect was electric' [Hanna, 1964: 15]) sealed
the bond between the vernacular and goal-directed collective emotion.

Such examples can be multiplied endlessly. One point that these
examples serve has already been made, namely, that vernacular literature
(oral and written) provides the masses with the emotionalized link between
language and nationalism that exists for élites at the level of ideological
and intellectual program. The beauty of the vernacular, the greatness of
the nationality, the purity of the common cause are grasped by many for
the first time — and thus associated with their personal emotional and
intellectual 'rebirth' — via the popular literature of nationalism. The
Finnish writer Estlander (early nineteenth century) realized this link when
he wrote 'No fatherland can exist without folk poetry. Poetry is nothing
more than the crystal in which nationality can mirror itself; it is the spring
which brings to the surface the truly original in the folk-soul' (Wuorinen,
1931: 69). Half a century later a Hindu nationalist expressed the same
thought, namely, that 'a nation[ality] could rise in its greatness only when
the literature of its motherland was well studied. It would certainly lead
to the love of national greatness and to the adoption of national habits and
manners' (from a letter to the editor, *Indian Mirror*, July 17, 1885; cited
by McCully, 1940: 255).

However, a second and related point still remains to be mentioned:
that the link between vernacular literature and nationalism provides yet
another avenue for the influence of nationalist sentiments and principles
upon language planning. The lexical, phonological, and grammatical forms
which become popularized and emotionalized via the moving literature
that is prompted by or contributory to the mass awakening of nationality
sentiments and nationalist activity have a subsequent directional grip upon

language planning which it may well be impossible to displace. Just as Lönnrot's reconstruction of the Kalevala 'revealed the startling resources of the Finnish language and came to play a decisive part in the development of modern Finnish both as a spoken tongue and as a literary vehicle' (Wuorinen, 1931: 75) so other inspirational literatures in periods of developing nationalism have influenced the subsequent development of languages all over the globe.[16]

Contrastive self-identification via language

The frequency with which vernaculars have become part and parcel of the authenticity message of nationalism (both directly and, again, indirectly, through their oral and written products) is certainly, in no small measure, due to the ease with which élites and masses alike could extrapolate from linguistic *differentiation* and literary *uniqueness* to sociocultural and political independence.[17] However, the latter extrapolation was not always made, to begin with, and was even explicitly rejected on some of the occasions on which it *was* made. Smaller and weaker nationalist movements were particularly likely to consider political independence as a surface phenomenon that might be here today and gone tomorrow. On the other hand, the uniqueness of folk-spirit and life-style that was represented by the vernacular was considered to be a truer and more lasting independence. 'If he had to choose between language and freedom,' De Valera told his friends of the early Gaelic League, 'he would choose language' (Bromage, 1956: 226); and so did the leaders of several other smaller nationalities, both then and now.

Nationalist leaders and masses frequently viewed the vernacular not only as the most undeniable indicator of uniqueness, but, precisely because it was so viewed, also as an indubitable nationality-contrastive or continuative device, depending on which view was felt to be in need of reinforcement. Obviously language had not always been so viewed among ordinary prenationalist ethnics. Nor was it always to be so among postnationalist cosmopolitans. 'Language may invite us to unite, but it does not compel us to do so' (Renan, cited by Singhal, 1967: 278). In the heat of nationalist awakenings, however, language is as basic a division as is the continental divide. It is the shibboleth that differentiates friend from foe. The anti-French tone of German nationalist thought ever since the middle of the nineteenth century[18] was repeatedly reflected in German views of the French language *per se* and of how German differed from it. Since the French (Franks) were originally a Teutonic people, one of their sins was that they forsook their native speech for a neo-Latin language. As a result they not only were guilty of treason to themselves, but also justifiably punished by inheriting all of the faults which led to the downfall of the Romans, namely, 'lack of seriousness about social relations, the idea of self-abandonment, and the idea of heartless laxity. Had they retained their original speech they would never have allowed such degradation to befall them' (Fichte, cited by Kedourie, 1961: 65). Although Herder was less invidious in his views, he was equally deterministic ('a so-called education in French must by necessity deform and misguide German minds. In my opinion this sentence is as clear as the sun at noon.' *Sämmtliche Werke*, Vol. 17, p.157) and, if anything, more striking in his rejection of French ('And you German, returning from abroad/Wouldst greet your mother in French?/Oh, spew it out before your door/Spew out the ugly slime of the Seine/Speak German, Oh you German!'; cited by Kedourie, 1961: 59). Jahn, a somewhat later German nationalist spokesman and activist, finally took the position that 'He who teaches his children to learn the French language, or permits them to learn it, is delirious; he who persists in doing this sins against the Holy Ghost; he who allows his daughter to study French is about as good as he who teaches his daughter the virtues of prostitution' (cited by Snyder, 1952: 28). The impact of such views on German language planning is not hard to find, e.g., in preferences such as the rejection of internationalisms from Graeco-Latin roots. Purification of the German language (through the substitution of German derivatives for 'borrowed words,' e.g. *Landshauptmann* for Gouverneur, *Befehlshaber* for Kommandant) was supported by many who did not necessarily support 'purification of the German race.'

Contrastive self-identification on the basis of language is a very ancient human proclivity.[19] However it is also a proclivity which in prenationalist days is unideologized and, therefore, conveniently bridgeable or forgettable. 'Even the linguistic distinction between Turks and Iranians was of little importance [in early twentieth century Central Asia]. The best proof of this is the existence of an ethnic group known as "Chagatay" consisting of both Iranian and Turkic language speakers who regarded themselves as very close to each other but different from other "Uzbeks" ' (Quelquejay & Bennigsen, 1961: 14). Language-and-nationality co-occurrences exist as widespread latent images of no activating or predictable significance. In the period of mass nationalism this co-occurrence becomes much more than a widespread image; it becomes a manipulable image, not merely with respect to the kinds of integration to which we have been referring, but with respect to the future of the vernacular itself. By rejection of English, the Irish and Indian nationalists, e.g. could not only establish their uniqueness[20] and not only conclude from "philological evidence" that their masters had really copied from *them*,[21] but could also operate directly upon a corpus of ethnic behavior and symbolism, a corpus that was (actually or potentially) at their very tongue and fingertips, that they were (actually or potentially) especially skilled to manipulate, and that was the (actual or potential) medium of the influence that they sought to exert. Thus the links between nationalism and the vernacular are many and mutually reinforcing. While they ultimately derive from the human dependence upon language to communicate and to channel experience, they derive more directly from the human tendency to 'seek for the "essence" or reality in the words used to designate this reality as experience' (Friedrich, 1963: 45). Nationalist beliefs, like all societally patterned beliefs, are language dependent. That nationalists recognize and exploit this dependence is, for our purposes, more noteworthy than the fact that, at times, it also comes into being without nationalism. As a result of such recognition, masses are tied into nationalist integration 'through their emotional investment in system symbols' (Katz, 1965: 361).

That the vernacular so commonly becomes such a symbol is (to review its sentimental component alone) partially a reflection of the fact that it is the *carrier* of all of the other notions and symbols advanced by nationalism ('. . . the people need the word to find a new way' [Pye, 1961: 219]; 'If a man is robbed of his earthly home he finds a spiritual home in his mother tongue, which is everywhere and always present to his senses, and can, therefore, at some time again become concrete and have an earthly home' [Vossler, 1932: 123]), partially a result of the fact that it is made into a prime symbol by 'intellectuals' and other influentials who more than any others are adept at its use and manipulation, and partially a result of its infinite interpretability as a symbol that stands for the entire nationality. Hence its surprising acceptability to the most varied inter-action networks who might easily differ as to other acceptable symbols of nationality. Nationalism is fundamentally a step toward modernization. As such it basically needs group symbols that are more *evocative* of the past than unyieldingly *anchored* (or anchoring) to it; more *indicative* of uniqueness than disablingly mesmerized by it. As other symbols of unity and authenticity become problematic because of their delimited and evaluatable nature the vernacular remains to be reinterpreted in accord with one's own most favored memories and longings, as well as in accord with what is considered most dear and laudable about the ethnic collectivity. ('In days of doubt, in days of gloom and anxiety about the fact of my motherland, thou alone art my support and my stay, oh great mighty, true and free Russian tongue ... It is unthinkable that such a language has not also been given to a great people' [Turgenieff, *Poems in Prose*; cited by Vossler, 1932: 129]). Through nationalism masses of people attain and maintain a new and a constantly renewed sense of identity and purpose. Their new (or old-new) songs, poems, slogans and proverbs, the moving phrases of their leaders and teachers, their national epics, and their national literatures, are all part and parcel of a sense of (re)birth, awakening, and mastery. ('Irish Irelandism helped to create something of the excitement of an intellectual discovery and an awareness among Irishmen that as a nation they were reborn ... it fostered self-confidence and self-reliance and cultivated a pride in national distinctiveness' [McCartney, 1967: 52]). But a (re)birth requires a bountiful mother and in the case of nationalism it is not surprising that this is so commonly the mother tongue (Daube [1940] records the earliest reference to 'Mueterlich deutsch' as occurring in 1349). Without the mother tongue, which too is viewed as reborn (see, e.g. Blach, 1883), it is clear that neither songs nor poems, nor slogans, nor proverbs, nor speeches, nor epics, nor books, nor schools, nor nationality, nor nation would have come into being, nor be what they are, nor what they could be; and, in a very real sense, this is so, both as a result of the 'accidents of history' and as a result of conscious planning.

Nationalism's need for language planning

The term *language planning* refers to the organized pursuit of solutions to language problems, typically at the national level (Jernudd & Das Gupta, 1971). Several investigators have enumerated rather similar types or kinds of language planning (see, e.g. Al-Toma, 1971; Gastil, 1959; Guitare & Quintero, 1968; Hamzaoui, 1965; Kirk-Greene, 1964; Heyd, 1954; Kurman, 1968; Minn Latt, 1966, Whiteley, 1969). Thus Neustupny (1970) has suggested (see Figure 9.1) that when the *problem* to be faced is that of *code selection*, *planning* is concerned with *official policy formation* by authorities in control of power. When the *problem* is that of *stabilizing the selected code* (in view of its variability over space, time, and experiential networks), *planning* is concerned with *codification* via dictionaries, grammars, spellers, punctuation, and pronunciation guides, etc. When the *problem* is that of rapidly *expanding* the number of available options (as a result of the addition of new functions for the selected code), *planning* is concerned with *elaboration* via nomenclatures, thesauruses, etc. When the *problem* is that of *differentiation* of one variety from another within any particular code, *planning* is concerned with *cultivation* via the preparation of style manuals, the subsidization of literary creativity in a variety of genres for various purposes and audiences. Neustupny clearly sees the above four *problem-planning correspondences* as normally standing at least in a rough sequential relationship to each other such that the least developed or least advanced speech-and-writing communities may need to be disproportionately concerned with *policy-formation planning*, whereas the most developed or most advanced communities are able to devote proportionately more attention to *cultivation planning*. Haugen's well known list of types or kinds of language planning (1966) includes norm selection, codification, elaboration, and implementation. The crucial difference between Haugen and Neustupny is easily reconciled since the one type of planning each uniquely includes might be regarded merely as an iterative procedure from the point of view of the other.

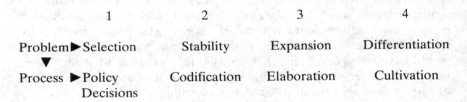

FIGURE 9.1 *Problem/process correspondences in language planning* (per Neustupny, 1970)

Neustupny's emphasis on cultivation (which he considers to be a concern that American students of language planning have tended to overlook — in comparison to Czech and Japanese students) might be from Haugen's point of view merely the reiteration of his four basic types in connection with successive varieties of any given code. On the other hand, Haugen's emphasis on implementation (an important emphasis indeed from the point of view of students of planned change in other-than-language) might be for Neustupny merely the reiteration or modification of decisions with respect to selection, codification, elaboration, etc.

If we accept Haugen's slightly simpler fourfold subdivision of language planning — at least for the purpose of giving initial organization to our review — it is interesting to note the extent to which nationalist movements have encouraged efforts in each of these divisions with respect to the actual or hoped for vernaculars of the population whom they sought to mobilize. Even where no unifying vernacular has immediately been available, nationalist movements have commonly set out to either find or create one, 'not only as a symbol but also as an agent in the diffusion of national sentiment among a wider segment of the population and in the growth of centralization' (Elsbree, 1953: 121).[22]

Code selection

The initial decision as to the 'proper vernacular' for the population under consideration is often far more complicated than either the concurrent or the subsequent picture presented by the nationalist leaders to their followers. To begin with, the ethnic identity of the population itself is often sufficiently amorphous, sufficiently continuous rather than discontinuous, that the drawing of a linguistic line is every bit as judgemental as is the act of drawing the ethnic line itself. Although there are often many 'talented and enthusiastic investigators' eager to 'demonstrate the unity and solidarity of the national language in spite of the variegated diversity of dialects' (Jaszi, 1929: 263–64), they frequently differ with one another in their definition of the outer limits of the nationality as well as in their preferences for the precise linguistic basis of its unification. Thus, some of the pioneers of the Slavic renaissance of the mid-nineteenth century dreamt of 'uniting all Slavonic peoples in one great Slav nation which would be the most numerous and powerful in the world. Some saw the best road to this aim in an amalgamation of all Slavonic languages in a common tongue' (Kahn, 1950: 88).[23] Where a variety of contending broader and narrower modernizing-authenticity movements compete for control over the same hitherto unideologized masses (see e.g. Zarevand, [1930] 1971) the link between language and nationalism cannot itself be closed until both limits of 'the language' and of 'the nationality' in question are themselves pragmatically determined. Little wonder then that 'prodigious philological research (repeatedly) accompanied nationalist agitation' (Barnard, 1965: 62).

However, even where the vernaculars and nationalities to be linked are essentially agreed upon, the utility of these vernaculars for the purpose of nationalism cannot be taken for granted. Such utility depends upon an accepted orthography, a reasonably uniform grammar, a sufficiently ample lexicon, a generally recognized phonology, not to mention the variety of 'styles' needed for technical and nontechnical, serious and humorous, formal and intimate communication. None of these are 'naturally' available to the 'natural' vernaculars of immobilized peasants and artisans and must be created before such vernaculars can serve the unifying, authenticating, and activating purposes of nationalism or of other mass movements. Obviously, most of the vernaculars utilized by mass nationalist movements during the past two centuries required substantial planning in order to *make* them simultaneously the unifying, authenticating, and modernizing tools that they were expected to be. However, the view that the perfection of vernaculars might, in some way, be created, planned, or produced by mere men rather than be entirely *god-given* was also to some extent *anti*nationalist in its assumptions. This may account, in part, for the resistance which such planning has encountered to this very day. It strikes some as presumptuous and others as impossible, as presumptuous and as impossible as it would be to artificially create the breath of life. As a result, language planning normally *merely* admits a resuscitating and invigorating role rather than any intention — let alone any attainment — along the lines of creation *de novo*.

Obviously, language planning had to be tried; for, not to do so would have meant to accept defeat on many even more crucial grounds. Not to standardize and enrich the vernacular would not only have meant that nationalist movements could not parsimoniously become mass movements (particularly so since most of them were so dependent on the inexpensively printed page and the itinerant lecturer for their more lasting and more massive impact), but it also would have meant that their vernaculars would forever remain in the intellectual and pragmatic shadows of others that had been fortunate enough to undergo slow but sure enrichment and standardization, both consciously and unconsciously, in prior generations. Obviously, neither of these alternatives has ever been acceptable to nationalist movements, no matter how much circumstances may have forced some to compromise with them.

When newly awakening English commercial and social élites began to throw off their dependence upon French and Latin, Roger Mulcaster (end of the sixteenth century) ventured a relativistic hypothesis:

'I do not think that anie language, be it whatsoever, is better able to utter all arguments, either with more pith or greater planesse, than our *English* tung is, if the English utterer be as skillful in the matter, which he is to utter, as the foren utterer is . . . It is our accident which restrains our tung and not the tung itself, which will strain with the strongest and stretch to the furthest, for either government if we were conquerers, or for cunning if we were treasurers, not anie whit behind either the subtile Greeke for couching close, or the statelie Latin for

spreding fair. Our tung is capable, if our people would be painful'
(cited in Whiteley, 1969: 95).

Two centuries later (1697) the great Leibnitz pointed to the unenviable
condition of his mother tongue, full of foreign expressions and con-
structions when used by the educated, and used arguments quite similar
to those of Mulcaster in rejecting the then common 'assertion that the
German language was unfitted to express higher thoughts' (Blackall, 1959:
4). However, unlike Mulcaster (but in accord with modern nationalist
thought), he also urged that *an institution be established* so that the
necessary terms and forms be made readily available and in *accord with
the spirit of the language*. 'Sein besonderer Zweck aber und das
Vornehmen (oder Objekt) dieser Anstalt wäre auf die Teutsche Sprach
zu richten, wie nehmlichen solche zu verbessern, auszuzieren und zu
untersuchen' (Blackall, 1959: 6).

At that time the French Academy was already 160 years old
(Robertson, 1910) and French was already firmly established as the only
'fully civilized' vernacular of Europe. 'Ennobling the language, defining
the usage of spoken and written language, classifying its vocabulary, and
giving uniformity to French phonetic and written forms ... [were]
regarded ... as a state and political concern' (Vossler, 1932: 126). No
wonder then that several German writers considered their mother tongue
to be in a sad state, and were eager to point out that 'it is mere prejudice
which leads us to consider languages that have been neglected or that are
unknown to ourselves, as incapable of being brought to a higher
perfection' (Friedrich Schlegel, approximately 1812; cited by Hayes, 1937:
54). This point has required constant reiteration from that day to this,
because although new proto-élites were often willing and eager to use, and
even to promote the vernacular for guidance of the masses, they and older
élites were often far from enthusiastic in their own utilization of the
vernacular, particularly for a number of their own higher intellectual and
cultural purposes. At stake in the upper reaches of society were those
long-established diglossia patterns which in themselves simultaneously
defined culture as well as its custodians. In the absence of mass nationalist
movements that could bring in their wake a revolutionary redefinition of
the basis of sociocultural integration, traditional diglossias continued in full
sway, particularly in the upper reaches of society. At the same time that
Janssaeus boasted that 'the French language has succeeded ... the Latin
and the Greek languages ... It has become so general that it is spoken
today throughout almost the whole of Europe, and those who frequent
society feel a kind of shame if they do not know it' (in his *La Véritable
Clef de langue française*, 1697; cited by Brunot, 1927, vol. V: 137), others

LANGUAGE AND ETHNICITY

had to plead for the creation of a 'literature en françois' (Claude de Seyssel, historian to Louis XII; cited by Kohn, 1944: 130) and for instruction in French within France itself.[24,25]

If such was the fate of the vernacular in the older state nations in which formerly diverse ethnic groups had already been fairly well integrated along sociocultural and political-operational lines, then the grip of traditional diglossia upon the intellectual life of the submerged nationalities on which modern mass nationalist movements focussed their attention was stronger yet. In the latter context the earlier trials and tribulations of languages now great but once also without honor among their own native élites are pointed to as an indication of how the worm can turn. It is now a Pilipino advocate who reminds us, via appropriate quotations, that 'Even English was barren of scientific terms as late as the 16th century . . . As late as 1532 Olivetan speaks of the French language as a barbarous jargon compared with Greek and Hebrew . . . Queen Elizabeth talked Latin with foreign ambassadors; Cromwell had Milton for his Latin secretary' (Rojo, 1937: 51–52) and that 'Tagalog or any other dialect can be expanded and modernized for scientific purposes within a generation or two, or sooner, given the proper determination and provided the additions are made on the advice of linguistic specialists' (Rojo, 1937: 55). As had been true in early periods so also in the cases of the latecomers: advocacy, use of development of the vernacular was regarded as (and was intended to be) rejective of traditionally ascribed statuses, of traditionally limited access to the languages of power and prestige, and of traditionally limited access to the roles of power and prestige. In many cases the rejected superposed languages were those of recognizably foreign conquerors and colonizers. However, in many instances the subjugation that was rejected had occurred in centuries past and had appeared to have become perfectly indigenized. When the Fennomen of 1863 raised the battle cry 'we must win Helsinki for the Finnish language' (Wuorinen, 1931: 130) and when Ziya Gökalp demanded that 'religious worship should be conducted in the language of the people, that is in Turkish instead of in Arabic . . . the whole liturgy with the exception of the fixed Qur'an recitation should be recited in the national tongue . . . the Qur'an should be taught in schools in the Turkish translation' (Heyd, 1950: 102–03), the sociocultural implications were easily as extreme (if not more so) as when Czechs rejected German; Slovaks, Hungarian; or Ukrainians, Russian. In each case, however, the language decision was inevitably linked to further language planning, precisely because nationalism was not only a movement of the masses and for the masses but, rather, also a movement to replace one élite with another, one sociocultural philosophy with another and one political-operational system with another. These replacements often required far more (and more prolonged) language planning than did the more obvious phase of nationalist massification alone.[26] Thus, we may well look to instances of traditional/traditionalized diglossia today (instances in which an intrenched élite utilizes a language of wider communication that does not really reach through to the masses) when we attempt to predict the settings from which future nationalistically guided pressures for language planning may come.[27]

Codification

Subsequent to language selection the variety of language planning tasks still to be faced are, nevertheless, legion. Even within the selected language the variety of spoken variants is likely to be great, whether because of the number of regional and historical variants, like those which complicated the growth of the nationalist movement in Greece,[28] or because of the number of social class variants, like those which complicated the nationalist movement in Hungary.[29] Even within the same social class a vernacular which serves primarily as a lingua franca for multitudes who know it only as a second language reveals irregularities which create bars to efficient communication.[30] Furthermore, where a written variety exists, the inevitable gap between the written and the spoken language must be coped with, else it may grow to such proportions that literacy is difficult to acquire even for native speakers.[31] All in all, an initial major task of nationalist-inspired language planning is 'that of linguistic organization, popularization and standardization' (Kahn, 1950: 243).[32] Each of these tasks is potentially fraught with great national danger or great national gain. Before language is highly ideologized minor differences are easily introduced which can later have major consequences (see, e.g. Omar, 1971). 'The Austrians got the Slovaks in the 1840s to standardize their spelling of a dialect which was remote from that of the Czechs and, therefore, made for two separate languages' (Deutsch, 1964b: 52–3). Similarly, initially minor similarities can later be put to great service. Thus, M. A. Castren, the first major grammarian of Finnish to appear during the period of early nineteenth century anti-Swedish-pro-Finnish nationalism wrote: 'I have decided to prove to the people of Finland that we are not a . . . nation isolated from the world and world history, but that we are related to at least one-seventh of the people of the globe. If the cause of this nation is thereby served, all will be well . . . Grammars are not objective, but without them I cannot attain my goal' (Wuorinen, 1931: 99).

Elaboration

So much for codification. But lexical expansion too is conscientiously pursued as a nationalist task of potentially monumental consequences. The users of developing languages are particularly aware of their lexical shortcomings. Leibnitz considered German 'rich in words denoting real objects, especially in words connected with occupations like mining, hunting and seafaring, but . . . lacking vocabulary to express those things not experienced by the senses, so that the scholar has been driven to Latin to describe such matters' (cited by Blackall, 1959: 5).[33] The developing language is always relatively impoverished when it comes to the more abstract subtleties of imported or recently innovated higher learning and fashionable society. One sign of the development of a language is its growth in exactly these respects. 'In his "Neology," published in 1801, [Sébastien] Mercier mentions over two thousand words unknown in the age of Louis XIV . . . "New words and expressions assailed the language in such numbers that newspapers and periodicals of that time could have been understood by Louis XIV only by means of a translation"' (Rocker, 1937: 291). However, modern nationalism is concerned not only with increasing the number of such new terms (including, of course, the fields of modern technology) but also with delimiting the source (and, therefore, the model) of their formulation, since 'the preservation of the language and the enthusiasm for serving it by reinvigorating its life through new styles and idioms' are not in themselves sufficient. These tasks must be accomplished in a manner that also provides 'proof that a nation[ality] has personality and self-respect' (Ahmad 1960: 103).

Thus, nationalist movements must not only fashion an apparently unified, authenticated, and modern-problem-oriented nationality out of the countless manifest interaction networks engaged in daily ethnic routines and beliefs, but they must fashion an equally apparently unified, authenticated, and modern-problem-oriented language out of the manifest diversity of phonological, lexical, grammatical, and semantic systems inherited from prenationalist speech networks. Nationalisms consciously undertake to produce self-consciously modern, authentic, and unifying standard languages, which are to be consciously employed and con-scientiously espoused, where previously there existed only regional and social varieties, unconsciously employed and unemotionally abandoned. Language planning is, therefore, a definite service to and by-product of the nationalist cause, and like that cause it may retire to the sidelines, at least temporarily, when its major goals *seem* to have been attained or are no longer at issue.

The dependence of nationalist-inspired language planning on élitist leadership is apparent at every step. Whether it be at the point of initial selection,[34] subsequent codification and elaboration[35] or final implementation,[36] the major forces at work seem to have been (and to be) élitist. They alternately *appealed* to each other to overtly take a hand at language planning[37] and *disguised* their efforts as being merely those of organizers of natural riches.[38] In all cases, however, as with most other nationalist activity, élites and their needs were instrumental in *bringing about* (rediscovering, disinterring, reassembling) the 'natural' uniqueness, and the unified pure language which nationalist theory and nationalist practice simultaneously assumed and required. Although we cannot today decisively pinpoint the factors responsible for either language planning successes or failures (see, however, Rubin & Jernudd, 1971), it is quite clear that new proto-élites also need(ed) language planning for the explicit purposes of élitist role behavior and power aspirations, and that the language planning in which they engaged was as much a *necessity* in the realization of their more purely instrumental goals, as it was a captive of *their unity and authenticity ideology.* If the one need provided the lion's share of the urgency, the other provided the lion's share of the direction.

Nationalist pressures on language planning

Language planning implies directed change toward a desired goal. The goal constrains and explains the activities engaged in on its behalf. Nationalist ideologies frequently provide such constraints and rationales for language planning. In so doing they provide a definition of the good or desirable language which language planning intends to bring into being, or, at least, to further and to strengthen. If we consider the linguistic self-perceptions and goal perceptions of various nationalist movements, it is not difficult to discern the differences separating them from linguistic self-perceptions of prenationalist (or postnationalist) speech communities. Like all self-perceptions nationalist language planning too tends to be, in part, a reflection of rationalizations after the fact and, in part, an indirect definition of a more desirable state of affairs yet to be attained in the future.

Language as an active agent

A major parameter of prenationalist (and postnationalist) evaluation of vernaculars in undoubtedly the esthetic. In 1599, S. Daniel's fond dream for the English language, namely that it might spread throughout the world, was justified merely on the basis of its supposed delicate beauty ('What worlds in th'yet unformed Occident/May come refind with th'accents that are ours?' cited by Whiteley, 1969: 95).

Subsequently

'Ronsard and the "Plèîde" . . . discovered in Italy the "canons" of ancient beauty . . . [and] viewed the French language only as a musical instrument to which new strings must be added if the new songs are to conform to the aesthetic principles of Greek and Roman beauty.

Tous ceux qui ces vers liront
S'ils ne sont Grecs et Romains,
Au lieu d'un livre ils n'auront
Qu'un pesant faix dans les mains.

. . . All were of the opinion that beauty and thought are subject to universal laws, and for this reason never hesitated to seek their inspiration beyond national frontiers' (Delaise, 1927: 188–90).

Coupled with this view, however, is frequently another which is purportedly related to it, namely correspondence to *natural* beauty, to the natural order of thought, to the natural state of events, objects, or ideas. Thus Bonald praised French for being 'a language which is simple without baseness, noble without bombast, harmonious without fatigue, precise without obscurity, elegant without affectation, metaphorical without conscious effort; a language which is the veritable expression of a perfected nature' (written between 1796 and 1819, published 1864: 329). His explanation for the widespread use of French was that it was 'the most perfect of modern languages and perhaps of all languages, . . . it follows most closely the natural order of things and their relationships, the objects of our thoughts, and it is the most faithful expression of the truest ideas' (p. 393).[39] This prenationalist view remained the dominant lay linguistic self-perception in France almost to this very day. When the French Academy, 'with all its authority and force . . . explains to the French people . . . how superior the French language is to any other', it does so in terms of 'the tradition that the French language is the clearest, most precise language in the world [and, therefore] the natural language of international diplomacy' (Hayes, 1930: 9 and 207). Obviously this view was not only initially a rationalization after the fact but it was also a reflection of France's long continental primacy as a state-nation.

'The beauty of modern French, as well as the attraction it exerts on cultivated minds, is due to its well-balanced blend of northern and southern elements. French of our day is the shrine in which the treasured remains of earlier centuries are still preserved. In it the sunshine of the south pierces with its warm rays the severity of northern earnestness. No other European language can boast of an equally happy composition' (Dominian, 1917: 11).

This view contains no clearly nationalist flavor or fervor, as is the case with many languages of more recent nationality-states and of nationalities still seeking cultural or political security. There is no indication that some typically or uniquely French behavior is fostered or facilitated by means of the French language. French is viewed as a gift to all of mankind, as an instrument of pure reason and as a creation of sublime and natural beauty, rather than as something parochially and primarily French. Not to use good French words in France, even given the antifranglais feeling of recent years, is merely to be gross and to show one's lack of good taste. Not to do so today in French Canada, however, is to reveal feelings of national inferiority (Bégouin, 1970).

In the case of German we can see both of these views in historical contrast. Schottelius's apologia for German (1663; 1466 pages plus introduction and index) is entitled (in part) 'Ausfuhrliche arbeit von der teutschen haubt sprache worin enthalten gemelter dieser haubt sprache uhrankunft/uhraltertuhm/reinlichkeit/eigenschaft/vermögen/invergleichlichkeit/grundrichtigkeit . . .'. Lest it appear that ethnic specificity is being stressed above, it should be pointed out that the author's intention was merely to claim for German the same desiderata as applied to the very few other 'haubt sprache' of the world (in whose company he dearly wanted German to be included). This becomes clearer, a century later, from Klopstock's 'Die deutsche Gelehrtenrepublik' (Hamburg, 1774) in which he still characterizes German as 'eine reichhaltige, vollblühende, fruchtschwere, tönende, gemesne, freye, bildsame, männliche, edel und vortrefliche Sprache.' However, the relative lack of recognition of German also leads him to conclude on a note of invidious comparison with other languages, on the ground that German 'Kaum die griechishce und Keine der andern Europäersprachen bieten darf' (p. 109; cited by Blackall, 1959: 326).

The need to justify German *vis-à-vis* French, and finally, the need to claim German superiority and particularity (i.e. 'Germanness') *vis-à-vis* French, becomes increasingly apparent as German nationalism continues to gather momentum. In 1794 Klopstock defends 'unsere männliche Sprache' against objections to its guttural sound. 'Töne, welche zu tief aus dem Halse heraufkommen, verrathen im [i.e. the Frenchman] Barbarey; und Tone, die man mit Selbstgeffalen in die Nase hinauftreibt, überfeine

Kultur' (in his *Grammatische Gesprache*; cited by Blackall, 1959: 327). By this time the view had already been expressed that German was superior to French (and to English and Italian as well) 'because it does not proceed from the mingling of the language of several peoples' (Gottsched; cited by Blackall, 1959: 119). It was therefore only a minor advance along the same front for Fichte to claim that the Germans were 'honest, serious, sober and speak a language which is shaped to express the truth' (cited by Reiss, 1955: 105).[40] Within a century this view had developed further to claim that the 'Nordics' superiority of physique fitted them to be vehicles of the superior language' (Childe, 1926: 211–12). Obviously within the framework of nationalism the vernacular not only makes its speakers authentic in thought and action, but it itself strains toward the authenticity which is inherent in it. The vernacular 'comes to be personified. The language, it is said, accepts or rejects foreign words' (Doob, 1964: 231).

The typically prenationalist and nationalist views of what was laudable about particular vernaculars are nicely contrasted if we compare Ribinyi's observations concerning Hungarian with Korais' concerning Greek. Writing in Latin, Ribyini, a teacher at the Lutheran school at Sopron, admitted in 1751 that 'Italian is pleasant, French beautiful, German earnest; but all these qualities are so united in Magyar that it is difficult to say wherein its superiority consists' (in his *Oratio de Cultura Linguae Hungaricae* 1751; cited by Marczali 1910: 236). However, for the nationalist spokesman, a century later, Greek was not merely endowed with 'exceptional charm,' it not merely influenced its speakers to become 'more eloquent and wise' but it influenced them to pursue political and cultural freedom. 'It is a rare thing for one to submit to . . . slavery if one has once managed to drink to the full the charm of the Hellenic language' (cited by Sherrard, 1959: 183). In the annals of nationalism the vernacular is not merely generally lovely. It is quite specifically powerful. Thus, with respect to Swahili 'Let us use it as a right, clerks and farmers, and though you may not believe it, English will move out. We don't want foreign languages. We feel they are a reproach. Swahili is a good language, our original language' (translated from Swahili by Whiteley, 1969: 161). With respect to Arabic it is necessary to 'comprehend its superior qualities over other languages and the special endowments which enabled it to achieve complete mastery over . . . vast regions' and it is desirable 'to discover the secret of this vitality and to lay our hands on the unique powers which our language represents *in order to utilize these powers in organizing our present and building our future*' (Costi Zurayq, 'Al-Wayi al Qawmi' [Nationality Consciousness], Beirut 1938: 38; cited by Nuseibeh, 1956: 70). Such unique vitality is more than just a metaphor of hyperbolic literati or an unreasoned stereotype of demagogic politicians. It is a view which frequently comes to be legitimized by whatever are the most responsible sources of legitimization available to a speech community. Given the total constellation of circumstances outlined above, few indeed will hesitate to remind all who will listen that 'the Anglo-Saxon language is the simplest, the most perfectly and simply symbolic that the world has ever seen; and that by means of it the Anglo-Saxon saves his vitality for conquest instead of wasting it under the Juggernaut of a cumbersome mechanism for conveyance of thought' (McGee, 1895: 280).

Nationalist language planning aims not at esthetics or euphonics (or parsimony or clarity) *per se* but at a definite cluster of overt, behavioral goals. Its image of language is an overt behavioral one as well. Nationalism intends that language use and language planning both should encourage and facilitate behaviors of broader unity, deeper authenticity, and various modern implementations of sociocultural and political-organizational integration. Nationalisms hold that it is part of the very nature of their vernaculars to advance their respective causes. It is this active, overt spirit of the language that language planning must, somehow, both observe and enhance. As ethnic fidelity alone is merely an incidental and superficial consideration *vis-à-vis* language in prenationalist periods — although it is an intermittently present consideration in such periods as well — so estheticism or parsimony alone are considered unworthy of socialized man in the age of nationalism. Beauty is only skin deep. It is what is below the surface that really counts and with respect to which language must be used and shaped.

Fostering unity and authenticity via differentiation from undesirable external linguistic influences

Nationalist language planning reveals a pervasive abhorrence of foreign influences. Whether this is viewed as merely an expression of a 'natural' abhorrence on the part of the language itself or whether it is acknowledged as a human evaluation aimed at human goals, it is encountered again and again in the directive pronouncements which serve as guides to official and unofficial guardians of the vernacular. Of course, an antipathy toward foreign elements and a preference for indigenous ones is certainly also found in prenationalist sources as well. Leibnitz, e.g. expressed this view ('Besser ist ein original von einem teutschen als eine copey von einem Franzosen seyn' [Blackall, 1959: 4]) but with little if any ideological or behavioral follow/up for this preference. However, such is no longer the case for those German writers who subsequently warned against foreign borrowings on the grounds that they ultimately denied a people its original and autochthonous character. Thus Fichte goes significantly beyond Leibnitz when he argues that 'Original, primitive languages are superior to composite, derived languages. German is an original language, its speech must be cleansed of foreign accretions and borrowings, since the purer the language, the more natural it is and the easier it becomes for the nation to realize itself and to increase its freedom' (Kedourie, 1961: 66–67).

Similarly, Bentham's views concerning English authenticity were merely based upon general principles of learning and understanding.[41] Noah Webster, however, in arguing for the development of an authentically American spelling of English a decade after the American Revolution, admitted that 'a capital advantage would be that it would make a difference between the English orthography and the American . . . I am confident that such an event is an object of vast political consequence . . . A national language is a bond of national union' (cited by Mencken, [1919] 1939: 10). 'As an independent nation,' he wrote, 'our honor requires us to have a system of our own, in language as well as in Government. Great Britain, whose children we are, and whose language we speak, should no longer be our standard; for the taste of her writers is already corrupted and her language on the decline' (cited by Bram, 1955: 56). Irish nationalists paraded the purity of Irish as further evidence of the wickedness of English. 'Of 100,000 English words not more than 33 percent are pure English or Teutonic, the rest being of classical or otherwise foreign origin; whilst of 100,000 Irish words, it is certain that 80 percent would prove to be pure Celtic' (Flannery, 1896: 97). Similarly focused 'antiforeign' emphases have characterized nationalist language planning of Finnish vis-à-vis Swedish (Wuorinen, 1931, 1954), of Estonian vis-à-vis Finnish (Kurman, 1968), of Turkish vis-à-vis Persian and Arabic (Heyd, 1950), or Urdu vis-à-vis Sanskrit, and of Hindi vis-à-vis Persian (Chatterji, 1943), etc., etc. Of course, parallel to cleansing the vernaculars of foreignisms in general (but of foreignisms derived from certain languages in particular), there goes the process of enriching these vernaculars from one's own most authentic sources. This process serves the same purposes of external separation and internal consolidation as does the cleansing process which it accompanies. '. . . With the ugly development of Hindu-Muslim communalism, High Hindi and Urdu became symbols of this conflict. Each is going its own way, intense Persianization [of Urdu] on the one hand and almost equally intense

Sanscritization [of High Hindi] on the other, so that in their more elegant forms one would be unintelligible to the speakers of the other' (Chatterji, 1943: 19).[42] While St. Stefan of Perm [fourteenth century] could consciously choose to utilize not that form of Komi which was considered '"purest" or "best" but one that [was] . . . spreading rapidly by the process of migration and urbanization' (Ferguson, 1968: 258), a modern nationalist language planner would also have found that the latter form was also the more authentic. At the very least nationalist language planning claims to press in the same direction as that which represents the genius of the language itself. 'The genius or language spirit of a nation is no mythological being; [rather] it is a force, a talent, a temperament. It is . . . the nature of genius to . . . be true and genuine, to remain true to itself . . . The true life of a national language is centripetal and inward, not centrifugal' (Vossler, 1932: 128–39). However, in crisis situations the genius of the language must not merely be followed but actively protected and abetted by language planning. 'Es verrät eine geringe Meinung von der Muttersprache, wenn man ihr nicht die Kraft zutrut, mut eigenem Mittein alles zu sagen . . . Und die heiligsten Rechte hat die Sprache in ihrer Eigenschaft als besondere nationale Sprache. Eine besonders schwere Sunde ist es darum, wenn man das echte, eigene Sprachgut mit fremden Wörtern durchsetzt' (Koppelman, 1956: 97–99).

A view such as the latter is common enough in nationalistically inspired language planning. However, it is often a correlate of a difficult struggle, not only against newly discovered linguistic 'strangers,' but also against those indigenous populations that have been particularly exposed to various 'foreign influences' (foreign names, foreign foods, foreign dress, foreign beliefs, and even 'such foreign and fantastic field sports as lawn tennis, polo, croquet, cricket and the like' [Beckett, 1966: 417]). Some of the linguistic by-products of such exposure may have become so completely indigenized as not to be foreign-marked in the eyes of most speakers and, indeed, as not to have indigenous synonyms. The protection of purity requires an attack against habits of speaking and against specified speech networks. It is not always a popular or a simple pursuit.

Fostering unity and authenticity via differentiation from internal linguistic alternatives

For nationalism, the enemy is not only without the gate; he has already, to some extent, crept inside as well and must now be expelled. In large measure, the enemy within is simply the same as the enemy without. Those varieties of the vernacular that have been most influenced by foreign models are, obviously, less preferred than those that have escaped such influences.[43] However, another enemy exists, namely the multiplicity of vernacular varieties *per se*, each pulling toward a different norm of pronunciation and spelling and, on occasion, of vocabulary and grammar as well. 'Citizens,' cried Bertrand Barère, a leading Jacobin, in 1794, 'the language of a free people ought to be one and the same for all' (cited by Hayes, 1931: 63). Internal diversity of usage is not only inefficient and potentially dangerous (for it fosters and protects behavioral and ideological disunity more generally), but it also invites invidious comparisons with favored and better established rivals. Thus, 'it was through the initiative of these [nationalist] congresses that the compilation of a great dictionary was undertaken in order to establish once and for all a standard for the Netherlandish language' (Clough, 1930: 79).

However, the selection or determination of a standard from among many available and competing varieties presupposes some model of the desirable. For nationalism ultimate desirability is coextensive with greater authenticity, even while the goals of unity and modern problem solving are being pursued. As for authenticity, where is it to be found? In the annals of nationalism, again and again, it is to be found in the past or in those regions or populations that have been least exposed to the contaminating influences of modern foreign forces (and, therefore, in those that remained most faithful to the purity of the past).

Fichte's view, that it was 'incumbent on a nation[ality] worthy of the name to revive, develop and extend what is taken to be its original speech, even though it might be found only in remote villages, or had not been used for centuries, even though its resources are inadequate and its literature poor — for only such an original language will allow a nation to realize itself and attain freedom' (Kedourie, 1961: 67), was widely shared and extremely influential among nationalist movements. A particularly frequent directive source of nationalist language planning, therefore, was the image of the noble and uncontaminated peasant who kept his language pure and intact, precisely as it had been in the golden past. It was the language of the inaccessible peasant (or of some other but equally sheltered population) that provided the linguistic *model* (the basic langue) upon which the elaboration, codification, and cultivation of the modern standard vernacular was to be performed and by which these processes were to be guided. In Ireland, De Valera, whose Irish was originally marginal, was urged by Pearse 'to do as Pearse himself had done, to seek out the people of the West [i.e. those furthest from English influences in particular and from modern, urban influences in general] as the fountainhead of Gaelic Ireland' (Bromage, 1956: 30).[44] In Finland, the 'unspoiled peasant' not only 'came to be considered as the embodiment of "national" traits and characteristics' but, even more strikingly, the model for 'vocabulary and idiom for the upbuilding of the new and "purer" national language' (Wuorinen, 1950: 47). In Estonia, the great linguistic reformer 'Aavik acknowledged a preference for "those linguistic forms in which the national characteristics of the language were best realized" ' (Kurman, 1968: 58) and, therefore, rural and historical forms rather than literary and more modern ones.

In the Slavic world this tendency to emphasize the rural and the distant past was particularly strong, because the recent urban past was so overwhelmingly colored by foreign influences. From the first, when 'Herder insisted on the rights of nationalities ... at a time when the Bohemians, Rumanians, Croatians and others had hardly any consciousness themselves of their nationality ... [and] at a time when their languages were no more than vernaculars spoken by illiterate peasants and deemed to be without future or dignity' (Kohn, 1944: 432), the richness of peasant speech has continued to be glorified. Thus, when Ljudevit Gaj sought to produce a common written language for the new southern Slav ideology of Illyrism 'he did not propose Croatian, his own language and that of the most numerous, historically most significant of the Austro-Slav peoples, as the basis of "Illyrian", but favored the primitive southern Dalmatian "Schto" ' (Kahn, 1950: 246).[45]

In the Islamic world the quest for purity and authenticity led Gökalp to prefer the Turkish 'used by the women, who had more than others preserved its native harmony and sweetness' (Heyd, 1950; 116). In the Arabic world, Lutfi, who 'did not believe ... that the spoken language should be adopted as a medium for literature,' nevertheless believed that 'languages lose their vitality when no longer rooted in the daily life of the people' (Ahmad, 1960: 104) and, therefore, urged that the classical language be simplified and vitalized in the direction of common speech which alone would be 'the natural source of its growth' (p. 104).[46] Thus, all in all, the quest for internal authenticity led repeatedly to the common folk, and, among them, to those who were assumed to have been in the most favored position to *maintain* the vernacular as it had been in the past, before foreign influences, foreign domination, foreign fads, and foreign models had begun to spoil the authentic and authenticating linguistic heritage bequeathed by generations of ancestors.[47] In its language planning theory, as in other matters, nationalism pursues modernization by beginning with the authenticity of long ago; it seeks the inspiration or drive required to meet urban needs by first returning to the pre-urban (if not the anti-urban) heritage. The return to origins, to purity, in language, is

part of a more general yearning for Gemeinschaft, part of a hope or
pretense that in the simplicity of Gemeinschaft may be found the solutions
to the complex problems of Gesellschaft. The long ago is a desirable point
of departure for several reasons. It is relatable to religious[48] and temporal
glories. ('Steket also in Teutschen Altertum und sonderlich ... der
Ursprung ... des uralten Gottesdienstes, der Sitten und Rechte des
Adels,' Leibnitz, as cited by Blackall, 1959: 460). It is uncontaminated by
the currently stigmatized anti-models. Finally for the man in the street,
any claims made for it are less confirmable and therefore, as a langue
model, it is infinitely more manipulable than those closer at hand.

Several basically conflicted tasks are obviously on the agenda of
nationalist-inspired language planning *vis-à-vis* the internal linguistic
scene. To begin with there is the same revolutionary (or anti-
establishment) turning of the tables, as is evident in connection with the
two previously discussed types of decision making: native language rather
than foreign language and vernacular of the people rather than classical
of the old élite. The foreign masters and the subservient old élites both
derided the language of the rural population as uncouth, impoverished,
and lawless. 'It was looked down upon as a vulgar dialect not deserving
the distinction of being called a language. For the most part only the lower
classes in the ... provinces spoke it and their accents varied from village
to village' (Clough, 1930: 56). However, it was (and is) precisely such a
variety that nationalist ideology most commonly purports to select (on the
basis of its avowedly greater purity, honesty, dignity and authenticity) as
a reflection and as a part of the national soul. However, unlike most
modern linguistic views which also consider the spoken language as 'the
only linguistic reality,' nationalist language planning proceeds to utilize the
preferred spoken variety in fashioning and deriving the basic language
model for a standard written language. This then is another conflicted task
for modern nationalist language planning. The spoken language (in all of
its regional and situational variability) is proclaimed as model but the
standard written language (for industry, education and government) is
definitely a major goal.

All of these internally contradictory tendencies of nationalist language
planning have elicited their share of derision among those who can afford
to be aloof. The pursuit of the 'genuinely authentic' has been characterized
as 'ein immer wiederkehrendes Irrtum des Nationalismus, und speziell des
kulturellen Nationalismus ... Nichts ist unnatürlicher als das dewusste
Streben natürlich zu sien' (Koppelman, 1956: 102). The imposition of
writing norms before the evolution of a written tradition was viewed as
a reversal of the natural order of things. 'English poets ... invested their

language with eloquence before orthographic or grammatical standardization took place. In Swahili the reverse occurred, the standardization
being effected on a non-literary dialect' (Whiteley, 1969: 95). The
dislocating impact of manufactured and standardized authenticity upon
any remaining truly authentic populations has been pointed to. 'Only those
members of the folk society who repudiate their own origin are admitted
. . . In this way the [newly] dominated group detaches people from their
original groups and at the same time rejects them from itself' (Ponsionen,
1962, 105). However, as with all contradictions seemingly implicit in
systems or between ideology and reality, the contradictions seemingly
implicit in nationalist language planning are such only when viewed from
without. From within they are viewed as an inevitable dialectic that serves
merely to test the ingenuity, the strength, and the faith of the faithful.

Planning for modernity with authenticity

Nationalist language planning must face two extreme positions in its
attempts to reconcile modernization and authenticity. At one extreme is
the view that such a reconciliation is *impossible;* at the other, that it is
unnecessary. One camp holds that the national language *cannot* (or should
not) be employed for modern purposes. 'A quiver of steel arrows, a cable
with strong coils, a trumpet of brass crashing through the air with two or
three sharp notes, such is Hebrew. A language of this kind is not adapted
to the expression of scientific results' (Renan, 1888; cited by Spiegel, 1930:
4). The other camp holds that the delays and the trials of nationalist
language planning (which optimally aims at expressing everything modern
via indigenous roots) are simply so much *wasted time and effort*. 'I would
personally like to encourage Hindustani to adapt and assimilate many
words from English . . . This is necessary, as we lack modern terms, and
it is better to have well-known words rather than to evolve new and
difficult words from Sanskrit or Persian or Arabic. Purists object to the
use of foreign words, but I think they make a great mistake' (Nehru, 1953:
456). But neither of the quoted opposing views is nationalist in inspiration.
The one is traditionalist; the other modernist. The nationalist *tour de force*
is to combine authenticity *and* modernism; indeed, to find that there is no
clash between them at all.

Both opposition to and trust in language planning, as an example of
conscious and organized intervention in language change and development, predate modern nationalism. However, both reveal a typical lack

of central concern for the ethnic, the authentic, the indigenously unique
spirit and form. When Robert Gruffydd (1697) has the language of
Cambria address the 'fond reader' with respect to the author's (that is his
own) labors on her behalf she merely claims that 'he hath endeavoured
to bestow upon me the privilege of Art . . . without even a moment of time
to adorn me as he would have wished' (W.R. Jones, 1966: 4). Even
Salisbury (1547?), recognizing that a Welsh capable of handling only rustic
experiences was doubly exposed to the danger of extinction, made no
ethnic claims and provided no ethnic guidelines for the conscious language
modernization that he favored. ('Do you suppose that ye need no better
words and no greater variety of expression to set out learning and to treat
of philosophy and the arts than you have in common use in daily
conversation, when you buy and sell and eat and drink . . .? And take this
as a warning from me — unless you bestir yourself to cherish and mend
the language, before the present generation is no more it will be too late'
(cited by W. R. Jones, 1966: 43). On the other hand, early opponents of
language planning are also predominantly nonnationalist in their views. A
common view is that of de la Ramée, predating the Academy itself and
anticipating a recurring reaction to professors who meddle with the
language: 'The people is the sovereign lord of its language and holds it as
a fief free of all obligations, and is obligated to no lord for it. The school
for this knowledge is not at all in the auditoriums of the Hebrew, Latin,
and Greek professors in the University of Paris, as some of our fine
etymologizers think; it is in the Louvre, in the Palais de Justice, in the
Halles, on the Place de Greve, on the Place Maubert' (1572, cited by
Guryceva, 1960: 30). Before he himself became a member thereof,
Montesquieu admitted (1690) that he had 'heard of a kind of tribunal
called the French Academy. There is none in the world less respected; for
no sooner has it decided than the people annul its decrees and impose laws
which *it* is obliged to follow. Some time ago, to fix its authority, it gave a
code of its judgements. That child of so many fathers was almost old when
it was born' (cited by Robertson, 1910: 209). A little over half a century
later Samuel Johnson was similarly sarcastic, but again without a trace of
the nationalist concern for authenticity. 'Academies have been instituted,
to guard the avenues of their languages, to retain fugitives and repulse
invaders; but their vigilance and activity have hitherto been in vain: sounds
are too volatile and subtle for legal restraints; to enchain syllables and to
lash the wind are equally undertaking of pride' (1755: v). Thus, we find
here repeated *vis-à-vis* language planning the same predominantly
different approaches that we previously encountered with respect to
language *per se*. The prenationalist view (whether positive or negative) is
primarily related to dimensions such as beauty, parsimony, efficiency,

feasibility, rather than to an ethnically authentic approach to any or all of the foregoing. The latter is typically a nationalist argument, if not always a consistent nationalist approach.

Writing during the period of intense nationalist efforts in Southern, Eastern, and Central Europe, Mauthner observed that nationalist movements might be reluctant to admit foreign *words* into their vernacular but they were not at all reluctant to admit modern (and, therefore, to a large extent foreign) *concepts* into their goals and methods. 'Before the intrusion of national consciousness, before the beginning of purist movements, the mass of the people borrowed freely from the treasure of foreign speech. Afterwards, such loans were avoided, but all the more numerously foreign concepts were brought into the language by translation. There are modern people of such touchy national feeling that they have driven purism to the utmost extreme (Neo-Greeks and Czechs). But they can isolate only their language, not their world concepts, their whole intellectual situation' (Mauthner, 1906: 55; cited by Rocker, 1937: 238).[49] Such is the view of an outsider. Seen from the inside the quest is for modernity ('Europeanization') *and* authenticity, simultaneously, for seeing the *world* but '*through our own eyes*,' for going to the *world* but '*in our own way*.' Nationalist language planning seeks and provides a rationale for the simultaneous attainment of what might seem (to uninvolved and unconcerned outsiders) to be disparate aims. In so doing, however, it is in the company of all modern ideologically guided social systems. Like them nationalist language planning is an organized self-fulfilling prophecy.

The favorite motto of Young Estonia (a group of early twentieth-century nationalist writers, intellectuals, and poets) was 'Let us be Estonians, but let us also be Europeans' (Kurman, 1968: 54). However, they were immediately faced with the 'regrettable fact that they could not create a national culture of high [i.e. European] quality with the underdeveloped literary language that they had inherited' (Kurman, ibid.). Language planning was an obvious necessity since 'the natural evolution of the language was, of course, unable to keep pace with the rapid progress of [European] ideas' (Raun, 1965: 9). A group of language enthusiasts, Aavik being the foremost among them, set about 'to remedy this shortcoming and guide Literary Estonian toward achieving parity with the "cultural languages" of Europe' (Kurman, 1968: 54). They followed three principles: 'aestheticism, phonological historicity and enlightened purism' (Kurman, 1968: 57), although maintaining, in general, that 'all of the sources, programs and rules necessary for the future development of Estonian can be found in the language itself' (p. 65). Thus, authenticity itself still permits and requires enlightened choice between contemporary alternatives, between contemporary and historical alternatives, between more esthetic and less esthetic alternatives, and between more indigenized and less indigenized alternatives. Nationalist language planning involves a constant interpretation and reinterpretation of authenticity such that sufficient flexibility is usually provided to accomplish what appears to be necessary and desirable. The vernacular, as a whole, is a means of symbolically indigenizing that which is materially and conceptually foreign and, as such, it can provide the means for indigenizing those aspects of itself which originate abroad.

Gökalp in particular, and the Turkish case in general, provide many illustrations of the rationales whereby nationalist-inspired language planning remains both authentic and enlightened. Gökalp's general position — in poetry and in other matters — was that it was 'the duty of Turkish poets to turn their backs on . . . foreign influences. They should learn only "technique" from the West, but poetical inspiration and aesthetic taste should come to them from the heritage of Turkish people — proverbs, legends and folk songs' (Heyd, 1950: 122). Thus, one opportunity for enlightening purism is to differentiate between that which is merely objective, physical, technical (and, therefore, ethnically inconsequential) and that which is subjective, spiritual and substantive (and, therefore, ethnically crucial). Furthermore, 'every word familiar to the people is a national asset.' Thus, 'there is no sense in rejecting [Persian and Arabic] words . . . which have become part and parcel of the vernacular, merely because they have been borrowed from foreign languages. To change these words for old Turkish words or for new words formed from Turkish roots would be equivalent to banishing from the language living elements and introducing into it words more strange and unintelligible to the common people' (Heyd, 1950: 116–17). The usage of the common people, therefore, on behalf of whose authenticity nationalism arises, also serves as a possible court of appeal when purism threatens to become non-functional.[50]

Gökalp summed up his goals 'in the matter of linguistic reform in the triple formula: modernization and Europeanization of the language in respect of scientific terms, and Turkification in respect of all other words and of grammar, syntax and orthography' (Heyd, 1950: 119). Obviously the indigenous heartland (ordinary words, syntax, and orthography) are to remain untouched. To the extent that lexical borrowings are needed for technical nomenclature, a preferred nonindigenous source is indicated. However, the realm of concepts is entirely unrestrained. There, the modern, the European may reign supreme without harming the authentic core.[51] Further, the definition of 'scientific terms' is also left open so that future interpretation and amplification of this realm remains possible. Indeed, the very establishment of a differentiation between the heartland and the periphery permits further differentiations and interpretations all of which claim to leave the heartland intact. Thus, during the less puristic days of Ataturk

> 'an ingenious cover and stimulant for linguistic adaptation was found in the theory of the Sun Language which, bolstering national pride, eased the pains of making Turkish a more useful modern instrument. Turkish, according to this theory ... [was] the mother of all existing tongues and "therefore any foreign term may be" re-adopted "provided it be given a Turkish assonance." Alien loan words and international technical terms could thus be incorporated in the language without jarring anyone's sensibilities' (Emerson, 1962: 138; citing, in part, Szabe, 1952).

Escape hatches

The enlightenment of nationalist purism in language planning thus proceeds along many well-trodden paths: the differentiation between ethnic core and nonethnic periphery, between technical and nontechnical, the differentiation between preferred and nonpreferred sources of borrowing, and, finally, the appeal to common usage among the masses. Thus, in India it is argued that 'native Hindi elements failing we should not go to a foreign country for words which can be supplied by Sanskrit; names of new *objects* and *processes* may be European and international; for *ideas* we should have our own words' (Chatterji, 1943: 29). Similarly in the Philippines it was foreseen that 'The [National Language] Institute shall use as a source primarily the Philippine tongues and then, if necessary, the Spanish and English, adopting from these languages such terms as are already familiar to the Philippine tongues, having been [in] general use in the same. Whenever it shall be indispensable to form new words these shall be taken principally from the classical languages such as Greek and Latin, especially for scientific literary and technical use. Foreign words thus newly formed shall be assimilated to Philippine phonetics and orthography' (Commonwealth Act no. 184: An Act to Establish A National Language Institute and Define its Powers and Duties, in Rojo, 1937: 64). Later, when Pilipino was more firmly intrenched, it was argued that 'names are arbitrary words and [so are] expressions used to denote ... things that can be felt and seen. In any language names are usually arbitrary ... [therefore], whenever it [is] necessary to borrow a foreign word . . . this [should] . . . be taken in, assimilated, and then regarded as a single morpheme . . . [On the other hand] terms expressing complex scientific concepts and relationships, and such abstractions, are best conveyed by words having a consistent and rational [i.e. Austronesian] morphology' (del Rosario, 1968: 10–11). It is in this fashion that nationalist language planning is able to go about its task of incorporating and of digesting the foreign in an enlightened (i.e. in an acceptable) way. When successfully accomplished the vernacular is not only expanded and strengthened but it has also retained the appearance of authenticity and the role of authenticator of experience. It is then still felt that a dictionary of the modernized language 'so far from being a mere list of unconnected words, reflects to a great extent the character of the people whose speech it is; . . . This is the kind of dictionary we want to see for our language and for our nation' (Flannery, 1896: 100).

Obviously, nationalist directed language planning does not proceed along a set, undirectional path that is universally accepted and admired by the target populations for whom it is intended. While it may be admired for 'preserving the purity and cohesion of the language . . . deliver[ing it] from the fate that befell ancient Latin, which passed out of use and was replaced by off-shoot languages such as French and kindred tongues, [by] devising new terms which our language needs, to denote new things and new ideas' (Jabri, 1953: 20–1), it is also criticized for the initial artificiality and unfamiliarity of its products. 'Not too long ago, when patriotic students in Bandung urged the teaching of certain courses in Indonesian, only two professors were able to comply; then, at the end of a fortnight the students had to reverse their petition because they could not understand the lectures' (Bro, 1954: 112). Even the planners themselves sometimes look askance at what they have done.

'Most of the Swahili contained in these books is correct grammatically, and may be defended on that ground. Grammatical accuracy, however, does not itself constitute a language, and it is perhaps this very exaggerated application of grammatical rules that has led us away from the real Swahili language and made us substitute something which is, at its best, lifeless though intelligible, at its worst, lifeless and unintelligible' (from the *Bulletin of the Inter-territorial Language Committee*; cited by Whiteley, 1969: 87).

Nevertheless, given the new functions that the language must fulfil, it must, perforce, acquire new units and structures. That being the case, it is a self-proclaimed and increasingly accepted responsibility of nationalist inspired language planning to guide the growth of the language and its involvement in new functions in such a way as 'to rid the language of bad influences and guide it along the proper road' (Government of Tanzania report 1965, cited by Whiteley, 1969: 104).

Nationalist-inspired language planning, like nationalist-inspired activity on all other fronts, escapes from the dilemmas and inconsistencies that always obtain between theory and practice, between ideology and implementation. Its royal roads are many. At times one or the other will be stressed; at times all will remain temporarily becalmed tension systems, waiting to spring in the direction of their dominant orientations. Ultimately, it not only works out a functional compromise between the new and the old, the regional and the national, the rural and the urban, the peripheral and the central, the foreign and the indigenous, the efficient and the authentic, but it does much more. Just as the state-into-nationality process requires time and stability to create the unified and natural entity of which it is so proud, so nationalist language planning pushes forward slowly, inexorably, when more rapid roads to its targets are not open. With the passage of time, and with the control over media and institutions of society, it converts the new *into* the old, the regional *into* the national, the rural *into* the urban, the foreign *into* the indigenous, the peripheral *into* the central and the merely efficient *into* the authentic.

In the realm of language planning, nationalism

'required that new words be consciously created to refer to operationally defined referents discovered or created [or borrowed] in the process of specialization . . . [Language planning is possible when men can] de-reify words, treating them as symbols, not as things in themselves; as secular not as sacred . . . [It] is not only a functional necessity for diffracted [i.e., modern, urbanized] systems, but is made possible only by a concurrent transformation in attitudes toward language' (Riggs, 1964: 141).

However the foregoing applies equally well to modernization-inspired language planning of any kind, rather than particularly to its nationalist variety. The latter goes beyond the former in that it constantly keeps an eye on the mirror of unifying authenticity. Indeed, it *must* do so since among the many inborn contradictions of nationalism is yet another which claims that authenticity is spontaneous and unrehearsed. In unabashedly proceeding to produce the spontaneous, nationalism keeps before itself a substantive image (flexible and alterable though it may be) of that which makes its vernacular 'richer, more limpid, warmer . . . abounding in metaphor, imagery, idiom, proverb,' that which makes it then 'truly unique,' that which provides it with 'the distinctive flavor of genius and authentic experience' (Talmon, 1965: 105; citing the views of Herder): the spirit of the nationality whose guardian and reflection it is. Nationalism brings new words into contact with this spirit of the nationality. It creates them in accord with the model of this spirit. Nationalism views itself as the guardian of the spirit rather than its creator. In the beginning there is the spirit and all else naturally follows therefrom, even if it must be planned.

Recapitulation: Early twentieth century European and more recent Southeast Asian language planning

In France

The classical example of language planning in the context of state-into-nationality processes is that of the French Academy. Founded in 1635, i.e. at a time well in advance of the major impact of industrialization and urbanization, the Academy nevertheless came after the political frontiers of France had long since approximated their current limits. However, complete sociocultural integration was still far from attained at the time, as witnessed by the fact that in 1644 the ladies of the Marseille(s) Society were unable to communicate with Mlle. de Scudéry in French, in 1660 Racine had to use Spanish and Italian to make himself undertood in Uzès, and even as late as 1789 half of the population of the South did not understand French. The unparalleled literary creativity in French under the patronage of Louis XIV could aim, at most, at a maximal audience of 2,000,000 literates (out of a total estimated population of 20,000,000). However, in actuality, no more than 200,000 participated in the intellectual life of the country and many of these considered Italian, Spanish and Occitan far more fitting vehicles for cultured conversation, whereas for publications Latin too was a common rival. All in all, the French Academy assumed an unenviable task — and one rather consistently ridiculed throughout several centuries — when it presumed to codify French vocabulary, grammar, and spelling for the purpose of perfecting refined conversation and written usage.

Several aspects of the Academy's approach reveal its premodernization goals and views. Far from seeking to provide technical nomenclatures for industrial, commercial, and other applied pursuits the Academy steadfastly refused to be concerned with such 'uncultured' and 'unrefined' concerns. Instead of attempting to reach the masses with its products the Academy studiously aimed its publication (at least for three centuries, if not longer) at those already learned in the French language. Finally, instead of appealing to anything essentially French in 'spirit,' in 'genius,' in 'essence,' or in 'tradition', it defended its recommendations via appeals to such purportedly objective criteria as euphonia, clarity, and necessity (redundancy). More than 200 years after its founding, when the Academy's continued lack of concern for the technical vocabulary of modernization had come to be accompanied by attacks on *anglomanie* and the tendency to *angliciser*, the worst that was said about overly frequent English borrowings was that they were unnecessary rather than that they were un-French:

'On n'entend que des mots à déchirer le fer,
Le railway, le tunnel, le ballast, le fender,
Express, trucks, wagons; une bouche française
Semble broyer du verre ou mâcher de la braise . . .
Certes, de nos voisins, l'alliance m'enchante,
Mais leur langue, à vrai dire, est trop envahissante!
Faut-il pour cimenter un merveilleux accord
Changer l'arène en turf et le plaisier en sport,
Demander à des clubs l'aimable causerie,
Flétrir du nom de grooms nos valets d'écurie,
Traiter nos cavaliers de gentlemen-riders?
Je maudis ces auterus dont le vocabulaire
Nous encombre de mots dont nous n'avons que faire.'

(Viennet, 1853)

In the nationality-into-state context the links between the authenticity component of nationalism and language planning, on one hand, and between the modernization-unification components of nationalism and language planning, on the other hand, are much more prominent and much more conscious. As a result, institutions and guidelines for language planning come into being very early in the mobilization process and remain in the foreground at least until authenticity, modernization, and unification seem reasonably assured. Here we are dealing with more highly pressured situations in which language planning is of top priority, not only because of ideological considerations but also because without it the new élites can neither communicate with each other about specialized élitist concerns while remaining within the limits of authenticity, nor can they move the masses toward greater unification, authentification, and modernization.

In Turkey

The Turkish language planning case is justifiably well known for the speed and the thoroughness with which it pursued modernization. As part of its overall post-World War I program of seeking a *new* Turkish identity (in contrast with the old Ottoman-Islamic identity), governmentally sponsored language planning conscientiously and vigorously moved to attain script reform (Roman in place of Arabic script), Europeanization of specialized nomenclatures (rather than the Arabic and Persian loan words hitherto used for learned or cultured purposes), and vernacularization or simplification of vocabulary, grammar, and phraseology for everyday conversational use (discarding the little understood and ornate flourishes patterned on Arabic or Persian).

Obviously Turkish language planning was a part of Ataturk's overall program of modernization. However, no nationalist movement can continue to push modernization without regard for authenticity. Thus the break with the holy Arabic script soon came to be defended on the ground that it was unsuited for the requirements of authentic Turkish phonology. Since even the prophet had clearly been an Arab before he was a Mohammedan he could hardly dispute the desire of Turks to put the needs of their Turkish authenticity first. The vast Europeanization of Turkish technical vocabulary had to be rationalized on the basis of the Great Sun Language Theory. On the basis of this authenticity-stressing theory it was claimed that all European languages were initially derived from Turkish. In that case all recent borrowings could be regarded as no more than reincorporations into the Turkish language of words or morphs that it had originally possessed but lost under the foreign impact of Arabic and Persian. Thus, the process of borrowing from European sources was ultimately not defended in public as a modernizing step, but, rather as an authenticating step! So too, and even more clearly, was the vernacularization and simplification of nontechnical Turkish. Here the language of the Anatolian peasant was held up as a model of purity and authenticity on the ground that it had been least contaminated by foreign influences and least corrupted by foreign fads.

Thus, on every front, language modernization decisions in Turkey were finally rationalized and legitimatized via authenticity sentiments and a way was found for these two components of nationalist ideology to reinforce common nationalist goals rather than to conflict with them or with each other. Such dialectic skill is by no means rare in the annals of language planning within highly nationalist contexts. On occasion modernization may appear to have the upper hand and, on occasion, authentification is stressed. In the longer run, however, what needs to be grasped is not so much the seesawing back and forth as the need to retain both components (actually all three components since uniformation too must not be lost) and to find a modus vivendi between them. Many examples of arriving at resolutions to the contradictory pressures built into nationalist language planning are to be found in the Estonian, Czech, Ukrainian, Greek, Turkish, and other relatively recent European language planning experiences. These examples deserve at least as much attention as do those drawn from more uncompromising periods in which one or another of three major components of nationalism was stressed.

Language planning in South and Southeast Asia

The lesser stress on ethnic authenticity in South and Southeast Asian nationalism thus far is reflected in the correspondingly greater roles of both indigenous and imported Languages of Wider Communication (rather than of vernaculars alone) as languages of central government and higher education. The well-nigh complete and rapid displacement of Latin, French, German, Russian, and Arabic which marked the end of Austro-Hungarian, Czarist, and Ottoman hegemony in Central, Eastern, and Southern Europe has had no parallel in South and Southeast Asia. Even the displacement of Dutch in Indonesia was conducted with a regional Language of Wider Communication in mind (a variety of Malay) rather than on behalf of a vernacular. Although some vernaculars have gained a level of recognition since independence that they never had in colonial days, the positions of English and French, on one hand, and of Hindi, Urdu, Malay, Indonesian, and Pilipino, on the other hand, are definite signs of the continued supra-ethnic stress of South and Southeast Asian language planning.

Indeed, the most central symbols and institutions of nationhood, the very processes of modernization and unification per se, are generally not related to vernaculars at all. Thus, as the nations of South and Southeast Asia progress along the path toward politico-operational integration, we may expect that the new sociocultural integration that they must seek to develop and the authenticity that they must seek to stress will also be supraethnic. In the language planning field this has taken the direction of protecting and increasing the authenticity of the non-Western Languages of Wider Communication that have come to be adopted for national unificatory purposes. In this sense the views of the language planning agencies of South and Southeast Asia are constantly becoming more and more similar to those of early twentieth-century Central, Eastern, and Southern Europe (even though they are not dealing as exclusively with vernaculars), and less and less like those of state-into-nationality contexts that originally provided them with models.

Romanization of script

Wherever classical literary traditions existed in preindependence South and Southeast Asia, romanization of script has been rejected (Fishman, 1972b). Although a modicum of romanization is practiced in conjunction with highly technical and advanced scientific work conducted in India, Pakistan, and Ceylon, e.g. the proposals to introduce romanization of script on a wider front — as an aid to literacy, modernization, or interregional communication — has been resisted as vigorously in those countries as it has been in China, Japan, or Israel outside of the area under consideration. The mass ideologization of this resistance is consistently in terms of indigenous authenticity vs. foreign artificiality.

Purification

The tendency to reject European or, more generally, 'international' lexical or morphological items, even for rather technical scientific or governmental work, is increasing through South and Southeast Asia. So is the tendency to limit the various vernacular influences on the national languages, even though such influences would tend to make these languages more widely understood. With respect to Hindi these tendencies take the direction of successively more extreme Sanskritization, ignoring the pleas of educators and statesmen alike that such treatment severely restricts the functional utility of the language. A similar process of Arabo-Persianization (and Islamization) is transforming High Urdu. In Malaysia, Indonesia, and the Philippines it leads to a growing emphasis on Austronesian derivatives, rather than on Graeco-Latin roots, in developing and in orthographically 'naturalizing' the specialized nomenclatures that Malay, Indonesian, and Pilipino increasingly require. In most of the earlier twentieth-century European cases of language planning the purification efforts were directed at one or another neighboring vernacular rather than at internationalisms as such. In South and Southeast Asia, given the general identification of internationalisms with Euro-American colonialism, purification shows tendencies of combating 'cultural colonialism' much more than neighboring vernaculars, all the more so since the latter have little if any competitive significance. The interest in indigenizing the national languages of South and Southeast Asia is a definite sign of the new and broader sociocultural integration that they must succeed in developing, to the end that a new supralocal ethnic authenticity will develop that will correspond to the broader unification and deeper modernization that can now be emphasized with increasing likelihood of success.

Language planning in South and Southeast Asia may be expected to be increasingly subjected to supraethnic authenticity goals on the part of governmental and intellectual élites. Whereas thus far language planning has been concerned primarily with such unification and modernization goals as mass literacy, participation, and productivity, the very focus on these goals has and must contribute, ultimately, to a redistribution of attention so that authenticity too will receive the recognition it has always required as one of the three equal-but-opposite partners in the inevitable triangle that nationalism represents.

Postscript

At the conclusion of an excursion such as ours, it is obvious that many problems remain to be solved; indeed, that there are more such than were initially apparent. Even if the wisdom of hindsight has been gained, and that is none too certain, the ability to put it to use — in subsequent theoretical and empirical analyses — remains to be seen. If it is true, as Kurt Lewin claimed, that 'nothing is as practical as a good theory,' then certainly I would add that nothing is as provocative for theory as practical problems and efforts. The recurring dimensions and sequences, with respect to nationalism and language planning, adumbrated in the previous pages, must now withstand their most serious test: attempts by others to apply them in the vast amount of archival and documentary research on the one hand and in the crucially necessary quantitative and multivariable research on the other hand, that remains and pleads to be undertaken. I am sure that much that I have outlined will need to be changed as a result of the work that will follow. The only satisfaction to which a student can legitimately look forward, other than the satisfaction of the work process itself, is that of having been considered, rather than ignored in the work of others.

For myself, I have learned a few lessons from the foregoing examination of the trials and tribulations, pains and pleasures, of successive clusters of nationalities throughout the globe. Most of the truths that I sense or acknowledge have been recognized before and in some instances, long ago. Perhaps all I can say is that I understand them better, more richly, for having derived them and arrived at them myself. It was 1893 when a little known spokesman for a little known nationality observed:

> 'Modern life is supposed to tend to break down all the barriers of nationality, of race and even of language, and to weld the nations of the earth into one mighty mass. That something like this may not be witnessed in a future stage of the world's history I am not prepared to deny ... However, ... side by side with the levelling tendency which annihilates distinctions and which would have one law, one language, one cosmopolitan character throughout, ... there is a counter tendency of a natural and involuntary character constantly emphasizing distinctions and building up local differences, tending to make languages' (Southall, 1893: 314–15).

I believe this observation to be correct; indeed to be even more correct in the latter part of the twentieth century, than it was in the latter part of the nineteenth when it was originally formulated. The need for identity, for community, to make modernity sufferable, is greater than it was and will become greater yet, and woe to the élites — in universities, governments, and industries — who do not recognize this or, even worse, who consider it to be only a vestigial remnant of nineteenth-century thinking.

The search for a rooted community, marked by uniqueness and by greatness, corresponds to a partial need, a postponable need, an over-lookable need, but to a basic social need for all that, a need to which all turn or return, at one time or another. A nation that does not recognize this about itself, and a scholarship that shuts this realization off from awareness, must, as a result, have less to offer modern man and modern science than is needed. It is for this reason that I am more fearful of the de-ethnicizing myths of the American and Soviet social sciences than I am of the myths of those still grasping for self-recognition and self-dignity. To call the latter 'irrational' and the former 'rational' (Myrdal, 1970), in unabashed oblivion of the fact that one's own so-called rationality (with its 'overkill' capacity) is the luxurious byproduct of a largely similar process once also dubbed 'irrational' (and worse), when it too began, is to be simultaneously dangerous, heartless, and uninformed. 'The significance of a social movement does not lie simply in the rationality of its ideas; nor in its success. To judge ... nationalism only by the logic of its ideas is to miss something crucial' (Marx, 1970: 32): its developmental necessity, its power, its creative potential. There is no maturity without adolescence — and adolescence is not only destructive and thoughtless, it is also tender and altruistic and intuitive and profoundly, humanly troubled, hopeless and hopeful at one and the same time.

It is foolish to predict the demise of adolescence, to deny its legitimacy, to ridicule it. It is doubly foolish to do so from the vantage point of an establishment bound to be counterridiculed. But it is also triply foolish, because the denyers are simultaneously denying themselves, their own inner selves, and offering this self-denial, at once stifling, self-congratulatory, and beside the point, to others who are in far different circumstances, as if it were the ultimate wisdom.

Nationalities will come and nationalities will go, but nationality behavior is here to stay and those attaining it for the first time, or attaining it anew at a broader level, will continually display the added sensitivity and insensitivity which always mark heightened experiences. This does not at all mean that the dream of 'one world' is an unattainable (not to say an unworthy) dream. Quite the contrary. It merely means that levels of kinship must be recognized and that these will continue to coexist as concentric circles, each adding to and enriching the human social identity provided by the others. Nor will national languages disappear. Quite the contrary; more and more national standard languages were predicted by Deutsch towards the beginning of World War II (1942) and his prediction has held up very well during the past three decades. However, the increasing number of standard national languages (the codification, elaboration, and cultivation of which are goals pursued via national language planning) does not forebode the doom of international languages or, ultimately, of even one language for the entire world. 'Narrower languages' and 'wider languages' have always coexisted, as have narrower and wider networks of sociocultural and political-operational integration. Indeed, the greatest force working for the voluntary acquisition of languages of wider communication in educated circles today (Denison, 1970), is the realization that one's national language is safe-but-insufficient (Fishman, 1969). Widespread diglossia patterns are re-emerging throughout the world today and nowhere as strongly as where speakers of small languages feel certain that their national and linguistic place in the sun is not threatened thereby.

When the fate of the world hangs in the balance, as it does today, only our faith in the emotional and intellectual capacity of man can carry the day. Nationalities and languages have been planned in the past and their bearers have subsequently gone on to other, more inclusive problems. This is happening again today. It will happen again in the future. It is part of the social drama of humanity. Would that we could help it happen with less wear and tear and with more mutual acceptance among all concerned.[53]

Notes to Chapter 9

1. See Chapter 4 of this volume for Part I of Language and Nationalism. The bibliography to Parts I and II is found on pp. 338–67.
2. Indeed, those pursuits and processes not influenced by such ideologies were long unconcerned with the vernaculars. Since political participation, e.g., was restricted to the nobility, the upper bourgeoisie, and the intellectuals, all of whom were suitably multilingual by virtue of also controlling a classical tongue and a prestige vernacular (even when they no longer maintained their original vernaculars), it was unnecessary 'before the end of the eighteenth century . . . [for] governments [to] regard the language of the people as a matter which concerned them . . . [Nor did they] attempt to destroy a language when they acquired new subjects through conquest or peaceful annexation' (Sulzbach, 1943: 48). There are, however, many pre-eighteenth century records of governmental use of vernaculars wherever contact with the masses *was* desired.
3. Learning (or relearning) the vernacular was an integral part of the re-ethnization of Czech, Slovak, Polish, Ukranian, Jewish, Rumanian, Estonian, and other latter nineteenth-century and early twentieth-century proto-élites drawn from middle-class (or better) sociocultural backgrounds. Thus, Arwiddson, a mid-nineteenth century leader of the pro-Finnish Swede-Finns held that 'the Finns could never become a truly united nation while the upper classes were separated from the lower by a linguistic gulf. The gulf could be bridged and the people united only by reversing the process which had made the upper classes increasingly Swedish. In a word they would have to adopt Finnish as their mother tongue' (Wuorinen, 1931: 53). A similar linguistic re-ethnization was frequently necessary in late nineteenth-century India. Chaudhuri recollects that during his childhood the nationalist leader Aurobindo Ghose 'spoke in English because having been educated wholly in England he could speak no Bengali at all when he came back to his country, and when he came to Kishorganj he had learnt just enough to carry on a simple conversation' (1951: 239).
4. Where the approximate vernacular is not that which is ideologically preferred (e.g. Sanskrit, classical Greek, classical Arabic, Irish, Hebrew), or where there are a great many mutually incomprehensible vernaculars without an established lingua franca (as, e.g. in parts of East and West Africa), the functional load of nationalism may be carried by other languages for longer or shorter periods. In most of these cases, however, there is considerable tension between two tendencies, on the one hand to revise nationalist ideology so that it will conform in a more stable fashion with the *actual* vernaculars, and, on the other hand, to augment the language planning and learning aspects of nationalist policy so that the vernaculars utilized will more quickly become

the ones that the ideology requires. The successes and failures of nationalism in the revival of so-called 'dead' languages or in the indigenization of distant languages is a fascinating topic which merits separate attention (see footnote 47, below).

5. In another context Kedourie observes quite correctly, that 'the reading of books [in the vernacular] became a political, a revolutionary activity' (1961: 103).

6. The earliest European arguments on behalf of *vernacular education* (rather than merely on behalf of more widespread literacy) can be traced back at least to the early fifteenth century. Nevertheless, such education long remained rare, indeed it was not until 1548 that 'Louis Le Roy first lectured in French at a university and became the first author of a treatise on metaphysics in the vulgar language' (Kohn, 1944: 132). Even then it was necessary to argue that there was no question of disregarding Hebrew, Greek, or Latin but only 'de cheminer plus seulement en sa voye domestique, c'est à dire escripre françoise, comme François que nou somme' (Geoffroy Tory of Bourges in his Champfleury 1529; cited by Kohn, 1944: 131). At roughly the same time the number of German books published annually in Protestant Germany was still only 116, i.e. half the number of Latin books (246). As late as 1714, the number of Latin books remained fairly constant although the number of German books published annually had increased to 419. In 1780 the two figures were 198 (Latin) and 1,917 (German) (see: Karl Biederman, *Deutschland im achtzehnten Jahrhundert* [Leipzig: Weber, 1859], vol. II, p. 504).

   By the end of the eighteenth century elementary education in the vernacular was becoming sufficiently common among the 'historic peoples' of Western Europe for coterritorial minorities to recognize the disadvantage under which their children labored and to agitate for change. 'Is it not strange that the Welsh differ in their method of teaching childen from every other nation in the world? There is no other country, to our knowledge, which does not first teach its own language to the children, apart from Wales' (Morgan John Rys 1793; cited by W. R. Jones, 1966: 39). A century later this identical argument had spread to Eastern Europe and half a century thereafter, to substantial parts of Africa and Asia. In all cases, however, the definition of the 'nation's own language' is ideologically rather than merely 'naturally' determined.

7. The educational use of the vernacular, particularly in higher education, seems, generally, to have lagged behind its use in particular legal pronouncements and in military announcements *intended to reach the common man*. Thus, 'in the 1360s King Edward III prescribed the use of English instead of Latin or French, in the lower courts of England' (Hayes, 1960: 60). Even earlier (842) the Oaths of Strasbourg presented significant evidence of the official use of the vernaculars for strategic purposes: 'Louis the German (King of the East Franks) and Charles the Bald (King of the West Franks) swore loyalty to each other. As they did, Louis used the *lingua romana* (Roman–French) so that his brother's retainers might understand him; and Charles spoke *lingua teudesca* (Deutsch–German) for the same reason. But these languages were certainly not yet . . . Kingdomwide in usage' (Shafer, 1955: 77). Nevertheless, such precedents did not always lead to consistent followups, due primarily to the fluctuating dependence of royal power upon popular support. In 1539

Francis I found it necessary to order that only French be used in legal acts
and pronouncements (thus excluding both Latin and regional languages such
as Provençal), although such orders had also been given by earlier monarchs.
Similarly, Philip II of Spain was advised during the century of Spanish world
power to use 'clear Castilian instead of an obscure and barbarous Latin' and
that civil law should be expressed 'en lengua común y popular' (Simón Abril
1550?; cited by Kohn, 1944: 153). The great and final decision on behalf of
the vernacular came with mass armies, mass involvement in political and legal
affairs, improved communication networks, and mass education systems,
rather than with any of the earlier precedents of the kinds mentioned above.

8. 'Furtherance of the modernization ideals requires the extended use of the
indigenous languages. No real 'emotional integration' of the new nations, and,
therefore, no secure national consolidation is possible as long as the members
of the tiny upper class in charge of administration, law enforcement and
modernized business and industry communicate in a European language and
the masses speak only their native tongue' (Myrdal, 1968: 81).

9. The objectively instrumental role of language in the reorganization of
economic and political systems is one of the major foci of Deutsch's *Social
Communication and Nationalism* (1953). His many indices of mobilization all
have in common the fact that they highlight exposure to vernacular communication from élitist groups attempting the activation and unification of
specific populations. More recently Myrdal has both indicated the indis-
pensability of the vernaculars in national modernization in South Asia, as well
as the problems of large-scale political integration likely to flow from their
utilization (1968: 81–89, 1639–40, etc.). Friedrich, among political scientists,
has consistently maintained the view that 'In any elaborate sense, community
means . . . language' since it conveys 'emotions, thoughts and other expressions of selfhood which bind . . . [interlocutors] into a community that is
continuously reborn through speaking and listening' (1963: 43 and 40). His
formulation contains echoes of the nationalist emphases on subjective
function, i.e. on the *particular* languages that are involved in the emotional
rebirth and in the authentic preservation of a nationality. The connection
between both kinds of functions is recognized (even if not stressed) by each
of the above mentioned authors, as well as by observers in the developing
nations *per se*. Chatterji, e.g., states '. . . we have the need for an [all-] Indian
language, which we must have for both utility and sentiment' (1943: 23).
Exactly the same point has been made by Ajarchukwu (1960), Ola (1960),
Whiteley (1969), Harries (1969), and others in Africa. Social science
recognition of the link between instrumental and sentimental interdependence, particularly in the work of Daniel Katz (1940, 1965) and others
of the University of Michigan group who have more recently been studying
'the national role' in individual behavior, has not yet been directed expressly
toward language, but could easily be so directed.

10. The vernacular also figured as a symbolic rallying cry (among several others
of a religious nature) in most of the premodern European efforts at broader
sociocultural integration beginning with the Arab invasion of the Iberian
Peninsula. Thus, under their military leader Jan Zizka, the Hussites went into
battle in 1420 with the [Catholic] Holy Roman Emperor and his allies in order
'to liberate the truth of the Law of God and the Saints, and to protect the
faithful believers of the Church, and the Czech and Slavonic languages' (cited

by Kohn, 1944: 111).

At similarly early dates the Catholic Churches of various countries recognized language as a natural indicator of nationality. Thus at the Council of Constance (1414), at which nation[ality] (rather than state) was the basis of representation, the English prelates claimed to represent a true nationality, as defined on the basis of 'peculiarities of language, the most sure and positive sign and essence of a nation in divine and human law' ['. . . diversitatem linguarum, quae maximam et verissimam probant nationem et ipsius essentiam, jure divino pariter et humano']. Conversely, the Portuguese objected to 'the inclusion of prelates from Sicily and Corsica with the Aragonese in the Spanish nation on the ground that, although subjects of the King of Aragon, they spoke another language and were therefore, "truly of a different nation"' (Loomis, 1939: 525–26). An even earlier example of the seemingly natural identity of separate peoplehood with separate language is found in Llywelyn II's thirteenth-century plea to Henry III ('I therefore seek, being a Prince, that I likewise shall have my Welsh law, and proceed according to that law. By common right, we ought to have our Welsh law and custom, as the other nations [*nationes*] in the King's Empire have — and in our language' [Jones-Pierce, 1950: 52]). Such examples can be multiplied almost without end both from even earlier periods as well as from after the Reformation, when language became an increasingly common referent in conjunction with minority efforts to differentiate between recognized states and unrecognized nationalities.

11. Language has undoubtedly appealed to many social scientists who have sought a more objective criterion of nationality than 'will,' 'consciousness,' or other common designata of nineteenth century nationalism. Thus, even in recent years, we find the view 'that the most conspicuous dimension of familiarity and difference, the dimension with the most points on it and the sharpest discontinuities, is language. [Therefore,] language is one of the most important factors in delimiting a national or ethnic group' (Rosenblatt, 1964: 37). The realization that language boundaries — particularly when we refer to spoken language — can be every bit as vague and as ambiguous as other sociocultural boundaries, has not penetrated far into social science circles.

A major pre-World War II review of nationalism in Europe concludes that 'all nationality movements on the continent [with the dubious exception of the Scottish] seem to be connected with language' (Chadwick, 1945, p. 2). Minogue's commentary on this conclusion would be widely accepted today, namely, that 'any single test of nationality breaks down . . . Yet in a metaphorical sense language remains the most promising candidate. A nation[ality] *does* consist of people who speak the same language' (1967, p. 31), thus once more, turning to the objective rather than facing squarely the subjective features of our concern.

If the sufficiency of language as a badge of nationality is questioned today, it is more likely to be partially due to the fact that language in and of itself does not unite England and the United States nor divide Switzerland, and partially on the grounds that people should not insist on being united politically on the basis of so inconsequential a factor as language. The 'linguistically neutral' Swiss federation (where strong language–nationality links exist within each of the cantons) arose in premodern days and has not been successfully copied in modern times. The first rejection confuses nationality and nation (or even state) and seems to argue unjustifiably that if two groups speaking the 'same' language do not clamor to be part of the same nation (or state) then their language cannot be a significant aspect of their respective groupness. The second rejection confuses the observer's values with those of his subjects.

In 1766 Turgot remonstrated with Du Pont de Nemours for having confounded the idea of the nationality with that of the state and went on to define 'nation[ality] as a community of language' (cited by Kohn, 1944: 229). Similarly, Stalin sought to reach a compromise between the demands of proletarian internationalism on the one hand and pro-Soviet nationalist appeals on the other, by stating that one of the characteristic features which distinguishes nationality from state is that 'a national[ity] community is inconceivable without a common language' of its own ([1913] 1942: 241). Whereas the bourgeois state was the enemy of the proletariat the nationality was not, since it *was* the proletariat.

12. Wilhelm von Humboldt expressed this view most succinctly, as follows: 'Their speech is their spirit and their spirit is their speech. One cannot express too strongly the identity of the two' (cited by Rocker, 1937: 228). The formalization of this view in more recent years has become known as the Whorfian (or the Sapir–Whorf) hypothesis (Fishman, 1960). Its original presentations are indicative of the nationalist contexts in which the conviction arose that language must be taken 'not merely as a set of words and rules of syntax, not merely as a kind of emotional reciprocity, but also as a certain conceptualization of the world' (Minogue, 1967: 120). Thus, Schleiermacher held that 'only one language is firmly implanted in an individual. Only to one does he belong entirely no matter how many he learns subsequently . . . [for] every language is a particular mode of thought and what is cogitated in one language can never be repeated in the same way in another. . . . Language, thus, just like the Church or state, is an expression of a peculiar [i.e. of a distinct way of] life' (cited by Kedourie, 1961: 63). That such views quickly lent themselves to sweeping invidious comparisons is obvious from Hamann's observations that 'Every people reveals its mode of thought through the nature, form, rules and mores of its speech . . . The legalism of the Jewish people, which rendered it so blind at the time of the divine visitation, is fully revealed in its language' (Johann Georg Hamann, Schriften, vol. II [Berlin: 1821]; cited by Baron, 1947: 132).

The continued emotional hold of this view, in the absence of confirmatory evidence, notwithstanding repeated efforts to provide such via controlled experiments, is evident from the fact that most cultural anthropologists today would doubtlessly agree with Vossler's intuitive claim that 'there rests in the lap of each language a kind of predestination, a gentle urge to this or that way of thinking' (1932: 137).

13. Although Herder's devotion to linguistic and cultural authenticity and diversity was certainly sincere, it was equally certainly anti-French, at least in origin (Barnard, 1969; Clark, 1955; Wells, 1959). It is interesting, therefore, to find a very similar view being expressed at approximately the same time by the French philosopher Limoge, who in a letter of 1790 to Bishop Gregoire of the National Assembly, observed that 'the spiritual wealth of the nation was stored in its language and could only be tapped by those understanding it; the

true spirit and character of a nation could only be expressed in the national tongue' (paraphrased by Shafer, 1955: 122). Certainly Herder was not alone in his recognition of the link between language and national authenticity. His contribution to this view and its subsequent espousal and intensification by generations of German philosophers and scholars must not be overlooked. Herder, Wilhelm von Humboldt, the Schlegel brothers, the Grimm brothers, Bopp, Schleicher, Dier, and many others '. . . established the attitude of the German mind to the language of its own people and to other languages. The whole of modern philology is essentially and almost exclusively a German product' (Vossler, 1932: 130). For continued German (post-Nazi) concern with such topics see Polenz (1967), Pielow (1967), Kochs (1966).

14. The unimportance of the distinction between languages and dialects, from the point of view of this argument, is revealed by the following claim on behalf of preserving Swiss-German: 'Unsere Mundart ist mehr als eine Verkehrs- und Umgangssprache: Sie ist Ausdruck einer ganz bestimmten Gesinnung. Sie wächst über andere Dialekte hinaus, weil in der Schweiz die Mundart dauernd die Umgangssprache aller Stände geblieben ist . . .; bei uns bildet sie ein Merkmal sozialer Einheit und ist Sinnebild unseres demokratischen Denken' (Sommer, 1945: 100). Thus, the same arguments utilized to distinguish between recognized varieties ('languages') were easily transferred to distinguish between less privileged ones, the status of the latter as languages (rather than as dialects) coming to be a reflection of the *societal success of the argument presented* rather than of the distance between any variety of reference and any other. Modern sociolinguistic theory takes full cognizance of the fact that the distinction between 'language' and 'dialect' is essentially linguistically arbitrary and societally reversible by treating both within one and the same theoretical framework (Fishman, 1971b).

15. The last two lines are rendered in a much subdued fashion in Chamberlain's widely known English translation, viz:
'That is thy land;
That, German, is thy Fatherland.'
(See J. F. Chamberlain, 'Literary Selections as an Aid in Teaching Geography,' *Journal of Geography* [September 1916], p. 12.) Arndt's German original may have been inspired in part by the last two lines of a poem entitled 'Now or Never' that appeared in the *Rheinishce Merkur*, No. 130, October 19, 1814: 'Und wo der Teutschen Sprache Laute tönen/Erblühe nur ein Reich des Kräftigen und Schönen!'

16. Where no indigenous literature is as yet being created in the vernacular the link between language, literature and nationalism is sometimes forged via well-planned translations from world literature. In this connection note Hodgkin's reference to translations from Racine and Marx in Wolof (1956: 176) and similar scattered references to such translations in Krio, Akan, and other smaller West African languages. Similar programs of creating nationalist literatures in translation have been conducted by the Soviets (e.g. see Wurm, 1954; Wurm, Waterson & Simpson, 1960).

Conversely, where earlier mass movements had succeeded, at least in part, on the basis of particularly moving and influential vernacular literatures, subsequent pan movements on behalf of a supranationality or state language may face unusual difficulty. Thus, 'the regional languages [of India] developed as the literary vehicles of a popular religious revival extending over centuries

... The *bhakti* movement which popularized Hinduism and made it intelligible to a mass public was a movement conducted in the language of each region ... a millenium ago ... The *bhakti* poets went out of their way to adhere to the native or *desi* meters characteristic of language as it was spoken and thereby capture its flavor and make more effective emotional contact with would-be devotees ... It was for this reason that the regional languages provided the obvious outlet for the burst of new cultural creativity which followed the 19th century influx of Western social and political thought ... [and which explains] the resistance to Hindi on the part of the votaries of other languages, notably Tamil, Bengali and Marathi, which have a far more impressive and more ancient literary heritage' (Harrison, 1963: 218–83). A very similar point is made for Irish in terms of the wealth of Irish literary (and other sociocultural) authenticity created in English over a span of centuries. As a result most Irishmen would prefer to cherish Irish 'as a museum piece, playing at most the role enjoyed by Latin in American colleges of a generation ago ... The utmost that can now be hoped for in reviving the use of Gadhalic would be the creation of a bilingual bureaucratic upper class, ruling over an English speaking mass — a paradoxical reversal of the conquest' (Clarkson, 1950: 46). A foreign (and foreign-speaking) ruling class, has been viewed as a particular misfortune since Biblical days: 'Lo, I will bring a nation upon you from afar, O house of Israel, saith the Lord; it is a mighty nation; it is an ancient nation, a nation whose language thou knowest not, neither understandest what they say' (Jeremiah 5: 15).

17. The major advocate of this extrapolation was Fichte, who not only championed the sociocultural distinctness of speech communities ('Those who speak the same language are linked together before human intervention takes a hand, ... they are by nature one indivisible whole' [Minogue, 1967: 64]), as did Herder and others, but also their political-operational distinctness. 'Just as it is true beyond doubt that, wherever a separate language is found, there a separate nation[ality] exists, which has the right to take independent charge of its affairs and to govern itself; so one can say, on the other hand that, where a people has ceased to govern itself, it is equally bound to give up its language and to coalesce with its conquerors' (Hayes, 1931: 215–16). The anti-French context of German language nationalism of the time is even clearer in Schlegel's statement that 'A nation[ality] that tamely looks on whilst it is being despoiled of its idiom forfeits the respect due to independence; it is degraded in the ranks of civilization' (Hayes, 1931: 225–26). German thought relating language to political integration went so far as to imply double political loyalty to bilinguals, viz. Ludwig Mises (1919). The struggle against French among English literati, coming as it did in premodern times, left many fewer scars (note: 'Theyr longage [French] In redynge is douse and dylycate./ In theyr mother tonge they be so fortunate./ They have the bybyll and the apocalypys of devynyte,/ with other nobyll bokes that in Englyche may not be' [Anon., *The Kalender of Shepherdes*, 1506]. 'Shall English be so poore, and rudely-base/ as not be able (through mere penury)/ to tell what French hath said with gallant grace,/ and most tongues else of lesse facunditie?/ God shield it should ...' [John Davies of Hereford, prior to 1618]).

18. Voltaire himself provides us with insight into the state of affairs in élitist German circles against which Fichte, Herder, and their associates cried out. 'When Voltaire was in Berlin as a guest of Frederick II he wrote to his friends

in Paris that he felt as though in France. French was spoken exclusively and German was only fit for the horses. The king's brother advised a Prussian nobleman to learn French since he surely could not want to be "a German beast"' (Hertz, 1944: 84). Frederick himself 'did not hide his contempt for German literature and German writers. In these, resentment against their lowly position became confounded with resentment against the French language and literature which the privileged classes and their imitators affected to cultivate. It was literary men, with literary preoccupations, who thus endowed language with political significance' (Kedourie, 1961: 60). If we extend the designation 'literary men' to include a variety of proto-élites it is obvious that the situation of Germany *vis-à-vis* France was long quite similar to that subsequently experienced by submerged nationalities in Central, Eastern, and Southern Europe, *vis-à-vis* Germany, Austro-Hungary, and Russia, or in parts of contemporary Africa and Asia today *vis-à-vis* the West.

19. Peoples throughout the world and in all ages have viewed themselves as uniquely possessing the gift of speech or, at least, of proper speech. The Greek designation of all non-Greeks as barbarians presumably 'had its source in the idea of stammering or inability to speak in a comprehensible way, the Greek word *barbaros* [being] akin to the Sanskrit expression *barbara*, which meant "stammering"' (Kohn, 1944: 7). Similarly the ancient Hebrews viewed their Egyptian masters as having been a 'stammering' or, at the very least, a 'wild-speaking' people (Psalms, 114: 1) from whom they were delivered because they (the Hebrews) had remained true to their names, their language, and their customs. 'The name *Slav* is derived from *slovo*, which, in all Slav languages, means "word" — they were the "worded ones," who could understand each other, whereas the Germans who merely mumbled (*mye-mye*), were *Myemtsy* ... dumb' (Namier, 1944: 102). The word *Hausa* (the self-name of a numerous people of Northern Nigeria) means 'language' in the vernacular of its native speakers, although there is the possibility that it refers to the fact that they adopted Arabic as their language of religion and higher learning rather than their vernacular. Both *Hausa* and *Bahasa* (Indonesia) probably share the Arabic root for *language* or *tongue*.

20. Compare 'I should also like to call attention to the illogical position of men who drop their own language to speak English, of men who translate their euphonious Irish names into English monosyllables, of men who read English books and know nothing about Gaelic literature' (Hyde; cited by Kohn, 1944: 147) with 'Is it not the chief object of our literary ambition, at present, to be able to compose an article in good English and to deliver an eloquent speech in the same language? And can we who have not even a smattering of the Aryan tongue honestly claim the denomination of Arya? Is it not a painful, a shameful necessity that compels me, at the present moment, to advocate the cause of Aryan learning in a foreign language' (A. Mitra, 1879–80; cited by McCully, 1940: 257). In our own day advocates of Swiss-German have similarly argued, *vis-à-vis* High German, 'Zukünftige Geschlechter werden uns Dank Wissen wenn wir ihnen diese lebendige Schutzwehr gegen fremdes Wesen und fremden Geist gesund erhalten' (Sommer, 1945: 101). Mazrui cites many such views (opposing the currently accepted Western languages of wider communication) by various African spokesmen (1973) and appends the full text of a statement of Obote (1967).

21. 'Philological research has proven beyond doubt a close relation between the

Greeks, Romans and Indo-Aryan peoples . . . This relationship existed also in thought . . . Indo-Aryans (now called Hindus) were the originators of civilization . . . Egypt, Greece and Rome were their pupils and recipients' (McCully, 1940: 247–48; paraphrasing an unsigned article in *The Arya* 1882–1883, I, 21–23). Somewhat later young Bengalis began to justify their use of Bengali (rather than English) for advanced, modern purposes on the ground that 'the English language was only a borrowing from Bengali' (Chaudhuri, 1951: 410). Note also the Great Sun Language theory whereby all (modern European) languages are derived from Turkish (Szabe, 1952).

22. Prior to the cited passage Elsbree observes: 'One of the characteristics of national movements in Southeast Asia has been that they have not developed out of native languages . . . The process in Southeast Asia clearly has been that of the state creating a national language rather than that whereby the national language forms the basis of the state' (1953: 120–21). The experience of India with Hindu, Malaysia with Malaysian, Indonesia with Indonesian, the Phillipines with Pilipino, and Pakistan with Urdu, are all of this type. However, this formulation would seem to be somewhat less applicable to Vietnam, Thailand, Burma, Ceylon, and one or two other nations with clearer ethnic preponderance (e.g. Korea, Cambodia, Laos). Thus, as earlier in Europe, both types of processes seem to be in evidence in Asian modernization and, again, they tend to be cyclically interrelated, the one flowing into and eliciting the other.

23. Perhaps the oustanding example of the flexibility of language planning and language decisions on behalf of largely unideologized populations is the Illyria movement of the mid-nineteenth century on behalf of the Southern Slavs. An Illyrian nationality was to be united, an Illyrian language was to be formulated, and an Illyrian nation was to be created out of the Croats, Slovenes, Macedonians, and several other smaller Balkan Slavic groups that shared a common ritual language. Napoleon had succeeded in briefly establishing an Illyrian duchy sixty years earlier, but it was not until the advent of pan-Slavism that an indigenous proto-élite discovered Illyria for its own purposes. Illyrianism easily attracted foreign intellectual support. 'Indeed, the interest of German romanticists in "Illyrian" literature was even greater than their attachment to Czech literary excavations. Southern Slav literature was even further off the main tracks of Western European literature, and, therefore, appeared still more romantic and politically more innocent' (Kohn, 1955: 419–20). However, the case of Illyria is not as unique as it might appear to be. The Dravidasthan movement which once sought to unite all southern (non-Aryan) India via a Tamil-based koine (McCully, 1940: 270) is also of this type, as is Sukarno's proposed union of Malaysia, the Philippines, and Indonesia into a single 'Malphilindo.' In each case the prior continuities and discontinuities were not sufficiently established or clear-cut to rule out a large number of alternative sociocultural and political-operational integrative possibilities, each of them with a language rationale among its components. The practical failure of many schemes is no more a real indication of their 'irrationality' than is the success of their competitors any valid indication of their 'rationality.' Success and objective rationality are two quite separate dimensions in sociopolitical behavior and history.

24. Seyssel goes on to 'admonish Louis XII to follow the example of Rome. 'What did the people and the princes of Rome do when they held the world empire

and aspired to perpetuate and eternalize it? They found no way as sure and as certain as that of magnifying, enriching and sublimating their Latin language, which at the beginning of the empire had been very meager and very crude' (Kohn, 1944: 130), thus turning the diglossia argument in his own favor. Latin was but a vernacular in its own day and age and if it too required cultivation in order to become the great instrument of culture that it subsequently came to be, might not a vernacular like French, which currently must live in the cultural shadow of Latin, aspire to the same greatness if it too were properly developed? This anti-diglossia argument we will see, was, subsequently, essentially repeated by adherents of other and still less recognized vernaculars. Thus Thomasius argued 'The Greeks had not written their philosophy in Hebrew nor the Romans in Greek — each of these great nations had used its vernacular because they rightly envisaged philosophy as a subject for all men. The French philosophers of recent times had followed the ancients in using the vernacular for their writings. Why should the Germans, by not doing so, suggest to other nations that philosophy and learning could not be written in their language?' (cited by Blackall, 1959: 13).

25. 'While French spread throughout the world as a universal language it had the greatest difficulty in gaining admission as a language of instruction in French schools even in the lower grades ... Even the few educators who accepted the demands for teaching French, however, did not regard it as a desirable end in itself; they saw in it an introduction and an aid to the better teaching of Latin. In the Collège de France it was explicitly forbidden to comment in French on Latin or Greek texts ... Even at the time of the Revolution no chair of French language existed [in any university in France]' (Kohn, 1944: 229 and 231). Little wonder then that when the jurist Christian Thomasius posted a German notice on the official bulletin board of the University of Leipzig (1687) stating that he proposed to offer a course in German, his act was viewed as 'a symbolic gesture reminiscent of Luther's nailing his theses to the door of the Church. Some 30 years later in looking back at this action, Thomasius declared that nothing had so horrified the University of Leipzig since its foundation and the screens [i.e. the bulletin board on which he posted his notice] might well have been reconsecrated with holy water as a result' (Blackall, 1959: 12–13). The revolutionary implications of disturbing the established diglossia patterns via offering education in the vernacular was at least implicitly recognized by many who advocated the vernacular. Thus the German linguist Gottsched (in 1739) attacked 'the "lovers of darkness" and the "enemies of the fatherland" who refused to countenance scholarly work in the vernacular. Like the ancient Egyptians they would make a mystery out of learning and so keep those who have not studied classical languages — that is to say the large mass of the nation — in bestial ignorance' (Blackall, 1959: 116).

26. Advocates of various pan-movements also recognized both the need for and the possible consequences of language planning. A modernized version of classical Arabic was advocated by some pan-Arabists as a crucial compromise between the uniform (but inaccessible and archaic) classical Arabic and the diverse (and diversifying) colloquial varieties (Nuseibeh, 1956: 74–76). Chinese communist recognition that a uniform written language (i.e., one not tied to the diverse spoken vernaculars) is of immense unifying value was anticipated, for their own pan-purposes, by early Christian missionaries such

as S. Wells Williams who cautioned that 'separate systems of writing would tend to break up the people into little clans and states,' and E. J. Eitel who pointed out that 'to tamper with the ideographs was tantamount to denationalizing the Chinese' (De Francis, 1950: 217–18). Recent Soviet pan-policy in Central Asia of developing selective integrative vernaculars but of stressing the unifying and leading role of Russian (see e.g. Allworth, 1965; Quelquejay & Bennigsen, 1961; Rakowska-Harmstone, 1970) was anticipated by the Finnish Social Democrats in 1906 when they declared that '(1) The development of Finnish into a fully satisfactory literary and educational medium and its elevation to the position of an official language has ever been and still is important for the educational, moral and material progress of the Finnish speaking workers . . .; (2) Swedish is indispensable for the advance of the Swede-Finn people in Finland. It is also an important channel through which educational influences and Social Democratic ideas may be brought to us . . . for these reasons the Party Congress favors the retention and further cultivation of Swedish; (3) . . . the Russian language . . . and modern Russian literature dealing with the ideal of liberty should be spread in Finland' (Wuorinen, 1931: 211).

27. '. . . The French used cultural relations as an object of low bargaining. We must refuse all bargaining. This refusal could lead to the reshaping of our programs. We may even have to envisage the use of a language other than French, and thus look toward other civilizations, countries, and friends' (Bourguiba 1961; published in Sigmund, 1963: 143).

28. 'Korais saw his task as two-fold: the revival of the Greek language and the education of the modern Greeks through the study of the works of their classical ancestors. The lack of linguistic homogeneity would be a stumbling-block to the unity of the Nation, since only when Greeks became aware of their ancient culture would they set about freeing themselves' (Sherrard, 1959: 182).

29. 'There were not only two [Magyar] nations [the noble and the peasant] but two Maygar languages: the language of the noble society full of foreign words which was scarcely understood by the peasants, and the popular Magyar tongue in its virginal purity and limitless capacity for development, looked down upon by the lord with a pitiful smile' (I. Acsady, 1903; cited by Jaszi, 1929: 263). Similarly, 'in 1790 the French national assembly published a manifesto which sought to arouse in all districts a holy emulation to banish jargons, the last remains of feudalism and monuments of slavery' (De Francis, 1950: 212).

30. '. . . there is a growing tendency for a local [industrial town] vernacular to be accepted as a worker's lingua franca — Wolof in Dakar, Bambara in Bamako, Yoruba in Lagos' (Hodgkin, 1956: 121). Compare this observation with Delgado de Carvalho's 'that the road net of the time [eighteenth century] constituted one form of the industrial movement. The circulation of workers brought on the disappearance of the dialects. Where workmen from different provinces congregated for great works, the use of French soon prevailed' (1962: 91). Nevertheless, French was initially primarily a lingua franca rather than a national standard.

31. For the extreme case note 'Lutfi's view [referring to Ahmad Lutfi al Sayyid the major Egyptian nationalist theorist of the nineteenth century] (that) Arabic had ceased to develop since the latter Abbasid period; its forms had

been fixed and the gap had widened between the written and the spoken language. Nothing less than a deliberate renovation (of the written language) was needed' (Ahmad, 1960: 103). A similar goal, but of less serious dimensions, was commonly espoused by European nationalist movements that initially found/created older written traditions and then proceeded to modify the modern (planned) written language in the direction of one or another spoken variety. For nationalist views *opposing* the approximation-uniformation of writing and speaking in instances where the two are much closer to each other than in the Arabic case note Chapter 7 ('Die Einwände der Reformgegner') of Lendle 1935.

32. This quotation, dealing as it does with Illyrian, was selected in order to stress the similarity between the planning problems faced by *Ausbau* languages (Kloss, 1952 and 1967) of greater and lesser differentiability. The quotation continues '. . . of developing the grammatical skeleton from the literary treasures of the past. There was a widespread conviction at that time that the Illyrian "mother tongue" already existed' (Kohn, 1955: 243).

33. Note the similarity of the condition of German in 1700 to that of Finnish in 1880. 'The absence of formal instruction in Finnish in the schools meant . . . that Finnish did not lend itself easily to the demands of polite society or of the world of letters . . .' (Wuorinen, 1931: 65). The popular emphasis on elaboration is formulated by Bentham in his 'list of the several qualities desirable in language' as follows: 'On the highest point stands *copiousness*. It is only in proportion as it is copious that a language contributes anything to its end' ([1820] 1962: 310).

34. 'Primarily due to the influence of Commonwealth President Manual Quezon, Tagalog — the language of his youth and of most Filipinos living in the environs of Manila — was selected as the basis for the national language to be known as Pilipino. Tagalog then was the native tongue only of some 19 percent of the population, as contrasted with Cebuano, which was spoken at home by one out of every four Filipinos' (Rauenholt, 1963: 192).

35. E.g. '[Leibnitz proposed] the establishment of what he called a "teutshgesinte Gesellshaft" whose function shall be to encourage the production of serious works (*Kernschriften*) in the German language' (Blackall, 1959: 4), or 'Composed of political leaders such as Sukarno and Hata as well as literary figures the [Indonesian language] Commission added to the language several thousand new terms [during the Japanese occupation period] many of them in the technical field in which all the languages of this area are weak' (Elsbree, 1953: 122–23).

36. 'In every country the diffusion of the *national* language was essentially a military necessity; it was imposed from above by means of compulsory education and, in many regions, it was nothing but an artificial creation' (Delaise, 1929: 165). Also, for an earlier period note Baron's contention that 'only Peter the Great's act of daring, followed by ruthless suppression of opponents, simplified alphabet and ritual so as to re-establish a measure of conformity between the religious and secular languages' (1947: 166).

37. 'We whose life is more peaceful, and who have more opportunity to cultivate letters, must use all our strength to enrich and to refine our language. In parliament and in country assemblies we must speak Magyar, and it is shameful that we cannot clothe fine thoughts in fine languages' (Ribinyi 1775; cited by Marczali, 1910: 236).

38. 'Meine Absichten sind nicht gewesen Neuerungen in unserer Sprache zu machen. Ich gehöre nicht unter die Zahl derer die sich einbilden, sie hätte Fähigkeit genug, ihre Muttersprache zu verbessern, andere einzurichten, und zu verschönern . . . Alles was also, meines Erachtens, ein Sprachlehrer thun kann, ist dieses, dass er die vorborgenen Schönheiten seiner Muttersprache aufsuche, entdecke, anpreise und bey seinen Landsleuten in Schwang bringen helfe' (Gottsched, in the introduction to his *Sprachkunst* 1748; cited by Blackall, 1959: 115).

39. 'Seventeenth-century French grammarians . . . claimed that the *ordre direct* was the "natural order" . . . as the 18th century unfolds we find Batteux and others recognizing emotional as well as logical order. It was pointed out that Latin order was different from that of French' (Blackall, 1959: 455).

40. Similarly, but with typically greater care to avoid invidious comparisons, Herder claimed that 'Germans, like all active peoples, preferred active verbs' (Minogue, 1967: 60).

41. In connection with foreign borrowings (which had been long opposed, but in vain, in the premodern development of English) Bentham observed 'When a word has thus been transplanted and naturalized in a single state, the conception entertained of its import, by persons altogether unacquainted with the cluster to which it belonged in the language from which it was borrowed, is always very obscure and imperfect in comparison with that which he has of a word which forms one of a cluster, more or less complete, originally of the growth of his own language, or fully rooted and naturalized in it' ([1820] 1962: 319). Southall employed this very same line of thought some seventy years later, but on behalf of Welsh language maintenance in the face of the rising tide of English: 'It is a simple fact that a man cannot express himself now in English concisely, or in an effective style; he can neither generalize nor specialize, without drawing into use words originating from extraneous sources' (Southall, 1893: 256). The ease with which this initially nonnationalist argument can be transformed for nationalist purposes is indicated by del Rosario who inveighs against foreign borrowing on the grounds that ' . . . consistent and intelligent modernization of their national languages would enable the Malaysians, the Indonesians and the Filipinos to overtake and eventually surpass in science and technology the Western nations, whose national languages are burdened with large numbers of terms derived from Latin and Greek, combining forms which are no longer consistent with the home and community languages spoken by their children. Japan, with her consistent Nippongo, is demonstrating that this can be done' (1968: 16).

42. Chatterji's reference to the 'more elegant forms' of Hindi and Urdu as most influenced by language planning should remind us that it is the more formal varieties in general, and the written language in particular (most particularly of all, written language for public governmental purposes), that are most directly exposed to language planning. Kloss has probably exaggerated the case in claiming that only written language is subject to *Ausbau* (1952, 1967). It is probably more accurate to say that official written language and the informal spoken language represent opposite extremes of a continuum of varieties with the former extreme being at the very vortex of language planning influences and the latter being most distant therefrom (see Fishman, 1973).

43. 'The literary Finnish then in use [about 1835, when Lönnrot's *Kalevala* first

appeared] . . . was based mainly on the West Finnish dialect . . . heavily freighted with Swedicisms. . . . One phase of the nationalist movement was the so-called "Finnization" of the literary Finnish, which meant that it should be purged of Swedish words and idioms so as to render it more national and more easily understood by the common man. The supporters of this demand looked to the richer eastern Finnish dialect as the future literary language' (Wuorinen, 1931: 75). The role of élites and of powerful literature in making and consolidating decisions with respect to such matters is indicated when Wuorinen observes, immediately following the above passage, that 'Lönnrot accepted the eastern dialect as his medium but made many important changes in it in favor of the western dialect . . . His choice . . . was decisive in determining the foundation upon which the Finnish language has rested since his day' (p. 76).

44. De Valera's reaction to this suggestion was to declare that 'he would willingly give up all he knew of English to talk like the natives' (Bromage, 1956: 30).

45. Gaj (1809–1871) not only held 'that this rather elementary idiom could serve as a better common denominator of Illyrian,' presumably due to its having remained closer to the 'proto' stage out of which (and away from which) the more accomplished southern Slav languages had developed, but his choice was also motivated by the hope 'that the factors of national rivalry could thus be eliminated from the reform work' (Kohn, 1955: 246–47). A similar consideration was also operative in the Indonesian elevation of Bazaar Malay to the position of Bahasa Indonesia. Thus instrumental considerations are often present from the very outset in locating the sentimental roots that nationalism requires, and particularly so in pan movements. For explicit recognition of this fact in connection with language planning see I. Kleivan 1969/70 who, not incidentally, also attends to the radio as a new instrumental factor in language planning.

46. The Arabic world popularly explains the revival and survival of their 'pure, original language,' after it had changed to Aramaic subsequent to the fall of Adam and Eve, by attributing the revival, on the one hand, to the miraculous powers of Ishmael, a son of Abraham, and the survival, on the other hand, to the loya'ty of the inaccessible Arabs of the Hejaz (Gallagher, 1963: 204). Lutfi's interest in reestablishing the link between written and spoken Arabic is similar to that of critics of the French Academy, such as Maurice Barrés [1862–1922], who held that 'words which spring from the soil represent nice distinctions and are employed by deeply rooted people with sharpened imagination and poetic feeling' (cited by Hayes, 1931: 196).

47. When no extant population remains that speaks the purported original vernacular then there may be no recourse but to seek broader unity and true authenticity by reviving a (classical) variety that has entirely ceased being a vernacular. Some of the efforts on behalf on Sanskrit or classical Arabic, and to an extent, those on behalf of Irish, Greek, and Hebrew, have been of this kind. All of these reveal the dangers that are hidden in the search for authenticity when a truly great past language is adopted even though it no longer is functional as a vernacular.

In the case of Hebrew the ideological and physical rejection of the diaspora plus the ingathering of exiles from all over the world made it possible for biblical, mishnaic, and medieval Hebrew (that had survived primarily as languages of liturgy, study, and writing) to give birth to a modernized (and widely accepted) vernacular. However, in Ireland, or more particularly, in Greece, neither of these antecedent ingredients were present. The Greek population still spoke a Greek vernacular when the nationalist movement began and it was therefore by no means without a useful indigenous vehicle of mass communication when that movement decided to adopt 'a slightly modernized version of ancient Greek, very different from the spoken idiom' as the national language, 'although it was familiar only to antiquarian scholars. They insisted upon it, because to them the rebirth of Hellas meant the rebirth of Classical Hellas, with its classical language, the language of republican freedom and of mankind's leading thought' (Kohn, 1944: 539). Here was a language — the parent of the living vernacular, never obsolete as the liturgical language of the Church, a link with the medieval splendor of Near Eastern civilization and with the greater ancient splendors of Hellenic civilization. The West admired Ancient Greece as much as Modern Greece admired the West and the ancient language, having sufficed in its day for a civilization which enlightened Westerners regarded as the equal of their own, would surely supply now the indispensable medium for a modern Greek variety of Western culture' (Toynbee, 1922: 20–21). After over thirty years of struggling with the adopted amalgam of modern and ancient Greek it was decided to return to the vernacular. However, by then the problem of 'how to express Western thought in Modern Greek without calling up reinforcements from the ancient language' (Toynbee, 1922: 21), had become much more emotionally and politically (and, therefore intellectually) involved and remains so to this very day, after several additional shifts in policy between more classical and more vernacular usage.

A similar danger, albeit in a less extreme degree, is involved in the ongoing efforts to Sanskritize Hindi. These efforts 'complicate what would in any case be the difficult task of choosing between words drawn from the different dialects [of Hindi] by insisting, with purist zeal, on virtually complete Sanskritization' (Harrison, 1963: 284). In this connection Nehru's plea that 'an effort must be made to discourage the extreme tendencies and develop a middle literary language on the lines of the spoken [Hindi] language in common use' (Nehru, 1953: 454) has been ignored due to the pull of the great tradition of Sanskrit authority and authenticity. 'In ancient and medieval India the unity of the entire sub-continent was preserved, such as it was, by just one factor: the existence of an élite of Brahmins who had a common culture throughout India and who spoke a common language — Sanskrit' (Naik, 1965: 103). Both Lutfi and Nehru were confident that mass education would inevitably force the written language in the direction of the spoken but, as yet, this has not happened to any great degree either in the case of written Arabic or in that of written Hindi.

Most nationalist movements of modern times have dealt with 'Great Traditions' of their own choosing, of their own definition, of their own shaping. The 'Great Tradition' was, in large part, a coproduct of the 'movement,' every bit as much as 'the movement' was a coproduct of 'the tradition.' The pliability of the preferred past was an undisguised blessing not available to those movements related to Great Traditions whose classical remains were widely known and highly regarded. Where real classical pasts of worldwide renown existed, the language problem was not one of choosing (or defining) the vernacular of the masses over the language of wider communication that had been adopted by assimilated élites but, rather, of choosing between a relatively indigenous (or indigenized) vernacular of the masses and the language of widely recognized and validated classical greatness and authenticity. In such cases the rejection of the immediate servile past led inexorably not to the reconstruction and elevation of a purer vernacular but of a real rather than metaphorical return to the language of authentic greatness. Such movements, therefore, are even more conflicted from the point of view of modernization than are those whose 'Great Tradition' is less evidential and more in need of interpretive recreation. In the strained dialectic between authenticity, unity, and modernity that characterizes all modern nationalist movements the hypnotic attraction toward a valid, classical tradition and classical (or classicized) language represents a possibly dis-functional victory for the first (and more immediately sentimental) over the two remaining (and more immediately instrumental) considerations. 'The language of a nation's youth is the only easy and full speech for its manhood and for its age. And when the language of its cradle goes, life itself craves a tomb' (Davies, 1945 [1845]: 70).

The Arabic world has certainly evidenced the most vocal recent concern for maintaining a classical versus any vernacular link to authentic greatness. '[Arabs] are conservative classicists, even purists in all that concerns their language. They do not want to facilitate the rules of grammar, they do not welcome foreign words, even those which have a modern scientific meaning. They invent words from Arabic roots for vitamins, hormones, automobiles . . . etc. This purism is the result of . . . more than thirteen hundred years of literary religious memories' (Moussa, 1955: 41–42). 'The Qur'an is accepted as the highest linguistic achievement of the Arabic language in every possible respect; nobody can possibly vie with it; everybody should try humbly to emulate it. Nothing should be written which does not comply with the linguistic, idiomatic, literary, and rhetorical conditions obtaining in the Qur'an. It would be considered almost treasonable if an Arab were to misspell a word or break one of the intricate numerous rules of Arabic grammar, especially if he were expected to have known the right form' (Shouby, 1951: 288–89). '[For] it is the Koran, the holy book of Islam, which will always remain our guide and our inspiration, and if we keep to the purity of the language . . . then indeed we shall have accomplished a renaissance of Arabic literature' (Nusuli, 1953: 23). 'The advocates of a classical or unadulterated Arabic have [therefore] won an overwhelming victory over those who would have liked very much to introduce some necessary reforms' (Chejne, 1969: 173). That this situation is subject to change is evident from the fact that 'a "medial" Arabic, neither rigidly classical nor fully colloquial . . . arose chiefly during the revolution in Egypt, starting with Naguib and Nasser . . . The masses . . . felt an unprecedented kinship with the new leadership . . . removing a profound psychological barrier separating the illiterate masses from the educated classes of society and creating on the political plane a new sense of unity and belonging' (Sharabi, 1966: 94).

48. The *reinforcement* of nationalist pressures upon language planning via religious influences is best indicated in conjunction with matters of spelling and orthography. Since language planning deals primarily with the written word it quickly trespasses upon that aspect of language use which has religious associations of the greatest stability. Little wonder then that religious

sanctions have so frequently been utilized for and against nationalist language planning.

The distinction between Serbian and Croatian was initially a script distinction between Roman Catholic (and, therefore, Latin script) Croatians and Eastern Orthodox (and, therefore, Cyrillic) Serbs. This distinction 'repeated itself in the Ruthenian cultural evolution between the Polish–Latin alphabet and the "old Ruthenian" Russian alphabet' (Kohn, 1955: 322–23), leading Ukrainians to finally opt for a Cyrillic alphabet even though a Latin one would have differentiated their language more fully from Russian efforts to absorb it. On the other hand, in the early nineteenth century, 'Count Sedlnitsky, the president of the Austrian police administration and one of the most influential officials under the Emperor Francis' regime after 1815, recommended the . . . restoration of the Czech written language' in Latin letter, specifically for the purpose of translating the Orthodox prayer book. 'Translation into the Western Slav languages in Latin letters appeared to the Austrian police state as an important device to fight the political danger of the pro-Russian Pan-Slav movement' (Kohn, 1955: 159–60; quoting materials from the archives of the Imperial Royal Ministry [Fischel, 1919: 57]). This use of Latin letters for a church text helped to firmly establish their hold on Czech and Slovak.

In the East 'the most powerful argument against a change in the script is that the sacred character of the divinely revealed Qur'an places Arabic and its script in a special category' (Nuseibeh, 1956: 73), for 'religion was as much the conveyor of the language as the language was the conveyor of religion' (Polk, 1970: xiv). Similarly, 'with the Persian script the Muslim feels his Urdu is an "Islamic language"; with the native Nagari it becomes a Hindu speech to which he cannot give his allegiance. The Hindu will not give up his national alphabet ['Hindi in Devanagari script . . . are *beati possidentes*;' Myrdal 1968, p. 88]. No compromise is possible between the two scripts, so fundamentally different are they from each other' (Chatterji, 1943: 25). 'Some of the greatest books in the *Devabhasha*, the language of the Gods in India [have been published] . . . in that script. This fact was responsible for the addition of the word *Deva*, i.e., "of the Gods, Divine, Holy," to the word *Nagari*, for the script. So Nagari became Devanagari, the script par excellence . . . [This view is] behind the widespread practice which has become established in present-day Hindi letters, according to which not only names of books and authors but also long quotation from English are given in Nagari letters, totally eschewing Roman script . . . as if it were something untouchable and not worthy of a place in the pages of Nagari Hindi' (Chatterji, in Anon. 1963: 10). On the other hand, those not willing to adopt such a position on the script issue are viewed as being 'unwilling to give an indigenous thing prominence' and 'like old Indian rulers . . . who invited alien powers to come and take over' (Raghavan, in Anon. 1963: 27).

Religious support has also been of great importance in the maintenance of traditional scripts for Chinese, Japanese, Armenian, Amharic, various Indian vernaculars, Irish, and Hebrew, with orthographic change also being resisted for religious reasons in several of these cases.

49. Instances of nationalist abandonment of traditional religious scripts are far fewer. The Turkish case is the most famous, of course, but equally interesting and far less known is the Rumanian 'adoption of the Latin alphabet, though

it is incapable of conveying all the sounds of the Rumanian language ...
[owing to] the ideology of their Latin origin ... In 1863 the use of Cyrillic was
forbidden' (Kolarz, 1946: 22). Ataturk's romanization of Turkish script was
motivated not only by a desire to modernize but also by an urge to separate
Turkey from her Ottoman cultural past. A similar dual function may be noted
in the forced cyrillization of Central Asian languages of Moslem, Buddhist,
and Confucianist populations in the Soviet Union (Quelquejay & Bennigsen,
1961; Wurm, 1954; Wurm, Waterson & Simpson, 1960).

Several references to religion-based difficulties encountered in script
revision and orthographic revision and in the planning of writing systems are
reviewed in Fishman (1971b). Quite similar religious involvements are to be
found in all other aspects of language planning from code selection through
codification and elaboration, to cultivation and implementation. Thus, just as
modern mass nationalism has had to grapple with religious loyalties (a
premodern and prenationalist basis of sentimental and functional integration)
and to learn to put such loyalties to its own use, so nationalist-based language
planning has had to overcome religious obstacles as well as to exploit religious
advantages in connection with its simultaneous goals of reinterpreted
authentification, unification, and modernization goals.

'It is amply clear that in premodern times religious élites not only
contributed to the ethnic authentification and unification of populations and
languages but, in addition, appealed to the latent sentiments of the speakers
of these languages in order to foster and strengthen their own positions as well'
(Cornish, 1936). A reciprocally reinforcing relationship was thus established
which could later be appealed to by both religionists and nationalists for their
particular purposes. The Western inspired need to choose between the two
is all the more painful in the East, where no indigenous rupture between them
has obtained. 'The circumstances of the invention of the 36 character alphabet
in AD 362, the role of the clergy in the adaptation and further development
of Armenian letters, and, above all, the persistent incursions and devastations
befalling Armenia as a nation clinging with tenacity to her ancient language
and her Mother Church in which that language remains enshrined, elevated
the language to a supreme altar of enduring distinction' (Dadrian, 1965: 377).
'In attempting in 1636 [the Council of Tarragona] to prevent the further
dissemination of Castilian from the pulpits, the Catalan clergy had made an
important move towards safeguarding Catalonia's existence as an independent
national entity' (Elliot, 1963: 321–22). 'The clergy ... had raised the
vernacular to the stature of a written language in the first half of the 16th
century. By the close of the eighteenth century the clergy represented, putting
it broadly, the only group among the educated that was still Finnish in speech'
(Wuorinen, 1931: 46). 'Luther ... perfected modern German and almost
created it out of the chaos of provincial dialect, because his aim was to bring
the word of God, the Bible, closer to us' (Vossler, 1932: 129). As a result of
such long-continuing associations between language and religion an aura of
antiquity (if not sanctity) is repeatedly discovered in modern vernaculars,
which blends with the authenticity ethos of modern nationalism. 'Y por siglos
y siglos rompían las olas del castellano sobre las santas playas, los profetas,
y todavía rompen sobre ellas en larga, interminable voluptuosidad de sueño
y de amor. Y de este modo, ¿en dónde habrá voz moderna, en dónde eco de
lengua actual qué más corra y se dilate por los espacios de las lenguas arcáicas'

(Capdevila, 1940: 164).

50. Similar to the appeal to common usage in combating excessive purism is the appeal to usage during earlier glorious periods. Thus, in the case of Arabic, Lutfi argued that 'in classical times the Arabs had accepted foreign words, and some of them found their way into the Qur'an . . . It [the Arab language] must do the same again' (Ahmad, 1960: 104).

51. Vossler (1932: 136), though far more sympathetic to nationalist language planning than Mauthner, also admits that realia are outside of the normal boundaries of the national. 'There is no national language that could be entirely national . . . In some way or another it must always be concerned with some factual or technical concepts.' This escape hatch, so frequently referred to in early stages of nationalist lexical elaboration, is often subsequently closed, fully or partially, either by insisting on indigenous morphs alone or by utilizing indigenous grammatical and phonological models (for pluralization, vowel harmony, etc.) to indigenize that which was initially permissibly foreign.

52. So salient and accepted is the quest for modernization of concepts in African and Asian nationalism that Lutfi is able to turn this quest into an argument on behalf of admitting European words and expressions into scientific Arabic. 'Those who rejected the European name for the European tool, he said, were really implying that it was unpatriotic to learn the modern sciences of Europe or utilize its inventions' (Ahmad, 1960: 116–17). Compare Lutfi's and Gökalp's eagerness for scientific terminology and lexical elaboration more generally with that of the third edition of the French Academy's *Dictionary* (1740): 'To the vocabulary was added a considerable number of words borrowed from the arts and sciences, which the Academy recognized as having become part of the mental equipment of many speakers and writers; but, conservative always, it murmurs a little against their too common usage' since its goal is to preserve 'France from a pernicious innovation in lexicography such as is encouraged in populous and fast-growing communities of uncritical readers where there is no such wholesome check' (Robertson, 1910: 216 and 223). Two centuries later, a historian of the French language reacted to the Academy's concentration upon the 'language of literature and correct conversation' (Robertson, 1910: 222) by stating that 'the civil engineers served the interests of the language more than many members of the Academy' (Brunot, 1924–37; cited by Delgado de Carvalho, 1962: 90).

53. When this volume was in final page-proof I came across the stimulating work of Anthony D. Smith (particularly his *Theories of Nationalism*. London, Duckworth, 1971). A first reading of his publications reveals many differences between my views and conclusions and his, as well as an even larger and more important array of similarities. The true significance of these differences and similarities must, of necessity, wait for a future occasion to receive proper consideration.

Bibliography

AAVIK, J. 1946–48, DerEntwicklungsgang der estnischen Schriftsprache, *Sprakvetensdapliga Sallskapets i Uppsala forhandlingar* 1946–1948, 93–111 (Bilaga F).

ABU-LUGHOD, I. 1967, Nationalism in a new perspective. In H. J. SPIRO (ed.), *Patterns of African Development; Five Comparisons*. Englewood Cliffs, N.J.: Prentice-Hall, pp. 35–62.

ABUN–NASR, J. 1963, The Salafiyya Movement in Morocco: The religious bases of the Moroccan Nationalist Movement. *St. Anthony's Papers* 16, 90–105.

ACTON, Lord (J. E. E.) 1907, Nationality. In J. N. FIGGIS & R. V. LAWRENCE (eds), *The History of Freedom*. London: Macmillan (originally published in *Home and Foreign Review*, 1862, July).

AGONCILLO, T. 1956, *The Revolt of the Masses*. Quezon City: Univ. of the Philippines.

AHMAD, J. M. 1960, *The Intellectual Origins of Egyptian Nationalism*. London. Oxford Univ. Press.

AJARCHUKWU, N. 1960, In quest of national language after independence. *West African Pilot*. Sept. 30.

AJAYI, J. F. A. 1960, The place of African history and culture in the process of nation-building in Africa South of the Sahara. *Journal of Negro Education* 30, 206–13.

AKZIN, B. 1964, *State and Nation*. London: Hutchinson Univ. Lib.

ALISJAHBANA, T. 1949, The Indonesian language, by-product of nationalism. *Pacific Affairs* 12, 388–92.

— 1962, The modernization of the Indonesian language in practice, in his *Indonesian Language and Literature: Two Essays*. New Haven: Yale Univ. Southeast Asia Studies, pp. 1–22.

— 1965, New national languages: A problem modern linguistics has failed to solve. *Lingua* 15, 515–30.

ALLWORTH, E. 1965, *Central Asian Publishing and the Rise of Nationalism*. New York: New York Public Library.

AL-TOMA, S. J. 1971, Language education in Arab countries and the role of academies. *Current Trends in Linguistics VI*, 690–720.

ANDERSON, E. N. 1939, *Nationalism and the Cultural Crisis in Prussia, 1806–1815*. New York: Ferrar and Rinehart.

ANON. 1963, *A Common Script for Indian Languages*. Delhi: Ministry of Scientific Research and Cultural Affairs.

APTER, D. E. 1965, *The Politics of Modernization*. Chicago: Univ. of Chicago Press.

ARENDT, H. 1945, Imperialism, nationalism, chauvinism. *Review of Politics* 7, 441–63.

— 1951, *The Origins of Totalitarianism*. New York: Harcourt.

ASHFORD, D. E. 1964, *Perspectives of a Moroccan Nationalist*. Totowa, N.J.: Bedminster Press.

AUMA-OSOLO, A. & OSOLO-NASUBO, N. 1971, Democratic African

socialism: An account of African communal philosophy. *African Studies Review* 14, 265–72.

AUNG, HTIN. 1953, Commentary on Rupert Emerson's 'The Progress of Nationalism.' In PHILIP W. THAYER (ed.), *Nationalism and Progress in Free Asia*. Baltimore: Johns Hopkins, pp. 82–95.

AUTY, R. 1953, The Evolution of Literary Slovak. *Transactions of the Philological Society* (London), 143–60.

AVTORKHANOV, A. 1965, Denationalization of the Soviet Ethnic Minorities. *Studies on the Soviet Union* 4, No. 1, 75–99.

BAILEY, F. 1960, *Tribe, Caste and Nation*. Manchester: Manchester Univ. Press.

BALANDIER, G. 1953, Messianismes et nationalismes en Afrique Noire. *Cahiers Internationaux de Sociologie* 14, 41–65 (in French).

— 1968, Political Myths of Colonization and Decolonization in Africa. In R. BENDIX (ed.), *State and Society*. Boston: Little, Brown, pp. 475–84.

BALD, M. A. 1925/26, The Anglicisation of Scottish Printing. *Scottish History Review* 23, 107–15.

— 1926/27, The Pioneers of Anglicised Speech in Scotland. *Scottish History Review* 24, 179–93.

BANTON, M. 1965, Social alignment and identity in a West African city. In HILDA KUPER (ed.), *Urbanization and Migration in West Africa*. Berkeley: Univ. of Calif. Press, pp. 131–47.

BARKER, E. 1932, The reformation and nationality. *Modern Churchman* 22, 329–43.

BARNARD, F. M. 1965, *Herder's Social and Political Thought: From Enlightment to Nationalism*. Oxford: Clarendon Press.

— 1969, *J. G. Herder on Social and Political Culture*. London: Cambridge Univ. Press.

BARON, S. W. 1947, *Modern Nationalism and Religion*. New York: Harper.

BARROW, R. H. 1949, *The Romans*. Baltimore: Penguin.

BARZUN, J. 1932, *The French Race*. New York: Columbia Univ. Press. (Reissued by Kennikat Press, 1966.)

BASCOM, Wm. R. 1962, Tribalism, nationalism and Pan-Africanism. *The Annuals* 342, 28–29.

BASKAKOV, N. A. 1960, *The Turkic Languages of Central Asia: Problems of Planned Culture Contact*. Translated with comments by Stefan Wurm. Oxford: Central Asian Research Centre, St. Antony's College.

BECKETT, J. C. 1966, *The Making of Modern Ireland, 1603–1923*. London: Faber and Faber.

Bégouin, L.-P. 1970, Les Franglophones. *Le Travaileur* October 6, 1.

Bell, Wendell, *et al.* 1967, *The Democratic Revolution in the West Indies: Studies in Nationalism, Leadership and the Belief in Progress.* Cambridge, Mass.: Schenkman.

Bellah, R. 1967, Civil religion. *Daedalus* 96, No. 1 (Winter), 1–21.

Bendix, R. 1964, *Nation-Building and Citizenship.* New York: Wiley.

Bentham, J. 1962, Essay on language. *The Works of Jeremy Bentham.* New York: Russell and Russell, Vol. 8, pp. 310–20. (Originally written about 1820.)

Berg, E. J. 1965, The economics of the migrant labor system. *Urbanization and Migration in West Africa.* In Hilda Kuper (ed.), Berkeley: Univ. of Calif. Press, pp. 160–84.

Besant, A. 1926, *India, Bond or Free?* New York: Putnam.

Bidwell, C. E. 1962, Language, dialect and nationality in Yugoslavia. *Human Relations* 15, 217–25.

Biederman, K. 1859, *Deutschland im achzehnten Jahrhundert*, Vol. 2. Leipzig: Weber.

Binder, L. 1964, Ideological foundations of Egyptian-Arab nationalism. In D. Apter (ed.), *Ideology and Discontent.* New York: Free Press, 128–54.

— 1966, Ideology and political development. In M. Weiner (ed.), *Modernization: The Dynamics of Growth.* New York: Basic Books, pp. 192–204.

Bin Ismail, Tuan Syed Narir. 1966, Strengthening linguistic links will hasten Malay unity. *Asia Magazine* (Manila), Oct. 9, 10–13.

Blach, J. 1883, *Die čechoslaven.* Wien and Teschen: Karl Prochaska.

Blackall, E. A. 1959, *The Emergence of Standard German as a Literary Language.* London: Cambridge Univ. Press.

Blond, G. 1960, *Admiral Togo.* Trans. Edward Hyams. New York: Macmillan.

Boehm, M. H. 1933, Nationalism: Theoretical aspects. *Encyclopedia of the Social Sciences* 11, 231–40.

Bolitho, H. 1954, *Jinnah: Creator of Pakistan.* London: John Murray.

Bourguiba, H. 1961, Bourguibism. (Speech delivered on October 12, 1961; translated and published by the Tunisian Secretariat of State for Information). In P. E. Sigmund, Jr. (ed.), *The Ideologies of the Developing Nations.* New York: Praeger, pp. 142–43.

Bram, J. 1955, *Language and Society.* New York: Random House.

Braunthal, J. 1946, *The Paradox of Nationalism.* London: St. Botolph.

Breton, A. 1964, The Economics of Nationalism. *Journal of Political Economy* 72, 376–86.

Bro, M. H. 1954, *Indonesia: Land of Challenge.* New York: Harper &

Row.

BRODA, R. 1931/2, Revival of nationalities in the Soviet Union. *American Journal of Sociology* 37, 82–93.

BROMAGE, M. C. 1956, *De Valera and the March of a Nation*. New York: Noonday Press.

BROWN, L. C. 1965, Changing cultures and new loyalties in North Africa. In Wm. H. LEWIS (ed.), *French-Speaking Africa: The Search for Identity*. New York: Waler, pp. 95–106.

BROWN, W. NORMAN. 1953, Script reform in modern India, Pakistan, and Ceylon. *Journal of American Oriental Society* 73, 1–6.

BRUNER, E. 1961, Urbanization and ethnic identity. *American Anthropologist* 63, 508–21.

BRUNOT, F. 1924–33, *Histoire de la langue française des origenes à 1900*. Vol. I–X. Paris: Colin (. . . *à nos jours*, in 14 parts, – 1953).

BUCK, C. D. 1916, Language and the sentiment of nationality. *American Political Science Review* 10, 44–69.

CADY, J. 1958, *A History of Modern Burma*. Ithaca: Cornell Univ. Press.

CAHNMAN, W. J. 1944, Religion and nationality. *American Journal of Sociology* 49, 524–29.

CAPDEVILA, A. 1940, *Babel y el castellano*. Buenos Aires: Editorial Bosada.

CARR, E. H. (Chmn). 1939, *Nationalism: A Report by a Study Group of Members of the Royal Institute of International Affairs*. London: Oxford Univ. Press.

CATALONIAN CULTURAL COMMITTEE. 1924, *Appeal on Behalf of Catalonia*. Geneva: Catalonian Cultural Committee.

CHADWICK, H. M. 1945, *The Nationalities of Europe and The Growth of National Ideologies*. New York: Macmillan.

CHAMBER, W. W. 1946, Language and nationality in German pre-Romantic and Romantic thought. *Modern Language Review* 41, 382–92.

CHAMBERLAIN, J. F. 1916, Literary selections as an aid in teaching geography. *Journal of Geography*, 15, 9–16.

CHATTERJI, S. K. 1943, *Languages and the Linguistic Problem*. London: Oxford Univ. Press.

— 1952, *Civilizations* 2, No. 1, 19–32 [no title over paper.]

CHAUDHURI, N. C. 1951, *The Autobiography of an Unknown Indian*. New York: Macmillan.

CHEJNE, A. G. 1965. Arabic: Its significance and place in Arab-Muslim society. *Middle East Journal* 19, 447–70.

— 1969, *The Arabic Language. Its Role in History*. Minneapolis: Univ. of Minnesota Press.

CHILCOTE, R. H. 1969, Development and nationalism in Brazil and Portuguese Africa. *Comparative Political Studies* 1, 501–25.

CHILDE, V. G. 1926, *The Aryans: A Study of Indo-European Origins.* New York: Knopf.

CHOWDHURY, M. 1960, The language problem in East Pakistan. *International Journal of American Linguistics* 26, No. 3, 64–78.

CLARK, S. D. 1938, The importance of anti-Americanism in Canadian national feeling. In H. F. ANGUS (ed.), *Canada and Her Great Neighbor.* Toronto: Ryerson Press, pp. 392–438.

CLARK, T. T., Jr., 1955, *Herder, His Life and Thought.* Berkeley: Univ. of Calif. Press.

CLARKSON, J. D. 1950, Big Jim Larkin: A footnote to nationalism. In E. M. EARLE (ed.), *Nationalism and Internationalism: Essays Inscribed to Carlton J. H. Hayes.* New York: Columbia Univ. Press, pp. 45–63.

CLOUGH, S. B. 1930, *A History of the Flemish Movement in Belgium: A Study in Nationalism.* New York: Smith.

COLEMAN, J. S. 1960, Conclusion: The political systems of the developing areas. In G. A. ALMOND and J. S. COLEMAN (eds.), *The Politics of the Developing Areas.* Princeton N.J.: Princeton Univ. Press, pp. 552–57.

— 1963, *Nigeria: Background to Nationalism.* Berkeley: Univ. of Calif. Press.

CONSTANTIN, D., PETROVICI, E., & STEFAN, G. 1963, *La formation du peuple roumaine et de sa langue.* Bibliotheca Historica Romaniae, I. Bucharest: Editions de l'Académie de la République Populaire Roumaine.

CORKERY, D. 1956, *The Fortunes of the Irish Language.* Cork: Mercier Press.

CORNISH, V. 1936, *Borderlands of Language in Europe and their Relation to the Historic Frontier of Christendom.* London: Sifton-Praed.

COULTON, G. G. 1935, Nationalism in the Middle Ages. *Cambridge Historical Journal* 5, 15–40.

CRABB, C. V., Jr. 1968, *Nations in a Multipolar World.* New York: Harper.

CURTIN, P. D. 1966, Nationalism in Africa. *Review of Politics* 28, 143–53.

DADRIAN, V. N. 1965, Major patterns of social and cultural change of the Armenians. *Year Book of the American Philosophical Society* pp. 375–79.

— 1967, Nationalism, communism and Soviet industrialization. A paper presented at the 62nd Annual Convention of the American Sociological Association, Aug. 28–31, San Francisco. Mimeo. 45 pp.

— 1968, The initial development of the Soviet posture on nationalities: A reappraisal of the roles of Lenin and Stalin. *Indian Sociological*

Bulletin 6, 1, 18–38.

DANIEL, S. 1599, *The Poetical Essays of Sam. Danyel*. London.

DAUBE, A. 1940, *Der Aufstieg der Muttersprache im deutschen Denken des 15 und 16 Jahrhunderts*. Frankfurt am M. -Diesterveg (*Deutsche Forschungen*, Vol. 34).

DAVIES, T. 1945, *Essays and Poems with a Centenary Memoir: 1845*. Dublin: Gill.

DAWSON, C. 1950, *The Revolt of Asia*. New York: Sheed and Ward.

DE BLAGHD, E. (BLUTHE, ERNEST). 1951, *The State and the Language*. Dublin: Comhdhail Náisiúnta na Gaeilege.

DE CAMPO, E. A. 1962, José Rizal. *Journal of Southeast Asian History* 3, 44–55.

DE FRANCIS, J. 1950, *Nationalism and Language Reform in China*. Princeton, N.J.: Princeton Univ. Press.

DE FREINE, S. 1965, *The Great Silence*. Dublin: Foilseacháin Náisiúnta Teoranta.

DECRAENE, Ph. 1961, *Le Panafricanisme*. Paris: Presses Universitaires de France.

DELAISE, F. 1927, *Political Myths and Economic Realities*. New York: Viking.

DE LA RAMÉE, P. 1572, *Grammaire* Paris: n.p.

DELGADO DE CARVALHO, C. M. 1962, The geography of languages. In L. WAGNER & M. W. MIKESELL. *Readings in Cultural Geography*. Chicago: Univ. of Chcago Press, pp. 75–93.

DEL ROSARIO, G. 1967, Consistency, not purity, is the important factor in language development. *Philippine Educational Forum* June, 1–11.

— 1968, A modernization-standardization plan for the Austronesian-derived national languages of Southeast Asia. *Asian Studies* No. 6, 1, 1–18.

DENISON, N. 1970, The use of English as a medium of communication in Europe. London: The Institute of Linguists. (Paper prepared for a conference on 'English — a European language' April, 1970.)

DEPRES, L. A. 1964, The implications of nationalist politics in British Guiana for the development of cultural theory. *American Anthropologist* 66, 1051–77.

— 1967, *Cultural Pluralism and Nationalist Politics in British Guiana*. Chicago: Rand McNally.

— 1968, Protest and change in plural societies. Paper presented at the 1968 annual meeting of the American Anthropological Association, Seattle, Washington.

DESHERIYEV, Y., KAMMARI, M. & MELIKYAN, M. 1965, [Soviet National Linguistic Policy Seen as a Model] *Kommunist* No. 13 (September)

55–56. (In English: *Current Digest of The Soviet Press* 1965, 17, No. 47, 14, 19).

DEUTSCH, K. W. 1942, The trend of European nationalism: The language aspect. *American Political Science Review* 36, 533–41.

— 1953, *Nationalism and Social Communication: An Inquiry into the Foundations of Nationality*. Cambridge, Mass.: MIT Press (second edition: 1966).

— 1956, *An Interdisciplinary Bibliography on Nationalism, 1935–1953*. Cambridge, Mass.: MIT Press.

— 1957, *Political Community in the North Atlantic Area*. Princeton, N.J.: Princeton Univ. Press.

— 1961, Social mobilization and political development. *American Political Science Review* 55, 493–514.

— 1964, Integration and the social system: Implications of functional analysis. In P. E. JACOB & J. V. TOSCANO (eds), *The Integration of Political Communities*. Philadelphia: Lippincott, pp. 179–208.

— 1964b, Communication theory and political integration. In P. E. JACOB & J. V. TOSCANO (eds), *The Integration of Political Communities*. Philadelphia: Lippincott, pp. 46–74.

— 1966, Nation-building and national development; Some issues for political research. In K. W. DEUTSCH & W. J. FOLTZ. *Nation-Building*. New York: Atherton. pp. 1-16.

DIOP, C. A. 1956, The cultural contributions and prospects of Africa. *The First International Conference of Negro Writers and Artists*. Paris: Presence Africaine, pp. 349–54; also in Kohn and Sokolsky, pp. 140–48.

DJARYLOGASINOVA, R. S. 1969, On the question of cultural convergence of the Koreans of the Uzbek SSR with neighboring peoples. *Soviet Anthropology and Archeology* 7, 26–35.

DOMINIAN, L. 1917, *The Frontiers of Language and Nationality in Europe*. New York: American Geographical and Statistical Society of New York.

DOOB, L. 1962, South Tyrol: An introduction to the psychological syndrome of nationalism. *Public Opinion Quarterly* 26, 172–84.

— 1964, *Patriotism and Nationalism: Their Psychological Foundations*. New Haven, Conn.: Yale.

DRAPER, T. 1970, *The Rediscovery of Black Nationalism*. New York: Viking.

DROZ, J. 1950, Concept français et concept allemand de l'idée de nationalité. *Europa und der Nationalismus, Bericht über das III internationale Historiker-Treffen in Speyer, 17 bis Oktober 1949*. Baden-Baden, pp. 111–33.

Du Bellay, J. 1948, *La défence et l'illustration de la langue françoyse*. Paris: Chamard (originally 1549).

Dubos, J. B. 1735, *Histoire critique de l'éstablissement de la monarchie française dans les Gaules*. 3 Vols. Paris: n.p.

Durkheim, E. 1933, *The Division of Labor*. Trans. G. Simpson. New York: Macmillan (originally published 1893).

Eastman, C. M. 1971, Who are the Waswahirli? *Africa* 41, 228–36.

Eddy, S. K. 1961, *The King is Dead*. Studies in the Near Eastern Resistance to Hellenism, 334–31 B.C. Lincoln, Neb.: Univ. of Nebraska Press.

Eisenstadt, S. N. 1966, *Modernization: Protest and Change*. Englewood Cliffs, N.J.: Prentice-Hall.

Ellmers, J. E. 1966, The Revolt of the Netherlands: The Part Played by Religion in the Process of Nation-Building. A paper presented at the 6th World Congress of the International Sociological Association, Sept. 4–11, Evian (France). 9 pp.

Elliot, J. H. 1963, *The Revolt of the Catalans; A Study in the Decline of Spain, 1598–1640*. Cambridge (Eng.).

Elsbree, W. H. 1953, *Japan's Role in Southeast Asian Nationalist Movements, 1940 to 1945*. Cambridge, Mass.: Harvard Univ. Press.

Emerson, R. 1962, *From Empire to Nation*. Boston: Beacon Press.

Engels, F. 1886, What have the working classes to do with Poland. *Commonwealth* March 24, March 31, May 5.

Epstein, A. L. 1967, Urbanization and social change in Africa (followed by comments and reply). *Current Anthropology* 8, 275–95.

Estienne, H. 1885, In P. Ristelhuber (ed.), *Deux dialogues du nouveau langage français, italianisé et autrement desguizé*. Paris: Lemerre (orig. pub. 1578).

Etzioni, A. 1965, *Political Unification*. New York: Holt.

Fallers, L. 1961, Ideology and culture in Uganda nationalism. *American Anthropology* 63, 677–86.

Farmer, B. H. 1965, The social basis of nationalism in Ceylon. *The Journal of Asian Studies* 24, 3 (May), pp. 431–40.

Fatemi, N. S. 1959, The roots of Arab nationalism. *Orbis* 2, 437–56.

Febvre, L. 1926, Langue et nationalité en France au XVIIIe siécle. *Revue de synthèse historique* 42, 19–40.

Ferguson, C. A. 1959, Myths about Arabic. *Georgetown University Monograph Series on Languages and Linguistics* 12, 75–82; also in *Readings in the Sociology of Language*. Ed. J. A. Fishman. The Hague: Mouton, 1968, pp. 375–81.

— 1968, St. Stefan of Perm and applied linguistics. In J. A. Fishman, C. A. Ferguson & J. Das Gupta (eds), *Language Problems of Developing Nations*. New York: Wiley, 253–66.

FERNANDEZ, J. W. 1962, Folklore as an agent of nationalism. *African Studies Bulletin* 2, 3–8.

FICHTE, J. G. 1807, *Addresses to the German Nation*. Trans. R. F. JONES & G. H. TURNBULL. Chicago and London, Open Court, 1922 (originally printed 1807–1808).

FISCHEL, A. 1919, *Der Panslawismus bis zum Weltkrieg*. Stuttgart/Berlin: Cotta.

FISHMAN, J. A. 1960, A systematization of the Whorfian hypothesis. *Behavioral Science* 5, 323–39.

FISHMAN, J. A. *et al.* 1966, *Language Loyalty in the United States*. The Hague: Mouton.

— 1968a, Nationality-nationalism and nation-nationism. In J. A. FISHMAN, C. A. FERGUSON J. & DAS GUPTA (eds), *Language Problems of Developing Nations*. New York: Wiley.

— 1968b, Some contrasts between linguistically homogeneous and linguistically heterogeneous polities. In J. A. FISHMAN, C. A. FERGUSON & J. DAS GUPTA (eds), *Language Problems of Developing Nations*. New York: Wiley, pp. 53–68.

— 1969, National languages and languages of wider communication in the developing nations. *Anthropological Linguistics* 11, 111–35.

— 1971a, *Bilingualism in the Barrio*. Bloomington: Indiana University Center for Language Sciences.

— 1971b, The uses of sociolinguistics [in connection with the creation and revision of writing systems]. In G. E. PERREN & J. L. TRIM (eds), *Applications of Linguistics: Selected Papers of The Second International Congress of Applied Linguistics,* Cambridge, 1940. Cambridge Univ. Press.

— 1971c, A multi-factor and multi-level approach to the study of language planning process. In R. KJOLSETH & F. SACK (eds), *Koelner Zeitschrift für Sociologie*.

— 1972a, Problems and prospects of the sociology of language. In N. HASSELMO *et al.* (eds), *Studies for Einar Haugen*. The Hague: Mouton, pp. 214–26.

— 1972b, Historical dimensions in the sociology of language. *Georgetown Univ. Monograph Series on Languages and Linguistics* 25, 145–55.

— 1973, Language modernization and planning in comparison with other types of national modernization and planning. *Language in Society* 2, 23–43.

FLANNGHAILE [FLANNERY], T. O. 1896, *For the Tongue of the Gael*. London: City of London Book Depot.

FONFRÍAS, E. J. 1960, *Razón del idioma español en Puerto Rico*. San Juan: Editorial Universitaria.

FRANKE, C. 1918, *Die Brüder Grimm, Ihr Leben und Wirken*. Dresden and Leipzig: Reissner.

FREEMAN, E. A. 1879, Race and Language, in his *Historical Essays*. London: Macmillan.

FRIEDLAND, Wm. H. 1968, Traditionalism and modernization: Movements and ideologies. *Journal of Social Issues* 24, 4, 9–24.

FRIEDRICH, C. J. 1963, *Man and His Government: An Empirical Theory of Politics*. New York: McGraw-Hill.

— 1966, *Nation-building*. In K. W. DEUTSCH & Wm. J. FOLTZ (eds), *Nation-Building*. New York: Atherton, pp. 27–32.

FURNIVALL, J. S. 1939, *Netherlands India: A Study of Plural Economy*. London: Cambridge University Press.

— 1956, *Colonial Policy and Practice: A Comparative Study of Burma and Netherlands India*. New York: NYU Press.

GADGIL, D. R. 1955, *Economic Policy and Development*. Poona: Sangam Press.

GALBRAITH, V. H. 1941, Nationality and language in Medieval England. *Transactions of the Royal Historical Society* 23, 113–28.

GALLAGHER, C. F. 1963, Language, culture and ideology: The Arab world. In K. H. SILVERT (ed.), *Expectant Peoples: Nationalism and Development*. New York: Random House, pp. 19–231.

GASTIL, R. 1959, *Language and Modernization: A Comparative Analysis of Persian and English Texts*. Cambridge, Mass.: Center for International Affairs of Harvard University.

GEISS, I. 1967, Notes on the development of Pan-Africanism. *Journal of the Historical Society of Nigeria* 3, 719–40.

GELLNER, E. 1964, *Thought and Change*. Chicago: Univ. of Chicago.

— 1965, Tribalism and social change in North Africa. In Wm. H. LEWIS (ed.), *French-Speaking Africa: The Search for Identity*. New York: Walker, pp. 107–18.

GENNEP, A. VAN. 1922, *Traité comparatif des nationalités*. Paris: Payot.

GERTEINY, A. G. 1967, The racial factor and politics in the Islamic Republic of Mauritania. *Race* 8, 263–75.

GLASKOW, W. G. 1971, The origin of the Cossacks. *East Europe* 20, No. 6, 25–29.

GLEZEREMAN, G. 1970, Class and nation. *Transactions of the Sixth World Congress of Sociology* 3, 309–18.

GLUNK, R. 1966, Erfolg und Misserfolg der nationalsozialistischen Sprachlenkung. *Zeitschrift fur deutsche Sprache* (Berlin) 22, 146–53.

GÖKALP, Z. 1914, Nation and Fatherland (Mittet ver Vatan). *Turk Yurdu*

6, No. 66. In N. Berkes (ed. trans.), *Turkish Nationalism and Western Civilization, Selected Essays of Ziya Gökalp*. London: Allen and Unwin, 1959.
— 1959, *Turkish Nationalism and Western Civilization*. Trans. N. Berkes. New York: Columbia Univ. Press.
— 1965, Turkish nationalism. In B. Rivlin & J. H. Szyliowiez (eds.), *The Contemporary Middle East*. New York: Random House, pp. 217–24.
— 1968, *The Principles of Turkism*. Trans. and annotated by R. Devereux. Leiden: Brill.
Goody, J. & Watt, I. 1963. The consequences of literacy. *Comparative Studies in Society and History* 5, 304–45.
Greenberg, J. H. 1965, Urbanism, migration and language. In H. Kuper (ed.), *Urbanization and Migration in West Africa*. Berkeley: Univ. of Calif. Press.
Greenough, J. B., & Kittredge, G. L. 1905, *Words and Their Ways in English Speech*. New York: Macmillan.
Gregory, A. J. 1967, African socialism, socialism and fascism on appraisal. *Review of Politics* 29, 324–53.
Grentrup, T. 1932, *Religion und Muttersprache*. Munster: Aschendorff.
Guetskow, H. S. 1955, *Multiple Loyalties*. Princeton: Center for Research on World Political Institutions.
Guitare, G. L., & Quintero, R. T. 1968, Linguistic correctness and the role of academies. *Current Trends in Linguistics* 4, 562–604.
Guryceva, M. S. 1960, The initial stage in the formation of the French national language. In M. M. Guxman (ed.), *Problems in the Formation and Development of National Languages*. Translated from the Russian original (published Moscow 1960) by the Center for Applied Linguistics, ms.
Haas, E. B. 1964, *Beyond the Nation-State: Functionalism and International Organization*. Stanford: Stanford Univ. Press.
Hadas, M. 1942, The religion of Plutarch. *Review of Religion* 6, 270–82.
— 1943, From nationalism to cosmopolitanism in the Greco-Roman World. *Journal of the History of Ideas* 4, 105–11.
— 1950, Aspects of nationalist survival under Hellenistic and Roman imperialism. *Journal of the History of Ideas* 11, 131–39.
Haim, S. 1962, *Arab Nationalism*. Berkeley: Univ. of Calif. Press.
Hajime, N. 1967, Basic features of the legal, political and economic thought of Japan. In C. A. Moore (ed.), *The Japanese Mind*. Honolulu: East-West Center Press, 143–63.
Hall, R. A., Jr. 1942, *The Italian questione della lingua: An Interpretive Essay*. Chapel Hill: Univ. of North Carolina Press.

HALPERN, B. 1961, Zionism and Israel. *Jewish Journal of Sociology* 3, No. 2, 155–73.

HAMZAOUI, R. 1965, *L'Académie Arabe de Damas et le problème de la modernisation de la langue arabe*. Leiden: Brill.

HANDMAN, M. S. 1921, The sentiment of nationalism. *Political Science Quarterly* 36, 104–21.

HANDELSMAN, M. 1929, Le rôle de la nationalité dans l'histoire du Moyen Age. *Bulletin of the International Committee of Historical Sciences* October, no. 7.

HANNA, S. A., & GARDNER, G. H. 1969, *Arab Socialism: A Documentary Survey*. Leiden: Brill.

HANNA, W. A. 1964, *Eight Nation Makers*. New York: St. Martin's.

HARDY, E. R., Jr. 1946, The patriarchate of Alexandria: A study in national christianity. *Church History* 15, 81–100.

HARRIES, L. 1969, Language policy in Tanzania. *Africa* [London], 39, 275–79.

HARRISON, S. S. 1960, *India: The Most Dangerous Decades*. Princeton, N.J.: Princeton Univ. Press.

— 1963, Hindu society and the state: The Indian Union. In K. H. SILVERT (ed.), *Expectant Peoples: Nationalism and Development*. New York: Random House, 267–99.

HARTZ, L. 1964, *The Founding of New Societies*. New York: Harcourt, Brace & World.

HATT, P. K. & REISS, A. J., Jr. (eds). 1957, *Cities and Society*. Glencoe, Ill.: The Free Press.

HAUGEN, E. 1966, Linguistics and language planning. In Wm. BRIGHT (ed.), *Sociolinguistics*. The Hague: Mouton, 50–71.

— 1966, *Language Planning: The Case of Modern Norwegian*. Cambridge, Mass.: Harvard University Press.

— 1968, Language planning in modern Norway. In FISHMAN, J. A. (ed.), *Readings in the Sociology of Language*. The Hague: Mouton, pp. 673–87.

HAYES, C. J. H. 1928, Two varieties of nationalism: Original and derived. *Association of History Teachers of the Middle States and Maryland: Proceedings*. No. 26, 71–83.

— 1930, *France, a Nation of Patriots*. New York: Columbia Univ. Press.

— 1931, *The Historical Evolution of Modern Nationalism*. New York: Smith (2nd ed., 1948).

— 1937, *Essays on Nationalism*. New York: Macmillan.

— 1942, The church and nationalism: A plea for further study of a major issue. *Catholic Historical Review* 28, 1–12.

— 1960, *Nationalism: A Religion*. New York: Macmillan.

HAZELWOOD, A. (ed.) 1967, *African Integration and Disintegration*. London: Oxford Univ. Press.

HERDER, J. G. 1877–1913, *Sämtliche Werke*. Berlin: B. Suphan, 33 Vols.

HERTZ, F. 1944, *Nationality in History and Politics*. New York: Oxford Univ. Press.

HETTLICH, E. L. 1933, *A Study in Ancient Nationalism: The Testimony of Euripides*. Williamsport, Pa.: Bayard.

HEYD, U. 1950, *Foundations of Turkish Nationalism: The Life and Teachings of Ziya Gökalp*. London: Luzac and Harvill.

— 1954, *Language Reform in Modern Turkey*. Jerusalem: Israel Oriental Society.

— 1968, *Revival of Islam in Modern Turkey*. Jerusalem: Magnes Press of the Hebrew University.

HIBINO, Y. 1928, *Nippon Shindo Ron: The National Ideals of the Japanese People*. Trans. A. P. MCKENZIE. London: Cambridge Univ. Press.

HITCHENS, K. 1970, The Rumanians of Transylvania and the congress of nationalities. *Slavonic and East European Review* 48, 388–402.

HODGKIN, T. 1956, *Nationalism in Colonial Africa*. London: Frederick Muller.

HOLL, K. 1908, Das Fortleben der Volkssprachen in Kleinasien in nachchristlicher Zeit. *Hermes* 43, 240.

HOURANI, A. 1946, Arab Nationalism, in his *Syria and Lebanon*. London: Oxford Univ. Press, pp. 96–104.

HUGHES, A. J. 1963, *East Africa: The Search for Unity*. Baltimore: Penguin.

HUGELMAN, K. G. 1931, Die deutsche Nation und der deutsche Nationalstaat im Mittelalter. *Historisches Jahrbach* 51, 1–29, 445–84.

HU SHIH. 1934, *The Chinese Renaissance: The Haskell Lectures, 1933*. Chicago: Univ. of Chicago Press.

HYDE, D. 1894, *Revival of Irish Literature and Other Addresses*. London: Fisher Unwin, 117–37.

INGELHART, R. F., & WOODWARD, M. 1967, Language conflicts and political community. *Comparative Studies in Society and History* 10, 27–45.

INKELES, A. 1960, Industrial man: The relation of status to experience, perception and value. *American Journal of Sociology* 6, 1–37.

IRELE, A. 1969, Negritude or black cultural nationalism. *Journal of Modern African Studies* 3 (no. 31).

IZZEDDIN, N. 1953, *The Arab World*. Chicago: Univ. of Chicago Press, pp. 19–21.

JABRI, C. 1953, Modern literary trends in Islamic countries. *Colloquium on Islamic Culture*. Princeton, N.J.: Princeton Univ. Press, pp. 19–21.

JACOB, P. E., & TEUNE, H. 1964, The integrative process: Guidelines for analysis of the bases of political community. In P. E. JACOB & J. V. TOSCANO (eds), *The Integration of Political Communities.* Philadelphia: Lippincott, pp. 1–45.

JAKOBSON, R. 1945, The beginnings of national self-determination in Europe. *Review of Politics* 7, 29–42.

JANOWSKY, O. I. 1945, *Nationalities and National Minorities.* New York: Macmillan.

JASZI, O. 1929, *The Dissolution of the Habsburg Monarchy.* Chicago: Univ. of Chicago Press.

JERNUDD, B. & DAS GUPTA, J. 1971, Towards a theory of language planning. In J. RUBIN & B. JERNUDD (eds), *Can Language Be Planned?* Honolulu: East-West Center Press.

JOHANNSON, A. 1892, Zu Noreens Abhandlung über Sprachrichtigkeit. *Indogermanische Forschungen* 1, 232–55.

JOHNSON, H. G. 1968, A theoretical model of economic nationalism in new and developing states. Chapter I in H. G. JOHNSON (ed.), *Economic Nationalism in Old and New States.* London: Allen and Unwin.

JOHNSON, S. 1755, *A Dictionary of the English Language.* 2 vols. London.

JONES, D. G. 1950, National movements in Wales in the 19th Century. In A. W. WADE-EVANS *et al., The Historical Basis of Welsh Nationalism.* Cardiff: Plaid Cymru, pp. 99–129.

JONES, R. F. 1953, *The Triumph of the English Language.* Stanford: Stanford Univ. Press.

JONES, W. R. 1966, *Bilingualism in Welsh Education.* Cardiff: Univ. of Wales Press.

JONES-PIERCE, T. 1950, The age of the princes. In A. W. WADE-EVANS *et al., The Historical Basis of Welsh Nationalism.* Cardiff: Plaid Cymru, pp. 52–59.

JOSEPH, B. 1929, *Nationality, Its Nature and Problems.* London: G. Allen and Unwin, Ltd.

JUMBA-MASAGAZI, A. H. K. 1970, *African Socialism, A Bibliography.* Nairobi: the East African Academy.

KAHL, J. A. 1959, Some social concomitants of industrialization and urbanization. *Human Organization* 18, 2, 53–75.

KAHN, R. A. 1950, *The Multinational Empire: Nationalism and National Reform in the Habsburg Monarchy, 1848–1918.* 2 vols. New York: Columbia Univ. Press.

KARPAT, K. H. 1964, Turkey: The mass media. In R. E. WARD & D. A. RUSTOW (eds), *Political Modernization in Japan and Turkey.* Princeton, N.J.: Princeton Univ. Press, pp. 282–85.

KARTODIRDJO, S. 1962, Some problems on the genesis of nationalism in

Indonesia. *Journal of Southeast Asian History* 3, 67–94.

KARVE, I. 1962, On the road. *Journal of Asian Studies* 22, 13–29.

KATZ, D. 1940, The psychology of nationalism. In J. P. GUILFORD (ed.), *Fields of Psychology*. New York: Van Nostrand, pp. 163–81.

— 1965, Nationalism and strategies of international conflict resolution. In H. KELMAN (ed.), *International Behavior: A Social Psychological Analysis*. New York: Holt, pp. 356–90.

KAUTSKY, J. H. 1962, An essay in the politics of development. In J. H. KAUTSKY (ed.), *Political Change in Underdeveloped Countries: Nationalism vs. Communism*. New York: Wiley, pp. 1–122.

KAZEMZADEH, F. 1968, Pan movements. *International Encyclopedia of the Social Sciences* 11, 365–70.

KEARNEY, R. N. 1967, *Communalism and Language in the Politics of Ceylon*. Durham, N.C.: Duke Univ. Press.

KEDDIE, N. R. 1969, Pan-Islam as proto-nationalism. *Journal of Modern History* 41, 17–28.

KEDOURIE, E. 1961, *Nationalism*. New York: Praeger, 1960 (revised, 1961).

KELMAN, H. C. 1969, Patterns of personal involvement in the national system: a social-psychological analysis of political legitimacy. In J. N. ROSENAU (ed.), *International Politics and Foreign Policy*. New York: Free Press, pp. 276–82.

— 1971, Language as an aid and barrier to involvement in the national system. In J. RUBIN & B. H. JERNUDD (eds), *Can Language be Planned? Sociolinguistic Theory and Practice for Developing Nations*. Honolulu: University of Hawaii Press, pp. 21–51.

KENDALL, P. L. 1956, The ambivalent character of nationalism among Egyptian professionals. *Public Opinion Quarterly* 20, 277–89.

KENNEDY, J. 1968, *Asian Nationalism in the Twentieth Century*. New York: Macmillan.

KERNS, O. P. 1954, The revival of Irish, a case re-stated. *The Irish Ecclesiastical Record*, March.

KHOURI, M. A. 1971, *Poetry and the Making of Modern Egypt (1882–1922)*. Leiden: Brill.

KILSON, M. L., Jr. 1957–58, The analysis of African nationalism. *World Politics* 10, 484–97.

— 1958, Nationalism and social classes in British West Africa. *Journal of Politics* 20, 368–87.

KINROSS, LORD (Balfour, Patrick; Baron Kinross). 1964, *Atatürk: The Rebirth of a Nation*. London: Weidenfeld and Nicolson.

KIRK-GREENE, A. H. M. 1969, The Hausa language board. *Afrika und Übersee* 47, 187–203.

KLEIVAN, H. 1969/70, Culture and ethnic identity: On modernization and ethnicity in Greenland. *Folk* 11–12, 209–34.

KLEIVAN, I. 1969/70, Language and ethnic identity: Language policy and debate in Greenland. *Folk* 11–12, 235–85.

KLOSS, H. 1952, *Die Entwicklung neuer germanischer Kultursprachen von 1800 bis 1950*. Munich: Pohl.

— 1967, Abstand languages and ausbau languages. *Anthropological Linguistics* 9, 7, 29–31.

KOCHS, T. 1966, Nationale Idee und nationalistisches Denken im Grimmschen Wörterbuch. In B. VON WIESE & R. HENSS (eds), *Nationalismus in Germanistik and Dichtung*. Berlin: Erich Schmidt, pp. 273–84.

KOHN, H. 1932, *Nationalism and Imperialism in the Hither East*. London: Routledge.

— 1944, *The Idea of Nationalism: A Study in Its Origins and Background*. New York: Macmillan (paperback: 1961).

— 1955, *Nationalism: Its Meaning and History*. Princeton: Van Nostrand.

— 1962, *The Age of Nationalism: The First Era of Global History*. New York: Harper.

— 1968, Nationalism. *International Encyclopedia of the Social Sciences* 11, 63–70.

KOLARZ, W. 1946, *Myths and Realities in Eastern Europe*. London: Lindsay Drummond.

KOPPELMAN, H. L. 1956, *Nation, Sprache und Nationalismus*. Leiden: Sijthoff.

KRADER, L. 1968, *Formation of the State*. Englewood Cliffs, N.J.: Prentice-Hall.

KUMAR, R. 1969, Community or nation? Gandhi's quest for a popular consensus in India. *Modern Asian Studies* 3, 357–76.

KUPER, L. 1965, *An African Bourgeoisie: Race, Class and Politics in South Africa*. New Haven: Yale University Press.

KURMAN, G. 1968, *The Development of Written Estonian*. Bloomington: Indiana University (*Uralic and Altaic Series*, Vol. 90, Research Center for the Language Sciences).

LA MOTTE-FOUQUÉ, F. DE. 1819, *Etwas über den deutschen Adel*. Hamburg.

LANDES, D. S. & TILLY, C. 1971, History as social science: Excerpts from the report of the history panel of the behavioral and social sciences survey. *Social Science Research Council Items* 25, no. 1, 1–6.

LANGLEY, J. 1969, Pan-Africanism in Paris, 1924–36. *Journal of Modern African Studies* 7, 69–94.

LEGUM, C. 1965, *Pan Africanism*. New York: Praeger.

LEMBERG, E. 1964, *Nationalismus*. 2 vols. Hamburg: Rowohlt.

LENDLE, O. C. 1935, *Die Schreibung der germanischen Sprachen und ihre Standardisierung*. Copenhagen: Levin and Munksgard.

LENGYEL, E. 1969, *Nationalism: The Last Stage of Communism*. New York: Funk and Wagnall's.

LEPAGE, R. B. 1964, *The National Language Question: Linguistic Problems of Newly Independent States*. London: Oxford University Press.

LERNER, D. 1958, *The Passing of Traditional Society*. Glencoe, Ill.: Free Press.

LEVINE, D. N. 1968a, Cultural integration. *International Encyclopedia of the Social Sciences* 7, 372–80.

— 1968b, The flexibility of traditional culture. *The Journal of Social Issues* 24, No. 4, 129–42.

LEWIS, G. 1972, *Multilingualism in the Soviet Union*. The Hague: Mouton.

LIEBERSON, S. 1970, Stratification and ethnic groups. *Sociological Inquiry* 40, 172–81.

LIEBNITZ, G. E. 1838, *Deutsche Schriften*, ed. by E. GUHRAUER. Berlin, vol. 1.

LINDMAN, K. 1963, Finland's Swedes: An introduction and a bibliography. *Scandinavian Studies* 35, 123–31.

LINZ, J. 1970, Early state-building and late peripheral nationalisms against the state: The case of Spain, ms. for the UNESCO Conference on Nation-Building, Cérisy, Normandie, August.

LIPSET, S. M. 1968, *Revolution and Counterrevolution: Change and Persistence in Social Structures*. New York: Basic Books.

LITTLE, K. 1965, *West African Urbanization: A Study of Voluntary Associations in Social Change*. London: Cambridge Univ. Press.

LLOYD, P. C. 1967, *Africa in Social Change*. Baltimore: Penguin.

LOCKWOOD, W. B. 1954, Language and the rise of nations. *Science and Society* 18, 245–52.

LOHIA, R. M. 1965, Hindi — here and now. *Seminar* 68 (April), 27–31.

LOOMIS, L. R. 1939, Nationality at the Council of Constance. *American Historical Review* 44, 508–27.

LONSDALE, J. M. 1968, Some origins of nationalism in East Africa. *Journal of African History* 9, 110–46.

MACPHERSON, J. 1966, *Fragments of Ancient Poetry (1760)*. Los Angeles: University of California at Los Angeles.

MADAN, I. N. 1965, Sanskritization. *Seminar* 68 (April), 24–27.

MAJUMDAR, R. C. 1961, Nationalist Historians. *Historians of India, Pakistan and Ceylon*. London: Oxford University Press, pp. 416–28.

MALÓN DE CHAIDE, P. 1794, *La Conversión de la Madalena, donde se ponen los tres estados que tuvo, de pescador, de penitente, i de gracia.* Valencia: Salvador Fauli (originally published: 1588).

MANNING, C. A. 1945, The menace of linguistic nationalism. *The South Atlantic Quarterly* 44, 13–22.

MARCZALI, H. 1910, *Hungary in the Eighteenth Century.* London: Cambridge Univ. Press.

MARKAKIS, J. 1967, Education and the emergence of nationalism in Africa. *Dialogue* 1, 9–20.

MARTIN, F. X. (ed.). 1967, *Leaders and Men of the Easter Rising: Dublin 1916.* London: Methuen.

MARX, G. T. 1970, Review of Theodore Draper's 'The Rediscovery of Black Nationalism.' New York: Viking. *Saturday Review* 4 July, p. 32.

MAUSS, M. 1956, La Nation. *Année Sociologique* 3rd series, 1953/54. Paris, P.U.F., pp. 5–68.

MAZRUI, A. A. 1963, On the concept of 'We are all Africans.' *The American Political Science Review* 57, 88–97.

— 1967, The national language question in East Africa. *East African Journal* 4, No. 3, 12–19.

— 1968, Some sociopolitical functions of English literature in Africa. In J. A. FISHMAN, C. A. FERGUSON & J. DAS GUPTA (eds), *Language Problems of Developing Nations.* New York: Wiley.

— 1969a, Violent contiguity and the politics of retribalization in Africa. *Journal of International Affairs* 23, 1, 89–105.

— 1969b, Pluralism and national integration. In L. KUPER & M. G. SMITH (eds), *Pluralism in Africa.* Berkeley: Univ. of Calif. Press, pp. 333–49.

— 1973, *The Political Sociology of the English Language.* The Hague: Mouton.

McCARTNEY, D. 1967, Hyde, D. P. Moran and Irish Ireland. In F. X. MARTIN (ed.), *Leaders and Men of the Easter Rising: Dublin 1916.* London: Methuen.

McCLELLAND, D. C. 1961, *The Achieving Society.* Princeton: Van Nostrand.

McCORMACK, W. 1959, The forms of communication in Vīraśaiva religion. In M. SINGER (ed.), *Traditional India: Structure and Change.* Philadelphia: American Folklore Society.

McCULLY, B. T. 1940, *English Education and the Origins of Indian Nationalism.* New York: Columbia.

McGEE, W. J. 1895, Some principles of nomenclature. *American Anthropologist* 8, 279–86.

McNEILL, Wm. 1963, *The Rise of the West*. Chicago: Univ. of Chicago Press.

MEHDEN, F. R. VON DER. 1968, *Religion and Nationalism in Southeast Asia*. Madison: Univ. of Wisconsin Press.

MEILLET, A. 1928, *Les Langues dans l'Europe nouvelle*. Paris: Payot. (Avec un appendice de L. Tesnière sur la statistique des languages de l'Europe.)

MENCKEN, H. L. 1936, *The American Language*. New York, Knopf (4th edition). First edition, 1919.

MENÉNDEZ-PIDAL, R. 1945, *Castilla, la tradición, el idioma*. Buenos Aires: Espasa-Calpe.

MERCIER, P. 1961, Remarques sur la signification du 'tribalisme' actuel en Afrique Noire. *Cahiers Internationaux de Sociologie* 31, 61–80.

MERKL, P. H. 1967, *Political Continuity and Change*. New York: Harper & Row, 1967.

MICHELET, J. 1946, *The People*. Trans. C. COOKS. London: Longmans (originally published in 1846).

MILL, J. S. 1910, *Utilitarianism, Liberty and Representative Government*. New York: Dutton.

MILLER, H. 1959, *Prince and Premier*. London: Faber.

MILNE, J. G. 1928, Egyptian nationalism under Greek and Roman rule. *Journal of Egyptian Archaeology* 14, 226–34.

MINER, H. M. 1965, Urban influences on the rural Hausa. In H. KUPER (ed.), *Urbanization and Migration in West Africa*. Berkeley: Univ. of Calif. Press, pp. 110–30.

MINN LATT, Y. 1966, *Modernization of Burmese*. Prague: Oriental Institute, Academia Publishing House of the Czechoslovak Academy of Sciences.

MINOGUE, K. R. 1967, *Nationalism*. New York: Basic Books.

MISES, L. 1919, *Nation, Staat und Wirtschaft: Beiträge zur Politik und Geschichte der Zeit*. Vienna: Manzsche Verlag.

MONTAGUE, R. 1952, The 'Modern State' in Africa and Asia. *Cambridge Journal* 5 No. 10.

MOORE, B., Jr. 1966, *Social Origins of Dictatorship and Democracy: Lord and Peasant in the Making of the Modern World*. Boston: Beacon Press.

MOORE, W. E. 1965, *The Impact of Industry*. Englewood Cliffs, N.J.: Prentice-Hall.

MOUSSA, S. 1955, Arab language problems, *Middle Eastern Affairs* 6.

MUSHKAT, M. 1971, Some characteristics of colonialism and its produce, African nationalism. *African Studies Review* 14, 219–41.

MYRDAL, G. 1968, *Asian Drama: An Inquiry into the Poverty of Nations*. 3 vols. New York: Pantheon.

— 1970, Cleansing the approach from biases in the study of under-developed countries. *Studium Generale* 23, 1249–66.

NAHIRNY, V. C. 1962, The Russian intelligentsia: From men of ideas to men of convictions. *Comparative Studies in Society and History* 4, 403–35.

NAHIRNY, V. & FISHMAN, J. A. 1965, American immigrant groups: ethnic identification and the problem of generations. *Sociological Review* 13, 311–26.

NAIK, J. P. 1965, *Educational Planning in India*. New Delhi: Allied.

NAIM, C. M. 1965, The consequences of Indo-Pakistani War for Urdu language and literature. *Journal of Asian Studies*, 269–83.

NAMIER, L. B. 1944, *1848: The Revolution of the Intellectuals* (from: Proceedings of the British Academy, Vol. 30.). London: Geoffrey Cumberlege, Amen House.

— 1952, Nationality and liberty. In L. B. NAMIER (ed.), *Avenues of History*. London: Hamish Hamilton. (Originally published as a paper of the Tenth Conference of the Accademia Nazionale de Lincei, Rome, 1948.)

NANDY, S. K. 1970, Is modernization westernization? What about east-ernization and traditionalization? *Transactions of the Sixth World Congress of Sociology* 3, 267–80.

NATARAJAN, S. 1956, Pertinent facts. *Seminar* 68 (April), 12–17.

NEHRU, J. 1953, *An Autobiography*. London: Bodley Head.

NEUSTUPNY, J. V. 1970, Basic types of treatment of language problems. *Linguistic Communications* (Monash University), 1, 77–100.

NEWTH, J. A. 1964, Nationality and language in Turkmenia. *Soviet Studies* 15, 4.

NIELSEN, E. W. 1964, Asian Nationalism. *Practical Anthropology* pp. 211–25.

NOREEN, A. 1892, Über Sprachrichtigkeit. *Indogermanische Forschungen* 1, 95–157. (Tr. from Swedish to German by Arnid Johansson, with substituted German examples.)

NOSS, R. 1967, *Language Policy and Higher Education*. (Vol. III, part 2 of a series entitled Higher Education and Development in South East Asia.) Paris: UNESCO and the International Association of Univ-ersities.

NUGROHO, R. 1957, The origins and development of Bahasa Indonesia. *PMLA* 72, 2, 23–28.

NUSEIBEH, H. Z. 1956, *The Ideas of Arab Nationalism*. Ithaca: Cornell Univ. Press.

NUSULI, M. 1953, Modern trends of literature in the Muslim countries, *Colloquium on Islamic Culture*. Princeton, N.J.: Princeton Univ. Press, 22–23.

OBOTE, M. 1967, Language and national identification. *East African Journal* 4, No. 3 (April), 3–6.

Ó CUÍV, B. 1969, The Gaelic cultural movements and the new nationalism. In K. B. NOWLAN (ed.), *The Making of 1916*. Dublin: Stationery Office.

O'HICKEY, M. P. 1898, The true national idea. Dublin: Gaelic League (Gaelic League Pamphlets, No. 1).

— 1909, *An Irish university, or Else—*. Dublin and Waterford: Gill.

OLA, C. S. 1960, Now is the time for one language. *Daily Express* (Lagos), 30 Sept.

OMAR, A. H. 1971, Standard language and the standardization of Malay, *Anthropological Linguistics* 13, 75–89.

O'REILLY, J. M. 1900, *The Threatening Metempsychosis of a Nation*. Dublin: Gaelic League (Gaelic League Pamphlets, No. 24).

OSTROWER, A. 1965, *Language, Law and Diplomacy*. Philadelphia: Univ. of Pennsylvania Press.

PADEN, J. N. 1968, Language problems of national integration in Nigeria: The special position of Hausa. In J. A. FISHMAN, C. A. FERGUSON & J. DAS GUPTA (eds.), *Language Problems of Developing Nations*. New York: Wiley, pp. 199–214.

PANIKKAR, K. M. 1955, *Asia and Western Dominance*. London: Allen and Unwin.

— 1962, *A Survey of Indian History*. Delhi: Asia Publishing House.

PARK, R. E. & BURGESS, E. W. 1924, *Introduction to Sociology*. Chicago: Univ. of Chicago Press.

PARKER, G. J. 1958, Indonesian images of their national self. *Public Opinion Quarterly* 22, 305–24.

PASSERIN D'ENTRÈVES, A. 1967, *The Notion of the State: An introduction to Political Theory*. Oxford: Clarendon.

PFAFF, R. H. 1963, Disengagement from traditionalism in Turkey and Iran. *Western Political Quarterly* 16, 79–98.

— 1970, The function of Arab nationalism, *Comparative Politics* 2, 147–68.

PFLANZE, O. 1966, Characteristics of nationalism in Europe, 1848–1871, *Review of Politics* 28, 129–43.

PHIPPS, Wm. E. 1908, The influence of Christian missions on the rise of nationalism in Central Africa. *International Review of Missions* 57, 229–32.

PIELOW, W. 1967, Nationalistische Muster im Lesebuch. In B. VON WIESE & R. HENSS (eds), *Nationalismus in Germanistik und Dichtung*. Berlin: Erich Schmidt, pp. 248–60.

PIETRZYK, A. 1965, Problems in language planning: the case of Hindi. In B. N. VARMA (ed.), *Contemporary India*. London: Asia Publishing

House, pp. 247–70.

PINSON, K. S. 1934, *Pietism as a Factor in the Rise of German Nationalism*. New York: Columbia.

— 1935, *Bibliographical Introduction to Nationalism*. New York: Columbia.

— 1936, Pietism — a source of German nationalism. *Christendom* 1, 266–80.

PILLSBURY, W. B. 1919, *The Psychology of Nationality and Internationalism*. New York: Appleton.

POLENZ, P. VON 1967, Sprachpurismus und Nationalsozialismus. Die 'Fremdwort' Frage gestern und heute. In B. VON WIESE & R. HENSS (eds), *Nationalismus in Germanistik und Dichtung*. Berlin: Erich Schmidt, pp. 79–112.

POLK, W. R. 1970, Introduction. In J. STETKEYYCH (ed.), *The Modern Arabic Literary Language*. Chicago: Univ. of Chicago Press.

PONSIONEN, J. A. 1962, *The Analysis of Social Change Reconsidered: A Sociological Study*. The Hague: Mouton.

POST, G. 1953, Rex Imperator. *Traditio* 9, 296–320.

POTEKHIN, I. 1958, The formation of nations in Africa. *Marxism Today* 2, No. 10, 308–14.

POTTER, D. 1962, The historian's use of nationalism and vice versa. *American Historical Review* 67, 924–50.

POWERS, G. C. 1927, *Nationalism at the Council of Constance (1414–1418)*. Washington, D.C.: Catholic University of America.

PURCELL, V. 1953, The crisis in Malayan education. *Pacific Affairs* 26, 70–76.

— 1953, The influence of racial minorities. In P. W. THAYER (ed.), *Nationalism and Progress in Free Asia*. Baltimore: Johns Hopkins, pp. 234–45.

PYE, L. W. 1961, Personal identity and political ideology. *Behavioral Science* 6, 205–21.

QUELQUEJAY, C. & BENNIGSEN, A. 1961, *The Evolution of the Muslim Nationalities of the U.S.S.R. and Their Linguistic Problems*. London: Central Asian Research Center.

RABELAIS, F. 1922, *Pantagruel*. Vol. III (ed. by A. LEFRANC). Paris: Champion (orig. published 1532).

RAKOWSKA-HARMSTONE, T. 1970, *Russia and Nationalism in Central Asia: The Case of Tadzhikistan*. Baltimore: Johns Hopkins.

RANGER, T. O. 1968a, Connections between 'Primary Resistance' movements and modern mass nationalism in east and central Africa. *Journal of African History* 9, 3, 437153, 4, 631–41.

— 1968b, Nationality and nationalism: The case of Barotseland. *Journal of the Historical Society of Nigeria* 4, 227–46.

RAUENHOLT, A. 1963, The spoils of nationalism: The Phillipines. In K. H. SILVERT (ed.), *Expectant Peoples: Nationalism and Development*. New York: Random House, pp. 178–95.

RAUN, A. & SAARESTE, A. 1965, *Introduction to Estonian Linguistics* (also: Ural-Altaische Bibliothek, XII). Wiesbaden: Harrassowitz.

REISS, H. S. 1955, *The Political Thought of the German Romantics, 1793–1815*. Oxford: Blackwell.

REISSMAN, LEONARD. 1964, *The Urban Process: Cities in Industrial Societies*. New York: Free Press, 1964.

— 1968, Urbanization: A typology of change. In S. F. FAUSS (ed.), *Urbanism in World Perspective*. New York: Crowell, pp. 126–44.

REMEIKIS, T. 1967, The evolving status of nationalities in the Soviet Union. *Canadian Slavic Studies* 1, 404–23.

RENDESSI, M. 1958, Pages peu connues de Djamal al-din al-Afghani. *Orient* 6, 123–28.

RIGGS, F. W. 1964, *Social Change and Political Development*. Bloomington: Indiana Univ. (Mimeo: Prepared for the Seminar on Political Behavior in Non-Western Countries. Ann Arbor, Michigan, July-August).

RJASANOFF, N. 1916, Karl Marx und Friedrich Engels über die Polenfrage. *Archiv für die Geschichte des Socialismus und der Arbeiterbewegung* (Leipzig), 6, 175–221.

ROBERTSON, D. M. 1910, *A History of the French Academy 1635 (4)–1910*. New York: Dillingham.

ROCKER, R. 1937, *Nationalism and Culture*. London: Freedom Press.

RODINSON, M. 1968, Sur la Théorie marxiste de la nation, *Voies Nouvelles* 2 (May), 25–30.

ROJO, T. A. 1937, *The Language Problem in the Philippines*. New York and Manila: The Philippine Research Bureau.

RONEN, D. 1968, Preliminary notes on the concept of regionalism in Dahomey. *Etudes Dahoméennes* 1, 11–14.

RONSARD, P. DE. 1952, *Oeuvres Complètes*, ed. by P. LAUMONIER. Paris: Lemerre (orig. pub. 1553–84).

ROSENBLATT, P. C. 1964, Origins and effects of group ethnocentrism and nationalism. *Journal of Conflict Resolution* 8, 131–46.

ROSENTHAL, E. I. J. 1965, *Islam in the Modern National State*. London: Cambridge Univ. Press.

ROSS, R. J. 1969, Heinrich Ritter von Srbik and 'Gesamtdeutsch' History. *Review of Politics* 31, 88–107.

ROTBERG, R. I. 1962, The rise of African nationalism: The case of east and central Africa. *World Politics* 15, 75–90.

— 1966, African nationalism: Concept or confusion? *Journal of Modern*

African Studies, 1, 33–46.

ROY, N. C. 1962, *Federalism and Linguistic States*. Calcutta: Mukopadhyay.

RUBIN, J. & JERNUDD, B. (eds). 1971, *Can Language Be Planned?* Honolulu; East-West Center Press.

RUSTOW, D. A. 1957, New horizon for comparative politics. *World Politics* 530–49.

— 1968a, Language, modernization and nationhood. In J. A. FISHMAN, C. A. FERGUSON & J. DAS GUPTA (eds), *Language Problems of Developing Nations*. New York: Wiley, pp. 87–106.

— 1968b, Nation. *International Encyclopedia of the Social Sciences* 11, 7–14.

SALMON, V. 1966, Language-planning in seventeenth-century England, its contexts and aims. In C. E. BAZELL, J. C. CATFORD, M. A. K. HALLIDAY & R. A. RUBINS (eds), *In Memory of J. R. Firth*. London: Longmans, pp. 370–97.

SAPIR, E. 1942, Language and national antagonisms. In A. LOCKE & B. J. STERN (eds), *When People Meet*. New York: Progressive Education Association, pp. 649–62. (Excerpted from his 'Language,' in *Encyclopedia of the Social Sciences* 9 [1933], 155–69.)

SAYIGH, R. 1965, The bilingualism controversy in Lebanon. *The World Today* 21, 3, 20–30.

SCALAPINO, R. A. 1964, Ideology and modernization — The Japanese case. In D. APTER (ed.), *Ideology and Discontent*. New York: Free Press, pp. 93–127.

SCHAECHTER, M. 1970, The 'Hidden Standard'; A study of competing influences in standardization. In M. HERZOG, W. RAVID, & U. WEINREICH (eds), *Field of Yiddish III*. The Hague: Mouton, pp. 284–327.

SCHMIDT-ROHR, G. 1932, *Die Sprache als Bildnerin der Volker: Eine Wesens und Lebenskunde der Volkstümer*. Jena: Eugen Diederichs Verlag (2nd ed., *Mutter Sprache*, 1933).

SCHORSKE, CARL E. 1968, The idea of the city in European thought: Voltaire to Spengler. In S. F. FAVA (ed.), *Urbanism in World Perspective*. New York: Crowell, pp. 409–24.

SCHWAB, W. 1963, Recent developments in applied linguistics. *Philippine Sociological Review* 11.

SEN, M. 1965, Role of the mother tongue. *Seminar* 76 (Dec.), 18–20.

SENGHOR, L. S. 1963, What is 'Negritude'? *West Africa* 4 Nov. 1961, also in P. E. SIGMUND Jr. (ed.), *The Ideologies of the Developing Nations*. New York: Praeger, pp. 248–50.

SETON-WATSON, H. 1965, *Nationalism Old and New*. Sydney: Sydney Univ. Press.

SHAFER, B. C. 1955, *Nationalism: Myth and Reality*. New York: Harcourt, Brace.

SHARABI, H. 1965. The transformation of ideology in the Arab world. *Middle East Journal* 19, 471–86.

— 1966, *Nationalism and Revolution in the Arab World*. Princeton, N.J.: Van Nostrand.

SHEPPERSON, G. 1953, Ethiopianism and African nationalism. *Phylon* 14, 9–18.

SHERRARD, P. 1959, *The Greek East and the Latin West*. London: Oxford Univ. Press.

SHILS, E. 1961, Centre and periphery. *The Logic of Personal Knowledge: Essays Presented to Michael Polanyi*. London: Routledge, pp. 117–30.

— 1971, Tradition. *Comparative Studies in Society and History* 13, 122–59.

SHOUBY, E. T. 1951, The influence of the Arabic language upon the psychology of the Arabs. *Middle East Journal* 5, 284–302.

SIGMUND, P. E., Jr. (ed.). 1963, *The Ideologies of the Developing Nations*. New York: Praeger.

SIEGMAN, H. 1962, Arab unity and disunity. *Middle East Journal* 15, 48–59.

SILVERT, K. H. (ed.). 1963, *Expectant Peoples: Nationalism and Development*. New York: Random House.

SIMMEL, G. 1957, The metropolis and mental life. In P. HATT & A. REISS (eds), *Cities and Society*. New York: Free Press, pp. 635–46.

SINGHAL, D. P. 1962, Nationalism and communism in South-East Asia. *Journal of Southeast Asian History* 3, 56–66.

— 1967, *Nationalism in India and Other Historical Essays*. Delhi: Oriental Publishers.

SIÒTHCHAÍN, MICHEÁL O. 1911, *A Call to Ireland*. Dublin: Gaelic League.

SITHOLE, N. 1959, *African Nationalism*. Cape Town: Oxford Univ. Press.

SJAHIR, S. 1947, *Out of Exile*. Trans. CHARLES WOLF, JR. New York: John Day.

SKINNER, G. W. 1959, The nature of loyalties in rural Indonesia. In G. W. SKINNER (ed.), *Local Ethnic and National Loyalties in Village Indonesia*. New Haven: Yale Univ. Southeast Asia Studies.

SMITH, D. H., & INKELES, A. 1966, The OM scale: A comparative sociopsychological measure of individual modernity. *Sociometry* 29, 353–77.

SMITH, W. C. 1954, *Pakistan as an Islamic state*. Lahore: Ashraf Press.

SNYDER, L. L. 1951, Nationalistic aspects of the Grimm brothers' fairy tales. *Journal of Social Psychology* 33, 209–23.

— 1952, *German Nationalism: The Tragedy of a People*. Harrisburg, Pa.: Stackpole.

— 1954, *The Meaning of Nationalism*. New Brunswick, N. J.: Rutgers

Univ. Press.
— (ed.) 1964, *The Dynamics of Nationalism*. Princeton, N.J.: Van Nostrand.
— 1968, *The New Nationalism*. Ithaca: Cornell Univ. Press.
SOMMER, H. 1945, *Von Sprachwandel und Sprachpflege*. Bern: Francke.
SOPHER, D. E. 1967, *Geography of Religions*. Englewood Cliffs, N.J.: Prentice-Hall.
SOREL, G. 1961, *Reflections on Violence*. New York: Collier.
SOUTHALL, J. E. 1893, *Wales and Her Language*. London: D. NUH.
SPIEGEL, S. 1930, *Hebrew Reborn*. New York: Macmillan.
SPRING, G., M. 1932, *The Vitalism of Count de Gobineau*. New York: Columbia.
STAAL, J. F. 1962, Sanskritization. *Journal of Asian Studies* 22, 261–75.
STALIN, I. (JOSEPH). 1942, *Marxism and the National Question*. New York: International Publishers.
STRAYER, J. R. 1940, The laicization of French and English society in the thirteenth century. *Speculum* 15, 76–86.
— 1966, The historical experience of nation-building in Europe. In K. W. DEUTSCH & Wm. J. FOLTZ (eds), *Nation-Building*. New York: Atherton, pp. 17–26.
STUBBS, W. 1874, *Select Charters and Other Illustrations of English Constitutional History from the Earliest Times to the Reign of Edward the First*. 2nd ed., Oxford: Clarendon Press.
STURZO, L. 1927, *Italy and Fascismo*. London: Faber and Gwyer.
SULLIVANT, R. S. 1967, The Ukrainians. *Problems of Communism* 16, No. 5, 46–54.
SULZBACH, W. 1943, *National Consciousness*. Washington: American Council on Public Affairs.
SUTTON, F. X. 1968, Languages and linguistics. Ford Foundation Representatives Meeting, Nairobi, June 6–8. (Mimeo.)
SYMMONS-SYMONOLEWICZ, K. 1965, Nationalist movements: An attempt at a comparative typology. *Comparative Studies in Society and History* 7, 221–30.
— 1968, *Modern Nationalism: Towards a Consensus in Theory*. New York: Polish Institute of Arts and Sciences in America.
— 1971, *Nationalist Movements: A Comparative View*. Meadville, Pa.: Meadville Press.
SZABE, L. 1952, Regression or new development? Twenty years of linguistic reform in Turkey. *Civilizations* 2, No. 1, 46–54.
TACHAU, F. 1964, Language and politics: Turkish language reform. *Review of Politics* 26, 191–204.
TAGORE, R. 1920, *Nationalism*. New York: Macmillan.

TALMON, J. L. 1965, *The Rise of Totalitarian Democracy*. Boston: Beacon.
— 1965, *The Unique and the Universal*. London: Secker and Warburg.
TAMBIAH, S. J. 1967, The politics of language in India and Ceylon. *Modern Asian Studies* 1, 215–40.
TIEDEMANN, A. 1955, *Modern Japan*. Princeton, N.J.: Van Nostrand.
TILLY, C. 1968, The forms of urbanization. In TALCOTT PARSONS (ed.), *American Sociology*. New York: Basic Books.
TOYNBEE, A. J. 1922, *The Western Question in Greece and Turkey*. London: Constable.
— 1953–54, *A Study of History*. Vols. VII–IX. London: Oxford Univ. Press.
TREVOR-ROPER, H. 1962, *Jewish and Other Nationalism*. London: Weidenfeld and Nicholson.
TURNER, R. H. & L. M. KILLAN (eds). 1957, *Collective Behavior*. New York: Prentice-Hall.
VAMBERY, R. 1944, Nationalism in Hungary. *Annals of the American Academy of Political and Social Science* 232, 77–85.
VAN DEN BERGHE, P. L. 1968, Language and 'Nationalism' in South Africa. In J. A. FISHMAN, C. A. FERGUSON & J. DAS GUPTA (eds), *Language Problems of Developing Nations*. New York: Wiley, pp. 215–24.
VENDRYES, J. 1925, *Language: A Linguistic Introduction to History*. New York: Knopf.
VICO, G. 1948, *The New Science*. Trans. T. G. BERGEN & M. H. FISCH. Ithaca, N.Y.: Cornell Univ. Press. (First published in Italian, 1725).
VOGT, H. 1967, *Nationalismus: gestern und heute; Texte und Dokumente*. Opladen: Leske.
VON FINKE, H. 1937, Die nation in den spätmittelalterlichen allgemeinen Konzilien. *Historisches Jahrbuch* 57, 323–38.
VON GRUNEBAUN, G. E. 1959, Problems of Muslim nationalism. In R. N. FRYE (ed.), *Islam and the West*. The Hague: Mouton, pp. 7–29.
— 1962, *Modern Islam: The Search for Cultural Identity*. Berkeley: Univ. of Calif. Press.
VOSSLER, K. 1932, *The Spirit of Language in Civilization*. London: Routledge.
WALLERSTEIN, I. 1960, Ethnicity et integration nationale en Afrique Occidentale. *Cahiers d'Etudes Africaines* 3, No. 1, 129–39.
WALSHE, A. P. 1970, Black African thought and African political attitudes in South Africa. *Review of Politics* 32, 51–77.
WARD, R. E. & DANKWART, A. R. (eds) 1964, *Turkey and Japan: A Comparative Study of Modernization*. Princeton, N.J.: Princeton Univ. Press.
WATERS, A. R. 1970, A behavioral model of Pan-African disintegration.

African Studies Review 13, 415–33.

WEINREICH, U. 1944, Di velshishe shprakh in kamf far ir kiyem. *Yivo-Bleter* 23, 225–48.

— 1953a, Di shveytser romantshn arbetn farn kiyem fun zeyer shprakh. *Bleter far yidisher dertsiung* 5, 68–76.

— 1953b, The russification of Soviet minority languages. *Problems of Communism* 2(b), 46–57.

WEISGERBER, L. 1933, Wesen und kräfte der sprachgemeinschaft. *Muttersprache* 48, 225–32.

— 1933, Martin Luther und das volkwerden der deutschen. *Mecklenburgische Monatshefte* 9, 552–54.

— 1938, Die macht der sprache im leben des volkes. *Mitteilungen des Universitätsbundes Marburg* 43–51.

— 1943, Die haltung der deutschen zu ihrer sprache. *Zeitschrift für Deutschwissenschaft und Deutschunterricht*, 1, 12–18.

WELCH, C. E. 1966, *Dream of Unity*. Ithaca: Cornell Univ. Press.

WELLS, G. A. 1959, *Herder and After: A Study of the Development of Sociology*. The Hague: Mouton.

WHEELER, D. L. 1969, Angola is whose house? Early stirrings of Angolan nationalism and protest, 1822–1910. *African Historical Studies* 2, 1–22.

WHITELEY, W. H. 1957, Language and politics in East Africa. *Tanganyika Notes and Records* Nos. 47–48, 159–73.

— 1968, Ideal and reality in national language policy: A case study from Tanzania. In J. A. FISHMAN, C. A. FERGUSON & J. DAS GUPTA (eds), *Language Problems of Developing Nations*. New York: Wiley, pp. 327–44.

— 1969, *Swahili: The Rise of a National Language*. London: Methuen.

WILDENMAN, R. & PARKALLA, H. 1966, *Nationalismus in Entwicklungpolitik*. Berlin/Mainz, Handbuch und Lexicon.

WILLIAMS, L. E. 1960, *Overseas Chinese Nationalism*. Glencoe, Ill.: Free Press.

WINDMILLER, M. 1954, Linguistic regionalism in India. *Pacific Affairs* 27, 291–318.

WIRTH, L. 1936, Types of nationalism, *American Journal of Sociology* 41, 723–37.

— 1938, Urbanism as a way of life. *American Journal of Sociology* 44, 1–24.

WOODWARD, E. L. 1916, *Christianity and Nationalism in the Later Roman Empire*. London: Longmans.

— 1946, The Patriarchate of Alexandria: A study in national Christianity. *Church History* 15, 81–100.

WOOLNER, A. C. 1938, *Languages in History and Politics*. London: Oxford

Univ. Press.

WUORINEN, J. H. 1931, *Nationalism in Modern Finland*. New York: Columbia Univ. Press.

— 1950, Scandinavia and the rise of modern national consciousness. In E. MEAD EARLE (ed.), *Nationalism and Internationalism: Essays Inscribed to Carlton J. H. Hayes*. New York: Columbia Univ. Press, pp. 454–79.

WURM, S. 1954, *Turkic Peoples of the U.S.S.R.* London: Central Asian Research Center.

WURM, S., WATERSON, N. & SIMPSON, C. G. 1960, *The Turkic Languages of Central Asia: Problems of Planned Culture Contact*. London: Central Asian Research Center.

YADAV, R. K. 1967, *The Indian Language Problem — A Comparative Study*. Delhi: National Publishing House.

YANG, C. K. 1961, *Religion in Chinese Society*. Berkeley, Univ. of Calif. Press.

ZANGWILL, I. 1917, *The Principle of Nationalities*. London: Watts.

ZAREVAND (= Nalbandian, Zavan, and Vartouhie). 1971, *United and Independent Turania; Aims and Designs of the Turks* (translated from the Armenian by V. N. DADRIAN).

ZARTMAN, I. Wm. 1965, Problems of Arabization in Moroccan education. *Confluent* 26 (1962) (in French), in B. RIVLIN & J. SZYLIOWICZ (eds), *The Contemporary Middle East*. New York: Random House, pp. 328–38.

ZATCHECK, H. 1936, *Das Volksbewusstsein: Sein Werden im Spiegel der Geschichtschreibung*. Brünn: Rohrer.

ZERNATTO, G. 1944, Nation: The history of a word. *Review of Politics* 6, 351–66.

ZNANIECKI, F. 1952, *Modern Nationalities*. Urbana: Univ. of Illinois Press.

10   On the peculiar problems of smaller national languages*

Most of the languages of the world are 'subnational' languages, i.e. they are not the national languages of the particular polities within which their speech (or speech-and-writing) communities reside. They may be utilized by large speech communities (e.g. such as Berber in Morocco and Algiers), they may even be languages of considerable literacy (as is Yiddish in the USSR or in Israel), but they are either only meagerly associated or entirely unassociated with the political power of a state apparatus and, therefore, with the rewards, blandishments and sanctions that such an apparatus can dispense. In any competition for functional stability with 'national' languages, it is clear that subnational languages must frequently come off second best. Indeed, their best defense is often to avoid competing with the national language at all, i.e. to withdraw into home, kin and intimacy functions and to leave the arenas of power and visibility to the national language.

From the perspective of subnational languages, the national languages are in enviable positions. They are viewed as controlling power, funds, jobs, prestige, etc. That national languages too have problems is often unrecognized by the adherents of subnational languages. Indeed, even sociologists of language have rarely indicated any awareness of such problems. It is the purpose of this paper to examine some of the problems that plague national languages, particularly those of national languages that may be designated as 'smaller' ones.

*Originally published in A. Gonzalea (ed.) 1984, *Panagani; Essays in Honor of Bonifacio Sibayan on his Sixty-Seventh Birthday*. Manila: Linguistic Society of the Philippines. 40–45; simultaneously published in *Philippine Journal of Linguistics*, 1983–84. Nos.2–1, 40–45.

All national languages are not equal

If I receive a letter in Russian, Chinese or Arabic, I am not surprised (as I would be if I received a letter in Berber). On the other hand, I feel no compulsion to answer letters that I receive in Russian, Arabic or Chinese in any of these same languages, as I would, for example, were the letters in French or in Spanish. For an American academician in this day and age not to know Russian, Chinese or Arabic is far less self-compromising than for him or her not to know French or Spanish. Not to be able to respond in French or Spanish is to reveal a lack of culture or education. Not to be able to respond in Russian, Chinese or Arabic is merely to reveal a lack of rare exposure or unusual background. Of course, all five are national languages of the first order (indeed, all five are also international languages in view of their UN roles), but, as my example reveals, even national languages of this first order are not equal. Nevertheless, although it is widely realized that American academics rarely know Russian, Arabic or Chinese, I still get a few letters in these languages every year, even from people that *know that I do not know* these languages. Someone translates these letters for me and I reply in English without any trepidation or discomfort. I confidently expect that my correspondents, the recipients of my English responses, read English fluently! It is a matter of national pride for them to write to me in their own national languages, and this is not regarded as unseemly pride since their national languages are not only 'larger' national languages but international languages as well.

However, not all national languages are languages that would be used for international correspondence, not even for one-way international correspondence. I have never received a letter in Pilipino/Filipino, nor one in Dutch, nor Greek, nor Indonesian, nor Polish, nor Swahili. What is more, I doubt that I ever will receive (or, in general, that Americans who have never been residents or nationals of the respective countries where the above languages are national languages have ever received or will ever receive) letters in the latter languages. The reason for my not receiving letters in Pilipino/Filipino is certainly not that I do not have friends and colleagues who can write letters in that language. The reason that I do not receive letters in Dutch is certainly not that it is rare for my Netherlandish and Flemish friends and colleagues to use that language for that function among themselves. The reason I do not receive letters in Indonesian or Swahili, from individuals who are perfectly capable of writing in those languages when they write to me (and who do use them when writing to each other) is not only that I am not expected to know these languages

(I am not expected to know Russian, Arabic or Chinese either), but that these are all languages that are currently not considered to be languages for international functions even by members of their own language communities.

Thus, there are several classes of national languages. A very few — the largest among them — also have *reciprocal* international functions. A few more have *unilateral* international functions. However, most national languages have no international functions at all. Indeed, most national languages (defined as any language considered to be ethnoculturally *integrative* rather than merely *official*) do not even discharge all *intra-*national functions either.

National languages with restricted intra-national functions due to internal minorities

The most obvious reason why some national languages fail to be employed for all *intra*-national functions is simply because there are many polities with *several official languages*. Official languages are languages that governmental authorities recognize and utilize in connection with delimited indigenous or foreign populations. English is an official language in many countries in which it is not a national language. French is an official language in Canada, and Spanish is in some parts of the United States mainland, although French is the national language of Quebec and Spanish is the national language of Puerto Rico. Similarly, Pilipino/Filipino does not discharge all intra-national functions in the Republic of the Philippines because there are various other Philippine languages that are officially recognized there for certain functions with certain populations. The same is true of Dutch in the Netherlands (a small but growing number of communities in the province of Friesland use Frisian and even the national and provincial governments sometimes do the same when serving those communities), of Hebrew in Israel, of Pashto in Afghanistan, of Hindi in India, etc. Indeed, we are living in an age when even non-democratic regimes are often willing to recognize a variety of regional languages as locally or nationally official, even if each such regime has one language which it actively fosters as national. Official languages that correspond to ethnocultural minorities limit the exclusive sway of national languages for intra-national functions.

Languages with intra-national restrictions due to external influences

However, many national languages fail to discharge all intra-national functions for reasons that are unrelated to indigenous ethnocultural minorities. While it is true that Swedish is also official in Finland and Finnish is also official in Sweden (i.e. both polities must provide for internal minorities), there are restrictions on the functions of Swedish in Sweden and restrictions on the functions of Finnish in Finland above and beyond those due to internal minorities. There are essentially no indigenous ethnocultural minorities in Portugal, nor in Norway, nor in Japan, and yet their own national languages do not discharge all available functions within those countries. In each and every one of them, English too discharges certain functions, precisely because Portuguese, Norwegian and Japanese are national languages without international functions. However, English is employed in these countries (and in many others as well) also for *intra*-polity purposes. This then is a restriction on the use of Portuguese, Norwegian and Japanese which is due neither to indigenous minorities nor to international conventions. It is this type of restriction to which we will devote our remaining discussion.

High technology, international culture, popular culture, youth culture and small national languages

Small national languages, i.e. national languages without international functions, are often avoided by their own mother tongue élites for highly technical and advanced topics, whether orally or in written form. Thus, English is used in advanced natural science and technological research/publication in Sweden, Holland, Israel and the Philippines. These languages *do* have terminologies for these functions, but these terminologies are much disregarded or are used for/adequate for *medium technology* pursuits only. Beyond the high school or elementary college textbook levels, their terminologies have not been developed to cope with the constantly expanding worlds of science and technology. Even at the popular technology level (where adequate native terminology does or could exist), English words are often clearly triumphant over the native terms that have either been coined or have been revived by local academies and language caretakers. This is particularly true in those pursuits in which popular technology and youth culture overlap: records, tape recorders, hi-fi, radio, television, pop-tunes and dance, motorcycles, automobiles, sports equipment, etc. In many respects, the seemingly enviable position of the smaller national languages *vis-à-vis* the sub-national languages in the very same polities (only *some* of the latter languages, at best, have official recognition) is actually fraught with problems. The smaller national languages do *not* discharge all of the functions in their own polities because of competition from 'below' (i.e. from subnational languages) as well as because of competition from 'above' (i.e. from supra-national or international languages). Indeed, in many ways, the life of smaller national languages is more complicated than is the life of subnational languages who face pressure from one direction (from above) alone.

Coping with competition from 'above'

The competition that small national languages face from below is for users rather than for uses. The fact that Cebuano is the mother tongue of many who live in a certain part of the Philippines does not make it into a rival for Pilipino/Filipino in most functions nor in most parts of the Philippine Republic. Nor do Cebuano words and structures unduly influence spoken Pilipino/Filipino in the Philippines as a whole. However, English not only competes with Pilipino/Filipino for certain uses, on the part of almost all users, but it is the constant source of borrowings, translation loans, interference and breakdowns in the Pilipino/Filipino system.

The natural tendency for a national language under attack is to resist and to counterattack. Irish purists can prohibit the use of anglicisms in their own circles. The arbiters of 'proper Norwegian' rail against English interferences in popular writing and speech. Members of the Israeli Knesset adopt angry resolutions against the flood of English signs and ads in Israel. Even the defenders of French have mobilized against the surge of franglais. But to little avail. It is only in well monitored print for well educated readers that 'the enemy of authenticity' can be kept at bay.

Actually, it is a 'stand-off'. English (or French or Russian) *cannot* displace indigenous national languages, small though some of them may be, but the latter also *cannot* rule out English influences in high culture, popular culture, youth culture and technology (most particularly: *not in* informal speech) by means of the formal sanctions that language planners control. To attempt to do so is to invite defeat, ridicule and loss of face.

If you can't defeat them, divide them

The complement to 'if you can't beat them, join them' is 'if you can't defeat them, divide them'. Language planning authorities for small national languages would benefit greatly from sociolinguistic sophistication so that they can tackle 'the enemy' where he is weak and avoid him where he is strong. What may well be regarded as 'terrible' usage in formal print may need to be laughed off as merely humor or sarcasm or playfulness or youthfulness or emotionality in informal speech. What may be taboo for schools and for church and for agencies of government *in print* (including certain radio/television 'talk' programs) may need to be ignored under other circumstances. It is worse to lose than not to fight at all. It is better to be the complete master of certain sociofunctional language realizations than to be half-master everywhere and complete master nowhere. Small national languages must judiciously select settings and functions that they can control completely and then utilize them like beachheads to expand their sway whenever possible. The big three public functions that can initially be largely controlled are internal government services, elementary education and mass media. Industry, technology and popular consumption may never be fully controlled, least of all by truly democratic regimes. To have only half a loaf may be a bitter pill for small national languages, but 'half a loaf is better than none'. If even large national languages have had to learn *that* lesson *vis-à-vis* languages of wider communication, then small ones must do so all the more.

Populations under stress

Certain segments of the population are particularly exposed to the ethos of national sovereignty and 'authenticity', on the one hand, and to influences from abroad, from international ideas, styles, visitors and artifacts, on the other hand. Urban élites and upwardly mobile or aspiring young folks are particularly likely to reflect and experience such a double exposure. Elites constitute the governing class, the influentials, the leadership. But they are also those who travel abroad most frequently, meet most often with foreigners both at home and abroad, read foreign publications, are most exposed to all foreign language media and, in general, understand and speak foreign languages most fluently. While it is they who formulate language planning policies and who master the most formal and 'correct' varieties of their small national language, it is also they who are most likely to make sure that their children attend schools conducted entirely, largely or at least partly in languages of wider communication and who are actually most likely to speak such languages at home in the circle of family, friends and visitors.

Upwardly mobile or aspiring young folks are also exposed to a variety of contradictory influences. They attend schools in which the national language is taught well and learned well. Nevertheless, these schools also stress the current language(s) of wider opportunity as does the entire youth culture to which such young people are inevitably exposed (via movies, TV, records, cassettes, comics and other realia), even when they socialize with one another in carefully supervised youth groups. There is a certain lability to both of these populations. They are the tone-setters. They have everything to gain from fostering the 'new authenticity' that the 'most correct' variety of the national language symbolizes, for they are its spokesmen, its tone-setters, its representatives and its chief beneficiaries and utilizers. On the other hand, they are also the ones who most fully recognize its limitations, its artificiality, its relative provinciality and the great, wide world 'outside' that languages of wider communication simultaneously are part of, index and symbolize. Either of these populations, élites and proto-élites, if disappointed or stymied, can become cynical or disinterested *vis-à-vis* their own small national language. They can psychologically and functionally demote it to a mere in-group secret code for the intermittent exclusion of foreign tourists, those same foreign tourists whose language(s) of wider communication the élites and proto-élites so admire and emulate.

The overlooked burdens of small national languages

It is the special burden of small national languages that they have 'almost made it' into the big leagues. They are, at best, 'almosts', 'never quites', 'solid mediocrities' and 'moral victors'. This is irking to their true believers who would like to see them safely, nobly and handsomely ensconced, beloved, honored and obeyed. The lives of most small national languages are actually far more precarious, if not beleaguered, than is commonly acknowledged or recognized. They are apt to be smirked at and condescended to and chuckled over, even by some who owe their bread and butter to them. However, their frailties do not elicit pity or sympathy, as do those of subnational languages. Small national languages are often secretly felt to 'deserve' the troubles they have because they also have the pomp and circumstance of nationhood as their compensation. Is there any wonder that, at times, their protagonists reveal a pettiness and even a meanness of spirit which bespeaks the never-ending pressures, the endless sniping, from above and from below, from without and from within, which is their lot?

The world generally pretends not to notice the discomforts of small national languages. Indeed, the usual pretense in 'polite society' is that these languages have no problems. On the surface, they are full members of the 'gentlemen's club' of standardized, national languages. They grace the letterheads of their chiefs of state, the philatelic and ceremonial paperwork of their state apparatuses. But below the surface, there is discontent, some protesting openly that they are used too little and too carelessly and others protesting more discreetly, that they are little better than frivolous, expensive and self-deluding games. What is even less fully appreciated, however, is that fact that Languages of Wider Communication come and go over the centuries but that local national languages, after these have been deeply implanted in symbolic literacy and religious production for the common citizen, have a staying power which may put LWCs to shame. When LWCs lose their H functions (usually due to competition from more aggressive and expansive alternative LWCs), they recede quickly and give way to their more rewarding competitor(s). When national languages undergo reverses, they retreat to home and hearth, to familiarity and informality, just as the more fortunate subnational languages manage to do, merely losing the literary flourishes and functions which once adorned them. The fact that the latter languages are frequently no more than 'almosts' and 'never quites' should not hide the fact that they generally live on to a ripe old age, whereas there is nothing as useless in a particular setting as a 'former LWC'.

11 Modeling rationales in corpus planning: Modernity and tradition in images of the good corpus*

The worm turns

Within the course of a decade a fundamental change has transpired within the ranks of students of linguistics *vis-à-vis* the very idea of corpus planning. In the late 1960s, when I and a small number of colleagues were enabled to spend a year at the East-West Center planning the *International Study of Language Planning Processes* (Rubin *et al.*, 1978), the most common reaction to our efforts on the part of linguists and linguists-in-training was 'It can't be done!' Corpus planning was viewed as akin to lashing the seas or chaining the winds at best, and to unsavory meddling in 'natural processes' at worst. The Hallian dictum 'leave your language alone' (Hall, 1950) still held sway and it reinforced, as well as expressed, the predominantly descriptivist bias of Western linguistics in general and of American linguistics in particular. Even those who were alarmed as to the continued decay of the English language — a constant matter of concern for the past century or more of English teachers and stylists — were far from believing that mere man either could or should intercede on an organized, centralized basis, to tamper with its fate or its form (see e.g. Newman, 1974; Graves & Hodge, 1979).

*Originally published in J. COBARRUBIAS & J. A. FISHMAN (eds), 1983, *Progress in Language Planning*. Berlin: Mouton 107–18.

That view, and all of the metaphors and alarms that it involves, is still with us, of course, and perhaps more so in the U.S.A. than in many other countries. I encounter it during visits to Israel among teachers who are fed up with the Academy's attempts to foster its brand of excessively proper, stilted, artificial Hebrew (*Ivrit shel shabat* [sabbath Hebrew], the opponents call it disapprovingly), *even now* when the language has been fully nativized and when its 'natural juices' appear to be fully activated and *self*-directive. I encounter it among anglophone linguists in Canada, convinced that the Office de la Langue Française is not only riding the wicked crest of Quebecois nationalism toward 'francization' but that it is arrogantly trying to change, improve, and modernize the French language even above and beyond Parisian splendor. I encounter it in the world of Yiddishists as well, whenever untraumatized youngsters (e.g. in the student journal *Yugntruf*) and unbowed oldsters (e.g. in the language-planning journal of the Yivo Institute for Jewish Research, *Yidishe shprakh*), employ neologisms that were clearly unknown to the critics' proverbial 'grandmother in [pre-World War II] Riga'. Nevertheless, the above opposition to corpus planning is clearly passé. It is fixated on local excesses (about which I will have more to say later), but these are the *excesses of success*. The continuing opposition to corpus planning, such as it is, can no longer successfully pretend that corpus planning cannot be done nor that it is impossible to do it well. It is, instead, even more drawn into discussions of *who* should do it, of *when* it should be done, and of *how* it should be done, rather than of whether it *can* or *should* be done at all.

Indeed, if a formerly biased notion (that corpus planning was inherently impossible or undesirable) is clearly waning — particularly among young linguists — the current danger seems to be from an equally biased but opposite view that considers it to be merely a rather simple, technical, linguistic exercise. One of my students at a recent linguistic institute put it in terms that seem to express the current (younger generation's?) relaxed view of the matter quite succinctly: 'It is nothing more than an exercise in lexical innovation or lexical substitution'. How the worm has turned in one decade! Unfortunately, however erroneous the predominant late-1960s view was, the waxing late-1970s view incorporates a triple error of its own.

A triple error

The tendency to view 'corpus planning' as nothing special, as just one more technical skill that a linguist should be able to pull out of his bag of tricks, is triply mistaken. It reveals a misunderstanding of lexicons *per se*, of corpus planning as a whole, and of the societal nexus of language planning more generally. Let me say a few words about each of these misunderstandings.

The snickering view that corpus planning is 'nothing more than lexical innovation or lexical substitution' reveals a profound downgrading of lexicons. This view, one which young linguists have probably taken over from their elders, implies that lexicons represent a somehow dispensable, trivial, and entirely uninteresting and expendable facet of the total language process. But lexicons are not that at all. They are not endless laundry lists, without rhyme or reason, without systematic links to each other and to all other facets of language. Lexicons are not interchangeable, dry, and dreary 'nuts and bolts'. Indeed, not only are they functionally indispensable and conceptually integrated aspects of the language process, but their successful planning involves tremendously complicated socio-cultural-political sensitivities that most linguists neither possess nor imagine. Actually, the current, more relaxed view (that corpus planning involves 'nothing more than lexical innovation') reveals ignorance not only of language planning and language behavior but of linguistics itself. However, for our immediate purposes here, suffice it to say that its downgrading of lexicons masks a downgrading of language/corpus planning by many of its purported friends and willing practitioners. The latter (corpus planning) is considered to be trivial because the former (lexicon) is considered to be trivial. Success with trivia is not considered to be success but, rather, to be trivia (as my Yiddish-speaking grandmother — not from Riga but from Soroke on the Dniester — used to say, 'May God protect me from such friends'. Her great-grandchildren today, when speaking English, topicalize this sentiment and render it, 'Friends like *that* we *don't* need!').

However, a more serious error than the foregoing downgrading of lexicons is the failure to recognize that corpus planning deals with far more than lexicons alone. Corpus planning has been extended to the development of entire stylistic varieties (e.g. nontechnical Somali prose), to number systems (e.g. converting a 'nine-and-thirty' system to a 'thirty-nine' system in Norwegian), to pronoun systems (e.g. the selections of nonhonorific second-person singulars in Japanese and Javanese), the simplification of verbal and phonological patterns (e.g. dropping feminine plural imperatives and complicated pointing/unpointing alternatives in modern Hebrew), etc. Thus, while the lion's share of corpus planning is certainly terminological (and all of my future examples here are unabashedly of this sort), there is, in principle, no reason why corpus-planning efforts should be denied (nor have they been) the 'tighter' linguistic systems that linguists and anthropologists are so proud of (for examples galore on other-than-lexical corpus planning, see Fodor & Hagege, 1983–1984).

Most serious of all, however, is the lack of recognition revealed by the 'merely lexicon' view of (1) the delicate and complex social context that commonly surrounds corpus planning, and of (2) the need for professional expertise with respect to *that* context if corpus planning is to succeed. It is a devastating mistake to assume that corpus planning merely requires the interplay and coordination of linguistic expertise and technological expertise, devastating certainly if one's goal is not merely to do corpus planning (i.e. not merely to *create* a nomenclature in chemistry, for example, or in some other modern technological area) but to have it *accepted* (i.e. to have it liked, learned, and used). If the *latter* is our goal (and anything less strikes me as a travesty), then cultural expertise in all of its ramifications is called for as well. Corpus planning, even when it is concerned with the elaboration and codification of nomenclatures, requires political/philosophical/religious sensitivity and expertise, particularly if the acceptance and implementation of corpus planning are not to be heavy-handed *ex post facto* impositions upon corpus planning but part and parcel of its ongoing activity from the very outset.

Modernization is not pursued in a vacuum

Every corpus-planning venture is conducted in a particular sociocultural context and that context is denied or ignored at the peril of the corpus planners, for it is that context that defines the parameters of acceptance, implementation, and diffusion. In this sense, modernization is both more than and less than modernization alone, for it constantly requires an amalgam of the old and the new in which the *proportions* of each and the *interpretations* of each must be frequently readjusted. Modernization, if it is to be broadly effective, rather than merely élitist and restricted or continually imposed from above, ultimately comes face to face with massive needs for sociocultural phenomenological continuity, stability, and legitimacy, regardless of how much econo-technical change occurs. The many examples of twentieth-century corpus planning in 'developing countries' reveal most clearly the dialectic between the modern and the traditional, the imported and the indigenous, but even corpus planning in the modernized Western world is by no means free of this dialectic (Berger, 1979; Connell, 1978).

Basically, modernization alone is just not enough to satisfy the cultural and philosophical needs of human populations (and, indeed, at times it is abhorrent to them). As a result, the language technician, the econo-technical technician, and the 'executive arm of power' in concert are also not enough to guarantee the success of corpus planning, particularly where at least a pretense of political and cultural independence and authenticity is maintained. Everyone wants a chemistry terminology of his own nowadays, at least for lower- and middle-level chemistry pursuits, but they generally want it to be *both* 'adequate for chemistry' *and* 'acceptable as their own'. Accordingly, many Israelis want 'theirs' to be faithful to the 'genuine oriental nature' of the Hebrew language. Many Hindi advocates want 'theirs' to reflect the perfection of classical Sanskrit. Filipino planners want 'their' chemistry terminology to be transparent, i.e. to utilize morphs that the young and the common man will understand. Nynorsk advocates want 'theirs' to derive from the uncontaminated Norse well. Katarevusa planners owe(d) allegiance to the pure Greek genius from which the entire world's democratic ethos has purportedly been derived. Many Arabic planners and teachers want to recognize Koranic exquisiteness in their chemistry terminology. Yiddish adherents want(ed) to avoid Germanisms, Anglicisms, Russianisms, or any other massive dependency on outside languages (Fishman, 1981). Of late, French authorities are, if anything, even more alarmed along these lines.

'Chemistry is chemistry; chemistry is universal', but chemistry terminologies are pulled in particularistic directions — by élites who seek to form, to lead, and to follow their masses, and by masses who are ever prone to return to deeply implanted local preferences when their revolutionary fugues and flirtations subside. Everywhere the planner encounters particularistic directions into which and through which 'universal modernization' must be channeled. The amount of pull will vary. The pullers and the pulled will vary. The interpretation of what is 'ours' and what is 'theirs' will vary. The general point, however, remains valid: modernization drives, goals, needs, and processes alone are not enough for corpus planning to succeed. Modernization repeatedly needs to be particularistically digested, legitimated, and domesticated or disguised (Nash *et al.*, 1976).

But the tradition is not enough either

If modernization has its limits (not to speak of its limitations), so, obviously does the local tradition. The tradition can rarely satisfy the linguistic needs of corpus planning if for no other reason than the fact that it cannot satisfy the compelling econo-technical needs of modernization. The tradition is inadequate both socioculturally and intellectually-conceptually. It lacks the paradigms, the theoretical parsimony, the conceptual systems that are both the resultants of and the contributors to modern expertise. Thus, the tradition can often provide no more than a vague outer limit, a rhetoric, an indigenous guiding principle, and, above all, a stabilizing identity to the process of modernization and to its corpus-planning counterpart. Like modernization, the tradition is both a comforter and a taskmaster. Like modernization it waxes and wanes in its power to constrain and to guide. Like modernization, it is constantly subject to varying interpretations (from $interpreter_1$ to $interpreter_2$ and from $time_1$ to $time_2$). Like modernization it tends to bite off more than it can chew, to claim more than it can deliver, to stake out more than it can control. The corpus planner needs help in order to gauge it accurately, to appreciate its hold and its significance, and to realize that its instability implies that *his* task is never done. The tradition also changes and develops, as does modernity, and the two interpenetrate and are at times interpreted as hostile, and at times as indifferent, and at times as harmonious with respect to each other.

Of course, all of the foregoing applies to the *sociopolitical auspices of modernization as a whole*, as well as to the status-planning context in which corpus planning is conducted. Even nationalistic modernization is far from being a genuine revitalization effort (Fishman, 1972). It is at least bimodal in outlook. Indigenous depth and historical legitimization are constantly used for *unprecedented purposes* and in *unprecedented ways* by nationalist movements. The old and the new may appear to the outsider to be odd bedfellows but they cohabit constantly. In each and every modernization experience we love them both and we despair of them both. We want to be in control of them both and wind up being controlled by them both. Corpus planning cannot long escape from their bipolarity. It must struggle to recognize and to integrate them both, and, like every other social pursuit, it is only indifferently successful in doing so for any length of time. For these very same reasons successful corpus planning is no simple thing.

Rationale and rationalizations

Corpus planning is faced by a dilemma — but yet it proceeds: chemistry terminologies continue to be prepared. They are launched under

382 LANGUAGE AND ETHNICITY

a variety of rationales and rationalizations. These are indispensable. The corpus planner needs to set out guiding principles for himself so that he will know what is 'good' and what is 'bad', what to seek and what to avoid. Even more crucial: the public or target audience also needs to be told why what is being offered to it is desirable, admirable, and exemplary. Critics too need to rationalize their opposition, qualms, or reluctance. For all of these reasons, therefore, models of the good and of the bad are formulated and expounded upon. In addition to extreme or polar solutions or positions, a number of compromise positions are also commonly advanced. They all seek to grapple with the old and the new, to combine them, and to differentiate between them, to find one in the other or to minimize or otherwise manipulate the gap between them.

Unabashed and undiluted rationalism à la Tauli (1968, 1974) (the 'good' is 'short', 'regular', 'simple', 'euphonious'), the unabashed and limitless importation or unabashed foreignisms, and the pursuit of neologisms on a completely *de novo* basis (i.e. via morphs without pedigrees) are also all resorted to on occasion and for special purposes, but these are rarely if ever rationalized as such or as national policy. Complete rationality is, after all, no more than a game played by intellectuals (and even then, only by intellectuals completely innocent of political aspirations or opportunities). To some extend the need to compromise with rationality is due to the limitations inherent in these solutions as solutions; to some extent it is due to their limitations as *approaches to solutions*. Thus, two equally rational principles often conflict (short terms are not necessarily euphonious, euphonious terms are not necessarily simple, simple terms are not necessarily short, etc.). Ultimately, even rationality is not an open-and-shut, completely objective matter and is subject to fairly substantial social and societal interpretation. As a result, even when rationality is appealed to it is commonly buttressed by or imbedded in other stated arguments or unstated assumptions.

The following examples (as are the others below) are from the journal *Yidishe shprakh*, published by the Yivo Institute for Jewish Research in New York (currently the only authoritative corpus-planning agency in the world of Yiddish).

Example 1: 'handout' (as at a scholarly conference or meeting). The anonymous *YS* spokesman recommends *tseteyl-bletl* and supports his recommendations as follows: 'Although it is a neologism, its composite structure, verb plus noun, is so productive and common that it sounds like a well-established term' (1973, 32 [1–3]: 32).

Note that the rationality of regularity (the structure is much employed and, therefore, has innumerable precedents) is clinched (rendered popularly irresistible) by assuring us that such a term sounds traditional rather than new. A neologism seems to require some sort of passport or apology. If it is new, it should at least *sound* old. It is clear that the recommender would rather have an old term to begin with wherever possible.

Example 2: 'pot roast'. The spokesman recommends *top-gebrotns* and explains why. 'This is not a made-up word. We find this word as far back as the writings of Mendele Moykher Sforim [1836-1917]' (1949,9: 61).

The recommender clearly recognizes the weaknesses of 'made-up' words. The fact that a word was used by a 'classicist of modern Yiddish literature' clearly establishes its legitimacy in his eyes, above and beyond that of the most rational neologism.

Compromises, compromises, compromises

Untempered rationality and undiluted traditionalism are extreme positions insofar as modelling rationales are concerned. More commonly, mixed rationales are employed. One such is to cite supporting usage among ordinary folk, speakers who cannot be suspected of partiality towards the corpus planner's recommendation. At times, this approach derives from serious ethnographic research in which large numbers of folk terms are collected and rescued from oblivion by being resurrected in a closely or metaphorically related meaning. This is a rationale that is not without its difficulties, however. Not all ordinary speakers, nor all widespread usages, are equally acceptable as precedents by corpus planners. Many man-in-the-street usages, indeed, are clearly unacceptable as barbarisms, vulgarisms, slang, archaisms, unjustified borrowings, etc. In modern Yiddish corpus planning, (New High) German influences (post-eighteenth century) are taboo, even if they have been popularly accepted (Schaechter, 1969). Thus, the appeal to popular currency normally involves an explicit or implicit set of assumptions as to *which* speech networks (often rural rather than urban, but often also from one region rather than from another), at which time in history (precontact, preinvasion, preoccupation, pre-floodtide-of-influence), are regarded favorably. A few examples may help:

Example 3: 'matching grant'. The authority recommends *akegngelt* and buttresses his recommendations as follows. 'We have noted *akegnshteln* for "to match" from Dr. Y. Gottesman, a countryman of ours from Sered, Southern Bukovina [Rumania during the Inter-War period; now in the USSR]; from Lifshe Shekhter-Vidmanm from Zvinyetchke, Northern Bukovina, we have "the inlaws [actually: mekhetonim, i.e. the kinship of in-laws *vis-à-vis* each other] give akegngelt"' (1972, 31 [2]: 56).

Example 4: 'poetry reading'. The authority recommends *poezye-ovnt* [= poetry evenings], even if the reading is during the day, since 'Polish Jews greet each other with *gutn-ovnt* [good evening] from mid-day on' (1975, 34 [1–3]: 78).

Note how approved individual speakers (perhaps because they come from the same region as the authority or are well known to him to be of unblemished speech) or even an approved region are cited. In both cases the usage referred to is pre-American and, in that sense, more authentic, uncontaminated. Thus the function is new but the world is old. The new is old; the old is new.

Another compromise solution is to find (whether through translation loans or through internationalisms) that 'theirs is ours'. Obviously this line of reasoning must also involve substantial flexibility and eclecticism, and care must be exercised that it not be carried to an unacceptable extreme. Ataturk's 'Great Sun Theory' is a well-known example of this approach. After the expulsion of foreign Arabisms and Persianisms it rationalized the importation of numerous Frenchisms/internationalisms on the ground that since all European languages were (purportedly) derived from Turkish, all borrowed Europeanisms were merely long-lost Turkish words returning to the fold, to their original home. Some less extreme examples of the 'theirs is ours' type are the following:

Example 5: What definite article should be used with the word '*loto*'; *der*, *di*, or *dos*? The authority replies, 'Certainly *not di loto*. There is an unfortunate tendency here [in the U.S.A.] always to use *di* with a foreign word . . . due to the influence of English *the* which is closer to *di* than to *der* or *dos*. [However] if *loto* were to be phonetically assimilated and if it were to change to *lóte* then, in such case, it would certainly be *di lóte*' (1950, 10 [2]: 63).

Seemingly, even a foreign borrowing becomes somewhat naturalized if an article is used with it that does not again reveal foreign influence. However, a subsequent stage of indigenization is reached with phonetic assimilation. At that point the term is fully 'ours' and therefore the usual grammatical paradigm then applies with respect to its article. Words ending in unaccented *e* are most feminine in Yiddish (some obvious exceptions: *der tate, der zeyde*) and, therefore, at that point the article would change from *der/dos loto* to *di lote*.

Example 6: Are words such as stimulate, formulate, emulate, etc., acceptable internationalisms? The authority replies, 'Just because an English word has a Latin root that doesn't necessarily make it an internationalism. That very word must occur in at least a few other major languages ('*kulturshprakhn*') for us to admit it into our language with a clear conscience. Each individual word needs to be considered separately. [*Stimulirn, formulirn* are quite acceptable internationalisms but] why do you need *emulirn* when you can simply say *nokhmakhn*?' (1963, 23 [2]: 63).

Note that a purported internationalism is acceptable as such if creditable others have already acted and accepted it as such. At that point it belongs to everyone (or to no one in particular) and, therefore, also to us. Prior to that point, it is a foreignism. However, even if it is an internationalism there may still be a 'simple' indigenous term that would obviously be preferable. Internationalisms are potential citizens but they are comparable to naturalized citizens. They are still not as authentic as the native-born variety.

Overdoing it

Corpus planners attempt to predict and to put into effect 'models of goodness' that target populations will like, learn, and use. However, the corpus planners are not themselves a random sample, either of 'the public' or of any of the more narrowly defined target populations at which corpus planners aim their corpus-planning products. They are commonly more ideologized than 'the public' in the sense of being more likely to reify the model that they are trying to implement. They are certainly more language-conscious (perhaps 'language-centered' is the term to use) relative to most target populations with which they have to deal. Other populations generally view language, at best, as only part of the pie, as only one aspect of the total social reality with which they are seeking to cope. Language planners as a whole, and corpus planners even more so, tend to overstress language as causal (Fishman, 1980), as crucial, as special, particularly so if their training is narrowly linguistic rather than broadly sociolinguistic. As a result, there is substantial risk that corpus planners will lose contact with the public and will not really have their fingers on the pulse of how the public is reacting to them, to their products, and to their once-valid model of the ever-changing and delicate balance between 'old' and 'new', between 'theirs' and 'ours', between neologistic and traditionalistic, that publics find acceptable. Because corpus planners *are* (or view themselves as) gatekeepers and custodians of the language, they tend to become overzealous defenders of their model of the good language. Their relative homogeneity in age, training, and background also contributes to the risk of being 'out of touch' at any particular time with what any particular target population will accept. 'Once-believers' of the same generation and 'nonbelievers' of a subsequent generation often view corpus planners as thick-skinned pachyderms at best, or as outlandish and outmoded remnants of an earlier age at worst. When corpus planners continue to do what they have always done, 'the public' (by then no longer the same in attitudes, interests, and needs as it formerly was) begins to consider them, the corpus planners, to be *over*doing it. Narrow-gauged corpus planners often become the butts of humor, sarcasm, and ridicule, unappreciated at best and vilified at worst.

'Notorious' failures

In such cases of credibility gap, of out-of-phaseness between corpus planners and their publics, anecdotes, jokes, and songs often appear whose goal is to tease, taunt, and otherwise deride the 'excesses' of corpus-planning products. The young native-born Israelis, tired of having old, diaspora-born 'authorities' tell them what proper Hebrew is, laugh endlessly at radio, television, and records that poke fun at the Academy (*Eych korim hatshuptshik al hakumkum?*). Francophone Quebecers gnash their teeth (and Anglophones slap their sides in exaggerated mirth) over the *stop* vs. *arret 'scandale'* in the government's 'francization' program. Yiddish speakers who have been none too observant of the Yivo's spelling strictures ridicule the gallons of ink (or is it blood?) spilled over whether the Yivo's own spelling rules require *fundestvegn* [nevertheless] to be spelled as one word or as three. Corpus planning that continues along its own mirthless path, oblivious of public sentiment and changes in the public model of 'the good language' (which must be internally differentiated for a variety of functions), is likely to find that its mirthlessness is increasingly the object of public mirth and merriment (not to speak of disdain and disregard). Many of the 'scandals' that come to public attention due to out-of-phaseness between corpus planners and target populations become 'fossilized' and continue to be cited for decades after the out-of-phaseness has been corrected.

A corpus planner's life is not an easy one (chorus: easy one): conclusions

Corpus planning is often conducted within a tension system of changing and conflicted loyalties, convictions, interests, values, and outlooks. One the one hand, authentification/indigenization of the new is admired and courted, but, on the other hand, it is often too limiting in reality and too rural/old-fashioned in image to serve or to be acceptable if uncompromisingly pursued. Successful corpus planning, then, is a delicate balancing act, exposed to tensions and ongoing change. All of this makes the corpus planner all the more dependent on disciplined social and societal sensitivity, theoretical and applied, in order to fully understand the drifts and pressures to which he must react. This is particularly true in newly modernizing contexts. It is also true in post-modern ones — whether they be democratic or totalitarian in nature. Totalitarian regimes may have more clout in the entire culture-planning area, but they too may run out of steam, particularly when it comes to influencing the spoken language, unless rapport is maintained with public sentiments and images of 'the good language', so that these can be either followed or shaped via massive institutions. Thus, it behooves corpus planning to engage in constant research and in ongoing evaluation, and this can only be done if social-research skills are either acquired or hired. A corpus planner's life is not an easy one (chorus: easy one), but then whose is?

References

BERGER, P. L. 1979, *Facing Up To Modernity: Excursions in Society, Politics and Religion*. New York: Basic Books.

CONNELL, J. 1978, *The End of Tradition: Country Life in Central Surrey*. London: Routledge and Kegan Paul.

FISHMAN, J. A. 1972, *Language and Nationalism*. Rowley, Mass.: Newbury House.

— 1980, The Whorfian hypothesis: varieties of valuation, confirmation and disconfirmation. *International Journal of the Sociology of Language* 26, 25–40.

— 1981, (ed.), *Never Say Die! A Thousand Years of Yiddish in Jewish Life and Letters*. The Hague: Mouton.

FODER, I. & HAGEGE, C. (eds) 1983–1984, *Language Reform*. Hamburg: Buske.

GRAVES, R. & HODGE, A. 1979, *The Reader Over Your Shoulder: A*

Handbook for Writers for English Prose. New York: Random House.

HALL, R. A., Jr. 1950, *Leave Your Language Alone!* Ithaca. (Reprinted 1960 as *Linguistics and Your Language*. New York: Doubleday-Anchor).

NASH, J., DANDLER, J. & HOPKINS, N. S. (eds) 1976, *Popular Participation in Social Change*. The Hague: Mouton.

NEWMAN, E. 1974, *Strictly Speaking: Will American Be the Death of English?* Indianapolis: Bobbs-Merrill.

RUBIN, J., JERNUDD, B., DAS GUPTA, J. *et al*. 1978, *Language Planning Processes*. The Hague: Mouton.

SCHAECHTER, M. 1969, The 'hidden standard': a study of competing influences in standardization. In M. HERZOG *et al*. (eds), *Field of Yiddish III*, 289–304. The Hague: Mouton. Also in Fishman, 1981: pp. 671–98.

TAULI, V. 1968, *Introduction to a Theory of Language Planning*. Uppsala: University of Uppsala Press.

— 1974, The theory of language planning. In J. A. FISHMAN (ed.), *Advances in Language Planning*. The Hague: Mouton, pp. 48–67.

12   Language spread and language policy for endangered languages*

Having contributed, over the course of many years, to the study of language spread, on the one hand, and to the study of language maintenance/language shift, on the other hand, it has generally been clear to me — and, I suspect, to others as well — that these two topical concentrations generally deal with quite different macro-level language situations. Language spread calls to mind the dynamic of English as an additional language, particularly in its role as the world-wide language of technology (both popular and advanced) and of huge chunks of youth-culture in most modern and modernizing contexts, the dynamics of Russian as an additional language in the Soviet Union (particularly among smaller Asian peoples who have no other means of access to the world of modern ideas and technology, but among all other Soviet peoples as well, for ideological and lingua franca purposes), the dynamics of Swahili as an additional language in East Africa, of French as an additional language among many anglophones (particularly young anglophones) in Canada, of Spanish as an additional language among enclaves of Latin American Indians, of Mandarin-Potinhua as an additional language among non-Han peoples in Mainland China, etc., etc. Many additional examples of language spread can be given, particularly if we go back in history (e.g. to the spread of Latin — initially as an additional language — in the Western Roman Empire and the partially contemporary and partially even earlier as well as later spread of Greek as an additional language for High Culture in Rome itself and throughout the Eastern Roman Empire). The common factor among all of these examples of language spread is that they focus upon contextually more-powerful languages whose spread is (or was)

*Originally published as the Opening Address to Georgetown University Round Table on Languages and Linguistics 12–14 March 1987.

facilitated precisely by the doors they can (could) open, the broader vistas they can (could) provide, the more statusful roles they are (were) associated with (at least potentially or referentially if not immediately), the promise they hold (held) to change the lives of their new speakers (initially: understanders and, ultimately, perhaps also readers/writers) in desired directions.

The mood in language spread studies is generally an 'upbeat' one, precisely because it takes its point of departure from the perspective of the spreading languages themselves and their sponsors. If we care to glance below this surface, however, the efforts related to language spread are also full of open or hidden tales of personal dislocation, of social dislocation and of cultural dislocation when viewed from the perspective of at least some of those to whom these languages spread. However, we tend to be so convinced that 'you can't fry omelettes without breaking eggs' that no other, less destructive metaphor occurs to us. We quickly, too quickly, place our hope in the ultimate beneficial effects of the socio-cultural revolutions that necessarily accompany language spread. We all love winners and the study of language spread is replete with accounts of their prowess in bringing new products, technologies, ideologies, curricula, appreciations, opportunities [including creative opportunities] to the populations exposed to them (more quickly to élites and more slowly to masses). We tend to (or want to) forget that 'spread' is one of those anesthetic terms that numbs us and lulls us from feeling or even recognizing the multitude of pains and of sins that it covers. If we add to our interest in 'spread' an interest in 'language policy', as I have been bidden to do in this paper, then we run the risk of overlooking another matter as well, namely, that spread not only involves conscious 'language policy', but unplanned spread as well, via Zeitgeist trends that can contribute as much or even more to spread than language policy *per se*. There is often a momentum to spread, a momentum to which social mobility aspirations contribute, as do the hungers for material and for leisure-time gratifications, as does the apparent stylishness of the pursuit of modernity itself. All in all, it is the complex processes of culture contact, cultural diffusion, culture change and culture conflict, and their dislocation of everyday life in all of its manifold activities, rather than language policy alone, that are involved in language spread. To reduce these manifold processes to the narrow parameters of language spread and language policy is, therefore, not only to impoverish our understanding of the broader context in which these parameters are implanted but also to impoverish our understanding even of these parameters themselves.

If the affective tone surrounding the study of language spread is a triumphalist one, then the mood surrounding the study of language shift often becomes quite sombre. We now focus on the sorrows of the losers, on their endangered languages and on their anguish, trauma and travail. We often sympathize with those whom history has defeated ('history' too, by the way, is a euphemism, otherwise we might have to admit that the cruel victors were flesh and blood, not only *like* us, but perhaps even our own forebears). However, as long as the vanquished are/were not flesh of our flesh and blood of our blood, we generally prefer to move on to less painful topics. Even the intellectualization of other people's pain (and intellectualization is the very heart of our enterprise, otherwise we may be taken for journalists or propagandists) is far from a happy or pleasant topic. There aren't many Nancy Dorians around who care to go back, time after time, to dying language communities, even for research purposes, although such communities contain the answers to many of the best, the most difficult and the most important questions: the questions of limits (of where and how to draw the line between dying and changing, between illness and health, between death and life). But, whether we attend to them or not, the endangered languages, i.e. languages with a large, sustained and uncontrollable negative balance with respect to the discrepancy between their inter-generational influx and their inter-generational outflux of speakers, are there and their number is legion, as any reader of *Cultural Survival Quarterly* or *Survival International News* can plainly see issue after issue, year after year.

Efforts to ameliorate the woes of endangered languages, to help them arrive at a *modus vivendi* (as opposed to a *modus 'morendi'*) with their more powerful competitors nevertheless go on, insufficient and thwarted though they may be. Often these efforts are in the hands of socio-linguistically untrained or only partially trained caretakers. Few language planning specialists read (or can read) what they write 'in those funny little languages of theirs' and comparative studies or theories of assistance to endangered languages (i.e. language policy on behalf of endangered languages) are few and far between. However, it seems to me that if we are sensitive to the loss suffered by our collective 'quality of life' on this planet when endangered animal species are further decimated, if we strain to do something on their behalf so that their natural habitats will be protected and their life-chances improved (like holding off the repair and replacement of the West Side Highway in New York for over a dozen years because certain species of fish would never recover if their current breeding grounds were destroyed), then the need to look steadfastly and act affirmatively in connection with endangered languages should be even more obvious. Theoretically there need be no conflict between language spread and language maintenance. Language spread may pertain to the acquisition of socio-culturally new ['modern'] functions, usually H-type functions, rather than to the displacement of speakers from their 'traditional' L-type functions. However, true though this may be theoretically, and I myself have testified many times to this theoretical truth, the complementary distribution of functions that it depicts is very often only an early and fleeting stage in a process which, if left unattended, easily develops into a subsequent stage in which that which is not theoretically necessary nevertheless, predictably, comes to pass: the spreading language initially associated with newer, more statusful roles and pursuits, soon competes with and also begins to erode the remaining functions originally allocated to the language(s) previously employed by the speech community. It is at this point that the danger begins.

The possibility of stabilization is there, of course. We call that possibility 'diglossia', namely, the co-presence within an ethnolinguistic community of a widely implemented, generally accepted and long-lasting complementary functional allocation of languages. We can all give examples of such consensual societal arrangements (even examples like Swiss German/High German, where no traditional religious props or social class advantages [like the monopolistic 'traditional' or pre-modern restriction of literacy] are available to provide the impetus for the continuation of such arrangements). But, after all is said and done, the diglossic solution to the problem of endangered languages is a very difficult one to arrive at under *any* circumstances, whether philosophically or empirically, all the more so under typically modern circumstances. And that brings me back to 'language policy'.

How can language policy be implemented so that endangered languages can find a safe harbor for themselves, tossed and battered as they soon are by the advancing functional spread of competitor languages associated with far greater status rewards? I know that there are those who take the view that 'survival of the fittest' should prevail in the language arena, as it does in the jungle. I know there are those who declaim against language policy on behalf of endangered languages, considering it useless, seeing in it tendencies toward excess and toward fostering and exacerbating inter-group tensions, an interference with the rights of the majority to rule and an implicit vote of 'no confidence' in the inherent fairness of the majority if left to its own devices (i.e. without imposing laws requiring the protection of endangered languages). However, I happen not to agree with these folks. I don't really believe in the 'survival of the fittest', precisely because it *is* the law of the jungle and I have always tried to follow a higher law than that. Although I don't fully put my trust in princes in order to even the scales between the strong and the weak, I also do not expect much 'inherent fairness' toward lambs on the part of wolves. I know that my advocacy of endangered languages will be interpreted as reflecting a vested interest on my part (I admit it; I feel aggrieved that my own mother tongue is an endangered language and I have vowed to do what I can on its behalf); nevertheless, I feel that I can make as much claim for acting in the public good as can my opponents, and I suspect that they too must have a vested interest or two up *their* sleeves (interests which they insist on not disclosing and even on hiding) in championing a majority that really needs no support. So I return with unbowed head to my original question: given that language spread is not an unmixed blessing, leading in many cases to language shift and to endangering the very existence of smaller languages engulfed by the processes of sociocultural change in which language spread itself is a co-participant, how can language policy be utilized on behalf of fostering a stabilized co-existence between the weak and the strong, between the lambs and the wolves?

Since considerable attention has already been directed at our Meeting toward the English Official/English Only movement in the U.S.A., a movement that seeks to utilize language policy on behalf of a powerful language (English in the U.S.A.) and against weaker languages in our country, I will attempt, at the particular request of our sponsors but hardly against my own will, to draw my examples from several other contexts that I have come to know rather well over the past few years, namely, the cases of Basque, Frisian, Irish and Yiddish, all of which raise in my mind questions of limits, i.e. are there stages of decline and conditions of endangerment beyond which the spread of a stronger competitor can no longer be contained? Or, to put it another way: can a better fit be engineered between language policy efforts on behalf of weaker languages and the *particular* functional circumstances in which such languages find themselves? In what follows, I ask you to keep in mind non-Western examples too, because although the specifics of my discussion will not apply to them, the general principles that I advance are, nevertheless, quite applicable.

The spread of endangered languages

If one examines the language status efforts on behalf of many endangered languages, one cannot help but be struck by the fact that they

generally attempt to fight fire with fire. Faced by the progressive encroachment of a competitor within the gates of their own ethnolinguistic
community, faced by the well nigh complete control of the domains of power
and modernity by this competitor, the loyalists to and the advocates of
endangered languages commonly (all too commonly) lay plans to capture
(or, in some cases, to recapture) 'the terrain of power and modernity'.
Basque advocates work on terminologies for the natural sciences in higher
education, because, presumably, that will advance the day when a
unilingually-Basque 'Basque Country' will arise again on both sides of the
Pyrenees. Irish protagonists lay plans for governmental offices and agencies
operating primarily in Irish, as befits 'the national and first official language'
of their country. Frisian loyalists seek to conquer the secondary schools and
the Town Councils and Yiddish protagonists, from at least the time of the
Tshernovits Language Conference of 1908 to this very day, are concerned
with dictionaries and grammars, modern poetry and belles-lettres, theatre
and intellectual journals, and with corpus planning at least for purposes of
popular science and inter-translatability with the New York Times.
Although it is clear to those who adopt such policies for themselves, and
to those who advocate them for others, that the time and effort invested
in spreading their endangered language into the uppermost functions of
modernity will (a) initially attract few who are both willing and capable of
using that language for these functions and (b) do little if anything to stem
the ongoing attrition with respect to the primary determinants of intergenerational language transmission (in Western or Westernized society:
home, neighborhood, elementary school, work-sphere, religious domain),
nevertheless, *such efforts continue unabated and represent major language
policy decisions*. Suggestions that a more modest target be aimed at, i.e.
that the primary intergenerational arena be focused upon and shored up,
are met with the scornful charge of 'folklorization', i.e. with accusations that
such a narrower focus would be tantamount to surrendering the power and
status related interactions of modern life (and, therefore, of language life)
and of opting for trivialization via a focus on the rural past (old wives' tales
and the folksongs and dances of a bygone age). The modern world, its
genres and pursuits, has a tremendous fascination for language policy
authorities, and understandably so, since they themselves are almost always
modernized élites who have been fashioned in the crucible of modern
tensions and aspirations.

The double 'approach-avoidance' dilemma

Actually, by the time a language is an endangered species, almost any proffered status planning solutions to its problems involve a high level of risk relative to the likely benefits to be gained thereby. Solutions that stress entry or re-entry into modernization pursuits and interactions imply a policy of direct competition and confrontation with a stronger (and often increasingly stronger) competitor. Understandably, relatively few ordinary individuals are ready, either linguistically or philosophically, to embark on such a confrontation, particularly when the forces that foster it are primarily linguacentric in nature. Studying (or teaching) astrophysics in Irish certainly proves that 'there is nothing deficient about our language; if we do not use it for astrophysics it is *we* who are at fault and not the language'. However, the huge amount of time, effort and funds necessary in order to reach that goal (both in connection with perfecting the necessary terminologies and texts, and in connection with getting teachers themselves to learn and to use them) and the small number of individuals who will ever use Irish (or Xish) for that purpose, seriously raises the question of whether *that* is a wise policy or not, particularly when at the very time that astrophysics is being stressed, the attrition on the 'home front' is still going on among many, many more individuals than will ever hear of astrophysics, let alone be enlightened by it. However, no sooner is the wisdom of pursuing such confrontational and multi-modern-functional priorities questioned and alternative emphases suggested focus-ing upon the family, the neighborhood and the elementary school, i.e. upon the very domains and role relations that are at the core of socioculturally patterned language acquisition and, accordingly, upon the domains and interactions that are central to inter-generational ethnolinguistic continuity, no sooner are such emphases suggested then the bugaboo of 'folklorization' raises its head. If Frisian and Yiddish are to be related only or primarily to the vernacular intimacy of hearth-and-home, if they are to be denied meaningful roles in the world of modern concerns, aspirations and statuses, then are they anything more than anachronistic spinning-wheels and pious formulas in an age governed by computers, rockets and the devil take the hindmost? Who wants spinning-wheel languages? Who needs them? Who stays with them after passing through adolescence and leaving home to find one's fortune in the big city? Isn't anything that might be won initially by this approach of shoring up the home front, ultimately lost in spades as the traditional and sheltered pre-modern world of parents and grandparents is left behind (even rejected) in a mad scramble to join the present and, better yet, the future?

Clearly, endangered languages and their custodians are damned if they do and damned if they don't, no matter *what* it is that they do or don't do in the language policy arena. Whether they fight language spread fire with fire or whether they fight it with water, the risks are apparently equally great and the outcomes equally dubious. They are buffeted by the double dangers of folklorization, on the one hand, and Irelandization on the other hand, and the more they seek to avoid the one, the more they risk gravitating toward the other. What can and what should a sociolinguistically informed language policy effort on behalf of endangered languages do? Is there any way out of their impasse?

Reasonable and reasoned compromise in language policy for endangered languages

If it is erroneous to pretend that 'nothing can be done for them by the time they are endangered', it also does not help to pretend that 'it is never too late' to rescue endangered languages, for indeed, it often *is* too late relative to the amount of social control that the policy planners who labor on their behalf either can or should exercise. However, it is *definitely not automatically too late* (as some misinformed observers would have it) merely because the 'endangered' stage has been reached. Even in our modern age, when speech-communities are so highly inter-related and inter-dependent, a judicious combination of direct community-building efforts (these are indispensable; *no language should be dependent on direct language policy efforts alone*), on the one hand, and direct language policy efforts, on the other hand, can (re-)stabilize speech-community networks and the borders between networks. However, as in the case of all 'emergency first aid', the hemorrhaging of the main arteries must be stopped first, well before major attention is devoted to poetry journals, to astrophysics and to the world of international power politics or even middle-level technology. However, the central domains of inter-generational mother tongue continuity must also not be defined too narrowly either; they include not only hearth and home but neighborhood [i.e. residential concentration], elementary schooling, worksphere and, often, the religious sphere as well. Taken together, these are the societal foundations that one inherits, that define community and that one hands on to the next generation on a societal rather than merely on an individual basis. Given the Euro-American focus that we have adopted for our discussion, these are the primary societal institutions and when a language is safe within them it has at least a generation's worth of breathing time and space. These are the initial institutions that transmit values and, therefore, these are the ones that transmit the values, loyalties, ideologies,

philosophies and traditions out of which a sense of community arises and
is maintained, from which the call to loyalty to the necessarily interpreted
ethnolinguistic past (as interpreted by the language loyalists) and the call
to custodianship *vis-à-vis* the desired ethnolinguistic future are derived, are
inculcated, are reinforced and are legitimated.

Material and materialistic beings though we be, we still have not
totally lost neither the capacity nor the need to live for ideals, for loved
ones, for collective goals. It is via the primary sociocultural institutions
that language is first related to the verities that make life worth living
and it is to these institutions that policy makers must turn if they are to
re-connect language with those verities. *Every language needs an idea —
a goal and a vision above the mundane and the rational — to keep it
alive.* The basic and minimally essential 'idea' is the imperative of
remaining a separate ethnolinguistic entity and a struggling language-
community must safeguard this idea before all others. In healthy
languages the 'idea' need not even be consciously recognized by the bulk
of the speakers; in struggling languages, consciousness of personal
responsibility for the language (the symbolic integrator of all that is
good and precious), needs to be developed early and stressed
repeatedly. The family, the neighborhood, the elementary school and
the church need to be urged, instructed, rewarded and guided to play
their irreplaceable roles in this connection. There is no substitute for
them, nor for the ideas that they can espouse from the very earliest and
tenderest years and, thereafter, throughout the life-span (ideas such as
the inherent *right* to continue, the *duty* to continue, the *privilege* of
continuing the language-in-culture association of any community's
historic preferred collective-self-realization), no substitute, certainly, if
vernacular functions are to be stabilized. These social functions are
absolutely necessary and they must be reconquered first, because
without them there are no vernacular functions at all that are intergenerationally transmitted, not even if quite a large number of people
study astrophysics in Basque. But the family, neighborhood and
elementary school are not enough. They are necessary but they are not
sufficient, least of all for 'moderns'.

'Man does not live by bread alone', the *Sayings of the Fathers* teach
us, but also 'If there is no bread there is no learning'. Just as corpus
planning without status planning is an empty game of silly linguists, so
mesmerization by hearth and home is a romantic infatuation of ethnic
innocents. Even while home and neighborhood are being re-
vernacularized (via language associations of parents active in
neighborhood nurseries and kindergartens, via language associations

related to shopping and to fishing, to knitting and to reading, via language-related local sports teams for toddlers and singing contests for adolescents, via prizes for language-championing essays at every grade level and pre-paid vacations for language-insistent and language-successful parents, via recognition in church and recognition in school in the many ways that dedication, piety and excellence are normally recognized by every self-respecting society, but in this context: in connection with language), at this very same time the work sphere — particularly the lower and entry-level worksphere — must also definitely be staked out early for language related recognition, rewards, promotions, raises and preferences of all kinds. The serious world of work and careers starts here and the bulk of the citizenry spends the bulk of its years in this world. This is the first area of language spread into which formerly endangered languages must be enabled (nay, must be shelteringly engineered) to expand. For many it will be the last significant language spread they will experience, particularly so if we count the world of mass entertainment (whether sports or performing arts) as normally falling within the secondary rather than within the primary institutions of language maintenance, i.e. within the institutional structures that are generally not societally or familially transmitted from one generation to the next, institutions with a weaker moralistic flavor and institutions that individuals generally enter only after adolescence.

The world of work has no limit. It goes from entry-level 'all the way up' and it is more likely than not that the further up it goes the more it will be dominated by the competing language of greater power. The weak are always more likely to be bilingual than the strong and those from the endangered language community who have the ability and seek the rewards related to the upper work-sphere will definitely need to show versatility in the intra- or inter-societally competing language of wider communication. There may, indeed, be room for a poetry journal or two in Yiddish or for an organic chemistry text in Frisian, but I seriously doubt whether these need to be priority concerns, until and unless we are no longer dealing with endangered languages but with communities of sufficient autonomy, above and beyond cultural autonomy, to provide the dynamics for language spread into many of the higher and more powerful reaches of society. In most cases, however, such autonomy is not only *not* a realistic early goal, but on the contrary, it is actually a counter-productive early goal for languages in the endangered state. To pursue the social and political policies that such a goal implies, when the language itself is still seriously struggling for its very existence and when the higher reaches of power and authority are still far outside of its grasp, rather than actually or even nearly within it, is to confuse the essential with the visionary, the immediate with the pot of gold at the end of the rainbow. It is also tantamount to providing ammunition to the opposition that is always waiting exactly for such errors in judgement in order better to be able to shoot down the entire restoration effort. It is tantamount to not recognizing that a functionally dislocated language needs generations of quiet and stability in the primary domains of intergenerational language continuity, rather than more turmoil, more dislocation and more disturbance of the intimate patterns of daily life which nurture both a distinctive ethnocultural pattern and its traditionally associated language.

The most important lesson to remember and, apparently, the most difficult one to learn initially, is the following one: *the intimate domains are also the most sheltered*; they nurture inter-generational continuity, even if these domains are not the major movers and shakers of the modern world. On the other hand, *the most powerful modern domains are also the most exposed* to the vicissitudes of power confrontation; they do *not* lay the foundations of community, precisely because their impact upon us comes developmentally later in life and their aim is higher and their grasp is of greater scope than that of the immediately experienced speech community. Endangered languages must assume control of the former — the intimate spheres of family and community — even though they may never attain control of the latter — the status spheres of supra-local power and authority. Assuming control of the home and community domains means (re-)building those domains via the endangered language, becoming inseparably interpenetrated by them, inextricably associated with them. In short, it means community build-ing, community policy, community well-being, community institutions, community life, community activity, rather than language policy alone, language policy *ad nauseam*, language fears and dreams and nothing more. Language always exists in a cultural matrix and it is this matrix that needs to be fostered via policy rather than the language *per se*. Not even linguists live by and for language alone; ordinary mortals are ever so much less capable of doing so. Language policy must maintain a fine balance between directness and indirectness, between figure and ground, between vinegar and honey. 'Lingua sana en communitas sana' is the only realistic goal for endangered languages; they must not become fetishes; rather, they must be intimately tied to a thousand intimate or small-scale network processes, processes too gratifying and rewarding to surrender even if they do not quite amount to the pursuit of the higher reaches of power and modernity.

400   LANGUAGE AND ETHNICITY

Conclusions

'A man's reach must exceed his grasp, or what's a heaven for?', Robert Browning opined, but that is a counsel that is tailor-made for those who can *afford* to fall flat on their faces if they reach too high. At the outset, and it is particularly the enfeebled outset that I am stressing because it is the stage of greatest risk, language policy for endangered languages *must* be more circumspect than that, more cautious, more calculating along risk-benefit lines. At the outset, before they acquire a dynamic of their own, all language policies must be sensitively harmonized with the functional profiles and the most crucial functional prospects of the languages on whose behalf they are formulated. Among endangered languages the hemorrhages in the realm of home and immediate community must be stopped first and quickly. The danger of folklorization, if, indeed, it exists (as in the rare case of 'nativization' movements), can be coped with later and more leisurely than can the danger of losing the remaining thinning ranks of mother tongue speakers. 'What profiteth it man to gain the world and lose his soul?' What profiteth it Irish or Basque to gain astrophysics and to lose the Gaeltacht or the casarías? The 'dangers of folklorization' become real only *after* the primary ethnocultural domains have been fully secured. Until such time, the dangers of Irelandization are infinitely greater than those of folklorization.

An exaggerated abhorrence of 'folklorization' (exaggerated, certainly, if this designation is pejoratively and indiscriminately applied to the necessity of giving priority to the pursuits of hearth and home [and of daily life more generally] for languages that are still threatened in these very functions) undercuts the very sense of uniqueness, the sense of ethnolinguistic authenticity and distinctiveness, that are at the experiential foundations of ethnolinguistic continuity. Our kith and kin, our neighbors and friends, our colleagues and clergy, our regular customers and employees, our child socialization patterns and our local collective memories, festivities, customs and traditions, these are the ultimately irrational *raison d'êtres* and building-blocks of separate ethnolinguistic existence. A computer and an atom-smasher by any other name are really exactly the same thing, but an ethnically encumbered interaction (such as the celebration of a festival, a birth, a birthday party or a marriage ceremony) in a language other than the historically associated one, signals a different family culture, a different everyday reality, a different interpretation of and involvement in the tangible past and a different view of the future. In short, as I first indicated twenty years ago in my *Language Loyalty in the United States* (1966), and as I subsequently theoretically elaborated in my *Language and Nationalism* (1972): a different language in the ethnoculturally encumbered interactions is indicative of a differently realized and implemented ethnocultural identity, a differently enacted and expressed ethnoculturally contrastive context, even if the same ethnic label is still utilized due to the elements of continuity that may remain even after language shift occurs.

Living cultures and languages are always changing, of course, but language shift is indicative of a culture's inability to control or significantly influence the rate and direction of its change. Efforts to foster endangered languages represent the will of endangered networks that are conscious of the dangers in which they find themselves and that are eager to influence yet other networks that are not yet conscious of those dangers, to hold on to and to increase the historically validated *content* of their lives, or some more traditional version and interpretation thereof, rather than just to their identity-metaphors devoid of such historically validated content, to maintain, significantly control, influence or guide their intercultural relations rather than to merely be the playthings, the by-products, the targets and captives of such relations under the control of others. Few of us, even the most powerful among us, are fully masters in our own homes; but none of us willingly settle for being strangers in our own homes, servants, dispossessed ghosts. It is not an ethnic label that we seek, but an ethnic content that strikes us as befitting the label, that seems to us to harmonize with it, that fits it in accord *with our own historic image* of 'goodness of fit' rather in accord with someone else's.

Language policy on behalf of endangered languages must assure the intimate vernacular functions first, and, if possible, to go on from there, slowly building outward from the primary to the secondary institutions of inter-generational mother-tongue continuity. The entry-level work sphere is a must; the more advanced work-sphere is a maybe. Diglossia is a must (with safely stabilized spheres exclusively for the endangered language); monolingual economic autonomy or political independence are maybes. Widespread reconquest of the vernacular intimacy functions is a must; language spread into the higher reaches of power and modernity is a maybe. The rationalization of language policy for endangered languages is a must; the maximization of results from such policies is, at best, a maybe, because under conditions of rapid social change and dislocation, there are always multiple other forces and other considerations to contend with, above and beyond language policy on behalf of such languages.

And of what value is this entire exercise for all of those, and, probably, for most of us, who may actually be more interested in English and in French, in Latin and in Greek, in Spanish and in Potinhua, in Swahili and in Hindi? Is talk of minor, endangered languages (who have a meager chance of surviving and even less chance of spreading) a fitting way to start off a conference on the unlimited horizons for language spread and language policy? *Indeed it is*, for just as illness teaches us about health, and just as psychopathology teaches us about what is normal in everyday mental life, so the problems of endangered languages teach us about the extreme delicacy of language policy and the extreme complexity of language spread. And while it behooves us to help these languages because they need our help most, because by doing so we become more human, we should also note that our involvement with them will also benefit us by making us more sensitive, more humble and more cautious language policy researchers and language policy implementers as well, researchers and implementers more likely to realize that for every gain there is a loss, for every self-satisfied smile, a despondent tear, for every glorious triumph a tragic defeat. And that, I hope and believe, is certainly a fitting note on which to start our explorations of the next two days.

13 Language policy in the U.S.A. past, present, and future*

Relative to the early 1960s, when I was at work on *Language Loyalty in the United States* (Fishman *et al.*, 1966), the total picture of language life in our country may be characterized by the adage *plus ça change, plus c'est la même chose*. On the surface a great deal has changed, but in my most pessimistic moments I wonder whether the change isn't mostly in our intellectual sophistication, sociolinguistic at its core, to discuss, analyze, and prescribe with respect to language in society. Basically ours is still a society whose peculiar genius is not along the lines of linguistic sophistication, sensitivity, or concern. Technology, productivity, standard of living, consumerism, populism, democracy, these and many other descriptions apply, but a concern for language is not generally among them. Neither language as an exquisite human gift, nor even English as an instrument or as a symbol, are part of the man-in-the-street's patrimony, his concept of what the United States is, what it stands for, what he or it is proud of, what he or it is stirred by, inspired by, committed to.

Even the exasperated know-nothingism of 'this is, after all, an English-speaking country' is cognizant only of two purported rewards resulting therefrom: political unity and communicational ease. English for our masses is a *lingua franca* rather than a thing of beauty, elegance, precision, purity, or greatness. 'It works'; it is an instrumentality; but as such, it is not an object of love, affection, devotion, emotion. For good or for evil, we have developed a civilization that is not sentimental about language, languages, or even about its own language. If our college youth is not heart-broken that the *Whorfian hypothesis* has, in its strong version,

*Originally published in C. A. FERGUSON & S. B. HEATH (eds), *Language in the U.S.A.* New York: Cambridge University Press, 515–26.

become decreasingly supportable (Fishman & Spolsky, 1977), neither is it thrilled by the worldwide spread of English. English is for them what it is for all but a small number of English teachers and 'professional Englishmen' in the U.S.A.: a modern Aramaic which all of mankind would adopt because of the material benefits to which it is an open sesame, rather than because of any internal spirit that animates it (Fishman, 1977a; Fishman, Cooper & Conrad, 1977). We are the ultimate *Gesellschaft*, never having had much collective *Gemeinschaft* to begin with. We are the ultimate modern society. The mysteries for which words are crucially needed, which language creates and which only language can solve — religion, philosophy, literature, ideology — are not the mysteries we dwell upon most. We glory in the least humanistic mysteries and there is precious little language and little language preciousness to be found among them. The state of language policy in the United States cannot but be a reflection of the above state of linguistic astigmatism that characterizes our national life more generally.

Language shift policy

The greatest American linguistic investment by far has been in the Anglification of its millions of immigrant and indigenous speakers of other languages. Without either constitutional or subsequent legal declaration or requirement that English is the *official* (let alone the *national*) *language*, a complex web of customs, institutions, and programs has long fostered well-nigh exclusive reliance upon English in public life. The result of two centuries of the foregoing is that literally hundreds of millions of Americans have been led, cajoled, persuaded, embarrassed into, and forced to forget, forego and even deny languages that were either their *mother tongues*, their *communal languages*, or their personal or communal additional tongues. The Soviet Union has attained universal Russification within sixty years, thus denying us the world's speed record with respect to *language shift*. However, the Soviet Union, as the inheritor *par excellence* of both Marx and Herder, has at least, thus far, only attained universal *familiarity* with Russian as a second language. Only a very minor proportion of the total ethnically non-Russian population has given up its own mother tongue for Russian (Lewis, 1972; Silver, 1974), even though just that shift is very noticeable among smaller nationalities, particularly those most urbanized and those most impacted by 'planned' (forced) migration into or out of their own areas. Thus language shift in the USSR, with its nationality republics, nationality regions, and nationality districts (all of them purportedly 'autonomous'), is primarily language displacement rather than language replacement. Language shift in the U.S.A. is quintessentially replacive. English as a second language has become English as a first language and the latter, in turn, has become English as an only language. No Herderian, Jeffersonian, or even ordinary 'little culture' protective institutions have been available to stem the tide. Certainly the cultivation of such has not usually been deemed a public responsibility, in the public good, to be paid for out of public funds.

Nevertheless, this picture is not exactly as it was in the early 1960s, the major difference being the *Bilingual Education Act* (Fishman, 1976). First funded in 1967–8, refunded in 1973–4, and again in 1979–80, the Act was primarily an act for the Anglification of non-English speakers and not an act for *Bilingualism*. Ironically, 'Bilingualism' has become a newspeak euphemism for 'non-English mother tongue.' 'Bilinguals' are thus non-English mother-tongue speakers; 'bilingual teachers' are those who teach them; 'bilingual programs' are those that Anglify them. This usage is uniquely American and barely disguises the negative semantic field to which it pertains. Under the aegis of the Bilingual Education Act, funds have been provided to state education departments, universities, and local school districts for experimental/demonstration programs that temporarily employ non-English mother tongues as co-media of instruction until (hopefully within three years or less),the pupil's English is good enough to become the sole medium of instruction. Thus, the act is basically not an act *for* bilingualism, but, rather, an act *against* bilingualism. It may contribute not merely to displacing non-English mother tongues from the instructional process, but to replacing them entirely (Kjolseth, 1973; Fishman, 1977b; Gaarder, 1977).

The Act provides for teaching the culture as well as the language of non-English-speaking students to students of 'limited English-speaking ability.' Guidelines of the Act also permit a small proportion of English-dominant students to participate in classes funded under the Act; however, realities of urban demography being what they are, such magnanimity does not go much beyond the co-presence of Blacks and Hispanics. Evaluation has invariably been in terms of English test-retest gains among the 'bilinguals' or non-English mother-tongue students. Quite predictably these gains have generally (i.e. on a nationwide scale) not proven themselves to be significantly higher than those of bilinguals not receiving *bilingual education* (American Institutes for Research (hereafter AIR) 1977). A simplistic approach to 'evaluating' bilingual education — whatever unknown mixture that may represent of teacher preparations, teaching methods, curricular materials, etc. — ignores the possibility of gains in other cognitive areas as well as in various noncognitive areas (including that of cultural security) for the bilingual child (not to mention the possibility of gains for participating Anglo children as well). Many careful local studies *have* revealed significant gains for 'bilinguals' receiving bilingual education (see e.g. Cohen, 1975, and various studies mentioned in Fishman, 1976). Contrasts between these studies and those which purport to show national trends underscore the peculiar double-bind of American public bilingual education in the late 1970s. It is damned if it does and damned if it doesn't. If it *does* bring about a rapid transition to English then it will no longer be needed. If it does *not*, it will also no longer be needed. This is hardly a context conducive to the development of educational expertise, stability, and achievement.

While *transitional bilingual education* has been increasingly faulted as insufficiently transitional (U.S. General Accounting Office (hereafter GAO), 1976; AIR, 1977; Epstein, 1977 a, b), other developments have tended to reinforce it. The U.S. Supreme Court's *Lau v. Nichols* decision (1974) has led to bilingual education in many school systems that might otherwise have done nothing in particular for their students of 'limited English-speaking ability,' or would have been content merely to offer them help in the acquisition of English *per se*. The Court's insistence that learning English and getting an equitable education were not the same thing, and that due process was denied when the latter was not forthcoming (even if the former was being pursued), has fostered bilingual education, frequently under threat of being found in noncompliance of federal law, as the remedy of choice. This remedy itself, however, has, at times, been called into question because of desegregation considerations (Teitelbaum 1977a, b) and bilingual education therefore finds itself confronted by a four-front war: (a) negative evaluatory evidence, (b) civil rights (desegregation) concerns; (c) union members fearful of losing jobs to 'bilingual' teachers; and (d) ethnic divisiveness sometimes headlined by the press (Epstein, 1977a; *New York Times* editorial 'Bilingual Danger,' November 22, 1976).

Language maintenance policy

Ethnic shift into the mainstream Anglophone middle class phenotype is the most common American minority experience. It epitomizes simultaneous social mobility, social integration, mass participation in the symbolic political institutions, and the setting aside of prior affect and intimacy. For these various reasons, the widespread re-ethnification or heightened ethnicity experiences of the past decade have been deeply worrisome to many, both at the grass-roots and the pseudo-intellectual levels, at the very same time that they have been espoused by an unprecedented number of others. A number of policy considerations have heightened the resulting tension and, as is usual in connection with ethnicity, language dimensions have quickly come to the fore, both for advocates and for opponents.

Sociological and sociolinguistic theory are both still too immature (with respect to what ethnicity is and how or why it is linked to language) to explain why it is that supposedly subdued and suppressed ethnicity sentiments blossomed forth all over the world in the late 1960s and early 1970s. The common American cocktail party variety of expertise blames it all on the Blacks (i.e. on contagion spread by the advocates of Black is Beautiful, Black pride, Black soul), but this is not only an ineffectual response to the worldwide nature of the phenomenon but it does nothing to explain even its American manifestations. Neither such notions as 'the bent twig' (a metaphor of Isaiah Berlin 1972), whereby repressed ethnicity must ultimately 'snap back,' nor the assumption of purely opportunistic alternation between purportedly 'rational class struggle' (Gellner, 1964; Glazer & Moynihan, 1975; Patterson, 1975) and 'irrational ethnicity' (Devereaux, 1975; Isaacs, 1975) are more than metaphor or bias in the face of the distribution of the ethnicity phenomenon historically, geographically, economically, and sociopsychologically. Three thousand years of Euro-Mediterranean social theory with respect to the nature of ethnicity, its recurring link to language, its developmental relationship to sociocultural change, its mutability and modernization, have been lost and are only now being retrieved (Fishman, 1977c, d). Modern capitalist, Marxist, and neutralist social theory with respect to ethnicity uniformly viewed it as a vanishing, irrelevant, or undesirable aberration in market-dominated Gesellschaft, and, in the processes of this self-serving astig-matism, lost sight of language in society as well. Little wonder then that the reappearance of both ethnicity and language in American public life has elicited the opposition of intellectuals who had predicted its doom and of journalists, union leaders, and ordinary folk who were themselves byproducts of the surrender and denial of the very attributes which others were now acclaiming.

Bilingual education has stumbled into the troubled waters of language and ethnicity, much to its own surprise. What began as a major effort to Anglify 'the last unfortunates' has come to be criticized as building a political and/or economic power base for ethnic proto-élites who purp-ortedly refuse to let their clienteles integrate into the mainstream.

Economic self-interest is presumably acceptable if pursued by the oil lobby, by the teachers' unions, and by our most reputable universities, but is considered meanly divisive if pursued by Hispanics, Native Americans, or other ethnics (Novak, 1972; Jaipaul, 1973). Political organizations and modern mass media channels of public influence are acceptable if adopted by mainstream Anglophones, but are disruptive if adopted by 'bilinguals.' Party politicians have a useful relationship and responsibility to the masses, but are merely self-seeking and power-hungry if they foster an ethnic base and seek to maintain its viability. Bilingual education is said to contribute to such a power base as is the general rebirth of ethnicity. Monolingual education is, on the other hand, seen as nonpartisan, and is equated with 'the public good' rather than with its own political power or self-interest.

It is hard to say what the ethnicity stress has contributed to non-English *language maintenance* in the United States. A new 'language loyalty' study would be needed to arrive at integrated empirical and theoretical understanding of this question. The few data-connected straws in the wind are hard to confirm and even harder to interpret. Obviously, many more people claimed non-English tongues in 1970 than did so in 1960, even in the absence of massive (non-Hispanic) immigration and contrary to all trends since 1930. Obviously ethnic studies programs at American colleges and universities have led to a mushrooming of language courses. Languages are now taught which were hardly represented (or entirely unrepresented) in university teaching a decade ago (Scanpresence, 1977). However, neither claiming a mother tongue nor enrolling in ethnic studies is extremely relevant to actual language use or language knowledge. It is most probably true that an attitudinal improvement (even halo-ization) has taken place, that mother tongues which were neither claimed nor studied before are now claimed and studied — but it also seems likely that such increased positiveness can be maintained and fostered for quite some time without any corresponding impact on either language knowledge or language use. Indeed, it is possible for language attitudes to improve in compensatory fashion as both use and knowledge decrease (Committee on Irish Language Attitudes Research, 1975). This may well be what is occurring for most non-English tongues in the U.S.A. It is not at all clear, particularly in the absence of further immigration from their respective home countries, what improved institutional bases they might reasonably hope for that would reintroduce and maintain them in families, neighborhoods, churches, organizations, and mass media. All of these have been already overwhelmingly Anglified quite a while back (Fishman *et al.*, 1966).

For Spanish, Native American languages, and for Vietnamese (the last merely representing a recent and non-recurring immigration), this situation is different. It is particularly so for the Spanish population which is numerically large, indigenized, and still growing as the result of legal and illegal immigration and a predictable birthrate. People who claim Spanish as their mother tongue constitute a huge proportion of all those in the U.S.A. who claim a mother tongue other than English. What is more, they use their language more than other groups, i.e. they contribute an even larger proportion of all those who primarily speak a language other than English. Understandably, Spanish bilingual education programs also account for the bulk of bilingual programs throughout the U.S.A., although, all in all, 68 languages were involved in 1976–7 and over 70 in 1977–8. Spanish, at the very least, seems destined to a lengthy — if not vigorous — life in the U.S.A.

Interestingly enough, while journalists, teachers' union representatives, and perhaps a good portion of U.S. citizens are concerned that bilingual education may 'build in' non-English enclaves into American political and social life, experienced students of American *hispanidad* fear just the opposite: that bilingual education will dissipate forces urging Spanish language maintenance in the U.S.A. (Kjolseth, 1973; Gaarder, 1977). No doubt, both arguments give too much credit to education as an independent causal factor in language shift and ethnic shift. As a distinctly secondary status system, education prepares an individual for participation in one or another primary status system whose impact on language maintenance is likely to be much more decisive than that of education *per se*. In modern Gesellschaft-like societies, the most powerful status system is that of the work-sphere. Thus, were our economy to be a rapidly expanding one, it would reward the participation of Hispanics and initially do so — as it did with the immigrant masses of the 1880–1920 period — even prior to their acquisition of English facility. The cycle thereupon established between higher economic reward and English fluency can continue to spiral upward at slightly below the rate at which the economy expands. In the absence of such expansion, prior knowledge of English may be individually facilitative, but can hardly have massive social mobility significance at a time when unemployment among monolingual English speakers is itself so widespread. The school simply cannot compensate for absence of economic opportunity in the society at large. It cannot 'prime the pump.' Schools most commonly require societal support in order to succeed, and this is certainly as true of bilingual education as it is of monolingual education. Moreover, schools are rarely independent causal forces with respect to the economy or society at large.

If the schools have probably not fostered non-English language maintenance in the U.S.A. — not even in their bilingual education guise — other factors have been equally inconsequential. Neither 'old country' sponsored efforts (tourism, visiting scholars and lecturers, subsidies for local cultural institutions, etc.), nor federally sponsored programs (e.g. the fiscally anemic and politically governed Ethnic Heritage Act, and the meager ethnic components of the National Endowment for the Humanities and the National Endowment for the Arts, etc.) seem to have had much impact on language maintenance in the U.S.A. In both cases the scale is too small and the stance taken is too conflicted for any major positive consequences to obtain (Fishman, 1980).

A number of court decisions may ultimately be more crucial, being both more forceful and more massive in their reach. Just as law has given a major impetus to regular (rather than demonstration) bilingual education programs, so several suits currently working their way through the courts may do for all government welfare programs what the Voting Rights Act has done for various non-English languages on the ballot. Just as such languages (usually Spanish and Native American languages, but also, here and there, Tagalog, Ilocano, Japanese, and others) are required to be on the ballot wherever more than 5% of the population in any election district is not literate in English, so these still pending suits may ultimately tend to require that all government services and programs be in the languages of those whom they serve. In the absence of such accommodation by government to the language of the populace, a *prima facie* case for inequity in delivery of government services is a distinct possibility. Given the Supreme Court's repeated unwillingness to declare English to be the obligatory language of public services, given the official status of Spanish in Puerto Rico (not to mention the co-official status of French in Louisiana and of Spanish in New Mexico), and given the continued growth of the Hispanic and Native American proportions of our population (as well as their continued spread into all urban areas), the likelihood that there will be increasing legal accommodation to their rights and needs is very great. Additional local statutes (such as that in effect in New York City requiring that the language of contracts and warranties/guarantees be the same as the language in which sales or agreements have been orally effected) will almost certainly add to the overall equity foundation for language maintenance in the United States. However, equity is a general principle rather than a language-focused policy in any substantive sense.

Language maintenance in the U.S.A. is not part of public policy because it is rarely recognized as being in the public interest. Until it can be so considered, it must be freed from the suspicion of divisiveness and incompatibility with progress, modernity and efficiency. Languages must be viewed as a precious natural resource rather than as a sword of Damocles. Like all resources, it can be squandered, put to reprehensible uses, or husbanded and developed for the greater general good. However, it may be impossible to arrive at this point of view and to formulate policies for such purposes in connection with languages other than English when the latter itself is so far from our consciousness and from our notion of the natural resources that we seek to protect and to cultivate. Too much of a spotlight on English may be contraproductive in this connection, but too little is also a handicap. Meanwhile I sense a striving and longing among most Hispanic graduate students and bilingual educators, as well as among many of their Native American counterparts, on behalf of language maintenance — a striving much more articulated, un-embarrassed, and moving than any that I came across in the early 1960s — but an even more pained and poignant inability with respect to how this goal can be attained.

The ethnicity movement may have freed many Hispanics and other ethnics from earlier complexes and fears, but it has not yet led them to effective new solutions or programs. It has resulted in the legitimization of smaller-scale bonds, interests, loyalties, and sentiments, and in the open verbalization of disenchantment with large-scale standardization (in government, industry, ideology, education, entertainment, dress, and diet) that was previously so admired as the wave of the future. For many, ethnicity interests, together with 'do it yourself,' environment and resource protection, urban neighborhood maintenance, and decentralization of government, represent a return to personal, direct, unique participatory involvement. The big establishments and even the big counter-establishments have failed to provide either peace, plenty, or participa-tion. But ethnicity is not the only smaller-scale force in modern life, and it is definitely not the only one seeking governmental support and recognition. However, alone among all of the other contenders, ethnicity is the only factor with a well-established negative semantic field associated with it, among both intellectuals and along America's 'Main Street.' When language and ethnicity maintenance are presented in their own right, as a natural right, they evoke images of Quebecization and Balkanization. What is for some 'a thing of beauty and a joy for ever' is for others regressive, explosive, and deceptive. There is no doubt in my mind that language and ethnicity in America can *not* make it on their own, in terms of public policy and at public expense, both because they are too weak (although stronger than in the early 1960s) and also because the opposition to them is ready-made and, therefore, ever ready. Ethnicity and

00

to them is ready-made and, therefore, ever ready. Ethnicity and bilingualism need to be retooled so that their 'image' will appear to be as much in line with the public good as is the image of other recognized self-interest groupings in American life.

Language enrichment policy

Both language shift policy and language maintenance policy are polar reactions to the language and ethnicity nexus. What the one seeks to overcome the other seeks to preserve. Although polar opposites, they are essentially engaged in a discourse that employs similar terms and reacts to similar concerns. It is the level of integration to be sought in society that separates them more than anything else. What is at stake is the validity of lower-order bonds and the desirability or possibility of higher-order ones that coexist with lower-order ones. The disagreement in this respect is nearly 2,000 years old. It springs from the Judeo-Greek (and Eastern Orthodox Church as well as early Islamic) rejection of the Western empire and the Western church view that universality was God's will and that lower-order bonds naturally fell away as mankind inevitably evolved toward one, higher, all-inclusive language and ethnicity. Not until the nineteenth century did this debate transfer to a different metaphor. Johann Gottfried Herder finally set aside the old debate (in which he too had engaged as champion of the suppressed Germans against the then imperial French) by adopting the view that the entire world needs to share and foster as many languages as possible.

Languages of Wider Communication (LWC) were of no interest to Herder for they were merely soulless lingua francas, pragmatic conduits for instrumental purposes (Fishman, 1978). The world always had and always would acquire these for the unavoidable mundane functions that they fulfilled. However, human dignity, ingenuity, love and kindness, idealism, altruism, sensitivity, hope and perseverance, and triumphs over travail — all of these reflections of what was most nobly and creatively and tenderly human — were preserved and fostered only by the variety of the languages that characterized all the peoples of the world. Herder raised the banner not so much of maintenance as of diversity. Diverse talents are needed to save the world from emptiness and mechanization and inhumanity, and these talents are the spontaneous gifts of various peoples, each animated by the spirit of its mother tongue. But languages can be shared. They can function not one at the expense of the other but one in addition to the other. A world made safe for little languages, through which people will feel deeply and think creatively, would be a better, more humane, more accepting and more innovative world for one and all. Herder's final years were spent advocating a world of many languages and, therefore, a world of many solutions to be shared across their original boundaries. A little over a century later, the American Benjamin Lee Whorf traveled pretty much the same path, beginning with the view that each truly different language sparked a truly different reality and world view among its speakers. By the end of his life, however, he had begun to argue that all of mankind and even natural science itself would benefit from the relative linguistic determinism that structurally diverse languages brought about. Different solutions require different inputs, and language is the ultimate input in all that is distinctly human about us.

What is it that Herder and Whorf can contribute to American language policy discussions and deliberations? They are spotlights of faith in language and languages amid the darkness of technology and mankind mechanized and insensitized. Languages must be shared as a common good but before they can be shared, they must be saved, loved, treasured. National policy toward this end finally lifts languages off of the ethnicity versus anti-ethnicity (lower ethnicity versus higher ethnicity) treadmill and sets them into a new universal orbit in which uniqueness serves not itself but the general good. Perhaps such a view could inform American language policy in the future. Congressman Paul Simon of Illinois seems to have this in mind when he suggests that languages need to be put back into the American economy rather than merely retired from active service. Recognizing the tremendous waste involved in eroding languages in homes and communities while trying to implant them anew via schools and colleges, he advocates federal support, including enrichment bilingual education, for their increased cultivation, study and instruction. Significantly, he views all of this not in terms of assistance to the poor, to the non-English-speaking or to the ethnics, but very distinctly as a contribution to the general diplomatic, commercial, intellectual, and aesthetic welfare of the country at large. We all need 'all those languages' in order to enrich our lives, our country, and our world (Simon, 1977).

It is too early to tell what will come of this very recent and largely unprecedented policy viewpoint (note its predecessor view in Fishman *et al.*, 1966: Chapters 1 and 5). It has its counterpart in the new Louisiana educational provision that while every non-Anglo child has a right to a state-funded education, partially via his mother tongue, every Anglo child has a corresponding right (a cultural right) to receive part of his education via another language in order to attain his maximal personal enrichment.

If both types of children can ultimately wind up in the same classroom, one motivated by transitional and maintenance considerations and the other by enrichment considerations, an optimal *modus vivendi* will have been attained. A secret long known to élites all over the world, that the education of their children provides them with greater opportunity, greater insight, deeper appreciations, greater sensitivity, additional aesthetic and cultural dimensions when it is conducted via more than one language of instruction (Lewis, 1976), is slowly being revealed to the public at large and is beginning to compete for public funds. As such it could become an alternative type of public education, available to the fortunate and gifted (fostering a new popular definition of 'bilinguals' and bilingualism in the American context), an approach that would do for American bilingual education what immersion did for the Canadian: yield outstanding results because those involved were self-selected to succeed. The experience of the Florida Dade County schools and of a multitude of bilingual private and parochial schools under the most diverse auspices all point to the success potential of enrichment bilingual education.

However, if enrichment language policy is limited or restricted to the schools alone, it will fail as surely as either transitional or maintenance policy when similarly restricted. What is needed is an enrichment policy that views the multilingualization of American urban life as a contribution to the very quality of life itself. Michael Novak has been calling for the creative preservation of our urban diversity (Novak, 1972) as has Monsignor Baroni (*New York Times*, April 20, 1977: B1). This cannot succeed without a language component but this component must have broader outreach as well. Neighborhoods live a life of their own in terms of most family, face-to-face experiences. However, neighborhood fairs can be shared, as can neighborhood pageants and parades. On the other hand a policy of support for non-English films, plays, television and radio, opera and song, press and poetry would stimulate generally shared enrichment experiences, but these would also trickle down to particular significance in particular neighborhoods.

Language policy involves a vision of America. A multilingual enrichment policy envisages a multilingual America as being in the public good. We support a multiparty system. We support a multilateral productive machine, i.e. one that operates both in the consumer and in the industrial capacity markets. Our anti-trust laws aim to diversify the economic market place. We can similarly diversify the cultural market place. Other countries do it. Ireland does it less successfully and Wales more successfully. Norway does it *vis-à-vis* two 'kinds' of Norwegian. Holland has begun to do it *vis-à-vis* Dutch and Frisian. Switzerland has long done so — not through bilingual education but through multilingual services of various kinds (McRae, 1964). Peaceful multilingual polities — where multilingualism is a public trust and a public good — are far from rare (Mackey & Verdoodt, 1975; Savard & Vigneault, 1975). We still have the possibility of opting for such a policy, particularly in conjunction with our Spanish language treasures. No fear of dissension is needed in order to frighten us into it. There is a vision of American magnanimity involved, but more than that, a vision of American possibilities, opportunities, appreciations, sensitivities, that we all should savour. 'Brotherhood' does not mean uniformity. A shared diversity can be the true meaning of the American promise: 'to crown thy good with brotherhood from sea to shining sea.'

Bibliography

AMERICAN INSTITUTES FOR RESEARCH (AIR) 1977, *Interim Report, Evaluation of the Impact of ESEA Title VII Spanish/English Bilingual Education Programs.* Palo Alto, CA: AIR.

BERLIN, ISAIAH 1972, The bent twig: a note on nationalism. *Foreign Affairs* 51.

COHEN, A. D. 1975, *A Sociolinguistic Approach to Bilingual Education: Experiments in the American Southwest.* Rowley, MA: Newbury House.

COMMITTEE ON IRISH LANGUAGE ATTITUDES RESEARCH (CILAR) 1975, *Report.* Dublin: CILAR.

DEVEREAUX, G. 1975, Ethnic identity: its logical foundations and its dysfunctions. In G. DE VOS & L. ROMANUCCI-ROSS (eds), *Ethnic Identity: Cultural Continuities and Change.* Palo Alto, CA: Mayfield.

EPSTEIN, N. 1977a, The bilingual battle: should Washington finance ethnic identities? *The Washington Post* June 5, C1.

— 1977b, *Language, Ethnicity, and the Schools: Policy Alternatives for Bilingual-Bicultural Education.* Washington, DC: Institute for Educational Leadership, George Washington University.

FISHMAN, J. A. 1965a, Who speaks what language to whom and when? *Linguistique* 2: 67–88.

— 1965b, *Yiddish in America: Sociolinguistic Description and Analysis.* Bloomington: Indiana University.

— 1966, Italian language maintenance efforts in the U.S. and the teacher of Italian in American high schools and colleges, *The Florida Foreign Language Reporters* 4: 3, 4, 26.

— 1972, Review of J. L. Rayfield, The Languages of a Bilingual Community. *Language* 48: 969–75.
— (ed.) 1976, *Bilingual Education: an International Sociological Perspective*. Rowley, MA: Newbury House.
— (ed.) 1977a, *Advances in the Creation and Revision of Writing Systems*. The Hague: Mouton.
— 1977b, *Bilingual Education: current perspectives, social science*. Arlington, VA: Center for Applied Linguistics.
— 1977c, Ethnicity and language. In H. GILES (ed.), *Language, Ethnicity, and Intergroup Relations*. New York and London: Academic Press.
— 1977d, Knowing, using, and liking English as an additional language. *TESOL Quarterly* 11.
— 1977e, Language, ethnicity, and racism. In M. SAVILLE-TROIKE (ed.), *Georgetown University Round Table on Languages and Linguistics 1977*. Washington, DC: Georgetown University Press.
— 1977f, *Language and Nationalism*. Rowley, MA: Newbury House.
— 1978, Positive bilingualism: some overlooked rationales and forefathers. In J. E. ALATIS (ed.), *Georgetown University Round Table on Languages and Linguistics 1978*. Washington, DC: Georgetown University Press.
— 1980, Ethnicity and language maintenance. In S. THERNSTROM (ed.), *Harvard Encyclopedia of American Ethnic Groups*. Cambridge: Harvard University Press.
FISHMAN, J. A. & HOFMAN, J. E. 1966, Mother tongue and nativity in the American population. In J. A. FISHMAN (ed.), *Language Loyalty in the United States*. The Hague: Mouton.
FISHMAN, J. A. & SPOLSKY, B. 1977, The Whorfian hypothesis in 1975: a sociolinguistic appreciation. In H. FISHER & R. DIAZ-GUERRERO (eds), *Language and Logic in Personality and Society*. New York: Academic Press.
FISHMAN, J. A. *et al.* 1966, *Language Loyalty in the United States*. The Hague: Mouton.
FISHMAN, J. A., COOPER, R. L., MA, R. *et al.* 1971, *Bilingualism in the Barrio*. Bloomington: Indiana University Press.
FISHMAN, J. A., COOPER, R. L. & CONRAD, A. W. 1977, *The Spread of English: The Sociology of English as an Additional Language*. Rowley, MA: Newbury House.
GAARDER, B. 1977, *Bilingual Schooling and the Survival of Spanish in the United States*. Rowley, MA: Newbury House.
GELLNER, E. 1964, *Thought and Change*. Chicago: University of Chicago Press.

GLAZER, N. & MOYNIHAN, D. P. 1975, Introduction. In N. GLAZER & D. P. MOYNIHAN (eds), *Ethnicity: Theory and Experience*. Cambridge, MA: Harvard University Press.

ISAACS, H. R. 1975, Basic group identity: the idols of the tribe. In N. GLAZER & D. P. MOYNIHAN (eds), *Ethnicity: Theory and Experience*. Cambridge: Harvard University Press.

JAIPAUL, 1977, *Politics of Ethnicity*. Philadelphia: Ethnic Heritage Affairs Institute.

KJOLSETH, R. 1973, Bilingualist education programs in the United States: for assimilation or pluralism? In P. R. TURNER (ed.), *Bilingualism in the Southwest*. Tucson: University of Arizona Press.

LEWIS, E. G. 1972, *Multilingualism in the Soviet Union*. The Hague: Mouton.

— 1976, Bilingualism and bilingual education: the Ancient World to the Renaissance. In J. A. FISHMAN (ed.), *Bilingual Education: An International Sociological Perspective*. Rowley, MA: Newbury House.

MACKEY, W. F. & VERDOODT, A. 1975, *The Multinational Society*. Rowley, MA: Newbury House.

MCRAE, K. D. 1964, *Switzerland: Example of Cultural Coexistence*. Toronto: Canadian Institute of International Affairs.

NOVAK, M. 1972, *The Rise of the Unmeltable Ethnics: Politics and Culture in the Seventies*. New York: Macmillan.

PATTERSON, O. 1975, Context and choice in ethnic allegiance: a theoretical framework and Caribbean study. In N. GLAZER & D. P. MOYNIHAN (eds), *Ethnicity: Theory and Practice*. Cambridge, MA: Harvard University Press.

SAVARD, J. G. & VIGNEAULT, R. (eds), 1975, *Multilingual Political Systems: Problems and Solutions*. Québec: Laval University Press.

SCANPRESENCE, 1977, *Action Conference on the Scandinavian Presence in America*. Minneapolis, MN: Scanpresence.

SILVER, B. 1974, The impact of urbanization and geographical dispersion on the linguistic russification of Soviet nationalities. *Demography* 11.

SIMON, P. 1977, Battling linguistic chauvinism. *Change Magazine* 9.

TEITELBAUM, H. & HILLER, R. J. 1977a, Bilingual education: the legal mandate. *Harvard Educational Review* 47: 138–72.

— 1977b, *The Legal Perspective*, Vol. III: *Bilingual Education: Current Perspectives*. Arlington, VA: Center for Applied Linguistics.

U.S. GENERAL ACCOUNTING OFFICE. 1976, *Bilingual Education: An Unmet Need*. Washington, DC: U.S. Government Printing Office.

SECTION 4:
Language and ethnicity in education: The bilingual minority focus

Ethnicity is a major component of mainstream education, and it is particularly so at the earlier levels. As a formal institution of socialization, education is necessarily also co-responsible for and engaged in sociocultural socialization, i.e. in socialization for ethnic membership and for ethnic consciousness. The elementary school's social studies curriculum, with its emphasis on national history, civics and geography, not to mention its rituals (salutes to the flag, patriotic assembly programs and commemorations of national holidays and great leaders), is essentially an explicit and implicit course in mainstream ethnic socialization or resocialization. Mainstream education is also an arena for the discussion and explication of values and moral issues, of national virtues and dilemmas, of national accomplishments and shortcomings, of supra-rational dedication, aspiration and concern. God and country, heritage and loyalty, these handmaidens and reflections of ethnicity are very much a part of the formal educational experience of the mainstream child. Is there any wonder then, that this is all the more so for the educational efforts that minority parents and minority community leaders focus (or attempt to focus) on the minority child? Indeed, when minority communities clamour for input into the educational system they are often merely revealing their awareness of the same concerns for early and sound ethnic socialization that their mainstream counterparts take for granted *vis-à-vis* mainstream (and, therefore, supposedly 'ethnically unmarked') children.

  Whether minority education is under minority community auspices entirely or whether it is a side-stream or infrequent (and, often, unwanted) guest within the mainstream system, its importance in the ethnic socialization and ethnolinguistic intergenerational continuity processes is difficult to exaggerate. For the minority community, particularly for one that is substantially ethnolinguistically 'marked' or 'different', and most particularly for one that is at the stage of conscious ethnicity, the formal educational process is often conceptually linked to language recovery, language maintenance and language planning — to both status planning and corpus planning — as well. Modern minority élites are likely to stress the role of formal education as an independent variable in bringing about the results that they seek in the entire arena of ethnocultural awareness, ethnocultural behavior and ethnocultural emotional saliency. This is not to say that exposure to and mastery of 'mainstream' skills, values and loyalties are necessarily rejected or even de-emphasized by minority communities and leaders. Whether or not this is so depends on the historical record and the historical context of intergroup relations and real (rather than mythical) access to mainstream rewards. Mainstream accommodation to minority ethnolinguistic goals in the educational arena are part and parcel of that record. Mainstream spokesmen often charge minorities with 'divisiveness', not realizing that from the minority perspective what is most often involved is the pursuit of stable bilingualism and biculturalism for themselves and their children, and the hope that such pursuit can be recognized as being in the general interest, rather than any rejection of the mainstream or any pursuit of political separateness. In either case, i.e. when political separateness is genuinely at issue and when it is merely spuriously charged (as a mainstream 'ethnic purification' witchhunt), the educational arena is very likely to be involved in the ensuing debate, precisely because education is a major rallying ground and forum for sociomoral clarification, implementation and evaluation in modern societies, whether mainstream or sidestream.

For minority ethnolinguistic communities the admission of their languages into the educational domain is often of both symbolic and concrete importance. Symbolically, it implies a functional recognition and promotion above and beyond the core domains of family, neighborhood and church. Elementary education, like the lower work sphere, is a broadening of intra-communal influence, a preliminary venture into the world of modernity, modern literacy and modern statuses within the purview of the minority community *per se*. Minority language literacy is also increasingly required to assure a future generation (particularly, a modernized generation) of intra-communal leaders, writers, poets, and religious functionaries. Finally, from the minority perspective, education provides an additional substantial block of time for influencing not only the younger generation but the parental generation as well. In modern environments and given modern life-styles, there are few other locales in which children and parents can be caused to gather, particularly given the decreased influence of religious institutions in modern urban life, and, accordingly, the school takes on an increased intra-communal function *vis-à-vis* the minority agenda in general and *vis-à-vis* the intergenerational ethnolinguistic continuity agenda in particular. Where these agendas are taken most seriously and where the mainstream authorities are lukewarm or obstructionist with respect to including sufficient minority ethnocultural emphases within the mainstream system, there is an understandably growing tendency to found schools under minority management, whether in lieu of mainstream public school attendance or supplementary to such attendance. This is a further indication of the major involvement of ethnolinguistic minorities in the educational domain.

However, after all is said and done with respect to the perceived importance of education for ethnolinguistic intergenerational continuity, there are also clear dangers in that connection that are less widely appreciated and must not be overlooked. Neither education nor the work-sphere are ever completely under minority ethnocultural control, neither in terms of ultimate power nor in terms of control of side-effects or unforeseen consequences. Except under the rare circumstances of cultural-autonomy within a larger political order, education (even ethnoculturally sponsored education) is always under superordinate control and influence. Because of the curricular requirements of such authorities, even minority-sponsored day-schools are required to teach the nationally 'integrating' language, history, political system and literature for a stipulated number of hours per week in every year of study. Thus, whereas mainstream spokesmen decry the 'intrusion' of sidestream concerns and curricular content within the general school program, it is not surprising that we also encounter sidestream educators, and parents too, who are concerned about the 'imposition' of mainstream regulations and requirements upon schools that are fully sponsored by and supported by minority ethnolinguistic communities *per se*. The result of the latter imposition is that instead of acting as a buffer or bastion of minority ethnocultural emphases, instead of providing some much needed breathing room in terms of, and behalf of, the minority ethnocultural system *per se*, the minority ethnolinguistic school itself becomes the purveyor of mainstream values and emphases, thereby giving them internal, rather than only external legitimization and, thereby, being co-opted to the further weakening of the very ethnocultural system that such schools are established and supported to foster. The problem is not that it is impossible to serve two masters, or, to put things less metaphorically, to design and implement a bicultural curriculum. The problem is that it is difficult to design and implement such a curriculum, so as to sufficiently compartmentalize the minority ethnolinguistic socio-educational goals from their general mainstream counterparts in order to permit the former to be as effectively pursued as the latter. This difficulty is even present at the conceptual level, because effective bicultural/bilingual education is still essentially unprecedented; in addition, however, the mainstream authorities that ultimately control the educational system also impose time and curriculum requirements which render it even more difficult for the minority ethnolinguistic school to pursue and attain its intra-communal goals. As a result, minority sponsored schools are often not only *not* the effective instruments of ethnolinguistic intergenerational continuity that they are touted to be, but, on the contrary, they are often contra-productive in that very connection. The de-ethnicized ethnic-community school is, in part, a byproduct of such tensions.

However, there are yet other (and perhaps even stronger) reasons why minority sponsored (minority responsive) education may ultimately not serve the goal of intergenerational ethnolinguistic continuity. On the one hand, modern education *per se* (particularly secondary and higher education) leads away from small and traditional reward systems and toward ever larger and more modern, ethnically 'unmarked' ones. It is of the very nature of modern knowledge to lead outward and it is only natural for those who have tasted the fruits of modernism to aspire to its greatest rewards, regardless of the pursuits and environments where these are to be encountered. Within relatively open and accepting ethno-ideological mainstream contexts, minorities always have major difficulties in establishing their own 'safe zones', areas of daily life where their own role-relations, places, topics, interaction networks and pursuits can dominate, where their ethnonational and ethno-linguistic distinctions have a fair chance of dominating and regulating the influences that surround them and stream in upon them. Those who are most highly educated have a particularly difficult time along these lines; their boundary maintenance capacity has been more weakened and the temptations to which they are exposed have been more strengthened, as a result of the very process of education itself.

The school and the educational process, even when both are under maximal intra-communal control, are two-edged swords from the point of view of intergenerational ethnolinguistic continuity. However, this is not only so at the higher levels of education (where the largest reward potential is so obviously under the control of the seemingly ethnically 'unmarked' mainstream). This is so at much lower levels of education also, wherever the integration between school and community is weak. To rely upon the school to do for language and culture what neither the family nor the neighborhood will or can do is to court disappointment and to avert one's eyes from the basic loci of ethnocultural and ethnolinguistic continuity. Schools need not merely reflect the dispositions of their constituencies; they may also seek to influence and to alter those dispositions. In either case, whether reflective or catalytic, schools must be closely linked to community processes of intergenerational ethnocultural and ethnolinguistic continuity if they are to live up to their expectations in this connection. Such linkages, via maximal parental involvement in school philosophy formulation, curriculum design, building management, classroom learning and teaching processes, hiring, budget-ing and fund-raising, serve to build schools that can rely upon, influence and activate parents and communities in connection with language-in-culture concerns. Without such linkages, the discontinuity between home/neighborhood and school produces the same ludicrous non-results as does a discontinuity between status planning and corpus planning. Schools under intra-communal ethnic auspices are not automatically constructive instruments of ethnolinguistic revival, survival or stabi-lization. To be such, they have to be planned and operated as such within a relevant speech-community context.

Finally, ethnic educators must not assume that they have con-stituencies at all. There are many speech-communities that are disinclined or opposed to having their vernaculars taught and fostered by schools, regardless of whether these are governmentally sponsored or intra-communally sponsored. The view that minority language X is not schoolworthy is not necessarily an outside, mainstream evaluation. Modernization and cultural democracy have fostered the view that all vernaculars are potentially schoolworthy, and this is undoubtedly true, but not all cultures accept this position, not even relative to themselves. Just as unthinking modernization of agriculture may lead to after-effects that are more dislocational than constructive, so the unreflective introduction of vernaculars into the educational process may be dislocative of tradi-tional religious and other authoritative role-relations. The gains and losses related to vernacular literacy are not everywhere the same and are not universally evaluated on a single scale whose calibration is recognized and accepted cross-culturally. Sometimes communities opt for school use of a traditionally recognized non-vernacular language with long established intra-communal religious functions. Sometimes communities opt for school use of a regional or even international lingua franca, rather than their own vernacular. These choices may strike the modernized reader as strange, if not bizarre, but they merely help emphasize our general point: without sociological and ethnocultural information, contextualization and insight one cannot prescribe the role of minority vernaculars in educational programs for and by ethnolinguistic minorities, not even when the goals of ethnocultural and ethnolinguistic maintenance are accepted by all concerned. Of course, all of these comments and cautions presume a minority perspective on language and ethnicity in education, a perspective which is all too rarely given either the intellectual or the applied attention that it deserves.

14 The sociology of bilingual education*[1]

The bulk of the current bibliography on bilingual education is either psychological (Lambert & Tucker, 1972; Lambert, Tucker & Anglejan, 1973; Mackey, 1972; Macnamara, 1966), educational (Andersson & Boyer, 1970; Andersson, 1971; Anon, 1971b, Gaarder, 1970; John & Horner, 1971; Lange, 1971; Noss, 1967; Special Subcommittee, 1967 and Swain, 1972) or linguistic (sections of Kelley, 1969; Saville & Troike, 1971) in nature. Although there has undoubtedly been *some* sociolinguistic impact on the foregoing (particularly in Anon, 1971a; Cohen, 1970; Fishman & Lovas, 1970; Kjolseth, 1972; Mackey, 1970; Macnamara, 1973; Ramos, Aguilar & Sibayan, 1967; Spolsky, 1972) an avowed sociology of bilingual education is still not at hand. This chapter represents an attempt in that direction, both theoretically and empirically. Among the byproducts to be hoped for from the development of a sociological component in this field are improved understanding, practice and evaluation with respect to the *thousands* of bilingual education programs now underway in the U.S.A. and elsewhere.

Historical and comparative perspective

The stress on *thousands* of programs immediately indicates that a world-wide perspective is in order if we are not to confuse *sociology* with *American society* and the particular constraints that it has imposed on bilingual education.[2] Of course we want to understand, implement and evaluate American bilingual education better, but in order to do so we must first realize wherein it is different than (and similar to) bilingual education elsewhere in the world. There are countries in which bilingual

*Originally published in *Etudes de Linguistique Appliquée* 1974: 112–24.

education is omnipresent and there is no other kind (e.g. Singapore). There are countries in which it is very widespread but in which there are other alternatives as well (e.g. Ireland). There are countries in which it is not very common but a recognized alternative (Wales, parts of non-Russian U.S.S.R.). There are countries in which it is rare and viewed as enriching for élites (e.g. Belgium, Switzerland), and others in which it is rare and viewed as compensatory for the poor (e.g. Andean Latin America). Certainly such macro-contextual societal differences should be built into a sociology of bilingual education, on the one hand, and promise to provide heuristic perspective for American bilingual education on the other.

Diachronic perspective is also likely to be needed, in addition to the comparative synchronic perspective just mentioned, in any sociology of bilingual education. From the earliest records of education in all classical societies we find ample evidence of the predominance of bilingual education (Lewis, 1976). Most often all formal education was élitist and, therefore, so was bilingual education. Most often the target or textual language differed from the process or mediating language. But, in any case, the variation to be noted across cultures, both in divising a sociology of bilingual education, on the one hand, and in benefiting therefrom for the purposes of American education on the other, requires scrutiny.

An initial sociological typology

From concern both for historical and comparative (i.e. synchronic and syncultural) perspective, an initial typology was derived based upon the interrelationship between four dichotomies, first to each other and then to rated success in the languages of primary and secondary emphasis.

Dichotomy 1: Language given primary emphasis vs. language given secondary emphasis (LPE-LSE)

Because languages are not functionally equal or identical almost all bilingual education programs devote more time to one than to another. It would seem, on intuitive sociological grounds, to be important to distinguish between the bilingual education *inputs* and *outputs* for LPEs and those for LSEs.

Dichotomy 2: Mother tongue vs. other tongue

Just as more bilingual education programs are 'unbalanced' as to the emphases the two languages receive, so are most classrooms within such programs as to the mother tongue-other tongue status of these languages for the students receiving bilingual education. It certainly appears sociologically advisable to examine the impact of this distinction on bilingual educational inputs and outputs.

Dichotomy 3: Minor vs. major language

The five official languages of the United Nations (English, French, Spanish, Russian and Chinese) were considered 'major' languages on the world scene, as was Arabic. The distinction between smaller and larger (broader and narrower) seems well worth considering in any sociological typology.

Dichotomy 4: Out-of-school formal institutions

A language of organized or official importance out of school (regardless of whether it is the mother or other tongue of students) obviously can have a far different claim on students, teachers and school authorities than a language that has no such out of school reinforcement. The sociology of bilingual education must be concerned with the power differentials of languages in the real world.

First preliminary findings

These dichotomies, in interaction with each other, result in 2^4 or 16 societal types of bilingual education contexts. These 16 contexts were 'applied to the literature', that is to say that I and several colleagues and advanced students (20 judges in all) rated jointly the 60 instances of bilingual education that we collectively knew best (whether on the basis of the published literature or case studies derived from our collectively shared and corroborated experiences). These ratings (averaged and rounded) were then used to predict criterion ratings that we jointly applied to each instance or case, these criteria being 'success relative to LSE and LPS goals' as rated on a four-point scale. The resulting multiple predictions may be viewed as a first approximation of the value of macro-societal contextual factors such as those that we have indicated thus far.[3]

Six-predictor ratings 'applied to the literature'

Notwithstanding the limitations which such data admittedly have, it would seem, nevertheless, that, as preliminary and provocative indicators, some importance can be ascribed to them and to the findings derived from them.

It is quite evident from Table 14.1 that our sample of cases is such that, insofar as attainments are concerned, a clear distinction must be made between the language of primary and the language of secondary attention. For the former (the language of primary emphasis) it is productive of greater rated success for the language to be the mother tongue (r = 0.41) and for it to be the language of important formal institutions outside of the school (r = 0.28). For the latter (the language of secondary emphasis) it is productive of greater rated success for the language to be the mother tongue (r = 0.35) and for it to be a major language on the world scene (r = 0.40). Note, however, the fact that the degree of rated success with respect to one language is substantially related to that with respect to the second.

Several interesting implications derive from the foregoing: unless both languages — or neither — can be societally viewed as mother tongues (not as much of a logical impossibility as is implied by our typology[4]), there would seem to be a built-in conflict within bilingual education in that both languages require mother tongue students to optimize success. However, rather than a conflict this state of affairs may actually be viewed as an equalization of educational success. Insofar as bilingual education is a reflection of the need to cater to two different mother tongue groups then it may be viewed as an opportunity to provide some appropriate degree of success to each. However, in addition, the language of primary attention must also be officially in evidence in society (i.e. it cannot merely be home and school based) and the language of secondary attention must also be of world-wide significance (it too cannot be merely of home and school relevance) for goal realization to be maximized.

All in all, in conclusion, we should note that this crude, 'first approximation,' sociological model yields multiples in the high forties and middle fifties. Thus, having accounted for 25% to 30% of the variance in 'rated success' we are encouraged to search for a more complex model.

A somewhat more advanced sociological model

Six more variables, each of them continuous, were also rated by the very same judges and at the very same time that the first six, above, were

TABLE 14.1 Six predictors and two criteria: Intercorrelations (N = 60)

x̄	Variables		1	2	3	4	5	6	7
1.53	1. Language of Primary Emphasis:	Other t=1, mother t=2	—						
1.62	2. Language of Primary Emphasis:	Minor =1, major =2	-.12	—					
1.48	3. Language of Secondary Emphasis:	Other t=1, mother t=2	-.97	.15	—				
1.47	4. Language of Secondary Emphasis:	Minor =1, major =2	.00	-.09	-.04	—			
1.48	5. Language of Formal Instit. :	Other t=1, mother t=2	.24	.01	-.20	.03	—		
2.61	6. Eval. of success re goal for LSE (hi=4, lo=1)		-.31	-.03	.35	.40	-.03	—	
3.42	7. Eval. of success re goal for LPE (hi=4, lo=1)		.41	-.07	-.38	.16	.28	.38	—

Cumulative Multiple Prediction:

LSE: Criterion 1(V7)

1. V4 = LSE : minor =1, major =2   R=.40
2. V3 = LSE: other t=1, mother t =2   =.54
3. V1 = LPE: other t=1, mother t =2   =.57

LPE: Criterion 2 (V8)

1. V1 = LPE : Other t=1, mother t=2   R=.41
2. V5 = LFI: Other t =1, mother t =2   =.45
3. V4 = LSE: Other t =1, mother t =2   =.47

rated for the 60 cases under review. One of these focused upon the language of *primary emphasis* and the language of *secondary emphasis* with respect to their goal intensivity (Fishman & Lovas, 1970). Another variable among the additional group of six pertained to the entire educational context as such, rather than to one or another of the languages of instruction *per se*, namely, it asked whether admission selectivity was high, medium or low. Finally, two quite provocative sociological variables were rated, namely (a) the extent to which either the language of primary or secondary emphasis was dependent on school instruction (rather than on more general societal participation) in order to be *learned* and (b) the extent to which there was nationalist or other heightened socio-political sentiment on behalf of either language of instruction. The general purpose of these latter two additional variables, as well as of the one dealing with 'selectivity-in' (the other side of the coin of 'drop-out') is to increase our sensitivity to the social nexus of education as a whole and to societal pressures upon the languages of instruction in particular. Certainly, schools in which there is either great selectivity as to who gets into bilingual education face a different type of task than those in which bilingual education is considered to be desirable for one and all. Similarly, where only the school is available to teach a particular language of instruction a far different task is at hand than when society at large and, most particularly, when organized forces within society, reinforce or stress that language (or those languages).

Twelve predictor ratings 'applied to the literature'

As the body of Table 14.2 (which follows) reveals the addition of six more predictor ratings yields several interesting results. Clearly both LSEs and LPEs are very widely school-dependent when they are *not* the students' own mother tongues (r = –0.66 and r = –0.59 respectively). Similarly, they are more likely to be supported by organized socio-political movements when they are themselves minor languages on the world scene (r = –0.37 and r = –0.39). Presumably, such movements are responsible for their being recognized by educational authorities to begin with. Finally, the two languages are likely to be school dependent in inverse degrees (r = –0.72), i.e. if one is, the other is not and vice versa. Thus, on the whole, bilingual education is frequently concerned with one societally-stressed language and one school-stressed language. The former is more likely to be the children's own language, regardless of whether it is major or minor. However, for a minor language to be present in the curriculum it is

THE SOCIOLOGY OF BILINGUAL EDUCATION 431

necessary to have organized socio-political support for it, regardless of whether it is the students' mother tongue or not. Presumably, without such support either one major language of two would be taught, even if neither were the students' mother tongue.

A glance at our criterion variables reveals that both LSEs and LPEs are rated less successful when *they* are school dependent (r = –0.44 and r = –0.53) and more successful when the *other* is (r = 0.42 and r = 0.38). In addition, LSE is rated more successful when it is more selective *vis-à-vis* admission (r = 0.34) and less successful when LPE goals are minimal. Thus, at this stage, we may add to our previous picture (see prior section, above), which implied that LSE success is rated high if the language of secondary emphasis is the students' own and is major, the additional proviso that it is rated high when it is not maximally school dependent and when maximal goals are pursued with respect to the language of primary emphasis. Nationalist movements as such, although they may be important determinants of whether LSEs are educationally utilized at all (particularly if they are minor languages), are not important determinants of whether LSE goals are successfully attained.

Insofar as LPE success is concerned we may add to our previous picture that such is rated high when it is the mother tongue of the learners and when out-of-school institutions also employ it, an additional under-scoring of the last mentioned. High school dependence of LPE instruction is definitely as contra-indicated as is high school dependence of LSE instruction, and, indeed, perhaps more so.

Finally, insofar as cumulative multiple predictions based upon our somewhat expanded model are concerned, it is quite obvious (from Table 14.2) that such prediction is substantially improved relative to the point at which we last examined it. From multiples in the high-40s and mid-50s we now find ourselves with multiples in the low and mid-70s. Note, however, that our earlier more primitive variables do not seem to hold up as well with respect to predicting LSE as they do with respect to LPE, once our additional predictors are permitted into the picture. Insofar as predicting LSE is concerned only the major status of the LSE continues to play a role, but not as important a one as whether LSE is school dependent. Finally, with the exception of the factor of selectivity all other significant multiple predictors deal with LPE (*its* goals, *its* school dependency and *its* nationalist roots.). Obviously, LSE success is largely dependent on LPE circumstances (whereas the reverse is slightly less so). Insofar as multiply predicting LPE is concerned, it is striking to note the extent to which similar, parallel or identical variables are called upon as are involved in multiply predicting LSE. Indeed, although their relative rankings are often different even this is not always so. Thus school dependency is once again the major independent variable and LPE goals and LSE major-minor status are still of cumulative importance. Once again, also, the *other* language's goals and its involvement in a nationalist movement are cumulatively important. Indeed, only two significant predictors really differentiate between the cumulative predictions of LSE and LPE. In the former case, selectivity; in the latter: that the learners' own language be that of formal institutions outside of the school.

On the adequacy of sociology alone

Thus far, we have examined sociological predictors alone. This has been quite legitimate insofar as we have sought to develop a sociology of bilingual education. In so doing, we have come up with a number of interesting and potentially important sociological findings (or in view of the fact that we are only interpreting other people's data, perhaps 'hypotheses' rather than 'findings'). The negative importance of school-dependency is clear: the more a language of instruction is entirely dependent on the school and lacking of counterparts outside of it, the less it is rated as successful in goal attainment, regardless of whether it is LSE or LPE. Related to this is the fact that the learners' own language must be that of *formal* institutions outside of the school if LPE goals are to be maximally attained, and that LSE benefits most from being a major world language.

By proceeding to add a few additional societal variables we have explained over half of the variance in rated LSE and LPE success. Although this is encouraging indeed it is appropriate to ask whether the addition of psycho-educational variables would result in a substantially different picture, quantitatively (i.e. in terms of magnitude of multiples) or qualitatively (i.e. in terms of variables contributing significantly to the cumulative multiple prediction).

As Table 14.3 reveals, the answer to both questions is negative insofar as LSE is concerned and positive insofar as LPE is concerned when adequacy of teaching methods/materials is introduced to reflect psycho-educational dimensions. In the former case the resulting cumulative multiple prediction is raised only from 0.75 to 0.77 and no predictors are brought into the final set that were not originally there (although two are displaced from it: V 4 (LSE: Minor-Major) and V 12 (extent to which LPE is school-dependent). On the other hand, in connection with LPE the

TABLE 14.2 *Cumulative multiple predictions (Based upon 12 societal predictors)*

	LSE = Criterion 1 (V 15)			LPE = Criterion 2 (V 16)	
1.	V7 Extent to which LSE is school-dependent,	R= .44	1.	V 12 Extent to which LPE is school-dependent	R= .53
2.	4 LSE: Minor — Major	.57	2.	15 Eval. of success of LSE	.60
3.	11 goal re LPE	.63	3.	3 LFI: Other-own	.65
4.	10 Selectivity	.69	4.	11 Goal re LPE	.67
5.	16 Eval. of success re LPE	.71	5.	8 Extent of nat. movt. for LSE	.68
6.	12 Extent to which LPE is school-dependent	.74	6.	1 LPE: Other-own	.71
7.	13 Extent of nat. movt. for LPE	.75	7.	4 LSE: Minor-Major	.72

TABLE 14.3 *Twelve sociological and two psychological predictors in conjunction with two criteria (R = .60)*

	Variables	$\bar{X}$
1.	Language of Primary Emphasis: other = 1, own = 2	1.53
2.	→ → → Secondary → : minor = 1, major = 2	1.62
3.	→ → → → : other = 1; own = 2	1.48
4.	→ → → → : minor = 1; major = 2	1.47
5.	→ → → Other formal institutions: other = 1; own 2	1.48
6.	Goal re LSE: 1 = trans. or monolit; 2 = partial; 3 = full	2.15
7.	Extent to which learning LSE is school dependent (1-3)	1.98
8.	Extent to which there is a nationalist movement for LSE (1-3)	1.52
9.	Adequacy of teaching methods/materials for LSE (1-3)	1.07
10.	Selectivity (academic stand.) for admission to BEP (1-3)	2.33
11.	Goal re LPE: 1 = trans. or monolit; 2 = partial; 3 = full	2.87
12.	Extent to which learning LPE is school dependent (1-2)	2.00
13.	Extent to which there is a nationalist movement for LPE (1-3)	1.52
14.	Adequacy of teaching methods/materials for LPE (1-3)	2.22
15.	Evaluation of success re goals for LSE (1-4)	2.62
16.	Evaluation of success re goals for LPE (1-4)	3.42

introduction of a psycho-educational predictor boosts the overall cumulative multiple from 72 to 83 and brings several other variables into the final set, namely V 2 (LPE: minor-major), V 7 (extent to which LSE is school-dependent) and 10 (selectivity). This is an interesting finding, implying as it does that LSE success is more societally determined and LPE more respondent to psycho-educational factors.

Note, however, that the fiscal set of cumulative predictors is still quite similar for both LSE and LPE, adequacy of school materials, extent of school dependency, and selectivity being important in both cases. Beyond this similarity LSE success is uniquely influenced (negatively) by intensity of LPE goals and (negatively) by the presence of a nationalist movement on behalf of LPE. On the other hand, LPE success is uniquely influenced (negatively) by being concerned with a minor language, by the extent to which LSE is school-dependent, and the extent to which LSE goals are successful. From the foregoing it should be clear that both psycho-educational and socio-educational manipulation may be required for successful bilingual education.

TABLE 14.4 *Intercorrelations**

VARIABLES	1	2	3	4	5	6	7	8	9	10	11	12	13	14	15	16
1	-															
2	12	-														07
3	97	15	-													
4	00	09	04	-												
5	24	01	20	03	-											
6	32	03	33	36	22	-										
7	62	01	66	09	05	10	-									
8	20	26	26	37	22	23	20	-								
9	08	05	08	64	12	34	09	03	-							
10	26	13	25	17	02	00	04	02	38	-						09
11	17	40	18	03	78	11	01	14	10	05	-					
12	59	25	62	07	07	06	72	16	17	17	05	-				
13	25	39	78	12	09	06	01	36	00	14	26	02	-		07	
14	14	42	10	18	35	30	04	34	37	05	32	12	34	-		
15	31	03	35	40	03	13	44	00	53	34	28	42	07	11	-	03
16	40	07	38	16	28	23	38	09	30	09	05	53	13	59	03	-

*Bold intercorrelations are significant. Intercorrelations *above* diagonal are not significant as zero orders but *are* significant in final cumulative multiple correlations.

TABLE 14.5 Cumulative multiple prediction of criteria (signif. variables)

LSE = Criterion 1 (V 15)		LPE = Criterion 2 (V 16)	
V9	Adeq. of Meths/Mats re LSE	R=.53	V14	Adeq. of Meths/Mats re LPE	R=.59
V2	Ext. to which learning LSE is school dependent	=.66	V12	Ext. to which learn LPE is school dep.	=.75
V11	Goals of LPE	=.74	V2	LPE: minor/major	=.78
V13	Ext. to which there is nat. mov. for LPE	=.76	V7	Ext. to which learn LSE is school-dep	=.81
V10	Selectivity re entering BEP	=.72	V15	Eval. of success re goals of LSE	=.82
			V10	Selectivity re entering BEP	=.83

Further empirical study, self-description and observation

Obviously we have gone as far as we should, if not beyond that, with deriving leads from the literature via quantitative or semi-quantitative methods.

The leads must now be refined and extended via empirical data. A beginning in this direction has been made via the International Study of Bilingual Secondary Education. It has, to begin with, established a register of some 1,200 bilingual secondary schools or school programs throughout the world. From this register it has selected 100 schools, in various settings, for intensive questionnaire follow-up in relation to all of the above-mentioned leads derived from the literature, as well as with respect to many other hunches derived from sociological and sociolinguistic theory more generally. In addition, some 10–12 schools will be studied in depth via personal visits and direct observation in order to further test the validity of the above-mentioned leads as well as to examine further the findings derived from the questionnaire responses. All in all, therefore, three types of data, at differing levels of abstraction and detail, will be compared. This, in itself, is an important undertaking since it will shed light on the constant suspicion that findings relative to bilingual education are limited due to sampling and methodological differences from one study to the next (Macnamara, 1973). A sociology of bilingual education must be even more concerned with such suspicions than must psychologically or pedagogically-oriented investigations. Since it seeks to systematize much of the situational and contextual variation that is otherwise regarded as error variance, it must be more certain that its situational and contextual data is wide-ranging and reliable. Whether or not the International Study of Bilingual Secondary Education can accomplish all that is needed in this connection, it is clear that a sociology of bilingual education is beginning to appear even from its early stages.

Notes to Chapter 14

1. The preparation of this report and the empirical work discussed therein were supported by a grant from the Research Section, Division of Foreign Studies, Institute of International Studies, USOE-DHEW (Contract DEC-0-73-0588).
2. Bilingual education is here defined as use of two or more languages of instruction with particular students (whether these be all or only some of a given cohort group), in subjects matter above and beyond language instruction *per se*. Whether this subject matter is closely allied to language (e.g. the literature or 'culture' uniquely encoded via a particular language) or basically unrelated to it (e.g. mathematics or physics) is itself a variable to be

investigated, just as are other questions prompted by this definition, e.g., the precise number of languages of instruction involved ('two or more') the proportion of all students involved,the number of years involved, the number of subjects involved, etc.

3. Two admissions are called for at this point. To begin with, the predictors ratings and the criterion ratings were made by the same raters (the last mentioned being made *before* the first mentioned by half of the judges and last by the others), thereby introducing an unknown degree of spurious consistency in the data which would tend to inflate the final multiple correlations obtained. Secondly, an approximately equal number of cases of each type were sought, thus effectively counterbalancing or ruling-out type itself as one of the possibly important factors in the success of bilingual education. Both of these limitations are overcome in more advanced research reported below.

4. Societies marked by widespread and stable diglossia may qualify on this score. In this connection see Fishman, 1967.

References

ANDERSSON, T. & BOYER, M. (eds) 1970, Bilingual Schooling in the United States, Washington, D.C., USGPO, 1970 (2 vols.); also (ANDERSSON), Bilingual education: The American Experience. *Modern Language Journal* 1971, 55, 427–40.

ANDERSSON, T. 1971, *Conference on Child Language*. Quebec: CIRB.

ANON 1971a, *Bilingual Education for American Indians*. Washington, D.C.: Office of Education Programs, United States Bureau of Indian Affairs.

—   1971b, *Razon de Ser of the Bilingual School*. Altanta: Southeastern Educational Laboratory.

COHEN, A. D. 1970, *A Sociolinguistic Approach to Bilingual Education*. Stanford (California): Committee on Linguistics, Stanford University, expanded, Newbury House, 1973).

FISHMAN, J. A., 1967, Bilingualism with and without diglossia; diglossia with and without bilingualism. *Journal of Social Issues* 23, no. 2, 29–38.

FISHMAN, J. A. & LOVAS, J. 1970, Bilingual education in sociolinguistic perspective. *TESOL Quarterly* 4, 215–22.

GAARDER, A. B. 1970, The first seventy-six bilingual education projects (Georgetown University) *Monography Series on Linguistics and Language Study* 23.

JOHN, V. P. & HORNER, V. M. 1971, *Early Childhood Bilingual Education*. New York: Modern Language Association of America.

KELLEY, L. G. (ed.) 1969, *Description and Measurement of Bilingualism*.

Toronto: UTP.

KJOLSETH, R. 1972, Bilingual education in the United States, for assimilation or pluralism. In B. SPOLSKY (ed.), *The Language Education of
Minority Children*. Rowley: Newbury House.

LAMBERT, W. E. & TUCKER, G. R. 1972, *Bilingual Education of Children*
Rowley (Mass.): Newbury; also

LAMBERT, W. E., TUCKER, G.R. & D'ANGLEJAN, A. 1973, Cognitive and
attitudinal consequences of bilingual education. *Journal of Educational Psychology* 65 141–59.

LANGE, D. L. (ed.) 1971, *Pluralism in Foreign Language Education*.
Chicago, Encyclopedia Britannica (*Britannica Review of Foreign
Language Education* vol. 3).

LEWIS, E. G. 1976, Bilingualism and bilingual education: the ancient world
of the Renaissance. In J. A. Fishman *Bilingual Education: An
International Sociological Perspective*. |Rowley,| Mass.: Newbury.
150–200.

MACKEY, Wm. F. 1970, A typology of bilingual education. *Foreign
Language Annals* 3, 596–608.

— 1972, *Bilingual Education in a Binational School*. Rowley: Newbury.

MACNAMARA, J. 1966, *Bilingualism and Primary Education*. London:
Edinburgh University Press.

— 1973, *The Generalizability of Studies in Bilingual Education*.
Montreal: McGill University. Mimeo.

NOSS, R. 1967, *Language Policy and Higher Education: Higher Education
and Development in South East Asia*. Paris: UNESCO and the
International Association of Universities.

RAMOS, M., AGUILAR, J. V. & SIBAYAN, B. P. 1967, *The Determination
and Implementation of Language Policy*. Philippine Center for
Language Study. Alemar-Phoenix, Quezon City.

Royal Commission on Bilingualism and Biculturalism. *Preliminary Report*,
1965, *General Introduction, Book 1: The Official Languages*, 1967;
Book II: Education, 1968. Ottawa: The Queen's Printer.

SAVILLE, M. R. & TROIKE, R. C. 1971, *A Handbook of Bilingual
Education*. (Rev. Ed.), Washington, D.C.: TESOL.

Special Subcommittee on Bilingual Education (United States Senate)
1967, *Bilingual Education: Hearings* — on S. 428. Washington:
UGPO (2 vol.).

SPOLSKY, B. (ed.) 1972, *The Language Education of Minority Children*.
Rowley (Mass.): Newbury.

SWAIN, M. 1972, *Bilingual Schooling: Some Experiences in Canada and the
United States*. Toronto: Ontario Institute for Studies in Education,
University of Toronto.

15 Philosophies of bilingual education in societal perspective*

Introduction

The voluminous literature on bilingual education reveals degrees of concern with three major goals: the political, the cultural, and the educational. These goals are not only pursued in various degrees of separation and combination, but they are variously evaluated by spokesmen of the different speech communities involved. The diversity of philosophical views on bilingual education is thus a result of each community's social diversity. Most complex societies normally reveal a variety of educational goals, even when monolingual education is the focus of attention. Bilingual education often presents an even more diversified philosophical scene, not only because it is commonly of more recent vintage (and, presumably, has had less time to achieve consensus) but also because it is much more commonly an intergroup enterprise. The groups involved in bilingual education often differ markedly in their resources, in their outlooks, and, therefore, in their goals. As a result, they favor or oppose bilingual education for different reasons. They want or fear different things. Where bilingual education has been in effect for many years (e.g. in Wales or in Dade County, Florida) there has been an opportunity for 'the dust to settle' and for the major dimensions and difficulties to be clarified, understood, and in large measure to be overcome. Thus, American 'viewers' must realize that the bilingual education around them is also philosophically far more 'unsettled' than it is in most other parts of the world.

---

*Originally published in E. J. BRIERRE (ed.) 1979, *Language Development in a Bilingual Setting*. Los Angeles: National Dissemination and Assessment Center, 36–47.

Marked and unmarked

Because of the greater recency of bilingual education, particularly in the public sector, as well as because of its more common intergroup character, it is recurringly obvious that one of the two languages involved would *not* be a medium of instruction were it not for bilingual education. That language which is utilized as a medium of instruction only because of the introduction of bilingual education will be referred to here as the *marked* language. The designation 'marked' implies special, unusual, different. However, it also implies problematic, most likely to be discontinued, most conflicted, less well established, and, therefore, at least temporarily weaker than the *unmarked* language. The distinction between marked and unmarked also applies to the populations involved in bilingual education. That population whose vernacular would not be recognized were it not for bilingual education will be referred to here as the *marked* population. This population is often a disadvantaged minority (e.g. Chicanos in the United States or Ultra-Orthodox Yiddish-speaking Jews in Israel), but it may be a disadvantaged majority (e.g. 'Bantus' in the Republic of South Africa) or even an advantaged minority (e.g. 'European' resident foreigners in Latin America). Marking is contextually determined in terms of power, precedence, and prevalence. However, marking is reversible. If hitherto marked groups become dominant (in governmental, economic, educational, or other spheres), they become unmarked; and unmarked languages that were hitherto the main or only media of education may become marked (e.g. English, today, in bilingual education in the Philippines) or even discontinued entirely.

The distinctions between marked and unmarked (languages, populations) permeate the philosophies of bilingual education as well as the frequent differences in views with which bilingual education is regarded by marked and unmarked spokesmen (Fishman, 1976).

The remedial goals of bilingual education

The most tangible (and perhaps the most common) goals of bilingual education entail a remedial reallocation of political and economic power. Disadvantaged populations often view bilingual education as a means of gaining entrée to better positions in the work force, to professional or technological expertise, and to greater participation in the political processes whereby societal priorities are set and resources are allocated. Unmarked spokesmen too often rationalize a long established lack of social mobility on the part of marked populations as being caused by a lack of unmarked language mastery on the part of those populations. Seemingly, both marked and unmarked spokesmen agree that bilingual education can provide a surer and a more humane route to unmarked language mastery than does unrelieved monolingual education in the unmarked language alone. As a result, the bulk of transitional/compensatory bilingual education in the United States is justified and rationalized on these manifest grounds. Nevertheless, as in most other areas of human endeavor, the manifest and the latent are not necessarily in agreement. Even in connection with the remedial goals of bilingual education, the views of unmarked and marked populations and their spokesmen are often in disagreement.

Unmarked spokesmen often suspect that bilingual education ostensibly undertaken for the purposes of fostering greater economic and political participation on the part of peripheral populations will really bring about not national integration but its opposite: the political and economic solidification of cultural discontinuities. Unmarked spokesmen often oppose bilingual education, even when its goals are avowedly transitional and compensatory, as having undesired side-effects in terms of cultural separatism and its politicization. In order to avoid such side effects, unmarked spokesmen usually advocate monolingual education in the unmarked language for disadvantaged minorities as a less threatening and more direct route to the amelioration of social problems encountered by marked populations.

If unmarked spokesmen fear marked cultural *resurgences* as unanticipated side effects of transitional/compensatory bilingual education, marked spokesmen commonly fear unanticipated cultural *dislocations* as a result of such education. Marked spokesmen accuse transitional/compensatory bilingual education of being no more than a palliative or placebo in the political-economic realm at the same time as it is viewed by them as disruptive and destructive in the cultural realm. While bilingual education is viewed as being too little and too late in bringing about any real re-allocations of societal power (marked spokesmen point out that populations acquire new languages if and when they are admitted to new social roles requiring these languages rather than vice-versa), it is considered a hidden subverter of the domains of intimacy (home, family, friendship, community), which are the last and only ones usually available to the marked language. Thus, marked spokesmen often view transitional/compensatory bilingual education as leading to a particularly crippling brand of double marginality: raising expectations that cannot be satisfied in the political and economic realm at the same time as undermining the ethno-cultural defenses of the marked community *vis-à-vis* its own 'internal life' (Gaarder, 1970; Kjolseth, 1973).

Transitional/compensatory bilingual education is thus not without its philosophical complexities and ambivalences. These, however, derive not only from the manifest or avowed goals of such bilingual education but from its putative latent goals or side effects in the cultural sphere interpreted in diametrically opposite ways by marked and unmarked spokesmen.

Marx vs: Weber: A classic disagreement

The philosophical suspicions pertaining to the cultural entanglements of transitional/compensatory bilingual education underscore the impossibility of treating bilingual education merely as a device for reaching remedial economic and political goals. Cultural questions are inescapable, not only because two different ethno-cultural constellations so commonly need to be recognized in bilingual education, but also because the causal priority of ethnic and economic resources is a well-established dilemma in Western social theory. Bilingual education planners and practitioners rarely realize that Karl Marx and Max Weber have very substantially anticipated their own concerns in this connection (Fishman, 1977). Thus, a review of the now-classical Marxian and Weberian theoretical positions may serve to clarify some of the philosophical disagreements that practitioners and planners so often encounter in connection with compensatory/transitional bilingual education.

The classical Marxian view claims that material resources are causally prior and primary in societal behavior (even above values and ideologies). The allocation or distribution of these resources elicits a cultural superstructure for their protection both between ethnic categories as well as within them. Thus, ethno-cultural grouping and the behaviors that distinguish them are considered to be merely epiphenomenal devices and defenses, secondary by-products created by the material facts of life. In bilingual education terms, this may translate either into a defense of transitional/compensatory programs (if they *do* assure access to new resources) or into an opposition to such programs (if they do *not* assure such access). In either case, it is that access to resources which is the basic desideratum from which the cultural consequences will flow. A genuine re-allocation and equalization of resources will lead to a necessary equalization of cultural identities. There are no inherent cultural advantages, as there are inherent material advantages. As soon as material advantages are equalized then there is no need for emphasizing cultural differences since the latter are merely resultants of the former rather than a reality in their own right. In both instances, those who favor the amalgamation of marked and unmarked populations should favor transitional/compensatory bilingual education; and those who do not, should not. But in both instances, *it is actual re-allocation of resources that is the crucial variable* rather than bilingual education *per se*; and for both the marked and unmarked groups, a class purpose and a class bias must be recognized. Thus, the Marxian view is basically that bilingual education in itself is useless for social mediation since such mediation requires direct action in the social (particularly in the economic/political) arena. Marxism and capitalism thus share a characteristic emphasis on material considerations.

The Weberian view as to the interaction between material and cultural dynamics is quite different from the foregoing. It does not so much attend to the chicken-and-egg problem of 'which comes first — material or cultural differences' as to the belief that cultural dynamics, once set into motion, cannot be considered epiphenomenal or derived. Indeed, Weber points out that ethno-cultural factors are fully capable of fashioning and altering the means of production and the directions of resource allocation. The classical Hindu, Chinese, and Judaic cultures produced very different and very characteristic treatments of resources, as did the Protestant ethic. All cultures generate their own resource allocation systems, as all resource developing systems generate their own cultural legitimations. From this point of view, transitional/compensatory bilingual education might very well have major remedial consequences, by design or by accident, precisely because of its ethno-cultural impact. Bilingual education should be supported or opposed not on the basis of any purported one-way model of necessary priorities in the relationship between material and cultural resources, but rather in the awareness that interactions and influences in both directions are constant and inescapable. These interactions and influences in both directions are responsive to planning. Those who oppose or favor cultural homogenization should oppose or favor transitional/compensatory bilingual education not because of any mistaken notion as to the putative primacy of material factors in societal life but on the basis of the impact of such bilingual education as *cultural planning*. The Weberian view thus holds out more hope than does the Marxian view that remedial bilingual education can be the beginning of social remediation. However, it also stresses that culture and politics are inescapably linked.

Herder and the ethno-cultural goals of bilingual education

If Marxism possibly leads to overstressing the material bases of social reality as a philosophical point of departure for bilingual education, then Herderism may overstress the ethno-cultural bases of social reality as an alternative philosophical point of departure. For Herder, ethno-cultural diversity is a supreme good that requires cultivation, protection, and devotion. Ethno-cultural uniqueness, originality, and authenticity are viewed as the very bases of societal functioning at a truly human level. These bases constantly require strengthening, particularly in view of the dehumanizing and leveling influences flowing from modern technology. Technologically disadvantaged languages and cultures are in constant danger of displacement and replacement by technologically stronger and more useful ones. Thus, while there is no gainsaying the *practical* utility of regional or international languages of wider communication such as English, French, Russian, Spanish, Arabic, or Chinese, these must never be permitted to displace languages of narrower communication, no matter how restricted an ethno-cultural validity they possess. Bilingual education, therefore, can become the means whereby these more powerful languages are acquired at the same time that marked languages are protected from oblivion, particularly for use in the spheres of ethnic intimacy and originality. Bilingual education for the purpose of language-and-culture maintenance thus becomes not only a major opportunity within the confines of alternative philosophies of bilingual education, but also a potential contributor to the betterment of modern life and to the very preservation of that which is most precious in human existence: ethno-cultural fidelity, creativity, and diversity (Fishman, 1972).

Not unexpectedly, the Herderian vision is not without its opponents. Even marked spokesmen are far from being unanimous adherents of language-and-culture maintenance. There are certainly many who consider bilingual education as being primarily justified by what it can 'deliver' in terms of superior unmarked language mastery rather than in terms of marked language maintenance. Indeed, there are marked language spokesmen who consider marked language maintenance as inherently unattainable as a school-based endeavor. They would much rather struggle against the obvious dangers of schooling entirely in the unmarked language than confront a school that claims interest in maintaining the marked language but which, under that guise, is successful only in advancing mastery of the unmarked language while fostering *varieties* of the marked language and *functions* for the marked language in conflict with or inconsistent with those of the marked home and community. Marked spokesmen have long pointed out that schooling is a two-edged sword with respect to the ethno-cultural continuity of marked speech communities (Fishman *et al.*, 1966). Even when schooling is fully under the marked community's own control, in terms of personnel, curriculum, and methodology (which is seldom the case in connection with remedial/bilingual education), it normally leads to greater exposure to unmarked functions and interactions. This becomes more evident when schooling is not under the marked community's control. Under these circumstances, its marked language emphasis easily becomes minimized and trivialized. The marked language becomes no more than 'words' — the marked culture becomes no more than 'things'. Thus, the delicate web of authentic beliefs, values, observances, and pursuits is lost and (even worse) caricatured by heavy-handed reliance on stock phrases and stereotyped foods. Thus, there are not only marked language spokesmen who are not greatly interested in pursuing bilingual education along Herderian philosophical lines but there are also some who oppose any such pursuit precisely on the grounds that bilingual education tends to subvert such principles even when it seeks to advance them. That being the case, it should certainly come as no surprise to find that there are unmarked spokesmen who oppose bilingual education oriented toward maintaining marked languages and cultures at public expense. The usual stance adopted by such opponents is that such an orientation is politically dangerous, culturally romantic, and fiscally frivolous. Basically, it is the Herderian glorification of diversity that is rejected and a counter-image that is enthroned: a world that is efficiently prosperous and pacified on the basis of a minimal number of major languages (preferably including — if not restricted to — the mother tongues of the unmarked opponents of Herderian thought). More surprising, perhaps, is the recurring appearance of unmarked spokesmen who *do* adopt the Herderian stance — in broader or narrower terms — and *do* champion the cause(s) of the marked language(s). Frequently, these unmarked spokesmen are themselves of marked background and their championship of the marked cause is part of a personal odyssey of returning to their own roots as well as part of their attempt to organize others to do so. However, there is also no dearth of genuinely unmarked spokesmen who have altruistically dedicated themselves to the advancement of marked languages and cultures and who have advocated and utilized maintenance-oriented bilingual education. Indeed, if there is today bilingual education for language-and-culture maintenance purposes involving Romansch in Switzerland, Navajo in New Mexico and Arizona, or Spanish in a few points in the Southwest, it is largely because of the efforts and the dedication of genuinely unmarked spokesmen of the Herderian ideal. On the other hand, language-maintenance oriented bilingual education programs in Ireland, Wales, among several American immigrant-derived populations, among Frisians in Holland, among Catalans in Spain, etc., are based, in large part, upon the efforts and devotion of re-ethnicized leaders who had previously experienced considerable 'unmarking.'

Although Herderians stand at the opposite extreme from Marxists, they recognize the potential contribution of politics and economic resources to their ethno-cultural goals. Whereas Marxists are still likely to deride Herderian arguments as objectively specious and logically inverted — thereby completely missing the Herderian point that life is more than materially based objectivity and logic — Herderians are by no means reluctant to admit the need for political and economic protection if language-and-culture maintenance is to succeed and if bilingual education for that purpose is to be effective (Gaarder, 1977). Herderian thought (historically influential among marked populations in Central, Eastern, and Southern Europe and spreading from there to marked populations throughout the world) is now coming into a new vogue among academic anthropologists, ethnographers, and ethnicity specialists in the United States and in Western Europe. Herderian concepts and Herderian ideals will obviously remain part of the permanent intellectual and emotional reservoirs of social philosophy and of bilingual education.

Educational enrichment goals

The Marxian–Weberian–Herderian debate attracts by far the lion's share of philosophically relevant attention within the bilingual education fold. As a result, an exploration of the strictly educational (as distinct from economic or cultural) goals of bilingual education may well become the sleeping beauty of this entire realm of discourse. A philosophical approach to bilingual education that views it from the point of view of education *per se* may well be crucial if unmarked populations are to be interested in bilingual education for themselves and their children. Since unmarked populations are already politically and economically dominant, the Marxian–Weberian debate is not really relevant to their concerns or interests. Furthermore, since unmarked populations are either ethno-culturally neutralized or ethno-culturally dominant, the Herderian pathos may be equally lost upon them. Thus, a distinctly unmarked approach to bilingual education is needed if it is to have anything to say to the unmarked population of the United States and of the world at large. Even those whose concern for bilingual education originated in a concern for marked populations should appreciate the tactical importance of co-opting unmarked support for bilingual education. However, such support is most assuredly attainable only if unmarked populations *themselves* have something to gain from bilingual education. If this view is to be developed, then bilingual education must justify itself philosophically as *education*, i.e. that it must justify itself as an alternative to monolingual education for the unmarked child, rather than as a factor in the social mobility or in the cultural protection of the marked child (Fishman *et al.*, 1977).

Overlooked though it may have been, the educational (as distinct from the political or cultural) philosophy of bilingual education is, nevertheless, not entirely an unplowed field. The approach commonly taken is akin to that frequently employed in foreign language instruction: an additional avenue for expansion of intellect, emotional capacity, aesthetic sensitivity, and communicative-intuitive development (Fishman, 1976). As a philosophical position, it is necessary to distinguish between the claim that any or all of the above desirable enrichment goals are more fully attainable via two (or more) media of instruction on the one hand, and Whorfianism on the other hand. This philosophical position distinguishes between grammar and culture. Whorfianism claims that the structural differences between languages lead to different cognitive styles or linguistic Weltanschauungen (Fishman, 1976). An enrichment philosophy of bilingual education claims that it is language, as the prime carrier of culture, that leads to distinctive sensitivities, values, appreciations, and understandings. Whorfianism claims that the ultimate determinants of human cognition — perception, thought, memory, and problem solving — are morpho-syntactic. Enrichment bilingual education claims that these ultimate determinants are found in the web of ethno-cultural creativity and usage to which languages are particularly attuned by virtue of being imbedded conveyors, expressors, and co-participants.

Enrichment bilingual education is certainly the traditional form of élitist education from time immemorial (Lewis, 1976) and is the type of bilingual education most widespread throughout the world today (Fishman, 1976). It is realized through special language schools in the Soviet Union and China, via immersion in French for Anglophone children in Quebec and Ontario, via expatriate schools throughout the third world for children of the indigenous middle class as well as the children of resident foreigners, via private schools stressing French (more rarely, Spanish, German, or Italian) for middle and upper class children throughout the West, etc. Just as with Russian princelings in an earlier era, and with Roman élites in an even earlier one, and with Sumerian élites in a still earlier one, bilingual education involving both a major local and a major extra-local ('world') language is viewed as providing an additional asset in life. Thus far, enrichment education has been available primarily to those who would *safeguard* the advantages of their favorable social status. It has rarely been made available to the masses during the past century in which public education has become predominant throughout the world. Nevertheless, there are already beginnings of bilingual education at public expense for unmarked children, and it is in this very context that the adherents of enrichment bilingual education see the major contribution that their philosophy can make. The movement toward 'one world' requires bilingual education so that all children can benefit from the 'additional window on the world' that bilingual education espouses. Indeed, enrichment bilingual education seeks to harmoniously interrelate the two most powerful educational trends of the post war era: the trend toward vernacularization and the trend toward internationalization. The first trend continues the nineteenth century European tendency to provide at least mother tongue education for all unmarked children. The second trend, in its most recent reincarnation, is intimately associated with the world-wide spread of English (just as it was formerly associated with the spread of French and other languages of wide communication) and reflects the growing realization of many new and struggling third world educational systems that vernacularization alone cannot solve the educational lag with which they are faced. However, the strongest barricades against enrichment bilingual education are encountered in the Western world where both vernacularization of education for unmarked populations and local technological control are both well established and well advanced. Under these circumstances (both characteristic of the United States), enrichment bilingual education receives its most dubious reception whereas it is precisely here that it requires acceptance.

The opposition to enrichment bilingual education in the United States (or in Britain, France, Italy, etc.) reveals the extent to which additional languages and cultural perspectives remain unreal for the unmarked mainstreams. The gains attributed to enrichment bilingual education are often viewed as marginal and minimal by the dubious. The expenses involved are considered disproportionately great for the benefits derived. The entire philosophical premise of enrichment bilingual education is simply disbelieved and reacted to as dealing with esoterica and exotica. This is not to say that enrichment bilingual education does not exist in these advantaged mainstream settings but that it has remained élitist in scope and orientation and that it appears destined to remain so until other languages and cultures become more widely recognized, experienced, and valued in the life of the advantaged unmarked citizenry. This *did* occur in antiquity and could occur again in modern times.

Ideal types and real cases

Philosophical distinctions have a tendency to gravitate toward ideal types. Such distinctions often engaged in a kind of 'distortion for the purpose of clarity' and the philosophical positions become increasingly purified and separated from each other. In the real world, however, syncretism is more common that orthodoxy. Types of bilingual education come into being that combine philosophical positions that are separate and different in theory, just as others come into being that make differentiations that seem to be philosophically unmotivated or unjustified. One and the same bilingual education program may serve transitional compensatory ends for some children and language maintenance ends for others. Similarly, one and the same program can very easily serve language maintenance purposes for certain students and enrichment purposes for others. Indeed, the three major philosophical positions discussed above often correspond to sequentially connected stages of bilingual education in practice. Thus, in recent years, bilingual education has frequently gotten underway as a remedial compensatory enterprise that unmarked authorities have instituted for the benefit of marked populations. Subsequently, as marked populations have come to enjoy upward political and economic mobility, they have exerted increased leverage upon the unmarked power structure to permit an alternative form of bilingual education to be made available, namely, one that had language-and-culture maintenance emphasis. A subsequent stage in the developmental cycle occurs, normally after still further growth in the political and economic power of the marked population, when members of the unmarked population seek enrichment bilingual education (involving the marked language as a co-medium) as an option for themselves at the same time that maintenance bilingual education is continued as an option for the marked population. The latter development is an about-face for the unmarked population, since the distance between offering bilingual education to marked populations as a way of overcoming their handicaps on the one hand, and desiring bilingual education for one's self and one's own children on the other hand, is a very considerable one in intellectual, emotional, social, political, and economic terms. The past decade of bilingual education in Canada and in Wales provides many examples of the sequence sketched above. If the socio-educational progression is viewed as a linear continuum with feedback, branching, and reversal possibilities, then it should come as no surprise that in actuality a large number of models exist in which several of the philosophies sketched above in their pristine purity are represented in varying practical proportions (Fishman, 1976). The transmutation of theory into practice is not only wondrous to behold but full of surprises as well.

References

FISHMAN, J. A. 1976, *Bilingual Education: An International Sociological Perspective*. Rowley: Newbury House.
— 1972, *Language and Nationalism*. Rowley: Newbury House.
— 1977, Ethnicity and language. In H. GILES (ed.) *Language, Ethnicity and Intergroup Relations*. New York: Academic Press. Also *This Volume*, Section I.
FISHMAN, J. A. *et al.* 1986, *Language Loyalty in the United States; the Maintenance and Perpetuation of Non-English Mother Tongues by American Ethnic and Religious Groups*. The Hague: Mouton.
— 1977, *Social Science Perspective on Bilingual Education*. Arlington: Center for Applied Linguistics.
GAARDER, B. 1970, The first seventy-six bilingual education projects. *Georgetown University Monograph Series on Languages and Linguistics*. Vol. XXIII, pp. 163–78.
— 1977, Political perspective on bilingualism and bilingual education. *Bilingual Schooling and the Survival of Spanish in the United States*. Rowley: Newbury House. pp. 95–128.
KJOLSETH, R. 1973, Bilingual education programs in the United States: For assimilation or pluralism? In P. R. TURNER (ed.) *Bilingualism in the Southwest*. Tucson: University of Arizona Press. pp. 3–27.
LEWIS, E. G. 1976, Bilingualism and Bilingual Education: The Ancient

World to the Renaissance. In J. A. FISHMAN (ed.), *Bilingual Education: An International Sociological Perspective*. Rowley: Newbury House. pp. 150–200.

16 Ethnic community mother tongue schools in the U.S.A.: Dynamics and distributions*[1]

Despite a previous national survey (Fishman, 1964; Fishman & Nahirny, 1966) and extensive current information it is not clear whether ethnic community mother tongue schooling in the United States has really changed greatly since the early 1960s. This particular quandary can be resolved only if ethnic community mother tongue schooling is more frequently and comparably studied. The picture that emerges from the most recent effort to probe this area reveals many surprises and things generally not known.

The dimensions of the universe of study

There may well be more ethnic community mother tongue schooling in the U.S.A. today than there was twenty years ago when the original Language Resources Project was conducted (Fishman et al., 1966). At the very least, significantly more such schools have been located in our current research (Language Resources II). In the early 1960s it seemed that '2,000 ethnically affiliated schools were operating in the continental United States' and, of these, 1,885 were located by the original Language Resources Project (Fishman & Nahirny, 1966: 94). At present, nearly 5,000 schools have been located (4,893 to be exact, including 91 in Puerto Rico, 65 in Hawaii, 24 in Alaska and 15 in Guam, none of these locations

*Originally published in International Migration Review 1980, 235–47.

having been within the purview of the original Language Resources Project), with perhaps as many as a thousand more remaining unlocated. Although the increase may be more apparent than real, simply because as more experienced investigators we may have located the schools much more effectively this time, the fact remains that it is a very large system, far larger than anyone seems to have imagined. Such schools have been located in every state of the Union, in the traditionally ethnic Northeast and Southwest, in the apparently anglified North Central (including the Midwest and the 'Cornbelt') states, with 1,088 such schools, and in the South, with 711 schools. This may be viewed as additional evidence that there is far more non-black and non-Anglo ethnicity in the United States than meets the eye; indeed, far more than some would care to see, including some journalists (Epstein, 1977), sociologists (Patterson, 1977) and social theoreticians (Gellner, 1964).

The true dimensions still remain to be discovered. The organizationally unattached schools; the Arabic schools that would not reveal themselves to a Jewish researcher operating out of a Jewish sponsored University; the Russian, Polish and perhaps other schools that would not reveal themselves to a project that was connected with the U.S. government; the various Buddhist maintained schools that so few Westerners have access to; the schools that may have been established by recently arriving Southeast Asian, smaller African, Asian, Latin American and even European language groups (Dutch, Bulgarian, Irish, Rumanian, Serbian or Turkish schools); all these remain essentially unlocated by the Language Resources II effort. Finally, all of these schools, as well as the nearly 5,000 that have been located, need to be studied periodically as well as exhaustively if demographic changes in their numbers and distributions are to be understood. For this to occur they must be viewed as a national resource not only by a few scholars, but by the granting agencies and governmental offices that have studiously ignored them in the past. They must be placed on the agenda not only of sociolinguistics but of sociology as a whole (particularly sociology of ethnicity), of educational sociology, of bilingual education and of language planning and applied linguistics more generally. These schools must be included in our educational, social and intellectual bookkeeping, more for the sake of our national well-being than for their sake, since even the United States cannot afford to overlook some 6,000 schools attended by as many as 600,000 children. All reports and plans concerning language policy, language learning and bilingualism in the United States (Eddy, 1979) are ludicrous if they do not mention these schools. Because these schools represent an old and proud American tradition, they will not quietly fold their tents and disappear. They are maintained, by and large, by ethnic communities that are competently English speaking. Often they are assiduously maintained by communities that are no longer, or that never were, speakers of the languages that these schools teach and in which they teach. These schools must be recognized as filling an important identity-forming and identity-providing function for millions of Americans. As such they deserve not only to be studied but to be understood and appreciated.

Dynamics: Ideological and pedagogical

The verities of ethnic community mother tongue schooling continue to be the traditional ones that were adumbrated in the 1960s. Language and ethnicity continue to be viewed as crucially and eternally interrelated (Fishman, 1977, 1978). The ethnic mother tongue, which may or may not be the personal mother tongue, is viewed as a causal dynamo from which ethnic greatness and authenticity are derived with certainty (Fishman, 1980). As a result of the foregoing convictions, language maintenance is viewed as a moral necessity rather than merely as a vital one (Fishman, 1979a). By means of such maintenance, stable ethnosocietal biculturalism is viewed as being attainable with certainty in the United States (Fishman, 1979b). Toward this end, therefore, an endless amount of planning, effort and devotion is applied to ethnic community mother tongue schooling (Fishman, 1979c). The ethnic community mother tongue school continues to be viewed as an independently effective agency that can attain, or by virtue of its own efforts significantly foster and augment, the attainment of language maintenance (Fishman, 1979d).

The foregoing assumptions may be suprarational; they fly in the face of much social science theory and evidence, but they contribute to community identity and viability and define an ethno-moral stance as well as an ethno-pedagogical goal. As a result, the foregoing beliefs and convictions have self-perpetuating consequences, far above and beyond their empirical validity or confirmability. The same can be said for the opinion that there has been a rebirth of ethnicity in their ranks since the mid 1960s. Schools that subscribe to this view not only believe that the ethnic behaviors and awareness of their pupils and parents have increased; they also report greater ethnic mother tongue attainment than do schools that do not subscribe to the rebirth of ethnicity *vis-à-vis* themselves (Markman, 1979). Ethnic mother tongue schooling constitutes a world particularly rich in faith, in feeling, in emotion and in dedication, and all these in turn contribute both to school continuity and to community continuity.

Greater ethnic mother tongue attainments are reported by schools whose programs are more than transitional in nature, i.e. by schools who do not merely use the ethnic mother tongue until pupils are competent in English; by schools whose students arrive already speaking the ethnic mother tongue at least to some extent; by schools that are marked by enthusiasm and innovativeness in relation to their ethnic mother tongue responsibilities and by schools that are organizationally sponsored, or derive from established community institutional linkages. All this (documented in detail in Markman, 1979) indicates that effective schools in this system are not operating on emotion alone. Their beliefs, community experiences and community involvements constitute a mutually reinforcing feedback system.

Language and states

The National Center for Education Statistics' 1976 Survey of Income and Education clarifies the state by state and the language by language data obtained by Language Resources II. The correlation between the total number of school age children (age 6–18) of non-English language background[2] in the various states (Table 16.1, column 5) and the total number of ethnic community mother tongue schools in the same states is 0.71. The correlation between the total number of persons (of all ages) of non-English language background in the various states (Table 16.1, column 2) and the total number of ethnic community mother tongue schools in the same states is even more substantial, namely 0.80. Although the differences between these two correlations support the opinion that these schools are agencies which involve the total community rather than just the children alone or even primarily, it is interesting to note that certain states have far fewer ethnic community schools than one would expect on the basis of their total (or school aged) non-English background population. In this category we find, among others, Louisiana (ethnic community schools for Cajuns are still few and far between), New Mexico (ethnic community schools for Native Americans and Chicanos are disproportionately few) and Texas (Chicanos have few schools of their own). Indeed, the entire Southwest (in the NCES study, includes Hawaii), where the bulk of our Native American and Hispanic populations are located, is underrepresented insofar as ethnic community mother tongue schooling is concerned.

TABLE 16.1 Estimates of total population and of persons with non-English language backgrounds and of total school age children, 6 to 18, and school age children with non-English language backgrounds in the United States, by region and state: Spring 1976 (numbers in 1,000's)[a]

Region and state	Total pop. (all ages)	Pop. with non-Eng. language backgrounds		Total school age children (6–18)	School age children with non-English language backgrounds	
		Number	% of total		Number	% of total
All states	211,317	27,985	13	50,326	5,032	10
Northeast	68,820	9,104	19	11,267	1,333	12
Connecticut	3,065	587	19	716	77	11
Maine	1,056	134	13	269	22	8
Massachusetts	5,751	952	17	1,346	109	8
New Hampshire	818	125	15	200	17	8
New Jersey	7,224	1,375	19	1,697	182	11
New York	17,833	4,433	25	4,073	758	19
Pennsylvania	11,670	1,292	11	2,656	140	5
Rhode Island	913	196	21	206	21	10
Vermont	469	46	10	114	(b)	6
Southeast	62,962	2,928	6	12,677	520	4
Alabama	3,589	50	1	886	(b)	1
Arkansas	2,126	43	2	503	(b)	1
Delaware	576	40	7	140	(b)	4
Florida	8,498	1,177	14	1,810	194	11
Georgia	4,910	103	2	1,200	27	2
Kentucky	3,375	52	5	829	(b)	(c)
Louisiana	3,746	624	17	1,000	140	14
Maryland	4,059	295	7	989	48	5
Mississippi	2,329	25	1	615	(b)	1
N. Carolina	5,383	88	2	1,291	22	2
S. Carolina	2,785	47	2	723	(b)	1
Tennessee	4,186	48	1	971	(b)	1
Virginia	4,915	240	5	1,168	38	3
West Virginia	1,793	42	2	407	(b)	(c)
District of Columbia	693	59	8	145	(b)	4

North Central	57,022	5,024	9	13,918	606	4
Illinois	10,994	1,473	13	2,655	223	8
Indiana	5,262	283	5	1,283	47	4
Iowa	2,873	152	5	690	16	2
Kansas	2,228	135	6	520	22	4
Michigan	9,077	852	9	2,318	91	4
Minnesota	3,890	405	10	988	26	3
Missouri	4,707	193	4	1,096	24	2
Nebraska	1,530	121	8	367	16	4
N. Dakota	622	98	16	162	(b)	4
Ohio	10,634	817	8	2,524	104	4
S. Dakota	672	61	9	166	(b)	3
Wisconsin	4,570	436	10	1,149	27	3
Northwest	8,094	655	8	1,940	106	5
Alaska	346	50	14	98	15	15
Idaho	828	36	7	208	(b)	6
Montana	747	60	8	191	(b)	4
Oregon	2,293	160	7	524	25	5
Washington	3,503	295	8	826	39	5
Wyoming	377	31	8	92	(b)	5
Southwest	44,619	10,237	23	10,524	2,468	6
Arizona	2,274	533	23	555	161	23
California	20,997	5,221	25	4,786	1,105	29
Colorado	2,537	360	14	616	82	23
Hawaii	843	293	35	206	53	13
Nevada	602	73	12	146	(b)	26
New Mexico	1,155	507	44	316	154	9
Oklahoma	2,681	128	5	624	36	49
Texas	12,308	3,041	25	2,952	846	29
Utah	1,222	83	7	322	19	6

Source: Survey of Income and Education conducted by the U.S. Bureau of the Census, Spring 1976.

Notes: [a] Detail may not add to total shown because of rounding.
[b] Less than an estimated 15,000 persons.
[c] Less than an estimated 0.3%.

On the other hand, certain states have more ethnic community mother tongue schools than might be expected on the basis ot their total (or school aged) non-English language background population. Among the latter we find Indiana and Nebraska (Amish and Hebrew schools) and North Carolina and Georgia (Hebrew and Greek schools). Certainly the Jewish and Greek Orthodox populations of the United States seem to support ethnic community schools that have crucial language teaching goals even when the constituencies involved are not of non-English language background.

When the demography of ethnic community mother tongue schools is approached from the perspective of the languages involved rather than from the point of view of the states involved, the NCES data is less helpful because non-English language background figures are reported only for seventeen languages. However, what is particularly interesting from an examination of these figures (Table 16.2) is the fact that the total number of ethnic community mother tongue schools correlates more highly with the number of native born school aged children of these 17 non-English language backgrounds (0.63) than it does with the number of foreign born school aged children of these backgrounds (0.07). Thus, again, it may be seen that ethnic mother tongue schools are by no mean oriented towards the non-English speaking, foreign born child. Quite the contrary, they are particularly attuned to the numbers of native born children of non-English language backgrounds and represent, above all, an attempt to avoid ethnic mother tongue loss among such children.[3] The entry of Chicano, Puerto Rican and Native American children into such schools is a sign of their 'Americanization'. Typically, these schools serve second, third and subsequent immigrant derived pupils today, and accordingly, there is a distinct paucity of such schools for recent immigrant children, particularly for those of Italian, Portuguese, Filipino and Vietnamese origin. Perhaps the latter are served by Title VII programs within the public education sphere. Both their own newness and the availability of Title VII may be responsible for the underdevelopment of their ethnic community efforts on behalf of mother tongue schools for their children. Their efforts in this direction will become intensified as the second generation increasingly comes onto the scene, as their inevitable disappointment with Title VII becomes articulated and as their community organization becomes more stable, sophisticated and encompassing.

The above point is given empirical grounding if the state by state school distribution for those of German background and those of Spanish background is examined. Both populations are served by schools in approximately half of the states. However, for those of German heritage

TABLE 16.2 Estimated numbers of persons age 6-18 with non-English language backgrounds in the United States, by language: Spring 1976 (numbers in 1000's)[a]

Non-English language background	Total all ages	Total Age 6-18	Age 6-18 Native born	Age 6-18 Foreign born
Total	27,985	5,032	4,051	981
Selected European languages	22,475	4,263	3,550	713
French	1,932	303	273	30
German	2,735	286	243	43
Greek	542	88	60	29
Italian	2,931	296	241	55
Polish	1,498	87	82	(b)
Portuguese	489	77	38	39
Russian	228	17	17	(b)
Scandinavian languages	661	29	23	(b)
Spanish	10,609	3,022	2,515	507
Yiddish	852	58	58	(b)
Selected Asian languages	1,842	301	131	170
Chinese	537	81	39	42
Filipino languages	522	103	56	47
Japanese	439	40	26	(b)
Korean	194	31	(b)	21
Vietnamese	150	46	(b)	46
Arabic	190	22	15	(b)
Navajo	159	54	54	(b)
Other languages	3,319	391	301	90

Source: Survey of Income and Education, U.S. Bureau of the Census, Spring 1976.
Notes:[a] Detail may not add up to total shown because of rounding. [b] Less than an estimated 15,000 persons.

the correlation between the number of ethnic community mother-tongue schools per state and the number of persons of German language background in the states shown in Table 16.3 is 0.74. For those of Spanish background, however, the corresponding correlation is only 0.58. Of the two, Spanish speakers are more frequently of recent foreign extraction, Title VII dependent and characterized by presently weak ethnic community organization.

The 'Americanness' of the ethnic community mother tongue school

The fact that ethnic community mother tongue schooling is primarily correlated with the number of American born children of non-English language background, as is increasingly becoming so for Chicanos and Amerindians as well, is an important finding for an understanding of language and ethnicity in the United States. It is with the second generation of immigrant derived ethnics that ethnicity generally becomes a matter of more conscious mobilization and that language maintenance arises as an aspect of conscious educational endeavor. Rather than reflections of foreignness, ethnic community mother tongue schools are actually reflections of dealing with both indigenousness and mainstream exposure. Together both provide our linguistic minorities with the security and the sense of urgency that foster mother tongue schooling under community auspices. Such schooling may, in turn, foster the indigenization of participatory ethnicity, i.e. the stabilization of a particularly American way of being ethnic, much more than they foster language maintenance. Attending an ethnic mother tongue school may well be an almost obligatory second generation ethnic experience in the United States; learning to speak, read and write the ethnic mother tongue with facility is clearly the exception rather than the rule. Just as being ethnic is now a legitimate way of being American (and this may be the greatest accomplishment of the ethnic revival), so attending an ethnic community mother tongue school, regardless of how little of the ethnic language is either taught or learned, is now the nonimmigrant ethnic child's unique way of being American, whether or not he/she is of non-English language background. Thus, the ethnic community mother tongue school moderates and modulates ethnic uniqueness at the same time that it channels Americanness via the community's own institutions. In both respects it makes a contribution that neither its internal nor its external observers expected.

TABLE 16.3 Estimated numbers of persons with non-English language backgrounds in states with 100,000 or more such persons, by totals and selected language groups: Spring 1976 (numbers in 1,000's)[a]

States with 100,000 or more non-English language background persons	Total persons with non-English language background	Selected European language background					Selected Asian language[c] background	All other non-English language backgrounds
		Total[b]	French	German	Italian	Spanish		
Northeast								
Connecticut	587	511	97	34	167	78	(d)	71
Maine	134	128	108	(d)	(d)	(d)	(d)	(d)
Massachusetts	952	821	187	26	139	87	21	110
New Hampshire	125	116	87	(d)	(d)	(d)	(d)	
New Jersey	1,375	1,159	28	112	357	378	14	183
New York	4,433	3,789	182	301	995	1,473	184	460
Pennsylvania	1,292	839	(d)	129	277	120	25	428
Rhode Island	196	184	63	(d)	52	(d)	(d)	(d)
Southeast								
Florida	1,177	1,070	64	71	79	684	32	74
Georgia	103	62	(d)	(d)	(d)	25	16	25
Louisiana	624	604	524	(d)		60	(d)	
Maryland	295	202	24	41	29	39	30	64
Virginia	240	135	25	24		63	42	62
North Central								
Illinois	1,473	1,150	29	231	105	401	67	256
Indiana	283	201	(d)	68	(d)	69	(d)	69
Iowa	152	106	(d)	63	(d)	18	(d)	42
Kansas	135	104	(d)	57	(d)	32	(d)	22
Michigan	852	630	53	127	88	85	37	185

Minnesota	405	(d)	114	(d)	20	17	82
Missouri	193	(d)	75	31	16	(d)	36
Nebraska	121	(d)	42	(d)	23	(d)	33
Ohio	817	41	186	115	87	30	225
Wisconsin	360	15	165	23	27	(d)	68
Northwest							
Oregon	107	(d)	30	(d)	34	29	25
Washington	195	(d)	50	(d)	68	48	52
Southwest and Hawaii							
Arizona	405	(d)	20	(d)	341	(d)	114
California	4,098	137	284	263	2,970	717	405
Colorado	312	(d)	52	(d)	219	(d)	34
Hawaii	21	(d)	(d)	(d)	(d)	(d)	31
New Mexico	410	(d)	(d)	(d)	391	242	95
Oklahoma	58	(d)	24	(d)	26	(d)	58
Texas	2,851	81	123	19	2,368	63	127

Source: Survey of Income and Education, U.S. Bureau of the Census, Spring 1976.

Notes:[a] Detail may not add up to total shown because of rounding.
[b] Includes French, German, Greek, Italian, Polish, Russian, Scandinavian languages, Spanish and Yiddish.
[c] Includes Chinese, Filipino languages, Japanese, Korean and Vietnamese.
[d] Less than an estimated 15,000 persons.

Notes to Chapter 16

1. Prepared under NIE Grant G–78–0133 (Project No. 8–0860).
2. 'Non-English language background' is defined in NCES (1976) as evinced by persons whose usual or second household language is not English, or, if over 14 years of age, whose mother tongue is other than English (whether or not the latter usually speak that mother tongue).
3. The last two correlations utilize the data for Yiddish (160 schools) rather than for Hebrew (2425 schools), and, therefore, avoid the major influence that the latter have on the other distributions and correlations reported here.

References

EDDY, P. A. 1979, Press conference on findings of a survey for the President's Commission on Foreign Languages and International Studies. *Linguistic Reporter* 22 (1, 2 and 11).

EPSTEIN, N. 1977, *Language, Ethnicity and the Schools*. Washington, D.C.: The George Washington Institute for Educational Leadership.

FISHMAN, J.A. 1964, The ethnic group school and mother tongue maintenance in the United States. *Sociology of Education* 37:306–17.

— 1977, Language, ethnicity and racism. *Georgetown University Roundtable on Languages and Linguistics*. Pp. 297–309. Aiso *This Volume*. Section I.

— 1978, Positive bilingualism: some overlooked rationales and forefathers. *Georgetown University Roundtable on Languages and Linguistics*. Pp. 42–52.

— 1979a, Language maintenance and ethnicity. In J. A. FISHMAN & B. R. MARKMAN. Also *This Volume*. Section II.

— 1979b, Bilingualism and biculturism as individual and as societal phenomena. In J. A. FISHMAN & B. R. MARKMAN. Also *This Volume*. Section II.

— 1979c, Bilingual education and language planning. In J. A. FISHMAN & B. R. MARKMAN.

— 1979d, Minority language maintenance and the ethnic mother tongue school. In J. A. FISHMAN & B. R. MARKMAN.

— 1979e, Ethnic mother tongue schools in the U.S.A.: What? Where? and how many? In J. A. FISHMAN & B. R. MARKMAN.

— 1980, The Whorfian Hypothesis: Varieties of valuation, confirmation and disconfirmation. *International Journal of the Sociology of Language*.

FISHMAN, J. A. *et al.* 1966, *Language Loyalty in the United States*. The Hague: Mouton.

464 LANGUAGE AND ETHNICITY

FISHMAN, J. A. & MARKMAN, B. R. 1979, *The Ethnic Mother Tongue School in America: Assumptions, Findings, Directory*. New York: Yeshiva University (Report to NIE re Grant G–78–0133, Project No. 8–0860).

FISHMAN, J. A. & NAHIRNY, V. 1966, The ethnic group school and mother tongue maintenance. In J. A. FISHMAN, *et al. Language Loyalty in the United States*. The Hague: Mouton. Pp. 92–126.

GELLNER, E. 1964, *Thought and Change*. Chicago: University of Chicago Press.

MARKMAN, B. R. 1979, Why do some ethnic mother tongue schools accomplish more than others? In J. A. FISHMAN & B. R. MARKMAN.

National Center for Educational Statistics. 1978, Geographic Distribution, Nativity and Age Distribution of Language Minorities in the United States, Spring 1976, Washington, D.C.

PATTERSON, O. 1977, *Ethnic Chauvinism: The Reactionary Impulse*. New York: Stein and Day.

17 Minority mother tongues in education*

For most native speakers of the 'state-building' or 'national' languages of the world, it is a foregone conclusion that their children should be educated (entirely or at least primarily) in their mother tongues. Since these mother tongues are often simultaneously demographically, politically, socially, culturally and economically dominant, it is also often crystal clear to their native speakers that other children (i.e. children for whom the official or national languages are not mother tongues) should also be educated in these languages because of their association with 'greater individual and collective advantage'. The latter, then, becomes the more generally avowed principle among those in a dominant position, and the issue of mother-tongue education is conveniently forgotten. Thus, when the issue of mother-tongue education arises, that is when it becomes an issue, it is very frequently merely a reflection of other issues: the establishment mainstream versus the sidestreams; the 'state-building' population versus 'peripheral minorities'; cultural integration versus cultural autonomy; political integration versus political separatism (or suspected separatist tendencies); progress, modernity and socio-economic mobility versus tradition, stability and insularity; and so on. In many instances, the above-mentioned underlying issues are exacerbated by immigrant status. If the native speakers of state-building languages are reluctant to provide long-term, community designed and regulated mother tongue education for the indigenous ethnolinguistic minorities within the polities that the former control, then they are doubly reluctant to provide such for immigrants and foreigners, 'interlopers from abroad'. Thus, the principled defence of mother-tongue education under all circumstances easily becomes a defence of 'the weak and disadvantaged' against the

*Originally published in *Prospects* (UNESCO) 1984, no. 1, 51–61.

strong and advantaged. Both 'plaintiffs' and 'defendants' adduce educational evidence in support of their views and convictions, but, since education is the servant of society rather than a free-floating force, the social issues and parameters that underlie the educational ones not only are but must be determining in the matter of mother-tongue education as well.

Exceptional contexts

There are two noteworthy exceptions to the above-mentioned minority/majority context when mother-tongue education becomes an issue. The first pertains to traditional education in which a religious classical language is at least the target language but may also be the process language. The second pertains to those settings in which the state-building (operational, official) language is almost no one's mother tongue (i.e. it does not correspond to any long-standing indigenous ethnolinguistic population) but, rather, is an administrative convenience inherited from earlier periods of political, cultural or commercial influence or control. Both of these exceptional contexts with respect to concern for mother-tongue use in education deserve a modicum of special attention, although the latter of the two can rather easily be subsumed under our more general (dominant/disadvantaged) discussion as well.

As for those polities in which the territorial principle is implemented (McRae, 1975), they too can easily be viewed as variants of the general dominant/disadvantaged case. This is so either because the territorial principle is, to a large extent, a legal fiction, and a single integrating language (which is also the mother tongue of one of the indigenous ethnolinguistic regions and populations) really rules the roost, or, because the various ethnolinguistic regions really have minorities within them for whom mother-tongue education is not fostered. Departures from the mother-tongue principle may derive not only from legal coercion but from pervasive social pressures and embarrassments as well.

The educational tip of the iceberg

Since the dominant/disadvantaged issue often surfaces in the educational domain, it is only right that we begin by addressing this domain, keeping in mind, however, that education is a socializing institution and must never be examined without concentrating on the social processes that it serves and the social pressures to which it responds.

The usual mainstream evaluation of the merits of minority mother-tongue instruction is from the point of view of whether such instruction facilitates acquisition and mastery of the socially dominant language. There is now more than enough evidence that this is indeed the case for certain types of student populations, namely those derived from low home and community literacy environments. It seems advisable to devote a large amount of time over a number of years to literacy in these students' mother tongues, thereby building up a strong foundation of native literacy skills upon which the edifice of second-language literacy can then be securely erected (Cummins, 1981). If this represents a *tour de force* for advocates of mother-tongue instruction for minority populations, it is, however, both illogical and productive of a number of new problems. The sense of moral and practical triumph is countered by a sense of intuitive doubt. How can more time devoted to the minority language (leaving less time for the dominant language) result in better achievement in the dominant language?

The latter query, and the incredulity that it reflects, can be and are being theoretically addressed. A model of cognitive development and functioning is involved, particularly a model of bilingual development and functioning, such that multiple languages are not displacively but facilitatively processed *en route* to literacy. The learner who arrives at school from a home and community environment in which literacy is 'in the air' (i.e. it is a widespread, intensively cultivated and highly respected and rewarded pursuit), arrives ready not only for first-language literacy but even for second-language literacy. However, the child who arrives without a prior foundation in literacy (and this is particularly likely to be the child from a culturally disadvantaged background) must first develop literacy-related socio-cognitive skills and dispositions and can do so most easily in his or her own mother tongue, i.e. in the language that is better known and more fully internalized.

The issue is not fully resolved, however, particularly since the range of circumstances to which the scenario sketched above applies is far from being fully delineated. How non-literate must the minority learner's environment be for initial mother-tongue-medium education necessarily to be the optimal approach from a purely psycho-educational point of view? Furthermore, if there is no adult literacy in a particular language, what functional sense can there be to beginning with child literacy in that language? What social reward can there be for childhood literacy in a language for which there is no corresponding community (adult) literacy? Clearly, the socio-pedagogic issue has not been fully worked out and the underlying models of cognition and language acquisition upon which it rests have been conceptualized and tested in too few and too un-differentiated social contexts. Nevertheless, these newer models do help explain why:

—Some indigenous/immigrant minority children obviously succeed with respect to dominant-language acquisition and mastery even without initial literacy in their own mother tongues.

—Many middle- and upper-class children do exceedingly well in schools operated in French or English, rather than in their respective mother tongues. Such children are clearly from home and community contexts in which mother-tongue literacy is omnipresent and referentially, if not overtly, implanted in the child prior to his or her arrival at school.

—Many children in non-Western religious communities seem to prosper in educational systems in which (classical) religious languages are the target or process languages (or both) of the school. In many such communities, adult religious literacy is much in evidence, though it may not be accompanied by writing or even by understanding.

Of course, it is quite possible that even in the above three examples most children would do better *vis-à-vis* dominant-language acquisition and mastery if they too were to first lay the foundations in their mother tongues. Finally, it must be stressed that if there are still doubts as to the psycho-educational advantage of initial instruction via the minority child's mother tongue, it is only because of the overwhelming concern for that acquisition of the societally dominant language rather than for his or her more pervasive intellectual, emotional and self-definitional development or for the future of his or her minority community.

Other dominant-culture subjects

It is common for representatives of dominant national cultures to consider mathematics and science to be ethnoculturally neutral. Nevertheless, this may not be how these subjects usually come across to the members of culturally disadvantaged communities. Be this as it may, the question still arises as to whether such subjects are best (most easily, rapidly, correctly) initially learned by students from the disadvantaged community in their own mother tongues or in the dominant language of their polities. To the extent that these subjects are truly quantitative rather than verbal, the previous line of argument may not obtain. However, on the whole, it would definitely seem to be best to rely upon a learner's strongest language as the medium of instruction in whatever subject area until the weaker language is fully strong enough to carry additional freight. This would seem to be even more so in connection with subjects that are initially highly verbal: history, civics, geography, health, etc.

The 'other learning'

Usually unevaluated in discussions of dominant versus disadvantaged languages of instruction are the 'other learnings' that could be acquired via the disadvantaged language. Since national educational policy is set by and evaluated by the dominant language community, it should come as no surprise that this is the case. Since the minority learner's continued membership and optimal functioning within the disadvantaged community and the cultural intactness of that community *per se* are rarely fully appreciated as national educational responsibilities, the other (ethnically encumbered) learnings are very rarely evaluated by the national educational authorities. The entire debate as to whether they would be better taught and learned in one language or another disappears in connection with them. It is realized that they are only taught when the disadvantaged language is used as the medium of instruction. Accordingly, there is no or little constructive interest among the central authorities in how well they are taught in their own language, since these learnings are not considered by national authorities to be really in the national interest. Nevertheless, even though it is often not possible to say how well they are taught and how fully they are learned, it is obvious that from the point of view of the disadvantaged communities some overall gain is both assumed and attained. In order to fully appreciate the disadvantaged view in this connection, the more general relationship between language and culture must be sketched, however briefly. Fuller treatments are available elsewhere (Fishman *et al.*, 1984; Fishman, 1984a).

Language and culture

The complex and intricate ties between a language and its associated culture are heuristically reducible to three major dimensions.

First, at any given point in time, every language indexes its associated culture more fully than others do. The distinctive artifacts, conventions, concerns, values and beliefs of any culture are more fully, easily and naturally expressed by its associated language than by others. Even the most accomplished and elaborate languages are suddenly inelegant, imprecise, unnatural and finally even ludicrous when put to the unfair task of expressing the nuances of a culture with which they have not been intimately identified. The disadvantaged language's inadequacy for fully coping with the advantaged culture is more than matched by the advantaged language's inadequacy when it is used to relate the distinctive behaviour and belief patterns of the disadvantaged culture.

Since disadvantaged cultures frequently lack numerous and intact institutions of socialization for the purposes of securing intergenerational cultural continuity, they are all the more likely to be eager to co-opt the school for this purpose. Accordingly, they are concerned that the school teach their children how to index their own minority culture as fully, effortlessly, naturally and accurately as possible. While it is true that the school by itself cannot accomplish its goal (intact family, neighborhood and other community institutions are vitally necessary for that purpose), modernizing and modern disadvantaged cultures nevertheless view themselves as dependent upon the school to contribute as much as possible towards enabling their children to index as much of their culture as possible (Fishman, 1984b).

Second, at any given point in time, every language symbolizes its associated culture more fully than others do. A language represents the associated culture of its native speakers. There is no mystery about why this should be so. Language is the most subtle and sensitive symbol system of the human species. It is no wonder, then, that it has come to symbolize — in and of itself — that which it conveys and of which it is a part. The part is not the whole, but it can represent the whole. The language represents the culture's existence, its vibrancy and its intergenerational continuity to all who use and listen to it. Disadvantaged populations are particularly dependent on this symbolism since they lack the full array of other public symbols that advantaged populations display. The use of the disadvantaged language in the school is a symbolic statement in and of itself. It says, 'We are here. We exist. We remain faithful to ourselves.' The use of the disadvantaged language in the schools is a statement of public legitimacy on behalf of populations that possess few other modes of symbolic entrée into the public realm.

Third, at any given point in time, every language enacts its associated culture more fully than others do. A language not only indexes and symbolizes its associated culture but it is part and parcel of that culture. Much culture is realized only through language. From law and religion to songs, tales, riddles and everyday greetings, every culture is not only language encumbered but language specific. At any given time, the culture cannot be properly enacted except through its associated language. Although there are a few cultures that have weathered the dislocation of language shift, they too have been much altered in the process and even they have been able to salvage only their most hallowed and ritualized treasures rather than the very warp and woof of their daily lives. Generally speaking, therefore, maintenance of the language is not enough for maintenance of the culture, but maintenance of a culture is impossible without maintenance of its language. Accordingly, disadvantaged populations, lacking as they do so many of the other means and props of cultural continuity, tend to focus upon the school (indeed, to an exaggerated extent) in their quest for such continuity. They intuitively recognize that their language enacts their culture. The school is a central language-related institution. Therefore, in their eyes, it is crucial that the school teach the language and teach through the language, thereby becoming an active agent in securing the continuity of the culture.

The minority school and community leadership

It goes without saying that schools alone cannot guarantee the continuity of cultures, if for no other reason than that schools are generally no more than intervening (serving) rather than independent (causal) variables with respect to such continuity. Schools require strong community support in order to accomplish even their more restricted cognitive and affective goals. Such support is all the more needed in connection with cultural continuity goals since much of the minority school's curriculum inevitably leads to the larger world: to its rewards, to its life-style, to its knowledge and to its language and culture more generally. Thus, the school serving minority-group children is in reality a two-edged sword, even when it is minority-community controlled. It leads away, out of and, in a sense, partially undermines the very community that it ostensibly serves. This is all the more so when the minority community really does not control the school, its staff, its curriculum or its more subtle messages.

However, there is also a definite sense in which the minority-group school may render genuine service to the quest for intergenerational cultural continuity: it may develop ethnolinguistic versatility and expertise among its students, and it may become an important employer of minority intellectuals and proto-élites. Without such versatility and expertise in the disadvantaged language and culture as well as in the advantaged language and culture, a new generation of effective minority leaders and negotiators will not be formed. Without the employment opportunities provided by the schools, the current generation of leaders and negotiators would either be forced into the general arena or deprived of intellectual status. They would, therefore, either be lost to the minority community as a whole, or to the process of influencing younger generations. The minority-group school is, therefore, an ambiguous factor. Its real thrust, at any time, depends on the contextual circumstances surrounding it and controlling it, i.e. forces far beyond its own control (Kloss, 1966).

Language and ethnocultural identity

If it is true, as I believe, that the mother tongue is not necessarily always the best medium of instruction (particularly if academic/cognitive criteria alone are evaluated), and if it is also true that the school cannot serve to maintain the disadvantaged language and culture unless other, stronger social and cultural institutions also pursue this goal, what then is the contribution of language to cultural identity and the contribution of the disadvantaged group's schools to that identity? At the most general level, the indexical, symbolic and enactive links between any language and its associated culture always make that language a prime factor in the formation of a corresponding cultural identity. However, given language consciousness and ethnic consciousness (both characteristics and goals of élites), it is all the more true that language forms ethnic identity (Fishman, 1972; Jacobson-Widding, 1984; Liebkind, 1979). Nevertheless, since disadvantaged populations are not fully in control of the processes through which the language and identity link is usually formed or fostered, anomalies are not uncommon. The disadvantaged language may be used and expropriated by the advantaged authorities as a tool against the disadvantaged community: to influence it, to misinform it and, indeed, to dissuade it from utilizing or valuing the disadvantaged language itself. Furthermore, the disadvantaged language may be altered, since its community does not have the power or the means to maintain language authorities of its own choosing. Hence, its writing system, its lexicon, its grammar and even its phonology are forced to take on massive characteristics that are foreign to, and even rejected by, the disadvantaged community (Kreindler, 1985).

When both the messages received via the disadvantaged language are hostile to the disadvantaged group's ethnocultural self-direction and continuity and the very corpus of the language (initially in its most formal written variant and, ultimately, in its informal spoken variants as well) has been brutalized, then the language may not only go into decline but may be rejected as well. Under such circumstances, the use of the mother tongue for minority education may not only be psycho-educationally unproductive, but it may be attitudinally rejected by the very community that previously supported such use. When a prime symbol and component of a culture is co-opted by that culture's opponents, then massive cultural dislocation is inevitable among the disadvantaged. In a sense, the disadvantaged language is being used against itself and against its natural home: its native speakers and their native culture. Although a sense of cultural identity may still be salvaged, this sense may be more attitudinal and affective than overt (i.e. than expressed in terms of ethnolinguistic continuity). 'Revivals' are still possible, of course, but unless the disadvantaged regain control over their own language, culture and institutions, these revivals may be fleeting and may fail to go beyond attitudes and feelings to cultural renewal *per se* (Fishman, 1984c).

Bilingualism and diglossia

Even where disadvantaged ethnolinguistic communities have sufficient political guarantees and cultural autonomy to manage their own ethnolinguistic fates, they are, nevertheless, of necessity bilingual. Even if their own language is and remains the sole language of initial instruction, the advantaged ('unifying', 'state-building', 'national') language must be increasingly taught as students progress through the grades. Even if their own relatively disadvantaged culture is fostered by the school, this is primarily via the 'soft' subjects of the humanities and the social studies. The sciences, technological fields, professions and government services are likely to be particularly dominated by the advantaged language and its culture both within the schools and without, because these are the true avenues of power in modern society. Disadvantaged ethnolinguistic communities, therefore, are always under strain, even where they are not under attack. They cannot stem the loss of talent from within their own ranks as their best minds are continually attracted to greater opportunities elsewhere. They cannot stem the influx of outsiders into their midst if their regions are rich in natural resources, scenic/tourist attractions, or of military importance due to proximity to frontiers. Even the most benign ethnolinguistic policies on behalf of disadvantaged ethnocultural groups may well be unable to stem the competition from 'outsiders' (Billigmeier, 1979).

Nevertheless, if something is to be done to foster ethnolinguistic intergenerational continuity for disadvantaged minority populations, it is clear that it cannot be done in the schools alone nor through a stated amount of mother-tongue medium instruction alone (Macnamara, 1971). A much more encompassing effort is needed involving: (a) neighbourhood institutions (schools, local religious units, mass media and other institutions of secular culture, such as clubs, libraries, choruses, camps); (b) minority-based regional economic planning and control; (c) minority-based political representation and control; (d) minority-based cultural (including educational) planning and control. In all the above-mentioned areas, bilingualism and biculturism must be an aspect of policy planning. The advantaged language and its functions must be controlled, just as much as the disadvantaged language and its functions must be fostered. The functional boundaries between the two must everywhere be known and safeguarded. The distinction between intragroup and intergroup bilingualism must be carefully pondered (Fishman, 1984d). While the latter may be easier to stabilize than the former, it may not really be an option, whether for historical or current pragmatic/political reasons. Stable and widespread intragroup bilingualism (diglossia) requires a difficult compartmentalization, either between domains (e.g. humanities primarily in the mother tongue and technology primarily in the other tongue) or within domains (popular interactions in the mother tongue and specialized interactions in the other tongue). Either type of compartmentalization is difficult to maintain under modern, secular auspices and in modern, secular life-styles. The best guarantee of disadvantaged ethnolinguistic continuity is, of course, a strictly enforced territoriality principle with a corresponding regulation of migration and economic control across territorial lines. However, barring military upheaval, it is futile to expect such arrangements to be arrived at where they do not already exist, precisely because they would be tantamount to the voluntary transfer of local power from the advantaged to the disadvantaged, a very unlikely scenario indeed. Thus, all that can be realistically expected — and even then not too often — are personality principle policies, on the one hand, and weak territoriality principle policies on the other. Neither provides the compartmentalization that is a prerequisite for diglossia. The use of disadvantaged mother tongues as co-media of instruction is a form of bilingualism, and instructional bilingualism cannot be stabilized when no societal stability for out-of-school bilingualism has been assured. Indeed, instructional bilingualism may lead to integration of minority children into the mainstream mould.

Tradition-based bilingualism

Our discussion thus far, focusing as it has exclusively on the problems and prospects of disadvantaged mother tongues as media of instruction, has nevertheless illuminated many general points. Above all, it should be clear that much more than educational attainment is at issue when use of the mother tongue as a co-medium of instruction is advocated or questioned. Issues of cultural integration, economic control and political power are usually involved (even if not discussed), and it is these issues, rather than the issue of educational attainment and its evaluation, that are at the crux of the problem, regardless of the democratic or authoritarian, capitalist or communist, religious or secular nature of the regime. To advocate the instructional use of disadvantaged mother tongues is to advocate, implicitly or explicitly, much more than that and much more than improved academic outcomes alone. Whereas positive academic outcomes may or may not necessarily be forthcoming, depending on the literacy level of the learners' preschool social environment, the socio-cultural and political implications of the use of disadvantaged mother tongues lead to some reform. It tends to lead to proto-élitist consolidation around the school and to movements on behalf of socio-cultural and political safeguards for disadvantaged groups, at least in their own areas of concentration.

Our entire discussion needs to be redirected, however, when we come to consider the instructional utilization of those disadvantaged languages that are involved in traditional diglossia arrangements of their own. In modern times, such arrangements, which always dignified the traditional intragroup religious/literacy/formality language at the expense of the traditional intragroup vernacular/informality language, have come under pressure in two respects: (a) to replace the traditional intragroup religious/literacy/formality language with some language of greater 'advantage' in the modern world, or (b) to replace the traditional intragroup religious/literacy/formality language with the traditional intra-group vernacular/informality language. The former pressures, when they succeed, immediately translate into a version of the disadvantaged in-group/advantaged-out-group scenarios that we have discussed above. The latter pressures, however, are of a substantially different sort and deserve some attention at this point. Pressures towards vernacularization in a traditional diglossia setting still involve advantaged and disadvantaged languages, but they involve only a single ethnolinguistic entity rather than two entities (we and they), as they did above. On the other hand, pressures towards vernacularization in a traditional diglossia setting do normally involve social-class differences, religious/secular altercations and traditionalist/modernist confrontations as well, all within the same ethnic fold. The absence of interethnic rivalry in this case reduces some of the potential for conflict but still leaves much of that potential unchanged. Displacement of the traditional language of religion/literacy/formality from its educational functions (whether as process, target or both) means the displacement of one set of élites by another. While initially posed as a problem in the humanistic domains of culture (religion, education, literature, and law), it ultimately involved at least some levels of all domains of socio-economic activity as well. What is initially presented as a democratization of high culture, a facilitation of understanding in religion and an acceleration of literacy and learning more generally is, if it succeeds, ultimately the destruction of an older status system built upon at least relatively restricted access to and mastery of the non-vernacular language of religion/literacy/formality (Fishman, 1981).

On rare occasions, the language of religion/literacy/formality has itself become fully or semi-vernacularized by modernization movements, rather than replaced from below. Such popularizations have occurred when the 'common people' have had a variety of different vernaculars and, therefore, when the language of religion/literacy/formality also served broadly unifying functions across regional or international boundaries, rather than merely the implied narrowly specific functions. However, even in the absence of such unifying functions, it is difficult to displace established intragroup languages of religion/literacy/formality. They are more easily compartmentalized against foreign borrowings and social pressures because of their longstanding indigenous status and their aura of sanctity (Altoma, 1969). Many of the school systems utilizing such languages have recorded considerable academic success and have also facilitated a modicum of social mobility across initial social class (DeFrancis, 1950). Such mobility may be clearly the exception rather than the rule, but its existence is often highlighted as proof of the basic fairness of the system *per se*. When the tradition of academic excellence and the possibility of social mobility via acquiring mastery of the language of religion, literacy and formality are weighed against the certain dislocation and interregional fragmentation that would follow if that language were replaced by a variety of vernaculars, it is easy to see why vernacular instruction may be rejected in favour of further popularization of the language of religion, literacy and formality (Lehmann, 1975). Once again, therefore, we note the predominance of extra-educational considerations in decision-making with respect to what is mistakenly taken to be a simple issue of educational achievement.

Multi-ethnic states

Many developing countries have entered upon the quest for universal education and literacy in a state of extreme internal linguistic diversity. Given lack of resources, on the one hand, and pressing problems both on the socio-political and technical fronts, on the other hand, it is easy to see why such polities should prefer the economies in cost and effort that a single language of instruction entails over the alternative of a multiplicity of such languages (Fishman *et al.*, 1968). Indeed, in such polities unifying language symbols, institutions and traditions may be a very urgent priority if progress along other fronts is to occur at all. The fact that many vernaculars have no literacy tradition of their own also militates against their use in school (beyond very initial stages or very informal functions) even among their own native speakers, not to mention the national authorities.

Further complications may exist in the path of vernaculars in such settings. If they are truly many in number, if none of them has been selected as the unifying language (thereby stimulating a sense of insulted pride among the others), if the outside (often colonial) lingua franca has very tangible and prestigious international functions, and if a great deal of interethnic mixture has occurred, particularly in the urban centres, it is particularly difficult to justify the additional costs that a seriously multilingual educational system must initially entail. Even where such a system is devised, it is often relegated to the earliest grades and to the softest subjects, so that the former integrating language can still be given considerable attention (Gorman, 1974; Pascasio, 1977). When traditional diglossia is dissolved, the former language of religion, literacy, formality is commonly retained at least in some lofty functions, and, therefore, with some school recognition as well. Similarly, when the integrating linguae francae of newly developing and highly multilingual polities are removed from their formerly exclusive sway in authoritative pursuits, it is still common to retain them at certain levels of administration and in certain high-culture functions. As a result, and once again, a new bilingual balance comes into being, both in the schools and in many socio-cultural domains more generally, rather than a move towards complete vernacularization. Thus, educational considerations are not nearly as powerful as other factors.

I have not discussed mother-tongue-medium education as a 'natural right' because it does not become such except where disadvantaged groups are sufficiently powerful not only to have their vernaculars constitutionally recognized but pragmatically protected as well. In three of the four contexts that we have discussed (in the case of revised or reformed traditional diglossia, in the case of highly diversified newly developing nations and in the case of integrated polities that recognize either the territorial or personality principle [or both] as a question of law), bilingual policies and practices come into being such that both the disadvantaged vernaculars and a more advantaged integrating/state-building/national language are employed, in education as well as in at least some other institutions of socio-political and technical significance. Only in the fourth case, in the case of already integrated polities in which no tradition of serious accommodation to disadvantaged vernacular exists as a matter of law, is the issue of bilingual education itself thoroughly conflictual. The recognition of disadvantaged vernaculars as co-media of instruction is suspected of leading to socio-political disintegration and to technical malfunctioning (Epstein, 1977). Disadvantaged languages as co-media of education are largely evaluated only from the point of view of how well they permit students to acquire and master the advantaged medium of instruction. Insufficient compartmentalization arrangements are instituted, which cannot foster intergenerational ethnolinguistic continuity. The school itself cannot attain that continuity. The disadvantaged vernaculars are often co-opted by foreign élites and used to discredit both the languages themselves and the ethnocultures with which they are associated.

To focus upon disadvantaged languages only as instructional co-media is to miss the point. Even as instructional media, such languages provide a purely instructional advantage only for an initial period and only for students derived from weak literacy contexts. But the real significance of using disadvantaged vernaculars as instructional co-media, particularly in polities in which prior integrating, state-building, advantaged languages and populations have enjoyed undisputed authority, is that such use symbolizes a lessening of relative disadvantage and, hopefully, an increase of the possibility of attaining ethnocultural autonomy, including technical and socio-political self-regulatory power. It is only under such circumstances that the use of disadvantaged languages as instructional established on a stable basis. It is only under such circumstances that such languages (and the cultures with which they are associated) can attain the compartmentalization that is necessary for their intergenerational continuity (a compartmentalization that state languages achieve by means of political frontiers). It is only under such circumstances that pupil achievement in and through disadvantaged languages is seriously evaluated by educational authorities. However, even under such circumstances, advantaged languages and their associated culture remain crucial factors in the lives of disadvantaged populations. Depending on the fluctuating absorptive capacities of advantaged reward systems (economic, social, political), the dependency of the disadvantaged upon the advantaged will require and reward various degrees of versatility in the advantaged language (Fishman, 1984e). Fluctuating though the mainstream absorptive capacity may be, it is the dependent population who must make sense out of bilingualism and biculturism and who must fashion both opportunities for mobility and opportunities for intergenerational ethnolinguistic continuity. This is a difficult task and one that should not be trivialized by evaluating merely the degree to which initial instruction via the disadvantaged language maximizes acquisition and mastery of the advantaged one. To do so is not only tantamount to adding insult to injury; it is also to lose sight of the true relationship between language, society and culture.

References

ALTOMA, H. 1969, *The Problem of Diglossia in Arabic*. Cambridge, Mass.: Harvard Middle Eastern Monograph Series.

BILLIGMEIER, R. H. 1979, *A Crisis in Swiss Pluralism*. The Hague: Mouton.

CUMMINS, H. 1981, *Bilingualism and Minority-Language Children*. Toronto: OISE Press.

DEFRANCIS, J. 1950, *Nationalism and Language Reform in China*. Princeton, N.J.: Princeton University Press.

EPSTEIN, N. 1977, *Language, Ethnicity and the Schools*. Washington, D.C.: Institute for Educational Leadership.

FISHMAN, J. A. 1972, *Language and Nationalism*. Rowley, Mass.: Newbury House.

— 1981, Attracting a following to high culture functions for a language of everyday life. In J. A. FISHMAN (ed.), *Never Say Die*! The Hague: Mouton, pp. 369–94.

— 1984a. Language and culture. In A. & J. KUPER (eds), *The Social Science Encyclopedia*. London: Routledge & Kegan Paul.

— 1984b, The significance of the ethnic mother tongue school. In J. A.

FISHMAN *et al.* (eds), *The Rise and Fall of the Ethnic Revival: Perspectives on Language and Ethnicity*, Chapter 11. Berlin: Mouton.
— 1984c, Epilogue: The rise and fall of the ethnic revival in the U.S.A. In J. A. FISHMAN *et al.* (eds), *The Rise and Fall of the Ethnic Revival: Perspectives on Language and Ethnicity*. Berlin: Mouton.
— 1984d, Bilingualism and biculturism as individual and as societal phenomena. In J. A. FISHMAN *et al.* (eds), *The Rise and Fall of the Ethnic Revival: Perspectives on Language and Ethnicity*, Chapter 4. Berlin: Mouton. Also *This Volume*. Section 2.
— 1984e, Language maintenance and ethnicity. In J. A. FISHMAN *et al.* (eds), *The Rise and Fall of the Ethnic Revival: Perspectives on Language and Ethnicity*. Berlin: Mouton, Chapter 5. Also *This Volume*. Section 2.
FISHMAN, J. A. *et al.* 1968, *Language Problems of Developing Nations*. New York: John Wiley.
FISHMAN, J. A. *et al.* 1984, *The Rise and Fall of the Ethnic Revival: Perspectives on Language and Ethnicity*. Berlin: Mouton.
GORMAN, T. P. 1974, The development of language policy in Kenya with particular reference to the educational system. In W. H. WHITELEY (ed.), *Language in Kenya*. Nairobi: Oxford University Press, pp. 397–454.
JACOBSON-WIDDING, A. (ed.) 1984, *Identity: Personal, Social and Cultural*. Uppsala: University of Uppsala Press.
KLOSS, H. 1966, German-American language maintenance efforts. In J. A. FISHMAN *et al.* (eds), *Language Loyalty in the United States*. The Hague: Mouton, pp. 206–52.
KREINDLER, I. (ed.) 1985, *Sociolinguistic Perspectives on Soviet National Languages: Their Past, Present and Future*. Berlin: Mouton.
LEHMANN, W. P. (ed.) 1975, *Language and Linguistics in the People's Republic of China*. Austin, University of Texas Press.
LIEBKIND, K. 1979, *The Social Psychology of Minority Identity*. Helsinki: University of Helsinki.
MACNAMARA, J. 1971, Successes and failures in the movement for the restoration of Irish. In J. RUBIN & B. H. JERNUDD (eds), *Can Language Be Planned?*. Honolulu: University Press of Hawaii, pp. 65–94.
MCRAE, K. D. 1975, The principle of territoriality and the principle of personality in multilingual states. *International Journal of the Sociology of Language* Vol. 4, pp. 33–54.
PASCASIO, E. M. (ed.) 1977, *The Filipino Bilingual: Studies on Philippine Bilingualism and Bilingual Education*. Quezon City: Ateneo de Manila University Press.

SECTION 5:
Élites and rank-and-file: Contrasts and contexts in ethnolinguistic behavior and attitudes

Modern, conscious and organized ethnicity requires leaders, much as does any other modern, conscious, organized social behavior. Like all leadership, ethnic leadership is in many ways similar to and in many ways different from those whom it leads. This is not an anomaly of ethnic leadership but, rather, of the very essence of leadership. If leaders were in no way different from the rank-and-file, then they could not provide the additional awareness, perspective, sensitivity and versatility that leadership requires and that leadership implies.

Minority ethnicity exists as a pattern of everyday life much before consciousness of such existence develops and is mobilized. The more fortunate and the more capable sons and daughters of ethnic minorities are often co-opted into the mainstream, particularly so in recent times, when mainstreams tend to define themselves and to present themselves as open-opportunity systems. Re-ethnification and re-linguification of the most capable is a common tactic whereby mainstreams deprive ethnolinguistic minorities of the internal leadership necessary to them if their autonomy is to be attained. Those minority sons and daughters with special skills, talents, aspirations and contacts are already different from the rank-and-file of their co-ethnics even at this initial stage, even before they assume any ethnolinguistic responsibilities, even when they are merely proto-élites, even when they are being courted and co-opted by the mainstream. If they were not different they would be of no use to the mainstream.

With or without such co-option, the intellectual experience of proto-élites is different than that of the rank-and-file. They are likely to be better educated, verbally more adept, with broader perspectives and more diversified experiences and interactions than those available to the rank-and-file. With or without co-option, but particularly with it, proto-élites are more likely to master the mainstream language, to be familiar with its history, literature and culture more generally, and to have more acquaintances within the mainstream; these are all natural resultants of greater ability and of the greater opportunities for cross-cultural study and contacts that such ability provides. It is not unusual, therefore, for the greater opportunity and reward system of the mainstream to tempt them, to influence them and even to alter their ethnic self-concepts, behaviors and allegiances. The co-option of minority élites is a form of 'white death' that, on the one hand, impoverishes minority ethnolinguistic groups, perpetuates their disadvantages and even threatens their very existence, and, on the other hand, it fosters self-confirming hypotheses pertaining to the 'natural inferiority' of such groups. Presumably they have no appreciable reward system of their own because they don't deserve one and couldn't manage one, for lack of talent and ability, even if they had one.

But all reward systems, even mainstream reward systems, have their absorptive capacities and the time inevitably comes when further co-option of minority proto-élites is impossible or sharply decreases in rate. Mainstreams also have their own agendas and priorities, including econotechnical and sociopolitical problems substantially unrelated to their 'peripheral' ethnolinguistic sidestreams. Thus, for a variety of reasons, the minority proto-élites that had heretofore been absorbed within the mainstream are no longer co-opted and may even be rejected, every bit as much as their less talented co-ethnics. Under such circumstances, disappointed proto-élites have few other alternatives than to return to their ethnolinguistic 'origins' and to seek their fortunes there, among their own 'kinsmen', close to their own 'roots'.

The process of élitist or proto-élitist 'return' is both painful and liberating. Its pain, above and beyond the pain of disappointment or betrayal vis-à-vis the mainstream, pertains to the admission of error and to the need to undergo (re-)enculturation once again, this time as a mature adult. The beginning of many ethnolinguistic consciousness raising and mobilization movements is characterized by the (re-)learning of the minority mother tongue and the (re)adoption of the minority folkways by élites and proto-élites that are returning to the minority fold and bringing to that fold the contrastively heightened awarenesses, the sense of frustration and of rediscovery, the consciousness of exploitation and of urgency, not to mention the energy and the talents, perspectives and contacts which are peculiarly theirs.

Are such re-ethnicized élites forcing their own aspirations upon the rank-and-file? Are they exploiting the rank-and-file, whipping up in it a false consciousness, only so that they, the élites, can obtain or recover positions of power and perquisites that they covet? It would be wrong to claim that such self-seeking behavior, dressed up in ethno-ideological garb, has never transpired. However, it would be equally if not more untenable to claim that such misuse of leadership is a particularly minority ethnic phenomenon or that it particularly typifies minority ethnic leadership/rank-and-file interaction. Indeed, such claims are easily as exploitative and as malicious as the very misbehaviors that they purport to discover in the generality of minority ethnic leadership; such charges are the very epitome of classical projection, of the pot calling the kettle black. Mainstream spokesmen who would prefer that either they themselves or other mainstream functionaries be the acknowledged leaders of a passive minority following, accuse ethnic leadership of inauthenticity and of self-aggrandizing pot-stirring.

Nevertheless, if we set aside the baseless charges of distinctively self-seeking manipulativeness, there is good reason to recognise that leadership/rank-and-file differences are manifold within the minority ethnolinguistic fold, even after an indigenous leadership arises, i.e. one that has not needed to go through a reconversion experience. Reconversion adds a poignancy, a heightened contrastivity, and an infusion of cross-cultural ability and sensitivity to the minority scene which it may subsequently lack, when its leadership is more thoroughly and indigenously authentic. However, even then, minority leadership can ill afford to be insular since the navigation of minority/mainstream policy, interaction and negotiation is its major responsibility. The ethnolinguistic minority's leadership remains substantially different in total life-style and cognitive style from that of the rank-and-file, and this difference is as often expressed in terms of greater behavioral and conceptual similarity to the mainstream as in terms of greater ideological awareness of the need to strengthen cultural boundaries and to foster areas of 'cultural breathing space' that will be largely or totally under minority ethnolinguistic auspices. The former atypicality of minority ethnolinguistic leaders *vis-à-vis* the rank-and-file is a byproduct of the leadership's educational superiority and negotiative responsibilities; the latter atypicality of minority ethnolinguistic leaders *vis-à-vis* the rank-and-file is a byproduct of the leadership's stewardship of the ethnolinguistic tradition. Both of these atypicalities have their definite counterparts among mainstream leaders.

It is a truism to point out that 'leadership leads' and, therefore, it must be at a different position, ideologically and behaviorally, than the position of those who are being led. Too great a discrepancy between the leaders and the led is non-functional, however, and results in changes of leadership or in waning of authority. Ethnolinguistic leadership is also internally highly diversified, whether viewed attitudinally, behaviorally or programmatically, so much so as to actually make it difficult for minority populations to achieve concerted action on their own behalfs. This means that stereotypes of ethnolinguistic leadership or of leadership/rank-and-file differences are inevitably false and that the true state of affairs in this connection constantly needs to be empirically established. The rank-and-file changes, minority-mainstream relations change, and the ethnic leadership changes. Any attempt to describe the latter alone, without both of the former as proper contexts for understanding the latter, is doomed to inaccuracy and to special pleading. All three are realities that are in constant and in intensive interaction and any attempt to define one as the constant and sole 'cause' and the others as mere 'effects' or consequences is to do a serious disservice to the difficult pursuit of understanding in an area already all too susceptible to bias and politicization.

18 Puerto Rican intellectuals in New York: Some intragroup and intergroup contrasts*[1]

A factor analysis of coded interview data on 20 Puerto Rican intellectuals in the New York City area yielded 5 item-factors (R) and 2 person-factors (Q). The R factors dealt with Spanish language dominance, ideological language maintenance, Puerto Rican cultural emphases, American aware-ness, and sociolinguistic sophistication. The Q groups differed meaning-fully and consistently on these 5 factors as well as on demographic background variables, particularly with respect to ideological vs. be-havioural Puerto Rican culture and language maintenance. In addition, intellectuals as a group were found to differ greatly and systematically from ordinary Puerto Rican males in having more ideological positions with respect to Puerto Rican culture and Spanish language maintenance in New York.

Two previous studies of the language maintenance efforts and attitudes of minority group intellectuals either concentrated on the demographic correlates of intragroup differences within this population (Fishman, 1965b; Fishman & Nahirny, 1966) or on contrasts between intellectuals of one minority group and ordinary members of other minority groups (Fishman, 1965a; Hayden, 1966). The present study attempts to go beyond previous attempts to gauge the language con-sciousness of minority group intellectuals primarily in two respects: (a) the intragroup differentiations are sought in terms of clusters of individuals reporting similar views and comments in free-ranging and lengthy bilingual interviews; (b) the intergroup differentiations are based upon views and

*Originally published in *Canadian Journal of Behavioral Sciences* (1969) No. 4, 215–26.

comments of ordinary members in the same minority group community obtained as a result of partially similar depth interviews. Both sets of interviews were conducted during the same three-month period of the summer of 1967.

More specifically, a representatively heterogeneous group of 20 Puerto Rican artists, writers, singers, musicians, and organizational leaders were interviewed as part of a larger study of Puerto Rican bilingualism in the greater New York area (Fishman, Cooper, Ma *et al.*, 1968). The interviews were designed to tap (a) claimed use of English and Spanish, (b) attitudes toward English and Spanish, (c) attitudes toward being Puerto Rican, and (d) attitudes toward being American. The interviews typically lasted more than two hours and were conducted for one hour or so in English and for another hour or so in Spanish. A report of the *prevalence* of various claims and views has appeared elsewhere (Fishman *et al.*, 1968). The present paper deals with the clusters of replies and the clusters of individuals noted among the intellectuals as well as with the differences between Puerto Rican intellectuals and ordinary Puerto Ricans in the greater New York area with respect to several of the topics probed by the interview. In general, our study of Puerto Rican intellectuals is related to a continued interest in determining when and why language and culture ideologies come to be present and elaborated among intellectuals as well as when and why these ideologies are (or are not) shared by ordinary members of minority communities.

Factor analysis of interview data

The 20 interviews completed with Puerto Rican intellectuals were subjected to a detailed content analysis which coded all comments in connection with 116 topics or questions, 48 of which were included in sufficient interviews to be usable for the purposes of an R factor analysis. The varimax orthogonal rotation procedure yielded a five-factor solution which seemed preferable to solutions based upon either fewer or more factors. (The intercorrelations between all 48 items, the complete rotated matrix, and the final factor loadings for each item are contained in Appendix II of Fishman *et al.*, 1968.) On the basis of a consideration of the items on each factor and their respective loadings, the factors were descriptively named as follows:

Factor I: *Spanish dominance and versatility* without rejection of English.
Factor II: *Ideological-activistic approach to Spanish-language maintenance*,

although English repertoire is available.

Factor III: In the context of Spanish positiveness, a *basic concern with Puerto Rican and American cultures as a whole* rather than primarily with languages.

Factor IV: *Familiarity with American behaviours and awareness of American pressures* on Puerto Rican adults and children in New York City.

Factor V: *Sociolinguistic sophistication: contextual communicative appropriateness* in the use of varieties of Spanish; intellectualization of language and Puerto Rican culture.

Given the fact that Puerto Rican intellectuals in the New York City area are far more skewed in their range of claims and attitudes than is the entire Puerto Rican speech community of which they are a part, the five factors would seem to reflect important nuances that may help us differentiate within the intellectual community.

From the point of view of sociolinguistic theory it is particularly interesting to note that the factor that pertains to Spanish dominance and versatility (I) does not imply the rejection of English. This co-existence of two languages is indicative of a bilingual community rather than merely indicative of individual bilingualism (Fishman, 1967). A further indication of societal bilingualism is the existence of a factor that deals with communicative competence (V). The ability to vary between 'folksy' and 'better' Spanish as well as the ability to vary between Spanish and English, and to engage in such variation in accord with the speech community's norms of communicative appropriateness, is the basic indicator of a bilingual speech community in which each language and variety has its legitimate functions.

It is interesting to find Spanish language dominance (actual use), ideology of Spanish language maintenance, and sophistication with respect to communicative appropriateness as separate factors on the one hand, and Puerto Rican cultural concerns plus American awareness as separate factors on the other hand. All in all, these five factors seem able to provide an encompassing picture of bilingual intellectual speech networks.

Factor analysis of individuals

A Q analysis of all individual replies yielded two maximally distinct clusters of intellectuals. Table 18.1 reveals the mean scores or percentages

TABLE 18.1 *Q-group differences on selected items*

Item	Factor	Item	Q_1 (n=11)	Q_2 (n=9)
4	1	Claimed repertoire in Spanish (3 = 1 variety; 4 = 2 varieties; 5 = 3 or more varieties)	3.73	4.33
9	1	Uses fewer varieties than aware of in English and not interested in mastering the others	0.82	0.56
10	1	Claimed Spanish repertoire > claimed English repertoire (latter = 1 variety only)	0.27	0.67
30	1	Use of English only where Spanish (or Spanish and English) is expected to be negatively interpreted	0.36	0.67
27	2	Ideological reasons for speaking Spanish only to bilingual Puerto Ricans	0.45	0.33
8	2	Personal repertoire in English (1 = 1 variety; 2 = 2 varieties, etc.)	3.18	2.44
15	2	Accepts personal responsibility for strengthening Spanish among 'Nuyorquinos' (1 = no; 2 = minor; 3 = yes: future; 4 = yes: current; 5 = yes: current + seeks more)	3.83	2.11
3	2	Bilingual Puerto Ricans to whom English is usually spoken: none	0.55	0.22
36	3	Actual or intended practice with children: Spanish only	0.18	0.44
28	3	Re: speaking Spanish only to bilingual Puerto Ricans: no concern	0.36	0.56
22	3	Can a creative Puerto Rican culture be maintained in New York? Yes, but only in Spanish	0.64	0.44
48	3	Conflict between Puerto Rican and American culture: yes, re: behaviors other than language	0.45	0.22
39	4	Why some 'Nuyorquinos' don't know Spanish: American pressures	0.18	0.56
46	4	Is Spanish important in being Puerto Rican? Yes, for obtaining Puerto Rican knowledge	0.27	0.56
45	4	What must an ordinary Puerto Rican do in order to remain Puerto Rican in New York? Behaviours (customs, language, organizations)	0.27	0.67
41	4	Number of Puerto Rican leisure time participations (1=1; 2=2; etc.)	2.00	3.22
31	5	To whom is better Spanish used: contextual variation	0.27	0.44

TABLE 18.1 (*Concluded*)

17	5	Evaluation of Spanish press, radio, and TV in New York: all negative	0.55	0.33
24	5	Bilingual Puerto Ricans to whom Spanish was spoken during past 2 days: work and ILA colleagues	0.27	0.44
43	5	Number of American leisure time participations (1 = 1; 2 = 2; etc.)	2.00	3.56

for these two groups on four items selected from each factor as being most in accord with the factor's major thrust.

On Factor I, Q_1 individuals claim a smaller Spanish repertoire, claim to use fewer English varieties than those of which they are aware, claim less difference between the size of their Spanish and English repertoires, and less frequently claim that their bilingual interlocutors would react negatively if they spoke English to them when Spanish alone or Spanish and English was expected. All in all Q_1 individuals score lower on Factor I ('Spanish dominance and versatility').

With respect to Factor II, Q_1 individuals are more ideological in explaining their use of only Spanish with bilingual Puerto Ricans, more frequently accept personal responsibility for strengthening Spanish among 'Nuyorquinos,' and more frequently claim that there are no bilingual Puerto Ricans with whom they speak English, all of the foregoing notwithstanding the fact that they claim a larger personal repertoire in English. In general, Q_1 individuals score higher on Factor II ('Ideological-activistic approach to Spanish language maintenance') even though they score lower on those factors that are more behaviorally than attitudinally focussed on language.

On Factor III the previously noted differences between Q_1 and Q_2 are further confirmed. Whereas Q_1 members less frequently claim to speak only Spanish with their children they more frequently claim that a creative Puerto Rican culture can be maintained in New York and that a conflict between Puerto Rican and American culture exists. The fact that Q_1 is less concerned about speaking only Spanish to bilingual Puerto Ricans is another indication among many that Q_1 members are less focussed upon language *per se* and more concerned with broader topics such as Puerto Rican culture with which Factor III is largely concerned.

As far as being aware of the pressures of the American environment

(Factor IV), Q_1 members less frequently blame the American environment for the fact that some 'Nuyorquinos' do not know Spanish. On the other hand, they claim fewer Puerto Rican leisure activities and less frequently make behavioral recommendations with respect to what ordinary Puerto Ricans must do in order to remain Puerto Rican in New York.

Finally, with respect to sociolinguistic sophistication and claimed contextual sensitivity (Factor V), Q_1 members again score lower. They less frequently claim contextual use of better Spanish and less frequently claim to have used Spanish with co-workers or with other Puerto Rican intellectuals during the two days prior to being interviewed. In addition, their reactions to all three Spanish mass media are more frequently negative.

To summarize, Q_1 members make fewer claims with respect to their own Spanish dominance and versatility and more frequent claims with respect to ideological Spanish language maintenance. They more frequently subscribe to items which imply a greater concern for Puerto Rican culture — as an intellectual-ideological construct — than for language. They claim greater familiarity with and acceptance of American behaviors and realities and less sociolinguistic sensitivity and sophistication. All in all, the distinctions between Q_1 and Q_2 seem to be along an ideological-behavioral continuum. Q_1 members are Puerto Rican primarily in ideological, intellectual, eclectic ways. In a sense, they are intellectuals, artists and organizers primarily and behavioral Puerto Ricans only secondarily. Q_2 members are practising Puerto Ricans, linguistically and behaviorally, without any rejection of American practices in the sphere of leisure activity. They are less strident ideologically and far less well known outside of the Puerto Rican community. They are primarily Puerto Ricans who serve their community as artists, writers, and organizers. They do not view their services or the pains and pleasures of being Puerto Rican in New York in sharp or grand ideological terms. They simply are Puerto Rican and, therefore, need not protest that they are or should be. Other evidence and theory indicate that, should sentiment for Puerto Rican separatism develop, its most strident leaders would primarily be drawn from the ranks of Q_1 individuals (Deutsch, 1966; Moore, 1965).

Demographic differentiation

The Q groups differ demographically (Table 18.2) as well as behavioral-attitudinally, and these two kinds of differences tend to reinforce and clarify one another. Q_1 individuals tend to be younger than

Q_2 individuals; they are more frequently American born, and, if Puerto Rican born, less frequently of small town or rural origin. A slightly larger proportion of Q_1 individuals has received higher education but a substantially larger proportion obtained their education in the continental U.S.A. Finally, Q_1 individuals have more frequently experienced positive social mobility in the U.S.A. *vis-à-vis* their father's occupation in Puerto Rico. All of these characteristics of Q_1 members (greater youth, American or large city birthplace, more education, American education, and greater occupational success) help explain the greater ideological and intellectual, but lesser behavioral, Puerto Rican culture and Spanish-language maintenance orientation of Q_1 members. It is primarily from the ranks of such partially marginal and mobile individuals that nationalist leaders and ideologists tend to be drawn.

TABLE 18.2 *Demographic differences between Q groups*

Demographic variables	Q_1 (n=11)	Q_2 (n=9)
Age		
−39	54%	33%
40–59	27%	56%
60–	19%	11%
Birthplace		
U.S.A.	18%	
San Juan	27%	22%
Large cities (›10,000 pop.)	45%	22%
Small cities or towns	9%	22%
Rural areas		33%
Education		
Elementary	9%	11%
Secondary	19%	22%
College	45%	45%
University	27%	22%
Education		
Continental U.S.A. (highest)	55%	33%
Puerto Rico	45%	67%
Occupational mobility		
Same as father's	45%	33%
Higher than father's	55%	56%
Lower than father's		11%

Some contrasts between ordinary Puerto Ricans and Puerto Rican artists, leaders, and intellectuals

Roughly 20% of the items discussed with our sample of 20 intellectuals were also included in a series of 32 interviews with Puerto Rican males living in a single Puerto Rican neighbourhood in the greater New York area (Hoffman, 1968). As a result, it is possible to compare several response distributions in these two very different populations, even though the respective factor structures in which these items were imbedded were quite different.

Contrasts pertaining to the Spanish language

In the intellectual sample (ILA) 60% of our respondents mentioned work and professional colleagues as being among those with whom they had spoken Spanish in the past two days; family, friends, and neighbors occupied a secondary place (40%). In the ordinary Puerto Rican (OPR) sample these two proportions are reversed. Spanish is primarily claimed as the language of family, friends, and neighborhood (59%) and far less frequently as the language of work. This difference, as obtained from formal interviews, is in agreement with differences disclosed by all other reports of the Bilingualism Configuration Study (census, word naming, word association, word frequency estimation, Spanish-usage rating, etc.) which disclose the dominance of Spanish in home and neighbourhood contexts rather than at work. However, it is not primarily the validity and reliability of the OPR data that is of interest at this point but the fact that for the ILA network within the New York Puerto Rican speech community Spanish has a major function that it does not have in the community at large. For Puerto Rican artists, community leaders, and intellectuals in the greater New York area, Spanish is not primarily the language of hearth and home, of family and friends, but, rather, the language of work, of professional activity, of association with others in task-oriented ways.

This difference in primary function, insignificant though it is in itself, accompanies many related differences in attitude and belief. Ordinary Puerto Ricans tend to define 'better Spanish' much more frequently in terms of vocabulary, grammar, and pronunciation (85%) than do artists, leaders, and intellectuals (55%). For the latter group 'better Spanish' is also thought of in terms of lack of interference and in terms of aesthetic qualities (45%), considerations that are almost lacking in the awareness of ordinary Puerto Ricans. Both groups agree, however, in specifying that they primarily attempt to use 'better Spanish' with educated interlocutors and with Latin Americans or Spaniards whose opinion of Puerto Rican Spanish is all too poor. Of course, the two groups differ greatly in the extent to which they claim to control a 'better Spanish' and in the extent to which they claim to use it contextually. Artists, leaders, and intellectuals claim to speak 'better Spanish' and 'folksy Spanish' with many of the very same interlocutors, depending on the requirements of situational and metaphorical use. Those ordinary Puerto Ricans who claim to control a 'better Spanish' claim to use it on a 'go-no-go' basis, that is, not to use it at all with their family and friends and to use it invariably with educated interlocutors and with non-Puerto Rican Hispanos.

Obviously, ILA members associate 'better Spanish' with open networks in which they interact both on a personal and on a transactional basis. Ordinary Puerto Ricans associate 'better Spanish' only with closed networks in which transactional interactions are available to them. This is indicative of the greater artificiality of 'better Spanish' as a construct or as a behavior system among ordinary members of the speech community under study.

Our two samples also differ markedly in the extent to which they report that knowing Spanish is necessary in order to be Puerto Rican (Table 18.3). This view, indicative as it is of conscious language loyalty and language ideology, is far more prevalent among the intelligentsia than among the common man. Of course 'knowing Spanish' may mean something quite different to these two non-overlapping networks of speakers. That this is the case is indicated by the responses obtained to our query as to whether there were many 'Nuyorquinos' who neither spoke nor understood Spanish. As Table 18.4 reveals, the vast majority of ordinary Puerto Ricans reported that most 'Nuyorquinos' speak and understand Spanish without real difficulty. At the same time an equally impressive majority of intellectuals reported that most 'Nuyorquinos' speak Spanish poorly.

TABLE 18.3 *Is it necessary to know Spanish to be Puerto Rican?*

Response	OPR (n=32)	ILA (n=20)
No	20(62%)	2(10%)
Yes	12(38%)	18(90%)

Thus the intellectual's position that knowing Spanish is needed in order to be Puerto Rican may be, in part, a critique of the level and purity of the Spanish controlled by most 'Nuyorquinos.' Be this as it may, we are still left with the obvious conclusion that ordinary Puerto Ricans may not only have a less demanding interpretation of what 'knowing' Spanish means, but that they also widely believe that 'knowing' Spanish, even at that more minimal level, is not absolutely necessary in order to be Puerto Rican in the New York City area.

Finally, our two samples also differ markedly in their view of how the mastery of Spanish might be improved among 'Nuyorquinos.' Among ordinary Puerto Ricans the most prevalent view is that 'it's up to the parents' (53%), followed closely by the view that 'no improvement is necessary or possible' (33%). Only 14% believed that the schools could help in this connection. Among intellectuals the most prevalent view is that 'it's up to the schools' (45%), with another 25% placing their hope in the activities of various Puerto Rican organizations. Only 30% reported that parents could be of much help in this connection. Thus, each group is focused primarily on the world that it knows and controls. Common folk place their trust in the family. Intellectuals place their trust in those institutions in the community that they actually or potentially control.

TABLE 18.4 *Are there many 'Nuyorquinos' who do not speak or understand Spanish?*

Response	OPR (n=29)	ILA (n=20)
Yes (many do not understand)	2(7%)	1(5%)
Most understand little and speak poorly	3(10%)	4(20%)
Most understand well but speak poorly	3(10%)	14(70%)
Most speak and understand without real difficulty	21(73%)	1(5%)

Contrasts pertaining to being Puerto Rican

As might be predicted, the common man replied to our inquiry as to 'What makes you a Puerto Rican?' by stressing the facts of birthplace and parentage (84%). Intellectuals, on the other hand, replied in terms of personal attainments. Most of them claimed that they were Puerto Ricans because of their attitudes, knowledge, sentiments, and behaviors (65%) rather than because of such ascribed characteristics as birthplace and parentage (35%). A related difference of opinion obtained in connection with our query as to whether there is a 'conflict between being Puerto Rican and being American.' Ordinary Puerto Ricans overwhelmingly replied that no such conflict existed (89%). Intellectuals replied almost as overwhelmingly that such a conflict did exist (75%).

Obviously, the ordinary Puerto Rican is less exclusive and less ideological all along the line. He does not believe that Spanish is absolutely necessary for being a Puerto Rican; he sees his being Puerto Rican as a simple fact of ascribed status; he sees no conflict between that ascription of birth and parentage and his (or his children's) attainment of Americanness. The naturalness of being Puerto Rican, on the one hand, plus the lack of conflict in also being American, on the other hand, may explain why ordinary Puerto Ricans are so split about resettling in Puerto Rico. Nearly half claim that they definitely will resettle in Puerto Rico (47%). Among intellectuals the corresponding percentage is only 10%, the vast majority indicating no more than 'maybe' or 'no' to this question. Intellectuals are obviously headed toward greater conflict. They more frequently intend to stay in the context where their opportunity potential is greater, but they are also more critical with respect to all aspects of this context. Thus, intellectuals tend to create some of the conflict that they experience.

Discussion

Puerto Rican intellectuals in New York are obviously more ideological and more demanding than the common Puerto Rican with respect to the needs of Puerto Rican cultural and linguistic self-maintenance in the New York City area. However, New York is also less frequently a way-station for them. Unlike the ordinary Puerto Rican they do not believe that they have come merely in order to save up some money or to improve their children's start in life. Their view is that they are in New York primarily for their professional advancement or for service to less fortunate members of their community. Many of them have outgrown the Island in terms of either professional or communal recognition. They are less likely to return and, perhaps therefore, are more demanding and more critical with respect to the language and the culture of Puerto Rican New York.

All in all, whereas language consciousness and language loyalty are generally at a rather low level among ordinary Puerto Ricans in the New York City area, it is higher among intellectuals than it is in the Spanish daily press (Fishman *et al.*, 1968) and it is higher in the Spanish daily press than it is among ordinary folk. The intellectual's concern for language maintenance and language purity — low-keyed though it is among Puerto Rican intellectuals in New York today — represents a conscious and ideological position that is available for future integrative or separatist development, as circumstances may dictate. This position is currently less pronounced and less coherent the further we depart from the small and rather exclusive circles of the intelligentsia and the closer we come to the Puerto Rican 'man in the street' and to the speech networks with which he interacts.

Notes to Chapter 18

1. Preparation of this paper was facilitated by the East-West Center, Institute of Advanced Projects, University of Hawaii, where the author spent the 1968–69 academic year as Senior Specialist.

References

DEUTSCH, K. W. 1966, *Nationalism and Social Communication* (2nd ed.) Cambridge: MIT Press.

FISHMAN, J. A. 1965a, Varieties of ethnicity and varieties of language consciousness. *Georgetown University Monographs in Languages and Linguistics*, pp. 18, 69–79.

— 1965b, *Yiddish in America*. Bloomington: Indiana University Research Center in Anthropology, Folklore and Linguistics.

— 1967, Bilingualism with and without diglossia: Diglossia with and without bilingualism. *Journal of Social Issues* 23, No. 2, 29–38.

FISHMAN, J. A., COOPER, R. L., MA, R., *et al.* 1968, Bilingualism in the Barrio. Final Report to DHEW under Contract OEC–1–7–062817–0297. New York: Yeshiva University.

FISHMAN, J. A., & NAHIRNY, V. 1966, Organizational interest in language maintenance. In J. A. FISHMAN *et al.*, *Language Loyalty in the United States*. The Hague: Mouton.

HAYDEN, R. 1966, Some community dynamics of language maintenance. In J. A. FISHMAN *et al.*, *Language Loyalty in the United States*. The Hague: Mouton.

HOFFMAN, G. 1968, Life in the neighborhood: A factor analytic study of Puerto Rican males. In J. A. FISHMAN, R. L. COOPER, R. MA *et al.*, *Bilingualism in the Barrio*. Final Report to DHEW under contract OEC–1–7–062817-0297. New York: Yeshiva University.

MOORE, W. E. 1965, *The Impact of Industry*. Englewood Cliffs (N.J.): Prentice Hall.

19 Attracting a following to high-culture functions for a language of everyday life: The role of the Tshernovits Language Conference in the 'Rise of Yiddish'*[1]

The 'spread of language' does not always entail gaining new speakers or users — whether as a first or as a second language. Frequently it entails the gaining of new functions or uses, particularly, 'H' functions (i.e. literacy-related functions in education, religion, 'high culture' in general, and, in modern times, in econotechnology and government, too) for a language that is already widely known and used in 'L' functions (i.e. everyday family, neighborhood and other informal/intimate, intragroup interaction). Wherever a speech community already has a literacy-related élite, this type of language spread inevitably involves the displacement of an old élite (the one that is functionally associated with the erstwhile H) by a new élite that is seeking a variety of social changes which are to be functionally associated with the prior L and which are to be instituted and maintained under its own (the new élite's) leadership.[2] The last century has witnessed the rise and fall (but not the complete elimination) of such efforts on behalf of Yiddish.

*Originally published in R. L. COOPER (ed.) 1980, *Language Spread: Studies in Diffusion and Social Change*. Bloomington: Indiana University Press, 291–320.

The traditional position of Yiddish in Ashkenaz (= the traditional Hebrew-Aramaic and Yiddish designation for Central and Eastern Europe, Jews living in or derived from this area being known, therefore, as Ashkenazim) was — and in many relatively unmodernized Orthodox circles still *is* — somewhat more complex than the H vs. L distinction usually implies. At the extreme of sanctity there was *loshn-koydesh*[3] alone, realized via its hallowed biblical and post-biblical *texts*. At the opposite extreme, that of work-a-day intragroup life, there was Yiddish alone: the vernacular of one and all, rich and poor, learned and ignorant, pious and less-than-pious. Although 'sanctity' and 'work-a-day' existed on a single continuum and were connected by a single overarching set of cultural values and assumptions, they were, nevertheless, clearly distinct overt, cognitive and emotional composites. In between these two extremes were numerous situations in which (a) *loshn-koydesh* and Yiddish co-occurred insofar as intragroup life was concerned, and less numerous ones in which (b) co-territorial vernaculars or written languages were employed insofar as intergroup activities involving the work-sphere, government and infrequent 'socializing' required.

The traditional intragroup intermediate zone resulted in a Yiddish oral literature of high moral import and public recognition (sometimes published in Yiddish but, at least initially, as often as not, translated into *loshn-koydesh* for the very purpose of 'dignified' publication). It also included the exclusive use of Yiddish as the process language of oral study, from the most elementary to the most advanced and recondite levels. And it included the exclusive use of Yiddish as the language of countless sermons by rabbis and preachers and as the language of popular religious tracts (ostensibly for women and uneducated menfolk). Thus, Yiddish *did* enter pervasively into the pale of sanctity and even into the pale of sanctity-in-print (hallowed bilingual texts — *loshn-koydesh* originals with accompanying Yiddish translations — had existed ever since the appearance of print, and, before that, as incunabula), but it never existed in that domain as a fully free agent, never as the sole medium of that domain in its most hallowed and most textified realizations, never as fully independent target medium but only as process medium underlying which or superseding which a single *loshn-koydesh* text or a whole sea of such texts was either known, assumed or created (Fishman, 1973, 1976).

As a result, when traditional Eastern European Jewry enters significantly into the nineteenth-century drama of modernization, *loshn-koydesh* and Yiddish are generally conceptualized, both by most intellectuals and by rank-and-file members of Ashkenaz, in terms of their

extreme and discontinuous textified vs. vernacular roles, their intermediate co-zones having contributed neither to the substantial
vernacularization of *loshn-koydesh* nor to the phenomenological
sanctification of Yiddish. As the nineteenth century progresses there are
increasing efforts to liberate Yiddish from its apparent subjugation to
Hebrew (the latter being metaphorically referred to as the noble daughter
of heaven, Yiddish being no more than her handmaiden), particularly for
more modern intragroup H pursuits. In addition, there were also
increasing efforts to liberate Yiddish from its inferior position *vis-à-vis*
co-territorial vernaculars in connection with modern learning and non-
traditional life more generally. It is with the former type of language
spread that this paper deals most directly (and with its implications for the
role of *loshn-koydesh*, which was also then being groomed for modern H
roles at the intragroup and at the intergroup levels), although the spill-over
from the former to the latter type of language spread was often both an
objective and an achievement as well. Obviously, when one component
of a traditional diglossia (here: triglossia) situation changes in its functions,
the societal allocation of functions with respect to the other(s) is under
stress to change as well.

The Tshernovits Language Conference: Success or Failure?

Three different positive views concerning Yiddish were clearly
evident by the first decade of the twentieth century and a fourth was then
increasingly coming into being.[4] The earliest view was a *traditional
utilitarian* one, and it continues to be evinced, primarily by ultra-Orthodox
spokesmen, to this very day. In accord with this view Yiddish was (and
is) to be utilized in print for various moralistic and halakhic[5] educational
purposes because it has long been used in this way, particularly in
publications for women, the uneducated and children. Any departure from
such use — whether on behalf of modern Hebrew or a co-territorial
vernacular — was/is decried as disruptive of tradition. Another view was
a *modern utilitarian* one, namely, that Yiddish must be used in political
and social education if the masses were ever to be moved toward more
modern attitudes and behaviors because it was the only language that they
understand. This view was, and to some extent still is, widely held by
maskilic[6] and Zionist/socialist spokesmen. A third view was also evident
by the turn of the century, namely, that Yiddish was a distinctly indigenous
and representative vehicle, and, therefore, it had a *natural role to play both
in expressing and in symbolizing Jewish cultural-national desiderata.*

Finally, we begin to find expressed the view that for modern Jewish needs Yiddish is the *only or major natural expressive and symbolic vehicle*.

In the nineteenth century the first two positive views (and the counterclaims related to them) were encountered most frequently, but the latter two were beginning to be expressed as well (see, particularly Y. M. Lifshits' writings, e.g. 1863, 1867; note D. E. Fishman's discussion [1980] of Lifshits as transitional ideologist). In the twentieth century the latter two views (and their respective refutations) came into prominence, and the former two receded and were ultimately almost abandoned.[7] The last public encounter of all four views was at the Tshernovits Language Conference. There the first two views were presented and strongly refuted whereas the last two remained in uneasy balance, neither of them appearing clearly victorious over the other.

Planning the Conference

The father of the idea to convene an international conference on behalf of Yiddish was Dr. Nathan Birnbaum (Nosn Birnboym) (1864–1936)[8] who came to the U.S.A. in 1907 with that very purpose in mind. Birnbaum, who had coined the word 'Zionism' (in German: *Zionismus*) and had conceptualized much of its mission in the early 1890s, had by then already broken both with Theodore Herzl (1860–1904) and with Herzlian Zionism on the grounds that to save Jews ('to solve the Jewish Question') without aiming at fostering Jewishness ('to solve the Jewishness Question') was tantamount to fostering assimilation under Jewish auspices. In the course of his own Jewish self-discovery he came to regard Yiddish as the vehicle of genuine, rooted Jewishness and, therefore, as the preferred vehicle of a kind of modernization that would also be particularly attuned to the simultaneous need for continuity of Jewish culture, traditions and values. He had begun to write in this vein by the beginning of the century in the German periodical *Selbst-Emancipation* (that he founded in Vienna in 1885) and continued doing so subsequently in his Yiddish weekly *Dokter birnboyms vokhnblat* that he founded in Tshernovits (Czernowitz, Czernowce, Chernovtsy, Cernauti),[9] to which he had moved at the invitation of university students in Vienna who hailed from Tshernovits, who were sympathetic toward Yiddish and who had come under the influence of his writings. However, Tshernovits did not give him the visibility (or the income) that he required, and he decided to visit the U.S.A. in pursuit of both and on behalf of

Yiddish, 'the world language of a world people'.

Birnbaum's initial host in the U.S.A. was the socialist-Zionist Dovid Pinski, already well known as Yiddish novelist and dramatist, who had read Birnbaum's articles in German and was eager to help him reach a wider pro-Yiddish audience. Immediately attracted to Birnbaum's cause was the socialist-territorialist[10] theoretician and philosopher Khayem Zhitlovski (for extensive bibliographic details see Roznboym, 1929). The three of them formed a curious troika (a neo-traditionalist on his way back to full-fledged orthodoxy, a labor-Zionist and a philosophical secularist), but together they issued a resolution for a world conference concerning Yiddish, composed in Pinski's apartment on Beck Street in the South Bronx (also signed by the playwright Yankev Gordon and the publisher Alex Yevalenko), and together they brought it to a less than massive public at two 'evenings' (Yiddish: *ovntn* although not necessarily transpiring in the evening) on the Lower East Side. Far more unforgettable than the arguments that they then marshalled for such a conference and more impressive than the proposed order of business suggested in connection with it was the fact that its chief architect, Birnbaum, spoke to the audiences in German (for he could not yet speak standard or formal Yiddish, although he had begun to write Yiddish articles in 1904). His addresses, although purposely peppered with Yiddishisms, struck most commentators as impressive but funny, funny but painful. The intelligentsia was learning its mother tongue so that the latter could fulfill new functions and thereby provide new statuses to masses and intelligentsia alike.

But there *was* an intended 'order of business' for Tshernovits, no matter how much it may have been overlooked at the *ovntn* or even at the conference itself. Birnbaum, Zhitlovski and Pinski agreed (primarily at the latter's insistence) to 'avoid politics' and 'resolutions on behalf of Yiddish' (Pinski, 1948), particularly since the political and ideological context of Yiddish differed greatly in Czarist Russia, in Habsburg Austro-Hungary and in the immigrant U.S.A. Thus they agreed upon a 'practical agenda' and a 'working conference' devoted to the following ten points:

1. Yiddish spelling
2. Yiddish grammar
3. Foreign words and new words
4. A Yiddish dictionary
5. Jewish youth and the Yiddish language
6. The Yiddish press
7. The Yiddish theater and Yiddish actors

8.   The economic status of Yiddish writers
9.   The economic status of Yiddish actors
10. Recognition for the Yiddish language.

The agenda starts off with four items of corpus planning.[11] Yiddish was correctly seen as being in need of authoritative codification and elaboration in order to standardize its usage and systematize its future growth. Major corpus planning efforts for Yiddish — though called for and attempted before — was a sign of its new importance. Point five recognized the dangers that modernization represented for the ethnic identity of the younger generation, particularly if it pursued education and advancement in co-territorial vernaculars to the exclusion of Yiddish. Points six to nine stressed press and theater — their quality and their economic viability — the massive means of bringing modern Yiddish creativity to the public. Finally, the last point recognized something that was certainly on Birnbaum's mind. Jews themselves — not to speak of gentiles — were unaccustomed to granting recognition to Yiddish, and, therefore, such recognition was often begrudged it even by democratic or democratizing regimes that gave some consideration to cultural autonomy or to officially recognized cultural pluralism (as did pre-World War I Austro-Hungary). As Pinski in particular feared, the entire agenda of the conference was 'subverted' by the tenth point and, indeed, was dominated by what was in reality only half of that point: *Jewish* recognition for Yiddish.

Why was the conference held in Tshernovits?

Tshernovits was only a modest-sized town (21,500 Jews out of a total population of 68,400) and of no particular importance *vis-à-vis* Jewish cultural, political, economic developments. It was clearly overshadowed by Warsaw, Vilna, Odessa and several other urban centers in the Pale of Settlement within the Czarist Empire. Nevertheless, the recent history of Czarist repressions may have made it undesirable (if no longer clearly impossible) to convene the Conference in one of those centers. Even within the Austro-Hungarian Monarchy, however, such Jewish centers as Kruke (Cracow), Lemberik (Lemberg, Lvov), and Brod (Brodie) were clearly of greater importance than Tshernovits. Tshernovits was of course easily accessible to Yiddish speakers in Austro-Hungary, Czarist Russia and Rumania, but its symbolic significance far surpassed its locational convenience and was two-fold: (a) Not only was it in *frantsyosefs medine*

but many segments of its hitherto significantly Germanized Jewish
intelligentsia were already struggling to revise their attitudes toward
Yiddish — a struggle that was particularly crucial for that period in
Austro-Hungarian cultural politics *vis-à-vis* Germans, Poles,
Ukranians/Ruthenians and Jews in the Bukovina and in Galicia as well —
and (b) Birnbaum had already decided to relocate there and had several
young followers there (many of whom were students at the University in
Vienna during the school year — and had there been influenced by
Birnbaum). These young followers could provide (on a volunteer basis and
during the summer vacation period in particular) the techni-
cal/organizational underpinnings of a world conference for Yiddish.
Indeed, these young followers constituted, with Birnbaum, the organizational committee that sent out the invitations to individual organizations
and committees, secured a hall (not without difficulty), planned a banquet
and a literary evening and disbursed the meager fees that the participants
in the Conference paid in order to be either delegates (5 Kronen) or guests
(1 Krone). Both of these factors (the convening of the Conference in
Tshernovits and Birnbaum's young but inexperienced followers there in
the grips of their own discovery of H-possibilities for Yiddish) influenced
the course of the Conference. The delicate balance of minority relations
in Galicia and Bukovina resulted in more widespread attention being paid
to the first Yiddish World Conference than its sponsors had bargained for.
The census of 1910 was already being discussed, and it was apparent that
the authorities again wanted Jews to claim either German (in Bukovina)
or Polish (in Galicia) as mother tongue (as had been done in 1890) in order
to defuse or counter-balance the growing pressure from
Ukranians/Ruthenians and Rumanians for additional language privileges
and parliamentary representation. Previously, Jews had been counted
upon to buttress the establishment out of fear that 'unrest' would lead to
anti-Jewish developments of one kind or another. It was equally apparent
that young Jews were disinclined to play this role any longer and that they
were threatening to claim either Yiddish or Hebrew, even though neither
was on the approved list of mother tongues and even though claiming a
language not on the list was a punishable offence.[12] Indeed so great was
the tension concerning the Conference that the President of the Jewish
Community (*kehile*) in Tshernovits refused to permit the Conference to
meet in community facilities for fear of incurring official displeasure or
worse. Clearly, a new within-fold status for Yiddish would have intragroup repercussions as well: upsetting the former within-group diglossia
system was also related to new intergroup aspirations as well, and these
were, of necessity, political and economic (or likely to be suspected of
being such), rather than merely cultural (no matter what the official

agenda of the Conference might be).

Moreover, meeting in Tshernovits also determined the very nature of the guests and delegates (a distinction that was soon ignored) that could attend, discuss, propose, vote upon and ultimately implement the Conference's deliberations and resolutions. The regional tensions in conjunction with national/cultural rights resulted in attendance by a more substantial number of students and ordinary folk, many in search of something spectacular or even explosive, than might otherwise have been the case. Similarly, because of the characteristics of Bukovinian Jewry *per se* there were more Zionists and fewer Bundists,[13] more traditionally religiously oriented and fewer proletarian-politically oriented delegates and guests than would have been the case elsewhere. Birnbaum's youthful admirers and assistants were quite incapable of rectifying this imbalance via such simple means as sending more invitations to more 'nationally conscious' circles. Indeed, for them, as for most Jewish intellectuals in Tshernovits *per se*, the idea of a Conference *on behalf of* Yiddish and conducted *in* Yiddish was not quite believable even as it materialized. Most local Jewish intellectuals were

> 'the mainstay of . . . daytshtum (Germanness), and of a *sui generis* daytshtum to boot, Bukovinian daytshtum. None of the socially and politically active local (Jewish) intellectuals imagined anything like speaking to the people in its language. Indeed, when Berl Loker, who belonged to the exceptions, then a young student, was about to give a lecture in Yiddish, he invited my wife to attend as follows: "Come and you will hear how one speaks pure Yiddish at a meeting!" The best recommendation for a speaker was the accomplishment of being able to speak to a crowd in lovely and ornate German' (Vays, 1937).

Thus, the lingering disbelief that Yiddish was suitable for H pursuits ('Is Yiddish a language?') *surrounded* the Conference and even found its way *into* the Conference, and did so in Tshernovits more than it would have in many other, more industrialized and proletarianized centers of Jewish urban concentration and modernization. Bukovinian Jewry and its modernizing élites were then both still relatively untouched by the more sophisticated pro- and anti-Yiddish sentiments that were at a much higher pitch in Warsaw, Vilna, Lodz or Odessa.

Who attended the Conference?

The invitations sent by Birnbaum's 'secretariat' were addressed to those organizations and communities whose addresses they happened to have. Many *unimportant* societies and clubs were invited, whereas many even more important ones were not. Personal invitations were few and far between. The writer and essayist Y. L. Perets (1852–1915), perhaps the major influence upon the younger generation of Yiddish writers and a conscious ideologist of synthesis between all Jewish values and symbols, modern and traditional, *was* invited and came with his wife (with whom he spoke more Polish than Yiddish). The two other 'classicists of modern Yiddish literature', Sholem Aleykhem (1859–1910) and Mendele Moykher Sforim (1836–1917), were also invited but did not come. Sholem Aleykhem at least claimed to be ill, but Mendele, in his seventies, offered no excuse at all, and, as a result, was sent no greetings by the Conference such as were sent to Sholem Aleykhem. Zhitlovski came but Pinski was 'busy writing a book' (Pinski, 1948). A young linguist, Matesyohu Mizes (Mathias Mieses), was invited (as were two other linguistics-oriented students, Ayzenshtat and Sotek) to address the Conference on the linguistic issues that apparently constituted forty percent of its agenda. Other than the above individual invitations, a general invitation was issued and broadcast via the Yiddish press and by word of mouth 'to all friends of Yiddish'. All in all some 70 showed up, and these were characterized by one participant (and later major critic) as having only one thing in common: 'They could afford the fare . . . Everyone was his own master, without any sense of responsibility to others' (E[ste]r, 1908).

The geographic imbalance among the resulting participants is quite clear:

From the Czarist Empire: 14; among this delegation were found the most prestigeful participants: Perets, Sholem Ash (still young but already a rising star), Avrom Reyzin (a well known and much beloved poet), D. Nomberg (writer and journalist, later a deputy in the Polish Sejm and founder of a small political party, *yidishe folkistishe partey*, stressing Yiddish and diaspora cultural autonomy), N. Prilutski (linguist, folklorist, journalist, later Sejm deputy), Ester (Bundist, later Communist [Kombund and Yevsektsiye] leader). Zhitlovski (though coming from the U.S.A.) and Ayznshtat (though then studying in Bern) were also usually counted with the 'Russians'.

From Rumania: 1; I. Sotek of Braila (an advocate of writing Yiddish with Latin characters and a student of Slavic elements in Yiddish).

From Galicia and Bukovina: 55; among them eight minor literary figures and 47 students, merchants, bookkeepers, craftsmen, etc., including one 'wedding entertainer' (*badkhn*). This group was the least disciplined and, on its home territory, least impressed and convinced by attempts to keep to any agenda.

'At the most crucial votes no more than forty members participated . . . In the vote on the resolution that Yiddish be considered a national [Jewish] language no more than 36 individuals participated. People always were arriving late to sessions. Some did not know what they were voting about. People voted and contradicted their own previous votes. In addition it was always noisy due to the booing and the applauding of "guests from Tshernovits". No one at all listened to Ayznshtat's paper on Yiddish spelling' (E[ste]r, 1908).

Nor was the banquet or the literary program any more orderly or consensual. When local Jewish workers arrived to attend the banquet

'it was discovered that they lacked black jackets and they were not admitted. They began to complain. Some of the more decently clad ones were selected and admitted without jackets. Some of the "indecently" clad workers took umbrage and protested so long that the policeman took pity on them and sent them away. As a result, the "decently" clad ones also decided to leave. After the opening remarks I called everyone's attention to what had occurred. It immediately became noisy and I was told to stop speaking. I left the banquet and a few others accompanied me' (E[ste]r 1908).

Attracting an élite to modern H functions for an erstwhile traditional L runs into problems due to the fact that prior and concurrent social issues have brought about allegiances and identities that are not congruent with those that further the interests of the new élite and the new functions. Reformulation of identities and regrouping of allegiances is called for and is difficult for all concerned.

The conference *per se*

The Conference lasted for a little under a week, beginning on Sunday August 30, 1908.

'A quarter after ten in the morning there walked onto the stage Nathan Birnbaum in the company of Y. L. Perets, S. Ash, Dr. Kh. Zhitlovski and other distinguished guests. . . . Dr. N. Birnbaum opens the conference reading his first speech in Yiddish fluently from his notes . . . He reads his speech in the Galician dialect' (*Rasvet*, Sept. 1908: quoted from *Afn shvel* 1968).

Birnbaum stressed the fact that this was the first worldwide effort on behalf of Yiddish, sponsored by its greatest writers ('respected even by the opponents of Yiddish') and the beginning of a long chain of efforts yet to come. These opening remarks caused a sensation among local Tshernovitsians.

> 'Everyone knew that he [Birnbaum] doesn't speak Yiddish and that the speech would be translated from German. However, all were eager to hear how the "coarse" words would sound coming from the mouth of Dr. Birnbaum who was known as an excellent German speaker . . . However at the festive banquet in honor of the esteemed guests . . . he spoke superbly in German, the way only he could' (Vays, 1937).

Indeed, a speaker's ability to speak Yiddish well and the very fact that Yiddish *could* be spoken as befitted a world conference, i.e. in a cultivated, learned, disciplined fashion in conjunction with modern concerns, never ceased to impress those who had never before heard it so spoken.

> 'Zhitlovski made the greatest impression on all the delegates and guests, both at the Conference and at the banquet (which was a great event for Yiddish culture that was still so unknown to most of those in attendance). "That kind of Yiddish is more beautiful than French!" was a comment heard from all quarters and particularly from circles that had hitherto rejected Yiddish from a "purely esthetic" point of view' (Vays, 1937).[14]

FIGURE 19.1 *A postcard printed soon after the Tshernovits Conference, showing left to right, A. Reyzin, Y. L. Perets, S. Ash, Kh. Zhitlovski, and H. D. Nomberg*

Yiddish used adeptly in an H function was itself a triumph for Tshernovits, almost regardless of what was said more substantively.

But of course a great deal *was* said substantively as well. The linguistic issues were 'covered' by Ayznshtat, Sotek and Mizes. Whereas the first two were roundly ignored, the third caused a storm of protests when, in the midst of a paper on fusion languages and their hybrid-like strength, creativity and vigor, he also attacked *loshn-koydesh* for being dead, stultifying and decaying. Only Perets' intervention saved Mizes' paper for the record as 'the first scientific paper in Yiddish on Yiddish' (Anon., 1931).[15] Obviously, the tenth agenda item stubbornly refused to wait its place in line and constantly came to the fore in the form of an increasingly growing antagonism between those (primarily Bundists) who wanted to declare Yiddish as *the* national Jewish language (Hebrew/*loshn-koydesh* — being a classical tongue rather than a mother tongue — could not, in their view, qualify as such) and those (primarily Zionists and traditionalists) who, at best, would go no further than to declare Yiddish as *a* national Jewish language, so that the role of Hebrew/*loshn-koydesh* — past, present and future — would remain unsullied.[16] In the midst of this fundamental argument more primitive views still surfaced as a result of the presence of so many ideologically unmodernized guests. One of the delegates recounts the following tale:

'... (T)here suddenly appears on the stage a man with a long, red beard, wearing a traditional black *kapote* (kaftan) and *yarmelke* (skull-cap). He begins speaking by saying "I will tell you a story". The hall is full of quiet expectancy. We all listened carefully in order to hear a good, folksy anecdote. The man recounts in great detail a story about how two Jews once sued each other in court because of a *shoyfer* (ritual ram's horn) that had been stolen from the *beysmedresh* (house of study and prayer). With great difficulty they explained to the gentile judge what a *shoyfer* is. Finally the judge asked: "In one word — a trumpet?" At this point the litigants shuddered and one shouted to the other: "Is a *shoyfer* a trumpet?" The assembled participants in the hall were ready to smile at this "anecdote" which had long been well known, when the man suddenly began to shout at the top of his lungs: "You keep on talking about language but is Yiddish (*zhargon*) a language?" ' (Kisman, 1958).

The compromise formulation penned by Nomberg ('*a* national Jewish language') was finally adopted, thanks only to the insistance of Perets, Birnbaum and Zhitlovski, over the vociferous opposition of both left-wing and right-wing extremists who either favored an exclusive role for Yiddish ('*the* national Jewish language') or who wanted no resolutions at all on political topics.[17]

Very little time was devoted to organizational or implementational issues such as whether the Conference itself should sponsor 'cultural work', convene a second conference within a reasonable time or even establish a permanent office (secretariat) and membership organization. Although the last two recommendations were adopted (the first was rejected due to unified left-wing and right-wing disenchantment with the Conference's stance re the *the* or *a* national language issue), and although Birnbaum and two young assistants were elected to be the executive officers and to establish a central office, very little was actually done along these lines. At any rate, the tasks entrusted to the secretariat were minimal and inoccuous ones indeed. In addition, Birnbaum soon moved ever closer to unreconstructed Orthodoxy and to its stress on matters 'above and beyond language'. (He subsequently continued to defend Yiddish as a bulwark of tradition but pointed out that it was the tradition rather than the language that really counted. He therefore metaphorically translated the prayer book phrase *roymemonu mikol loshn* not, as it was usually understood, 'Thou hast raised us above all other languages', but rather, 'Thou hast raised us above all languages', Birnbaum [1946].) At any rate, he was not an administrator/executive but an ideologue. He was, as always, penniless, and the funds that were required for an office and for his salary never materialized. Zhitlovski returned to America and threw himself into efforts there to start Yiddish supplementary schools and to restrain Jewish socialists from sacrificing their own Jewishness and the Jewish people as a whole on the altar of Americanization disguised as proletarian brotherhood. Perets did undertake one fund-raising trip to St. Petersburg where Shimen Dubnov (1860–1941), the distinguished historian and ideologist of cultural autonomy in the diaspora and himself a recent convert to the value of Yiddish, had convened a small group of wealthy but Russified potential donors. The latter greeted Perets with such cold cynicism that he 'told them off' ('our salvation will come from the poor but warm-hearted Jews of the Pale rather than from the rich but cold-hearted Jews of St.Petersburg') and 'slammed the door'. Thus, for various reasons, no office was ever really established in Tshernovits and even the minutes of the Conference remained unpublished (although S. A. Birnbaum helped prepare them for publication by editing out as many Germanisms as possible), and were soon misplaced or lost and had to be reconstructed more than two decades later from press clippings and memoirs (Anon., 1931).

Intellectuals (and even an intelligentsia) alone can rarely establish a movement. Intellectuals can reify language and react to it as a powerful symbol, as the bearer and actualizer of cultural values, behaviors, traditions, goals. However, for an L to spread into H functions more concrete considerations (jobs, funds, influence, status, control, power) are involved. Only the Yiddishist 'left' had in mind an economic, political and cultural revolution that would have placed Yiddish on top. But that 'left' did not even control the Tshernovits Conference, to say nothing of the hard, cruel world that surrounded it.

American reactions to the Tshernovits Conference

The increasingly democratic, culturally pluralistic and culturally autonomistic pre-war Austro-Hungarian Empire was the model toward which mankind was moving insofar as the leading figures at Tshernovits were concerned. One of the areas of Jewish concentration in which this was most clearly not the case — and where the very concept of a symbolically unified, modernized, worldwide Jewish nationality with a stable, all-purpose vernacular of its own was least understood, accepted and actualized — was the U.S.A. No wonder then that the Tshernovits Conference was generally accorded a cool reception here and even a derisive one.[18] The idea of teaching people how to spell or write or speak Yiddish 'correctly' was viewed by one journalist as being no less ridiculous than the idea of teaching people to laugh correctly, grammatically (Sambatyen, 'A falsher gelekhter, gor on gramatik', *Yidishes Tageblat*,[19] Sept. 1, 1908). The *Tageblat* was an Orthodox-oriented paper, and in its editorials before and after the conference it stressed that *loshn-koydesh* alone was of value for Jewishness while English (or other co-territorial vernaculars elsewhere) met all of the general and citizenship needs that Jews might have. To elevate Yiddish to H functions was not only ridiculous but blasphemous.

> 'If the resolutions of the conference declare ... that all Jewishness will be found in Ash's drama "God of Vengeance" and in Perets' "*Shtrayml*" ... will anyone care? Our people decided long ago that we are a nationality and that our national language is none other than that in which the spirit of the Jewish people developed ... the language in which the Bible is written, the Book that has made us immortal' (Sept. 20, 1908).

If the Orthodox-bourgeois *Tageblat* was unfriendly toward the Conference, to say the least, the secular-socialist *Forverts* (still publishing

to this very day and now in its 82nd year) was almost every bit as much
so. Its correspondent Moris Roznfeld (a famous Yiddish laborite-poet in
his own right) wrote from Galicia just a few days before the Conference
opened.

'I know that with just a few exceptions there is not much interest in
America in this Tshernovits Conference for many reasons. First of all,
most believe that nothing practical will come of it. Secondly, the
American Yiddish writer, as well as the Yiddish reader, is not terribly
interested in rules of grammar. What difference does it make whether
one writes

גײן ,גײהן

or

גאײן

[all pronounced geyn/gayn depending on speaker's regional dialect],

יוד ,ייד, איד

or even

יאהודי

[the first three pronounced id/yid and the last — utilized only
ironically/contrastively in Yiddish — Yahudi, and therefore not really
an orthographic variant in a continuum with the first three], as long
as it can be read and understood . . .? Among the majority of even
our good writers, Yiddish is regarded merely as a ferry that leads to
the other side, to the language of the land, which each of us must learn
in the land in which he finds himself.

But these views, objectively and impartially stated, apply only to
America. Here, in Galicia, they are more than merely grammatical
issues. Here it is a political issue, an issue of life itself . . .

. . . If it were to be officially decided that *loshn-koydesh* is the
Jewish language, then the Jewish masses would lose their power and
their vernacular would be ignored. Only the Jewish snobs, the
aristocratic, "let-them-eat-cake" idealists, would gain thereby. Therefore, the eyes of the real friends of the people and of the friends of
the workers in Galicia and even in Russia are turned toward
Tshernovits. Therefore the conference there has major, historical
importance. I don't know from what point of view the Conference will

treat the language issue ... The Conference might even be of an academic, theoretical nature ... Nevertheless, the Conference will have strong reverberations on Jewish politics in Galicia.'

Note Roznfeld's total disinterest in either the linguistic portion or any possible American validity of the Tshernovits agenda. In 1908 few American Yiddish writers, few even among the secular laborites among them, aspired to H functions for Yiddish. In their eyes Jews, as workers, were destined to be part of the greater American proletariat, and English would, therefore be its language for higher socialist purposes and, ultimately, its brotherly interethnic vernacular as well. The Bund's 1905 Declaration and its positing of Jewish cultural autonomy in Eastern Europe, with Yiddish as the national language of the Jewish proletariat, was considered, at best, to be a politically relevant platform for Eastern European Jewry alone, but one that was irrelevant for those who had immigrated to 'the Golden Land'. Thus, if neither the linguistic nor the political potentialities of the Conference applied here then the Conference as a whole was merely a distant echo, and either a somewhat funny one or a clearly sacreligious one at that. If it was difficult to assign H functions to Yiddish in its very own massive heartland, where its stability was less threatened (so it seemed) and where all agreed as to its utility, how much more difficult was it to do so in immigrant-America where its transitionality was assumed by secularists and traditionalists alike? If the brunt of American commentary on the Conference was negative, that in Eastern Europe was initially equally or even more so, and on three grounds. As expected, the Hebraist and extreme-Zionist reaction was unrelentingly hostile. In their eyes Yiddish was a language that demoted Jewry from its incomparable classical heights to the superficiality and vacuousness of such illiterate peasant tongues as Ukranian, Lithuanian, Rumanian, etc. To foster Yiddish struck J. Klausner, Z. Epshteyn and many other Hebraists as being laughable, if it were not so sad; an exercise in self-impoverishment and self-debasement. A considerable number of those who shared their view urged that a massive counter-conference be convened (and, indeed, the First World Conference for the Hebrew Language *was* convened in Berlin in 1910) and that an even more massive propaganda campaign be launched to attack Tshernovits and its infamous resolution. However the veteran Hebraist and philosopher Ahad Ha-'am (1856–1927) argued vehemently against such efforts on the grounds that they would give Tshernovits more visibility than it could ever attain on its own. According to Ahad Ha-'am the Jewish people had already experienced two great philosophical disasters in the diaspora: Christianity and Hasidism.[20] Both of these had mushroomed precisely because Jews themselves had paid too much attention to them by dignifying them with unnecessary commentary. This sad lesson should now be applied to Tshernovits and to Yiddishism as a whole. They were *muktse makhmes miyes* (*mukze mehamat mius*), *loathsomely ugly*, and the less said about them the better.

If the right-wing opposition generally elected to counter Tshernovits with a wall of silence, the left-wing opposition apparently decided to drown it to death in a sea of words. From their point of view Tshernovits had been a 'sell-out' on the part of those who were willing to water down, render tepid and weaken the position *vis-à-vis* Yiddish of 'the broad folk-masses' and 'the Jewish proletariat', in order to curry favor among the bourgeosie via adopting an uninspired and uninspiring 'all Israel are brothers' approach. The modern, secular, socialist sector of the Jewish people, 'the revolutionary and nationality-building sector', had, by then, already surpassed the meager goals and the luke-warm resolutions of Tshernovits. They, therefore, refused to be compromised and whittled down by a conference that was 'an episode instead of a happening' (Kazhdan, 1928) and whose resolution was no more than 'a harmful illusion' (Zilberfarb, 1928) and 'a mistake that must not be reiterated' (Khmurner, 1928).

'The Tshernovits Conference was converted into the opposite of what its initiators had projected. Its isolation from the Jewish labor movement took its revenge upon the Conference ... The great masters of Yiddish literature did not possess the magic to convert the Jewish middle class and the bourgeois intellectuals into co-combatants and partners with the Jewish workers in the latter's greater national role of limitless loyalty to the Yiddish language. Yiddish cultural life therefore far surpassed the Tshernovits Conference ... Neither at the Teachers Conference in Vilna, nor at the organizational convention of the Central Yiddish School Organization (*Tsisho*), nor at the Tsisho Convention of 1925 where the founding of the Yivo [=Yiddish Scientific Institute; today: Yivo Institute for Jewish Research] was proclaimed, nor at any of the many other [Yiddish] teachers conferences in Poland was there even a word spoken about the Tshernovits Conference ... Today, 60 years after Tshernovits we know: Tshernovits was not destined to have any heirs ... There was really nothing to inherit' (Kazhdan, 1969).

Even now, over three decades after the Holocaust — when most commentators tend to wax lyrical about Jewish Eastern Europe and to remember it in somewhat rosy terms — there remain Bundist leaders who remember Tshernovits only as a flubbed opportunity.

Even those who were quite satisfied with Tshernovits in symbolic terms soon realized that it was a fiasco in any practical organizational terms. As soon as World War I was over (and, indeed, in the very midst of the War in anticipation of its conclusion) various Yiddish writers and cultural spokesmen began to call for 'a world conference for Yiddish culture as a result of purely practical rather than demonstrative and declarative goals. We have outgrown the period of mere demonstrations and theoretical debates. There is much work to be done!' (Sh. N[iger], 1922). Zhitlovski himself (1928) called for 'an organization to openly unfurl the flag on which it will be clearly written: Yiddish, our national language, our only unity and freedom ... a "Yiddishist" organization with the openly unfurled flag of our cultural liberation and national unity'. Others repeatedly reinforced and repeated this view (e.g. Lerer, 1928; Mark, 1968; Zelitsh, 1968). As a result, most subsequent major non-partisan or supra-partisan international efforts to organize Yiddish cultural efforts more effectively have viewed themselves as the in- strumental heirs of the Tshernovits Conference (e.g. YIKUF-yidisher kultur farband, 1937; Yidisher kultur kongres, 1948; Yerushelayemer velt konferents far Yidish un Yidisher kultur, 1976). Clearly, however, the realities facing Yiddish after World War I were far different than those that Tshernovits assumed. The multi-ethnic Austro-Hungarian Empire had been split into several smaller states, each jealously protective of its particular national (=state building) language and quick to set aside the Trianon and Versailles guarantees to Yiddish (Tenenboym, 1957–1958). The former Czarist 'pale of settlement' was either in the same situation as the foregoing (insofar as Poland and the Baltic states were concerned) or, ultimately, under even more powerful Russificatory control than before (in White Russia and in the Ukraine). Despite Bundist grievances, a good part of the spirit of Tshernovits lived for two post-war decades in the Yiddish schools, youth clubs, theaters and cultural organizations of Poland, Lithuania and Rumania and, despite Communist attacks, in their regulated counterparts in the U.S.S.R. However, by just prior to World War II the former were economically starved and politically battered (Eisenstein, 1949; Tartakover, 1946), whereas the latter were being discontinued under duress of Russification fears and pressures (Choseed, 1968). After World War II Jewish Eastern Europe was no more. It became incumbent on Yiddish devotees in the U.S.A. and in Israel, i.e. in two locales where Yiddish was originally not expected to benefit from the spirit of Tshernovits, to defend it if possible.

Re-evaluating the Tshernovits Conference: Shadow or substance

Notwithstanding Kazhdan's lingering negative evaluation in 1968, distance has made the heart grow fonder insofar as the majority of commentators is concerned. Those few who initially held that the symbolism of Tshernovits had been substantial, i.e. that it had raised Yiddish to the status of an honorific co-symbol, regardless of what its practical shortcomings might have been (for example, Mayzl, 1928; Prilutski, 1928; Pludermakher, 1928), finally carried the day. The views that are encountered today in Yiddishist circles are very much like those that began to be heard when the first commemorative celebrations in honor of Tshernovits were organized in 1928. (In September 1918 World War I had technically not yet ended and celebrations were presumably not possible). 'Yes Yiddishism is a young movement, but it is not at all that poor in traditions. One of the loveliest traditions of Yiddishism is the memory of the Tshernovits Conference. No memoirs, pedantry or arguments can darken the glow of that bright cultural dawn's early light that is known by the name: The Tshernovits Conference of 1908' (Pludermakher, 1928). Perhaps it was and perhaps it wasn't necessary to compromise in connection with the crucial resolution. In either case, no one was fooled by the compromise. 'The Tshernovits Conference was recorded on the morrow immediately after the last session as the Yiddishist revolt — and that is the only way in which the opponents of the Yiddish language *could regard* it' (Prilutski, 1928) for even to claim H *co*-functions *alongside* of Hebrew/*loshn-koydesh* was a devastating rejection of what these opponents were aiming at. As a result, Tshernovits deserved to be viewed as 'the first mobilization' (Mayzl, 1928) on behalf of Yiddish.

Seventy years after Tshernovits, Yiddishist opinion with respect to it is, if anything, even mellower. Living as they do with the constant if quiet anxiety produced by the continual attrition of Yiddish, Tshernovits has come to be viewed not merely as a milestone in the millenial struggle of Yiddish for symbolic recognition, but as symbolic of the best that Eastern Europe Jewry as a whole achieved and can offer to its far-flung progeny today. Tshernovits is viewed increasingly as a by-product of the confluence of the three organized movements in modern Jewish life: Jewish socialism, Zionism and neo-Orthodoxy. At Tshernovits representatives of all three recognized the significance of Yiddish. Tshernovits was the by-product of a confluence (and, therefore, it disappointed those who wanted it to be all theirs). It was a momentary confluence that quickly passed and from that day to this, no one has been able to 'put them together again'. Indeed, absence does make the heart grow fonder.

> 'They were three, the convenors of the Tshernovits Conference: the champion of Jewish cultural renaissance and consistent Zionist, Dovid Pinski. He came to the land (of Israel) in advanced old age and died here. Khayem Zhitlovski, one of the first Jewish socialists who, after countless reincarnations in search for a solution to the Jewish question, in his old age, sought to attach himself to the 'Jewish' Autonomous Region, Birobidjan. And Nathan Birnbaum, the ideologist of Zionism and nationalism, who, after various geographic and ideological wanderings, after various apostasies and conversions, finally reached the shores of Jewish eternity. He waited for the Messiah all his life and suffered terribly the pangs of His delayed coming . . . He sowed everywhere and others reaped. He gave up this world for the one to come. All three of them served the Jewish people, each in his own way, and as such they [and Tshernovits] will remain in our historical memory' (Roznhak, 1969).

Theoretical recapitulations

The late-nineteenth/early-twentieth century efforts to gain and activate intellectual and mass support for Yiddish, and the Tshernovits Conference of 1908 in particular, illustrate several of the problems encountered in a particular type of language spread: the spread of a former L into H functions in High Culture (education, literature, scholarship), government, technology and modern literacy-dependent pursuits more generally.

1. Many of those most active on behalf of advocating, rationalizing and ideologizing this type of language spread will, themselves, have to learn how to use the erstwhile L in H functions and, indeed, may have to learn the L *per se*. In this respect the spread of an L into H functions poses similar problems for those who are already literate (and who may, indeed, be the gate-keepers or guardians of literacy) as does the spread of any new vernacular into H functions. Nationalist language-spread movements that are not derived from an intragroup diglossia context (e.g. the promotion of Czech, Slovak, etc. in pre-World War I days or of Catalan, Occitan, Irish, Nynorsk, etc. more recently), also often begin with intelligentsias that do not know or master the vernaculars that they are championing. In the Yiddish case many intellectuals of the late-nineteenth century were not only *oriented* toward Hebrew/*loshn-koydesh* as H for Jewish cultural affairs but *also toward* either German, Russian or Polish as H for modern

purposes. Thus Ls existing within a traditional diglossia setting may face double opposition in seeking to attain H functions.

2. One set of factors hampering the spread of Ls into H functions is their own lack of codification (e.g. in orthography, grammar) and elaboration (in lexicon). However, there is a tension between such corpus planning, on the one hand, and status planning needs, on the other hand. It is difficult to turn to serious corpus planning while status planning is still so unsettled (or opposed), and it is difficult to succeed at status planning (particularly insofar as attracting ambivalent or negative intellectuals and literacy gate-keepers is concerned) on behalf of an L that is clearly deficient in terms of corpus characteristics that might render it more suitable for H functions.

3. The vicious cycle that exists between lack of corpus planning and lack of status planning is most decisively broken if a status shift can be forced (by legal reform, revolution or disciplined social example). The Tshernovits Conference's gravitation toward the 'political (status planning) issue' was a spontaneous recognition of this fact, so often pedantically overlooked by language technicians and 'experts' who are oriented toward the relatively easier corpus planning task alone.

4. The very same intragroup and intergroup status and power reward systems that previously lead intellectuals to seek/acquire literacy and position via one or more Hs subsequently hinder the spread of Ls into these H functions. Any such language spread would imply a major dislocation or a change in intellectual and econo-political élites and prerogatives. If Yiddish had achieved H intragroup functions in the cultural-intellectual realm this would have threatened rabbinic/traditional and modern Zionist/Hebraist hegemony in that sphere. In addition, the spread of Yiddish into H functions would not only have meant the displacement of one power/status élite by another but the popularization/massification/democratization of intragroup political participation and a de-emphasis on élitism as a whole. This, too, is similar to the dynamics and consequences of many modern nationalist advocacies of vernaculars except that the cultural-political opposition faced in the case of Yiddish may have been more variegated insofar as 'preferred' language is concerned, since not only Hebrew/*loshn-koydesh* but Russian, German and even Polish were its rivals for H functions throughout the Pale.

5. However, just as modern recognition of Ausbau languages (see footnote 2, below) derives more from their adoption for non-belletristic than for belletristic functions, so it is the spread into econo-political functions that is particularly crucial in this century if status planning for erstwhile Ls is

to succeed. In connection with Yiddish, only the Bundists seem to have glimpsed this truth before, at, or soon after Tshernovits (subsequently the Jewish Communists — many of them ex-Bundists — did so as well, but with quite different purposes and results), and even they spoke of Yiddish more commonly in terms of cultural autonomy. Ultimately, however, their design foresaw a socialist revolution: the complete displacement of religio-bourgeois econo-political control and the recognition of separate but interrelated/orchestrated culturally autonomous populations *each with control over its own immediate econo-technical apparatus*. Although the political representation of Yiddish-speaking Jews *as such* (i.e. as a nationality with its own national [mother] tongue) in the co-territorial parliaments was advocated also by some Labor Zionists, by minor Jewish parties such as the Folkists and the Sejmists and even by (some) ultra-Orthodox spokesmen (e.g. those of Agudas Yisroel), only the Bundists had a real economic realignment in mind with educational, political and cultural institutions deriving from and protected by firm Yiddish-speaking proletarian economic control.

6. The weak representation of Bundists at Tshernovits led to the complete neglect of the economic basis of Yiddish as either *a* or *the* Jewish national language and to a complete preoccupation with cultural ideology, cultural symbolism and cultural rhetoric. As a result there also arose the view that the Conference itself might be an ongoing moving force — either because it would have an executive office for 'cultural work' or because it simply had convened and sent forth its resolutions into the world. However, languages are neither saved nor spread by language conferences. Ideology, symbolism and rhetoric are of undeniable significance in language spread — they are consciously motivating, focusing and activating — but without a tangible and considerable status-power counterpart they become — under conditions of social change — competitively inoperative in the face of languages that do provide such. They may continue to be inspirational but — *particularly in modern times* — they cease to be decisive, i.e. they ultimately fail to safeguard even the intimacy of hearth and home from the turmoil of the econo-political arena. The ultimate failure of Tshernovits is that it did not even seek to foster or align itself with an econo-political reality that would seek to protect Yiddish in new H functions. The ultimate tragedy of Yiddish is that in the political reconsolidation of modern Eastern Europe its speakers were either too powerless or too mobile. They were the classical expendables of twentieth-century Europe and, obviously, no language conference or language movement *per se* could rectify their tragic dilemma. Unfortunately, few at Tshernovits were sufficiently attuned to broader econo-political realities

to recognize that. Instead of being en route to a new dawn for Yiddish they stood more basically before the dusk of the Central and Eastern European order of things as it had existed till then.

7. However, it is the delicate *interplay* between econo-political and ethno-cultural factors that must be grasped in order to understand both success and failure in language spread. Any attempt to pin all on one or another alone is more likely to be doctrinaire than accurate. The Yiddish case, because it involves a diglossia situation and multiple possibilities for both L and H functions in the future, is particularly valuable because it makes the co-presence of both sets of factors so crystal clear. Econo-political factors alone are insufficient to appreciate the internal rivalry from *loshn-koydesh*/Hebrew and the fact that the latter was undergoing its own vernacularization and modernization at the very same time that Yiddish was being championed for H functions. On the other hand, no amount of internal ethno-cultural insight can explain the allure that German and Russian (and, to a smaller degree, Polish) had for the Jewish bourgeoisie and intelligentsia. Finally, as a capstone to what is already an insuperable burden of opposition, there comes the linguistic relationship between Yiddish and German — the extra burden of all weak Ausbau[21] languages — and the cruel compound of moral, esthetic and intellectual caricature and self-hatred to which that lent itself. After being exposed to such an array of internal and external overkill for well over a century, is it any wonder that the 1978 Nobel Prize for literature awarded to the Yiddish writer I. B. Singer often elicits only a wry smile in what remains of the world of Yiddish.[22,23]

Notes to Chapter 19

1. Prepared originally for presentation at the Ford Foundation and Center for Applied Linguistics sponsored Conference on Language Spread, University of Aberstwyth, Wales, September 12–14, 1978, and revised for publication in the conference proceedings *Language Spread: Studies in Diffusion and Social Change*, Robert L. Cooper, ed., published in 1980 by the Center for Applied Linguistics, Arlington, Virginia and simultaneously, in *Never Say Die! A Thousand Years of Yiddish in Jewish Life and Letters* (Fishman 1980). Preparation of this study was supported by a grant from the Memorial Foundation for Jewish Culture, New York City.
2. The traditional co-existence of a non-vernacular language of high culture (H) and a vernacular of everyday life (L), the former being learned through formal study and the latter in the context of familial intimacy, was dubbed *diglossia* by Ferguson (1959): 325–40). Such contexts and their similarity and dis-similarity *vis-à-vis* other multilingual and multidialectal contexts have been

examined by several investigators, among them Gumperz (1964: 137–53) and in Fishman (1967: 29–38).

3. Throughout this paper the distinction will be adhered to between the traditional amalgam of Hebrew and Aramaic, referred to by Yiddish speakers as *loshn-koydesh* [Language of Holiness] and Modern Hebrew, as developed in Palestine/Israel during the past century as a language of all of the functions required by a modern econo-political establishment. Where the distinction between Hebrew and *loshn-koydesh* is not clear or is not intended they will be referred to jointly.

4. For a full treatment of each of these four substantively distinct but also interacting views of Yiddish, see Fishman (1980).

5. Halachic, an adjective derived from halaha (Yiddish: *halokhe*), refers to the entire body of Jewish law (Biblical, Talmudic and post-Talmudic) and subsequent legal codes amending, modifying or interpreting traditional precepts under rabbinic authority.

6. Maskilic, adjective derived from *haskala* (Yiddish: *haskole*), an eighteenth-nineteenth-century movement among Central and Eastern European Jews, associated in Germany with the leadership of Moses Mendelssohn (1729–1786), designed to make Jews and Judaism more modern and cosmopolitan in character by promoting knowledge of and contributions to the secular arts and sciences and by encouraging adoption of the dress, customs, economic practices, educational programs, political processes and languages of the dominant non-Jewish co-territorial populations. For observations as to differences between the haskole in central and eastern Europe, see Fishman (1980).

7. Both Zionists and socialists increasingly shifted from the second to the third positive view at or around the turn of the century. In 1889 the Zionist leader Sokolov defended Yiddish merely as a necessary vehicle of mass agitation and propaganda (Roznhak, 1969), and even Herzl, who knew no Yiddish, founded a weekly (*Di velt*) in 1900 in order to reach the Eastern European masses. Similarly, socialist spokesmen such as Arkadi Kremer merely advocated the use of Yiddish in order to attain their mass educational purposes in 1893 and organized *zhargonishe komitetn* (Yiddish-speaking committees) in order to foster literacy and to spread socialist publications among Jews in the Czarist Empire. Soon, however, a new (the third) tune began to be heard. In 1902 the Zionist editor Lurye (co-editor with Ravnitski of the well known periodical *Der yid*) wrote that Yiddish must not only be considered as a means of propaganda but as 'a national-cultural possession which must be deveoped to play the role of our second national language' (Roznhak, 1969). In 1905 the Bund adopted its declaration on behalf of Jewish national–cultural autonomy with Yiddish as the language of the Jewish proletariat and of the intellectuals that serve and lead that proletariat. Scholarly literary organizations in the field of Yiddish began to arise soon thereafter: (a) 1908, The Yiddish Literary Organization (St. Petersburg), (b) 1909, The Yiddish Historical-Ethnographic Organization (St. Petersburg), (c) 1908, The Musical-Dramatic Organization (Vilna).

8. The Yiddish advocacy of Nathan Birnbaum (Birnbaum being a major protagonist of the latter half of this paper) deserves special mention and, indeed, further investigation in connection with the topic of re-ethnification of élites. Such re-ethnification and accompanying re-linguification is a

common process in the early stages of very many modern ethnicity movements (see Fishman, 1972) and exemplifies both the proto-élitist return to (or selection of) roots (often after failure to transethnify 'upwardly' in accord with earlier aspirations), as well as the masses' groping toward mobilization under exemplary leadership. However, modern ethnicity movements are essentially attempts to achieve *modernization*, utilizing 'primordial' identificational metaphors and emotional attachments for this purpose. Thus, they are not really 'return' movements (not really nativization or past-oriented). They exploit or mine the past rather than cleave to it. Partially transethnified élites can uniquely serve such movements because of their own double exposure. Birnbaum is therefore exceptional in that he ultimately rejected this secularized, Germanized, Europeanized milieu on behalf of a 'genuine return' to relatively unmodernized Orthodoxy. By the second decade of this century he had rejected Jewish modernization (in the guise of socialism, Zionism and diaspora nationalism, all of which he had once charted) as hedonistic and as endangering Jewish (and possibly world) survival. There is about the late Birnbaum a Spenglerian aura foretelling the 'decline of the West' and cautioning Jews that their salvation (and the world's) would come only via complete immersion in traditional beliefs, values and practices (Birnbaum, 1918: 1946). He viewed Yiddish as a *sine qua non* in that connection, rejecting its use for modern, hedonistic purposes such as those which he himself had earlier espoused, both immediately before and after the Tshernovits Language Conference of 1908. This rare combination of complete Orthodoxy and uncompromising defense of Yiddish within an Orthodox framework have made Nathan Birnbaum into something of a curiosity for both religious and secular commentators. Such *genuine returners* to roots also exist in the context of other modernization movements (for example, in the nineteenth- and twentieth-century Greek, Arabic, Slavophile and Sanscrit contexts) and represent a vastly overlooked sub-class within the study of ethnicity movements. Even in their case it would be mistaken to consider them as no more than 'spokes in the wheels of progress' merely because they frequently represent an attempt to attain modernization without Westernization. A contrastive study of Birnbaum and other such 'genuine returners' would be most valuable for understanding this sub-class as well as the more major group of 'metaphorical returners'. Note, however, that Birnbaum remained a committed advocate of Yiddish (although not in any functions that would replace *loshn koydesh*) even when he embraced ultra-Orthodoxy, whereas 'true returners' in other cases embraced their respective indigenized classic tongues. To revive Hebrew was long considered anti-traditional and was not possible except in speech networks that were completely outside of the traditional framework — ideologically, behaviorally (in terms of daily routine) and even geographically. The dubious Jewish asset of complete dislocation and deracination was denied the unsuccessful advocates of Sanscrit and classical Greek, Arabic or Irish.

    For a more detailed examination of Nathan Birnbaum's life and thought see Fishman (1987).

9.   Tshernovits is currently located in the Moldavian SSR. Between the two World Wars it was in Rumania. At the time of the Language Conference, and ever since the Austrian occupations in 1774 (after defeating the Ottoman Turkish occupants), it was in a section of the Austro–Hungarian Empire

known as Bukovina (until 1848 administratively a part of Galicia with which Bukovina remained closely connected as far as 'Jewish geography' was concerned).

10. Territorialism acknowledged the need for planned Jewish resettlement in an internationally recognized and protected Jewish territory, but did not consider Palestine to be the only or the most desirable location for such resettlement in view of the conflicted claims and geopolitical perils associated with it. Various territorial concentrations in Eastern Europe itself, in Africa (Angola, Cirenaica, Uganda), in South America (Surinam), in North America (Kansas-Nebraska), in Australia (Kimberly Region) and elsewhere have been advocated since the latter part of the nineteenth century. At one point Herzl himself was not convinced that a homeland in Palestine and only in Palestine should be adamantly pursued and was willing to consider a 'way-station' elsewhere. Most territorialists split with the Zionist movement and set up an organization of their own in 1905, when the Seventh Zionist Congress rejected an offer by the British government to create an autonomous Jewish settlement in Uganda.

11. Corpus planning is one of the two major branches of language planning: the authoritative allocation of resources (attention, funds, manpower, negative and positive sanctions) to language. Corpus planning entails modifying, enriching or standardizing the language *per se*, often via publishing and implementing orthographies, nomenclatures, spellers, grammars, style manuals, etc. Its counterpart is status planning, i.e. attempts to require use of a language for particular functions: education, law, government, mass media, etc. Corpus planning is frequently engaged in by language academies, commissions or boards. Status planning requires governmental or other power-related decision-making and sanctions-disbursing bodies: political religious, ethno-cultural or economic. The two processes must be conducted in concert if they are to succeed and take hold across a broad spectrum of uses and users. Yiddish has constantly suffered due to deficiencies in the status-planning realm and, as a result, its corpus-planning successes are also limited, although several can be cited (Shekhter, 1961). For a detailed empirical and theoretical review of language planning, see Rubin *et al.* (1978).

12. Vays reminisces as follows (1937, i.e. 30 years after the Conference): 'As is well known, Yiddish was not recognized in Austria as a language, just as the Jewish people was not recognized as such. At the university, e.g. it was necessary to fill out a rubric "nationality" and no Jew was permitted to write in "Jew". The nationalist-oriented Jewish students, not wanting to cripple the statistical distribution in favor of the ruling nationality to the detriment of the minority nationalist-oriented Jewish students, sought various ways of forcing the authorities to recognise the Jewish nationality. Some wrote the name of a nationality that happened to occur to them. There was no lack of entries of "Hottentot" mother tongue and "Malay" nationality'. This context for the Conference led the Yiddish *Sotsyal demokrat* of Cracow to greet the Conference as follows: 'The significance of the Conference is augmented by the fact that it takes place in Austria where Yiddish is closest to official recognition' (Kisman, 1958). Tshernovits itself also impressed the delegates and guests from abroad (primarily from the Czarist Empire) not only with its ethnic heterogeneity but with its 'air of relative democracy, where at every step one could feel European culture' (Kisman, 1958).

For Eastern European Jewry the late-nineteenth-early-twentieth century Austro-Hungarian Empire represented Western-style democracy plus nationality-cultural rights, both of which were still sadly lacking in the Czarist Empire and both of which were foundational to the Conference's goals, although neither was explicitly referred to at the Conference itself.

13. The Bund (full name: Jewish Workers Bund [= Alliance] of Russia, Lithuania and Poland) was organized in Vilna in 1897, the same year as the first Zionist Congress was held in Basel. Always socialist, it adopted a Jewish cultural-autonomist, Yiddish-oriented platform in 1905, as a result of which it clashed with Lenin, Trotsky and other early Bolshevik leaders. The Bund became the mainstay of secular Yiddish educational, literary and cultural efforts in interwar Poland. For further details and entrée to a huge bibliography, see Mendelsohn (1970) and Kligsberg (1974).

14. The 'esthetic point of view' is dealt with at length by Miron (1973). Although not unknown in connection with other supposedly inelegant vernaculars during the period of struggle to legitimize them for H functions, the vituperation heaped upon Yiddish in terms of its claimed esthetic shortcomings clearly seems to border on the hysterical. Loathsome, ugly, stunted, crippled, mangled, hunchbacked, gibberish were commonplace. 'Away with dirt, with spiderwebs, with *zhargon* and with all kinds of garbage! We call for a broom! And whom the broom of satire will not help, him will we honor with the sticks of wrath! Quem medicamenta non sanant, ferrum et ignis sanant!' (*Jutrzenka*, 1862, no. 50: 428). Note, however, that the esthetic metaphor (e.g. the German Jewish historian Graetz refused to 'dirty his pen' with Yiddish or to have his works translated into that 'foul tongue'), interesting though it may be in and of itself, must not obscure from analysis more basic social, cultural and political goals and loyalties of those that express them. The Yiddish proverb *nisht dos is lib vos iz sheyn, nor dos is sheyn vos iz lib* (We do not love that which is lovely, rather we consider lovely that which we love) applies fully here. By the time of Tshernovits the full force of invective had begun to pass (although it can be encountered in Israel and elsewhere to this very day, see, e.g. Fishman & Fishman, 1978) and the countertide of positive hyperbole had begun to rise, assigning to Yiddish not only beauty but virtue, subtlety, honesty, compassion, intimacy and boundless depth.

15. While it is certainly inaccurate to consider Mizes' comments as 'the first scientific paper in Yiddish on Yiddish', it is not easy to say whose work does deserve to be so characterized, primarily because of changing standards as to what is and is not scientific. One of my favorites is Y. M. Lifshits', *Yidish-rusisher verter bikh* [Yiddish-Russian Dictionary] (Zhitomir, Bakst) and his introduction thereto, both of which remain quite admirable pieces of scholarship to this very day. Other candidates for this honorific status abound, several of considerably earlier vintage.

16. Somewhat positive Zionist stances toward exilic Jewish vernaculars had surfaced from time to time well before Tshernovits. Reference is made here not merely to utilizing such vernaculars for immediate educational/indoctrinational purposes, such usage being acceptable to almost the entire Zionist spectrum, but to allocating intimacy-related and even literacy-related functions to them, both in the diaspora and (even) in Erets Yisroel on a relatively permanent basis. Herzl himself (in his *Diary* 1885), suggests a parallel with Switzerland, such that Hebrew, Yiddish and Judesmo [=

Judeo-Spanish] would be recognized. Except in Labor Zionist circles such views were very much in the minority and remained little developed or concretized but yet provided the basis for claims at Tshernovits that since many Zionists/Hebraists had been careful not to reject Yiddish, so Socialists/Yiddishists should do nothing to reject Hebrew/*loshn-koydesh*.

17. Interestingly enough, the Balfour Declaration, issued by the British government on November 2, 1917, favoring 'the establishment in Palestine of a national home for the Jews, but without prejudice to the civil and religious rights of existing non-Jewish communities' also used the *in*definite (a) rather than the definite article (the) as a compromise between opposite extreme views in the Foreign Ministry.

18. Several of the references and citations in this section are originally found in Rothstein, 1977.

19. Just as Yiddish books commonly carried *loshn-koydesh* titles until rather late in the nineteenth century, so Yiddish periodicals commonly bore either *loshn-koydesh* or German titles even into the present century. The diglossic implications are manifold even at an unconscious level. The people of 'The Book' was (and in the more unreconstructed Orthodox circles still is), accustomed to encounter serious H-level writing (and particularly such on intragroup concerns) in *loshn-koydesh*. Thus, a Hebrew title for a Yiddish book is, in part, a visual habit, in part a cultural signal and in part a disguise (*vis-à-vis* rabbinic criticism and other possibly hostile authorities). Similarly, a relatively ephemeral periodical dealing with the wide world of modern secular events is entitled in German for much the same reasons. Neither *forverts* nor *yidishes* nor *tageblat* were parts of commonly spoken Eastern European Yiddish by well before the nineteenth century. Nevertheless these were perfectly acceptable components of a journalistic title of those times, particularly in the U.S.A.

20. Hasidism: a Jewish movement founded in Poland in the eighteenth century by Rabbi Israel Baal Shem Tov and characterized by its emphasis on mysticism, spontaneous prayer, religious zeal and joy. The various hasidic leaders or masters (singular: *rébi*, plural: *rebéyim*, as distinguished from *rov*, *rabonim* among non-Hasidim typically instructed their followers via tales. Yiddish was, therefore, their crucial medium, and their tales became an early major component of popular Yiddish publishing (many also being published — first, simultaneously or soon thereafter — in *loshn-koydesh*). Although much opposed by most rabbinic authorities for almost two centuries (the latter and their followers being dubbed *misnagdim*, i.e. opponents), hasidism finally became generally accepted as a co-valid version of Jewish orthodoxy and is a vibrant (and the more numerous) branch thereof, as well as a major (but largely unideologized) source of support for Yiddish, to this day.

21. Ausbau languages are those that are so similar in grammar and lexicon to other, stronger, previously recognized languages that their language authorities often attempt to maximize the differences between themselves and their Big Brothers by multiplying or magnifying them through adopting or creating distinctive paradigms for neologisms, word order and grammar, particularly in their written forms. Thus Ausbau languages are 'languages by effort', i.e. they are consciously built away from (= ausbau) other, more powerful and basically similar languages so as not to be considered 'mere dialects' of the latter, but rather, to be viewed as obviously distinctive

languages in their own right. The Ausbau process is responsible for much of the difference between (Landsmal) Nynorsk and Bokmal, Hindi and Urdu, Macedonian and Bulgarian, Moldavian and Rumanian, Byelo-Russian and Russian. For the particular difficulties faced in finding, creating and maintaining Ausbau differences, including examples from the Yiddish vs. German arena, see Wexler (1974). The original formulator of the term Ausbau (and of its contrast: Abstand) is Kloss (1967).

22. Some additional useful secondary sources concerning the Tshernovits Language Conference are Goldsmith (1977), Passow (1971), and Lerner (1957). A literally endless list of other journal articles (pre-1928 and primarily post-1928, this being the date of the Yivo's twentieth anniversary volume (Anon. 1931) remains to be exhaustively catalogued.

23. For their helpful criticism of an earlier draft of this paper I am indebted to Robert L. Cooper, David E. Fishman and, most especially S. A. Birnboym. I alone assume responsibility for any errors of fact or interpretation that still remain and hope to correct them in future studies of the Tshernovits Conferents, of Nathan Birnbaum and of other issues in the late functional and structural modernization of Yiddish.

References

ANON. 1931, *Di ershte yidishe shprakh-konferents* [The First Yiddish Language Conference]. Vilna: Yiddish Scientific Institute — Yivo.

BIRNBAUM, N. 1908, Di konferents far der yidisher shprakh; efenungs rede, *Dokter Birnboyms vokhnblat*, 1 [1]:3–7. Reprinted in Anon 1931, 3–4, *Di ershte yidishe shprakh-konferents* [The First Yiddish Language Conference]. Vilna, Yiddish Scientific Institute — Yivo. Also reprinted 1968, Afn shvel 4 (185):3–4.

— 1918, *Gottes volk*. Vienna: Löwit.

— 1946, *Selections from His Writings*. London: Hamagid.

CHOSEED, B. 1968, Reflections of the Soviet nationalities policy in literature: The Jews, 1938–1948. Ph.D. dissertation, Columbia University. (University Microfilms, no. 69–15, 665.)

E[ste]r [Ester Frumkin] 1908, Di ershte yidishe shprakh konferents [The First Yiddish Language Conference]. *Di naye tsayt* 4:89–104.

EISENSTEIN, M. 1949, *Jewish Schools in Poland, 1919–1939*. New York: King's Crown.

FERGUSON, C. A. 1959, *Word* 15:325–40.

FISHMAN, D. E. 1980, Di dray penemer fun yehoshue mordkhe lifshits [The three faces of Yehoshue Mordkhe Lifshits]. *Yidishe shprakh* 38.

FISHMAN, J. A. 1967, Bilingualism with and without diglossia: Diglossia with and without bilingualism. *Journal of Social Issues* 23(2).

— 1972, *Language and Nationalism*. Rowley: Newbury House.

— 1973, The phenomenological and linguistic pilgrimage of Yiddish: Some examples of functional and structural pidginizaton and depidginization. *Kansas Journal of Sociology* 9:127–36.

— 1976, Yiddish and *loshn koydesh* in traditional ashkenaz: the problem of societal allocation of macro-functions. In A. VERDOOST & R. L. KJOLSETH (eds), *Language in Sociology*. Louvain: Peeters, 39–74.

— 1980, The sociology of Yiddish: a foreword. In J. A. FISHMAN (ed.), *Never Say Die! A Thousand Years of Yiddish in Jewish Life and Letters*. The Hague: Mouton.

— 1987, *Ideology, Society and Language: The Odyssey of Nathan Birnbaum*. Ann Arbor: Karoma.

FISHMAN, J. A., & FISHMAN, D. E. 1978, Yiddish in Israel: a case study of efforts to revise a monocentric language policy. In J. A. FISHMAN (ed.), *Advances in the Study of Societal Multilingualism*. The Hague: Mouton, 185–262.

GOLDSMITH, E. S. 1976, *Architects of Yiddishism*. Rutherford: Fairleigh Dickenson. (See particularly the chapters on Birnboym, Perets, Zhitlovski and the Tshernovits Conference *per se*.)

GUMPERZ, J. J. 1964, Linguistic and social interaction in two communities. *American Anthropologist* 66 (6) part 2.

KAZHDAN, Kh. Sh. 1928, An epizod anshtot a gesheyenish (20 yor nokh der tshernovitser konferents) [An episode instead of an event (20 years after the Tshernovits Conference)]. *Undzer tsayt* 7:73–77.

— 1969, Tshernovits — Kholem un vor [Tshernovits: dream and reality]. *Undzer tsayt* January: 17–21.

KHMURNER, Y. 1928, Vegn a feler vos khazert zikh iber [About an error that is being repeated]. *Bikhervelt* 7:1–6.

KISMAN, Y. 1958, Tsum fuftsikstn yoyvl: di tshernovitser shprakh-konferents [On the fiftieth anniversary: The Tshernovits Language Conference). *Undzer tsayt* July/August: 8–13.

KLIGSBERG, M. 1974, Di yidishe yugnt-bavegung in poyln tsvishn beyde velt-milkhomes (a sotsyologishe shtudye) [The Jewish Youth movement in Poland between both World Wars (a sociological study)]. In J. A. FISHMAN (ed.), *Shtudyes vegn yidn in poyln* 1919–1939. New York: Yivo Institute for Jewish Research, 137–228.

KLOSS, H. 1967, 'Abstand languages' and 'Ausbau languages'. *Anthropological Linguistics* 9 (7) 29–41.

LERER, L. 1928, Tsayt tsu shafn a kultur-gezelshaft [Time to organize a culture society]. *Literarishe bleter* 26:500-501, 509.

LERNER, H. J. 1957, The Tshernovits Language Conference: a milestone in Jewish nationalist thought. Master's Thesis, Columbia University.

LIFSHITS, Y. M. 1863, Di fir klasn [The four classes]. *Kol mevaser*

21:323–28 and 23: 364–66. (Also see the editor's [Alexander Tsederboym's] comments: 375–80 and 392–93.)

— 1867, Di daytsh-yidishe brik [The German-Jewish bridge]. *Kol mevaser* 5 (31):239–241. (See nos. 32, 33, 34, 35 and 41 or subsequent comments.)

MARK, Y. 1968. 60 yor nokh der shprakh-konferents in tshernovits [60 years after the language conference in Tshernovits]. *Forverts* August 25, Section 2: 11–15.

MAYZL, N. 1928, Di ershte mobilizatsye [The first mobilization]. *Literarishe bleter* 35:681.

MENDELSOHN, E. 1970, *Class Struggle in the Pale*. Cambridge, Mass.: Harvard University Press.

MIRON, D. 1973, A language as Caliban. *A Traveller Disguised*. New York: Schocken, 34–66.

N[iger], Sh. 1922, A yidisher kultur kongres [A Congress for Yiddish culture]. *Dos naye lebn* 1 (2):1–4.

PASSOW, D. 1971, The first Yiddish language conference. In I. D. PASSOW & S. T. LACHS (eds), *Gratz College Anniversary Volume*. Philadelphia: Gratz College.

PINSKI, D. 1948, Geburt fun der tshernovitser konferents; a bletl zikh-roynes [Birth of the Tshernovits Conference; a page of memories]. *Tsukunft* Sept.: 499–501.

PLUDERMAKHER, G. 1928, Di tshernovitser konferents un di ufgabn fun itstikn moment [The Tshernovits Conference and the current task]. *Literarishe bleter* 40:777–78.

PRILUTSKI, N. 1928, Nokh di tshernovitser fayerungen [after the Tshernovits celebrations]. *Literarishe bleter* 4:797–99.

ROTHSTEIN, J. 1977, Reactions of the American Yiddish press to the Tshernovits Language Conference of 1908 as a reflection of the American Jewish Experience. *International Journal of the Sociology of Language* 13:103–20.

ROZNBOYM, M. M. 1929, Zhitlovski-bibliografiye. In Y. N. SHTEYNBERG & Y. RUBIN (eds), *Zhitovski zamlbukh*. Warsaw: Bzozhe, 461–79.

ROZNHAK, SH. 1969, Hebreyish-yidish (bamerkungen tsu un arum der tshernovitser shprakh-konferents) [Hebrew-Yiddish (comments on and about the Tshernovits Language Conference)]. *Goldene keyt* 66: 152–69.

RUBIN, J. *et al.* 1978, *Language Planning Processes*. The Hague: Mouton.

SHEKHTER, M .1961, Mir shteyen nit af an ort [We are not standing still]. *Yiddish*. New York: Congress for Jewish Culture. 351–63.

TARTAKOVER, A. 1946, Di yidishe kultur in poyln tsvishn tsvey velt-milkhomes [Jewish culture in Poland between two World Wars].

Gedank un lebn 4(1): 1–35.

TENENBOYM, Y. 1957–1958, Di yidishe shprakh af der tog-ordenung fun der sholem-konferents in pariz, 1919 [The Yiddish language on the agenda of the peace conference in Paris, 1919]. *Yivo-bleter* 41:217–29.

VAYS (Slonim), SH. 1937, Oys di tsaytn fun der tshernovitser konferents [From the times of the Tshernovits Conference]. *Fun noentn over* 1:57–63.

WEXLER, P. 1974, *Purism and Language*. Bloomington: Indiana University Language Science Monographs.

ZELITSH, Y. 1968, A tsveyte konferents far der yidisher shprakh — 60 yor nokh tshernovits [A second conference for the Yiddish language — 60 years after Tshernovits]. *Afn shvel* 185 (4):2–3.

ZHITLOVSKI, KH. 1928, Tshernovits un der yidishizm: tsu dem tsvantsik yorikn yoyvl-yontev fun der tshernovitser konferents [Tshernovits and Yiddishism: In honor of the twentieth anniversary celebration of the Tshernovits Conference]. *Tsukunft* December: 735–37.

ZILBERFARB, M. A. 1928, A shedlikhe iluzye [A harmful illusion]. *Bikhervelt* 8:38–43.

20 Ethnic activists view the ethnic revival and its language consequences*[1]

Introduction

According to 1979 census figures for the United States as a whole, nearly 38 million individuals out of a total population of 217 million (i.e. roughly 17% of the population) claimed a language other than English as their mother tongue. This figure is proportionately higher than its counterpart in various decades prior to 1970. An 'ethnic revival' of similar or greater dimensions has been documented throughout much of Western Europe in the mid-sixties and early seventies (Allardt, 1979; Beer, 1980). In the United States, a somewhat similar phenomenon made itself felt by giving rise to an increased awareness of 'roots' in many ethnic groups (Novak, 1973). How this awareness is manifested and explicated by several samples of ethnic 'activists' is the subject of this paper.

We have chosen to interview a cross-section of organizationally or otherwise communally active respondents from three different language groups whose communities are located in five different areas of the country. We will refer to them all as 'activists'; although they differed appreciably in their views, behaviors and actual involvements in ethnolinguistic maintenance. The nature of these differences *between* them (between groups) and *among* them (within groups) constitutes the focus of this report. We interviewed French 'activists' in Louisiana and in New England; Spanish 'activists' in California, Florida and New York City; and Yiddish 'activists' also in New York City. The interviewees were selected (with the help of local site-coordinators) to represent a wide variety of

*Originally published (co-authored with Esther G. Lowy, Michael H. Gertner, Itzek Gottesman & William G. Milan) in *Journal of Multilingual and Multicultural Development*, 4:236–69.

backgrounds, occupations, educational levels, knowledge and use of their 'ethnic' mother tongue (hereinafter EMT), age, birthplace and interpretation of the ethnic heritage itself. The interviews were conducted in both languages wherever possible, the extent of the use of the EMT depending on the ease and competence of the person being interviewed. Linguistic analyses of the English and EMT usage of the respondents are planned for future publication.

Five general areas of interest were explored via our interviews: (i) the ethnic revival, (ii) EMT maintenance, (iii) domains for use of EMT and/or English, (iv) stability or change in the EMT itself, and (v) hopes and expectations for the future of the EMT in the United States.

Site selection

Since not all Franco-Americans come from the same country of origin or live under the same sociohistoric contextual circumstances, two sites as maximally different as possible were picked for our interviews: (a) Lafayette, Louisiana and the surrounding area in the heart of Acadiana, where the French speakers are divided among *Cajuns* and *Creoles* (Allain, 1978; Hallowell, 1979; Rushton, 1979; Thibodeaux, 1977; Waddell, 1979) and (b) Nashua, New Hampshire, a centrally located 'Franco-Canadian' community, permitting the researcher also to collect data in nearby Lowell, Massachusetts and Manchester, New Hampshire, as well. Both of the latter towns and the surrounding countryside were centers of the textile industry where many French-Canadians came to work and settled at the beginning of the century (Hendrickson, 1980).

The Hispanic population is by far the largest non-English-speaking group in the United States today and since Spanish speakers come from a variety of different countries of origin, we chose three widely separated sites, corresponding to three major Hispanic cultures. Chicanos ('Mexican-Americans') were interviewed in Los Angeles, California (Metcalf, 1974; Thompson, 1974), Cuban-Americans in Miami, Florida (Argüelles & MacEoin, 1980; Solé, 1979, 1982) and Puerto Ricans in New York City (Wolfram, 1973; Zentella, 1981).

The greatest concentration of Yiddish speakers in the United States is in New York City. Therefore, that city was chosen as the site for interviews in Yiddish (Fishman, 1965).

Sample selection

We attempted to interview between 20 and 30 individuals at each site. Restrictions of funding, time and availability, both of the subjects and researchers, account for the slightly varying numbers of individuals actually interviewed in each group. All in all, 142 interviews were conducted, 23 with Franco-Americans in Louisiana (Fr1), 21 with Franco-Americans in New England (Fr2), 22 with Chicanos in California (Sp1), 22 with Cuban-Americans in Miami (Sp2), 24 with Puerto Ricans in New York (Sp3) and 30 with Yiddish speakers in New York (Y).

The interviews

The interviews were conducted, whenever feasible, in both languages, suited to the ability and ease of the person being interviewed. A conversational pattern was established, geared to the interests and background of the speaker, and directed around five general topic areas grouped approximately according to the questions listed, but not necessarily in that order (depending on the natural flow of respondent interest).

I. Ethnic revival

1. Was there an ethnic boom?
2. Did it increase *respondent's* EMT use?
3. Did it improve *respondent's* attitudes toward EMT?
4. Did it renew *respondent's* customs of culture?
5. Did it increase EMT use in the *community*?
6. Did it improve attitudes toward EMT in the *community*?
7. Did it renew customs of culture in the *community*?
8. What caused revival?   INTERNAL FORCES?
9.   local group?
10.   local person?
11.   national group?
12.   national figure?
13. What caused revival?   EXTERNAL FORCES?
14.   govenment funded programs?
15.   other ethnic movement?
16.   legislation? (bilingual education, voting rights,
                            civil rights, fair employment practices, etc.)
17.   other?

II. EMT maintenance

18. Can your group maintain its ethnicity without EMT?
19. Would it be a LOSS if group ceased to be separate?
20. Is there a GAIN from separateness?
21. Are there more important problems than EMT maintenance?
22. Do you know other people who feel this way?
23. Has another group been more successful in EMT/ethnic maintenance?
24. Do you know why?
25. Can it be copied?

III. Domains of EMT/English use

26. Are there domains for ENGLISH?
27. Are there domains for ENGLISH *WITHIN* ethnic community?
28. Are there domains for EMT?

IV. Stability or change in the EMT

29. Has EMT changed recently?
30. Has it improved?
31. Has GRAMMAR improved?
32. Has PURITY improved?
33. Is change related to boom?
34. Should change be counteracted?
35. Do changes inhibit communication?
36. Should there be a standard?
37. Value-judgements on variety?

V. The future of EMT in the United States

38. Exclusively EMT?
39. Equality of EMT and English?
40. Positive EMT attitude among ethnics?
41. Positive EMT attitude by outsiders?
42. Linguistic assimilation?

The conversations were taped with the agreement of the subjects so that the interviewers took very few notes and were able to create a freer atmosphere of informal conversation. Our hope was to elicit natural speech patterns in the EMT rather than the formality of the standard language.

The interviews were conducted by three different researchers, a native Spanish speaker, a native Yiddish speaker, a native French speaker fluent also in Spanish and Yiddish. All three were fully bilingual and able to switch back and forth between English and the EMT in accord with interviewee preference and facility.

The analysis

Responses were coded on a 'yes/no/don't know' basis, for the purpose of *this* report. However, since the interviews were invariably in the form of conversations, statements and replies were usually qualified or explained. Such qualifications were noted while 'scoring' the tapes for the purpose of the report and form the source of all descriptive comments cited below.

General attitudes and expectations

Do activists believe that there was an ethnic boom? If so, did it affect their own attitudes and did it cause any kind of change in their community? Did it increase the use of the EMT or change people's attitudes towards their ethnicity? Interviews were initiated by asking whether subjects believed that an ethnic revival had occurred during the 1960s and early 1970s and if so, whether it had affected their own attitudes/behaviors and/or those of their own community. Overall, 83.1% (Q1/GT/T)[2] of all respondents said that there *was* an increased awareness in their own community, though they were not always sure what was happening elsewhere. In general, attitudes, reactions and perceptions differ substantially between different ethnic groups. As can be seen at various points in Table 20.1, the Hispanic activists are generally most optimistic and felt strengthened by recent political gains and new immigrational influx. The French activists have long felt isolated, seem depressed, saw very minor gains and did not feel that any ethnolinguistic help provided by the government was meant for them, since they have been in the United States for a long time and are not disadvantaged immigrants. Among most Yiddish activists, Yiddish is not viewed as the most important factor in keeping either overt or attitudinal ethnicity alive among Jews, despite the fact that in some segments of the Jewish population it was 'always' used and goes hand-in-hand with the maintenance of religious and cultural practices, on the one hand, or participation in a secular literary-theatrical-educational subculture, on the other hand.

Individual vs. community

There is often a substantial difference between what respondents say they themselves do and what they perceive is happening in their community. This can be consistently seen when we examine the tabulated responses for questions 2 through 7.

	Individual Totals	Community Totals
Did 'ethnic revival' increase EMT use?	Q2:41.6%	Q5:59.2%
Did 'ethnic revival' improve attitudes?	Q3:62.0%	Q6:69.0%
Did 'ethnic revival' renew customs?	Q4:40.1%	Q7:55.6%

The same three questions also reveal marked inter-ethnic group differences:

	Individual Totals	Community Totals
Spanish EMT	Q2:54.4%	Q5:80.9%
Spanish EMT	Q3:73.5%	Q6:88.2%
Spanish EMT	Q4:66.2%	Q7:82.8%
Yiddish EMT	Q2:23.3%	Q2:60.0%
Yiddish EMT	Q3:30.0%	Q3:80.0%
Yiddish EMT	Q4:13.3%	Q4:53.3%
French EMT	Q2:34.1%	Q2:25.0%
French EMT	Q3:43.7%	Q3:31.8%
French EMT	Q4:18.2%	Q4:15.9%

Whereas in the Spanish and Yiddish samples our respondents viewed their respective communities as changing in a more 'positive' direction more often than they themselves (our respondents often viewed themselves as having been 'positive' *even before the revival*), we find the opposite situation among the French EMT sample. The individual French activist increased EMT usage and came to feel more secure in being 'French'

TABLE 20.1 *Positive replies to each question by sample and nativity* (NB = Native-born; FB = Foreign-born)

QUESTION		FRENCH			SPANISH				YIDDISH	GRAND TOTAL
		Fr1 (1)	Fr2 (2)	Fr tot (3)	Sp1 (4)	Sp2 (5)	Sp3 (6)	Sp tot (7)	Y tot (8)	(9)
I										
1. Was there an ethnic boom revival?	NB	63.6	73.7	68.3	92.9	100.0	77.8	88.0	87.5	78.0
	FB	100.00	50.0	66.7	100.0	95.0	93.9	95.4	78.6	90.0
	T	65.2	71.4	68.2	95.4	95.4	87.5	92.6	83.3	83.1
2. Did it increase respondent's EMT use?	NB	31.8	42.1	36.6	78.6	50.0	55.6	68.0	43.8	47.6
	FB	00.0	00.0	00.0	37.5	45.0	53.3	46.5	00.0	33.3
	T	30.4	38.1	34.1	63.6	45.4	54.2	54.4	23.3	41.6
3. Did it improve respondent's attitudes toward EMT?	NB	45.4	47.4	46.3	85.7	100.0	88.9	88.0	50.0	59.8
	FB	00.0	00.0	00.0	50.0	60.0	80.0	65.1	7.1	65.0
	T	43.5	42.9	43.2	72.7	63.6	83.3	73.5	30.0	62.0
4. Did it renew respondent's customs of culture?	NB	4.6	36.8	19.5	92.9	50.0	44.4	72.0	18.8	35.4
	FB	00.0	00.0	00.0	75.0	75.0	40.0	62.8	7.1	46.7
	T	4.4	33.3	18.2	86.4	72.7	41.7	66.2	13.3	40.1
5. Did it increase EMT use (community)?	NB	13.6	42.1	26.8	85.7	100.0	66.7	80.0	62.5	50.0
	FB	00.0	00.0	00.0	75.0	95.0	66.7	81.4	57.1	71.7
	T	13.0	28.1	25.0	81.8	95.4	66.7	80.9	60.0	59.2
6. Did it improve attitudes toward EMT (community)?	NB	27.3	42.1	34.2	92.9	100.0	100.0	96.0	87.5	63.4
	FB	00.0	00.0	00.0	87.5	80.0	86.7	83.7	71.4	76.7
	T	26.1	38.1	31.8	90.9	81.8	91.7	88.2	80.0	69.0
7. Did it renew customs of culture (community)?	NB	4.6	31.6	17.1	85.7	100.0	66.7	80.0	56.2	43.9
	FB	00.0	00.0	00.0	100.0	95.0	60.0	83.7	50.0	71.7
	T	4.4	28.6	15.9	95.4	95.4	62.5	82.8	53.3	55.6

		(1)	(2)	(3)	(4)	(5)	(6)	(7)	(8)	(9)
8. What caused revival? INTERNAL FORCES?	NB	72.7	52.6	63.4	78.6	100.0	77.8	80.0	87.5	73.2
	FB	100.0	00.0	33.3	75.0	75.0	80.0	76.7	57.1	70.0
	T	73.9	47.6	61.4	77.2	77.3	79.2	77.9	73.3	71.8
9. local group?	NB	68.2	31.6	51.2	78.6	00.0	11.1	48.0	6.2	41.5
	FB	00.0	50.0	33.3	75.0	40.0	13.3	37.2	7.1	30.0
	T	65.2	33.3	50.0	77.3	36.4	12.5	41.2	6.7	36.6
10. local person?	NB	40.9	00.0	22.0	14.3	00.0	11.1	12.0	18.8	18.3
	FB	00.0	00.0	00.0	25.0	10.0	6.7	11.6	00.0	8.3
	T	39.1	00.0	20.4	18.2	9.1	8.3	11.8	10.0	14.1
11. national group?	NB	00.0	00.0	00.0	14.3	00.0	11.1	12.0	6.2	4.9
	FB	00.0	00.0	00.0	50.0	15.0	33.3	27.9	14.3	21.7
	T	00.0	00.0	00.0	27.3	9.1	25.0	20.6	10.0	12.0
12. national figure?	NB	4.6	00.0	2.4	42.9	00.0	00.0	24.0	00.0	8.5
	FB	00.0	00.0	00.0	50.0	10.0	6.7	16.3	7.1	13.3
	T	4.4	00.0	2.3	45.4	9.1	4.2	19.1	3.3	10.6
13. What caused revival? EXTERNAL FORCES?	NB	00.0	21.0	9.8	00.0	00.0	44.4	16.0	31.2	15.8
	FB	00.0	00.0	00.0	12.5	30.0	53.3	34.9	28.6	31.7
	T	00.0	19.0	2.3	4.6	27.3	50.0	27.9	30.0	22.5
14. government program?	NB	9.1	5.3	7.3	7.1	00.0	11.1	8.0	00.0	6.1
	FB	00.0	00.0	00.0	12.5	15.0	6.7	11.6	00.0	8.3
	T	8.7	4.8	6.8	9.1	13.6	8.3	10.3	00.0	7.0
15. other ethnic movement?	NB	9.1	31.6	19.5	92.9	100.0	55.6	80.0	25.0	39.0
	FB	00.0	00.0	00.0	87.5	70.0	73.3	74.4	14.3	56.7
	T	8.7	28.6	18.2	90.9	72.7	70.8	76.5	20.0	46.5
16. legislation?	NB	45.4	10.5	29.3	64.3	50.0	88.9	72.0.	00.0	36.6
	FB	00.0	00.0	00.0	12.5	90.0	60.0	65.1	00.0	46.7
	T	43.5	9.5	27.3	45.4	86.4	70.8	67.6	00.0	40.8

TABLE 20.1 (*Continued*)

QUESTION		FRENCH Fr1 (1)	Fr2 (2)	Fr tot (3)	SPANISH Sp1 (4)	Sp2 (5)	Sp3 (6)	Sp tot (7)	YIDDISH Y tot (8)	GRAND TOTAL (9)
17. other?	NB	22.7	42.1	31.7	42.9	00.0	66.7	48.0	62.5	42.7
	FB	100.0	00.0	33.3	12.5	60.0	46.7	46.5	50.0	46.7
	T	26.1	38.1	31.8	36.4	54.6	54.2	47.1	56.7	44.4
II										
18. Can you have ethnicity without EMT?	NB	18.2	36.8	26.8	50.0	00.0	66.7	52.0	56.2	40.2
	FB	00.0	100.0	66.7	37.5	25.0	20.0	25.6	57.1	35.0
	T	17.4	42.9	29.6	45.4	22.7	37.5	35.3	56.7	38.0
19. A LOSS if group ceased to be separate?	NB	68.2	84.2	75.6	100.0	100.0	100.0	100.0	75.0	82.9
	FB	00.0	100.0	66.7	100.0	100.0	100.0	100.0	64.3	90.0
	T	65.2	85.7	75.0	100.0	100.0	100.0	100.0	70.0	85.9
20. Is there a GAIN from separateness?	NB	4.6	5.3	4.9	64.3	50.0	33.3	52.0	6.2	19.5
	FB	00.0	00.0	00.0	50.0	80.0	60.0	67.4	21.4	53.5
	T	4.4	4.8	4.6	59.1	77.3	50.0	61.7	13.3	33.8
21. More important problems than EMT maintenance?	NB	63.6	73.7	68.3	100.0	100.0	44.4	80.0	68.8	72.0
	FB	100.0	100.0	100.0	87.5	90.0	73.3	83.7	85.7	85.0
	T	65.2	76.2	70.4	95.4	90.9	62.5	82.3	76.7	77.5
22. Do you know other people who feel this way?	NB	54.6	68.4	61.0	92.9	100.0	44.4	76.0	56.2	64.6
	FB	100.0	100.0	100.0	87.5	75.0	80.0	79.1	57.1	75.0
	T	56.5	71.4	63.6	90.9	77.3	66.7	77.9	56.7	69.0
23. Another group more successful in EMT ethnic maintenance?	NB	31.8	52.6	41.5	64.3	00.0	88.9	68.0	56.2	52.4
	FB	00.0	00.0	00.0	62.5	65.0	73.3	67.4	42.9	58.3
	T	30.4	47.6	38.6	63.6	59.1	75.0	67.6	50.0	54.9

		(1)	(2)	(3)	(4)	(5)	(6)	(7)	(8)	(9)
24. Do you know why?	NB	22.7	42.1	31.7	57.1	100.0	55.6	60.0	37.5	41.5
	FB	00.0	00.0	00.0	25.0	75.0	53.3	58.1	42.9	51.7
	T	21.7	38.1	29.6	45.4	77.3	54.2	58.8	40.0	45.8
25. Can it be copied?	NB	9.1	10.5	9.8	21.4	50.0	44.4	32.0	00.0	14.6
	FB	00.0	00.0	00.0	00.0	30.0	20.0	20.9	7.1	16.7
	T	8.7	9.5	9.1	13.6	31.8	29.2	25.0	3.3	15.5
III										
26. Are there domains for ENGLISH?	NB	72.7	84.2	78.0	100.0	100.0	100.0	100.0	81.2	85.4
	FB	00.0	100.0	66.7	87.5	100.0	100.0	97.7	78.6	91.7
	T	69.6	85.7	77.3	95.4	100.0	100.0	98.5	80.0	88.0
27. Domains for ENGLISH *WITHIN* ethnic community?	NB	22.7	42.1	31.7	64.3	100.0	44.4	60.0	93.8	52.4
	FB	100.0	00.0	33.3	25.0	50.0	73.3	53.5	64.3	55.0
	T	26.1	38.1	31.8	50.0	54.6	62.5	55.9	80.0	53.5
28. Are there domains for EMT?	NB	81.8	68.4	75.6	92.9	100.0	100.0	96.0	87.5	84.2
	FB	100.0	100.0	100.0	87.5	100.0	100.0	97.7	78.6	93.3
	T	82.6	71.4	77.3	90.9	100.0	100.0	97.1	83.3	88.0
IV										
29. Has EMT changed recently?	NB	40.9	52.6	46.5	100.0	100.0	77.8	92.0	81.2	67.1
	FB	100.0	50.0	66.7	100.0	95.0	100.0	97.7	85.7	93.3
	T	43.5	52.4	47.7	100.0	95.4	91.7	95.6	83.3	78.2

TABLE 20.1 (*Continued*)

QUESTION		FRENCH			SPANISH				YIDDISH	GRAND TOTAL
		Fr1 (1)	Fr2 (2)	Fr tot (3)	Sp1 (4)	Sp2 (5)	Sp3 (6)	Sp tot (7)	Y tot (8)	(9)
30. Has it improved?	NB	4.6	26.3	14.6	28.6	50.0	11.1	24.0	12.5	17.1
	FB	100.0	00.0	33.3	00.0	10.0	00.0	4.6	35.7	13.3
	T	8.7	23.8	15.9	18.2	13.6	8.3	11.8	23.3	15.5
31. Has grammar changed?	NB	4.6	00.0	2.4	7.1	00.0	11.1	8.0	6.2	4.9
	FB	00.0	00.0	00.0	00.0	20.0	00.0	9.3	7.1	8.3
	T	4.4	9.5	2.3	4.6	18.2	4.2	8.8	6.7	6.3
32. Has purity changed?	NB	4.6	10.5	7.3	00.0	00.0	11.1	4.0	12.5	7.3
	FB	00.0	00.0	00.0	00.0	15.0	00.0	7.0	14.3	8.3
	T	4.4	9.5	6.8	00.0	13.6	4.2	5.9	13.3	7.8
33. Is change related to boom?	NB	4.6	26.3	14.6	35.7	50.0	55.6	44.0	37.5	28.0
	FB	100.0	00.0	33.3	12.5	45.0	46.7	39.5	14.3	33.3
	T	8.7	23.8	15.9	27.2	45.4	50.0	41.2	26.7	30.3
34. Should it be counteracted?	NB	22.7	15.8	19.5	57.1	50.0	11.1	40.0	12.5	24.4
	FB	00.0	50.0	33.3	100.0	75.0	80.0	81.4	28.6	66.7
	T	21.7	19.0	20.4	77.3	72.7	54.2	67.6	20.0	42.2
35. Do changes inhibit communication?	NB	00.0	00.0	00.0	00.0	00.0	22.2	8.0	6.2	3.7
	FB	00.0	00.0	00.0	25.0	35.0	6.7	23.3	7.1	18.3
	T	00.0	00.0	00.0	9.1	27.3	12.5	16.2	6.7	9.9
36. Should there be a standard?	NB	45.4	57.9	51.2	85.7	100.0	66.7	80.0	37.5	57.3
	FB	00.0	100.0	66.7	100.0	95.0	100.0	97.7	28.6	80.0
	T	43.5	61.9	52.3	95.4	95.4	87.5	91.2	33.3	66.9

	(1)	(2)	(3)	(4)	(5)	(6)	(7)	(8)	(9)
37. Value judgements on variety?									
NB	00.0	00.0	00.0	21.4	00.0	11.1	16.0	6.2	6.1
FB	00.0	00.0	00.0	00.0	30.0	00.0	14.0	7.1	11.7
T	00.0	00.0	00.0	13.6	27.3	4.2	14.7	6.7	8.4
V Wish for EMT in the future:									
38. Exclusively EMT?									
NB	00.0	00.0	00.0	00.0	00.0	00.0	00.0	12.5	2.4
FB	00.0	00.0	00.0	00.0	00.0	00.0	00.0	00.0	00.0
T	00.0	00.0	00.0	00.0	00.0	00.0	00.0	6.7	1.4
39. Equality of EMT and ENGLISH?									
NB	63.6	36.8	51.2	92.9	100.0	77.8	88.0	75.0	67.1
FB	100.0	50.0	66.7	87.5	90.0	93.3	90.7	78.6	86.7
T	65.2	38.1	52.3	90.9	90.9	87.5	89.7	76.7	75.4
40. Positive EMT attitude among ethnics?									
NB	63.6	79.0	70.7	50.0	00.0	77.8	56.0	68.8	65.8
FB	100.0	100.0	100.0	25.0	50.0	40.0	41.9	42.9	45.0
T	65.2	81.0	72.7	40.9	45.4	54.2	47.1	56.7	57.0
41. Positive EMT attitude by outsiders?									
NB	40.9	73.7	56.1	50.0	00.0	88.9	60.0	00.0	46.3
FB	00.0	50.0	33.3	37.5	50.0	66.7	53.5	14.3	43.3
T	39.1	71.4	54.6	45.4	45.4	75.0	55.9	6.7	45.1
42. Linguistic assimilation?									
NB	00.0	5.3	2.4	00.0	00.0	00.0	00.0	00.0	1.2
FB	00.0	00.0	00.0	00.0	00.0	00.0	00.0	00.0	00.0
T	00.0	4.8	2.3	00.0	00.0	00.0	00.0	00.0	00.0
Total NB	22	19	41	14	2	9	25	16	82
Total FB	1	2	3	8	20	15	43	14	60
TOTAL	23	21	44	22	22	24	68	30	142

overtly, but did *not* as often see such changes transpiring in the ethnic community. Wherever substantial generational differences obtain, the native generation's view is more positive than the foreign-born generation's view in these connections (in agreement with nation-wide statistical findings reported in Fishman *et al.* (1985). Among Yiddish activists in particular, the individual figures appear proportionately rather low. This can be accounted for by the fact that the 19 individuals (out of 30 in our sample) who answered that their use of the EMT had not increased, qualified their statement by saying things like, 'It didn't increase because it never decreased;' 'I personally have always spoken Yiddish.' This view obtained even more commonly among those who were Orthodox (i.e. among 6 out of 8 self-styled Orthodox Jews) than it did among those who were conscientious secular Yiddishists (13 out of 22). For a similar reason, we note that the largest claimed *increase in Spanish use* is among Chicanos with 63.6% (Q2/Sp1/T), i.e. among those who have been exposed to the influence of English the longest, whereas those who qualified their negative statements saying, 'I never stopped speaking Spanish,'; 'In the family we always speak Spanish' were primarily Cubans and Puerto Ricans. There was and is both in Florida (Sp2) and in New York City (Sp3) a constant influx of new monolingual Spanish speakers, either from Puerto Rico itself or, in the case of Miami, from different Caribbean, Central and South American countries. They also come either as tourists or to do business, and 'we are, of course, forced to speak Spanish to them since *they* don't speak English.' Thus, all in all, it is the more Americanized ethnic 'activists,' those less exposed to newcomers or traditional enclaves, whose personal behavior, linguistic and cultural attitudes changed the most during the 'ethnic revival.' The re-ethnization of a hitherto de-ethnicized (proto-)élites has previously been documented as a recurring aspect of ethnic reawakenings (Fishman, 1972; Allardt, 1979; Beer, 1980).

Internal vs. external causation of ethnic revival

Did internal or external forces cause the revival? Only 22.5% (Q13/GT/T) of our respondents suggested that *external* forces brought about the revival, whereas 71.8% (Q8/GT/T) felt that this had been achieved by the efforts of the community itself. It was often admitted, however, that there was a general atmosphere conducive to success and that the time to push was 'now.' The younger generation of all groups, i.e., those born in the United States, with the exception of the Cuban young people (Q17/Sp2/NB) brought up such reasons for the prevailing atmosphere as opposition to the Vietnam War, 'Our parents and grandparents have been pushed around long enough,' and, among young Jews, a desire to fight back as a reaction to the Holocaust. Only the French in Louisiana often indicated that a particular local group and individual were instrumental in bringing about new awareness (Q9/Fr1/NB and Q10/Fr1/NB). Hispanics in general were the only ones to report frequently being influenced by 'another ethnic movement' (Q15/SpT/T:76.5%), which was usually identified as the Black Civil Rights Movement, with Chicanos comparing Caesar Chavez to Martin Luther King (Q15/Spl/T:90.9%). Similarly, a Hispanic role in the 'ethnic revival' was, at times, mentioned by the French and Yiddish activists, who attributed the strength of the Hispanics to 'sheer numbers.' Interestingly enough, the Spanish activists more frequently report that they know *why* 'the other ethnic movement' succeeded (Q24), and, also, that they believe that 'the other group's success strategy' can be copied (Q25).

Ethnicity without EMT?

Is ethnicity without EMT possible? This question prompted a good deal of emotion, soul-searching and ambivalence. Most respondents were adamant that such a combination was *not* possible, and the 38% who admitted that it was feasible (Q18/GT/T) qualified their statement by saying, 'Of course, it would not be the same kind of ethnicity!' 'It would not be the real thing!' Yiddish activists tended to be most permissive in this connection (Q18/T/T); 56.7% of the Yiddish activists saying that Jewish ethnicity could survive without Yiddish. Both French and Spanish activists almost invariably spoke of the EMT as being an integral part of the culture, 'It is the expression of the soul,' 'Our culture without it would be like a body without a heart,' 'You cannot express your really intimate feelings in any other language,' 'It is the language that gives warmth and love to our family unit.' Many young people talked of learning or relearning their EMT, of regret that their parents, for reasons they well understood, had not taught them the language, of their pride and interest in their heritage and of the value of possessing two languages: 'L'homme qui parle deux langues vaut deux hommes' (a man who knows two languages is worth two men), while their elders recollected the suffering they had experienced as children when they were punished for speaking another language on the school grounds. They were relieved that their children 'would not have to go through that' and were pleased that their children and grandchildren were more and more interested and dedicated to their ethnolinguistic background (Hansen, 1938). Spanish activists tended to be the most convinced that 'another ethnic group' has been more successful on behalf of its own ethnic interests than they themselves had been. The French activists were least convinced of this. The former usually pointed to the Blacks; the latter, to the Hispanics (as did the Yiddish activists). This is doubly interesting because the Hispanics were also the most emphatic with respect to their own gains while the French activists were least so. Seemingly, the French activists were simultaneously most isolated with respect to the ethnic revival as a general phenomenon and least impressed by it as an intragroup occurrence.

All respondents reported that it would be a great loss if their group ceased to be separate (Q19/GT/T:85.9% of all respondents — i.e. 100% of the Spanish activists, 75% of the French and 70% of the Yiddish), citing loss of identity of the group as well as part of the self. This is almost equally important to both native-born and foreign-born activists. Clearly, total assimilation was unwanted and the melting pot was not invoked as an ideal.

Despite the above sentiment, 77.5% of the activists (Q21/GT/T) allowed that there were problems for many of their communities that *were more pressing than the maintenance of the EMT*. Economic mobility and acceptance in the larger Anglo-community were the most often cited, and if giving priority to English was what such mobility and acceptance demanded, it was very regrettable, but understandable, if in so doing some part of one's ethnicity (such as language) fell by the wayside. In all groups, maintaining one's EMT without learning English was rarely preferred and, indeed, was equated by the younger native-born activists with backwardness and poverty.

Domains of EMT and English

Where and when does one speak in the EMT and where and when in English? Is there a place for English within the ethnic community itself? Eighty-eight percent of all activists (Q26/GT/T) replied that there *were* separate domains for English and for the EMT. Whether English would be used by them within the ethnic community was qualified by 53.5% as depending on the subject matter under discussion, and generally also the age of the speakers (Q27/GT/T), with significantly more English reported as being spoken by the native-born than by the foreign-born (Q27/NB:Fr/T;Sp/T;Y). Matters pertaining to business and professional activity, as well as those relating to school and studies, were very often reported as being discussed in English because that is the language in which these activities are transacted, and frequently the speaker does not command the necessary vocabulary in the EMT. However, on the other hand, young Puerto Rican activists in New York, often more fluent in English than in Spanish, explained that *they* were studying the EMT in college for pragmatic reasons. They felt that they needed to improve their EMT mastery because the language is needed in order to communicate with the older generation in the community and to render services to those recent arrivals who had not yet learned English. Most of these young people were preparing to work in service fields and felt that knowing both English and Spanish was an asset which would yield practical benefits for the community *as well as for themselves*.

EMT change

Has the EMT changed recently? Many of the activists pointed to what all linguists know: that all languages change over time. 'If we don't adapt and accept the changes, the language will not be alive, it will become like Latin, a dead language only found in books and that no one speaks any more.' Many of the 78.2% of our respondents who said that their EMT had indeed changed recently (Q29/GT/T) qualified this by saying that it has not changed for the better, an opinion most often expressed by the older foreign-born respondents in all groups. Thus, although many French activists said that more Franco-Americans were learning the language and attempting to attain standard French (Q36/Fr/T — 52.3%), they also commonly reported (as did other activists) that a great deal of English had crept into daily speech, even into the media, where it 'definitely has no business being,' and 'even teachers use it,' which is wrong, because 'children should be taught correctly in school at least.' Some respondents were purists and felt that there should be an English-free standard, even if not everyone will or can use it. Highly mixed varieties known as *Franglais*, *Yinglish* and *Spanglish* are resented by many and definitely anger some (Varo, 1971). Most activists, however, make no value judgements on the variety spoken; in fact even the French activists don't care very much about *how their neighbors speak it*, the important thing being to speak it, to use it and keep it alive.

Hopes for the future

And what of the future? Almost none of the activists wants a self-contained ethnic group where only the EMT would be used and almost none wants linguistic assimilation either. The ideal for many would, of course, be some stable form of bilingualism and biculturism, and 45.1% (Q41/GT/T) hope for respect and acceptance of their language and culture by outsiders and for a supportive attitude from their own people (Q40/GT/T:57%). Only an extremely small percentage, merely 0.7% (Q42/GT/T), fear that linguistic assimilation is in the cards for the future, because 'English is a powerful language which is spreading all over the world.'

Dimensional summary

Activists of the three American ethnolinguistic groups studied have in common a conscious and strong desire to maintain their particular ethnicity alongside their Americanism and consider the EMT to be its most vital and visible expression. They are concerned about teaching it to their children and generally refuse to admit that it could entirely die out in the U.S.A. Some mixture of the EMT and English is generally considered inevitable and the price one has to pay to keep one's language alive in an Anglo/English-dominated environment (Rayfield, 1970), particularly since it causes no problems of intragroup communication.

The French activists are just beginning to sense new possibilities for fostering intracommunal use of their EMT and most frequently relate their efforts to feelings of pride in their background and love for the 'elegant beauty' of their language. The Yiddish activists have relatively modest aspirations, given the prevalent view even among them that Jewish culture is ultimately not based on the Yiddish language and can therefore survive without it if need be. The Hispanics are far more numerous than the other two groups and Spanish activists are savoring the strength of numbers. Their language will never die out, they say, since even when English is spoken within the community (and even within the family), the EMT will prevail, constantly renewed by new immigration and frequent visits to the mother country.

The French activists in Louisiana have very recently become more vocal and are encouraged by bilingual educational laws in their state. The latter have enabled them to make some small gains in the use of their EMT despite the fact that they are still fairly isolated from the mainstream of French speakers (Gold, 1980). In the New England states, no such legislative assistance is available to activists, but the close proximity to

French Canada, and the constant visiting of relatives and friends there, both helps to keep language sentiment alive (even if it does not actually strengthen its use very much) and, on the whole, keeps it at a more *consciously* positive level than in Louisiana.

The Chicanos are the most EMT-positive of the Hispanic groups. Claiming to have taken their cue from the Black civil rights movement, they feel that they have made substantial gains in ethnic awareness, which in turn may have encouraged the Puerto Ricans, the least EMT-positive Hispanic group, to start organizing themselves to take greater advantage of federal occupational and educational programs with language 'possibilities.' The language positiveness of the Cubans is still largely a reflection of immigrational recency plus political sophistication.

French and Yiddish activists point to 'Hispanics' as the ultimate source of the ethnic revival within their own communities. Thus, an implicit chain of influence is revealed in popular wisdom: from Blacks to Hispanics, and from Hispanics to other ethnics. The empirical confirmation of this chain of influence is not yet at hand (and may even be more a product of popular fantasy than of historical reality), but its attitudinal reality is nonetheless impressive.

There are a few generational differences which show the native-born activists (and particularly the hitherto most Americanized among them) to have positive EMT attitudes/expectations/evaluations more commonly than do the foreign-born, e.g. the native-born more commonly attribute increased *personal* EMT use to the ethnic boom, they more commonly attribute the ethnic boom to internal forces, and they more frequently anticipate even more positive EMT circumstances in the future, both among insiders and outsiders. On the other hand, native-born activists are less commonly inclined to be satisfied with intra*community* improvement in EMT use or attitudes, less likely to interpret ethnic separateness as an unambiguous asset for language maintenance and are less commonly concerned about a puristic standard of EMT usage. All in all, the 'ethnic revival' views of language activists reveal complex inter-ethnic and intra-ethnic *differences*, as well as many inter-ethnic and intra-ethnic *similarities,* and the interaction between all of the factors involved will require much additional scrutiny.

Notes to Chapter 20

1. We acknowledge with gratitude the assistance of the following local site-coordinators: Philippe Gustin, CODOFIL, Lafayette, LA; Père Jean-Marie

Jammes, St. Martinville, LA; Claire Quintal, Assumption College,
Worcester, MA; Normande Dubé, Nat. Materials Development Center,
Bedford, NH; Carmen Silva-Corvalan, University of Southern California,
Los Angeles, CA; Rosa Castro Feinberg, LAU Center, University of Miami,
FL; Lisandro Garcia-Marchi, NYC Board of Education, New York, NY; José
Cruz-Matos, Hostos Community College of City University of New York,
New York, NY; Silvia Burunat, The City College of the City University of
New York, NY.
2. *QI/GT/T-Question 1*, Grand Total *Column*, Total *row*. This notational form
will be used repeatedly, below, with ethnolinguistic specification (French,
Spanish, Yiddish or native-born, foreign-born) indicated as necessary.

Bibliography

ALLAIN, M. 1978, Twentieth Century Acadians. In G. R. CONRAD (ed.),
The Cajuns: Essays on Their History and Culture. Center for
Louisiana Studies, University of Southwestern Louisiana, Lafayette,
LA.

ALLARDT, E. 1979, Implications of the ethnic revival in modern, industrialized society: A comparative study of the linguistic minorities
in Western Europe. *Commentationes Scientiarum Socialium*.
(Helsinki).

ARGÜELLES, L. & MACEOIN, G. 1980, El Miami Cubano. *Areito* 7, No. 28,
4–15.

BEER, W. R. 1980, *The Unexpected Rebellion: Ethnic Activism in
Contemporary France*. New York: New York University Press.

BULLIVANT, B. M. 1982, Are ethnic schools the solution to ethnic children's
accommodation to Australian society? *Journal of Intercultural Studies*
3, 17–35.

ECKSTEIN, A. 1982, What is the role of ethnic schools in education for a
multicultural society? *Journal of Intercultural Studies* 3, 48–69.

FISHMAN, J. A. 1965, *Yiddish in America: Sociolinguistic Description and
Analysis*. Bloomington: Indiana University Press.

—— 1972, *Language and Nationalism*. Rowley, MA.: Newbury House.

FISHMAN, J. A., COOPER, R. L., MA, R. *et al*. 1971, *Bilingualism in the
Barrio*. Bloomington: Indiana University Press.

FISHMAN, J. A., GERTNER, M. H., LOWY, E. G. & MILÁN, W. G. 1985,
Ethnicity in action: the community resources of ethnic languages in
the United States. In J. A. Fishman *et al*. *The Rise and Fall of the
Ethnic Revival*. Berlin: Mouton, 195–282.

GOLD, G. L. 1980, *The Role of France, Quebec and Belgium in the Revival
of French in Louisiana Schools*. Quebec, International Center for
Research on Bilingualism.

HALLOWELL, C. 1979, *People of the Bayou — Cajun Life in Lost America*. New York: E. P. Dutton.

HANSEN, M. L. 1938, *The Problem of the Third-Generation Immigrant*. Rock Island, IL: Augustana Historical Society.

HENDRICKSON, D. 1980, *Quiet Presence: The True Stories of Franco-Americans in New England*. Portland, ME: Guy Gannett Publishing Co.

LEWINS, F. 1982, The political implications of ethnic schools. *Journal of Intercultural Studies* 3, 36–47.

METCALF, A. A. 1979, The study of California Chicano English. *International Journal of the Sociology of Language* 2, 53–58.

NORST, M. 1986, Ethnic schools: What are they and what would they like to be? *Journal of Intercultural Studies* 3, 6–16.

NOVAK, M. 1973, *The Rise of the Unmeltable Ethnics*. New York: Macmillan.

RAYFIELD, J. R. 1970, *The Languages of a Bilingual Community*. The Hague: Mouton.

RUSHTON, W. FAULKNER 1979, *The Cajuns: From Acadia to Louisiana*. New York: Farrar, Straus, Giroux.

SOLE, C. A. 1979, Selección idiomática entre la nueva generación de Cubano-Americanos. *The Bilingual Review* 6, No. 1, 1–10.

— 1982, Language loyalty and language attitudes among Cuban-Americans. In J. A. FISHMAN & G. KELLER (eds), *Bilingual Education for Hispanics in the U.S.A*. New York: Columbia University Press.

THIBODEAUX, J. S. 1977, *Les Francophones de Louisiane*. Paris: Editions Entente.

THOMPSON, R. M. 1974, Mexican-American language loyalty and the validity of the 1970 Census. *International Journal of the Sociology of Language* 2, 7–18.

VARO, C. 1971, *Consideraciones Antropológicas y Políticas en Torno a la Enseñanza del 'Spanglish' en Nueva York*. Río Piedras, PR, Ediciones Libreria Internacional.

WADDELL, E. 1979, French Louisiana: An outpost of *L'Amerique Française*, or another country and another culture? *Projet Louisiane*, No. 4, McGill University, Université Laval, York University, Canada.

WOLFRAM, W. 1973, *Sociolinguistic Aspects of Assimilation: Puerto Rican English in New York City*. Arlington, VA: Center for Applied Linguistics.

ZENTELLA, A. C. 1981, Language variety among Puerto Ricans. In C. A. FERGUSON & S. BRICE HEATH (eds), *Language in the U.S.A*. Cambridge: Cambridge University Press, 218–38.

21　Nathan Birnbaum's view of American Jewry*

Nathan Birnbaum (1864–1937), one of the giants of modern Jewish thought and the founder of not one but of fully three modern Jewish movements (Zionism, Yiddishism, and the Return-to-Orthodoxy), has been far too little remembered and even less understood by committed Jews of today, all of whom are in one way or another, the direct beneficiaries of Birnbaum's manifold and herculian efforts. His struggle against assimilationist tendencies among 'Jewish moderns', the term he used in referring to Jews who were fully in touch with Western European culture and values, was unending and literally all-consuming. Now, on the occasion of his 50th *yortsayt*, we not only owe *him*, but we owe *ourselves*, the distinct pleasure of reacquainting ourselves with his endlessly original and scintillating views, views which span all of the concerns that still engulf us today as we continue to struggle with modernity, either in order to domesticate it along Jewish lines or in order to escape from its clutches.

'Original' is actually too tame a designation for Nathan Birnbaum; perhaps 'revolutionary' is more appropriate, if we can set aside its usual left-wing implications. Even before his Zionism was fully articulated, indeed, at the tender age of 19, he shocked the world of Germanized Jewish university students in his home-town, Vienna, via public lectures and self-published brochures addressed to 'so-called Germans, Slavs, Hungarians, etc., of the Mosaic Confession, by a student of Jewish nationality'. He attacked their 'drive toward assimilation' (Assimilationssucht) as unworthy, self-impoverishing and doomed to failure because it fostered rather than calmed the worst fears of anti-semites. Immediately thereafter, in 1883, i.e. nearly a dozen years before the Dreyfus affair in France which belatedly wakened the Jewish sensitivities of Theodore Herzl, Birnbaum literally coined the word

*Originally published in *Judaica Book News* (1987), 18, No. 1, 10–11 & 68–70.

'Zionism', both in German and in Hebrew, organized the first university-linked Zionist student organization, *Kadimah*, and single-handedly founded, edited and published its journal *Selbst-Emancipation!*. Although he was later forced to accept Herzl's organizational leadership in order to remain within the Zionist organization, he became the first Western Zionist to call for a positive reassessment of the role of Yiddish in modern Jewish life and in the cultural authenticity of millions of Jews, an authenticity that Western Zionists must not only safeguard but one that they must increasingly incorporate into their own lives. Later, as 'the first among equals' in Yiddishist ranks, and as the originator and organizer of the greatest Yiddishist 'event' to date, the First World Conference for the Yiddish Language (Tshernovits, 1908, see below), he opposed any down-grading of Hebrew and of traditional Judaism in Jewish life, thereby eliciting the ire of left-wing Yiddishists. Finally, as the first really eminent, Western rediscoverer of unreconstructed Orthodoxy, he issued a call and started a movement for less routinization and more beauty, more deeply felt Jewish experiences and a more intense personal commitment to ushering in the Messiah. In this, his last phase, he was the first in Orthodox ranks to call for an exodus from Holocaust-bound Europe, beginning in the early 1920s, and for resettlement in small, preplanned all-Jewish settlements 'elsewhere', so that Jews could live in accord with their own culture and be free of the urban disarray and mercantilism that had plagued them for so many centuries.

As I have tried to demonstrate in Fishman (1987), *Ideology, Society and Language, The Odyssey of Nathan Birnbaum*, the many phases which he so meteorically traversed are integrated via Birnbaum's constantly restless searching for a definition of his own Jewishness, his unhappiness with the Jewish situation and his continual planning for ways and means to remedy that situation. His entire adult life constitutes an integrated whole, notwithstanding the fact that many of his specific views changed from one phase to the next, because certain themes never disappear from his agenda. One of these integrating themes is 'America', a topic that he touches upon in each one of his phases. As a result, his views about America are much more original and much more fully developed than those of his contemporaries. Neither Herzl, nor Akhad Ha-'am, nor Zhitlovski (even though the latter lived for more than a score of years in North America, see below), nor the Gerer Rebe ever really articulated a fine-grained picture as to 'How is America different from all the other lands of dispersion?' Only Birnbaum managed to do so and this should make him doubly intriguing for American Jewry.

How did Birnbaum come to be so familiar with America, in general, and with Jews in America, in particular? His familiarity begins with a 1907–1908 five month long lecture tour here (during the very zenith of his Autonomist/Yiddishist stage), a tour in which his three phases came together, his past, his present and even his future, more so than they had done in Central Europe itself.

Birnbaum ostensibly came to America in order to lecture about Zionism (predictably, he stressed the need for 'Zionism as a culture-building movement', a view that represented his uniqueness *vis-à-vis* the Zionist movement in general[1] and the more politically oriented Herzl in particular). These lectures enabled him to visit a substantial part of the country, reaching far into the West and into the South. Indeed, they enabled him to visit parts of the country that most resident Jewish leaders and Yiddish writers knew very little about. These lectures also enabled him not only to cover his expenses, but even to 'put a little aside', this being a rare occurrence for Birnbaum whose life usually hovered just below the line of genteel poverty.

But his visit to America also permitted Birnbaum to meet face to face with Dovid Pinski, already a major figure both in Zionist and in Yiddish literary circles, and to explore with him one of Birnbaum's pet projects: convening the 'First World Conference for the Yiddish Language.' Their meetings on this matter took place in Pinski's apartment on Beck Street, in the South Bronx, where they were immediately joined by Khayem Zhitlovski, whose contributions to Yiddishist and Diaspora Autonomist thought were also already well known. The only obvious puzzle about these meetings in the Bronx, a puzzle thus far overlooked by scholarship on Yiddishism, is why Birnbaum waited until this 1907 visit to America — a locale so far away from his usual haunts — in order to issue the first call to what became the famous Tshernovits Conference of 1908. America was then still far from being at the center of the world of Yiddish and Birnbaum, as we have implied above, had actually come up with the idea of such a conference on behalf of Yiddish as far back as 1905, i.e. more than two years before his visit to America took place, at a talk that he gave in Tshernovits itself. At that earlier time he adumbrated almost the entire agenda of such a conference, the very agenda that he, Pinski and Zhitlovski itemized in their late 1907–early 1908 meetings on this very matter, as well as in the call to the conference that they then issued: sessions on a standardized modern orthography, on assistance to writers and actors, on literature and theater, on the preparation and publication of practical grammars, dictionaries and text books, and finally, sessions on fostering the societal recognition of the language *per se*, particularly among the young (Birnbaum, 1905).

Given that he already had such a fully itemized and well established view of what the conference agenda should be, there were dozens of Eastern European 'stars' in the firmament of Yiddish (e.g. Y. L. Peretz, A. Reyzen, Sh. Ash, H. D. Nomberg), all of whom Birnbaum knew well and most of whom he had partially translated into German, and introduced at literary 'evenings' that he had organized and chaired in Vienna and throughout Galicia, whom he could have approached. Why did Birnbaum wait for more than two years, and until he was in far away America, in order to bring his ideas to the attention of a number of *American* Yiddishists and in order to get their particular support? It may be, of course, that Birnbaum had especially warm feelings for Pinski and Zhitlovski and that they, too, were particular admirers of Birnbaum. He knew Pinski well from his own, prior, Zionist stage. Among Zionists, Pinski was the major, active Yiddish writer, just as among Yiddish writers, Pinski was the most outspoken and uncompromising Zionist. Pinski knew very well who this German-speaking, German-writing Viennese was, what his erstwhile contributions to Zionism had been and how justified his criticism was of a Zionism that focused on *shtadlo"nes* and *shnorera"y* (intercessions with non-Jewish political authorities and fund-raising). With Zhitlovski, Birnbaum shared a diaspora-autonomistic weltanschauung. However, in both cases, Birnbaum could easily have found first-rate Eastern European counterparts (and found them substantially earlier to boot) for the purposes of attracting and mobilizing the world of Yiddish on behalf of his conference plans. We are forced to conclude, it seems to me, that Birnbaum preferred to wait until he could approach Pinski and Zhitlovski for their support in far away America *precisely because they were in America*. Their residence in America meant that they could not 'take away' from him either the Yiddishist movement or the conference on behalf of Yiddish as (in Birnbaum's view) Herzl had done a decade before in connection with Zionism and as the Eastern European 'stars' could possibly still do in connection with Yiddishism. Once burned, twice shy.

After releasing the first call to the conference from New York, Birnbaum concluded his lecture tour and took a boat back to Europe. On the high seas he experienced an unforgettable realization of the presence of God, in the air round about him, in the waves that surrounded him, an anticipation of his coming phase, when, in his own words, he was transformed from being a doubter (*apiko'yres*) to being a believer (*ma'min*). All in all, all three of his phases had met and intersected in connection with his American visit.

But for us today, the most important and most curious accompaniments of Birnbaum's first visit to America[2] are *not* his reiteration of his long-standing differences with Herzl's Zionism, *nor* his attracting Pinski and Zhitlovski to the notion and to the sponsorship of the Tshernovits Conference, *nor* even his experience of the presence of God. What is most noteworthy and most unusual is that this trip enabled him to closely observe America, Americanism and American Jewry and to think deeply about these new and interconnected phenomena. As a result of this trip, Birnbaum expressed a number of original views concerning the pluses and minuses that he observed in this new nexus and their implications for Jews and *yi*"*dishkayt* in the new world.

While still in America, Birnbaum (1908) published (in the Viennese *Jüdische Zeitung*) four letters from America. These letters are chiefly concerned with immigrant life on the East Side, with Yiddish theater (of which Birnbaum had long been an avid admirer and vigorous champion from the time of the first visit of A. Goldfaden, with his theater-troupe, to Vienna and their presentation there of *Di kapri*"*zne moyd* [The Capricious Lass]), with the palpable tensions between Germanized Jews (from which Birnbaum himself stemmed) and Eastern European Jews (with whom he so identified) in America — a topic whose European and, particularly, Austro-Hungarian, manifestations Birnbaum never tired of analyzing, and even with tourism pure and simple (e.g. the Congressman from the Lower East Side, Goldfogel, introduced Birnbaum to Theodore Roosevelt, then still President of the United States, who struck Birnbaum as being similar, in many respect, to Kaiser Wilhelm). However, the immediate upshot of all these letters, in Birnbaum's view, was that the future of American Jewry, whether politically, economically or culturally, was far from certain. A year later (1909), having had additional time to reflect on his American observations and experiences, Birnbaum authored his more considered analysis of the entire configuration of Jews in America, doing so under the title 'Americanism and the Jews.' By then Abraham Cahan's *Yekl: A Tale of the New York Ghetto* (1889) had already appeared, but Cahan was still far from being the authoritative figure that he later became and no fictionalized metaphors about the immigrant generation in New York (which designation also applies to Hutchins Hopgood's the *Spirit of the Ghetto* [1902]) could be the equal to Birnbaum's diagnosis and prognosis, which were both exceptionally innovative as well as prophetic.[3]

In his 1909 article, at a time when the melting pot was still a very popular notion, Birnbaum attacked this 'ideal' as a grave danger, both for Jews and for America. At that time, the New York Yiddish press was full of praise for Israel Zangwill's *The Melting Pot*, partially on the strength of Roosevelt's publicized, positive evaluation thereof. Birnbaum's view, however, was that the Yiddish papers were merely senselessly reflecting general American rhetoric, without realizing that the 'melting pot' was not the same thing as 'freedom'. The true and simple consequence of the 'melting pot' for Jews was the destruction of *yi*dishkayt*. Birnbaum fully appreciated the fact that the persecution of Jews in Europe had awakened among Jewish immigrants a ravenous hunger for freedom and equality, but he urged his readers to realize that Jews in America were living under far different circumstances than those that governed their lives in Europe and that they could understand neither themselves nor America in European terms.

Superficially, it might appear that America was socioculturally quite similar to the Russian and the Austro-Hungarian monarchies. (Of the latter, Birnbaum had long been a great champion.) True, they all revealed numerous minorities and the overarching and integrating role of a single language and culture in the comprehensive orchestration of all social processes, whether those between the various minorities themselves or those between the minorities and the central authorities. However, Birnbaum warned that this apparent similarity disappears on closer analysis and that neither the Jewish problems nor the solutions to these problems were the same in Europe and in the United States.

Birnbaum sees the main difference between Europe and the United States, insofar as ethnolinguistic minorities are concerned, neither in the lack of legal recognition of the minorities in the U.S.A., nor in their huge numbers here, nor in their recency of arrival, nor even in their lack of deeply historical, territorial concentration. The main difference in Birnbaum's eyes, lies in the fact that in America the 'center' itself is not yet consolidated and lacks depth. All residents are encouraged to learn English, of course, but not in order to become Englishmen. Englishmen, *per se*, cease to be Englishmen in America, even though they already know English when they arrive.[4] Indeed, in America everyone does learn English, sooner or later, but no deeper ethnocultural tradition is directly forthcoming as a result. Americanism, as a historical, intergenerational culture, as a culture with its own philosophy of life, still does not really exist. That fact constitutes the major difference facing minorities in the United States, when compared with minorities confronting German (or Hungarian) in Austro-Hungary or *vis-à-vis* Russian (or Polish) in Czarist Russia.

Jews who pursue the languages of government there, in Europe, arrive in the heartland of a foreign culture (actually, Birnbaum believes, they only 'half-arrive', because to really 'arrive' one must also be

Christian, because at the very heart of Germanness or Russianness there is an inescapable Christian component which even the majority of Jewish assimilationists are not willing to accept). On the other hand, Jews who pursue the language of government in America can arrive only at something unformed, something unfinished. Who really knows what American culture is and who has the proper ordination to issue edicts and to render authoritative opinions in connection with it?

Birnbaum anticipates Horace Kallen when he argues in 1909 (fully 15 years prior to the appearance of Kallen's (1924) *Culture and Democracy in the United States*), that a fully implemented American culture ('Americanism') implies, on the one hand, loyalty to democratic laws and institutions. On the other hand it requires a renewed flowering of the major customs, values and wisdoms of the cultures that were so often persecuted across the seas and that had only competitive associations with each other there. Finally, Birnbaum concludes that it is precisely because the 'melting pot' destroys the prior ethnocultural patterns of the immigrant, that it is actually the antithesis of Americanism, the enemy of Americanism, given that it impoverishes, cancels out and tears down, without even having replacements for that which it destroys. Jews, as a collectivity, do not appear to understand this and bow down to the golden calf of the melting pot, but every immigrant father, as an individual, understands this thoroughly and spontaneously, when his own child laughs at him and scorns his ways and his values.

Birnbaum discusses at length the alienations of American Jewish youth *vis-à-vis* the language and the customs of their immigrant parents. Of course, others have done so as well, both before and after Birnbaum, but Birnbaum also has something original to say in this connection, as in almost every other. He opines that the insecurity of the immigrants themselves is the major cause of both their lack of opposition to the 'false and empty Americanism of the melting pot', on the one hand, and the negative attitudes with which their own children, the members of the second generation, view them, on the other hand. If the parents were not immigrants, were not uprooted from the familiar rounds and contexts of their daily life, they could be exemplars of a proud Judaism and return their children to the proper path of authenticity. However, in their immigrant dislocation, it is not uncommon for parents to applaud and to say 'bravo' when the younger generation is derisive toward and escapes from their influence. Instead of the parents raising the children, the children are often in control and, thereby, further intensify the insecurity of the parents.

So what can be done to ameliorate this sorry situation? How can *yi'dishkayt* escape from the vicious and destructive circle that surrounds it? In all of his phases, Birnbaum was a believer in deeds: an advocate, originator and implementer of plans, organizations, publications. This trust in *mitsvesd'se* (affirmative commandments) came to his assistance even in the early 1920s, when he raised the alarm that a great calamity was on its way — the greatest of all the calamities of Jewish history — to annihilate *yi'dishkayt*. Again in the 1930s when he chastized Dutch Jewry, in whose midst he lived (as a refugee from Nazi Germany), that they were as sheep and oxen who calmly move on, slowly chewing their cuds, en route to the slaughterer, even then he firmly held that proper steps could still be taken to avoid the desolation that he foresaw.

But Birnbaum was also always a firm believer in mystic, instinctive forces of the Jewish soul and in the collective memory and good common sense of the Jewish people.

He applied these two very different (but also, very complementary) approaches to solving the problems of American Jewry and American Judaism. On the one hand, he suggested massive attempts to rouse American Jews so that they would be more conscious of their ancient as well as of their more modern cultural treasures. If he had remained here he probably would have turned to concrete details, as well as to long-range plans, in accord with this approach.[5] Most probably he would have organized yet another youth organization (as he had initially done during his Zionist and Yiddishist stages and as he did, once more, in his Orthodox stage[6]), convened conferences, established publications and initiated far-flung informational efforts in order to awaken and activize American Jews on behalf of preserving and fostering their own identity in America. However, since he realized that he was not destined to roll up his sleeves here, he relied primarily on his firm adherence to the second path: the path that was derived from a deep conviction in Jewish eternity. He trusted in Jewish fate not to permit false Americanism to triumph. A new generation would arise, he predicted, one thoroughly at home with and secure in the ways of America. That generation would have new American-born leaders, new and original ideas, new methods, and, above all, a new will to build Jewish life, a new readiness to be different from the mainstream of American life and, in addition, a new readiness to be different from their frightened fathers, a readiness to return to the healthy certainties of their grandparents and to build the future on those foundations. These ideas, that were developed by Marcus Hanson only in 1946, in his *The Immigrant in American History*, Birnbaum already formulated in 1909. Even before he himself became a *bal-tshu've* (a penitent returnee to

Orthodoxy), he prophesized that a return to more classical origins would become a mass-movement among an entire generation of American Jews.

Interestingly enough, Birnbaum did not preach cultural autonomy to or for American Jews of his day and age. He held that they were not ready for that, just as he had held at an earlier stage, that until Westernized, Germanized Jews of all kinds re-established their ties with Jewish culture and *yi"dishkayt*, they would be unfit and unready for *aliya"h* to *Erets Yisroel*. Whereas Shimen Dubnov still scolded Salo Baron during the 1930s for not foreseeing an age of cultural autonomy among American Jews, Birnbaum, as far back as 1909, already understood that American Jews required extensive re-Judaization before cultural autonomy or any other specific long-term solution to their dilemma could be given useful consideration.

Like Herder (from whom much of Birnbaum's pre-Orthodox imagery is derived), Birnbaum constantly believed that every people, individually, and all of humanity, collectively, is better off, more creative in its own problem solving and more contributory to world culture, when the authentic and deeply unique culture of its heritage is fostered and further developed. In connection with his rejections of 'false Americanism' at the beginning of this century, Birnbaum was far ahead of most others in believing that an intergenerationally intact and authentic *yi"dishkayt* in America would render both Jews and America more cultured and more rooted. He most definitely believed that those who are of the opinion that Jews are no longer capable of finding the way back to themselves and of developing their culture further, from that point of departure, 'underestimate the deep forces that live on within the Jewish people'.

Nathan Birnbaum was among the first (and, perhaps, even the very first) to be a philosophical 'Americanist' among Central and Eastern European Jewish leaders. In his autonomist stage he recognized that America was a new phenomenon in Jewish history and that the Jews in this new nation (in Lipset's (1963) terms: 'the first new nation') would witness and demonstrate not fewer but even more miracles than did their ancestors of old.

Notes to Chapter 21

1. 'Der Zionismus als kulturbewegung, Referat gehalten auf dem Zionistenkongresas am Basel, August 29, 1897', and published the following year in Birnbaum (1898).

2. Birnbaum's second (and final) visit to America occurred in 1921, when he came as a member of an Agudes Isroel delegation in which he, a *bal-tshuʰve* among Orthodox giants, was definitely a junior senator. Birnbaum never wrote about this second visit, true to the 'junior senator' model of reticence. Upon the return of the Agude delegation, Birnbaum resigned from his recently appointed position as Executive Secretary, although he remained a member of the organization until his death.
3. This article is translated into English for the very first time in Fishman (1987).
4. From his very first to his very last stage, Birnbaum continued to make comparisons between English and Yiddish, ultimately stressing that Yiddish had no more need to be embarrassed about its multi-componentiality than did English. In his article, Birnbaum (1908) comments that American English is definitely not British English and has few caretakers and arbitors, insofar as correctness or standardization are concerned.
5. When Birnbaum wrote this article he was still the avid champion of Yiddish and of autonomous, governmentally supported Yiddish schools. Accordingly he cannot keep from criticizing the fractured Yiddish of American Jews, even though he himself still needed to speak to them in German during his visit to the U.S.A., and was often laughed at by his listeners exactly when he wanted to be taken most seriously. During this visit he also decried the negative impact of the American public school on the Jewishness of American Jewish homes, much as he had decried similar influences of German, Russian, Polish and Hungarian schools in Central and Eastern Europe.
6. A few years after resigning his position with the Agude, Birnbaum founded his own organization, *Oyʰlem* (ascenders), to foster intensified, cultivated and less routinized Orthodox piety. For a statement of his goals, see Birnbaum (1927).

References

Birnbaum, N. 1898, *Zwei Vorträge über Zionismus*. Berlin.
— 1905, Ostjüdische Aufgaben, Separatdruk: *Bukowiner Post*. Czernovitz.
— 1908, Briefe aus Amerika. *Jüdische Zeitung*. Wein, v.II, 20 January, 7 February, 20 March, 10 April.
— 1909, Der Americanismus und die Jüden. *Die Welt*. v.XIII, 1 January, 8 January.
— 1927, Aufruf. ('Orden der Aufsteigenden [Aulim]'). *Israelit* 22 December.
Cahan, A. 1889, *Yekl: A Tale of the New York Ghetto*. New York.
Fishman, J. A. 1987, *Ideology, Society and Language: The Odyssey of Nathan Birnbaum*. Ann Arbor: Karoma Publishers.
Hansen, M. L. 1946, *The Immigrant in American History*. Cambridge, Mass.: Harvard University Press.

HOPGOOD, H. 1902, *Spirit of the Ghetto*. New York: Funk & Wagnalls.

KALLEN, H. M. 1924, *Culture and Democracy in the United States*. New York: Bonn and Liverright.

LIPSET, S. M. 1963, *The First New Nation: The United States in Historical and Comparative Perspective*. New York: Basic Books.

SECTION 6:
Ethnolinguistic homogeneity and heterogeneity: Worldwide causes, consequences and aspirations

Ours is a world of many peoples and many tongues. It is inevitable that there be a degree of competition and conflict between them, even more so than that there be co-operation and concord between them. Even in the 'global village' that characterizes many aspects of international life, ethnicities still tend to have a very substantial life of their own (very much as families do in a real village). Ethnicities and their associated cultures, languages and religions not only continue to provide the major dimension of early enculturation and socialization, but they themselves differ greatly in size, in resources, in priorities, in philosophies, in their histories and in their values. It is no wonder then that the propensity to conflict which is part of inter-human behavior (even between two members of the same family) should also be a recognizable part of inter-ethnic behavior as well. Unfortunately however, from the very beginning of speculative social theory in the circum-Mediterranean area to this very day, ethnicity has been primarily associated with its debits, rather than with its assets. This is as ludicrous a state of affairs as would obviously be the case if social theorists were to be fixated on the negative, conflicted and aggressive aspects of individual or family behavior, to the virtual exclusion of their positive, constructive, altruistic and nurturative aspects. In the mainstream of the Western tradition positive ethnopluralists are few and far between and viewed as romantics rather than as hard-headed realists and objectivists. No wonder then that the number of negative myths about the implications of ethnolinguistic diversity is as large as it is and as resistant to modification on the basis of either factual information, on the one hand, or pluralistic philosophy, on the other.

The view that ethnolinguistic diversity is itself nothing but a byproduct of poverty and backwardness is a recurring theme in both modern liberal and conservative thought. Both of these perspectives are uniformizing, one for the benefit of activating the downtrodden and fractionated proletarian masses and the other for the benefit of a more rational and productive market place. The attractiveness of uniformation and its seeming congruence with the growing communicational inter-connectedness of all parts of the globe seems to obscure and befog appreciation for the co-existence of larger and smaller bases of aggregation among all human populations. The family, close friends, the neighborhood, the local institutions (churches, clubs, schools) continue to function and to wield appreciable influence in daily life even in an age of global telecomunication and intercultural contact. Neither of the major sources of sociocultural influence, the traditional and the ultra-modern, are self-sufficient or fully replacive of the other and the traditional sphere is 'alive and well' even in the most modern circles. Modern élites support and cultivate ethnonational differences — in their funerals and in their birthdays, in their marriages and in their anniversaries, in their holidays and in their commemorations — as much as they foster international commerce, amusements and technology. However, befogged or not in the modern mind, ethnolinguistic diversity persists and is not directly or appreciably related to major economic or political grievances.

The same demystification is much needed in terms of such oft-advertised consequences of ethnolinguistic diversity as civil strife. When the maximal number of other social, economic, political, historical and cultural concurrents are considered simultaneously, alongside of ethnolinguistic diversity, as possible causal circumstances leading to civil strife, ethnolinguistic diversity *per se* clearly and obviously makes no contribution at all to clarifying, explicating or predicting the latter.

Why then are such destructive myths so hard to combat? Myths are vested interests and vested interests produce their own intellectual blinders, even when they are entertained and adopted by folks who are modern, progressive and even 'intellectual'. An ethnopluralistically appreciative and supportive world, both on an inter-polity and on an intra-polity level, is still a long way off today; indeed, as far off as it has been at any time during the post-World War II era. Even though scores of 'New (and ethnolinguistically diverse) Nations' have arrived on the world scene, nations that have been and remain relatively unplagued by separatism, and even though separatism itself is a relatively low level issue on the world scene, ethnolinguistic diversity is viewed suspiciously and dubiously, even by most democratic polities. Power is a scarce commodity

and power-sharing is never engaged in voluntarily. Ethnolinguistic aggregates are suspected of power aspirations and ethnolinguistic pluralism
is considered a bad risk, insofar as potentially fostering such aspirations
rather than overcoming them. Cultural democracy does not necessarily
accompany political democracy and even where such a co-ocurrence is
encountered it is often surrounded by legalisms and delays that make it
more fictive and non-operative in actuality than either the theory or letter
of the law imply.

The most stable pluralistic solutions have been territorial ones (e.g.
Switzerland, Finland, Yugoslavia), although the recent policies in
Australia and in Anglo-Canada (*vis-à-vis* the non-founding languages)
along 'personality principle' lines are also highly promising. However,
territorial solutions have been accompanied by their fair share of problems
(e.g. in India, Belgium, Spain, U.S.S.R.) and even 'personality principle'
solutions are far from being non-controversial (viz. the success of the
'English Official' movement in the U.S.A. in raising the specter of
'divisiveness', not in connection with its own scare tactics but in connection
with governmental services in the languages of non-English speaking
newcomers). Peoples have not yet learned to live together harmoniously,
any more than people have. Nevertheless, particularly when viewed from
a minority perspective, the dream lives on. Even if it is an impossible
dream, on a worldwide scale it will continue to attract the dedication of
those who refuse to believe that only the strong, the many and the rich
deserve to be themselves, to impose themselves on others and to claim that
they are even implementing justice thereby. The dream of real cultural
democracy remains one of the major unrealized (and often even unspoken) dreams of the twentieth century. For all that, it remains a
desideratum that will not go away, a challenge that remains to be solved
and not at the expense of the minorities who have already paid such a
heavy price for the insensitivity of those on whose sense of justice and
acceptance they depend.

22   Whorfianism of the third kind: Ethnolinguistic diversity as a worldwide societal asset*

We are currently witnessing a revival of Whorfianism in linguistics and anthropology, and it is a wondrous sight to behold (see, e.g. Alford, 1978; Friedrich, 1979; Silverstein, 1979; Kay & Kempton, 1984). This revival is all the more a phenomenon worth pondering, given that previously some two generations of researchers (primarily working within research traditions that come closest to replicating natural science paradigms within the social sciences) had overwhelmingly passed negative judgements upon what they considered to be the most crucial as well as the most stimulating hypotheses of Benjamin Lee Whorf. Indeed, for some 25 years (at least from the late 1950s to the late 1970s) it was exceedingly hard to find a good word on behalf of Whorf in hard-nosed, quantitative, experimental social-science circles *per se*, or in the philosophical-theoretical circles derived from and influenced most directly by such social sciences. During many of these years only a few courageous stalwarts among the leading lights of the language-related disciplines (Dell Hymes first and foremost among them [1966]), kept the faith insofar as Whorf and Whorfianism are concerned; but even they obviously did so in conjunction with more holistic and nonquantitative 'poetic' perspectives than the empirical tradition of American hypothetico-deductive science is either accustomed to, comfortable with, or impressed by. What was generally overlooked during this long period of widespread skepticism or outright rejection of Whorfianism was that his defenders and his detractors were not always

*Originally published in *Language in Society* (1982) 11, pp. 1–14.

reacting to the same facets of Whorf's thinking, were not apparently always concerned with exactly the same theories and, finally, were therefore not impressed by the same data, proofs, or tests.

Methodological differences: Interpretational differences

Now, as the worm turns (or begins to do so), it seems clear to me that for a quarter century many of us in the language-related disciplines have been so mesmerized (positively or negatively) by two theories commonly associated with Whorf (the *linguistic relativity hypothesis*, which I will call W_1, i.e. 'Whorf-sub-one,' and the *linguistic determinism hypothesis*, which I will call W_2, i.e. 'Whorf-sub-two')[1] that the rest of Whorf's work remained correspondingly obscured. It was all the more difficult to recognize that much of Whorf was being substantially neglected in the process, when not only were W_1 and W_2 recurringly found wanting, but when they were so found by what was then a new breed of researchers who themselves initially represented and expressed a significant expansion of what the language-related disciplines had formerly been. Let us remember that the 1950s and 1960s (and even the 1970s) constituted a time in which a definite methodological tradition matured and diversified within the language-related disciplines: the tradition of quantitative experimentation following classical independent variable-dependent variable lines of inquiry, proof and argumentation. This tradition, let us also remember, was drastically different from the more text-analytic, descriptive-anecdotal, ethnographic, holistic, and nonlinear commentary and analysis that Whorf had employed and that most of his adherents preferred (and prefer to this very day). Given these major differences as to the nature of evidence and the nature of proof that obtained between Whorf and his critics (and, more recently, between his staunchest defenders and his critics), it is now evident, insofar as W_1 and W_2 are concerned, that not only do the critics and the defenders disagree as to what has been proven but that they also disagree as to what Whorf's hypotheses were to begin with.

Clarification of 'what Whorf really meant' is no easy matter. It is complicated by the fact that Whorf died in 1941 at the regrettably early age of 44. All of his professional writing transpired between 1925 and 1941. Thus, he has now been dead for almost two-and-a-half times as many years as he had available to clarify and finalize his own hypotheses. During his own life time he was aware of some doubts and misunderstandings — even in the circle of his friends and admirers, including Sapir — and began to

revise, restate, and reinterpret his own views and eliminate the inconsistencies that inevitably were to be found among them, given the fact that
they were always evolving rather than fixed and final in his own mind.
Nevertheless, he was granted very little time for such revisions and
emendations, and as a result, left us only the equivalent of one slim volume
of professional writings (totaling under 300 pages). Interpretations, tests,
and evaluations of W_1 and W_2 are by now obviously much more
voluminous than Whorf's work itself. Although he has become a legend
(hero or failure, as the case may be), that status had added nothing to
either the clarity of his own writings or to the uniformity of interpretations
to which they have been subjected.

The critique of criticism

Increasingly, current-day defenders of Whorf attack his detractors as
either never having read his work, or vulgarizing him. The 'never having
read Whorf' criticism seizes upon the extensive anti-Whorf literature and
accuses the critics of having largely read one another, thereby merely
contributing exegeses of each other's texts, rather than having examined
Whorf's original views. Whether justified or not in this particular case,
there is an obvious danger for methodologically different traditions to be
ideologically disinclined to read each other. This disinclination stems not
only from the formalized and avowed higher level differences that separate
them, but also from the fact that reading each other's literature is often
a truly aggravating and unenlightening experience, given that it is
accompanied every step of the way by lower-level disagreements as to
what is *data*, what is *interpretation*, and what is *demonstration*. The
'vulgarization of Whorf' criticism is also precedented in the annals of
cross-methodological and cross-philosophical/ideological debate. Not unlike criticism of Marx or Freud, much criticism of Whorf has been labeled
simplification, reductionism, atomization, distortion, and so on (e.g. note
Alford's 1978 criticism of Brown, 1976; Berlin & Kay, 1969; Cole &
Scribner, 1974; Slobin, 1971; on the other hand, note the critiques of
Whorf in each of the above-mentioned sources. For an exhaustive list of
quantitative-experimental criticisms of Whorf in connection with W_2 in
particular, see Sridhar, 1980). Similarly, the defenders of Whorf have not
escaped unscathed, having been dubbed mystics, romantics, dogmatists,
and anecdotalists.

The underlying point here is one of wide significance, its implications going far beyond Whorfian hypotheses W_1 and W_2, and even beyond linguistics or the language-related disciplines. The problems sketched above with respect to defining and confirming various theories may be expected to multiply rather than to diminish, precisely as a by-product of disciplinary growth and inter-disciplinary stimulation. The broader and the more inclusive a field of enquiry becomes — and the language-related disciplines taken together are certainly among those that have experienced the most remarkable flowering and expansion during the past quarter century — the more likely just such problems are to arise. What is data, what constitutes proof, what is disconfirmation — indeed, just what is the problem — these all become less rather than more consensual as interdisciplinary perspective increases. Indeed, this is the price we pay (and that work on the Whorfian hypotheses has paid) whenever we focus disparate methodological perspectives on the same problem. Different methodologies are different languages. They are not duplicates of one another. They intertranslate only roughly, rather than exactly. They are different *Weltanschauungen* and, therefore, rather than being articulated in any fine-grained manner, they are immediately valuable precisely because they highlight different aspects of reality. Ultimately, a type of bilingual/bicultural accommodation may be attainable between them, but that takes more time, effort, and good will than science or scientists can frequently spare. W_1 itself would have predicted that maximally different methodological languages would be maximally divergent in defining and discussing W_1 and accordingly in deciding on its validity.

Quite understandably, the rise (or return) during the past decade of ethnography, holism, linguistics of intent, and anthropology of meaning has resulted in a new view of Whorf's work and in new hope among those who are intuitively or philosophically 'attuned' to him, not to mention those few who stood by him during the long dry spell from the 1950s through to the late 1970s. For many others, however, the recent change in *Zeitgeist* (*Methodengeist*?) has left the basic issue either unresolved or in a distinct state of contention — and particularly so with respect to W_2 — not only as to the truth of the matter (i.e. as to what has or has not been proven), but even with respect to the issue itself (i.e. as to what Whorf himself did or did not claim in that connection). While I will not dwell upon my own views on these matters here,[2] I will briefly reiterate my considered opinion that regardless of what our (or posterity's) personal judgement with respect to the above matters may be, the past quarter-century's intellectual struggle with these hypotheses has been eminently worthwhile. Not only have W_1 and W_2 been reexamined and possibly rehabilitated, but more importantly, the struggle has stimulated and even fathered a number of related fields of unquestioned worth and vitality. Such fields as language universals (at least in their Greenbergian realizations, see Ferguson, 1978), ethnosciences (including ethnotypologies and ethnocognition as a whole) and socio-linguistics might all be weaker today if some of their leading formulators and adherents had not quite consciously been either struggling with or for Whorf (i.e. with or for W_1 and/or W_2), as they rightly or wrongly understood him. Even if W_2 in particular were ultimately to be discarded as untenable, the stimulation that it has provided, both to its erstwhile supporters and its erstwhile detractors — not unlike the stimulation provided by certain unconfirmed hypotheses of Freud and Marx — will have resulted in permanent gains for the disciplines on either side of the issue that have considered it seriously. This too, should be a lesson to us for the future: the interaction between *Zeitgeist* in methodology of the social sciences, on the one hand, and *Zeitgeist* in the sociology of knowledge, on the other — inescapable though it may be — may nevertheless be worthwhile. Every orthodoxy, being simultaneously an orthodoxy in both of the above respects (i.e. in respect to what is known and in respect to how knowledge may be pursued) — whether this be Chomskyism, ethnomethodologism, ethno-graphism, or natural scientism in the language-related disciplines — leads away from certain topics, sensitivities, and questions as well as toward others. If we are lucky, the gain may equal or exceed the loss, and if we are wise, no orthodoxy — not even our own — will remain unchallenged for very long.

Yet another side to Whorf: The value of ethnolinguistic diversity

As mentioned earlier, interdisciplinary and intermethodological struggles with and about W_1 and W_2 have tended to obscure from sight another aspect of Whorf. I am referring to Whorf as a neo-Herderian champion (linked to Herder by the usual intellectual linkage system of students and teachers and the teachers, in turn, to their teachers, and in this particular case via Sapir, Boas, Wundt, and von Humboldt — this complete linkage system not yet being fully confirmed but quite clearly reasonable, see Y.M. 1974) of a multilingual, multicultural world in which 'little peoples' and 'little languages' would not only be respected but valued (Fishman, 1978). The advisability of such a world order has long been a bone of contention in Euro-Mediterranean thought in which for some three-and-a-half thousand years distinctly opposite views with respect to this issue have been recurringly restated and reexamined. The two poles mentioned above were occupied, on the one hand, by ancient Hebrew and Greek prophets and social philosophers, and, on the other, by spokesmen for the Western Roman Empire and the Western Catholic Church. As I have indicated elsewhere (Fishman, 1982), and as I still hope to show some day in all the detail that it entails, the former conceived of the world ethnocentrically, perhaps, but yet ethnopluralistically, viewing ethnolinguistic diversity as part and parcel of the fundamental nature of human society, ethnolinguistic stability or the intactness of any ethnolinguistic collectivity as sanctified (and, if 'properly' enacted, i.e. enacted in accord with the highest mission or design that existed for each and every people, as eternal). In accord with this view, transethnification and translinguification were viewed as cataclysmic tragedies, whereas ethnolinguistic intergenerational continuity, if 'properly' enacted, was viewed as its own reward: ennobling, authentic, fulfilling, humanizing. This tradition, initially encoded via classical Judaism, Eastern Orthodox Christianity and early Islam — all of which yielded systems of thought and valuation which are still generally in accord with these views to this very day — first reached Central Europe via Slavic (i.e. Eastern Orthodox) influences on Czech and German medieval social philosophers (Jakobson, 1945). It was then available — with ever increasing stress on a language aspect of authenticity — to become an ingredient of early Reformation thinking, and, subsequently, has had numerous Western as well as Central and Eastern European spokesmen and defenders (Deutsch, 1942).

Meanwhile, the Western Empire and the Church that it adopted (and that finally became its major heir), had developed a theory of language and ethnicity more in accord with their own needs, opportunities, and much greater technical capacities. From their point of view, small and localized ethnolinguistic collectivities were quite natural and even desirable early stages of social organization, but no more than that. As greater opportunities, rewards, understandings and benefits (spiritual as well as material) became available, populations were expected to re-ethnify and relinguify accordingly, in pursuit of their own best interests. Thus, except for lags attributable to temporary breakdowns in the reward system and to the self-seeking stubbornness of local leaders (always accused of being afraid of being deprived of their prerogatives), what the East viewed as sanctified and eternal the West viewed as open, changeable, and reward-determined. Any particular ethnolinguistic boundary came to be viewed in the West as no more than a functional and possibly temporary reflection of the authoritative flow of rewards in the past, and, therefore as naturally and even joyfully invalidated by newer, more effective, more beneficial reward arrangements. The outer limit of this process — both for the

Western Empire/Church and its more modern, secular substitutes and replacements — was a unified mankind within a single unified realm, subscribing to a universal value system and, as a result of all the foregoing, speaking a universal language (see St. Augustine in his *City of God*). Thus, what has come to be viewed by some as the epitome of rational self-interest and enlightened pan-human concern — including predominant present-day liberal, statist, Marxist, and neutralist sociological schools of thought — is viewed by others (usually operating on a more local and intimate scale) as the epitome of dehumanization and self-destruction. Many modern societies — including the U.S.A. and the U.S.S.R. — have simultaneously inherited major segments of both of the above traditions and, therefore, are *internally* conflicted as well as being conflicted with viewpoints from outside their own borders. In this respect, as in many others, Whorf is an avowed Easterner rather than a Westerner. To show this clearly requires another brief detour in order that we may review Herder's major premises. Herder's major premises.

Johann Gottfried Herder (1744–1803): Praeceptor slavorum[3]

Herder's unique contribution to the above-sketched arena of competing values and purposes was to sidestep either extreme — or to co-opt them both — via the view that the entire world needs a diversity of ethnolinguistic entities for its own salvation, for its greater creativity, for the more certain solution of human problems, for the constant rehumanization of humanity in the face of materialism, for fostering greater esthetic, intellectual, and emotional capacities for humanity as a whole, indeed, for arriving at a higher stage of human functioning. It is precisely in order to arrive at this higher stage and in order to participate more fully in it that less powerful ethnolinguistic collectivities must be protected, respected, and assisted, because it is they who have the most vital contribution to make to these desirable goals.

While he shared the Hebreo-Greek view that loyalty to one's authentic tradition is a *sine qua non* that inevitably brings its own rewards, he went beyond that tradition in two major respects. Within any authentic tradition he stressed the authentic language as constituting the very center on which all else depended. Furthermore, he considered the rewards of fidelity to language and to way of life to be available not only to the community in which these originated but to all of mankind. For Herder, and for genuine pluralists since Herder, the great creative forces that inspire all humanity do not emerge out of universal civilization, but out of the individuality of separate ethnic collectivities — most particularly, out of their very own authentic languages. Only if each collectivity contributes its own thread to the tapestry of world history, and only if each is accepted and respected for making its own contribution, can nationalities finally also be ruled by a sense of reciprocity, learning and benefiting from each other's contributions as well. In this fashion Herder encompasses both the particular and the universal. He considers political and economic arrangements that unite and that transcend individual peoples as possible and desirable, but only if they are built upon and derive from a genuine prior cultivation of ethnolinguistic individuality, because it is only the latter that can render the constituent parts active, creative, contributing, self-respecting and other-accepting members of any supranational design. For Herder, the two levels, the smaller and the larger, are ultimately simultaneously ongoing, rather than the latter displacing the former.

Even from the above brief paraphrasing it should be clear how much of current thinking (and how much more of current feeling) in the language-related disciplines is Herderian in origin. Members of these disciplines are often deeply saddened to learn of mother-tongue loss and of cultural assimilation on the part of small and powerless ethnolinguistic entities. Indeed, in deeply unconscious and prescientific ways, convictions such as these are among the very ones that brought many of us to linguistics, to anthropology, to bilingual education, and to a variety of ethnic studies. It is Herder who most clearly and forcefully formulated these views. He did not wince at their romanticism, as many of us do now, for, unlike us, rationalists at least in our professional guises, he firmly believed that it was at the level of the intuitive or prerational that the most profoundly human and creative experiences were to be encountered. Nevertheless, though our science clothes our prerationality far more fully than did Herder's literary, historical esthetic, and folkloristic interests, most of us can still recognize in him hidden parts of ourselves. If we are also attracted to Whorf on some prerational, intuitive level, it is because Whorf, too, is an unabashed Herderian. Via his hypotheses W_1 and W_2 he seeks to control and tame or discipline the Herderian passions within him. But the passions are there nonetheless, and, scientific or not, it is high time we looked at that part of Whorf directly rather than indirectly.

Whorf and Herder: Overlooked similarities in basic values

Herder's defense of backward Slavic Europe, a defense which stresses the untutored refinement and wisdom of peoples that have not capitulated to the massive blandishments of Western materialism, who experience life and nature in deeply poetic and collectively meaningful ways, is paralleled by Whorf in his defense of Native-Americans in particular and of non-Western wisdom and perspective in general. For Herder, the specter of uniformation hovering over Europe appears in a French guise; for Whorf, the danger that approaches is predominantly Anglo-American and English in nature. It is not only that he views the Hopi language as revealing '. . . a higher plane of thinking, a more rational analysis of situations than our vaunted English . . . (which) compared to Hopi is like a bludgeon compared to a rapier' (1956 [1936]: 85), but that he recurringly finds the West in general, and the English-fostering West in particular, to be conceptually inferior, intellectually biased, and interculturally overly proud, even haughty. Whorf's view that the Greeks 'debased' linguistics after the Hindus (Pānini) had founded it at an exceptionally advanced level (1956 [1940]: 232) is too well known to require citing here. Less well known is his view that

> . . . the ideal of worldwide fraternity and cooperation fails if it does not include ability to adjust intellectually as well as emotionally to our brethren of other countries. The West . . . has *not* bridged the intellectual gulf; we are no nearer to understanding the types of logical thinking which are reflected in truly Eastern forms of scientific thought or analyses of nature. This requires . . . the . . . realization that they have equal scientific validity with our own thinking habits (1941:21).

Here we find not only Herder's theme that the universal is a fraud, a mask for the self-interest of the dominating over the dominated, but an insistence on putting the case precisely in terms of science itself. This, indeed, is one of Whorf's major themes: that science itself must accept the non-West as an equal and must come to view itself as no more obviously rational and objective than the so-called mysterious East. The West is highly irrational in Whorf's eyes, particularly Western science, since it tends to confuse power with insight and understanding.

> . . . (Do) our cultivated wheat and oats represent a higher evolutionary stage than a rare aster restricted to a few sites in the Himalayas (?). From the standpoint of a matured biology it is precisely the rare aster which has the better claim to high evolutionary eminence: the (Western) wheat owes its ubiquity and prestige merely to human economics and history. The eminence of our European tongues and thinking habits proceeds from nothing more (1956 [1936?]: 84).

As with Herder, therefore, there is a sharp anti-establishment bite to Whorf. Herder attacked French and Francofied interests in Europe as a whole and among Germans in particular; Whorf points his finger at the West as whole and at Anglo-American imperialism in particular. In so doing, both Herder and Whorf not only are opposing long-standing (taken-for-granted) intellectual assumptions, but they are also foregoing the safety and patronage that normally come from siding with the social and political establishment. Whorf's digs at the English language are particularly noteworthy if we consider that Anglo-American and other Western linguists were (and often still are) hard put to detach themselves from its purported superiority.[4] Not only was Whorf completely free of any such popular wisdom *vis-à-vis* English, but he was particularly dubious about schemes to foster Basic English or some other natural or artificial auxiliary language as the basis of world unity. There was no easy road to world unity as far as Whorf was concerned, and the best that native speakers of English (particularly scientists who were native speakers of English) could do in pursuit of that goal was to supplement their English with 'the point of view of multilingual awareness' (1956 [1941]: 244). More generally he warned that,

> ... those who envision a future world speaking only one tongue whether English, German or Russian, or any other, hold a misguided view and would do the evolution of the human mind the greatest disservice. Western culture has made, through language, a provisional analysis of reality and, without correctives, holds resolutely to that analysis as final. The only correctives lie in all those other tongues which by aeons of independent evolution have arrived at different but equally logical, provisional analyses (1956 [1941]: 244).

Although Whorf's overriding interest in language and cognition permeates all of his writing — even most of that which is of a semipopular or lay nature (and which we also tend to overlook today, even though he was immensely involved in such writing as a public service) — his Herderian stress on diversity, on 'all those other tongues,' on genuine universality being attainable only via a 'multilingual awareness' which accepts and utilizes the languages and perspectives of non-Western peoples, shines through and underlies all that he writes. Like Herder, he believes that the world's little languages and peoples are a treasure trove of wisdom and refinement. Only if this human treasure is valued and shared can biases be set aside and a genuine (rather than a self-serving imperialistic) universal perspective be attained. It is no wonder that among American linguists Hymes has been the most outspoken opponent of the impoverishment that would result from seeking universals based on

English alone (1970 [1974]), doing so precisely by invoking Herder.

The Whorf of W_3 is directly linked to much of the social consciousness of the language-in-society-related disciplines. As such he is related to pluralistic language policies, to cultural democracy and language maintenance efforts, to enrichment bilingual education, and to sympathy and assistance for the Third World in efforts to attain pan-human sanity and salvation. Whorf died still hoping against hope that a bilingual awareness might arise to reform the misguided Western world before it was too late, before 'the impending darkness' (1956 [1942]: 270) that he feared would descend upon us all — including the world of science — without such an awareness. It is Whorf's abiding faith in the benefits of linguistic diversity that attracted many of us to him and to the language-related disciplines and that may well continue to do so for others, regardless of the fate of W_1 and W_2.

Coming full circle: The scientific status and methodological implications of W_3

Can the Herder-Whorf vision of a better world based upon sharing a multiplicity of little languages and appreciating a variety of little peoples be tested, confirmed, or revised and refined? Does it have a scientific rather than 'merely' a humanistic or philosophical future? I think so, because even though neither Herder nor Whorf was marked by much econopolitical sophistication (which, of course, is not to say that they were apolitical, much less to deny that their views have political consequences; see Bernard, 1983), they might nevertheless both have been right (or wrong) on an empirical sociopsychological level alone. Much of the recent and ongoing work on global consciousness and international understanding has consistently demonstrated that active and advanced multilingualism is a significant independent variable in their prediction (Barrows, Clark & Klein, 1980). In addition, much of Wallace Lambert's work on the greater cognitive flexibility of bilinguals (Lambert & Peal, 1962; Lambert et al., 1973) is in direct agreement with the W_3 school of thought. There has thus far been no explicit link between W_3 and either of the above research endeavors, but that is largely because W_1 and W_2 have substantially hidden W_3 from sight. However, if that were no longer to be the case and if a veritable ground-swell of interest in W_3 were to develop, I predict that the consequences would be manifold, quite independently of their directionality in any substantive sense.

Some W_3 researchers will doubtless seek to render the status of this hypothesis more precise by operationalizing quantitative measures of its independent and dependent variables and by assigning subjects to randomly constituted, maximally contrasted treatment groups for the purposes of controlled experimental comparison. Other researchers, however, will quite definitely take a quite different and more qualitative route toward testing W_3. The two approaches may well disagree with respect to some of their findings, interpretations, and, indeed, with respect to their claims of fidelity to the original W_3 hypothesis. Still other researchers will continue to believe (or, indeed, to disbelieve) in W_3, entirely as a matter of devotion, as a value, regardless of what the findings might be, since the language-related disciplines, like all disciplines, are themselves also value systems (and in the West, internally conflicted value systems). As such, they are protective of kindred values and of those who subscribe to them. Finally, midway between the more internally consistent approaches to W_3 mentioned above, there will be those who will seek to combine both this world and the next, that is, to refine their 'values' via 'science' and to guide their 'science' via 'values.' The hypothesis as such is necessarily too broad ('necessarily' because it derives not from science *per se* but from values more basic than science), and science as an enterprise is too variegated to entertain only a single interpretation, operationalization, or formulation thereof. It is consistent with the entire spirit of W_3 to conclude that such must be its fate in any free scientific climate.

The legacy of W_3 for linguistics as a science

The past quarter-century's experience with W_1 and W_2, and the coming quarter-century's experience with W_3 can serve to remind linguistics-as-a-science that linguistics is also very significantly a humanities field and an applied field as well. As a result, even more so than were linguistics to be a science and only a science, it corresponds to certain pervasive, soul-satisfying, meaning-and-value needs of its 'members.' These needs can also have dignifying and protective value for the discipline *qua* science. Our frequent advocacy of the weak and as yet unappreciated peoples and languages upon which W_3 focuses, dignifies not only them but us, safeguards not only them but us, for it keeps us from following (or straying) in the footsteps of Hitler's professors (Weinreich, 1946) along a path which glorified W_1 and W_2 without experiencing the tempering impact of W_3.

Certainly, linguistics as a science and linguists as scientists cannot and should not try to escape from the values and loyalties, dreams and intuitions, visions and sensitivities that move them and that touch them. If these prerationalities are not self-aggrandizing (and neither Herder's nor Whorf's were, if they lead to greater assistance, appreciation and dignity for the world's little peoples and little languages), then these are prerationalities to be proud of. If we each of us will but carry them on our sleeves within our own country rather than merely *vis-à-vis* someone else's — whether our own country be the U.S.A. or Israel, Egypt or Mexico, Canada or Yugoslavia, China or the U.S.S.R. — then these are prerationalities that will be good for us as individuals, good for linguistics as a discipline, and good for mankind as our common concern. That, ultimately, was the very kind of linguistics that Whorf envisioned.

Notes to Chapter 22

1. I do not consider it necessary, at this late date, more than to mention the well-documented fact that neither W_1 nor W_2 were hypotheses original to Whorf. Others in Whorf's immediate circle of colleagues had acknowledged interest and sympathy for these views prior to Whorf's focus upon them, and such views had been articulated for approximately two centuries by various European (particularly German) thinkers (e.g. Herder, von Humboldt, and Wundt, to name only a few), and the basic notions in one or both of these hypotheses occur several times throughout two-and-a-half thousand years of Euro-Mediterranean language-related speculation (Culjak, 1968; Fishman, 1980) and are probably of at least similar vintage in India, China, and perhaps even elsewhere. Nevertheless, today we not only parsimoniously but also rightfully call these hypotheses 'Whorfian,' because it was precisely Whorf's stimulating focus upon them that returned them to modern debate and inquiry, particularly in the United States. To call these hypotheses *Whorfian* is, therefore, as technically mistaken as to call the Western Hemisphere *The Americas* (after Amerigo Vespucci) but, at the same time, it is also equally justified and, by now, equally traditional to do so.
2. My documented view (Fishman, 1960, 1978, 1980) is that Whorf did entertain both of the hypotheses here referred to as W_1 and W_2, although he was considerably less certain and less consistent with respect to the latter than the former. Furthermore, my evaluation of the empirical literature leads me to the conclusion that W_1 has been confirmed over and over again, not only by Whorf and since Whorf, but prior to Whorf, whereas W_2 has not been confirmed as a stable phenomenon at the lexical level by methods that recognize the independent variable-dependent variable distinction and the canons of publically confirmable reliability and validity. Even less confirmation of W_2 has been forthcoming in accord with the above research paradigm at levels higher than the lexical. (See Haugen, 1977 for recent further confirmation of this conclusion.) If investigators following ethnographic, holistic, and nonlinear research strategies were to become fully convinced of the validity of W_2 (I do not sense any such conviction among them at this time; indeed, I sense a

tendency among such researchers to ascribe W_2 not to Whorf himself but, rather to those who misunderstand him, e.g. Alford, 1978; Silverstein, 1979). I would conclude that the two different interpretations/operationalizations of the hypotheses involved were responsible for the difference in findings. These methodological differences might or might not prove reconcilable. As long as they were not, I would tend to consider the hypothesis contested or unconfirmed (but, hopefully, in a state of productive tension) regardless of my own preferences in the matter.

3. Since a paper on Whorf is hardly the right place for extensive quotations from Herder, I will satisfy my urge to use such quotations by summarizing Herder's views on various topics and referring the reader to the original sources where these views can be found. The best account of Herder's life is Haym, 1877–85. For a fine account and interpretation of Herder's manifold direct and indirect interests in language and ethnicity/nationality, see Ergang, 1931. It is directly to Herder's *Sammtliche Werke* (1877–1913) that the reader must turn for the full treatment of the view that there is nothing more central than language in the life of any ethnic collectivity (*Volk*) (see e.g. XI 225, XVII 58, XVIII 337 and 384); neither individual nor collective creativity are possible if the authentic ethnic language is lost (see e.g. XVI 46, XVII 59 and 288–89, XVIII 387); learning from other peoples and languages poses no problem if one does it without forgetting or dishonoring one's own (see e.g. I 407, VI 217, VIII 336); early and consistent education in the mother tongue is a necessity regardless of whatever else one learns (see e.g. I 380–81 and 406, IV 301, XXX 129); the universal can be participated in fruitfully (rather than slavishly) only through the authentic (see e.g. XIV 448, XVII 211–12, XVIII 248). A typical formulation of the latter view urges: 'Let us contribute to the honor of our nationality — and learn incessantly from and with others — so that together we can seek the truth and cultivate the garden of the common good' (XVII 211–12); also 'Let us, therefore, be German, not because Germans are superior to all other nationalities, but because we are Germans and cannot well be anything else and because we can contribute to humanity at large only by being German' (Ergang, 1931: 265).

4. Whorf's lack of positive hyperbole with respect to English is all the more remarkable given sentiments such as the following which were nurtured by linguistic culture just prior to his time: (a) 'The Anglo-Saxon language is the simplest, the most perfectly and simply symbolic that the world has ever seen . . . [B]y means of it, the Anglo-Saxon saves his vitality for conquest instead of wasting it under the juggernaut of cumbersome mechanism for conveyance of thought' (McGee, 1895). (b) 'The English language is a methodical, energetic business-like and sober language that does not care much for finery and elegance, but does care for logical consistency and is opposed to any attempt to narrow-in life by police regulation and strict rules, either of grammar or of lexicon. As the language is, so is the people . . . It must be a source of gratification to mankind that the tongue spoken by two of the greatest powers of the world is so noble, so rich, so pliant, so expressive and so interesting' (Jespersen, 1938 [1905]: 235). Ironically, the latter author's laudatory view that 'as the language is, so is the people' would probably be characterized in recent days as revealing 'extreme Whorfianism,' whereas Whorf's sharply critical views insofar as English is concerned have nevertheless not spared him from being similarly characterized.

References

ALFORD, D. K. H. 1978, The demise of the Whorf hypothesis (A major revision in the history of linguistics). *Proceedings of the Fourth Annual Meeting of the Berkeley Linguistics Society*. Berkeley: Berkeley Linguistics Society, pp. 485–99.

BARROWS, T., CLARK, J., & KLEIN S. 1980, What students know about their world. *Change* 12: 10–17 and 67.

BERLIN, B. & KAY, P. 1969, *Basic Color Terms*. Berkeley: University of California Press.

BERNARD, F. M. 1983, National culture and political legitimacy: Herder and Rousseau. *Journal of the History of Ideas* 44: 231–54.

BROWN, R. 1976, Reference: In memorial tribute to Eric Lenneberg. *Cognition* 4: 125–53.

COLE, M. & SCRIBNER, S. 1974, *Culture and Thought: A Psychological Introduction*. New York: John Wiley and Sons.

CULJAK, M. 1968, The Theory of Linguistic Weltanschauung and B. L. Whorf's Hypothesis: Historical Sources and Critical Assessment. Ph.D. Dissertation, University of Delhi.

DEUTSCH, K. W. 1942, The trend of European nationalism: The language aspect. *American Political Science Review* 36: 533–41.

ERGANG, R. R. 1931, *Herder and the Foundations of German Nationalism*. New York: Columbia University Press.

FERGUSON, C. A. 1978, Historical background of universals research. In J. H. GREENBERG, C. A. FERGUSON & E. A. MORAVCSIK (eds.), *Universals of Human Language*. Stanford: Stanford University Press.

FISHMAN, J. A. 1960, The systematization of the Whorfian hypothesis. *Behavioral Science* 5:323–79.

— 1978, Positive bilingualism: Some overlooked rationales and forefathers. In J. E. ALATIS (ed.), *Georgetown University Round Table on Languages and Linguistics 1978*. Washington, D.C.: Georgetown University Press.

— 1980, The Whorfian hypothesis: Varieties of valuation, confirmation and disconfirmation I. *International Journal of the Sociology of Language* 26: 25–40; also Chapter 14, *This Volume*.

FREIDRICH, P. 1979, Poetic language and the imagination: A reformulation of the Sapir hypothesis. In P. FREIDRICH (ed.), *Language, Context and the Imagination*. Stanford: Stanford University Press.

HAUGEN, E. 1977, Linguistic relativity: Myths and methods. In W. C. MCCORMACK & S. A. WURM (eds.), *Language and Thought: Anthropological Issues*. The Hague: Mouton.

HAYM, R. 1877–85, *Herder nach seinem Leben und seinen Werken dargestellt*. 2 vols. Berlin.

HERDER, J. G. 1877–1913, *Sammtliche Werke*, ed. by B. SUHAN, E. REDLICH *et al*. 33 vols. Berlin.

HYMES, D. 1966, Two types of linguistic relativity (with examples from Amerindian ethnography). In W. BRIGHT (ed.), *Sociolinguistics: Proceedings of the UCLA Sociolinguistics Conference, 1964*. The Hague: Mouton.

— 1970, Bilingual education: Linguistic vs. sociolinguistic bases. *Georgetown University Monograph Series on Languages and Linguistics* 23: 69–76. (Revised in his *Foundations in Sociolinguistics*. Philadelphia: University of Pennsylvania Press, 1974.)

JAKOBSON, R. 1945, The beginning of national self-determination in Europe. *The Review of Politics* 7: 29–42.

JESPERSEN, O. 1938 [1905], *Growth and Structure of the English Language*. 9th edition. Garden City, N.J.: Doubleday.

KAY, P. & KEMPTON, W. 1984, What is the Sapir-Whorf hypothesis? *American Anthropologist* 86, 65–79.

LAMBERT, W. E. & PEAL, E. 1962, The relation of bilingualism to intelligence. *Psychological Monographs* 76: No. 27 (Whole No, 546).

LAMBERT, W. E., TUCKER, G. R., & D 'ANGLEJAN, A. 1973, Cognitive and attitudinal consequences of bilingual education. *Journal of Educational Psychology* 65: 141–59.

McGEE, W. J. 1985, Some principles of nomenclature. *American Anthropologist* 8: 279–86.

SILVERSTEIN, M. 1979, Language structure and linguistic ideology. *Proceedings of the Chicago Linguistics Society*. Chicago: Chicago Linguistics Society, pp. 193–247.

SLOBIN, D. I. 1971, *Psycholinguistics*. Glenview, Ill.: Scott, Foresman.

SRIDHAR, S. N. 1980, Cognitive determinants of linguistic structure: A cross-linguistic experimental study of sentence production. Ph.D. Dissertation. Champaign-Urbana: University of Illinois.

WEINREICH, M. 1946, *Hitler's Professors: The Part of Scholarship in Germany's Crimes Against the Jewish People*. New York: Yiddish Scientific Institute-Yivo. (Yiddish version: 1947).

WHORF, B. L. 1941, A brotherhood of thought. *Main Currents in Modern Thought* 1: 13–14.

— 1956, *Language, Thought, and Reality: Selected Writings of Benjamin Lee Whorf* ed. by J. B. CARROLL. New York: Wiley.

Y. M. 1974, Editorial comment: a Herder-Humboldt-Sapir-Whorf hypothesis? *Romance Philology* 28: 199.

23 Utilizing societal variables to predict whether countries are linguistically homogeneous or heterogeneous

Introduction

Psycholinguists are accustomed to studying linguistic homogeneity as an *individual* repertoire variable, i.e. to view it as a dimension that can vary in degree, along the entire range linguistically very narrow- to linguistically very broad-ranged individual repertoires. Via such studies one can seek answers to questions about the relative important of other individual characteristics that tend to make for, or be predictive of, broader or narrower individual linguistic repertoires. Sociolinguists, on the other hand, are accustomed to studying linguistic homogeneity/heterogeneity as a *societal* repertoire variable, i.e. to view it as a dimension that can vary in degree, along the entire range from very homogeneous to very heterogeneous speech networks or speech communities. Via such studies one can seek answers to questions about the relative importance of other speech-network or speech-community characteristics that tend to make for, or be predictive of, broader or narrower speech-network/speech-community repertoires. The present study is in the latter tradition, except that it is focussed on larger societal units than sociolinguists commonly study, namely on polities, i.e. on political entities most of which are self-governing. It will try to explore linguistic homogeneity as a characteristic of polities, i.e. to view linguistic homogeneity/heterogeneity as a dimension that can vary in degree, along the entire range from linguistically very homogeneous to very heterogeneous polities. It is hoped that this study will contribute to answering questions about the relative importance of other polity-characteristics that tend to make for, or be predictive of, more or less linguistically homogeneous polities. If there were a recognized inter-disciplinary area of specialization known as 'politilinguistics' this study might be assigned to it; since no such area of specialization is generally recognized, we will consider this to be study of a macro-sociolinguistic kind and one that should be of interest not only to sociologists and political scientists but to all who have a live interest in political affairs and processes.

Just as it is true that all individuals and speech communities have their very own, individual experiential histories that fully explain their particular degrees of linguistic homogeneity, so this is true with respect to individual polities. Nevertheless, in a study comparing many individuals or many speech communities we consensually set aside purely individual ('clinical') circumstances and seek overall, actuarial answers. We are interested in factors of a generalizable sort, factors that are relevant to the vast majority of individuals or speech communities, so that our analyses and conclusions too can have the broadest relevance. We are willing to come up with answers that may not be maximally informative or predictive with respect to individual X or speech community Y (they will have to be investigated via 'clinical' studies focussed directly on them and on them alone), in order to be able to attain answers that have the greatest explanatory or predictive power for the total sample of individuals or the total sample of speech communities that have been or might be studied. Similarly, when engaged in studies at the inter-polity level, we must set aside a full-scale inquiry into Belgium or India *per se* and seek to locate the polity level characteristics that will provide the most powerful explanatory or predictive account of inter-polity variation in linguistic homogeneity/heterogeneity for our total sample of polities. There *is* a theoretical link between individual clinical research and large sample actuarial research. Many studies of the one kind provide hypotheses and clues to be investigated via future studies of other kind. But at any particular point in time, any piece of research is inevitably of one kind or the other. The present study is based on a large sample of polities (n=130) and seeks to be maximally explanatory or predictive at that level, i.e. with respect to the inter-polity variance in linguistic homogeneity/heterogeneity.

Prior research on this topic

The groundbreaking study of this type, examining a large number of variables in a large number of polities in connection with linguistic homogeneity/heterogeneity was that by Fishman (1966; slightly revised: 1968), although he was admittedly inspired in this direction by earlier work by Deutsch (1966). Fishman's study contrasted 52 polities that were relatively homogeneous (i.e. those in which *fewer than 15%* of the population did not share the dominant mother tongue in the country) with 62 polities that were relatively heterogeneous (i.e. polities in which *more than 15%* of the population did not share the dominant mother tongue of the country), doing so in connection with a very large number of historical, demographic, social, cultural, political and economic variables (198 in all), in order to determine which, if any, of all of these variables significantly differentiated between the two major types of polities focussed upon by his study. The data Fishman worked with was primarily that provided in the cross-polity handbook of Banks & Textor (1963) and, secondarily, that provided in a similar handbook by Russett *et al.* (1964). Fishman's major conclusions were twofold: (a) the manifold differences encountered between relatively homogeneous and relatively heterogeneous polities are overwhelmingly characterizable as differences between richer and poorer polities more generally, and (b) when the basic economic differences are statistically controlled for or partialed out, then only two of the prior manifold differences between linguistically more homogeneous and linguistically less homogeneous polities still remain, namely *political enculturation* (in connection with which case the relatively more homogeneous polities are more numerous) and *sectionalism* (in connection with which the relatively less homogeneous polities are more numerous). Fishman takes leave of this study, not without listing many empirical and methodological caveats indicative of the need for better and more cross-polity data in general and language-related data in particular, by posing a major problem for future research, namely, to determine the direction of causality between the major variables related to his findings, i.e. did certain polities tend to remain economically more underdeveloped, politically less enculturated and more extremely sectionalistic because they were *already* linguistically more heterogeneous or, vice versa, did they remain linguistically more heterogeneous because they were economically less developed, politically less enculturated and characterized by more extreme sectionalism. Fishman's own interpretation, perhaps more a wish than a demonstrated conclusion, was that it was not impossible to pursue (via modern planning methods) *both* economic development *and* ethnolinguistic heterogeneity together, as joint rather than as mutually exclusive goals.

Pool turned to Fishman's questions as to the direction of causality and the possibility of simultaneously maximizing both ethnolinguistic heterogeneity and economic development (1969; reprinted with slight revisions in 1972) with a more elegant statistical analysis, on the basis of which he concluded that 'a planner who insists on preserving cultural-linguistic pluralism had better be ready to sacrifice economic progress . . . [because] at the extremities of linguistic diversity there is at present not a single country able to serve as a model (or living proof of the danger) of economic-development-*sans*-assimilation-in-language; (1969: 151–52). However, the dangers of arriving at conclusions based only upon data from the extremes of any distribution, as Pool had done, led McRae (1983) to focus on the *two largest language groups in any polity* for the purpose of defining linguistically more homogeneous and linguistically less homogeneous polities. His conclusion, somewhat more in line with Fishman's hopes than with Pool's findings, is that

> 'high levels of political and economic development are compatible
> with the existence of two (or possibly more) significant language
> communities, but probably not with extreme linguistic fragmentation.
> In other words, efficiency of communication may indeed be correctly
> identified as a prerequisite to development, but this efficiency need
> not rest upon exclusive use of a single language; it may be achieved
> on the basis of two languages and perhaps three' (p.15).

Although the exact nature of the research question had inevitably been changing from study to study, from an exploration of the differences between relatively homogeneous and relatively heterogeneous polities, to an exploration of the direction of causality between ethnolinguistic homogeneity/heterogeneity and economic development, to an exploration of the possibility of having one's cake and eating it too, the dependence on the original Banks & Textor data *vis-à-vis* relative linguistic homogeneity, on the one hand, and the lack of a conclusive answer to Fishman's initial question ([how] do linguistically more homogeneous and less heterogeneous countries differ?), on the other hand, remained constant throughout. In this same tradition of cumulative, even if not definitive, research, one more study remains to be reviewed.

Since linguistic homogeneity/heterogeneity *per se* is often a reflection of underlying (or accompanying) racial or religious homogeneity, Gurr (1972) provided a cross-tabulation that made it possible for McRae to determine whether relative linguistic homogeneity was a predictor of level of civil strife, within and across various degrees of racial and religious homogeneity. McRae's analysis of Gurr's cross-tabulation of polities

classified simultaneously on all three of these dimensions (the basic data
being, once again, from Banks & Textor, 1963) revealed that all three
dimensions were important predictors of civil strife, but that *the difference
in mean level of civil strife was greatest when comparing polities on the
relative linguistic homogeneity dimension* (with relatively homogeneous
polities scoring lower on civil strife than strongly heterogeneous ones). In
discussing his results, McRae did not raise either the issue of controlling
economic variables or of utilizing any of the hundreds of other cross-polity
variables that could be utilized in accounting for cross-polity variance in
civil strife. It may very well be that such controls or other variables would
significantly decrease, or even reverse, the apparent prominence of
relative linguistic heterogeneity in accounting for inter-polity differentials
in level of civil strife. This, indeed, is a topic to which we have also
addressed ourselves in a separate study (Fishman & Solano, in press and
this volume, Chapter 24).

We complete this review of the relevant prior literature with the
observation that all prior studies are ultimately characterizable by two
weaknesses: (a) they are all still dependent on Banks & Textor's indices
of relative linguistic homogeneity which date back to the early 1960s and
which must be considered both imprecise for their own time and
out-of-date for ours, and (b) they are all methodologically simplistic in that
they handle only 2-3 variables at a time (via zero-order correlations,
comparisons between means or chi-squares) rather than attempting to
locate the optimal sub-set of cross-polity predictors of linguistic
homogeneity/heterogeneity via more powerful, parsimonious and cumulative statistical approaches. We ultimately hope to overcome both of these
limitations but will address only the latter of the two in this paper, leaving
the former for the near future (Fishman, McConnell & Solano, in press).
By separating these two issues, we hope to more clearly indicate the
interplay of methodological and substantive issues in conjunction with
linguistic homogeneity/heterogeneity as an independent and as a dependent variable.

Independent variable examined in the present study

Two hundred and thirty-eight cross-polity variables are scrutinized in
the present study in attempting to return on a more rigorous basis to
Fishman's questions originally raised in the mid-1960s, namely, (i) to what
extent and in what ways are relatively linguistically homogeneous polities,

as a sub-set of all of the world's polities, different from relatively heterogeneous ones, i.e. to what extent can the most powerful and parsimonious sub-set of all available cross-polity variables predict relative linguistic homogeneity across all polities and (ii) what is the substantive composition of that sub-set? In order to answer this question the cross-polity data provided by the following sources was utilized:

194 variables provided by Banks & Textor (1963),
  4 variables provided by Russett et al. (1964),
 15 variables provided by Gurr in Feierabend & Feierabend (1972) or by the Feierabends themselves, and
 25 variables provided by Sivard (1977).

A complete enumeration of these 238 variables will be provided on request, but it seems unwarranted to take the space that such a list would require here because our analytic method, presented below, immediately scales this huge list down to one less than 10% as long and consisting of the only variables actually needed in order to maximally predict relative linguistic homogeneity across 130 polities. In comparison to previous studies, the present study is based upon more cross-polity variables and involves more polities [1,2] than any undertaken before. Our dependent variable remains the tried and true (or, at least, tried and traditional) Banks & Textor dichotomy between relatively linguistically homogeneous and relatively linguistically heterogeneous polities, but to the familiar demographic, historic, social, cultural, political and economic predictors that Banks & Textor, on the one hand, and Russett et al., on the other hand, provided a quarter century ago, we are now adding the anger, violence and strife variables provided by Gurr (in the Feierabend text) as well as the military and social expenditure variables provided by Sivard. While it is true that some of the independent variables that we will use post-date the dependent variable to be used, this minor lapse from strictly causal thinking is excusable (as well as unavoidable until better linguistic heterogeneity data is forthcoming), requiring merely that we assume that the Banks & Textor dichotomy on the dependent variable is still reflective of a roughly accurate grouping of the countries of the world into two sub-groups.

The statistical methods to be employed in the present study

Modern statistical procedures are well suited to the methodological problem posed by our study (and, indeed, to the problem faced by

Fishman, Pool and McRae in earlier years), namely, that one has a great deal (indeed, a surfeit) of data that *might* be pertinent to a particular dependent variable and what is needed is a parsimonious way of sifting all that data so as to come up with the smallest sub-set thereof that can most powerfully (i.e. most fully, most completely, most exhaustively) account for the variance in the dependent variable. One such approach is known as 'cumulative multiple prediction' and it was first introduced by Fishman & Herasimchuk into sociolinguistic research in 1969 (for other examples of the same vintage see Fishman, Cooper & Ma, 1971), a few years after it had found its way into psycho-educational research faced by the same problem of picking the most powerful and parsimonious sub-set of predictors from a much larger set of available and 'potentially interesting' ones (Cohen, 1968; definitely restated: Cohen & Cohen, 1975). Cumulative multiple prediction proceeds by first finding the largest single zero-order correlation with the dependent variable (in our case, the dependent variable is the dichotomy 'relatively linguistically homogeneous vs. relatively linguistically heterogeneous') in the entire matrix of correlations which include 237 correlations with that variable. It then proceeds to find that particular additional independent variable that will correlate least with the one that has just been located while correlating most with the dependent variable, in other words, that additional independent variable that has the largest partial correlation with the dependent variable after its correlation with the prior independent variable has been set aside. Having found this optimal second variable (from now on, we will call all of these selected independent variables 'predictors'), it now proceeds to find the best third predictor that correlates least with the two that have come before it and most with the dependent variable. It will continue this search for additional predictors only as long as there are additional predictors that do significantly add to the cumulative multiple prediction of the dependent variable that has already been achieved by the combined set of previously selected predictors. Once there are no such variables to be found in the entire data-set that will add significantly to the cumulative prediction of the dependent variable, the procedure ends. All else in the matrix is predictively superfluous, redundant or irrelevant, 'interesting' though it may appear to be to the uninitiated, in so far as our initial question is concerned: to what extent can the dependent variable be accounted for by all of the predictors utilized by the study and what is the most powerful and parsimonious sub-set of these predictors that can predictively accomplish by themselves as much as can the entire assembled battery of independent variables?

Clearly, this approach is well suited to overcome the problem of working with variables only two or three at a time, an approach which, given the large number of independent variables that the field of cross-polity research has provided, possesses neither the conceptually integrative power nor the quantitative integrative capacity of cumulative multiple correlation.

The optimal sub-set of predictors of relative linguistic homogeneity

Tables 23.1 and 23.2 list the 18 (out of a possible 233) predictors[3] that are the only ones needed in order to arrive at the highest prediction of 'relative linguistic homogeneity' in the 130 polities for which sufficient information was provided so that they could be retained in the study. Table 23.1 names these variables and identifies the sources from which they were derived. Table 23.2 shows the intercorrelations *between* these 18 variables (listed in the order of their importance, i.e. in the order of their entry into the forward selection procedure) and also shows their zero-order correlations with the dependent variable (CP) itself.

It is evident from Table 23.1 that none of the Russett *et al.* and Gurr or Feierabend & Feierabend variables 'make it' into our current analysis and that only 2 of the Sivard variables are selected. Thus we are left essentially with Banks & Textor predictors in order to predict the Banks & Textor dependent ('criterion') variable.

Preliminary conceptual integration of the optimal sub-set of predictor variables

We have mentioned, above, that we had two goals in this paper, namely, (i) to determine the extent to which cross-polity differentials in relative linguistic homogeneity could be accounted for or predicted, and (ii) to attempt to conceptually integrate or understand that particular sub-set of predictor variables that most powerfully and parsimoniously predicted our dependent variable. We will now begin to attempt the latter goal, at least preliminarily, and then return to it again later after we have also attempted the former goal.

The major surprise in Table 23.1 is that it includes neither Gross National Product nor Per Capita Gross National Product, variables found in both the Bank & Textor and the Sivard data-sets and variables related

TABLE 23.1 Intercorrelation matrix: Linguistic homogeneity (CP) and the sub-set of 18 optimal predictors***

	CP	CK	CR	AY	AM	AE	DA	CW	ER	DE	IA	EJ	CB	HW	HJ	HE	FS	DK
CK	515*	—																
CR	514*	362*	—															
AY	254*	138	-064	—														
AM	075	-292*	014	-047	—													
AE	302*	551*	508*	261*	-161	—												
DA	-314*	-419*	-168	007	180**	-276*	—											
CW	228*	643*	205*	162	-184**	353*	-465*	—										
ER	-507*	-748*	-449*	-053	229*	-546*	313*	-505*	—									
DE	-165	-198**	-116	032	154	-109	-219**	-064	156	—								
IA	184*	215*	-003	153	-099	162	-030	230*	-235*	186**	—							
EJ	-441*	-330*	-348*	000	055	-127	174*	-247*	335*	037	093	—						
CB	379*	652*	440*	204**	-154	537*	-297*	489*	-669*	-038	391*	-285*	—					
HW	036	-025	-096	062	-081	-113	-035	028	059	221**	328*	186**	208**	—				
HJ	-258*	-364*	-053	-213**	245*	-200**	465*	-488*	286*	-061	-126	133	-315*	-056	—			
HE	-231*	-343*	-138	-181**	140	-408*	-032	-234*	345*	157	-227**	212**	-401*	024	008	—		
FS	033	245*	-076	-076	-071	-071	039	157	-002	-049	436*	055	085	206**	-089	-222*	—	
DK	343*	542*	339*	192*	-080	585*	-179**	480*	-528*	-020	334*	-173	572*	-014	-292*	-473*	305*	—
FH	219**	456*	183*	228*	-104	411*	-121	480*	-410*	-071	251*	-231*	401*	-048	-202**	-508*	151	653*

* Decimal points omitted in this as well as in subsequent tables.

** For n=125 (the nearest tabled value to d.f.=n-2=128): *p.01 = .228 and **p.05= .174

to the first Fishman study (1966) which launched this entire area of inquiry. On the other hand, many of the variables in the optimally predictive and parsimonious sub-set are indirectly economic in the sense that they are the modernization, westernization and development variables that the social sciences have long pointed to as being economically linked. This may become clearer if we subdivide the list constituting Table 23.2 into two sub-lists, one including only positive predictors of linguistic homogeneity and the other, only negative predictors of this criterion, i.e. variables more closely related to relative linguistic heterogeneity. This has been done in Table 23.3, based upon the first column of Table 23.2, with the variables

TABLE 23.2 *The sub-set of 18 optimal predictor variables in accounting for variance in 'linguistic homogeneity'*

From Banks & Textor (1963):

AE = Polities located in Scandinavia or Western Europe.
AM = Polities located in North Africa or the Middle East.
AY = Polities whose population density is very high or high.
CB = Polities where newspaper circulation is 100 or more per thousand.
CK = Polities where the predominant religion is Christianity.
CR = Polities that are also racially and religiously homogeneous.
CW = Polities that are historically Western or significantly Westernized.
DA = Polities that were formerly dependencies of Britain or France, rather than Spain.
DE = Polities where the type of political modernization is non-European autochthonous.
DK = Polities whose ideological orientation is conventional rather than doctrinal, situational, etc.
EJ = Polities where sectionalism is extreme or moderate, rather than limited or negligible.
ER = Polities where interest articulation by non-associational groups is significant or moderate, rather than limited or negligible.
FH = Polities where interest aggregation by the legislature is significant, moderate or limited rather than negligible.
FS = Polities where the party system is broadly aggregative, rather than personalistic, situational or ad hoc.
HE = Polities where the role of the police is politically significant.
HJ = Polities where the character of the religious system is Muslim or partially Muslim.

From Sivard (1977):
HW = Area in sq. km. IA = Health Expenditures.

TABLE 23.3 *Positive and negative zero-order correlations of the optimal sub-set of predictors and linguistic homogeneity**

i. Positive Correlations with Criterion	ii. Negative Correlations with Criterion
CK= Polities where the predominant religion is Christian 515	ER= Polities where interest articulation by non-associational groups is significant or moderate −507
CR= Polities that are also religiously and racially homogeneous 514	EJ= Polities where sectionalism is extreme or moderate −441
CB= Polities where newspaper circulation is 100 or more per thousand 379	DA= Polities that were formerly dependencies or Britain of France, rather than Spain −314
DK= Polities whose ideological orientation is conventional rather than doctrinal, situational, etc. 343	HJ= Polities where the legal system is Muslim or partially Muslim −258
AE= Polities located in Scandinavia or Western Europe 302	HE= Polities where the role of police is politically significant −231
AY= Polities whose population density is high or very high 254	DE= Polities where the type of political modernization is non-European autochthonous −165
CW= Polities that are historically Western or significantly westernized 228	

TABLE 23.3 *(Continued)*

i. Positive Correlations with Criterion	*ii. Negative Correlations with Criterion*
FH= Polities where interest aggregation by the legislature is more than limited or negligible 219	
IA= Health Expenditures 184	
AM= Polities located in North Africa or the Middle East 075	
HW= Area in sq. km. 036	
FS= Polities where the party system is broadly aggregative rather than personalistic, situational or *ad hoc* 033	

*For n=125, p.01 = .228 and p.05 = .174

being rearranged in both columns in the order of descending magnitude of zero-order correlation with linguistic homogeneity.

The nature and flavor of the variables in column i, Table 23.3, is heavily northern and western European: religious and racial homogeneity, usually (although not exclusively) under the auspices of Christianity and westernization; high literacy, high population density plus more substantial health-related appropriations, and interest aggregation via the legislature (rather than via the armed forces, for example), many of these being not only indicators of democratization but, very definitely, of development. Even the non-significant predictors (non-significant at the zero-order level but, as we will soon see, making significant incremental contributions to the cumulative multiple prediction of our criterion, linguistic homogeneity) support some of this same flavor. On the other hand, the apparent thrust of the variables in column ii, Table 23.3, is quite different.

The variables that tend to make for linguistic heterogeneity (i.e. to undercut linguistic homogeneity) are non-Western, non-modern (e.g. non-associational interest articulation), and, generally non-interactive (e.g. sectionalism and police involvement in politics). Thus, on the whole, a good part of the picture initially presented by Fishman in 1966 is reproduced, even though the types of data-analysis *per se* have been substantially altered and even though the data set has been substantially augmented. This is reassuring, because it implies that the earlier findings were not entirely artifacts of a particular data set nor of a particular statistical analysis. The reoccurrence of 'sectionalism' as a major predictor of linguistic heterogeneity is also of major importance, in this connection, precisely because of the non-reoccurrence of 'per capita GNP'. The presence of the former may well be a more basic and less easily remediable accompaniment of continuing linguistic heterogeneity than are deficiencies with respect to the latter. Note that our 1966 data for 'per capita GNP' was that provided by Banks & Textor while our current data on this variable is that provided by both Banks & Textor and Sivard. These two data sets are separated by points in time at least 15 and probably 20 years apart. By the mid-1970s, the inter-polity range in 'per capita GNP' may have decreased, relative to its range in the early 1960s, and, as a result, that variable may have become a less powerful predictor in and of itself, i.e. the Developing Countries may well have improved their 'per capita GNP' standing, in the short run, without either materially decreasing their linguistic heterogeneity, on the one hand, or duplicating the long-term social consequences that earlier development brought about in Western life. As appealing as this minor explanatory effort may be, there is really no need to explain (as well as no adequate way of explaining) the *non-occurrence* of a predictor and it must suffice to say that when considered jointly and competitively with all other variables in our data set GNP (whether per capita or as a sum-total) does not wind up in the optimal sub-set of predictors because it does in and of itself account for any independent variance in inter-polity linguistic homogeneity/heterogeneity, as 18 other optimal predictors enter into the cumulative multiple prediction of that dependent variable.

Let us now briefly set aside our initial efforts to render conceptually meaningful the optimal sub-set of cross-polity predictors of linguistic homogeneity and turn to our other major question, namely, *to what extent* (to what degree) has this entire data-analytic enterprise really succeeded in accounting for the cross-polity variance in linguistic homogeneity/heterogeneity? Certainly, it does not pay to invest too much interpretative effort in this enterprise at this point, interpretation being relatively easy, at any rate, since it is to such an extent a self-confirming argument 'after the fact' (i.e. after the facts are at hand), unless we can successfully demonstrate that we have accounted for a sufficiently impressive portion of the inter-polity variance in linguistic homogeneity/heterogeneity to make further interpretative efforts really worthwhile. We turn, therefore, to the cumulative multiple correlations of our optimal sub-set of predictors.

Cumulative multiple prediction of the criterion variable

Table 23.4 indicates the order-of-entry of the variables in the optimal sub-set of predictors in accounting for unexplained variance in the criterion variable. Starting off with predictor variable CK (=Polities where the dominant religion is Christian), which yields a correlation of .5151 with the criterion, a final cumulative multiple correlation of .8819 is attained with the entry of FH (=Polities where interest aggregation by the legislature is significant, moderate or limited rather than negligible or absent). FH is the last variable in the original data-set, a set consisting of 233 other predictors, to enter into the cumulative multiple equation via producing a significant increment in the criterion, relative to the particular cumulative multiple correlation that had been obtained before its entry. Obviously, a multiple correlation of slightly more than .88, accounting as it does for somewhat more than three-quarters (.7777% to be exact) of the cross-polity variance in linguistic homogeneity/heterogeneity is well worth taking note of and discussing further.

One new ingredient revealed by Table 23.4 needs to be set aside before proceeding to discuss the order-of-entry itself, that order being the next most important information presented by the Table. Four variables, BZ, CA, CO and FJ, figure briefly in the cumulative multiple correlation only to be removed. Had we specified that we were interested only in the *eleven* most optimal predictors of linguistic homogeneity, BZ would have been one of them; had we specified that we wanted no more than *thirteen*, CA would have been one of them, but BZ would not. Had we specified that we were interested only in the *fourteen* most optimal predictors of linguistic homogeneity, CO and FJ would have been among them, but BZ and CA would not have been. However, since we were looking for the optimal sub-set of predictors of our criterion, cross-polity variance in linguistic homogeneity, without the size of that sub-set being limited, *a priori*, to any particular number of predictors (indeed, our only prior

TABLE 23.4 *The cumulative multiple prediction of the criterion by the optimal sub-set of predictor variables*

Variable Entered	Removed	Multiple R	R²	Change in R²	F Enter	T Remove	No. of vars included
CK		5151	2653	2653	46.22		1
CR*		6235	3887	1234	25.65		2
AY		6643	4413	0526	11.86		3
CO		7001	4901	0488	11.97		4
BZ		7243	5247	0345	9.01		5
AM		7414	5497	0250	6.83		6
FJ		7551	5702	0205	5.81		7
AE		7665	5875	0174	5.10		8
CA		7789	6067	0192	5.85		9
DA		7888	6222	0155	4.88		10
CW		8058	6493	0272	9.15		11
	BZ**	8019	6431	−0063		2.11	10
ER		8121	6595	0164	5.69		11
DE		8217	6752	0158			12
IA		8305	6896	0144	5.38		13
	CA**	8275	6848	−0048		1.81	12
EJ		8405	7064	0216	8.53		13
CB		8477	7186	0122	4.99		14
	CO**	8436	7117	−0069		2.83	13
	FJ**	8390	7040	−0077		3.10	12
HW		8504	7232	0192	8.06		13
HJ		8576	7355	0123	5.36		14
HE		8642	7469	0114	5.13		15
FS		8707	7582	0113	5.27		16
DK		8769	7689	0107	5.18		17
FH		8819	7777	0088	4.39		18

* If CR is excluded from entering into the cumulative multiple prediction, on the grounds of its possible redundancy with the criterion, the resulting total cumulative multiple correlation is .8182 (attained in 13 steps) and is reached as follows: CK=.5151; EJ=.5896; AM=.6303; AY=.6612; FJ=.6837; EJ=.7036; CW=.7230; DA=.7440; CE=.7566; IB=.7725; (Delete CK=.7664); DE=.7815; (delete FJ=.7816); HW=.7911; EE=.8016; FT=.8110; BO=.8182. The only new variable involved are the following four:

CE= Polities where the religion is Catholic (r with CP=.452*)
IB= Foreign economic aid (million US dollars) (r with CP=.227**)
EE= Polities where political enculturation is high (r with CP=.228*)

BO=   Polities whose economic development status is highly developed (r
        with CP=.188**)

The discussion below will clearly indicate that the above optimal sub-set of
predictors is conceptually fully commensurate with the optimal sub-set that obtains
when CR remains in the analysis.

**Identification of four variables that initially entered the cumulative multiple
   prediction but were subsequently removed in order to enable additional optimal
   predictors to enter the equation:

BZ=   Polities where freedom of the press is complete or intermittent
        rather than absent (r with Criterion =-.096)

CA=   Polities where newspaper circulation is 300 or more per thousand (r
        with Criterion =.297)

CO=   Polities that are racially homogeneous (r with Criterion =-.121)

FJ=   Polities where the party system is quantitatively one party dominant
        (r with Criterion =.141)

stipulations were that (i) only a variable that can make a significant
incremental contribution to the prior amount of criterion variance already
accounted for be admitted at each step, and (ii) that no more variables
be admitted when no such significant increments were forthcoming). Since
the cumulative multiple correlation procedure searches for the best next
variable to admit at every step in order to assemble the optimal sub-set
of predictors *at that step*, it only accepts variables that are optimal for that
step, some of which may not be optimal later on, in more subsequent steps.
Although the mathematics of this entire procedure is too advanced for our
discussion here, it still is worth pointing out (and confirmable on
inspection) that the four variables that initially entered and were later
removed are very similar in nature to (and, indeed, are sometimes partially
redundant with) some of those that we discussed previously, in connection
with Tables 23.1, 23.2 and 23.3 above.

   It is quite clear from Table 23.4 that the order-of-entry of variables
into the cumulative multiple correlation is not the same as the order of
magnitude of the zero-order correlations of these variables with the
criterion. Indeed, the difference between these two orders generally
increases as one proceeds further down the list of successive additions to
the list of optimal variables for inclusion in the cumulative multiple
prediction of the criterion. It is also quite clear that the top half of the list
carries the brunt of the predictive load. This is necessarily so, since the
very design of this approach is such as to find the most important
predictors first (important in the sense of accounting for the largest

possible amount of still unexplained variance in the criterion variable). If we look at the first seven variables that finally wind up in the most optimal sub-set (the first seven in the 'variable entered' column in Table 23.4) we see that they attain a cumulative multiple correlation of .8058 (out of the maximum of .8819 that will be reached 11 variables later) and that some 65% of the criterion variance has already been accounted for (out of some .78% that will ultimately be accounted for when the entire optimal sub-set is constituted). Although the increase in predictive power provided by the final 11 variables is certainly not to be sneezed at, and although it is exactly that increase over and above the major predictive capacity of the top seven variables that marks the clear and foremost superiority of the technique we have been using in comparison to the earlier techniques that were incapable of examining more than two or three variables at a time in conjunction with each other, it still remains true that the top seven carry the lion's share of the predictive and explanatory burden *vis-à-vis* cross-polity variance in linguistic homogeneity/heterogeneity and should be clearly recognized for doing so.

A brief, final return to the conceptual integration of the optimal sub-set of predictor variables

The top seven predictors referred to above, all of which were selected for inclusion in the cumulative multiple equation before any originally selected variables had to be excluded so that the process of selecting the optimal sub-set of predictors could run its full course, definitely reinforce our earlier impressions that linguistic homogeneity on the world scene is a byproduct of the racial, religious and cultural homogeneity that is related to Christian, Western European, more generally Western and North African/Near Eastern experiences. What were or are these experiences, as they *currently* manifest themselves? The second set of predictors, the eleven that follow the first seven, are the indicators and metaphors that imply what these experiences are and/or might have been.

Having already attempted a verbal and impressionistic approach to conceptually integrating the sub-set of optimal predictors of linguistic homogeneity, we will now attempt a more quantitative approach, namely via factor analysis. Factor analysis begins with a correlation matrix between all of the variables being studied (in our case, a huge matrix of 28,203 [i.e. $n(n-1)/2$] intercorrelations). It then mathematically extracts from this huge number of intercorrelations the smallest number of maximally different mathematical dimension (to be called 'factors') that can reproduce as much of the total variance in the matrix as possible (for more details as to this method, consult any advanced statistics text or Cattell, 1978). Our huge matrix was reduced in this fashion (just as the plethora of independent variables had been reduced previously via the cumulative multiple correlation method) to a smaller and more manageable, more conceptually integratible sub-set of 'factors', yielding the results shown in Table 23.5. Forty-three unrotated ('orthogonal') factors were required to account for all of the variance in the original 238×238 matrix, the first five of which account for 52% of that variance, the first ten of which account for 67% of that variance and the first 20 of which account for 83% of that variance. Clearly, there is a great deal of overlap between the dimensions in our original data-set and factor analysis renders

TABLE 23.5 *Factor structure of the optimal sub-set of predictor variables*

Predictor Variable	Loads Highest on Factor No.	(Loading)	Loads Next-Highest on Factor No.	(Loading)
CP	I	(425)	XV	(283)
CK	I	(743)	IV	(−399)
CR	I	(388)	V	(−297)
AY	XX	(−399)	I	(317)
AM	IV	(590)	IX	(452)
AE	I	(694)	V	(−298)
DA	II	(399)	I	(−321)
CW	I	(701)	III	(308)
ER	I	(−689)	IV	(282)
DE	XIII	(−369)	VI	(301)
IA	V	(568)	I	(439)
EJ	IV	(397)	V	(342)
CB	I	(768)	XXV	(−199)
HW	V	(388)	XXXIX	(311)
HJ	I	(−425)	VII	(307)
HE	I	(−525)	II	(−508)
FS	V	(420)	XXII	(296)
DK	I	(776)	II	(218)
FH	I	(638)	III	(321)

considerable service when reducing that data-set to the least number of maximally different factors.

Table 23.5 reveals several other interesting findings that enable us to go beyond our previous point of conceptual integration. Our criterion variable, linguistic homogeneity, loads most highly on Factor I. This is the General Factor in our data-set, the one that accounts for a greater proportion of the variance in our data-set (51%) than any other. Several of the members of the optimal sub-set of predictors, indeed, 10 out of 18 (CK, CR, AE, CW, ER, CB, HJ, HE, DK, and FH), also have their highest loading on this same factor. Additionally, three other members of the optimal sub-set of predictors, AY, DA and IA, have their next highest loading on Factor I. Clearly, Factor I is of crucial conceptual importance for understanding both our criterion variable and the optimal sub-set of variables available for predicting it. Other frequently occurring factor memberships pertain to Factor V (highest loadings for IA, HW, and FS; next highest loadings for CR, AE and EJ) and Factor IV (highest loadings for AM and EJ and next highest loadings for CK and ER). These three factors alone account for nearly 3/4 (74%) of the cumulative variance in the complete 238 variable matrix. Let us therefore turn to an examination of these *three* factors *per se*, since they best summarize or characterize fully 16 out of the sub-set of 18 optimal predictors of linguistic homogeneity. Table 23.6 assists us in doing just that, by listing the 10 variables that load highest on each of these three major factors, whether or not they are among the optimal sub-set of 18 best predictors of linguistic homogeneity that we have examined before.

TABLE 23.6 *Variables that load highest on the three factors that best characterize the optimal sub-set of predictors*

Factor I	Factor IV	Factor V
IR= Life expectancy 841	AN= Polities located in the Middle East 668	BF= Polities whose GNP is very high or high 648
EL= Polities where interest articulation by associational groups is significant or moderate 819	AM= Polities located in North Africa or the Middle East 590	ID= Number of teachers 631

TABLE 23.6 (*Continued*)

Factor I	Factor IV	Factor V
IM= Literacy rate 819	CF= Polities where the dominant religion is Muslim 493	HX= GNP 607
II= Per Capita Gross National Product (GNP) 804	AF= Polities located in the Caribbean, Central America or South America −413	IC= Size of armed forces 600
FG= Polities where interest aggregation by the legislature is significant or moderate 800	DD= Polities where political modernization is European or European derived −413	HZ= Education expenditures 600
AB= Polities located in Western Europe, Scandinavia, North America or Australasia 798	CM= Polities where the dominant religion is Catholic rather than Muslim −425	HV= Population 583
GY= Polities where the bureaucracy is modern or semi-modern 796	CE= Polities where the dominant religion is Catholic −491	IE= Number of physicians 584
IJ= Public expenditures per capita on education 789	GN= Polities where the legislative-executive structure is presidential −475	BL= Polities whose international financial status is very high or high 579
CX= Polities that are historically Western rather than Westernized through a colonial relationship 786	GV= Polities where the legislature is unicameral −485	AW= Polities whose population is very large or large 580
IQ= Infant mortality rate −834	FI= Polities where the party system is quantitatively one-party −495	IA= Health expenditures 568

optimal predictors of linguistic homogeneity. Table 23.6 assists us in doing just that, by listing the 10 variables that load highest on each of these three major factors, whether or not they are among the optimal sub-set of 18 best predictors of linguistic homogeneity that we have examined before.

None of the 10 highest loading variables with respect to Factor I are variables that we have encountered thus far, i.e. they are not redundant with the optimal sub-set of variables for predicting linguistic homogeneity. As a result, these high loading variables enable us to further flesh-out and render meaningful the very Factor that best characterized our criterion and most of its optimal predictors. This factor consists of the attributes of modern, western, developed, and democratic polities. Factor V on the other hand, though very similar to Factor I conceptually, is more indirectly concerned with economic circumstances or with the types of personnel or expenditures that economically more affluent polities can better afford or more easily maintain. Since this is only the second most powerful factor represented in our sub-set of optimal predictors, it does not come through strongly in accounting for cross-polity variation in linguistic homogeneity. Finally, when we turn to Factor IV, the third most powerful factor represented among the optimal sub-set of predictors of linguistic homogeneity, we find a mix of positive and negative loadings that add up to a 'have not' syndrome *vis-à-vis* Factors I and V: polities of the Middle East, North Africa, outside of the Americas or Europe, Muslim or Catholic, with non-presidential executives, and with non-European political modernization. All in all, the factor analytic detail confirms and quantifies the major impressions about the nature of the optimal sub-set of predictors of linguistic homogeneity that we had arrived at early, including the distinct message that economic considerations are definitely present, even if not overwhelmingly or directly so. The factors and the optimal sub-set of predictors must not be confused and they cannot be interchanged in our discussion. Both are arrived at via the utilization of reductionistic mathematical approaches to masses of quantitative data, but the former (factor analysis) provides a conceptually richer context for interpreting the latter, both in manifest and in latent terms, and we have utilized the latter (cumulative multiple correlation) for predictive purposes.

Conclusions

We have returned to a 1966 question with both better data and better methods of data analysis, methods that are more appropriate for the large data sets that have been available to sociolinguists (but generally not exhaustively analyzed) for the past quarter century. As a result, we have not only arrived at findings that are empirically and theoretically better supported, but we have been able to examine the extent to which earlier findings were dependent upon the methods utilized to obtain them, rather than more generally tenable. Out of a data-set of nearly 240 cross-polity variables we have been able to parsimoniously select the optimal sub-set that best predicts relative linguistic homogeneity. This optimal sub-set of variables yields a cumulative multiple correlation of .8819, accounting for 78% of the cross-polity variance in relative linguistic homogeneity. Previous methods of data analysis, handling, as they did, only two or three variables at a time, provided no inkling of the total power of the data-set to elucidate the criterion under study. An understanding of the conceptual nature of the optimal sub-set of predictors has also been advanced by the present study. Both intuitive (*a priori*) and factor analytic (*post hoc*) analyses indicate that the criterion itself and the lion's share of its optimal predictors pertain to modernization, democratization, westernization and development, on the one hand, and, more indirectly than was previously assumed, to economic advancement phenomena, on the other hand. Future research on this topic is in need of better and more recent criterion data in order to determine whether the findings reported in the present study are replicable when relative linguistic homogeneity is measured as the continuum it really is, rather than as the dichotomy that it has been taken to be ever since Banks & Textor's 1963 cross-polity characterizations were first presented.

Inevitably, our approach has not answered all questions that have been posed by investigators of the relationship between socio-cultural dimensions and relative linguistic homogeneity; thus the issue of the direction of causality between linguistic homogeneity/heterogeneity and the many widely admired and desired attributes of economically more advanced polities is still not conclusively resolved. It is unlikely that this question can be fully answered from current-status data alone and without the construction of cross-polity data-sets of a longitudinal ('diachronic') nature. However, we ourselves are now undertaking a partial approach to the issue of directionality, by examining the role of linguistic homogeneity/heterogeneity as a *predictor* of economic development when a truly extensive set of other potential predictors of cross-polity economic differentials are also utilized (Fishman & Solano, in press b). If economic well-being and modernization are importantly predictive of linguistic homogeneity/heterogeneity, on the one hand, but linguistic homogeneity/heterogeneity are not importantly predictive of economic development, on the other hand, we will at least have made some progress in connection with the issue of direction of causality. As matters stand now, it is clearer than before that even though no manifestly economic variable enters into the optimal sub-set of predictors of linguistic homogeneity, that most of the variables that do make it into this subset (particularly those in Factors I and V) are economically suffused and encumbered. While it remains possible that future and more enlightened planning can seek to safeguard linguistic heterogeneity (thereby advancing cultural democracy) while pursuing maximal economic development, it is now even clearer than before that these two goals have generally not gone hand in hand before in the polities that are extant today. This finding highlights the problem of safeguarding minority languages. Modern polities — *and even modern, regionally autonomous groups* — all pursue the very processes and goals that have made for linguistic homogeneity 'toward the center' in the past, and that tend to undercut the very processes of linguistic heterogeneity at the polity level. In connection with 'threatened languages', in particular, the intervention of *appropriate* language-and-culture planning (Fishman, 1988), therefore becomes even more urgent than it has been heretofore. My friends in the Basque Country, in Friesland and among the defenders of Yiddish, Irish and other threatened languages might well want to take this admonition to heart.

Notes to Chapter 23

1. The four data-sources actually provide some information on 171 polities, but for the following 41 the available data were too sparse to merit their inclusion in the current study: Andorra, Antigua/Barbuda, Bahamas, Barbados, Belize, Bhutan, Brunei, Cape Verde, Comoros, Djibouti, Dominica, Equatorial Guinea, Fiji, Grenada, Guinea Bissau, Kiribati, Kuwait, Lesotho, Liechtenstein, Malawi, Maldives, Malta, Monaco, Nauru, Papua New Guinea, Puerto Rico, Q(u)atar, St. Kitts & Nevis, St. Lucia, St. Vincent & the Grenadines, San Marino, Sao Tome & Principe, Seychelles, Solomon Islands, Surinam, Swaziland, Togo, Tuvalu, Vanuatu, Vatican, Western Samoa. Polities established after 1976 and constituent republics of the Soviet Union are not included in the data-base. Clearly, our results might well have been different had it been possible to include any sizeable number of the above polities in our analyses.
2. The main reason why Banks & Textor's dichotomous data on linguistic homogeneity is utilized in this study rather than the continuous data provided by Russett *et al.* is that the former is available for more than twice as many polities than is the latter.
3. There are only 233 predictors of CP because 4 predictors that also represented degrees of linguistic homogeneity/heterogeneity (as reported by either Banks & Textor [1963] or Russett *et al.* [1964]) were barred from being included in

the cumulative multiple prediction since their redundancy with CP would have produced a speciously high value of R and R^2.

References

BANKS, A. S. & TEXTOR, R. B. 1963, *A Cross-Polity Survey*. Cambridge, MA: MIT Press.

CATTELL, R. B. 1978, *The Scientific Use of Factor Analysis*. New York: Plenum.

COHEN, J. 1968, Multiple regression as a general data analytic system. *Psychological Bulletin* 70, 426–43.

COHEN, J. & COHEN, P. 1975, *Applied Multiple Regression/Correlation Analysis for the Behavioral Sciences*. Hillsdale, NJ: Erlbaum.

DEUTSCH, K. W. 1966, *Nationalism and Social Communication; An Inquiry into the Foundations of Nationality*. (2nd ed.) Cambridge, MA: MIT Press.

FEIERABEND, I. K. & FEIERABEND, R. L. (eds) 1972, *Anger, Violence and Politics: Theories and Research*. Englewood Cliffs, NJ: Prentice-Hall.

FISHMAN, J. A. 1966, Some contrasts between linguistically homogeneous and linguistically heterogeneous polities. *Sociological Inquiry* 6, 146–58. Reprinted in (1968) J. A. FISHMAN, A. FERGUSON & C. A. DAS GUPTA (eds), *Language Problems of Developing Nations*. New York: Wiley, 53–68.

— 1988, Language spread and language policy for endangered languages. *Georgetown University Round Table on Languages and Linguistics*. Also in *This Volume*, Section III.

FISHMAN, J. A., COOPER, R. L. & MA, R. *et al.* 1971, *Bilingualism in the Barrio*. Bloomington, IN: Indiana University Language Sciences.

FISHMAN, J. A. & HERASIMCHUK, E. 1969, The multiple prediction of phonological variables in a bilingual speech community. *American Anthropologist* 71, 648–57.

FISHMAN, J. A., McCONNELL, G. & SOLANO, F. R. in press, Utilizing better criterion data in exploring societal factors predictive of linguistic heterogeneity at the inter-polity level.

FISHMAN, J. A. & SOLANO, F. R., in press a, Cross-polity perspective on the importance of linguistic heterogeneity as a possible 'contributory cause' of civil strife. Also, *This Volume*, Chapter 24.

— in press b, The other side of the coin: is linguistic homogeneity/heterogeneity an important predictor of economic development at the cross-polity level?

GURR, T. R. 1972, A causal model of civil strife: a comparative analysis using new indices. In I. K. FEIERABEND & R. L. FEIERABEND (eds), *Anger, Violence and Politics: Theories and Research.* Englewood Cliffs, NJ: Prentice-Hall, 184–222.

McRAE, K. D. 1983, *Conflict and Compromise in Multilingual Societies.* Waterloo, Ontario: Wilfred Laurier University Press, 5–33 (See pp. 24–25 in particular).

POOL, J. 1969, National development and language diversity. *La Monda Lingvo-Problemo* 1, 140–56. Slightly revised (1972) in J. A. FISHMAN, (ed.), *Advances in the Sociology of Language.* The Hague: Mouton, 213–30.

RUSSETT, B. M., ALKER, H. R., Jr., DEUTSCH, K. W. & LASSWELL, H. D. (eds) 1964, *World Handbook of Political and Social Indicators.* New Haven, CT: Yale University Press.

SIVARD, R. L. 1977, *World Military and Social Expenditures, 1977.* Leesburg, VA.: WMSE Publications.

24 Cross-polity perspective on the importance of linguistic heterogeneity as a 'contributory factor' in civil strife*

Introduction

The brunt of the small body of worldwide cross-polity research in sociolinguistics, if we interpret 'worldwide' as applying to studies that attempt to determine trends that are applicable to all the polities in the world (or as close to 'all' as the availability of data will permit), has attended to the concomitants of linguistic homogeneity/heterogeneity (Deutsch, 1966; Fishman, 1966 [1968]; Pool, 1969; Rustow, 1968; McRae, 1983; Fishman & Solano, in press and this volume, Chapter 23). This body of research sometimes treats the cross-polity differences in linguistic homogeneity/heterogeneity as a dependent variable, asking 'what factors make for greater or lesser linguistic homogeneity?'. On the other hand, sometimes the cross-polity differences in linguistic homogeneity/heterogeneity are treated as an independent variable and the question that is posed is 'what are the resultants of greater or lesser linguistic homogeneity?'. Overall, the former emphasis is somewhat stronger than the latter and the present study, emphasizing as it does the latter type of question, is, therefore, one of the very few studies explicitly looking at cross-polity linguistic homogeneity/heterogeneity as an independent or predictor variable.

Almost all of the earlier cross-polity studies of either kind, whether

*Originally presented at the Conference on Language and National Development; The Case of India. Hyderabad, India, January 4–8, 1988.

they deal with linguistic homogeneity/heterogeneity as a dependent or as an independent variable, suffer from two debilitating considerations: (i) the largest data-pool as to linguistic homogeneity/heterogeneity (Banks & Textor, 1963) is one that treats this variable as a dichotomy, distinguishing between polities with linguistic minorities that constitute less than 15% of the population (=homogeneous), on the one hand, and polities with linguistic minorities that constitute more than 15% of the population (=heterogeneous), on the other hand; and (ii) the manifold other variables that are investigated concomitantly with linguistic homogeneity/-heterogeneity are analyzed only two or three at a time, thereby providing no estimate at all of either the *relative power* of the *cumulative nature* of the huge number of variables available for examination. The present study seeks to overcome the second of these two limitations by addressing newer quantitative analytic techniques to the huge number of descriptive cross-polity variables (numbering literally in the hundreds) that political scientists have perfected during the past quarter century. Thus, we hope to go beyond such questions as 'do linguistically homogeneous and heterogeneous polities differ significantly on X (civil strife)?', and even beyond such questions as 'does the difference between linguistically homogeneous and heterogeneous polities with respect to X still obtain when Y (e.g. racial homogeneity) and Z (e.g. religious homogeneity) are partialed out?', to turn to the questions 'to what extent can inter-polity differences in X be explained? (i.e. what proportion of the total inter-polity variance in X can be accounted for?)' and 'what is the substantive nature of the optimal sub-set of variables that accounts for the greatest proportion of the inter-polity differences in X and is linguistic homogeneity/heterogeneity among them?' The latter questions require that we analyze all cross-polity variables simultaneously and contrastively by utilizing techniques that will locate the most powerful and parsimonious sub-set of independent variables or predictors *vis-à-vis* the dependent variable that we are focusing upon: civil strife. Obviously, the latter questions are more complex and more demanding than the former, both in terms of maximal utilization of multivariate data as well as in terms of recognizing the cumulative power of the few variables that are ultimately selected out of the many (indeed, breath-takingly many) that have now become increasingly available to us thanks to the data collection efforts of our colleagues in political science.

The data-set

Our data-set consists of 238 cross-polity variables on each of 130 polities.[1] These variables deal with linguistic homogeneity/heterogeneity, total magnitude of civil strife and 236 other social, cultural, economic, demographic, geographic, historical and political descriptors drawn from a variety of now readily available sources, more than three-quarters of which stem from Banks & Textor (1963) and the remainder of which are from Russett *et al*. 1964; Gurr, 1972; Feierabend & Feierabend, 1972, and Sivard, 1977. Our dependent variable, total magnitude of civil strife (hereafter, simply 'civil strife'), is one perfected by Gurr and consists of an index derived from a logarithmic combination of three basic forms of strife: conspiracy, internal war and turmoil, each of which has been weighted for frequency, duration and intensity. Gurr himself has used this variable as a dependent variable in connection with a much smaller data-set than the one we intend to employ, below, while McRae (1983) has also made use of it provocatively in conjunction with linguistic homogeneity/heterogeneity (based on Banks & Textor, 1963) and only two other variables. Ours will be the first study that will utilize a huge data-set of independent variables (including linguistic homogeneity/heterogeneity in conjunction with this particular dependent variable.

Since most linguists, even most sociologists, are not very accustomed to dealing with political science variables, their accuracy and manner of derivation deserve some attention. Many variables are based upon information provided by international bodies, most of them affiliated with the United Nations but some of them operating independently. These inevitably rely on information provided by governmental agencies, political authorities and individual scholars in the various polities of the world. Some of these sources of information are biased and inaccurate, but several of these sources of error-variance have either been corrected by confrontation with other sources, corrected by the compilers of the sources themselves, or treated as random error-variance relative to any particular research purposes to which the data will be put. Other variables are constituted via the considered professional judgements of panels of political scientists who are familiar with large numbers of polities. Where experts disagree with respect to one country or another additional expertise is sought or mean ratings are used. All in all, the data is far from perfect, but this is the state of affairs with respect to psycho-socio-cultural data in general (including much linguistic data, if we are totally honest about it) and, at any rate, it is the best that is currently available for the exhaustive study of worldwide cross-polity phenomena. As cross-polity data increases, improves and changes, sociolinguistic analyses thereof will need to be replicated and/or updated. At any point in time, however, optimal approaches to multivariate analysis will need to be pursued. The present study may well provide a methodological approach that will continue to be of interest long after the data *per se* has been superseded.

The statistical methods to be employed in the present study

Certain newer statistical procedures are well-suited to the methodological problem posed by our study, namely, that one has a great deal (indeed, a surfeit) of data that *might* be pertinent to a particular dependent variable and what is needed is a parsimonious way of sifting all that data in order that one may come up with the smallest sub-set thereof that can most powerfully (i.e. most fully, most completely, most exhaustively) account for the variance in the dependent variable. One such approach is known as 'cumulative multiple prediction' and another is known as 'factor analysis', both of which were first introduced into sociolinguistic research by Fishman, Cooper & Ma in 1972 (after the 1969 introduction of the former method alone by Fishman & Herasimchuk, almost immediately after the method *per se* was perfected [Cohen, 1968]), and both of which will be utilized in the present study. Cumulative multiple prediction proceeds by first finding the largest single direct correlation (referred to as a 'zero order correlation') in the entire matrix of intercorrelations of the dependent variable with the entire array of independent variables. In our case, there will be 235 such intercorrelations with the dependent variable ('civil strife').[2] It then proceeds to find the particular additional independent variable that will correlate least with the one just previously located while correlating most with the dependent variable, in other words, that additional independent variable that has the largest 'partial correlation' with the dependent variable after its correlation with the prior independent variable has been set aside or 'partialed out'. Having found this optimal second variable (from now on, we will call all of these selected independent variables 'predictors'), it now proceeds (i) to provide the 'cumulative multiple correlation' that the two of them *taken together* have with the dependent variable and then (ii) to find the best third predictor that correlates least with the two that have come before it and that correlate most with the dependent variable. It will continue this cumulation and search for additional predictors only as long as it can locate additional predictors that can significantly add to the cumulative multiple correlation with the dependent variable that has already been achieved by the combined set of previously selected predictors. Once there are no such additional predictors to be found in the entire data-set whose partial correlations with dependent variable, after setting aside their correlations with all of the prior independent variables that have been selected, produces a significant increment in the cumulative multiple prediction of the dependent variable, the procedure ends. All other available zero-order correlations with the dependent variable are predictively superfluous, redundant or irrelevant ('interesting' though it may appear to be to the uninitiated) insofar as our guiding questions are concerned: (i) to what extent (i.e. to what degree) can the dependent variable ('civil strife', in our case) be accounted for by the variables available to us in our data-set and (ii) what variables constitute the most powerful and parsimonious sub-set of these variables, i.e. what is the substantive nature of the optimal sub-set of variables (and, in our case, is linguistic homo-geneity/heterogeneity among them?) that can attain the highest cumulative multiple prediction of civil strife? Once this sub-set of independent variables has been located and once it has been judged to yield a sufficiently high cumulative multiple correlation to merit our further attention, we can then return to our entire matrix of intercorrelations and use factor analysis, a method about which we will comment briefly in a subsequent section, to provide additional conceptual richness and in-tegration to our understanding of the deeper and more pervasive nature or 'meaning' of this particular sub-set.

Clearly, this approach of cumulative multiple correlation and factor analysis is well suited to overcome the approach of working only with two or three variables at a time that characterized almost all prior sociolinguistic research on the large number of independent variables that the field of cross-polity inquiry has provided, an approach that possessed neither the conceptually integrative power nor the quantitative integrative capacity of cumulative multiple correlation and factor analysis. If we pursue the question of the possible independent significance of linguistic homogeneity/heterogeneity in accounting for cross-polity differences in civil strife via the older methodology of examining two or three variables at a time, we will never be able to investigate (and conceptually integrate) all of the possible combinations of over two hundred variables in order to arrive at a conclusion as to the relative significance of linguistic homogeneity/heterogeneity in such an extensive data-set. Linguistic heterogeneity is commonly pointed to, particularly in the popular press and by political spokesmen, as a dangerous condition *vis-à-vis* the level of civil strife and we need an approach that can come to a conclusion as to whether it deserves to be so considered relative to all of the other inter-polity characterizations that are simultaneously operative as inde-pendent variables, all of which have their own possible consequences for civil strife.

The optimal sub-set of predictors of inter-polity differences in magnitude of civil strife

Tables 24.1 and 24.2 list the 13 (out of 235 available predictors) that are *the only ones needed in order to arrive at the highest multiple prediction of Magnitude of Civil Strife* in the 130 polities for which sufficient information was provided so that they could be retained in the study.[3] Table 24.1 names these variables and identifies the sources from which they were derived. Table 24.2 shows the intercorrelations *between* these 13 variables (listed in the order of their importance, i.e. in the order of their entry into the cumulative multiple forward selection procedure, and also shows their zero-order correlations with the dependent variable (HT) itself.

TABLE 24.1 *The sub-set of 13 optimal predictor variables in accounting for variance in 'civil strife'*

From Banks & Textor (1963)
BA = Polities whose population density is medium.
BZ = Polities where freedom of the press is complete or intermittent rather than absent.
DI = Polities whose ideological orientation is developmental.
EB = Polities where the electoral system is competitive or partially competitive.
ET = Polities where interest articulation by anomic groups is frequent.
FH = Polities where interest aggregation by the legislature is significant, moderate or limited rather than negligible.
FN = Polities where the party system is quantitatively one-party rather than two-party.
FT = Polities where the party system is qualitatively Latin American liberal-conservative.
HE = Polities where the role of the police is politically significant.

From Feierabend & Feierabend (1972)
IU = Persisting deprivation.
IX = Short term deprivation.

From Sivard (1977)
IH = Population per soldier.
IZ = Coercive potential.

TABLE 24.2 Intercorrelation matrix: civil strife and sub-set of 13 optimal predictors[a]

	HT	IX	IU	IZ	ET	BZ	BA	FT	DI	FN	EB	IH	FH	HE
IX	492*	—												
IU	336*	053	—											
IZ		-461*	-413*	—										
ET	322*	119	170	-130	—									
BZ	133	035	009	-063	-145	—								
BA	060	-063	-152	112	000	120	—							
FT	255*	166	-005	083	049	-114	-120	—						
DI	271*	132	011	-182**	-006	-108	-049	-037	—					
FN	226**	-117	-137	-355*	-082	-310*	173	-131	324*	—				
EB	-180**	-015	-278*	-041	-220**	177**	-075	120	022	-307*	—			
IH	017	068	083	099	-038	-086	-135	-030	472*	146	032	—		
FH	-049	-053	-264*	-347*	-243*	-296*	-053	148	-179**	-396**	660*	-115	—	
HE	150	184	221**	-205**	163	-204**	-046	177**	006	263*	-630*	-159	-508*	—

[a]For n=125, *p.01=.228 and **p.05=.174

It is obvious from Table 24.1 that linguistic homogeneity/heterogeneity does not appear at all among the optimal sub-set of predictors of civil strife, thereby answering (without yet fully clarifying) one of our major questions. We will have to return to the issue of why this is so later, below. For the moment let us also note that most of the optimal sub-set of predictors stems from Banks & Textor, with the Feierabends and Sivard also being represented, but only barely so.

Preliminary conceptual integration of the optimal sub-set of predictor variables

We have specified at the outset that we had two major goals in this paper, namely, (i) to determine the extent to which cross-polity differentials in civil strife could be accounted for and (ii) to attempt to conceptually integrate or understand that particular sub-set of predictor variables that most powerfully and parsimoniously predict civil strife in order to better grasp why it is that linguistic homogeneity/heterogeneity is or is not among them. We will now begin to address the latter goal, at least preliminarily, and then return to it again later, after we have also attempted the former goal.

In order to grasp the extent of the non-overlap or unrelatedness between linguistic homogeneity/heterogeneity and civil strife it should be pointed out that the zero-order correlation between them is merely minus 120 (−120) and that a comparison with Fishman & Solano (in press and this volume) reveals that these two variables, when each is subjected to its own cumulative multiple prediction, share only two optimal predictors: BZ (Polities where freedom of the press is complete or intermittent) and HE (Polities where the political role of the police is significant). Both of these predictors correlate *negatively* with linguistic homogeneity (i.e. they are more characteristic of heterogeneous than of homogeneous polities, the correlation being significant at the .01 level for HE) and *positively* with civil strife (neither being significant at the .05 level). BZ finally drops out of the cumulative multiple prediction of linguistic homogeneity/heterogeneity entirely because subsequent predictors enter the equation and attain a higher cumulative multiple prediction after BZ is deleted. Essentially, therefore, we are left with only one shared predictor, HE, a predictor which is negative and significant in predicting linguistic homogeneity but positive and non-significant in predicting civil strife. If linguistic homogeneity/heterogeneity were significantly related to civil strife then the bulk of the predictors of linguistic homogeneity/-heterogeneity would also tend to be the predictors of civil strife; however, this is not so. The two are essentially predicted by an almost completely different set of predictors. So much for a statistical indication of the unrelatedness of linguistic homogeneity/heterogeneity and civil strife. Let us now turn to a more conceptual delineation of this same issue. The substantive nature of the optimal predictors of HT (=civil strife) may become somewhat clearer if we subdivide the list and constitute Table 24.1 into two sub-lists, one including only positive predictors of civil strife (i.e. variables that tend to imply more civil strife) and the other containing only negative predictors of this criterion (i.e. variables that tend to imply less civil strife). This has been done in Table 24.3, based upon the first column of Table 24.2, with the variables being rearranged in both columns in the order of descending magnitudes of positive zero-order correlation with linguistic homogeneity.

The nature and flavor of the significant variables in column i, Table 24.3, is strongly focussed on deprivation, coalitions of anomic groups, emphases on resource development rather than on basic human needs. Police involvement in politics, freedom of the press being at least partial, population density being merely moderate, and the proportion of soldiers to civilians being relatively low, all tend to add up to an explosive situation that can neither be controlled nor effectively ameliorated. We will return later to a more detailed, more quantitative and more integrative attempt at understanding exactly what it is that characterizes the sub-set of optimal predictors of civil strife. Let it suffice here to say, whatever it is that characterizes that sub-set, that it is clearly different from what characterizes the optimal sub-set of predictors of linguistic homo-geneity/heterogeneity, the flavor and nature of the latter being western-ization, modernization, democratization, all based upon long-standing positive economic characteristics.

We will now briefly set aside our initial efforts to render conceptually meaningful the optimal sub-set of cross-polity predictors of civil strife (and to understand why linguistic homogeneity/heterogeneity is not among them) and turn to our other major question, namely to what extent (i.e. to what degree) has this entire data-analytic enterprise really succeeded in accounting for cross-polity variance in civil strife? Certainly, it would be unwise to invest much more interpretative effort in this enterprise, with respect to how we can best understand the optimal sub-set of predictors of civil strife and why linguistic homogeneity/heterogeneity is not among them if we cannot successfully demonstrate that this optimal subset does, indeed, account for a sufficiently impressive portion of the inter-polity

TABLE 24.3 *Positive and negative zero-order correlations of the optimal sub-set of predictors and civil strife*[a]

i. Positive Correlations with Criterion		ii. Negative Correlations with Criterion	
IX= Short term deprivation	492*	IZ= Coercive potential	−461*
IU= Persisting deprivation	336*	FN= Polities where the party system is quantitatively one-party rather than two-party	−226**
ET= Polities where interest articulation by anomic groups is frequent	322*	EB= Polities where the electoral system is competitive or partially competitive	−180**
DI= Polities where the ideological orientation is developmental	271*	FH= Polities where interest aggregation by the legislature is more than negligible	−049
FT= Polities where the party system is qualitatively Latin American liberal-conservative rather than social revolutionary	255*		
HE= Polities where the role of the police is politically significant	150		
BZ= Polities where freedom of the press is complete or intermittent	133		
BA= Polities where population density is medium	060		
IH= Population per soldier	017		

[a]For n=125, *p.01=.228 and **p.05=174

variance in civil strife to make further interpretive efforts really worthwhile. Interpretative efforts in the social sciences tend to be self-confirmatory and self-gratifying. We can almost always manage to render meaningful anything that we find. Accordingly, it is better to be sure that what we have found out is significant before we launch into extensive interpretative efforts with respect to it.

Cumulative multiple prediction of the criterion variable

Table 24.4 indicates the order-of-entry of those variables that constitute the optimal sub-set of predictors in accounting for unexplained variance in the criterion variable. (For an advanced mathematical

TABLE 24.4 *The cumulative prediction of the criterion (civil strife) by the optimal sub-set of predictor variables*

Variable Entered	Removed	Multiple R	R^2	Change in R^2	F to Enter	F to Remove	V No.
IX		4915	2416	2416	40.77		1
IU		5815	3381	0965	18.52		2
IZ		6323	3998	0617	12.95		3
ET		6690	4476	0478	10.81		4
BZ		6944	4822	0346	8.28		5
BA		7144	5103	0282	7.08		6
FT		7379	5445	0341	9.14		7
DI		7599	5775	0330	9.45		8
FN		7759	6020	0245	7.39		9
EB		7916	6266	0246	7.86		10
EU		8052	6483	0217	7.27		11
IH		8144	6633	0150	5.23		12
FH		8219	6755	0121	4.34		13
	EU*	8155	6651	–0104		3.70	12
HE		8225	6765	0114	4.07		13

*Identification of variables that initially entered the cumulative multiple prediction but were subsequently removed in order to enable additional optimal predictors to enter the equation:
EU = Polities where articulation by anomic groups is frequent or occasional (r with Criterion = .180**)

discussion of this method see Cohen & Cohen, 1975.) Starting off with
predictor variable IX (=Short term deprivation), which yields a correlation of .492 with civil strife, a final multiple correlation of .8225 is
ultimately attained with the entry of HE (=Polities where the role of the
police is politically significant), the last variable in the original 235-
predictor data-set to enter into the cumulative prediction as a result of
producing a significant increment in the criterion, relative to the particular
cumulative correlation that had already been obtained before its entry.
Clearly, a multiple correlation of slightly more than .82, accounting as
it does for somewhat more than two thirds (.6765% to be exact) of the
cross-polity variance in civil strife is well worth taking note of and
discussing further.[4]

It is quite clear from Table 24.4 that the order-of-entry of variables
into the cumulative multiple correlation is by no means exactly the same
as the order-of-magnitude of the zero-order correlations of these
variables with the criterion (as shown in Table 24.2). It is also clear that
the top half of the order-of-entry list carries the brunt of the predictive
load. This is necessarily so, however, since the very design of the
cumulative multiple correlation approach is such as to find the most
important predictors first (important in the sense of accounting for the
largest possible amount of still unexplained variance in the criterion
variable). If we look at the first six variables that wind up in the optimal
sub-set of predictors (the first six in the 'variable entered' column of
Table 24.4) we see that they attain a cumulative multiple correlation of
0.7144 (out of the maximum of .8225 which will be reached seven
variables later) and that some 51% of the criterion variance has already
been accounted for by these same six variables (out of some .68% that
will ultimately be accounted for after the entire optimal sub-set of
predictors is constituted). Although the increase in predictive power
provided by the final six variables that enter the equation is certainly not
to be sneezed at, and although it is exactly that increase over and above
the admittedly major capacity of the top six variables that represents the
clear and foremost superiority of the technique we have been using, in
comparison to the earlier techniques that were incapable of examining
anything more than two or three variables at a time in conjunction with
any criterion variable, it still remains true that the top six predictors
carry the lion's share of the predictive and explanatory burden *vis-à-vis*
cross-polity variance in civil strife and that they should be clearly
recognized for doing so.

A brief, final conceptual return to the conceptual integration of the optimal sub-set of predictor variables

The top six predictors referred to above definitely reinforce our earlier impressions that civil strife is related to the *combination* of deprivation-coercion-anomic groups, at least intermittent freedom of the press and medium population density. This seems to be a dangerously explosive combination of need, lawlessness, punitiveness-plus-permissiveness and population dispersion. Looking at the last seven predictors too, we find that the above mentioned punitiveness-plus-permissiveness contradiction is paralleled by the one party-plus-competitive electoral system contradiction, implying factors within the dominant party, by the contradiction between a significant police role in politics, on the one hand, and interest aggregation via the legislature, on the other hand, as well as by the contradiction between coercive potential and a negligible inverse relationship between population size and number of soldiers. The previously mentioned deprivational syndrome is reinforced via the developmental emphasis. All in all, we are confronted by a very contradictory constellation indicative of discordant pressures and opposing tendencies in a context of deprivation and expenditures for long-range developmental goals that are not calculated to ease the deprivation issue in the near future.

This picture is impressionistically different than that which characterized the optimal sub-set of predictors of linguistic homogeneity (Fishman and Solano, in press), the latter being impressionistically more 'harmonious' and more 'positive' by far.

Having twice attempted brief verbal and impressionistic approaches to conceptually integrating the sub-set of optimal predictors of civil strife — the better to understand why linguistic homogeneity/heterogeneity is not among them — we will now attempt a more quantitative approach, namely via factor analysis. Factor analysis begins with a correlation matrix between all of the variables available for our inquiry (in our case, a huge matrix of $n(n-1)/2$ or 28,203 intercorrelations, when $n=238$). It then mathematically extracts from this huge number of intercorrelations the smallest number of maximally different mathematical dimensions (to be called 'factors') that can reproduce as much of the total variance in the matrix as possible. (For more details as to this method, consult any advanced statistics text or Cattell, 1978.) Our huge matrix was reduced in this fashion (just as the plethora of independent variables had been reduced previously via the cumulative multiple correlation method) to a

TABLE 24.5 *Factor structure of the optimal sub-set of predictor variables*

Predictor Variable No. (Loading)	Loads Highest on Factor No. (Loading)		Loads Next-highest on Factor	
{ HT	VIII	(445)	IX	(336) }
IX	IX	(404)	V	(365)
IU	I	(–388)	IV	(364)
IZ	I	(497)	III	(–280)
ET	VIII	(386)	XXXVIII	(302)
BZ	XXVIII	(295)	I	(283)
BA	II	(–356)	XI	(–316)
FT	III	(356)	VI	(253)
DI	II	(482)	I	(–456)
FN	III	(–568)	IV	(–491)
EB	I	(590)	II	(460)
[EU	I	(–590)	XVII	(212)]
IH	II	(496)	I	(–386)
FH	I	(638)	III	(321)
HE	I	(–525)	II	(–508)

much smaller and more manageable, more conceptually integratable sub-set of 'factors', yielding the results shown in Table 24.5. The factor structure that was obtained in this fashion is necessarily the very same as that reported previously in our study of the determinants of linguistic homogeneity/heterogeneity, since it is derived from the same inter-correlation matrix of 238×238 variables that was also factor analyzed for the purposes of that study. Forty-three unrotated ('orthogonal') factors were required to account for *all* of the variance in the original 238×238 matrix, the first five of which account for 52% of that variance, the first ten of which account for 67% of that variance, the first 20 of which account for 83% of that variance and the first 28 of which (in view of the fact that the highest factor that will come up in our discussion will be Factor number 28) account for 91% of that variance. Clearly, there is a great deal of overlap between the 238 dimensions in our original data-set and factor analysis renders considerable service in reducing that data-set to the least number of maximally different factors.

Table 24.5 reveals several interesting findings that enable us to go beyond our previous point of conceptual integration. Our criterion variable, civil strife (=HT) loads most highly on Factor VIII, the same factor on which ET (=Polities where interest articulation by anomic groups is frequent) also has its primary loadings. This co-occurrence of HT and ET gives us some of the additional flavor of what civil strife actually amounts to. The factor that is characterized by the largest numbers of variables in the optimal sub-set of predictors is Factor I, represented by EB, FH, HE [negative loading], IU [negative loading] and IZ. The next most frequent factor within the sub-set of optimal predictors of HT is Factor II, represented by BA [negative loading], DI and IH. Finally, we come to Factor III which is represented by FN [negative loading] and FT. These three factors are also the ones that characterize the next to highest factor loadings of most of the optimal subset of predictors of civil strife, as well as accounting for 88% of the cumulative variance in the complete 238 variable matrix. Obviously, we should turn to these three factors *per se*, given that they substantially involve over three quarters of the optimal sub-set of predictors of civil strife, in order to better conceptualize the nature of that sub-set. Table 24.6 assists us in doing just that, by listing the ten variables that load highest on each of these three major factors, whether or not they are among the optimal sub-set of the 13 optimal predictors of civil strife that we have examined before.

None of the 10 highest loading variables with respect to Factor I are variables that we have encountered thus far, i.e. they are not redundant with the optimal sub-set of variables for predicting civil strife. As a result, these high loading variables enable us to further flesh-out and render conceptually more meaningful the very factor that characterizes the largest number of the optimal predictors of civil strife. This factor, in very broad-brush terms, consists of the attributes of modern, western, developed, and, on the whole, democratic polities. The optimal sub-set of variables for predicting civil strife have, at best, only moderate loadings on this factor, two of which are negative (HE, which should, therefore, be interpreted, as 'Polities where the police do *not* play a significant role in politics', and IU, which should be interpreted as '*Absence of* persistent deprivation'). All in all, therefore, while this factor is frequently related to civil strife, it is not strongly related to it, reminding us, perhaps, that some of the more advanced (and economically advanced) countries also suffer from civil strife, rather than only the developing/poorer ones.[5] What most clearly differentiates between this factor *vis-à-vis* civil strife and this factor *vis-à-vis* linguistic homogeneity/heterogeneity is that the precise

TABLE 24.6 *Variables that load highest on the three factors that best characterize the optimal sub-set of predictors*

Factor I	Factor II	Factor III
IR= Life Expectancy 841	GD=Polities where political leadership is élitist −689	CY= Polities that have been significantly Westernized through a colonial relationship 727
EL= Polities where interest articulation by associational groups is significant or moderate 819	FB= Polities where interest aggregation by political parties is other than negligible 682	AF= Polities located in the Caribbean, Central America or South America 726
IM= Literacy Rate 819	EN= Polities where interest articulation by institutional groups is very significant −686	FN= Polities where the party system is quantitatively one party 568
II= Per Capita Gross National Product 804	DQ=Polities where the status of the regime is constitutional or or authoritarian rather than totalitarian 669	HH=Polities where the character of the legal system is civil law rather than common law 567
FG= Polities where interest aggregation by the legislature is significant or moderate 800	QB= Polities where the legislature is functioning 644	FW= Polities where the party system is stable −535
AB= Polities located in Western Europe, Scandinavia, North America or Australia 798	HL= Polities that are communist −632	HF= Polities where the character of the legal system is civil law (rather than Common or Muslim) 526
GY=Polities where the bureaucracy is modern or semi-modern 796	FD= Polities where interest aggregation by the executive is significant 616	DU=Polities where governmental stability is generally present −485

TABLE 24.6 (*Continued*)

FACTOR I	FACTOR II	FACTOR III
IJ= Public expenditures per capita on education	DN=Polities where the system style is mobilizational	CE= Polities where the dominant religion is Catholic
789	−608	470
CX= Polities that are historically Western, rather than Westernized through a colonial relationship	FE= Polities where interest aggregation by the executive is more than negligible	DY= Polities where the representative character of the regime is pseudo-polyarchic rather than non-polyarchic
786	570	−488
IQ= Infant mortality rate	AK=Polities located in Central and South Africa	EM= Polities where interest articulation by associational groups is more than negligible
−834	555	442

items that load highest on this factor are quite different in these two contexts (overlapping only FH and HE, but with signs reversed: police role in politics being negatively correlated with linguistic homogeneity and positively correlated with civil strife, and vice-versa, interest aggregation by the legislature being positively correlated with linguistic homogeneity and negatively correlated with civil strife). All in all, therefore, it may help to think of this factor as present in both linguistic homogeneity and civil strife, but weaker and more negatively tinged in the latter than in the former. Countries with civil strife may also be moving ahead with respect to modernization, Westernization, economic development, etc., but more slowly, with more negative concomitants as well, and with progress itself being dislocative and, therefore, contributory to civil strife. In addition, it should be noted that CP (linguistic homogeneity/heterogeneity), a variable that also has a moderate sized 'highest loading' on Factor I, is by no means significantly represented either in the optimal sub-set of predictors or in the factor structure of civil strife. Finally, it is significant that whereas CP itself loads highest on Factor I, HT (civil strife) does not do so at all.[6]

Factor II is characterized by many oligarchic or authoritarian features, notwithstanding lip service for a modicum of 'representative government' window-dressing. Thus, although there is a functioning legislature and little élitism, interest aggregation by political parties and institutional groups is negligible, interest articulation by the executive branch is predominant and activization (mobilization) of the population on behalf of national causes is absent. There is a repressive and anti-communist, authoritarian tinge to this factor which places it in conflict with many of the tendencies represented by Factor I.

Factor III is marked by political instability *per se*. It is characterized by westernization via long-standing former colonial relationships and by a one-party system that is only pseudo-polyarchic rather than really representative of the interests of different associational groups. Both Factors II and III have a strong Latin American constituency, whereas Factor I is strongly North-West European, North American and Australian in its make-up.

Although the optimal sub-set or predictors and the factorial structure clarify each other, they must not be confused with one another. We have used the latter merely to flesh-out and render more conceptually meaningful the former, which we have preferred for predictive precision at a level more proximate to the data *per se*. Both of these approaches, the optimal sub-set of predictors arrived at via cumulative multiple prediction and the factor structure of the variables as a whole, are arrived at by means of powerfully reductionistic data-analytic methods. These methods are admirably suited to what is becoming a growing problem in the social sciences, namely, more data than can be coped with by ordinary statistical methods, or, quite frankly, by the human brain. Cumulative multiple prediction and factor analysis, utilized together, can sift through a mountain of data, find the variables that are predictively most powerful and non-redundant relative to the criterion and, finally, render those variables more meaningful by placing them within a richer conceptual framework. We hope that our use of these two methods in this paper will provide not only interesting findings but a worthwhile methodological model for others in the sociolinguistic enterprise.

Conclusions

The widespread journalistic and popular political wisdom that linguistic heterogeneity *per se* is necessarily conducive to civil strife has been shown, by our analysis, to be more myth than reality. In addition, when a very varied and extensive set of predictors is contrastively analyzed as potential independent variables in connection with civil strife, other cultural factors, such as religious and racial homogeneity/heterogeneity, also do not seem to play independently significant roles as predictors of cross-polity differences in civil strife. However, our analysis has not only debunked a cruel and misleading myth. It has also tried to clarify the factors that *do* contribute independently to civil strife. These seem to be the combination of deprivation, authoritarianism and modernization. When these are co-present, then linguistic and other types of cultural heterogeneity may be exploited for mobilizational purposes attending civil strife, but, presumably, when these are absent, civil strife does not as readily occur and the role of linguistic homogeneity/heterogeneity is even more negligible than otherwise.

Out of a data-set of 235 cross-polity variables we have been able to parsimoniously select the optimal sub-set that best predicts civil strife. This optimal sub-set, consisting of 13 predictors, yields a cumulative multiple correlation of .8225, accounting for .68% of the cross-polity variance in civil strife. Previous methods of data analysis, focussing, as they did, on only a handful of predictor variables at the same time as they considered linguistic homogeneity/heterogeneity, provided no inkling of the total power of the total data-set available to elucidate the criterion under study, nor of the true role of linguistic homogeneity/heterogeneity in the optimal prediction of civil strife. As additional and better cross-polity data becomes available in the years ahead (most in need of improvement is the linguistic homogeneity/heterogeneity data *per se*), the methods we have utilized (or modifications and improvements of methods along similar lines) should prove useful in pushing ahead with further research on this general topic. Of one thing we remain quite confident, namely, that just as linguistic homogeneity/heterogeneity cannot be considered a major independent predictor or moderator of economic development (even though the opposite direction of causality does find some support in our data; see Fishman & Solano, in press, and this volume, Chapter 23), so linguistic homogeneity/heterogeneity cannot be considered an important independent predictor of civil strife when an extensive panoply of deprivational, modernizational and non-ideological authoritarianism predictors are also considered.

We hope that our many friends in India will be among those who might well be most interested in this inter-related cluster of findings, although India, *per se* must, of course, be described and explained, first and foremost, in terms of its own incomparable individual history.

Notes to Chapter 24

1. The four data-sources utilized for this study actually provided information on 171 polities, but for the following 41 the available data was too sparse to merit their inclusion in our analyses: Andorra, Antigua/Barbuda, Bahamas, Barbados, Belize, Bhutan, Brunei, Cape Verde, Comoros, Djibouti, Dominica, Equatorial Guinea, Fiji, Grenada, Guinea Bissau, Kiribati, Kuwait, Lesotho, Liechtenstein, Malawi, Maldives, Malta, Monaco, Nauru, Papua New Guinea, Puerto Rico, Q(u)atar, St. Kitts & Nevis, St. Lucia, St. Vincent & the Grenadines, San Marino, Sao Tome & Principe, Seychelles, Solomon Islands, Surinam, Swaziland, Togo, Tuvalu, Vanuatu, Vatican, Western Samoa. Polities established after 1976 and the constituent republics of the Soviet Union are not included in the data-base. Clearly, our results might well have been different had it been possible to include any sizable number of the above polities in our analyses.

2. There are only 235 (rather than 238) predictors of civil strife because 3 other predictors (provided by Gurr) that represent components of civil strife were barred from being included in the cumulative multiple prediction since their redundancy with the criterion variable (HT) would have produced a speciously high value of R and R.[2]

3. Gurr civil strife indices and Banks & Textor liguistic homogeneity/-heterogeneity classifications are available for only 114 polities. For 16 additional polities we felt confident in making linguistic homogeneity/-heterogeneity classifications based on our own familiarity with them. For these 16, no civil strife indices were available. In general, missing data, on any variable for any polity not included in the Banks & Textor/Gurr data-sets, was handled by entering the mean of the total distribution on that variable. The result of this method of handling missing data is to decrease the variance on any variable that is significantly plagued by missing data. Such variables then prove to be less effective predictors or less predictable criteria. This implies that HT would really be more predictable than we have demonstrated it to be, were individual civil strife estimates to become available for the 16 polities for which uniform mean values were utilized.

4. The later removal of EU, after its entry at step 11 of the forward selection procedure, is due to the fact that after step 11 the procedure searches for the best 12 and then the best 13 predictors of HT, as long as there are any predictors left that can make significant incremental contributions to the prior amount of criterion variance already accounted for at any particular step. Since the cumulative multiple correlation procedure searches for the best next variable to admit at every step, in order to assemble the optimal sub-set of predictors *at that step*, it accepts variables that are optimal for that step, some of which may no longer be optimal later on, at higher steps. Although the mathematics of this entire procedure is too advanced for our discussion, it is, nevertheless, worth pointing out that the variable removed, EU, is very similar to (and, indeed, somewhat redundant with) ET, which entered earlier and was retained in the entire forward selection procedure.

5. One strong indication that cross-polity variance in economic circumstances is not itself directly predictive of civil strife is obtained via barring all economic indicators (there are four such in our data-set) from being available for the forward selection procedure. When this is done, the cumulative multiple

prediction of HT increases from .8225 to .8654 and the proportion of explained variance in HT rises from nearly 68% to nearly 75%. Thus, rather than contributing to the predictability of civil strife, economic variables actually decrease the predictability of civil strife, another way of saying that similar degrees of civil strife may occur in polities that are at markedly different point of the continuum of economic well-being.

6. HT loads highest on Factor VIII. Other high loading variables on this factor are as follows:

HR=	Magnitude of internal war	393*
ET=	Polities where interest articulation by anomic groups is frequent	386
HU=	Magnitude of predicted civil strife	310*
IX=	Short term deprivation	284
AT=	Polities located in East Asia, South Asia and South-east Asia	312
EI=	Polities where sectionalism is extreme	350
AZ=	Polities whose population density is very high or high	370
HS=	Magnitude of turmoil	301*
EZ=	Polities where interest aggregation by political parties is significant	−328

*This variable is a constituent or transformation of total civil strife and, accordingly, was barred from entering into the cumulative multiple prediction of HT.

Factor VIII is multi-party (but, on the other hand, non-significant interest aggregation by political parties), interest articulation by anomic groups, short term deprivation, South, East and Southeast Asian, extreme sectionalism and very high/high population density. Since only ET is also encountered in the sub-set of optimal predictors of HT the other permissible predictors loading high on this factor do not account for significant independent variance in HT, in comparison with variables that have their highest loadings on other factors (see Tables 24.4 and 24.5), presumably because they correlate more highly with each other than they do with HT.

References

BANKS, A. S. & TEXTOR, R. S. 1963, *A Cross-Polity Survey*. Cambridge, MA: MIT Press.

CATTELL, R. B. 1978, *The Scientific Use of Factor Analysis*. New York: Plenum.

COHEN, J. 1968, Multiple regression as a general data analytic system. *Psychological Bulletin* 79, 426–43.

COHEN, J. & COHEN, P. 1975, *Applied Multiple Regression/Correlation Analysis for the Behavioral Sciences*. Hillsdale, NJ: Erlbaum.

DEUTSCH, K. W. 1966, *Nationalism and Social Communication: An Inquiry into the Foundations of Nationality*. Cambridge, MA: MIT Press (2nd edition)

FEIERABEND, I. K. & FEIERABEND, R. L. (eds) 1972, *Anger, Violence and Politics: Theories and Research*. Englewood Cliffs, NJ: Prentice-Hall.

FISHMAN, J. A. 1966, Some contrasts between linguistically homogenous and linguistically heterogeneous polities. *Sociological Inquiry* 6, 146–58. Reprinted (1968) in J. A. FISHMAN, A. FERGUSON & J. DAS GUPTA (eds), *Language Problems of Developing Nations*. New York: Wiley, 53–68.

FISHMAN, J. A., COOPER, R. L., MA, R., *et al.* 1972, *Bilingualism in the Barrio*. Bloomington, IN: Indiana University Language Sciences.

FISHMAN, J. A. & HERASIMCHUK, E. 1969, The multiple prediction of phonological variables in a bilingual speech community. *American Anthropologist* 71, 648–57.

FISHMAN, J. A. & SOLANO, F. R. In press and this volume, Chapter 23.

GURR, T. R. 1972, A causal model of civil strife: a comparative analysis using new indices. In I. K. FEIERABEND & R. I. FEIERABEND (eds), *Anger, Violence and Politics: Theories and Research*. Englewood Cliffs, NJ: Prentice-Hall, 184–222.

McRAE, K. D. 1983, *Conflict and Compromise in Multilingual Societies*. Waterloo, Ontario: Wilfrid Laurier University Press (see pp. 5–33, in particular).

POOL, J. 1969, National development and language diversity. *La Monda Lingvo-Problemo*. 1, 140–156. Slightly revised (1972) in J. A. FISHMAN (ed.), *Advances in the Sociology of Language*. The Hague, Mouton, 213–30.

RUSSETT, B. M., ALKER, H. R., JR., DEUTSCH, K. W. & LASSWELL, H. D., (eds) 1964, *World Handbook of Political and Social Indicators*. New Haven, CT: Yale University Press.

RUSTOW, D. A. 1968, Language, modernization and nationhood — An attempt at typology. In J. A. FISHMAN, C. A. FERGUSON & J. DAS GUPTA (eds), *Language Problems of Developing Nations*. New York: Wiley, 87–105.

SIVARD, R. L. 1977, *World Military and Social Expenditures, 1977*. Leesburg, VA: WMSE Publications.

25   Toward multilingualism as an international desideratum in government, business, and the professions*

Multilingualism and the Zeitgeist

The term 'multilingualism,' or any of its partial synonyms and correlates (such as 'bilingualism' or 'bilingual education'), refers to so complex a field of phenomena that it should really be no surprise that it is defined or clarified in much the same way as are the constituent items of a projective test: more in accord with the latent internal dynamics of whatever 'moves' the definer than in accord with the manifest external characteristics of the defined. Not only is this true if we move from culture to culture and seek to discover the dominant views about 'multilingualism' in a variety of ethnocultural traditions, but it is also true if we focus on any one context, particularly one that is highly exposed to the assets and debits of rapid social change, such as the one we are in presently in the United States, and we seek to discover the dominant view about 'multilingualism' from one period of time to another. Under both types of contrastive circumstances we quickly discover that 'multilingualism is a sometime thing'; i.e. it is a variable rather than a constant. It is interpreted and reinterpreted, by all segments of society, in accord with larger issues, more pressing priorities that shape these segments, that move them, worry them, force them to alter their priorities. Yes, 'multilingualism is a Zeitgeist thing' and 'the times, they are a-changing,' particularly in the U.S.A. and the rest of the Western democratic world.

*Originally published in *Annual Review of Applied Linguistics* (1985), 6, 2–9.

'Multilingualism' is not only perceived differently as a result of these changes but, in addition, its adherents and advocates must become adept at recognizing these changes and putting a *different* best foot forward, as the times dictate, for in truth, multilingualism *is* many-faceted, and aspects of it that are overlooked or underemphasized at particular times (places) deserve to be recognized and emphasized at other times (places).

'Multilingualism: as a euphemism for 'you know what'

In the U.S.A. in particular, but probably in much of the Western democratic world more generally,[1] we have recently come to 'the end of an era' with respect to multilingualism in social policy perspective. During this past period, multilingualism was treated better than it had hitherto been (viz., the vastly increased availability of bilingual education, bilingual ballots, bilingual health and social services, bilingual legal proceedings, etc., when comparing 1980 with 1970), particularly in connection with the low-men on the social totem-pole: relatively recent, relatively poor, and relatively unwesternized/unmodernized immigrants. This greater availability of services in the languages these newcomers understand may have masked the fact that the improvement in services did not, generally, signify any corresponding improvement in underlying attitudes to such recipients of public assistance. Most of us knew this, or at least sensed this, but hoped that the latter would ultimately flow from the former; i.e. that laws requiring a vast variety of multilingual services would foster changes in the social behaviors and attitudes of those engaged in and maintaining these services. There is good social-psychological theory for such expectations ('mechanisms become drives,' Gordon Allport taught us long ago) given sufficient stability of the services *per se*. The entire state-into-nationality cycle derives precisely from the stability of such services and the affective bonds that it ultimately establishes between the servers and the served (Fishman, 1972).

However, few 'usually well-informed sources' stopped to ask what the underlying problem was. Why was the movement on behalf of linguistic diversity so suspect and why was such diversity itself viewed as being so problematic, even by many of those who provided the services, let alone by others who only learned of them indirectly, through the media? Intellectual diversity was fully respectable within the Western democratic tradition. So was aesthetic diversity. So was philosophical diversity. Religious diversity was not only accepted but constitutionally protected. Why, then, should linguistic diversity be any different? Why should it alone have such rough going and such poor reviews in the media and among intellectuals and community influentials? Perhaps our very success in having the issue labelled as dealing with multilingualism, our very success in getting it *called* 'multilingualism,' was, in part, responsible for our lack of sensitivity to the fact that in popular parlance this term was no more than a stylish euphemism. Multilingual diversity is generally viewed as a sign of and as the basis of *ethnocultural diversity*. When the lay public and its leadership ponder the purported assets or debits of multilingualism they are really pondering the assets and debits of its ethnocultural origins, concomitants, and consequences. They are really asking themselves, 'Is that the kind of reality we want for ourselves in our own backyard? In our own city? In our own country?' In the Western tradition of sociology of knowledge with respect to ethnocultural diversity, such diversity generally smacks of conflict, of social and political turmoil, of worrisome calls for power-sharing along inter-generationally continuous ethnocultural lines — all of these being not only partially true but also universally frightening possibilities for vested interests and their referential allies. Our penchant and preference, as language teachers, as linguists, as sociologists and anthropologists of language, to focus on the linguistic side of the issue has its parallels among lawyers (who tend to see 'legalities' rather than society and its manifold vested interests), among physicians (who tend to see 'diseases' rather than health care systems as reflections of social values and priorities), and among other professionals too. By too narrowly professionalizing an issue we desocialize it and, thereby, lessen our own understanding of it as well as society's.

The 'Second American Revolution'

However, what was a consensually acceptable euphemism in the late 1960s and 1970s has obviously become decreasingly useful as a euphemism in the 1980s. Furthermore, many of the most widespread rationales *for* multilingualism may recently have done it more harm than good. Our continued advocacy of cultural democracy, of ethnocultural pluralism as being in accord with the true spirit of an America in which the melting pot *did* not, *could* not, and *would* not triumph, all of these claims, true as they are, have increasingly begun to do us a disservice given the new Zeitgeist which I call the 'middle-class revolt' and which our President calls the 'second American revolution.' The 'great society' of Lyndon B. Johnson, in whose administration much of the fundamental legislation pertaining to multilingualism in the U.S.A. was initiated, was itself a direct lineal offspring of the Rooseveltian 'New Deal' of the early depression thirties. It viewed our economy as capable of limitless growth, and our goals as sharing this growth (with at least some pretense of equity) with all segments and classes of society. The poor and the weak not only deserved to be helped but they could and would be helped because America was strong and rich, would always be so, and there was more than enough to go around. A country that can afford to pursue civil rights for all can afford a little cultural democracy too. A country that can afford to invest in outer space as a potential resource for mankind can also afford to invest a little in its own inner space and in the cultural resources that go unrecognized there. Nixon did not signal any departure from this approach to multilingualism. Johnson was defeated by our defeat in Vietnam. Humphrey was defeated by his inability to reject our continued presence there. Nixon was defeated by Watergate. Carter was defeated by the hostages in Iran. During all of these years American economic circumstances, and those of the Western democracies more generally, changed greatly from affluent growth to stagnation, inflation, and skyrocketing national deficits. Middle-class 'magnanimity' turned increasingly inward, self-centered, and self-protective. Nevertheless, our own rationales for multilingualism did not keep up with these changes. As the dominant middle- and upper-classes of our own societies changed their views and priorities, we language-focussed-folk continued to address them in the spirit of the 'great society,' of the Voting Rights Act, of Lau, of the Fair Employment Practices' Act, of the Civil Rights Act, of Jefferson and Kallen, of Herder and Whorf. In a sense, we chose to be right rather than to be effective, to be responsible rather than flexible in the pursuits of our goals. Practical wisdom is not made of such stuff.

The middle-class revolt and the image of multilingualism

The 'Roosevelt Revolution' (much more deserving of the name 'Second American Revolution' than the Reagan administration's worship of supply side economics above all other sanctities), let us remember, was not by any means merely a triumph of labor, of the working class. The depression had been profoundly frightening and destructive for the middle- and upper-middle-classes as well. Businesses and banks went bankrupt. Fortunes were lost. Empires were shattered. Successful breadwinners were ruined. City and state governments ran out of funds.

Mortgages were foreclosed on hundreds of thousands of homes and farms. In addition to the 'third of the nation' that was 'ill fed, ill clothed, and ill housed,' the 'middle third' (many of those members were less than a generation away from immigrant status and had just become accustomed to 'living comfortably') was also shaken to its innermost depths. The 'Roosevelt Revolution' could not have succeeded without the 'middle third's' active support and acceptance, and much of that was a by-product of its own resolve that such things must no longer happen to it, must not threaten it, must not endanger it again. For that 'middle third' the 'Roosevelt Revolution' was an amalgam of altruism and pragmatism, decency and insurance, love thy neighbor, and charity begins at home. Little by little, however, the coalition that Roosevelt had stitched together came apart. The Reagan Revolution is merely one more indication that the mood of the middle-class has changed profoundly relative to 1930–1940. The middle-class is no longer willing to pay substantially and endlessly for 'other people's benefits,' particularly given the type of 'other people' and the prevalence of 'other people' that characterize American society today and that make it a very different America than it was in 1930–1940. Adherents of multilingualism must learn to appeal in new ways, along new dimensions, along self-interest dimensions, to the class that has always held power in the U.S.A. (and other Western capitalist democracies as well) but that has come to see its needs and priorities much differently in the 1980s than in the 1930s.

The trouble with multilingualism in Reaganistic perspective

The long-term Western negativism toward permanently multilingual-multi-cultural-multi-ethnic arrangements, negativism which I have shown elsewhere (for complete references see Fishman, 1985a, b, c) to be deeply embedded in the political, moral, and social philosophy of the Western Empire, the Western Church, and the Commercial and Industrial Revolutions culminating in capitalist universalism, on the one hand, and socialist universalism, on the other hand, is only partially responsible for the revision or 'correction' in middle-class sentiments in this connection. A major component in this change-of-heart was the fact that the U.S.A. itself was seen as having changed in undesirable and potentially explosive ways since the 1930s and 1940s. Indeed, from its own parochial, middle-class perspective, the U.S.A. today, after two centuries of efforts toward this goal, is still further away from the consolidation of an 'American people' as a homogeneous ethnocultural entity than at any prior time during this century. During the formative childhood years of today's middle-class adults, our country seemed well on its way toward unification. Today, diversification is running rampant, not only ethnoculturally but in sexual preferences, in family 'types,' in dress codes, and in respect for authority and propriety in general. In the 'good old days' (let us take 1940–1960 as the lower limits of that halcyon time) the total population *expanded* by 36%, the English mother-tongue population *grew* by 60%, and the non-English mother-tongue population *decreased* by 12% (or, discounting the growth in Spanish, by fully 25%). However, from 1960–1979, 'everything changed' (Fishman, 1985b). The total U.S. population grew by only 25% and the English mother-tongue segment thereof grew by only 22%. On the other hand, in those same fateful years the non-English mother-tongue population increased by roughly 100% (becoming 17%, or so, of the entire population!), and even without the preponderant Spanish contribution to that growth its increase was still in the neighborhood of 73%. Obviously, the ethnocultural makeup of America had been profoundly changed before our very eyes.

Indeed, not only had the relative incidence of non-English mother-tongue claimants surpassed its pre-World War I level, but the diversity of these claimants had also become far greater and less promising than before. Our earlier non-English mother-tongue claimants were primarily of European extraction. They were largely at least white and Christian. Today's non-English mother-tongue claimants speak more Asian, Pacific, and African languages than European ones and represent peoples and cultures with whom the 'middle third' of America is less familiar and less comfortable. Finally, even though the immigration 'then' was primarily white, Christian, and European, that flood too had had to be withstood, and a policy of restrictive immigration was instituted by the mid-1920s. Now, when the numbers of newcomers are far larger, their relative proportion of the total population greater and rising, and their ethnic make-up far less attractive, 'something simply has to be done about it.' The 'middle third' of America, the decisive third in terms of the public decision-making alignment, is worried about its own future, and the multilingual policies of the recent past are among the very things that it thinks should be changed so that its worries can be assuaged. Facilitating and encouraging 'those people's' multilingualism, 'paying for it out of our pockets,' is easily the most expendable luxury in the current budget. Unfortunately, this is almost the only association with multilingualism that the 'middle third' has, and it is this constriction of view, a totally unnecessary and impoverishing restriction, that the friends of multilingualism now need to counteract. In this they will be joined by the spirits of Whorf and Herder, for these two 'forefathers of positive bilingualism' (Fishman, 1985c) were convinced that the mastery of two or more languages was an asset for all of society, for its majority as well as for its minorities.

Multilingualism: What's in it for M.E. (Middle Elite)?

Credit must be given to José Llanes, then Director of the Multilingual-Multicultural Program at the University of San Francisco, for recognizing the importance of this line of argument on behalf of bilingual education in the Bay Area as early as the mid-1970s. He was the first, as far as I know, to convene a conference on bilingualism in government, industry, and the professions, doing so even before the conservative trend had become so clear that we could all recognize it. Unfortunately, the proceedings of his conference could not find a publisher then. For the entire idea of proper, white, middle-class Americans seriously learning Spanish, Russian, Chinese, Arabic, and Hindi had to fight a two-front war: against Rooseveltian solicitude for the non-English and limited-English proficient, on the one hand, and against white, middle-class parochialism on the other hand. But every idea has its day, and the time has finally arrived when Llanes' inspired but premature idea may yet get a serious hearing. The time is ripe because the middle élite, supporting the Reagan Revolution ostensibly on behalf of middle-class liberation (this time, from lower-class oppression), wants to know, above all else, 'what's in it for ME?' Let me try to reconstruct now some of the ideas that I first expressed then (and which I have continued to express off and on for the past decade), not because I am an inveterate champion of the Middle Elite, but because I think that it would be suicidal for the meager forces for multilingualism in the U.S.A. to try to push ahead on any other basis in the near future.

Transitional or maintenance for 'them' vs. enrichment for M.E.

We have impaled multilingualism on the horns of the ethnocultural diversity dilemma. It is time we liberated it from that no-win situation, freed it from a nexus that has, for at least some 3,000 years of recorded history, remained conflicted in the Euro-Mediterranean World (the world which provides a major part of our American intellectual, philosophical, political, and social thought to this very day). Multilingualism also contributes world-wide to another area of discourse, to the area of governmental, industrial, and professional functioning and to the humanistic as well as technical skills without which these functions simply cannot be successfully discharged in today's world. The multilingual civil servant, the multilingual corporation employee or officer, the multilingual professional; they are all stronger, more likely to be effective and successful practitioners in their respective areas of expertise than are their monolingual counterparts. They can communicate more successfully with more people. They can serve more people. They can 'sell' more people. They can elicit confidence in more people. They can understand more people. They can be more flexibly assigned. They require less back-up support. They are exposed to more different ideas and, as a result, come up with fresher solutions or, at least, with more seasoned perspectives. In short, they are a greater asset. Their multilingualism is all gain and no loss. It is no more politicized than mathematics or chemistry. It is a type of multilingualism that can be built into our national book-keeping, as we go about planning our needs for leadership in one corporate area or another, in one professional field or another, in one governmental area or another. It can be built into training programs, on-campus and off-campus, done in-house and contracted out, provided through pre-service or in-service, but it must be taken as seriously in our national book-keeping as arithmetic or English if it is to be there *when* needed and *to the degree* needed for it to 'pay off.' Engineering education cannot wait until college for students to study arithmetic, nor can it wait until college for some of them to study Spanish, others Chinese, still others Russian, Arabic, or Xish.

When I flew in to testify at San Francisco's Board of Education hearings on the Lau Remedies that it was suggesting (1975), my testimony elicited little attention from the assembled Board members. I was an academic, a foreign academic and a foreign academic that represented no new voting bloc in San Francisco. Board members, therefore, left their seats, or talked to each other, or dozed, or read their newspapers while I spoke to the applause of those who had brought me and who hardly needed to be convinced that multilingualism was good for the soul and good for democracy. However, the speaker after me, both to my delight and my chagrin, was listened to much more attentively. He was not a more famous professor from a more distinguished university, but, rather a ten-year-old blond headed little boy who spoke fluently (and, I was later told, faultlessly) in Mandarin telling the Board members that he was delighted to be in a Chinese bilingual education program because he planned to be a sailor and to visit China when he grew up. Of course he was listened to! He represented a possible new constituency, a possible Anglo-mainstream, middle-class constituency that the majority of the Board knows, respects, and is largely drawn from itself.

And, indeed, who among us is to open up China to American commercial and industrial ventures? Would not Chinese-speaking negotiators have an infinite advantage in doing so over English-only counterparts. And what about Russia? And what about Japan? And what about Latin America? Isn't our reception a better one, *even where English is 'known'* (which often means no more than 'semi-known'), when the local language is also known by 'our man' there (even if only semi-known, but particularly if used with a modicum of wit and grace)?

Two-way bilingual education: Enrichment for M.E.

For a decade I have been hammering away at the thought that enrichment bilingual education (combining, in one program, pupils who know Xish but little or no English and pupils who know English but little or no Xish) was the optimal program for gaining support for bilingual education under 'American circumstances.' Such a combination avoided the constant polemics that surround the other major types of bilingual education, transitional and maintenance, with their built-in conflictual associations. Such a combination would attract middle-class support and, therefore, hopefully stable and ample support. Such a combination would counteract the fallacious view that bilingual education was no more than another poverty program, a social service 'for them' ('you know who'). Such a combination would counteract the view that the only legitimate function of bilingual education was to teach English (or, as more commonly put: to 'make them learn English and forget Xish)'. I cannot say that my colleagues welcomed my views any more than they did those of Llanes, mentioned above. It was all 'pie in the sky'; it would dilute the efforts directed at the minority child. The fact that I predicted the middle-class revolt and the inability of minorities to carry the day for bilingual education by their own numbers, talents, and resources was certainly a prediction that upset more people than it convinced. But there may have been even more to my prediction than I myself expected.

I am proud to say that my own state, New York, has just come forth with a million dollars to support ten experimental programs scattered around the state in what is now called 'two-way bilingual education' combining either Spanish and English or Chinese (Mandarin) and English. These programs are in trouble, but it is the kind of trouble we like and the kind newspapers don't write about: they do not have sufficient room to admit all of the 'Anglo pupils' whose parents want them to be admitted! And, miracle of miracles, the Bureau of Bilingual Education (under Carmen Perez's expert leadership) has awarded these grants only to school districts able to engage in comprehensive evaluation; i.e. not only to evaluate English, but Xish too, and subject-area progress too, and even the elusive 'affective domain,' all aspects of education that AIR, Epstein and de Kanter and Baker somehow overlooked when 'only' the minority child was the focus of our bilingual education attention. It took us a decade of fumbling with transitional bilingual education for Cummins-type research to set us finally on a path of doing it effectively. It will take us several years, I am sure, before two-way bilingual education becomes effective in connection with optimal mix of children, with allocation of time to languages, with languages to curricular areas, with curricula and materials, with cognitive and affective outcomes, etc., etc.

These new programs should not be prematurely oversold. They are not panaceas, and they are certainly not 'cheapies.' Good language teaching programs need many years before learners become proficient. One thing is clear, however: the societal implications of such programs are 'different.' They include the English-proficient middle-class child. They answer the middle-class taxpayers' question 'what's in it for me, for my children?' They are attuned to national problems that are recognized, even given the conservative nature of our day and age — problems of international governmental concern, problems of international industrial and commercial concern, and problems of professional outreach and income for a variety of American helping professions. It is an approach whose time has come. Let us, therefore, be among those who help initiate such programs. Let us help find support for them. Support for exciting programs with middle-class pupils is often easier to find because school boards do not expect 'someone else to pay for that.' Let us discover the best programs of this type. Let us publicize the best programs. Let us encourage young middle-class parents to demand such programs in the school that their children attend. Remember, every such program also serves n/2 ethnic minority children as well. They are *needed* by the very nature of these programs. They are the real, live speakers of Xish, thanks to whom the English mother-tongue pupils get extra reinforcement, extra motivation, extra assistance in connection with their learning of a skill that will be useful to them in the real world, in the market place, in the job market, in the diplomatic arena, in connection with the myriad tasks, skills, and interests that are meaningful and fitting for middle-class America. Through such programs (and possibly others, too, that serve middle-class America, e.g. immersion programs) multilingualism may finally be admitted into the pale of skills that are of service to America. It has taken us a long time to get such recognition. Let's do our best not to let it slip away!

Note to Chapter 25

1. Most of my examples deal with the U.S.A. and I will refer to the U.S.A. throughout this paper. Nevertheless, with minor variation, most of my arguments apply also to much of Canada and Western Europe. It would take up too much space to point out these parallels, which are left to the informed reader to insert as he/she reads along.

References

FISHMAN, J. A. 1972, *Language and Nationalism*. Rowley, MA: Newbury House.
— 1985a, Language, ethnicity and racism. In J. A. FISHMAN *et al. The Rise and Fall of the Ethnic Revival*. Berlin: Mouton, 3–14.
— 1985b, Mother-tongue claiming in the United States since 1960: Trends and correlates. In J. A FISHMAN *et al. The Rise and Fall of the Ethnic Revival*. Berlin: Mouton, 107–94.
— 1985c, Positive pluralism: Some overlooked rationales and forefathers. In J. A. FISHMAN *et al. The Rise and Fall of the Ethnic Revival*. Berlin: Mouton, 445–56.

26   Bias and anti-intellectualism: the frenzied fiction of 'English Only'

With the adoption of the English Language Amendment proposition in California in November, 1986, and with the margin in favor of that adoption being nearly three-to-one (73.2% vs. 26.8%), it is doubtless true that, for the first time in American history, a language policy issue has come to the fore as a prominent internal issue in the U.S.A. It was not by any means the first, nor, probably, the last, triumph for the 'English Official/English Only' nativism of the 1980s, but it was a triumph in one of our most populous, economically developed and modernistically oriented states. This was a triumph that signaled that gone were the days when I and other language status specialists would have trouble explaining to American academic and lay audiences why there were those among the Irish and the Welsh, the Jews and the Poles, the Flemings and the Frisians, the Catalans and the Basques, and among various and sundry other 'emotional nationalities that get so upset about and make such an issue over' their language, whereas Americans are too solid, secure, rational and realistic to get involved in anything like that. To most Americans, 'before California', language always seemed to be such a trivial issue relative to seemingly 'real issues', issues pertaining to the economy and to foreign policy, to sports and to the weather next weekend. The prevailing stereotype in this connection, one almost equally prevalent among academicians and the lay public, was forcefully brought to my attention in 1968, when I co-edited a volume entitled *Language Problems of Developing Nations*. A colleague who chanced to see a copy of this book on my shelf chided me for the redundancy in the title. 'It's like giving a book the title "The Smallness of Midgets"; only midgets are small and only undeveloped nations have language problems. You're indulging in a tautology with a title like that!' he said. How noteworthy then, that the U.S.A. has joined the ranks of the 'developing nations', or, alternatively, that there is greater realization that no tautology is involved at all. There are many developing nations without language problems (e.g. El Salvador and Rwanda) as well as many developed ones with language problems (e.g. Belgium and Spain). Clearly, something has happened of late in the U.S.A. to bring the status of English into controversial prominence and I would like to ask what that is, why now and why in the U.S.A. However, first of all, I would like to start at the end and ask, 'What difference would it make?', i.e. what would really change in the daily operation of government and in the daily rounds of every-day life in our country if English Official legislation continues to be adopted and is even enacted at the national level?

What difference would it really make?

In a recent issue of the *International Journal of the Sociology of Language* (1985, No.60), David Marshall attempts to pursue this topic in detail by examining the impact of a federal English Official amendment on the operation of six states: California, Hawaii, Texas, New Mexico, Maine and Illinois. Since there is still no definitive wording of any such amendment, he takes H.J.R 96 and S.J.R. 167 of the 99th Congress as his basic texts. He cannot be sure just how these texts would be implemented or interpreted, were they ever to be adopted, but he generally concludes that, if taken seriously, they would require 'a great deal of [prior] law to be rewritten', whereas if left as a pious gesture, as such laws currently are in most of the states that have adopted them, they would have no impact at all on governmental services. In Illinois, e.g., the passage of a law making English the 'official' language of the state in 1969 (a revision of a 1923 law that had made 'American' the official language of Illinois, a remarkable 'denomination' but one that hails back to Noah Webster's recommendation of 1790, in order to get around the Supreme Court's ruling that had invalidated the Nebraska state law that very same year!) has not hindered the Illinois [State] Educational Development Board from requiring that:

> 'Agencies having direct contact with substantial numbers of non-English speaking or otherwise culturally distinct citizens shall establish occupational titles for persons having sufficient linguistic ability or

cultural knowledge to be able to render effective services to such
citizens' [Ill. Ann. Stat. ch. 127 Par. 63b 109 (6)]

Accordingly, Illinois continues to provide services to the public, ex-
aminations for applicants for state civil service positions and courses for
its current employees in languages other than English. In this particular
instance, Marshall concludes, 'one wonders whether it means anything for
Illinois to have an official language' (Marshall, 1986: 57). This conclusion
is bolstered by the fact that the law in Illinois has been on the books since
1923 (or since 1969 at the latest), permitting sufficient time to elapse for
observers to judge how it is being enforced and what it is taken to mean.
In all other states with 'Engish Official' laws (as of April 1987: Hawaii,
Tennessee, Indiana, Kentucky, Nevada, Virginia, Georgia, California,
Arkansas, Mississippi and North Dakota) no such time perspective is
available and only two, Nebraska and California, have included such laws
as amendments to their state constitutions, i.e. adopted them in a way that
makes these laws relatively difficult to scrap or change. Note, however,
that Nebraska has done just that, effectively repealing its 1920 'English
Official' act in 1987, and that in Hawaii, a state in which the official status
of English is usually ignored by English Only advocates, Hawaiian too is
official and, indeed, is also designated the state's 'native' language (Hawaii
Rev. Stat. Sec. 5–6.5 [1983]). Just to round out the picture, before looking
into the 'English Official/English Only' effort *per se*, it should be pointed
out that it suffered significant defeats in 14 states in 1987, namely, in
Arizona, Colorado, Florida, Maryland, Montana, Nebraska, New
Hampshire, Louisiana, New Mexico, Oklahoma, South Dakota, Texas,
Washington, West Virginia and Wyoming. 'English Official/English Only'
legislation is still pending in 16 other states, leaving only Maine, Oklahoma
and Oregon untouched, one way or the other, at this time.

Frankly, it is not really possible to say what difference English Official
laws would make at either the state or the national governmental levels.
The various bills and laws that have been formulated thus far differ in their
intent and in their wording. Even where these are similar, they still differ
in their implementation. In no case has their implementation been subject
to a court ruling, although court cases are now being planned in California
and, perhaps, also in other jurisdictions. All in all, given the decentralized
nature of the American legal process, both with respect to law making,
law enforcing and law interpreting, we can expect a great deal of variation,
including patterned law avoidance, even where such laws are enacted or
adopted. The same is also true internationally. Of the many countries with
monolingual 'Official Language' legislation (Turi, 1977), many are extremely liberal in so far as using additional languages in order to

adequately serve populations which require languages other than the official one. 'Official' language is often interpreted as 'language of official record' and although most countries with designated and single official languages cannot be *required* to use other than those languages they, nevertheless, frequently do so, as a matter of tradition, sense of decency, or dictate of pragmatism.

All in all, therefore, my remarks thus far add up to the propositions that (a) we don't really know yet how 'English Official' laws will be formulated, interpreted and implemented (even if the courts ultimately find them to be legal) and, therefore, (b) there is no reason yet to consider such laws to be calamities, 'worst scene scenarios', or the beginning of 'a new order' and the end of the outgoing and accepting America that we know and love. As in Illinois, most states may consider their 'official language' laws as merely being as decorative and as innocuous as the 'official flower' and the 'official bird' laws that most states have adopted.

Of course, the law in itself is not all that counts. *Leges sine moribus vanae*, the Romans realized, just as much as *leges mori serviunt*. Laws require a certain tradition, a certain inborn sense of right and wrong, in order to be either adoptable or enforceable. It is hard to tell how the current English Official movement would turn out in these respects. On the one hand, when referendums are being debated and appeals to justice and pragmatism are highlighted, various advocates of the English Official position claim to exclude (transitional) bilingual education and emergency health, police and fire protection services from the purview of their bills, propositions, laws and/or amendments. On the other hand, at various times and in various places, even such innocuous and governmentally unencumbered matters as Spanish language advertising by McDonalds and Burger King and bilingual customer services by Pacific Bell are attacked, by some of them, as practices that 'tend to separate our citizens and our people by language' and 'lead to dangerous divisiveness' (*Louisville* [KY] *Times*, 12/23/85; *Up. date* 1986). Although Gerda Bikales, the Executive Director of U.S. English, claims that her organization 'is not targeting advertisers, nevertheless', she adds, 'the national group is not discouraging individual members from doing so.' The lack of any such discouragement leads me to suspect that the Burger King and Pacific Bell protests do not merely represent the views of a few loony extremists, but that what they are saying openly expresses the underlying unstated (hidden?) goal of the movement: to move from English Official to English Only, i.e. from English only in government to English only in society.

Since bilingual education is the largest and the most omnipresent

non-English language effort of the federal and of various state governments, its adherents have every right to feel nervous about its future, even
when it is explicitly excluded from any particular English Official agenda.
Just as English Official legislation, even when adopted, can remain
unimplemented, so there can be a 'handwriting on the wall' ripple effect,
leading to budget cuts, foot-dragging, obstructionism and negative attitudes toward non-English language services that are clearly outside of the
purview of any particular legislation. The more exacerbated the debate
becomes, the more likely it is to move public sentiment in the latter
direction. There is cause for worry, if not for alarm, whenever the *Zeitgeist*
leans in the direction of seeing diversity as an *ipso facto* threat to unity.
Obviously, the current American *Zeitgeist* itself needs to be examined, i.e.
the cultural milieu as a whole, because more than the letter of the law is
involved (and necessarily so) in bringing law into being, in interpreting law
and in enforcing law. Law itself is a by-product, a dependent variable, even
more than it is *primum mobile* or an independent variable. So, if I have
stressed before that 'English Language Amendments' need not be
calamities, that they need not be as bad practice as they may seem to be
in theory, then it is also possible to suspect, on the other hand, that the
initial legislation is merely an entering wedge, that it really masks much
worse developments and much more negative and restrictive goals *vis-à-vis*
the future. It will take a while for us to know which of these two
alternatives will more generally carry the field. In either case, it behooves
us to ask our next question: why has a concern for English Only/English
Official surfaced in the U.S.A. and why at this particular time in our
national history? Let us consider these questions one at a time.

Why in the U.S.A. and why now?

In what has been referred to as the 'century of English' (Fishman,
Cooper & Conrad, 1977), at a time when English is the world's most
prestigious, most effective and most sought-after vehicle of communication
the world over (Kachru, 1982), when political careers in non-English
mother tongue countries are made or ruined partially on the basis of
whether candidates for national office there can handle English effectively
(in order to negotiate with Schultz or with Reagan or appear before the
American Congress [none of whom can handle any language other than
English] when they visit Washington, D.C.), when English is still
spreading and gaining uses and users in the entire non-English mother

tongue world, why should a concern for its functional protection arouse so much interest in the wealthiest, most prestigious and most powerful core-English-mother-tongue country of the world, a country in which fully 85% of the population is of English mother tongue and where anywhere between 94% and 96% of the population is English speaking (Fishman *et al.*, 1985)? It does not really seem to me that the very ubiquity of English, whether worldwide or in the U.S.A. *per se*, can be appealed to as an explanatory vehicle in answering this question. It cannot merely be that the American defenders of English, flushed by the victories of their dearly beloved tongue on a world scale, have become enraged at the 'slights' to the hegemony of English in its own, American backyard. No similar legislative effort to redress the internal insults to English, real or imaginary, have surfaced in other core countries of English such as England, Australia or New Zealand, all of which have substantial non-English mother-tongue populations of their own. The general view toward non-English languages in governmental use in each of these countries is quite benevolent (re England, see Garcia & Otheguey, 1986; Linguistic Minorities Project, 1982; re Australia: Australia: Commonwealth Department of Education; Clyne, 1985; Pauwels, 1988) and even supportive in ways undreamt of in the U.S.A. At government expense, certain Australian radio and television channels are devoted exclusively to non-English broadcasting, ethnic community schools are provided with significant government subsidies and the teachers for these schools are trained at state universities, government offices and services are provided in literally dozens of languages, etc., etc. In all of these countries there is at least as much concern for the future of English in the world, for its continuation as the *de facto* official language of record within these countries, and for a good standard of English mastery in the schools and for proper English usage thereafter as in the U.S.A. with actual school achievement in English being at least as high and probably higher there than in the U.S.A. Even Anglo-Canada, with all of its wounded pride at the hands of a recalcitrant (and, at times, triumphalist) francophone Quebec, is more accommodating to its language minorities, francophone and non-francophone alike, than would be considered either seemly or likely in the U.S.A. (Churchill & Smith, 1986, McRae & L'Allier, 1986). No, any purported American or 'English Only' self-image as the 'true keeper of the English flame' cannot really hope to account for the phenomenon we are trying to explain. It is not English-centeredness itself (love of the language, mastery of nuances of the language, fascination with the beauty of the language *per se*) that seems to be the crucial variable. I have yet to hear of English Only advocates mustering votes to increase the anemic budgets so as to expand the currently small number of TESOL programs that cannot begin to accommodate the non-English and limited–English students (at the child, adolescent and adult levels) that are clamoring for admission. I have also never seen an Anglo-American parent cry at the beauty of his/her child's English, or of Shakespeare's either for that matter, although I have seen francophone and hispanophone and other parents do so, both in the U.S.A. and abroad, *vis-a-vis* their respective mother tongues and the verbal virtuosity and virtuosi to be encountered in those languages. What does seem to be crucial are certain characteristics of the recent (post-Vietnam) American experience more globally, more centrally than any preoccupation with language *per se*.

When English Only/English Official advocates tell us that our linguistic minorities 'are getting the wrong message' when the U.S. government addresses or serves them in languages other than English, presumably a message that it is not necessary to learn English in order to live and prosper in the U.S.A., I sense a wounded *amour propre*. Otherwise, why the utterly ridiculous paranoia about the possible inability of one part of the country being able to communicate with the other?; why the nightmares of bloodshed or social conflict because of language differences? Is there any internal evidence at all to confirm such fears? Aren't the comparisons to Sri Lanka or India not only far-fetched and erroneous but completely removed both from the reality of the U.S.A. as well as from the reality of those countries? And, to top things off, aren't the problems even of these countries fundamentally unrelated to linguistic heterogeneity (Fishman & Solano 1988a, and this volume, Chapter 24)?

No, there is a seriously wounded self-concept involved insofar as mainstream America yearns for English Official/English Only to salvage its sense of propriety and law and order. Otherwise, why the imperviousness to the data on language maintenance and language shift with respect to our non-English mother tongue population? Why are facts so useless in the discussion? Why is it so irrelevant to English Official/English Only advocates that with the exception of isolated and self-isolated groups, such as certain Amerindians, the German speaking Old Order Amish and Hutterites, the Russian speaking Old Believers and Yiddish speaking Khasidim [none of whom would be in the least bit affected by English Official/English Only legislation], all other *ethnolinguistic minorities in the U.S.A lose their ethnic mother tongues completely by their second or third generations of encounter with American urban life*. Not only do they become 'English usually' speakers; they become 'English only' speakers by then (Veltman, 1983; Fishman *et al.*, 1985). Hispanics are no exception to this 'iron law' as far as learning English is concerned. Their only exceptionality pertains to their slightly longer retention of Spanish as well (a one generational difference at most), due to the continued influx of monolingual Spanish speakers into their urban barrios. As a result of this influx the concentration of Spanish speakers remains high and the economic value of Spanish remains substantial for the denizens of the barrios (Heath, 1985) for one generation beyond the general immigrant norm. Accordingly, many second and third generation Hispanics who haven't learned any Spanish at home, from parents and siblings who stopped speaking it themselves or who could have spoken it to them but didn't, learn it from life in the immigrant impacted neighborhood, an impactedness that the new immigration policy of 1986 seems to be on the way to counteracting.

Instead of rigidly perseverating on recent arrivals who need governmental services in Spanish if their health, education, welfare and political rights are to be safeguarded, English Only/English Official advocates should be asking themselves 'why are those second and third generation Hispanics — who usually or only speak English by now — still living in those barrios where previously their parents and grandparents lived and where now the new immigrants concentrate?' But to ask this question would lead to yet another unknown, undesired and/or rejected data-set, namely one that shows that mastery of English is almost as inoperative with respect to Hispanic social mobility as it is with respect to Black social mobility. A racist society experiencing little sustained economic growth during the past few decades has no way of massively rewarding anglophone Hispanics. Twenty-five per cent of Hispanics today live at or below the poverty level, a rate that is easily two or even three times as high as the proportion of Hispanics that are not English speaking. Among the older immigrants English was acquired, their immigrant cultures were destroyed and their social mobility was their payoff or reward for the dislocation experienced. Among Hispanics, Asians and Pacific Island immigrants of the last two decades only the first two steps in this equation have been realized (due more to the dynamics of urban dislocation and mobility aspirations than to any governmental program whatsoever).

What signs of 'getting the wrong message' are there and what would the wrong message be? Are there any signs of 'separatism', of 'ethnic political parties', of 'ethnic militancy', of 'anti-Americanism', of 'ethnic terrorism'? The Black political party that surfaces during presidential primaries is certainly of no direct relevance to English Official advocates since it is supported by the most uniformly anglified population in all of American society, the Black Americans (35% of whom live at or below the poverty level and 70% of whose males are predicted to be either in jail, on drugs or in the throes of alcoholism by the year 2000 if current trends continue unabated). Why does the anglo-oriented middle-bourgeoisie feel as much or more abused by government services in languages other than English than the ethnic poor and immigrants themselves feel by the rapidly diminishing scale of such services? A higher proportion of middle class, anglo-oriented Americans have been turned off by multilingual ballots than there are non-English mother tongue voters who have used such ballots. More anglo-oriented Americans have been turned off by the very notion of bilingual education than there are Limited English Proficient children who have received bilingual education. The 'why should we pay for them?' syndrome, the 'why didn't my grandparents get such benefits?' syndrome, the '*we* know what's good for them' syndrome, the '*we* only want to liberate them from their ethnic self-imprisonment [because when we follow our leaders that is free choice but when they follow their leaders that is capitulating to demagoguery]' syndrome, these all boil down to the 'who's in control here anyway; we who deserve to be or those riff-raff and upstarts?'. These attitudes are all sublimations of the sense of being abused, of being taken advantage of, of being denied one's own rightful place in the sun and in the scheme of things that seems to plague so much of anglo-oriented America today. The English Only/English Official movement may largely represent the displacement of middle-class anglo fears and anxieties from the difficult if not intractable *real* causes of their fears and anxieties to mythical and simplistic and stereotyped scapegoats. If those with these fears are successful in passing English Official amendments, this would represent another 'liberation of Grenada' rather than any mature grappling with the really monumental economic, social and political causes of conflict, unrest and contention in either America or in the world at large today.

'English Official/English Only' advocates continue to stress the problems 'out there', due to and among non-English speaking Americans. They refuse to admit to any problems 'in here', i.e. among themselves and among middle class anglified Americans more generally. There can be no doubt that such problems exist, given that it has proven to be so relatively easy for the holders of power to launch a witch-hunt in the 1980s, a patriotic 'purification' campaign against 'foreign elements', akin today to the anti-Catholic, anti-immigrant, anti-Black and anti-hyphenated- American campaigns of past eras in American history. Indeed, the campaign against 'foreign contaminants' has attracted an odd mix of adherents, among them conservation/natural resources proponents, those who fear that Hispanics are plotting to force the Anglos to learn Spanish as the nation's first language (a case of the pot calling the kettle black, if there ever was one), and supporters of a large variety of traditional conservative causes (e.g. 'the right to life' [=anti-abortion] and anti-gun-control). Finally, having discovered that it is an issue that excites the baser instincts, it has been exploited as a fund-raising and voter mobilization ploy for conservative candidates, causes and referenda reaching far beyond the English issue *per se*. In political parlance, it is a 'stampeder', an issue whose importance far transcends its own limits. The insecurity of the relatively secure and those who wishfully identify with them shouts out from above and around this odd assembly of defenders of middle class good-and-welfare. It is this insecurity that needs to be examined, more than anything else, in order to understand the English Only/English Official appeal on the current American political scene.

And why is anglo-oriented, middle-class America particularly insecure and upset by 'these foreigners' in its midst who are getting government services in languages other than English? Perhaps because it is America that has lost more relative leverage on the world scene than any other major power during the past two score years; perhaps because it is the American economy that has performed less glamorously than its own mythology and built-in aspirations and expectations had led its prior beneficiaries to expect; perhaps because the ethnic revival led to multi-cultural mutterings that finally frightened more of the mutterers and their listeners than it satisfied, gratified or influenced in any way (Fishman *et al.*, 1985); perhaps because this is the first anglo-American generation that has had to face the possibility that it and its children would not rise socially to a station in life higher than that of their parents, etc., etc. The new insecurities of anglo-mainstream-oriented American middle class life, combined with the widespread disappointment in the liberal ameliorative promise of the Roosevelt to Johnson era, have led to the English Only/English Official 'solution', a 'cheap thrill' if there ever was one. It solves none of the problems leading to the above-mentioned insecurities (indeed, it does not even recognize any of those problems), and, therefore, still leaves the way open for various other vindictive displacements of 'unloadings' of insecurity in the future. It is the classical wrong solution to the wrong problem. Indeed, even were English in America being threatened by other languages, the English Only/English Official forces have failed to recognize that such a language conflict, like all other language conflicts wherever they arise, merely represent(s) the tip of the iceberg of inter-ethnolinguistic conflict based upon economic, political and cultural grievances. These grievances represent the real problems and not their linguistic concomitants. If inter-ethnolinguistic divisiveness is a real threat to America, which I firmly believe it is not (that charge being no more than a currently fashionable form of nativistic witch-hunting), then English Only/English Official efforts are wasting our time, leading us away from real solutions to the causes of this threat and orienting us to the pursuit of mere symptoms and byproducts of the threat. Thus, even in terms of its own definition of what ails America, English Only/English Official is an abysmal failure in getting down to basic causes and, therefore, at suggesting effective solutions. By manufacturing the myth of 'giving our new arrivals the wrong message' (which, like all myths, is shrouded in vague and unspoken mysteries and allusions), it must wind up with an unreal solution. Myths, as Barthes (1976) and Woolard (1986) remind us, do not simply hide the truth, they distort it. The truth is that English Only/English Official efforts cannot hide the fact that the power-class (and those anglos and non-anglos who aspire to join its ranks) feels insecure about its own leadership-role and its power-prerogatives in American society; the distortion arises when others (those who are presumably 'getting the wrong message' by thinking that they too deserve some power in American life) are blamed for these insecurities and for the power-class's difficulties in finding genuine solutions to them.

The profile of English Only supporters revealed by the June 1986 nationwide poll of the New York Times/Columbia Broadcasting System reveals an age, education and income progression. The older the age, the higher the income and the higher the education the greater the support for 'English Only', with relatively little support coming from either Blacks, Hispanics or other minorities (Asians, Amerindians). This is an alarming alignment of power *vs.* its absence, except for an equally alarming minor reversal of this trend at the lowest end of the [white] income distribution (family income below $12,000/yr) where English Only sentiment outpolls that among those whose family income is at the very top of the scale (above $50,000/yr). It is this latter identification of Whites desperate for the taste of power — and for disassociation from non-White immigrant minorities — with those who already 'have made it' that carries with it a potentially dangerous explosive charge. Note should also be taken of the atypicality of those relatively few Hispanics who are active in mainstream politics in the U.S.A. when interpreting the tendency of the Hispanic middle-class (from whose ranks the new Director of the Office of Bilingual Education and Minority Language Affairs, Alicia Coro, and the New Director of U.S. English, Linda Chavez, are drawn) to vote for English Only. The Hispanic middle class is obviously faced by a 'no win' situation. Either they must reject the charge of anti-Americanism or they must confirm it and the only way is to vote for English Only far more frequently than do other

Hispanics (29%). Hispanics pay their own price, a doubly heavy price, for their membership, or membership aspirations, in the American establishment.

Of times and tides in American history

Although we have tried to grapple with the question of 'Why Now?', our answer, above, should not hide the fact, already alluded to, that this is not the first time in American history when immigrants and their languages have been considered suspect by significant segments of the establishment. In the early years of the Republic, Benjamin Franklin railed against the Pennsylvania Germans due to his inability to influence them during election campaigns because they understood no English and he, no German. Anti-Catholicism and anti-immigration biases were prominent in the 1880s and, appropriately enough, were referred to (by adherents and detractors alike) as constituting the 'Know Nothing' party (a designation that would be quite appropriate for the ELA ideologists today). During and after World War I, we witnessed a spate of anti-hyphenation, anti-foreigner, anti-foreign language agitation and legislation (the legislation all being found unconstitutional by the end of that decade). And here we are again, in a period of retreat from affirmative action, anti-immigration legislation, budget-cutting with respect to health, education and welfare programs and serious threats to social security and Medicare. As before, the threat to cultural democracy and to continually renewed and self-maintaining ethnolinguistic diversity comes from the right of the American political spectrum, such as it is. However, as Arthur Schlesinger Jr. has recently pointed out, 'both conservatism and reform degenerate into excess'. Just as liberal reformism produced problems by *its* solutions, so our current conservative binge is producing problems, fiscal, moral and military, by its policies and priorities. Accordingly, as the debits of conservatism begin to clearly outweigh its assets, there should come, 'shortly before or after the year 1990 . . . a sharp change in the national mood and direction . . ., [when power should pass to] the young men and women who came of political age in the Kennedy years' (Schlesinger, 1986). Unfortunately, it is not absolutely clear that Schlesinger is a good prophet in this particular connection, recent polls having indicated a growing conservatism (rather than a growing liberal inclination) among America's younger population. Nevertheless, their Kennedy/Vietnam/Youth Revolt experiences of the 1960s and 1970s may still leave them more accepting of minorities and ethnic differences and contributions than their parents were or are to this very day.

Schlesinger takes comfort from this cyclical nature of American politics, because he believes that 'the two jostling strains in American thought ... [are] indissoluble partners in the great adventure of democracy'. I agree and find consolation in the idea that no political establishment is likely to become so established as to permanently foreclose philosophical opposition and pragmatic cost-effectiveness accounting in the electorate. But another comment by Schlesinger also strikes me as basically correct and gives me greater concern in my sociolinguistic capacity. Schlesinger reminds us that 'in the American republic, conservatism and reform ... agree more than they disagree'. This is nowhere truer than in the realm of language.

The two-front war: Fostering ethnolinguistic diversity as a national good

My basic opposition to the English Only/English Official efforts is that I would like my government to actively foster and value ethnolinguistic diversity. If Australia can declare that every child that has one should be encouraged and assisted to maintain an ancestral language other than English, and every child who does not have (or no longer has) one should be encouraged and assisted to acquire and maintain a community language other than English, then I am strengthened in my conviction that the American mind and the American heart and soul are sufficiently accepting and encouraging to make a similar statement. In pursuit of such a goal of government activity on behalf of fostering ethnolinguistic diversity as a national desideratum, I find myself stymied by the residual lack of language consciousness (certainly lack of positive language consciousness) that we have acquired from our British intellectual and legal heritage, on the one hand, and by the uniformationism that is similarly shared by conservatism and liberalism, on the other hand. There is as much opposition to ethnolinguistic diversity in Marx, Engels, Roosevelt and Hart as in Lord Acton, Ronald Reagan, Jacques Barzun and Senator Hayakawa. The left (or the so called 'liberal center') fantasizes an ethnically uniformized America as much as does the right, even if it does not act-out its fantasies quite so openly and so fully. The one conceives of ethnolinguistic diversity as bourgeois nationalism that sunders the unified proletariat and the other conceives of it as subversive extremism that destroys the established order. Both associate it with pure emotionality or even irrationality, since both see in it values and priorities that are unrelated to the maximization of productivity in the economic sphere. The mild (practically inaudible) language maintenance stance of the National Association for Bilingual Education, of the Smithsonian's annual festivals of American folklife (even that of the 1987 Festival, with its emphasis on 'America's many voices' [=languages]), of the National Council of Teachers of English, of the National Council for Black Studies, of the Linguistic Society of America, of the Conference on College Composition and Communication, of the Center for Applied Linguistics, of the National Council of the Churches of Christ in the U.S.A. and of the American Jewish Committee's Institute of Human Relations, does not begin to redress the imbalance, for most of them are merely being tolerant, rather than vibrant, with respect to fostering the non-English language resources in the U.S.A., and others of them are engaging in special pleading, which is equally, if not more, ineffective (Smitherman-Donaldson, 1987). Nor is the constant academic call for 'More research' (note the study on 'English Language Concerns in American Life: Historical and Contemporary Dimensions', headed by Prof. Guadelupe San Miguel, of Education and Chicano Studies, University of California, Santa Barbara with very modest Ford Foundation support) anything like a goal or an effective lever. We are a long, long way from a positive language policy, such as the ones the Australians have just adopted calling for an active second language (either English or a Community Language Other Than English) for every Australian; indeed, so far away that it would be not only premature but dangerously self-defeating to engage, at any now-forseeable date, in the requisite discussion out of which such a policy might ultimately flow. The disentanglement of linguistic pluralism from civil strife and from debits in connection with per-capita gross-national-product has only just begun even in academia (Fishman & Solano, 1988a) and it will be a long time before the implications of that disentanglement trickle down to the lay public and its leaders.

As an unabashed linguistic pluralist, I have not only the English Only/English Official forces to contend with but also all those forces, whether on the right or on the left, that deny the Herd-erian/Whorfian/Kallenian vision (and, I might add, of the Hebrew prophetic vision of 'seventy peoples and seventy languages' even 'in the end of all days' when the earth will be full of the glory of God), a vision of ethnolinguistic pluralism as a value in its own right. So yes, I will continue to struggle for bilingual education (stressing its enrichment potential for all children, rather than merely its transitional use *en route* to English Only in the school, a compensatory use that I predicted a dozen years ago would be self-destructive for bilingual education [Fishman,

1973]). Only enrichment bilingual education will gratify the social and cultural mobility goals of the middle class for its children and turn that class into allies, rather than sullen enemies, of bilingual education. I will oppose the terribly, destructively misguided English Only/English Official efforts, although I think they may yet experience some further local victories in the short run, before the courts and the new *Zeitgeist* that is coming will catch up with them. But I will also continue to oppose American uniformationism under any guise, political, ethnic, religious or philosophical. If a turn toward reform is coming, and every time I read the headlines it seems to me to be simultaneously overdue, impossible and inevitable, then I hope to have introduced enough Herderian/Whorfian/Kallenian thought into the awareness of a younger generation of students and colleagues (see, e.g. Fishman, 1982) to convince the reformers that it is not enough to be *anti*-English Only or *anti*-English Official. Ethnolinguistic diversity is something I hope they will be *for*, as a public good (as it is in Australia, where the personality principle is just as dominant and the territoriality principle is just as inoperative as they are in the U.S.A.), as something that is in the national interest and in the interest of all our children, and, therefore, as something that reform needs to champion when it again finds it place in the sun, just as conservatism should, both being 'indissoluble partners in the great adventure of [American] democracy'.

Neither major partner in the American idea and the American experience has done right in so far as fostering linguistic pluralism is concerned. Each has to be taught that in the American tradition *unum* and *pluribus* go hand in hand. The *unum* grows out of *pluribus* but does not replace it! The *unum*-ideal and the *unum*-reality pertain to our love and loyalty to America and to its fundamental political institutions and commitments. The *pluribus*-ideal pertains to our substantive values, to our religious commitments, to our problem solving approaches, to the living ethnic heritages, the co-streams of American life and American vision that remain alive for millions upon millions of our citizens. In a system of checks and balances, it is the *pluribus*-ideal that counterbalances the *unum*-ideal. Each saves the other from its excesses and it is the *pluribus*-ideal that requires bolstering in America today. The 'protectors of *pluribus*' must rally their forces of conviction and of persuasion, because pluralism is the very genius of America: pluralism of political jurisdictions, pluralism of educational jurisdictions, pluralism of religious faiths (most of which, by the way, are ethnically focussed as well) and pluralism of intellectual and philosophical outlooks. It is this broad-minded and good-hearted pluralism that has made America great and no mean-

spirited, ghost-battling, witch-hunting, frightened bully-boys can long
deflect it from the patrimony of *pluribus* that has made it great in the past
and that will keep it so in the future.

Bibliography

AUSTRALIA: COMMONWEALTH DEPARTMENT OF EDUCATION 1982, *Towards a
    National Language Policy*. Canberra: Australian Government Print-
    ing Service.
BARTHES, R. 1972, *Mythologies*. New York: Hill and Wang.
CHURCHILL, S. & SMITH, A. 1986, The emerging consensus. *Language and
    Society/Langue et société*. no. 18. 5–11.
CLYNE, M. G. (ed.) 1985, *Australia, Meeting Place of Languages*.
    Canberra: ANU Pacific Linguistics.
FISHMAN, J. A. 1973, Bilingual education: What and why? *The Florida FL
    Reporter*. Spring/Fall, pp. 13–14, 22, 43.
—   1982, Whorfianism of the third kind: Ethnolinguistic diversity as an
    international societal asset. *Language in Society* 11, 1–14.
FISHMAN, J. A. *et al.*, (eds.) 1968, *Language Problems of Developing
    Nations*. New York: Wiley.
FISHMAN, J. A. *et al.* 1977, *The Spread of English*. Rowley, MA: Newbury
    House.
FISHMAN, J. A. *et al.* 1985, *The Rise and Fall of the Ethnic Revival*. Berlin:
    Mouton.
FISHMAN, J. A. & SOLANO, F. R. 1988a, Cross-polity perspective on the
    importance of linguistic heterogeneity as a 'contributory factor' in civil
    strife. *Proceedings of the Hyderabad Conference on Language and
    National Development. The Case of India*. Hyderabad, Osmania
    University; also *This Volume*, Chapter 24.
—   1988b, Cross-polity perspective on the importance of linguistic
    heterogeneity as a 'contributory factor' in per capita gross-national-
    product. In press.
GARCIA, O. & OTHEGUY, R. 1986, The education of language-minority
    children: impressions of London from a New York perspective.
    Primary Teaching Studies 2, 81–94.
HEATH, S. B. 1985, Language policies: patterns of retention and
    maintenance. In WALKER CONNER (ed.), *Mexican–Americans in
    Comparative Perspective*. Washington: Urban Institute Press. 257–82.
KACHRU, B. B. 1982, *The Other Tongue: English Across Cultures*. Urbana:
    University of Illinois Press.

LINGUISTIC MINORITIES PROJECT 1983, *Linguistic Minorities in England*. London: University of London Institute of Education.

MARSHALL, D. F. 1986, The question of an official language: Language rights and the English language amendment. *International Journal of the Sociology of Language*. no. 60, 7–76. (Marshall's article is followed by comments by 18 sociolinguists from a variety of countries.)

MCRAE, K & L'ALLIER, J.-P. 1986, Youth speaks out. *Language and Society/Langue et société*. no. 18, 12–19.

PAUWELS, A. (ed.) 1988, The Future of Ethnic Languages in Australia. *International Journal of the Sociology of Language*. (#72, entire issue).

SCHLESINGER, A. M., Jr. 1986, *The Cycles of American History*. Boston: Houghton Mifflin.

SMITHERMAN–DONALDSON, G. 1987, Toward a National Public Policy on Language. *College English*, 49, 29–36.

TURI, G. 1977, *Les dispositions juridico-constitutionnelles de 147 états en matière de politique linguistique*. Quebec City: International Center for Research on Bilingualism.

VELTMAN, C. 1983, *Language Shift in the United States*. Berlin: Mouton.

WEBSTER, N. 1790, *A Collection of Essays and Fugitiv* [sic!] *Writings*. New Haven.

WOOLARD, K. A. in press, Sentences in the language prison: The rhetoric of an American language debate. {Presented at the American Anthropology Association annual meeting, December 1986, Philadelphia}.

27   The rise and fall of the 'ethnic revival' in the U.S.A.*

The sociological imagination faces a riddle

There is a vast amount of evidence pointing to the conclusion that an 'ethnic revival' of sorts occurred in the U.S.A. between the mid-1960s and the mid-1970s and that it had significantly declined by the late 1970s. The evidence for the revival consists of 'across the board' increases in non-English mother-tongue claiming (even for mother tongues experiencing neither immigrational nor natural increases; Fishman, 1985); increases in the number of ethnic community mother-tongue periodical publications (Gertner et al., 1985; García et al., 1985); increases in the number of ethnic mother-tongue schools (Fishman et al., 1985); increases in the number of ethnic community local religious units utilizing languages other than English in some part of their total effort (Fishman et al., 1985); increases in the number of radio stations and television channels broadcasting in languages other than English (Fishman et al., 1985); all of the former increases involving 1960–1970 comparisons, as well as increases in ethnic studies (courses, departments) at American colleges and universities (Gambino, 1976); ethnic awareness on the part of minority leaders and community members (Lowy, et al., 1985); ethnic pageants and festivities (Esman, 1982; Esterik, 1982); and, not least of all, increased ethnic concerns in the mainstream press and other mass media as well as increased ethnic 'sensitivity' on the part of the mainstream political parties. An Ethnic Heritage Act was passed by the Federal government

*Originally published in J. A. FISHMAN (ed.) 1983, Journal of Intercultural Studies, 1983, 4: 5–46.

(1974: see *Congressional Record*, v. 118. no. 168, Oct. 17, 1972), and an ethnic heritage question was asked by the Census Bureau (1979). Within a period of 10 to 12 years, sidestream ethnicity became a more publicly visible and openly presentable aspect of local and national life, whether in advertising, entertainment or education. However, by the late 1970s and early 1980s, the 'ethnic boom' seemed to have subsided very considerably. Although it was not as quiescent an area as it had been in the early 1960s, another public agenda had come into prominence (depression/inflation in the economy, the nuclear/missiles arms race, the oil shortages, oil gluts and energy problems more generally), and several of the above-mentioned indicators of an 'ethnic revival' now showed a downturn (Fishman, 1985).

Both the 'revival' and the subsequent 'decline' deserve considerable attention, not only because they had their counterparts throughout the Western capitalist democracies (Allardt, 1979; Olzak, 1983), but because they pertain to a major blind spot in the modern social sciences: the nature of ethnicity and the factors influencing it as a dependent variable (Rosen, 1980). The ethnicity revival of the mid-1960s was totally unanticipated, both as to time and place by the very disciplines presumably best equipped to do so. To social theoreticians, open, post-industrial societies seemed to be the last ones in which sidestream ethnic revivals would occur (Beer, 1980). Generally favorable economic trends seemed equally contra-indicative insofar as 'reversions' to ethnicity were concerned. The established sociological imagination, focussed as it was (and as it largely still is) on social class and economic factors as the prime forces (and only legitimate, 'rational' bases of aggregation) in modern society (see e.g. Patterson, 1974 and 1977; Steinberg, 1981), could not envision ethnicity as either a constructive or as an effective force in modern society, least of all in those very societies in which the recent ethnic revival proclaimed its presence (Ra'anan, 1980). Not having predicted nor understood its 'revival,' it is similarly unenlightened with respect to its renewed relative quiescence. However, it is basically ethnicity as such, as a social process, that is not really understood. Its rise and fall cannot be grasped in the absence of understanding the 'thing itself.' The immigrant-minorities context of the lion's share of the language-related revival in the United States poses an additional complexity over and above all of the above (Gilbert, 1982), and one that should certainly not be overlooked.

Two misconceptions have monopolized the mini-theories that pertain to the ethnic revival. One of these considers it 'nothing more than nostalgia'; the other: 'nationalism' or, what is worse, 'chauvinist tribalism.' Neither of these explains either the rise or the decline, since they are both more inclined to *explain away* than to explain the matters that should interest us. Not only have neither of these mini-theories coped with the issues of time and place, mentioned above, but they have not even recognized such related issues as co-occurrence throughout the Western capitalist democracies, likelihood of recurrence, possible differences between indigenous and immigrant ethnic minorities, political-cultural and other possible goals of the revivals, etc.

The ethnic revival: An exercise in 'nostalgia'

The ethnic revival as 'mere nostalgia,' mocking put-down though it be, deserves a few words of serious criticism. Although 'nostalgia' is obviously not a technical social-science concept, its connotations deserve our attention, not only for what they tell us about how the revival is viewed by those who seize upon this term, but for what they tell us about the viewers themselves. 'Nostalgia' implies past-orientedness to begin with, i.e. it is a state of being out of touch with current realities and, in that sense, an irrationality, albeit usually of a trivial kind. However, above and beyond past-orientedness and triviality *per se*, 'nostalgia' connotes a lacrimous ineffectiveness, a romantic longing for the setting sun *after the sun has set*, a hopelessly ineffectual intellectual or practical posture, a pitiful confusion of substance and shadow, a fascination with things dead that should be over with and forgotten rather than remembered, respected, activated or celebrated (Plumb, 1970).

Interestingly enough, in his *Human All Too Human*, Friedrich Nietzsche formulates an aphorism which not only pertains to nostalgia but which does so in the context of minority ethnicity as well. It would be difficult, I think, to find a better example of the nostalgia point of view with respect to the ethnic revival:

'We call to mind that Greek city in southern Italy, which once a year still celebrates its Greek feasts, amid tears and mourning that foreign barbarism triumphs ever more and more over the customs its people brought with them into the land; and nowhere has Hellenism been so much appreciated, nowhere has this golden nectar been drunk with so much delight, as amongst these fast-disappearing Hellenes (Nietzsche, 1879, quoted from a 1974 English translation).'

The 'nostalgia' view of the ethnic revival — a view encountered at every academic cocktail party but never in the technical literature — starts off with the premise that American ethnolinguistic minorities are fast disappearing and inevitably doomed (the prevalence of this view is documented by Metzger, 1971). It is then further assumed that these nearly extinguished aggregates engaged in a final and futile gasp of self-recognition and self-assertion in the mid-1960s (Steinberg, 1981). Without any research to guide the conclusion, and without any theory to structure it, even this purported last gasp was viewed as doomed to be unproductive, self-indulgent and passing, rather than as part of a process with long-term origins and implications. The insinuations of 'nostalgia' are meant to be at least faintly funny, as if those who could no longer engage in sex could do no more than talk of it, think of it, remember it. Nietzsche's discussion is in terms of 'the afterglow of art.' The nostalgia view of the ethnic revival considers what occurred from the mid-1960s to the mid-1970s to be the afterglow of ethnicity: merely a pale shadow, a memory (perhaps even figment) of 'the real thing.' Indeed, there is one school of thought that even questions whether 'the real thing' exists or *should* exist. It despises ethnicity and, even more so, any implied 'nostalgia' for that phenomenon. This view constituted the liberal counterpart to racist 'myths of the blood' (Biddiss 1966, 1970a, 1979; Field, 1981; Hoffman, 1983). It is itself a myth propagated by those who usually debunk myths, particularly myths that depend on suprarational notions such as intuition and spontaneous longing.

The nostalgia view has achieved no empirical basis whatsoever. It is a case of fighting romanticism with romanticism. Why should nostalgia (which is, after all, a distinctly human behavior that 'lower orders' of life are incapable of) obtain at all, and, more specifically, why should it have obtained in the mid-1960s, in the particular places and populations where it was manifest? Has it occurred before? Will it recur? Or is it strictly a one-shot affair? Was it stronger in some ethnolinguistic groups than in others? Was it generationally patterned? Was it related to social class, and if so, how? We look almost in vain for research on ethnic nostalgia (note, however, Raspa, 1984). It is a fuzzy, woolly term that leaves us just as unenlightened in the end as it found us at the beginning. It is a nonanswer, a nonexplanation, an evasion of intellectual responsibility. In addition, it is a negatively loaded term. While its negativism may be justified or unjustified, it is certainly necessary to marshall evidence and theory before judgements are passed. To call the ethnic revival 'an exercise in nostalgia' is to be judgemental prior to evidence and smacks of opposition to the need for evidence. Those who use the term need no evidence, for they know 'intuitively' that the ethnic revival cannot and should not be enduring. They lack both the objectivity and the discipline necessary in order to refine their private wisdom and, possibly, to convert parts of it into publicly confirmable evidence and theories.

The ethnic revival from the perspective of 'nationalism'

If 'nostalgia' provides an unresearched, judgemental and anti-intellectual perspective on the ethnic revival, then the perspective derived from inquiries into 'nationalism' provides an embarrassment of riches. Here we are dealing with a perspective that has produced a rich harvest of historical, sociological and political science treatises, empirical and theoretical, quantitative and qualitative, by scholars all over the world. (Indeed, the exhaustive bibliographies of such studies, e.g. Winkler & Schnabel, 1979 or Bentley, 1982, the annual bibliographic supplements of the *Canadian Journal of Studies in Nationalism* and the topical bibliographies of language and nationalism *per se*, e.g. Fishman, 1972a; Fishman, 1984, not to mention such magisterial general surveys as Seton-Watson, 1977, commonly list more research than any one person can possibly follow, let alone digest and integrate.) Thus, our problem in this connection is how best to be parsimonious and yet locate the most relevant works that can give us maximum insight into what this topical area might possibly contribute to an understanding of the ethnic revival.

Early research on nationalism

The continental divide separating early from modern studies of nationalism is probably Karl Deutsch's *Nationalism and Social Communication* (1953; second edition 1966). Prior to that time, most publications stressed either the ideas of noteworthy nationalist spokesmen and intellectuals, on the one hand, or the differences between separate ideological, chronological and geographic co-occurrences, on the other hand. A distinction was frequently drawn between the 'good nationalism' (rational, voluntarist, contractual) of Western Europe and the 'bad nationalism' (irrational, 'organic,' aggressive) of most other parts of Europe. Whereas the former was derived from the libertarian traditions of the French revolution and from the free association of citizens in order to accomplish popular participation in national sovereignty, the latter was derived from German and Italian experiences initially, and from Eastern Europe subsequently, each with its legacy of totalitarianism, extremism and abandonment of democratic freedoms. It is particularly the latter brand of nationalism that has come to stand for the total phenomenon in the eyes of many of the modern liberal and Marxist critics of the ethnic revival as well (for a critique of this view see Rothschild, 1981). The leap from Frisian demands for use of their own language in local administrative jurisdictions, or from Chicano mobilization on behalf of bilingual education, to charges or suspicions of 'racism,' 'chauvinism' or 'nazism' is quickly and unjustifiably made (for a critique of this view see van den Berghe, 1981), perhaps because of the common romantic stress on inherited ethnic identity, responsibility and continuity in each of these instances.

Although it is common to find the modern origins of 'organicist' nationalism in Herderian imagery (thereby reinforcing the German nature of such nationalism), the stress on innate authenticity, on the desirability of discontinuity between one ethnocultural aggregate and another, and on the imperatives of such discontinuity, is much older than Herder or his immediate intellectual progenitors (Fishman, 1982). Indeed, it is older than the medieval snippets that have often been grudgingly conceded by nonhistorians (Symmons-Symonolewicz, 1981), as amply demonstrated by Kantorowicz 1950–51 and Armstrong 1982 and even older than the early Eastern Christian accommodations to Balto-Slavic realities (Jakobson, 1945). Its earliest sophisticated Euro-Mediterranean attestations are Greek (Fishman, 1977; Jüthner, 1923; Dickinson, 1896) and Hebrew (Hengel, 1980; D. E. Fishman, Mayerfeld & J. A. Fishman, 1985) and probably reflect the sanctification of small-scale econotechnical and sociocultural establishments. Since such establishments were originally the rule throughout the world, they were undoubtedly sanctified and stabilized elsewhere as well, but research on ancient Southeast Asia, Sub-Saharan Africa and the Americas is lacking in this connection. Our Euro-centeredness — both in building theories of ethnicity and in critiquing those that have been advanced by others — leads us to overstress our own intellectual, ideological and sociopolitical origins in these respects (as well as in many others). Similarly, the notion of a rationalist compact (and, therefore, of rational re-ethnization in the direction of greatest mutual advantage) does not really originate in revolutionary France. It has definite Alexandrian (Toynbee, 1981), Roman (*civis romanus sum*), Western Christian (Galatians 3:28; McNair, 1982) and triumphant Islamic precursors as well (Baali & Wardi, 1981).

Modern Western students of nationalism have only recently recognized the extremely varied and heterogeneous nature of the forms that it can take. Organic and political; rational and irrational; contractual and inherited; left and right; democratic and authoritarian; secular and religious; stable and changeable; conflictual, competitive and co-operative — these are all possibilities within the nationalist mix, and contending possibilities at that. To relate the 'ethnicity boom' of the mid-1960s to mid-1970s to this entire area of discourse is therefore merely to relate it to a *particular* stress on ethnicity rather than to necessarily similar goals or levels of intensity.

The objective reality of nationalism, nationality and nations

Most of the commonly attributed characteristics of nationalism posited in the early studies of this phenomenon can now be recognized as merely pertaining to a restricted sub-set of its possible (and at times incidental) sociofunctional 'colorations.' Like all other social categories and processes, nationalism has more situational characteristics than it has fixed ones. American familiarity with our two major political parties, and their constantly shifting ideological grounds for accomplishing practical ends, should have made American students of ethnicity more attuned to this very aspect of nationalism than it evidently has. And do not social scientists realize that religious systems are highly changeable and con-textual in their beliefs and emphases and that they are, in essence, much more invented and created than discovered or received? Is this not even more true of social class as a force in American political life? Instead of expecting one class or another to have a certain interest or a certain level of awareness eternally, we now generally recognize that class is just one of several crosscutting allegiances and that it cannot be expected to be predictably on one side or another of issues that arise. Certainly, the distinction between class and class-*consciousness* is universally made and the lack of correspondence between the two is not taken to imply that one or the other is 'false' or 'useless' or 'base'.

> 'Although few abstract concepts have more strongly influenced modern social theory and ideology than the notion of class, in advanced countries the theoretical concept is rarely transformed into an actual consciousness of class solidarity strong enough to overcome the effects of other attachments, more primordial and often more parochial, formed out of the experiences of daily life.'
>
> (Dahl, 1982: 64)

However, the fact that class does not have the power that some would wish (or that some have predicted it would have) in American life, has not only *not* invalidated the concept but has led to more refined understandings of its situationality.

Yet in connection with nationalism-related phenomena, their

situationality and subjectivity not only came as a great surprise but, for some, have seemed to question the very tenability of the concept. For Kedourie, 'nationalism is a doctrine invented in Europe at the beginning of the 19th century' (1961: 20). For Turner, 'nations are not so much discovered as created by the labours of the intelligentsia' (1978:55). Similar statements can be cited from most other major syntheses, commentaries and critiques of earlier work on nationalism, including my own (Fishman, 1972a). Nevertheless, the subjective and situational nature of nationalism, however much it has come to be accepted and understood within the field of nationalism research itself (e.g. Hobsbawm, 1977; Lonsdale, 1977; Moerman, 1965), still exacts a high price of opprobrium when it is rediscovered in connection with American ethnicity phenomena.

Seemingly, the authenticity claim, on the one hand, and ongoing ideological, artifactual and behavioral innovation and syncretism, on the other hand, make not only difficult but odd bedfellows. It is as if critics were saying: 'A movement that advocates 'authenticity' is nothing more than a hoax if it is other than authentic.' The unauthenticity of pro-authenticity movements then becomes an intensifier of the nostalgia charge. The ethnic revival is charged not only with pining for a past that is over, done with and irretrievably lost, but (which is worse) of pining for the past that never even was. However, aside from the fact that the creation of self-fulfilling prophecies and the formulation of usable pasts are part and parcel of all social movements and social institutions (Lazzerini, 1982), it seems to me that what should be of concern to us is not so much that this activity also typifies authenticity quests, as much as that such quests occur and recur and require satisfaction. Furthermore, manufactured authenticity is commonly as moving, as stirring and as commanding as 'the real thing.' This is no more than testimony to the symbolic needs and symbolic capacities of the human species. The very strongest symbols apparently deal with 'primordial' and 'parochial' experiences that are (purportedly) derived from and that (purportedly) validate everyday life (Shils, 1957, 1981; Mazrui, 1982). To the 'ordinary member' (as distinct from the social scientist), it is often not the empirical objective validity but the emotional subjective validity that counts. During the mid-1960s to mid-1970s, the *felt*-validity of their sidestream ethnicity counted more than it previously had for many people, and we must try to understand why, rather than ask whether the symbols that were honored at that time were 'really real.' The latter is a technical, factual matter and reveals a detached, external perspective, rather than an insightful idea. The phenomenon that we are trying to explain, moreover, is largely a subjective one and requires, at least in part, an appreciation of internalized feelings and goals rather than merely the external dating of customs and social boundaries.

The Deutschian contribution to studies of nationalism

Karl Deutsch's main contribution to the study of nationalism (a contribution that has, of course, exacted its own price) was first and foremost to take it out of the hands of historians primarily and to place it more squarely in the hands of social scientists, particularly social scientists with quantitative inclinations (Calvert, 1982). However, even more substantively important (and even more pertinent to our own sociolinguistic interests), was Deutsch's interpretation of nationality as 'the ability to communicate more effectively and over a wider range of subjects' (1953:96), among a 'large number of individuals from the middle and lower classes, linked to regional centers and leading social groups by channels of social communication and economic intercourse' (1953: 101), thereby altering the focus from intellectual positions and historical events to social processes more generally and to language and communication in particular. His stress on 'the middle and lower classes . . . linked to leading social groups' would probably be restated nowadays in ways that would be less oriented toward late-nineteenth and early-twentieth century Central and Eastern Europe, but his stress on 'ability to communicate effectively,' 'regional centers,' 'leading social groups' and 'economic intercourse' have become the building blocks of most theories and studies since his own appeared. Just below the surface in his stress on 'social communication' are the basic notions of urbanization (core and periphery), dislocation (social and cultural change), élites (change agents) and economic interests (material modernization), all of them ingredients which figure in my own as well as in many other recent theories of nationalism (e.g. Wallerstein, 1974; Hechter, 1975; Chirot, 1976; Weber, 1976, etc.). Others since have introduced other formulations or refinements (mobilization, modernization — e.g. Gellner, 1964; Nairn, 1977) and I myself have tried to pay particular attention to 'ethnic consciousness' as the crucial distinction between ethnicity and nationalism (Fishman, 1972a), but basically we have all merely rearranged, documented and expounded upon (revised and explained) one or more of the original Deutschian notions. It is thanks to these notions and their revisions that we can now demonstrate the cultural and ideological innovation and consciousness-raising that literally create a nationality where before there was only a passive, unrealized, unactivated ethnic potential.

In the above-mentioned process, language is not only inevitably used, but it becomes *symbolic* of the mobilization on behalf of which it is used, as well as the *natural arbiter* of those who can be reached and included. Of course, nationalism involves *a new use of language* (for new purposes), as well as *new varieties of language*, but the result is that the most sophisticated symbol system normally available to us becomes both symbolic of, as well as an ingredient and index of, the mobilized, modernized consciousness on behalf of which it is employed. The part (language) not only stands for the whole, but renders the whole conscious, binds the whole together and implements the whole. In the process of doing so (a process that takes time and effort and is far from being as inevitable, 'natural' and unidirectional as it appears in retrospect to be), an awareness of identity is created that often overrides the other interests (religious, economic and political) of the population involved. Once created, a nationality may be self-perpetuating (which, of course, does not mean fixed or unchanging) until it is overcome by forces greater than those that it has mobilized.

Critique of Deutschian and Neo-Deutschian theory

There are several alternative (and, in part, complementary) versions of Deutschian theory today, among which the Hechterian is currently most popular (see, e.g. Beer, 1980; Khlief, 1979). Hechter (1975) is primarily concerned with the mobilization along ethnic lines of late modernizing peripheral areas. His data pertains to Welsh and Irish nationalism and its varying and wavering electoral appeal over a period of generations to its potential constituencies. He interprets their support of nationalist efforts as constituting a belated awareness and rejection of their 'internal colonialism'. Thus, ethnic revivals of the Hechterian type are basically responses of peripheral and late modernizing ethnic groups whereby they undertake to struggle for the rectification of their basically economic grievances with respect to the established 'ethnic diversification of labor.' Hechter's interpretations of ethnic revivals are clearly Deutschian, but (at least until their very recent and unexpected revision: Hechter *et al.*, 1982) they were, if anything, more 'conflict'-oriented than were Deutsch's, the latter's views being rather more 'competition'-oriented. Hechter also stresses the earlier stages of industrialization-urbanization-modernization as being most conducive to ethnic revivals, whereas Deutsch himself, Fox, Aull & Cimino (1978), Eisenstadt (1971) and others stress later stages. Much research on the most recent period of the ethnic revival among

Belgian Flemings (see the review by Nielsen, 1980) reveals that Flemish causes appeal most to those that are urban middle class and professionals rather than to workers (for similar conclusions about earlier periods see van Alboom, 1982; Jansegers, 1982). They imply that stalled, urban mid-modernization (rather than late-peripheral modernization) provides the dynamics for mobilizing along ethnic lines in order to advance basically economic goals. At the other end of the modernization continuum, we find Eisenstadt's analysis (1971) which focusses on ethnic revivals in various African settings in which modernization has been 'defeated.' The economic and technological collapse of modernization results in a return to regional ethnic identities over and above the prior thin veneer of integrative national identity.

The Deutschian studies, regardless of the particular stage in the modernization process on which they focus and regardless of their conflict-competition differences, all rely on a basically economic dynamic. They view ethnic revivals as élitist-manipulated programs for attaining economic goals. Undoubtedly, *such* revivals do obtain and, even more undoubtedly, economic goals and grievances do play a role in ethnic movements (e.g. Blauner, 1969; Bonacich, 1972; Fenwick, 1982; Glazer, 1983; Keyes, 1981; Rothschild, 1981) and in ethnic survival (Bonacich & Modell, 1981; Melville, 1983), just as they do in religious and secular movements and experiences of all kinds. Many ethnic groups are obviously class-defined as well ('ethclasses', as Milton Gordon calls them) and, equally obviously, ethnicity has to mean something different for middle and lower class Chicanos, Poles, Italian, etc. What is more dubious, however, is the implication that economic issues are somehow at the core of the human drama in general and of ethnic revivals and experiences in particular (note the disappointment of Olzak, 1982 when such is *not* found to be the case and the constant need of most confirmed empiricists to ponder other variables, e.g. Reitz, 1974; Lieberson, 1981). Those who posit economic primacy *a priori* (not unlike those who claim that ethnicity is imaginary and that only social class is real;) inevitably wind up viewing ethnicity as a 'mere by-product of more basic forces' and, therefore, as expendable if not entirely unnecessary and even undesirable (Stein & Hill, 1977; Steinberg, 1981). Culture *per se* becomes an epiphenomenon! Unfortunately, 'Marx and Engels left no clear theoretical guidelines for conceptualizing the phenomenon of nationalism' (Turner, 1978: 60) and, therefore, their followers are left with 'no explanation of how to deal theoretically with the ethnic divisions of mankind when confronted with divisions based on class' (Kolakowski 1979: 48), and few of their disciples have had the temerity to strike out on their own to seek out an explanation (note, however, Nairn, 1975; Lowy, 1976; Jakubowicz, 1981; among others calling for more initiative along these very lines and the variety of views covered by Davis [1973] and others.). Instead of seeing ethnicity as a factor in interaction with others (class, sex, age, religion), influencing others and being influenced by them in complex fashions that always required *empirical* elucidation, ethnicity becomes 'something' merely to be explained away as an economic residue. This view, of course, is in conflict with Berlin's diametrically opposed view (1972), according to which the ethnic revival of the mid-1960s to mid-1970s was a rejection of the heartless, soulless economic determinism in modern life and its requirement that we disguise our true feelings and beings for the sake of maximizing the efficiency of the modern marketplace. Most seriously, however, the economic emphases that derive from Deutschian studies (as well as the countless Marxian and neo-Marxian studies whose ultimate appreciation of ethnicity is infinitely less than that of the Deutschian school) do not agree with the basic thrust of our evidence-anchored view (arguable though it may still be) of the ethnic revival in the United States, namely, that it was basically a generalized response over and above any economic differences between the groups that manifested it (Fishman, 1985).

The non-American, non-immigrant contexts of the Deutschian and neo-Deutschian research reviewed above present yet further hurdles in successfully applying it to the ethnic revival in the U.S.A. Instead of modernization problematics, we are dealing in the U.S.A. primarily with post-modernization problematics (Etzioni, 1968). Instead of indigenous minorities wavering back and forth between central integration and peripheral autonomy, we have primarily immigrant minorities reassessing their original identities in a country with no deeply historical, 'indigenous' ethnic center, indeed, in a country in which immigrational diversity *is* the center. Instead of a Deutschian programmatic and politicized opportunity, the ethnic revival in the U.S.A. was more a diffuse reaction to mainstream characteristics and blandishments (rather than restrictions), in the context of particular events and opportunities. Instead of a Deutschian ideological and cultural innovation and transformation, the recent ethnolinguistic revival in the United States was primarily a rearrangement of identificational priorities and components. Instead of being the by-product of Deutschian proto-élite initiatives, the non-English-language-related ethnic revival in the United States was largely an instance of leaderless drift. Instead of a Deutschian stress on autonomy in matters of language, religion, education and economy, its stress was on self-understanding, self-righteousness, self-acceptance and, perhaps, even self-indulgence.

Instead of a progression from ethnicity to nationality to nation (which I first clarified in 1968 and which has since then become widely accepted in studies of nationalism; see, e.g. Magocsi, 1978), we generally find no more than an acknowledged interest in ethnicity that remains far below the level of intensity that would be necessary for the nationality and nation stages to obtain.

Indeed, if the ethnic group-into-nationality transition is usually rather dubious in the case of the ethnic revival in the U.S.A., then the nationality-into-nation stage is almost always entirely absent, both in ideological as well as in concrete organizational or practical terms (Sagarin & Moneymaker, 1979; McCord & McCord, 1979). Even the virtual absence of much feared ethnic politicization (Foster, 1980; Bruckner, 1980) in connection with the ethnic revival in the U.S.A. (which is *not* to say that there was no ethnic politics, a veritable staple of the American scene since the days of Benjamin Franklin; see Estrada, 1983; Heath, 1977; Lucas, 1980; Waltzer, 1980; Glazer, 1982; Spinrad, 1983) cannot be attributed to the factors usually involved in the absence or presence of politicized nationalism in Deutschian theory. Normally, such politicization is attributable to the impenetrability and hostility of the established power structure (Mayer, 1980; Pristinger, 1980). However, it would be more accurate to say that in the American case the absence of serious ethnic politicization (see Parenti, 1967 and note his critique of Wolfinger, 1965) was due to the basically non-instrumental nature of the ethnic revival *per se* and to the weak role of any intelligentsia in the revival as a whole, notwithstanding the general rise in ethnic saliency that transpired.

Although ethnic studies at colleges and universities grew amazingly, and although this growth was a crucial aspect of the revival *per se*, these programs did not prepare 'new men' to join with already-politicized proto-élites in the acceleration and expansion of nationalist activism in the manner so convincingly demonstrated by Hobsbawm (1962, 1977) for various European settings. The third-generation-derived college students of most ethnolinguistic backgrounds were hardly 'new men' and, at any rate, higher education, on the whole, may have remained the enemy of ethnicity and of sidestream ethnic continuity that it traditionally has been in America. Rather, the ethnic revival entailed a detachment on the part of 'ethnolinguistically interested' students from the total higher education experience of pre-professional training, just as the revival *per se* entailed their detachment from the values, goals and processes of the mainstream more generally.

Even among Hispanics or Amerindians, where more 'new men' *did*

come into being and where a new leadership *was* trained on American
college campuses (a leadership far different in make-up than that which
preceded it), frustrated careerism was hardly an ingredient in the overall
make-up of these new leaders (Limón, 1982). Unlike the Deutschian
models, their protest was not against a mainstream or central system that
excluded them (as detailed by Smith, 1981; Khlief 1982a and many others
who 'overdo' the role of disappointed élites and proto-élites in ethnicity
movements), but, on the contrary, against one that eagerly included them
as exemplars of 'affirmative action,' an establishment that transethnified
more than it gratified in any material way.

Instead of breaking with internal traditional forces (ethnic churches
and ethnic schools), the revival ultimately dug in around these very
institutions of daily life. As a result, none of the three stages proposed by
Hroch (1968) with respect to the life of all nationalist movements (small
groups of ideologically innovating intellectuals, wider networks of patriots-
agitators and, finally, serious popular mobilization) usually obtained and
the latter two, by and large, were totally absent. The revival occurred
during a period of relatively easy social advancement, rather than during
one of curtailment, and it was, therefore, partially a rejection of such
advancement as the be-all-and-end-all of meaningful life. 'Righting the
balance of uneven development' (Nairn, 1977) does not seem to have been
widely involved. Indeed, neither the absence nor the experience of social
mobility may have been widely involved as much as the downgrading of
such mobility from its previous position as the pinnacle of triumph and the
attainment of the good life. The revival was neither a 'liberal education
for traditional individuals' nor 'a kind of professional education for
individuals on the move into the bourgeiosie' (Womack, 1980). It was
neither a questioning of loyalty to America nor a search for a higher
loyalty. Indeed, it was far too innocent and unfocussed even to be an
enduring ethnic revival.

All in all, therefore, our review of Deutschian and neo-Deutschian
concepts and theories has been helpful largely because it has helped
highlight our contention that the ethnic revival in the United States
represented a different type and intensity of ethnic process than that which
has hitherto been explored in the fameword of nationalism research.
Exploring this revival further may throw light on various, as yet
little-understood, aspects of ethnicity transformations — particularly those
going on in post-modernization, immigration-based contexts — aspects
and transformations that call into question several relatively unquestioned
assumptions concerning the relationship between sidestream ethnicity and
social class, liberalism-conservatism, élites, ethnic-consciousness, social

conflict and political activism (Newman, 1973). Indeed, our inquiry into the ethnic revival in the U.S.A. may ultimately help us better understand some aspects of modern minority ethnicity everywhere.

Situational aspects of ethnic saliency

A major problem with the Deutschian and neo-Deutschian approaches to variation in ethnic saliency is that they are overly categorical or macro-oriented. Even at the macro-level, however, they have been criticized as insufficiently predictive (e.g. it is difficult to explain *when* ethnic competition/conflict will occur relative to the onset of consciousness of disadvantage, internal colonization or change in central priorities). Accordingly, it is to the level of middle-range specificity — i.e. a level of analysis that is neither overly macro- nor micro-level in orientation — to which we now turn, doing so, admittedly, in terms that parallel sociolinguistic theory as it has been developed during the past two decades.

Immigrant-derived ethnicity in the United States today (and also Chicano, Amerindian and indigenous minority ethnicity in many settings throughout the world), implemented as it largely is in a context characterized by inter-ethnic contact and by culture change more generally, is largely a repertoirial phenomenon. By this I mean to say that it coexists together with a number of 'varieties' of socially-patterned behaviors, some of which are sidestream ethnicity-derived, others of which are mainstream ethnicity-derived, and yet others of which bear the stamp of modern generality that is not (or is no longer) indicative of any particular ethnicity whatsoever within its context. The first and second generational pangs of conflict and double marginality, documented so tellingly in the 1930s and 1940s (e.g. Child, 1943), are still present in some cases, but they are much more muted and mellowed. Relative to earlier periods and to the concerted Americanization pressures that were formerly applied by both mainstream and sidestream institutions, it is now not only possible to 'be American' in a variety of different ethnic ways, but sidestream ethnicity *per se* has also become much more modern and American. The spirit of the times is different and the vast majority of Americans reveal sidestream ethnicity-associated ways of doing, feeling and knowing within their total repertoire of social behaviors. An American ethnicity, too, is coming into being (Hraba, 1979), slowly but massively, for ethnogenesis is occurring in America too, rather than merely elsewhere (Grigulevich & Kozlov, 1981; Jones & Hill-Burnett, 1982), but it is criss-crossed by minority ethnic realizations, just as the latter are totally criss-crossed by American doings, feelings and knowings. The total repertoire is increasingly experienced as a highly integrated whole (rather than as bits and tatters of disparate cloth), although it is made up, as are all modern cultures, of old and new threads of diverse ages and origins. It is the totality of these threads which constitute the total repertoire, but they are never implemented totally, all at the same time. As with repertoires more generally, the ethnic repertoire is selectively (i.e. contextually) implemented, on the basis of socioconsensual principles of appropriateness and in pursuit of individual goals within a framework of social norms and expectations. Identity is a matter of social location, Berger (1961) tells us. Accordingly, particular combinations of threads ('varieties' of behavior) are selectively implemented, sometimes combining sidestream and mainstream ethnicity, and sometimes combining old (arguably 'authentic') and new aspects of either or both. Old bread and new wine are constantly brought together (Gallo, 1981) and, as a result, newness is less overwhelming and disorienting. The principles of selection between the myriad of possible combinations are both macro- and micro-determined.

The contextualization of sidestream ethnicity

Several approaches have been advanced from the point of view that ethnicity is first and foremost situational (e.g. Handleman, 1977, Moerman, 1965; Paden, 1971). In accord with principles that have now been well-established for the utilization of one language/variety or another within a bilingual community (Fishman, Cooper, Ma et al., 1975), the implementation of one ethno-behavioral variety or another can be conceptualized at various corresponding levels of abstraction. At the most micro-level, we can recognize ethno-*acts* and ethno-*events*. The transitions of birth, death, marriage, coming of age, etc. (Hareven, 1978; Fried & Fried, 1980) may well be more heavily characterized by sidestream ethnicity behaviors (including more snatches of ethnic mother-tongue use) than are most other acts, events or 'scenes' of modern urban life. Certain *persons* are particularly likely to be interacted with in terms of shared sidestream ethnicity: grandmother, the parish priest, the community poet, the teacher of the local ethnic mother-tongue school. Similarly, certain *places* and their congruent *topics* and *role relationships* (the three together being the building blocks of *situations*) are also markers of sidestream ethnicity, particularly if they are ritualized (highly predictable or formalized). If getting grandfather to do you a favor when interacting with him privately at the big table in the family dining-room is a recognizable sidestream-ethnicity-stressing situation (Gallo, 1981), then conducting the Passover seder with the immediate family at the same table is even more likely to be so (Schneider, 1972; Shils, 1981).

However, it is not necessary to conceptualize sidestream ethnicity episodically (even though that may be the level of preferred data collection or of disciplinary reward). Entire slices of social life (*domains*) may be more colored by sidestream identity and its implementation than are others: religion more than work, home/family more than street/-neighborhood, school more than entertainment, etc. (Fishman, 1972b). Domains, related as they are to the major institutional channels of society, constitute parsimonious cognitive, affective and overt behavioral boundaries in the organization of social life. It is not necessary to insist that they always obtain as clearcut and exclusively sidestream or mainstream situational aggregations in order to recognize that they might very well be exactly that for some networks and in some historical junctures. Clearcut and uniform or not, they may nevertheless appear to be so phenomenologically for 'actors' and they may well constitute legitimate investigatory targets for researchers.

Network types may also usefully differentiate between sidestream and mainstream ethnicity behaviors or particular combinations thereof. In certain *closed* networks, i.e. networks in which individuals are united by bonds of intimacy and shared experience that transcend and override status differences (and, therefore, ones in which they are relatively inhospitable or closed to outsiders), sidestream ethnicity may be particularly salient, relative to its salience in *open* networks. Similarly, in *personal* interactions (in which shared qualities of the participants are stressed, rather than the transactional or instrumental goals of their particular encounter), sidestream ethnicity may come to the fore ever so much more than in interactions focussed upon practical outcomes (Barth, 1969). Finally, at the very highest level of generality, there are cultural value clusters that contextualize socially-patterned behavior. Whereas *Gemeinschaft* and *Gesellschaft* most certainly coexist in modern life, they are not equally salient on each and every occasion. Values of intimacy, primary relationships, feelings of sympathy, or co-responsibility, of interest and involvement in one's fellows, of face-to-face experience and emotional commitment to 'those of one's own kind' (Boas, 1909; Fischer, 1982), with whom one can really 'let one's hair down', may be ever so much more associated with sidestream ethnicity than are all of the powerful, efficient, productive and competitive interactions that constitute the effective achievement-oriented component of modern life (Findling,

1972). Not surprisingly, the former context may reveal far more sidestream ethnic being, feeling and knowing (as well as ethnic mother-tongue use or semi-use) than the latter.

Other aspects of the ethnicity repertoire

The contextualization and interpenetration of ethnicities of one kind or another (as distinct from categorical 'all or none' ethnicity throughout) does not exhaust the notion of ethnicity repertoire. It merely gets to the issue of *when*. There are other repertoirial issues (even above and beyond the issue of *why*, an issue to which we will soon come). One of these is the issue of *repertoire range*. How many and how disparate are the sidestream ethnicity contexts that are societally recognized? For some, they will be limited to family contexts alone or to family and religious ritual. That would constitute a smaller repertoirial range than one that realized sidestream ethnicity in the educational and occupational domains as well. An even more fundamental issue is that of *repertoire compartmentalization*, i.e. the extent to which mainstream and sidestream ethnicity may be implemented in one and the same contexts (acts, situations, etc.). Where sidestream ethnicity and mainstream ethnicity are jointly permissible in one and the same situation (i.e. where compartmentalization is absent or very meager), the blending of the two will proceed more rapidly than where specific situations are allocated to either one ethnicity or the other and the two are kept studiously apart. The compartmentalization of dual ethnicity is generally difficult to maintain in modern, interactive urban contexts (Fishman, 1980; 1985). As a result, not only does di-ethnia seldom obtain at the societal level, but ethnic discontinuity also becomes rare. The daily or festive rounds that typify one ethnicity are increasingly found in the other that is co-present with it in time and place, and this redundancy or parallelism both reflects and fosters the lack of compartmentalization and the ongoing melding that has been mentioned above. While modernization of once-rural sidestream ethnicities increases their ability to cope with urban American social, economic and political realities, it also increases the melding potential between modernities even if they stem from two different ethnocultural sources or points of origin, precisely because boundary maintenance (Haarman, 1986; Strassoldo, 1982; Paulston & Paulston, 1980) on a *cultural* basis is difficult when one modernity faces another. Ethnocultural boundary maintenance may be anathema to the liberal disposition with its penchant for untrammeled interaction. However, boundary maintenance is a minimal characteristic of all life, from the most elementary to the most complex. It entails the basic need and right to define one's own system and the circumstances under which others may enter it. Without boundary maintenance the crucial ability to exercise 'controlled acculturation', that even certain tiny pre-modern societies such as the Old Order Amish and the Hasidim can engage in (Eaton, 1952a; Thompson, 1981), becomes impossible even for much larger groups such as most Hispanic-Americans, German-Americans and Italian-Americans. For modern urban minorities, *primary* institutions are the very sinews of boundary maintenance (Hechter *et al.*, 1982; Breton *et al.*, 1980). As recent Hispanic experience reveals, numbers alone merely facilitate but do not by any means guarantee boundary maintenance (Massey & Mullan, 1984) on behalf of intergenerational cultural continuity.

Similarities and differences between narrowly ethnolinguistic and broader ethnocultural transitions

Language is both part of, indexical of, and symbolic of ethnocultural behavior. As ethnicities meld, change or absorb and replace one another, it is inevitable that the languages of these ethnicities will be modified as well. Language change, *per se*, in the usual linguistic sense of alteration in lexicon, semantics, syntax and phonology, is, of course, always ongoing, particularly between languages in contact (Weinreich, 1953), even without the problematic context which we are here examining of the overlap and co-occurrence of ethnic realizations. Of course, ethnocultures too are constantly changing, notwithstanding the authenticity claims and the authenticity experiences of their members. But what I am interested in at this point is not so much change as replacement or substitution, i.e. the adoption of what is consensually regarded as a new or different language in conjunction with a particular ethnic identity or behavioral realization. Essentially, therefore, what I am referring to is the possibility of language *shift* and its co-occurrence with apparent or experienced ethnocultural *constancy*. Such co-occurrences, contra-indicated though they may be in nationalist dogma, do occur and have occurred massively in the U.S.A., and they need to be examined for what they imply for language and ethnicity as well as for language and culture more generally.

For students of the American ethnolinguistic scene, it has been clear for nearly a quarter century that although both language and ethnicity are capable of repeated transformation, these need not occur in tandem.

Indeed, of the two, language, on the one hand, and its associated total ethnicity package, on the other hand, the former is the far more labile of the two (Fishman, 1966). The subsystems of language, as well as given languages as wholes, are capable of change and of being exchanged far more rapidly and discontinuously than is the total ethnicity constellation (although it, too, is constantly subject both to change and to exchange). Up to a certain point, the language associated with a given sidestream ethnicity is considered to be merely *influenced* by the language of mainstream ethnicity. After that point, a sense of real transition obtains and the language of the mainstream may be utilized for sidestream ethnicity, in addition to all its other uses. This point is reached more definitively and more consciously in print than in speech. In either case, however, it is indicative of the fact that no matter how all-embracing language is experienced to be as the vehicle or as the symbol of the total ethnocultural package (Fishman, 1972a), it is really only a part, and a detachable part at that, rather than the whole of that package. This is all the more so when, as in the case of the American ethnic revival, language ideologies and language movements *per se* are almost entirely lacking (Svensson, 1974; Sagarin & Moneymaker, 1979), when those for whom language itself takes the place of the country they have left are vanishingly few and considered off-beat even by their closest friends and neighbors. All the more reason, therefore, why ethnocultural experiences as inter-connected ways of doing, feeling and knowing have been phenomenologi-cally much more robust than their linguistic accompaniments. The former may and do change and meld tremendously and yet they can be experienced (and interpreted by outsiders) as 'authentic' and as intact continuity phenomena.

A few salient rituals, a few foods, a transition commemoration here and there, a dance, a melody, these may be enough to maintain the sense of ethnocultural continuity in the midst of far-flung social change and ethnocultural innovation and melding (Alba & Chamlin, 1983). The 'authentic' community cannot be 'saved' but neither need it be 'lost' (Tsai & Sigelman, 1982). The ethnocultural self-concept, the notion of group identity, can remain intact and unchanged far beyond any similar experience with respect to language. Indeed, in the case of language, detachments occur, and often consensually so, and yet the total ethnocultural experience — traumatized though it may temporarily be — can recover a sense of stability and continuity. Thus, I am *not* saying that the replacement of one language by another does not exact a huge price in terms of ethnocultural authenticity and continuity and in terms of societal organization and stability as a whole. What I *am* saying is that the price is contingent on the degree of internal management and control of the total change process and that ultimately, after the worst is over, a sense of basic ethnocultural continuity and authenticity can be recaptured, notwithstanding the linguistic detachment and replacement that has occurred and notwithstanding the overall ethnocultural innovation and melding that has transpired. Learning the ethnic mother tongue as a second language and camouflaging mother-tongue loss by institutional 'gains' at very modest levels of intensity of second-language use (Fishman *et al.*, 1985) are powerful examples of the simultaneity and confoundability of mother-tongue loss *and* ethnocultural continuity and change.

The experience of language continuity and the experience of ethnic continuity are both highly attitudinal; however, the latter is a much more robust attitude than the former. It is particularly for written language that discontinuity and detachment are clearly evident. For spoken languages, the continuity-discontinuity transitions are not as sharp but the morpho-syntactic and phonological systems can bend only so far before they are considered to be 'something else.' The combination of relative linguistic inflexibility and relative ethnocultural flexibility finally results in the triumph of overall ethnocultural continuity experiences over ethno-linguistic discontinuity experiences, if the latter can be brought under ultimate control. The hammer is experienced to be the same even though on one occasion the head was replaced and on another the handle. Ethnolinguistic and ethnocultural continuity in the U.S.A. are both far greater at an attitudinal level than at an overt behavioral one, whether viewed experientially (from within) or evaluationally (from without). In addition, the latter (ethnocultural continuity) is greater than the former (ethnolinguistic continuity). The ethnic revival consisted of a rise in the saliency of both and at both levels, even though the former was already much weakened and the latter much transformed, from an external evaluation point of view. The revival did not compensate for or overcome either the weakness, on the one hand, nor the transformations on the other. That it occurred at all is its claim to fame, rather than that it triumphed or that it stabilized. It did neither, and yet it was an unexpected and significant occurrence. On the language front, it was generally related to increased *institutional* concern for language and increased retrospective mother-tongue acquisition (second-language learning at best) rather than to genuine language movements or renativization. However, some of the most traditional communities proved capable of the most 'radical' steps on behalf of language maintenance via boundary maintenance (Calhoun, 1983; St Clair & Leap, 1982).

The ethnic revival in America: When and why

The ethnic revival in the United States between the mid-1960s and the mid-1970s co-occurred with somewhat similar phenomena in many other parts of the democratic capitalist world. Although most of the other occurrences involved indigenous minorities (Welsh, Irish, Scots, Bretons, Alsatians, Frisians, Catalons, Basques, etc.,) several immigrant settings also revealed a quickening of minority ethnocultural effort: e.g. among *Gastarbeiter* immigrants in Western and Northern Europe, among 'non-Founding' minorities in Canada, among Euro-immigrants in Australia, etc. Any theory of the ethnic revival in the U.S.A. must cope, therefore, with its co-occurrence in time with both indigenous and immigrant revivals in many and quite separate parts of the Western world. That is to say, it must be enlightening in the specific case but yet be based on generalized theory.

Let us remind ourselves of what the mid- to late-1960s were like, particularly in the U.S.A. The Vietnam War was continually intensifying and eliciting the opposition of liberals and the young. The Civil Rights movement had ground to a halt even before the assassination of Martin Luther King in 1968, adding to the general disenchantment with the Anglo-establishment and to the Black conviction that Black (and Black alone) was beautiful. The rising tide of Black pride should not be ignored as a stimulant for the White ethnic revival, but neither should it be overstressed. The two circles overlap only in part, have essentially their own dynamics and their own course, intensity, focus and time frame (Lowy *et al.*, 1985). The 'flower children' and the hippies expressed the disenchantment of broad segments of American youth (including ethnic American youth) — a disenchantment with big business, big labor, big government and the entire fixation on material or financial success. Most strikingly, however, was the fact that *these* young people were not the only ones gripped by a counter culture. 'Do it yourself,' 'small is beautiful,' environmental protection of air, water and nature against the inroads of a rampant profit motive, were widely acceptable and implemented indications of alienation from previously uncritically agreed-upon mainstream practices and values. It was an affluent period. Unemployment was low; inflation, minor. Funds were apparently available for any and all ventures. The space program was in high gear and so were city-center efforts in education and urban renewal. Nevertheless, or, perhaps, therefore, with all of the verve that the times revealed, there was a deep and abiding youth and young adult disaffection which clearly expressed the questioning and even the rejection of mainstream values, priorities and processes. Indeed, many of those that appeared to be most disaffected were exactly from backgrounds which were most comfortably middle class and Anglo or anglified-third-generation (Bender & Kagiwada, 1968). Much before sociologists began to do so (Shils, 1969; Riesman, 1981), untold ordinary citizens began to re-examine and even question the dream of mere abundance. Several of the other causes that they later championed related to those who had long been slighted by the mainstream: women, homosexuals, Blacks, followers of various alternative lifestyles, of new departures in music, art and culture more generally (Martin, 1981) and of religious fundamentalism. In this context, it was quite natural for many of them also to liberate and dignify ethnic aspects for their own identities as well.

What took the form of campaigns for local cultural autonomy in Europe took the form of advocacy of ethnic studies programs and invocation of ethnic dress, food, hairdo, song, dance and music in the U.S.A. Both were 'anti-central' expressions, rejective of the power and the ethos, the values and priorities, the rewards and the blandishments of mainstream cultures and their constituted arbiters and authorities (Fox, Aull & Cimino, 1981). However, the American version of this luxuriant growth was, if anything, more anarchic. It generally lacked political program or sophistication. It was often incoherent rather than merely inchoate. On the 'left', it covered the waterfront from revolutionary activism to principled inactivism, from 'Weathermen' to 'flower children,' with greater overall similarity in levels and manners of sexual gratification and drug-culture tolerance than in political platforms, programs or analyses. Among some, anyone over thirty was suspect and the number of years under thirty is extremely finite and fleeting. On the 'right', a return to 'true religion' began to spread. Distancing from the mainstream was, therefore, bi-directional: that of the liberal counterculture and that of a budding fundamentalism among those shocked by the mainstream's permissiveness (Harrell, 1975; Kelly, 1972; Liebman & Wuthnow, 1983; Sandeen, 1970; Shupe & Stacey, 1982). The ethnic revival in America was part and parcel of two counterculture 'movements,' and like these 'movements' it was more an expression of mainstream alienation than of serious analyses of mainstream evils or serious intent to force or manipulate the mainstream into a new accommodation with sidestream ethnicity. It was not a 'youth rebellion' or even a 'youth movement' in the classic sense in which such phenomena have been described and analyzed previously in the sociological literature (Eisenstadt, 1978). Given the American context, the ethnic revival both failed and succeeded far more drastically than its protagonists themselves ever imagined; it influenced the mainstream more than an outright rebellion would have, but it was co-opted more fully and more quickly than would have been possible if a full-blown breach had occurred.

In terms of our contextualization discussion, the ethnic revival in the United States succeeded in bringing sidestream ethnicity out of the family and neighborhood closet (Mangione, 1981) and made it salon-worthy. It could be revealed (and gratified) in college and in church, in public places rather than merely in private ones. It could present itself as being for the general good (e.g. in the case of bilingual education). Its little personal networks — restaurants, theaters, churches, radio/television programs, neighborhood clubs and schoolhouses — came to be viewed as the spice of life without which all would be anglobland, tasteless and inert (Gans, 1965; Fischer, 1982; Greeley, 1977). The ethnic revival, as part of the total counterculture experience of the times, represented an expansion, both in the public as well as in the private spheres of life, of the sidestream ethnicity repertoire. At the same time, its compartmentalization and ideologization remained as weak as it had been. While third generations never really return to the life of the first (Bender & Kagiwada, 1968; Goering, 1971; Nahirny & Fishman, 1965), the ethnic revival was not even an attempt along such lines.

Although, on the one hand, it spilled over into everything, on the other hand it remained low in intensity and nonspecific in goals, very much as the total counterculture movement of which it was a part. When the latter dissipated, so did it, leaving a vague but recognizable imprint on the general tone and tenor of American life to the effect that there was no 'one model American' (Lopez & Vogel, 1979). Before the 'revival,' minority ethnicity was peripheral to, but connected with, the larger developments and forces of co-territorial social history (Chirot, 1976). In the revival it became part and parcel of that history.

The ethnic revival and the formation of the American people

The ethnic revival in the U.S.A. shares certain characteristics with most of the other ethnic revivals of approximately the same time. *It reflected a pervasive (but ultimately muted) alienation from the central ethos and institutions of mainstream society*. However, given the shallower depth and greater plasticity of 'American ethnicity,' it was also a formative experience in the ongoing saga of the formation of the American people (Gans *et al.*, 1979). Out of thousands of religions, there has arisen an unestablished American view of religion that places religion on a pedestal.

Religion is nonspecific, nonfunctional or nongoal-oriented for *American society as a whole* but yet it is all-pervasive, comforting and altogether approved and desired by the vast bulk of Americans and, therefore religion is an integrative force notwithstanding the diversity of religions (Berger, 1961; Fenn, 1972; Hammond, 1963, 1964). Religion in America is neither lower class nor upper class; it is neither liberal nor conservative. It no longer controls law, nor education, nor government, nor health, nor business, nor culture; yet it is a recognizable ingredient and determinant of all of them and in the daily lives, happiness and well-being of the bulk of the population. Without controlling very much, it has become a verity. Americans expect each other 'to be religious'; *any* religion will do and all religions are equally valid (Greeley, 1972). Religion (rather than any particular religion) has become part of the common, overarching 'American experience.' To have no religion is, in the eyes of most Americans, to be both suspect and impoverished simultaneously. Some religions are more exotic than others, but, in contrast to earlier days (Moore, 1982), any religion is distinctly better than none in popular estimation. De Tocqueville's analysis in this connection rings truer today than when he originally wrote it: 'If it be of the highest importance to man, as an individual, that his religion should be true, it is not so to society . . . Provided the citizens profess a religion, the peculiar tenets of that religion are of little importance to its [American society's] interests' (de Tocqueville, [1835] 1945: 314).

Thanks to the revival, sidestream ethnicity has come to play a public role very similar to that of religion in American life (Schneider, 1972). A sidestream ethnicity is recognized as being not only 'natural' but as being humanizing and strengthening in some very general sense, and those who implement or display it situationally are not outsiders in urban America (Sibley, 1969). It controls no domain of behavior completely but it is 'a good influence' and makes for a more interesting, colorful, rooted life. It is family-stability-related, neighborhood-stability-related, personal-stabililty-related. Americans now expect each other to have some sidestream ethnicity; any sidestream ethnicity will do and all ethnicities are equally good (well, almost all) because their role is no longer to help or hinder 'being a success in America' (Sowell, 1981) but to provide 'roots': meaningful cultural depth to individual and family life. Thus a sidestream ethnicity as part of one's background (rather than any particular sidestream ethnicity) has become part of an enriched and overarching *American* experience in ways adumbrated by Handlin (1957) and Greene (1975). There is no need to hide it. In fact, it would be churlish and putting on false airs to do so. What is worse, it would be denying an aspect of

American identity (Shanabruch, 1981; Alba & Chamlin, 1983).

But, of course, a shared, 'common American' ethnicity is growing too (just as is the shared American civil religion), particularly among the young (Gleason, 1980). The liberal dream of a modern society, in which ethnicity is secondary to the central social processes and individual aspirations and involvements, is being approximated via innumerable and mighty mainstream forces. This is, of course, a case of ethnogenesis (Bromley, 1974; Gallagher, 1974; Salamone, 1975; Singer, 1962), rather than of the 'disappearance of ethnicity,' as liberals had mistakenly hoped and believed because of their association of ethnicity with the sidestream alone. It proceeds via the fact that the two, the sidestream and the mainstream, are not greatly compartmentalized and, indeed, are co-present not only in most domains but in most situations as well. The family and the church, the school and the mass media, all are appropriate contexts for implementing, combining and innovating either or both. As a result, the extent of overlap and parallelism between the two streams increases. The boundaries between the two are far less clear than they would be in a European context where historically deep indigenous ethnicities come into contact. In addition, the plasticity of the concept of 'American ethnicity' is still quite substantial and, as a result, the sidestream more easily becomes part of the mainstream. Indeed, they become tributaries and variants or versions of the mainstream itself, rather than arriving at a stable, diglossic/di-ethnic compartmentalization *vis-à-vis* the mainstream (Kutsche, 1979). The ethnic revival in the U.S.A. has therefore contributed to a simultaneous broadening of the permissible limits of the notions of 'American' and of sidestream ethnicity, making both notions more all-inclusive, more all-embracing, more similar than they were heretofore.

The ethnic revival has hastened ethnic change rather than halted it (Banton, 1981). Instead of becoming a major arena of conflict, in fact, instead of being assumed to be a major source of conflict (a charge — as Dubnow revealed long ago [1906/1970] — usually made by establishments against aggrieved minorities), ethnicity has become just one legitimate interest among many. In modern America, ethnicity is most often a behavior/attitudinal repertoire experience rather than an all-or-none boundary or category. Increases in its saliency or implementation involve hardly any corresponding 'identity' changes or accommodations elsewhere in the repertoire. The two streams are symbiotically rather than dis-placively implemented in the lives of multitudes who are in the mainstream rather than apart from it. Bromley (1983) believes that in the U.S.S.R. the various nationalities have become more similar to each other while still retaining their individuality. The ethnic revival simultaneously brought about both of these conditions in the U.S.A. Ethnicity became an open, visible part of social identity, but it remained no more than that, i.e. it remained only *part* of social identity (Gleason, 1983) and, therefore, became more modern than primordial in nature.

On the language front, the ethnic revival in the United States from the mid-1960s to the mid-1970s accomplished even less, *in any overt sense*, than it did on the broader front of ethnocultural behaviors more generally. Non-English language use did not increase and there was no more concerted approach to non-English language maintenance than there had been before the revival. There were no language 'struggles' (at least none that would not have occurred without the revival), no real language movements, no surge *to* language consciousness or *beyond* language consciousness to language *use*. However, at the attitudinal level, so closely allied with identity definition, non-English mother-tongue claiming did rise dramatically and practically across the board in the late sixties. But non-English mother-tongue claiming was heritage claiming, family-roots claiming, mainstream de-identification. It was an attitudinal gesture with only indirect and institutional consequence. By the mid-to-late 1970s, it too was largely dissipated among the grandchildren and great-grandchildren of older immigrant extractions. It could return, but even if it did, that would still be a long step away from any increase in non-English language use.

It is hard to imagine that the mid-1960s and mid-1970s were only a decade apart. From a time of plenty and conspicuous rejection of the establishment on the part of the young, the United States had entered a period of new concerns: gasoline shortages and gluts, high unemployment, substantial inflation and a new seriousness (and new materialism) on the part of the young. College cohorts became more grade-conscious, more job-conscious and more propriety-conscious in dress and in public behavior. Public ethnicity emphases withdrew somewhat into their former private recesses. In the early 1980s a bill to establish a National Commission for Utilization and Expansion of Language Resources (H.R. 4389) in order to 'utilize the more than 28 million people in our nation' who speak languages in addition to English (Gonzale, 1981), died in committee and the entire bilingual education Title VII edifice was threatened (S. 2412). Mainstream comforts, positions, rights and privileges became more salient again, particularly among the very age groups that had previously deprecated them, perhaps because their availability was now uncertain. Non-English mother-tongue claiming plummeted, most particularly in those groups in which its attitudinal base was furthest removed from overt language-use experience (Fishman, 1985). There is once more the danger of stylish liberal predictions regarding the 'end of ethnicity' (Fishman, 1982), temptations to trumpet the 'triumph of straight-line theory' (Gans, 1979, reclaimed but endlessly qualified in Gans, 1980), and the uselessness of an ethnicity that is 'purely symbolic.' Apparently, the cultural time, the cultural space, sense of history and quest for unique dignity of minorities are not easily appreciated or kept in mind. Most social theoreticians simply have different functional expectations of ethnicity than do the ethnic minorities themselves, and without sympathetic sensitivity the 'death wish' *vis-à-vis* ethnicity will once again come to the fore. Most social scientists are uncritical liberals; unfortunately, few of them have sensed that 'what is *illiberal* is homogenization in the name of liberalism' (Novak, 1977), something that Dubnow (1906) and other minority spokesmen realized many decades ago.

The future of sidestream language and ethnicity in America

It is difficult to predict the future of sidestream ethnic phenomena because they carry within them the seeds of their own regeneration. Functioning, as they do in the United States, at the private and attitudinal levels (even more so than at the public and overt behavioral levels), it is easy to assume that they have ceased to exist merely because they are not visible to the outside (particularly to the unsympathetic outside) observer. Furthermore, since they flourish in direct proportion to distancing and alienation or detachment from the mainstream (but not only because of unmet economic or career expectations, as claimed by the Marxist, Deutschian and their derivative schools), there is a major historical or unique component in their occurrence. Will a period crystalize again when indigenous and immigrant minorities in Europe and ethnic as well as counter-culture identities in the United States will be treated in very similar ways, and in which sidestream identity will be publicly proclaimed again as more colorful, touching, praiseworthy and decent than losing one's self in the mainstream? Who can tell? But to the extent that massive disappointment is inevitable in modern urban life (Berman, 1981), to the extent that modernization is its own worst enemy (as all of the great founders of modern sociology have claimed), to the extent that *Gemeinschaft* has learned to cope with and to 'work around' *Gesellschaft*, to the extent that the adversity of *Gesellschaft* is itself a prime factor in the pursuit or creation of *Gemeinschaft* (Levin, 1980; Gallo, 1981), to the extent that ethnic social institutions and structures remain (indeed, even increase) when cultural assimilation obtains (and, therefore, the former continue to provide channels for cultural memories, aspirations and revivals, far more than has been generally appreciated, viz. Gordon, 1964; Stryker, 1981; Taylor, 1981, particularly given the intellectual penchant to artificially separate structure from culture), to *that* extent the seeds of sidestream ethnicity will bloom not only again, but again and again (Castile & Kushner, 1981). Berlin's metaphor of the pent-up force of 'the bent twig' (1972) that ultimately snaps back all the more forcefully (to break loose from the oppressive mainstream pressures of modern life), may on occasion be quite appropriate. On the other hand, ethnic revivals need not be the backlash that Berlin implies, any more than they need be economically inspired in the trite Marxist sense. They can be unfocused, unchanneled, unpoliticized and relatively unexploited in any material sense. That they can still occur three and more generations after immigrant incorporation into a relatively open and mobile society has begun is testimony to the emotional depths which revivals plumb, and to the length of the hibernation that even remnants of sidestream ethnicity can survive (Berger *et al.*, 1973).

But perhaps the major lesson of the ethnicity revival in America is that terms such as 'emotion' and 'hibernation' are basically unjustified. Ethnicity revivals are precisely ethnicity repertoire changes: changes in repertoire saliency, range, compartmentalization and discontinuity or contrastivity. They are not a return to life of that which was dead. In that sense, they are really not revivals at all. They are awakenings and reforms (or at least reformulations) in a very long and honorable progression of revivals, awakenings and reforms that have led to new visions of America (McLoughlin, 1978). The social-science vocabulary of references to sidestream ethnicity has tended toward conceptually impoverished good-bad, active-passive (live-dead) polarities. Obviously fresher, more diversified and conceptually more integrated approaches are needed, both with respect to indigenous as well as with respect to immigrant minorities (Weinberg, 1976; Petersen, 1980). This is particularly so since so much of sidestream ethnicity is situational, attitudinal and private, constantly interacting with the mainstream and changing it, as well as being changed by it. The 'American Dream' has included both the promise of assimilation (Rodriguez, 1981; Mann, 1979), the promise of ethnolinguistic self-maintenance (Deloria, 1970), and the promise of freedom to choose between them (Pratte, 1979). However, when major shocks, disappointments and barriers to cultural syncretism occur (as they must, even in relatively open and affluent societies), the private often becomes more public, the attitudinal: overt, the quiescent: active, the interactive:

exclusive, the accepting: the rejective, the background: salient. Periphery
and core, sidestream and mainstream *always* co-exist and many factors
(rather than just one) are capable of changing the focus from the one to
the other. When viewed in worldwide perspective, the limits and
intensities of ethnicity in the United States remain innocent indeed, and
I would predict them to remain so, gaining thereby far more than they lose.

To predict the future course of sidestream language and ethnicity in
the United States would require us to do the impossible: to predict
America's future. That is clearly a task that is beyond anyone's capacity.
The number of possible intervening variables between characteristics of
the sidestreams and characteristics of the mainstream are simply too
numerous to contemplate. Historical contingencies and cohort influences
represent the unpredictable borderline between humanistic and social-
scientific endeavor (Cherlin, 1981). But given the special nature of
mainstream 'American ethnicity,' its historical shallowness, plasticity and
permissiveness, it would certainly seem safe to say that it will be host to
and influenced by myriad sidestream ethnicities rather indefinitely. While
non-English languages may generally be expected to play rather weak
functional roles in most sidestream ethnicities on the American scene past
the first generation (in this connection, racially recognizable and recent
Hispanics, South and Southeast Asians and Pacific Islanders may constitute the chief exceptions for the rest of this century), such languages,
nevertheless, can continue to be present massively at an attitudinal level
(and, consequently, they are the recipients of community institutional
attention), given particular historical junctures. Sidestream ethnicity has
been projectively discounted and given a short lease on life all too often
in the past. Indeed, it is virtually impossible for those who desire and
predict the death of minority ethnicity — and this has included most of
the major lights of modern liberal sociology — to be more than surprised
at what they consider to be mere 'momentary blips' rather than indications
that their conceptions of ethnicity are fundamentally mistaken. Otherwise
it would be apparent to them that to predict once again the general
'straight line' demise of minority ethnicity is not only a mistaken view, and
not only a statement about the prognosticators, but a blinder that hides
from vision part of the process that needs to be better understood.

Sidestream ethnicity is a phoenix in modern life; it constantly arises
anew from its apparent ashes. But the ashes are more apparent than real.
If Western Europe can accommodate both increased regionalism and
increased extra-regionalism (not only in terms of the E.E.C. but in terms
of increasingly being the periphery to an America-centered Western world
[Khlief, 1982b]), then America itself can accommodate both its own

sidestreams and its mainstream as interactive systems. If we recognize sidestream ethnicity as situationally governed (rather than as categorical or all-or-none in nature), as a continuing and often innovative cultural process of boundary maintenance and reconstruction (Horowitz, 1977), as going through stressed and quiescent phases (with *either* direction of development being possible — as per Leach, 1954 and Keyes, 1979 — rather than merely the progression from quiescent to stressed that the Deutschian school has fixated upon), as also being purposefully rational, comforting, reassuring, orienting in culturally meaningful time and space and, therefore internally stabilizing (de Vos & Romanucci-Ross, 1975; Hsu, 1979; Greene, 1975), rather than primarily irrational, manipulative, combatitive or externally destabilizing (e.g. Parot, 1981; Holli, 1981; Chrislock, 1981; Tudjman, 1981), as reflecting sidestream-mainstream relations in generalized and affective terms, rather than only in focused and instrumental respects (Cohen, 1974), as being cultural-identity and cultural-democracy-related (Chrisman, 1981; Klein & Reban, 1981), rather than only incivility- and conflict-related, then we can better appreciate both its longevity as well as the difficulty faced in predicting its future. Ethnicity is 'a far more durable and powerful phenomenon than is usually depicted, ... it draws on far deeper historical roots and sociological conditions' and, here one might add, goes through many more transformations, overt and attitudinal 'than many would allow' (Smith, 1981). This would not be nearly so surprising if modern, liberal thought had not pretended to the contrary for so many years (and not only in the United States but in Europe as well, as Krejci & Velinsky have shown, 1981), and if, like Isaiah Berlin, it had developed pluralistic rather than monistic models of the future (Manent *et al.*, 1983; see particularly the essay on Berlin and 'liberal pluralism' by Hausheer).

Most probably there is no 'non-ethnic tomorrow' in the offing, not even in the 'post-separatist world'; only a tomorrow in which the ethnic and the supraethnic (the sidestreams and the mainstreams) will be more intimately linked (Boulding, 1979), as they are in the United States today. Furthermore, just as its stress in recent European history has rarely aimed at political separatism (Allardt, 1979; Williams, 1982), so its recent quiescence in the United States does not presage its demise (Rollins, 1981). Minority ethnicity is constantly restructuring and recreating itself and its future, all around us (Benkin & De Santis, 1980; Crispino, 1980), well into and beyond the third generation. It is because so many social scientists — particularly sociologists and political scientists — have recognized only one extreme of sidestream ethnicity or the other (*either* political separatism strivings and disturbances of civility *or* amalgamation into the mainstream and total disappearance) that most of the more moderate and subtle dimensions of post-modern sidestream ethnicity have been so little understood (Cohen, 1978; Hsu, 1979). Like most other aspects of culture, ethnicity waxes and wanes and changes in response to more powerful and encompassing developments. Like most other aspects of culture, it does *not* follow a straight line. If our attention to the ethnic revival in the U.S.A. of the mid-1960s to mid-1970s has highlighted some of these generally overlooked dimensions, if it has spotlighted the pan-human nature of symbolic and attitudinal, nonprogrammatic ethnicity, and if it has placed the complexity and subtlety of such ethnicity more squarely on the agenda for further empirical attention and theoretical elaboration, then it has been an eminently worthwhile effort.

References

ALBA, R. D. & CHAMLIN, M. B. 1983, A preliminary examination of ethnic identification among Whites. *American Sociological Review* 48, 240–47.

ALLARDT, E. 1979, *Implications of the Ethnic Revival in Modern Industrialized Society*. Helsinki: Societas Scientiarum Fennica.

ARMSTRONG, J. A. 1982, *Nations Before Nationalism*. Chapel Hill: University North Carolina Press.

BAALI, F. & WARDI, A. 1981, *Ibn Khalden and Islamic Thought-Styles: A Social Perspective*. Boston: G.K. Hall.

BANTON, M. 1981, The direction and speed of ethnic change. In C.F. KEYES (ed.), *Ethnic Change*. Seattle: University of Washington Press, 31–52

BARTH, F. 1969, *Ethnic Groups and Boundaries*. Boston: Little-Brown.

BEER, W. R. 1980, *The Unexpected Rebellion: Ethnic Activism in Contemporary France*. New York: New York University Press.

BENDER, E. I. & KAGIWADA, G. 1968, Hansen's law of 'third generation return' and the study of American religio-ethnic groups. *Phylon* 29, 360–70.

BENKIN, R. L. & DE SANTIS, G. 1982, Creating ethnicity: East European Jews and Lithuanian immigrants in Chicago. *Sociological Focus* 15, 231–48.

BENTLEY, G. C. 1982, *Ethnicity and Nationality: A Bibliographic Guide*. Seattle: University of Washington Press.

BERGER, P. L. 1961, *The Noise of Solemn Assemblies*. Garden City, NY: Doubleday.

BERGER, P. L., BERGER, B. & KELLNER, H. 1973, Modernity and its discontents. In P.L. BERGER, B. BERGER & H. KELLNER, *The Homeless*

Mind. New York: Random House.

BERLIN, I. 1972, The bent twig: A note on nationalism. *Foreign Affairs* 51, 11–30.

BERMAN, M. 1981, *All That is Solid Melts into Air: The Experience of Modernity*. New York: Simon and Schuster.

BIDDISS, M. D. 1966, Gobineau and the origin of European racism. *Race: Journal of the Institute of Race Relations* 7, 225–70.

— (ed.) 1970a, *Gobineau: Selected Political Writings*. London: Cape.

— 1970b, *Father of Racist Ideology: The Social and Political Thought of Count Gobineau*. London: Weidenfeld and Nicholson.

— (ed.) 1979, *Images of Race*. New York: Holmes and Meier.

BLAUNER, R. 1969, Internal colonialism and ghetto revolts. *Social Problems* 17, 463–72.

BOAS, F. 1909, Race problems in America. *Science* 79, 839–49.

BONACICH, E. 1972, A theory of ethnic antagonism: The split labor market. *American Sociological Review* 37, 547–59.

BONACICH, E. & MODELL, J. 1981, *The Economic Basis of Ethnic Solidarity: Small Business in the Japanese American Community*. Berkeley: University of California Press.

BOULDING, E. 1979, Ethnic separatism and world development. *Research in Social Movements, Conflicts and Change* 2, 259–81.

BRETON, R., REITZ, J. & VALENTINE, V., 1980, *Cultural Boundaries and the Cohesion of Canada*. Montreal: Institute for Research on Public Policy.

BROMLEY, Y. Y. 1974, *Soviet Ethnology and Anthropology*. The Hague: Mouton.

BROMLEY, Y. 1983, Ethnic processes in the modern world. *Social Sciences* (Moscow) 14, 98–114.

BRUCKNER, D. J. R., (ed.) 1980, *Politics and Language: Spanish and English in the United States*. Chicago: University of Chicago Center for Policy Study.

CALHOUN, C. J. 1983, The radicalism of tradition: community strength or venerable disguise and borrowed language. *American Journal of Sociology*. 88, 886–914.

CALVERT, P. 1982, Karl Deutsch and political science. *Political Studies* 30, 445–48.

CASTILE, G. P. & KUSHNER, G. 1981, *Persistent Peoples: Cultural Enclaves in Perspective*. Tucson: University of Arizona Press.

CHERLIN, A. J. 1981, Explaining the postwar baby boom. *Social Sciences Research Council Items* 35, 57–63.

CHILD, I. L. 1943, *Italian or American? The Second Generation in Conflict*. New Haven: Yale University Press.

CHIROT, D. 1976, *Social Change in a Peripheral Region*. New York:

Academic Press.

CHRISLOCK, C. H. 1981, *Ethnicity Challenged: The Upper Midwest Norwegian-American Experience in World War I*. Northfield, Minn.: Norwegian-American Historical Association.

CHRISMAN, N. J. 1981, Ethnic persistence in an urban setting. *Ethnicity 8*, 256–92.

COHEN, A. 1974, The lesson of ethnicity. In A. COHEN (ed.), *Urban Ethnicity*. London: Tavistock ix–xxiv.

COHEN, R. 1978, Ethnicity: problem and focus in anthropology. *Annual Review of Anthropology 7*, 379–403.

CRISPINO, J. A. 1980, *The Assimilation of Ethnic Groups: The Italian Case*. Staten Island, N.Y.: Center for Immigration Studies.

DAHL, R. A. 1982, *Dilemmas of Pluralist Democracy: Autonomy vs. Control*. New Haven: Yale University Press.

DAVIS, H. B. 1973, *Nationalism and Socialism: Marxist and Labor Theories of Nationalism to 1917*. New York: Monthly Review Press.

DELORIA, V. Jr. 1970, *We Talk, You Listen: New Tribes, New Turf*. New York: Macmillan.

DEUTSCH, K. 1953, *Nationalism and Social Communication*. Cambridge: MIT Press (Revised 1966).

DE TOCQUEVILLE, A. 1945, Principal causes which tend to maintain the democratic republic in the United States. In A. DE TOCQUEVILLE, *Democracy in America*, V.I 1835. New York: Vintage Books/Random House.

DE VOS, G. & ROMANUCCI-ROSS, L. 1975, Ethnicity: Vessel of meaning and emblem of contrast. In G. DE VOS & L. ROMANUCCI-ROSS (eds), *Ethnic Identity: Cultural Continuities and Change*. Palo Alto: Mayfield, 363–90.

DICKINSON, G. L. 1896, *The Greek View of Life*. London: Methuen.

DUBNOW, S. 1970, The ethics of nationalism [1906]. In S. DUBNOW, *History: Essays on Old and New Judaism* (Edited, with an introductory essay, by Koppel S. Pinson). New York: Atheneum.

EATON, J. W. 1952, Controlled acculturation: A survival technique of the Hutterites. *American Sociological Review 17*, 331–40.

EISENSTADT, S. N. 1971, Sociological analysis and youth rebellion. In S. N. EISENSTADT *From Generation to Generation*. New York: Free Press, vi–xlix.

— 1978, *Revolution and the Transformation of Societies*. New York: Free Press.

ESMAN, M. R. 1982, Festivals, change and unity: The celebration of ethnic identity among Louisiana Cajuns. *Anthropological Quarterly 55*, 199–210.

ESTERIK, P. VAN 1982, Celebrating ethnicity: Ethnic flavor in an urban festival. *Ethnic Groups*. 4, 207–28.

ESTRADA, L. F. 1983, Language and political consciousness among the Spanish-speaking in the United States: A demographic study. In D. J. R. BRUCKNER (ed.), *Politics and Language: Spanish and English in the United States*. Chicago: University of Chicago Center for Policy Study, 13–22.

ETZIONI, A. 1968, *The Active Society*. New York: Basic Books.

FENN, R. K. 1972, Toward a new sociology of religion. *Journal of the Scientific Study of Religion* 11, 16–32.

— 1973, Talking past one another: Notes on the debate. *Journal for the Scientific Study of Religion* 12, 353–59.

FENWICK, R. 1982, Ethnic culture and economic structure: Determinants of the French-English earning inequality in Quebec. *Social Forces* 61, 1–23.

FIELD, G. G. 1981, *Evangelist of Race: The Germanic Vision of Houston Stewart Chamberlain*. New York: Columbia Univ. Press.

FINDLING, J. 1972, Bilingual need affiliation, future orientation and achievement motivation. In J. A. FISHMAN (ed.), *Advances in the Sociology of Language*, vol.II. The Hague: Mouton, 150–74.

FISCHER, C. S. 1982, *To Dwell Among Friends: Personal Networks in Town and City*. Chicago: University of Chicago Press.

FISHMAN, D. E., MAYERFELD, R. & FISHMAN, J. A. 'Am and goy as designations for ethnicity in selected books of the Old Testament. In J. A. FISHMAN (ed.), *The Rise and Fall of the Ethnic Revival*. Berlin: Mouton, 15–38.

FISHMAN, J. A. 1966, *Language Loyalty in the United States*. The Hague: Mouton, 15–38.

— 1968, Nationality-nationalism and nation-nationism. In J. A. FISHMAN, C. A. FERGUSON & J. DAS GUPTA (eds), *Language Problems of Developing Nations*. New York: Wiley, 39–52.

— 1972a, *Language and Nationalism: Two Integrative Essays*. Rowley: Newbury House.

— 1972b, Domains and the relationship between micro- and macro-sociolinguistics. In J. J. GUMPERZ & D. HYMES (eds), *Directions in Sociolinguistics*. New York: Holt, Rinehart and Winston, 435–53.

— 1977b, Language, ethnicity and racism. *Georgetown University Roundtable on Languages and Linguistics*, 297–309.

— 1980, Bilingualism and biculturism as individual and as societal phenomena. *Journal of Multilingual and Multicultural Development* 7, 3–15.

— 1982, The lively life of a 'dead' language, or 'everyone knows that

Yiddish died long ago.' *Judaica Book News* 13, no.1, 7–11.
— 1984, Studies of language as an aspect of ethnicity and nationalism (A bibliographic introduction). *Sociolinguistics* 14, no.2, 1–6.
— 1985, Mother-tongue claiming in the United States since 1960. In J. A. FISHMAN (ed.), *The Rise and Fall of the Ethnic Revival*. Berlin: Mouton, 107–94.
FISHMAN, J. A., GERTNER, M. H., LOWY, E. G. & MILAN, W. G. 1985, Non-English ethnic mother-tongue institutions in the United States: Demographic and functional characteristics. In J. A. FISHMAN (ed.), *The Rise and Fall of the Ethnic Revival*. Berlin: Mouton, 195–282.
FISHMAN, J. A., COOPER, R. L., MA, R. *et al.* 1975, *Bilingualism in the Barrio* (= *Language Sciences Monographs 7*). Bloomington: Indiana University 1971, 1975 (Second edition).
FOSTER, C. R. (ed.) 1980, *Nations Without a State: Ethnic Minorities in Western Europe*. New York: Praeger.
FOX, R. G., AULL, C. & CIMINO, L. 1978, Ethnic nationalism and political mobilization in complex societies. In G. N. KENNEDY (ed.), *Proceedings of the Southern Anthropological Society No.12: Interethnic Communication*. Athens: University of Georgia Press.
— 1981, Ethnic nationalism and the welfare state. In C. F. KEYES (ed.), *Ethnic Change*. Seattle: University of Washington Press, 198–245.
FRIED, M. N. & FRIED, M. H., 1980, *Transitions: Four Rituals in Eight Cultures*. New York: Norton.
GALLAGHER, J. T. 1974, The emergence of an African ethnic group: The case of the Ndendeule. *International Journal of African Historical Studies* 7, 1–26.
GALLO, P. J. 1981, *Old Bread, New Wine: A Portrait of the Italian-Americans*. Chicago: Nelson-Hall.
GAMBINO, R. 1976, *A Guide to Ethnic Studies Programs in American Colleges, Universities and Schools*. New York: Rockefeller Foundation (Mimeo).
GANS, H. J. 1965, The Italians of the West End: place, class, culture and social structure. In H. J. GANS, *The Urban Villagers: Group and Class in the Life of Italian-Americans*. New York: Free Press, 17–39.
— 1979, Symbolic ethnicity: The future of ethnic groups and cultures in America. In H. J. GANS *et al.* (eds), *On the Making of Americans: Essays in Honor of David Riesman*. Philadelphia: University of Pennsylvania Press, 193–220; also, abbreviated, in *Ethnic and Racial Studies* 2, 1–20.
— 1980, Preface. In J. A. CRISPINO, *The Assimilation of Ethnic Groups: The Italian Case*. Staten Island, N.Y.: Center for Immigration Studies, v–x.

GARCÍA, O., FISHMAN, J. A., BURUNAT, S. & GERTNER, M. H. 1985, The Hispanic press in the United States: content and prospects. In J. A. FISHMAN (ed.) *The Rise and Fall of the Ethnic Revival*. Berlin: Mouton, 343–62.

GELLNER, E. 1964, *Thought and Change*. Chicago: University of Chicago Press.

GERTNER, M. H., FISHMAN, J. A., LOWY, E. G. & MILAN, W. G. 1985, Language and ethnicity in the periodical publications of four American ethnic groups. In J. A. FISHMAN (ed.), *The Rise and Fall of the Ethnic Revival*. Berlin: Mouton.

GILBERT, V., 1982, Current bibliography on immigrants and minorities: monographs, periodical articles and theses, 1971–80: U.S.A. *Immigrants and Minorities* 1, 89–141 and 200–32.

GLAZER, N. 1982, Politics of a multiethnic society. In L. LIEBMAN (ed.), *Ethnic Relations in America*. Englewood Cliffs, NJ: Prentice-Hall.

— 1983, *Ethnic Dilemmas, 1964–1982*. Cambridge: Harvard University Press.

GLEASON, P. 1980, American identity and Americanization. *Harvard Encyclopedia of American Ethnic Groups*. Cambridge: Harvard University Press, 31–58.

— 1983, Identifying identity: a semantic history. *Journal of American History* 69, 910–31.

GOERING, J. M. 1971, The emergence of ethnic interests: A case of serendipity. *Social Forces* 49, 379–84.

GONZALEZ, H. B. 1981, National Commission on Foreign Languages. *Congressional Record* August 4, E 3902.

GORDON, M. 1964, *Assimilation in American Life: The Role of Race, Religion and National Origins*. New York: Oxford University Press.

GREELEY, A. M. 1972. *Unsecular Man: The Persistence of Religion*. New York: Schocken.

— 1977, The ethnic miracle. In A. M. GREELEY, *Neighborhood*. New York: Seabury.

GREENE, V. R. 1975, *For God and Country: The Rise of Polish and Lithuanian Ethnic Consciousness in America, 1800–1910*. Madison: State Historical Society of Wisconsin.

GRIGULEVICH, I. R. & KOZLOV, S. Y. (eds), 1981, *Ethnocultural Processes and National Problems in the Modern World*. Moscow: Progress

HAARMANN, H. 1986, The role of language in processes of ethnic fusion and fission. In H. HAARMANN, *Language in Ethnicity*. Berlin: Mouton, 37–82.

HAMMOND, P. E. 1963, Religion and the 'informing' of culture. *Journal for the Scientific Study of Religion* 3, 97–106.

— 1964, Religious pluralism and Durkheim's integration thesis. In A. W. EISTER (ed.), *Changing Perspectives in the Scientific Study of Religion*. New York: Wiley, 115–42.

HANDLEMAN, D. 1977, The organization of ethnicity. *Ethnic Groups*. 1, 187–200.

HANDLIN, O. 1957, *Race and Nationality in American Life*. New York: Little Brown.

HAREVEN, T. K. (ed.), 1978, *The Family and the Life Course in Historical Perspective*. New York: Academic Press.

HARRELL, D. E. Jr. 1975, *All Things are Possible: The Healing and Charismatic Revivals in Modern America*. Bloomington: Indiana University Press.

HAUSHEER, R. 1983, Isaiah Berlin and the emergence of liberal pluralism. In P. MANENT *et al.*, *European Liberty*. The Hague: Martinus Nijhoff.

HEATH, S. B. 1977, Our language heritage: A historical perspective. In J. K. PHILLIPS (ed.), *The Language Connection: From the Classroom to the World*. Skokie: National Textbook Co.

HECHTER, M. 1975, *Internal Colonialism: The Celtic Fringe in British National Development, 1536–1966*. London: Routledge & Kegan Paul.

HECHTER, M., FRIEDMAN, D. & APPELBAUM, M. 1982, A theory of ethnic collective action. *International Migration Review* 16, 412–34.

HENGEL, M. 1980, *Jews, Greeks and Barbarians*. Philadelphia: Fortress.

HOBSBAWM, E. J. 1962, *The Age of Revolution*. New York: World Publishing Co.

— 1977, Inventing traditions in nineteenth century Europe. In E. J. HOBSBAWM (ed.), *The Invention of Tradition in Past and Present Society*. Cambridge: Cambridge University Press, 1–24.

HOFFMAN, R. C. 1983, Outsiders by birth and blood: racist ideologies and realities around the periphery of medieval European culture. *Studies in Medieval and Renaissance History* 6, 3–34.

HOLLI, M. G. 1981, Teuton vs. Slav: The Great War sinks Chicago's German *Kultur*. *Ethnicity* 8, 406–51.

HOROWITZ, D. L. 1977, Cultural movements and ethnic change. *The Annals* 433, September, 6–18.

HRABA, J. 1979, *American Ethnicity*. Itasca: Peacock.

HROCH, M. 1968, *Die Vorkämpfer der nationalen Bewegung bei den Kleinen Völkeren Europas*. Prague: Universita Karlova.

HSU, F. L. K. 1979, The cultural problem of the cultural anthropologist. *American Anthropologist* 81, 517–32.

JAKOBSON, R. 1945, The beginnings of national self-determination in Europe. *Review of Politics* 7, 29–42. (Reprinted in J. A. FISHMAN (ed.), *Readings in the Sociology of Language*. The Hague: Mouton, 1968,

585–97).
JAKUBOWICZ, A. 1981, State and ethnicity-multiculturalism as ideology. *Australian and New Zealand Journal of Sociology* 17, 4–13.
JANSEGERS, L. 1982, Onmachtspositie van het Brusselse flamingantisme (1884–1895). *Taal en Sociale Integratie* 6, 107–40.
JONES, D. J. & HILL-BURNETT, J. 1982, The political context of ethnogenesis: an Australian example. In M. C. HOWARD (ed.), *Aboriginal Power in Australian Society*. Honolulu: University of Hawaii Press, 214–46.
JÜTHNER, J. 1923, *Hellenen und Barbaren*, Das Erbe der Alten. Leipzig: Neue Folge VIII.
KANTOROWICZ, E.H. 1950-51, Pro Patria Mori in medieval political thought. *American Historical Review* 56, 472–92.
KEDOURIE, E. 1961, *Nationalism*. London: Hutchinson.
KELLY, D. M. 1972, *Why Conservative Churches Are Growing: A Study in Sociology of Religion*. New York: Harper and Row.
KEYES, C. F. (ed.), 1979, *Ethnic Adaptation and Identity: The Karen on the Thai Frontier with Burma*. Philadelphia: Institute for the Study of Human Issues.
— (ed.), 1981, *Ethnic Change*. Seattle: University of Washington Press.
KHLIEF, B. B. 1979, *Language, Ethnicity and Education in Wales*. The Hague: Mouton.
— 1982a, Ethnicity and language with reference to the Frisian case: Issues of schooling, work and identity. In K. ZONDAG (ed.), *Bilingual Education in Friesland*. Franeker: Wever, 175–203.
— 1982b, Ethnicity and language in understanding the new nationalism: The North Atlantic region, *International Journal of Comparative Sociology* 23, 114–21.
KLEIN, G. & REBAN, M. J. (eds) 1981, *The Politics of Ethnicity in Eastern Europe*. Boulder, CO: East European Monographs.
KOLAKOWSKI, L. 1979, Marxist philosophy and national reality: Natural communities and universal brotherhood. *Round Table* no.253, 43–55.
KREJCI, J. & VELIMSKY, V. 1981, *Ethnic and Political Nations in Europe*. London: Croom-Helm.
KUTSCHE, P. (ed.), 1979, *The Survival of Spanish-American Villages* (= *Colorado College Studies* 1979, no.15). Colorado Springs: Colorado College.
LAZZERINI, E. J. 1982, Ethnicity and the uses of history: The case of the Volga Tatars and Jadidism. *Central Asian Survey*. 1, no.2/Ç, 67–70.
LEACH, E. R. 1954, *Political Systems of the Highland Burma*. London: Bell.
LEHMAN, F. K. 1979, Who are the Karen, and if so, why? Karen ethnohistory and a formal theory of ethnicity. In C. F. KEYES (ed.),

Ethnic Adaptation and Identity: The Karen on the Thai Frontier With Burma. Philadelphia: Institute for the Study of Human Issues, 215–53.

LEVIN, H. 1980, The struggle for community can create community. In A. GALLAHER JR. & H. PADFIELD (eds), *The Dying Community*. Albuquerque: University of New Mexico Press, 257–78.

LIEBERSON, S. 1981, *A Piece of the Pie: Blacks and White Immigrants Since 1960*. Berkeley: University of California Press.

LIEBMAN, R. C. & WUTHNOW, R. (eds), 1983, *The New Christian Right*. New York: Aldine.

LIMÓN, J. E. 1982, El meeting: history, folk Spanish and ethnic nationalism in a Chicano student community. In J. AMASTAE & L. ELIAS–OLIVARES (eds), *The Spanish Language in the United States*. Cambridge: Cambridge University Press, 301–32.

LONSDALE, J. M. 1977, When did the Gusli (or any other group) become a 'tribe'? *Kenya Historical Review* 5, 123–33.

LOPEZ, T. R. & VOGEL, A. W. (eds) 1979, *No One-Model American*. Toledo: University of Toledo, College of Education.

LOWY, E. G., FISHMAN, J. A., GERTNER, M. H., GOTTESMAN, I. & MILAN, W. G. 1985, Ethnic activists view the ethnic revival and its language consequences. In J. A. FISHMAN (ed.), *The Rise and Fall of the Ethnic Revival*. Berlin: Mouton; also *Journal of Multilingual and Multicultural Development*. 1983, 4, 237–54.

LOWY, M. 1976, Marxists and the national question. *New Left Review* no.96, 81–100.

LUCAS, I. 1980, Political demands of Spanish-speaking communities in the United States. In D. J. R. BRUCKNER (ed.), *Politics and Language: Spanish and English in the United States*. Chicago: University of Chicago Center for Policy Study, 133–54.

MCCORD, A. & MCCORD, W. 1979, Ethnic autonomy: A social-historical synthesis. In R. L. HALL (ed.), *Ethnic Autonomy: Comparative Dynamics*. New York: Pergamon, 426–36.

MCLOUGHLIN, W. G. 1978, *Revivals, Awakenings and Reform: An Essay on Religion and Social Change in America, 1607–1977*. Chicago: University of Chicago Press.

MCNAIR, R. F. 1982, A universal language. *The Plain Truth*. January, 7–9.

MAGOCSI, P. R. 1978, *The Shaping of a National Identity: Subcarpathian Rus', 1848–1948*. Cambridge: Harvard University Press.

MANENT, P. *et al.* 1983, *European Liberty*. The Hague: Martinus Nijhoff.

MANGIONE, J. 1981, *Mount Allegro: A Memoir of Italian-American Life*. New York: Columbia University Press.

MANN, A. 1979, *The One and the Many: Reflections on American Identity*. Chicago: University of Chicago Press.

MARTIN, B. 1981, *A Sociology of Contemporary Cultural Change*. Oxford: Blackwell.

MASSEY, D. S. & MULLAN, B. P. 1984, Processes of Hispanic and Black spatial assimilation. *American Journal of Sociology* 89, 836–73.

MAYER, K. 1980, Ethnic tensions in Switzerland: The Jura conflict. In C. R. FOSTER (ed.), *Nations Without a State: Ethnic Minorities in Western Europe*. New York: Praeger, 189–208.

MAZRUI, A. A. 1982, Africa between nationalism and nationhood: A political study. *Journal of Black Studies* 13, 23–44.

MELVILLE, M. B. 1983, Ethnicity: an analysis of its dynamism and variability focusing on the Mexican/ Anglo-Mexican interface. *American Ethnologist* 30, 272–89.

METZGER, L. P. 1971, American sociology and Black assimilation. *American Journal of Sociology* 76, 627–47.

MOERMAN, M. 1965, Ethnic identification in a complex civilization: Who Are the Lue? *American Anthropologist* 67, 1215–30.

MOORE, R. L. 1982, Insiders and outsiders in American historical narrative and American history. *American Historical Review* 87, 390–412.

NAHIRNY, V. & FISHMAN, J. A. 1965, American immigrant groups: Ethnic identification and the problem of generations. *Sociological Review* 13, 311–26.

NAIRN, T. 1975, The modern Janus. *New Left Review* no.94, 3–30.

— 1977, *The Break-Up of Britain: Crisis and Neo-Nationalism*. London: NLB.

NEWMAN, W. M. 1973, A theory of social conflict. In W. M. NEWMAN, *American Pluralism: A Study of Minority Groups and Social Theory*. New York: Harper and Row.

NIELSEN, F. 1980, The Flemish movement in Belgium after World War II. *American Sociological Review* 45, 76–94.

NIETZSCHE, F. 1974, *Human All Too Human*. [1879] New York: Gordon Press.

NOVAK, M. 1977, *Further Reflections on Ethnicity*. Middleton, Pa.: Jednota Press.

OLZAK, S. 1982, Ethnic mobilization in Quebec. *Ethnic and Racial Studies* 5, 253–75.

— 1983, Contemporary ethnic mobilization. *Annual Review of Sociology* 9, 355–74.

PADEN, J. N. 1971, Urban pluralism, integration and adoption of communal identity in Kano, Nigeria. In R. COHEN & J. MIDDLETON (eds), *From Tribe to Nation in Africa*. Scranton: Chandler, 242–70.

PARENTI, M. 1967, Ethnic politics and the persistence of ethnic identification. *American Political Science Review* 61, 717–26.

PAROT, J. J. 1981, *Polish Catholics in Chicago, 1985–1920: A Religious History*. DeKalb: Northern Illinois University Press.

PATTERSON, O. 1974, Context and choice in ethnic allegiance: A theoretical framework and Caribbean case study. In N. GLAZER & D. P. MOYNIHAN (eds), *Ethnicity: Theory and Experience*. Cambridge: Harvard University Press 305–49.

— 1977, *Ethnic Chauvinism: The Reactionary Impulse*. New York: Stein and Day.

PAULSTON, C. BRATT & PAULSTON, R. G. 1980, Language and ethnic boundaries. *Language Sciences*. 2, 1(51), 69–101.

PETERSEN, W. 1980, Concepts of ethnicity, in *Harvard Encyclopedia of American Ethnic Groups*. Cambridge: Harvard University Press, 234–42.

PETRELLA, R. 1980, Nationalist and regionalist movements in Western Europe. In C. R. FOSTER (ed.), *Nations Without a State: Ethnic Minorities in Western Europe*. New York: Praeger.

PLUMB, J. H. 1970, *The Death of the Past*. Boston: Houghton Mifflin.

PRATTE, R. 1979, *Pluralism in Education: Conflict, Clarity and Commitment*. Springfield: Thomas.

PRISTINGER, F. 1980, Ethnic conflict and modernization in the South Tyrol. In C. R. FOSTER (ed.), *Nations Without a State: Ethnic Minorities in Western Europe*. New York: Praeger, 153–88.

RA'ANAN, U. (ed.), 1980, *Ethnic Resurgence in Modern Democratic States*. Elmsford: Pergamon.

RASPA, R. 1984, Exotic foods among Italian-Americans in Mormon Utah: food as nostalgic enactment of identity. In L. K. BROWN & K. MUSSEL (eds), *Ethnic and Regional Foodways in the United States*. Knoxville: University of Tennessee Press, 185–94.

REITZ, J. G. 1974, Language and ethnic community survival. *Canadian Review of Sociology and Anthropology* 11, 104–22 (Special issue).

RIESMAN, D. 1981, The dream of abundance reconsidered. *Public Opinion Quarterly* 45, 285–302.

RODRIGUEZ, R. 1981, *Hunger of Memory: An Autobiography. The Education of Richard Rodriguez*. Boston: Godine.

ROLLINS, J. (ed.) 1981, *Hidden Minorities: The Persistence of Ethnicity in American Life*. Washington, DC: University Press of America.

ROSEN, P. 1980, *The Neglected Dimension*. Notre Dame: University of Notre Dame Press.

ROTHSCHILD, J. 1981, *Ethnopolitics: A Conceptual Framework*. New York: Columbia University Press.

SAGARIN, E. & MONEYMATTER, J. 1979, Language and nationalist, separatist and secessionist movements. In R. L. HALL (ed.) *Ethnic Autonomy:*

Comparative Dynamics. Elmsford: Pergamon, 18–45.

SALAMONE, F. A. 1975, Becoming Hausa: ethnic identity change and its implications for the study of ethnic pluralism and stratification. *Africa* 45, 410–25.

SANDEEN, E. R. 1970, *The Roots of Fundamentalism*. Chicago: University of Chicago Press.

SCHNEIDER, D. M. 1972, What is kinship all about? In P. REINING, (ed.), *Kinship Studies in the Morgan Centennial Year*. Washington, DC: Anthropological Society of Washington, DC, 32–64.

SETON-WATSON, H. 1977, *Nations and States*. London: Methuen.

SHANABRUCH, C. 1981, *Chicago's Catholics: The Evolution of an American Identity*. Notre Dame: University of Notre Dame Press.

SHILS, E. 1957, Primordial, personal, sacred and civil ties. *British Journal of Sociology* 8, 130–45.

— 1969, Dreams of plentitude, nightmares of scarcity. In S. M. LIPSET & P. ALTBACH (eds), *Students in Revolt*. Boston: Houghton Mifflin, 1–35.

— 1981, *Tradition*. Chicago: University of Chicago Press.

SHUPE, A. & STACY, W. A. 1982, *Born-Again Politics and the Moral Majority*. New York: Edwin Mellen Press.

SIBLEY, D. 1981, *Outsiders in Urban Societies*. Oxford: Blackwell.

SINGER, L. 1962, Ethnogenesis and Negro-Americans today. *Social Research* 29, 419–32.

SMITH, A. D. 1981, *The Ethnic Revival*. New York: Cambridge University Press.

SOWELL, T. 1981, *Ethnic America : A History*. New York: Basic Books.

SPINRAD, W. 1983, The politics of American Jews: an example of ethnic group analysis. In J. B. MAIER & C. WAXMAN (eds), *Ethnicity, Identity and History: Essays in Memory of Werner J. Cahnman*. New Brunswick, NJ: Transaction Books, 249–72.

ST. CLAIR, R. & LEAP, W. 1982, *Language Renewal among American Indian Tribes: Issues, Problems, and Prospects*. Rosslyn, VA: National Clearinghouse for Bilingual Education.

STEIN, H. F. & HILL, R. F. 1977, *The Ethnic Imperative: Examining the new White Ethnic Movement*. University Park: Pennsylvania State University Press.

STEINBERG, S. 1981, *The Ethnic Myth*. New York: Atheneum.

STRASSOLDO, R. 1982, Boundaries in sociological theory: A reassessment. In R. STRASSOLDO & G. DELLI-ZOTTI (eds), *Cooperation and Conflict in Border Areas*. Milan: Franco Angeli, 245–71.

STRYKER, R. 1981, Religio-ethnic effects on attainments in the early career. *American Sociological Review* 46, 212–31.

SVENSSON, F. 1974, Language as ideology: The American Indian case.

Etudes de Linguistique Appliquée 15, 60–68.

SYMMONS-SYMONOLEWICZ 1981, National consciousness in medieval Europe: some theoretical problems. *Canadian Review of Studies in Nationalism* 8, 151–66.

TAYLOR, P. A. 1981, Education, ethnicity and cultural assimilation in the United States. *Ethnicity* 8, 31–49.

THOMPSON, W. E. 1981, The Oklahoma Amish: Survival of an ethnic subculture. *Ethnicity* 8, 476–87.

TOYNBEE, A. 1981, *The Greeks and Their Heritage.* New York: Oxford University Press.

TSAI, Y-M. & SIGELMAN, L. 1982, The community question: A perspective from national survey data — the case of the U.S.A. *British Journal of Sociology* 33, 579–88.

TUDJMAN, F. 1981, *Nationalism in Contemporary Europe.* Boulder, CO: East European Monographs.

TURNER, B. S. 1978, *Marx and the End of Orientalism.* London: Allen and Unwin.

VAN ALBOOM, R. 1982, Aspecten van de Waalse beweging te Brussel (1877–1914). *Taal en Sociale Integratie* 6, 3–106.

VAN DEN BERGHE, P. L. 1981, *The Ethnic Phenomenon.* New York: Elsevier-North Holland.

WALLERSTEIN, I. 1974, *The Modern World System.* New York: Academic Press.

WALTZER, M. 1980, Pluralism in political perspective. *Harvard Encyclopedia of American Ethnic Groups.* Cambridge: Harvard University Press, 781–87.

WEBER, E. J. 1976, *Peasants into Frenchmen: The Modernization of Rural France, 1870–1914.* Stanford: Stanford University Press.

WEINBERG, D. E. 1976, *Ethnicity: A Conceptual Approach.* Cleveland: Cleveland State University.

WEINREICH, U. 1953, *Languages in Contact.* New York: Linguistic Circle of New York.

WILLIAMS, C. H. (ed.), 1982, *National Separatism.* Vancouver: University of British Columbia Press.

WINKLER, H. & SCHNABEL, T. 1979, *Bibliographie zum Nationalismus.* Göttingen: Van den Hoeck and Ruprecht.

WOLFINGER, R. E. 1965, The development and persistence of ethnic voting. *American Political Science Review* 59, 896–908.

WOMACK, J. M. 1980, Marxism and nationalism. *Marxist Perspectives* 3, 170–74.

Taking leave: Concluding sentiments

This volume constitutes an involved but nevertheless selective tour through the countryside of 'minority perspectives on language and ethnicity'. Any tour through this area *must* be involved and *should* be selective. Involvement, whether more or less positive or more or less negative toward the minority perspective, is an inevitable byproduct of the interaction between the observer and the topic observed which characterizes the social sciences as a whole. Any disclaimer to the contrary is deluding with respect to the observer *vis-à-vis* him- or herself, as well as with respect to the observer *vis-à-vis* his or her audience. The posture of science, in the social sciences, surely requires that this involvement be admitted and that it be carefully watched in order to note (rather than to deny) the biases that this interaction introduces. Some of these biases can be counteracted and eliminated, at least in part, and others can only be replaced or confronted by counter-biases. The confrontation of biases provides the patient student with opportunities to weigh and compare and, thereby, to arrive at a more considered (although still not impartial) point of view.

Selectivity too is a reflection of point of view, just as is involvement, but it is also required by the voluminous nature of the data and by the need to find parsimony or focus. This need is not given in nature, nor is it an obvious by-product of science (whether social or natural) *per se*, notwithstanding its pursuit for over six centuries (ever since William of Occam's razor). Selectivity and parsimony in intellectual endeavors constitute a particularly Western esthetic principle of cognitive style, a principle which has demonstrated great power, but which has, at the same time, never produced any great curiosity as to the price that it exacts, i.e. what is lost thereby. Its penchant for demystification has fostered a disregard for mysteries, a disrespect and even derision for the supra-rational, speculative and romantic behaviors and values that are part and parcel of human experience, individual and social. As a result, social science has contented itself with demystifying ethnicity and the presumed language and ethnicity link, rather than trying to understand the experience of this linkage which continues to inform and guide the lives of millions throughout the entire world. In this sense, therefore, social science has confused the canon of objectivity, although it is not fully attainable, with a disregard for and a depreciation of behavior that is not objective, even though it is everywhere in evidence. This has been a self-impoverishing confusion for the social sciences, including sociolinguistics, a confusion of methodological aspirations which are themselves of the order of 'impossible dreams', on the one hand, with the need for delicate substantive curiosity for the dreams of all people at some times and some people at all times, on the other hand. I do not believe that the one should replace the other, but, rather that both should be pursued simultaneously.

The pleasure and anguish of language and ethnicity constitute a supra-rational concern and devotion particularly for minorities who have precious few other pleasures to celebrate, and it has been the goal of my work, as exemplified by this volume, not to demystify or debunk it, thereby degrading it, but to approach it respectfully, even with awe, as one approaches any sanctity of humankind (whether or not one accepts it as such in one's own experiential world). There is also a lesson for humanity and a lesson for social science in the ability to take sanctity *per se* and other people's sanctities, in particular, more dispassionately and more even-handedly. William James' *Varieties of Religious Experience*, still in print and still a subject of scholarly (not to mention popular) commentary after three quarters of a century, is much more of a contribution to social science and to humanity, precisely because it approaches religious experience with sympathy and curiosity and a never-ending concern for its contextual and inter-personal variation, than in any of the thousands of volumes published during the same time-period that have merely attempted to translate such experiences into mental disturbances and material insufficiencies. The world without mysteries is not a demonstrably better world than the world with them, and social science that cannot stand the mysteries that motivate and activate human behavior is not a better social science than social science that attempts to approach these mysteries without destroying them.

However, the selectivity due to the acceptance of mystery as a legitimate object of study is not the only selectivity that marks this volume. Since both language and ethnicity pertain to the daily rounds of life, to almost all of everyday life itself rather than only to its heightened ideological, religious, political and High Culture processes and experiences, it would be very desirable to examine them both in the context of socialization experience, of family life, of play and of work. If I have done so insufficiently, stressing, instead, topics that are more related to ethnic survival and to organized ethnic institutions, this is a reflection both of my own interests and of the brunt of conscious ethnic concerns and efforts. To the extent that I have not exhausted the topic that, of rights, should be within the purview of this volume, this is obviously an indication that the topic needs additional attention. However, it has not been my intention to be definitive but, rather, to make a further contribution to a field which has also had some productive attention paid to it by others and that would now seem to require an infusion of additional talented and tolerant attention. Will such attention be forthcoming? While I hesitate to add prophecy to mystery, I must say that the straws in the wind, at least in the U.S.A., are decidedly contradictory in nature. On the one hand, there is the undeniably growing conservative nature of American youth, as revealed both by recent, nationwide social science research and by the recent political preferences expressed by the younger generation itself. Such conservatism bodes ill for societal tolerance of and for social science concern for minority language and ethnicity phenomena. On the other hand, minority ethnicity in the U.S.A. is still experiencing the vibrancy and the intellectual ferment that the 'revival' of the mid-1960s to the mid-1970s together with the fact of ongoing immigration into the U.S.A., including ongoing immigration of intellectuals, have undeniably produced. In the long run, the former trend must overcome the latter, but the long run is exactly what we cannot foresee and where every effort to do so reveals more projection than insight.

From an American vantage point it is even more difficult to foresee the future of tolerant curiosity for minority language and ethnicity phenomena abroad. Positive indicators seem to predominate from Australia, Spain and the Netherlands, just to take a few examples of political and intellectual climates that currently seem propitious to minority language and ethnicity phenomena, but these are only a few points on a map and even they are sometimes in doubt. Minority ethnicity is generally beleaguered, problematic, under stress and strain, experiencing circumstances that cannot be controlled, problems that cannot be solved, grievances that cannot be adequately redressed. Only occasionally do glimmers of hope and tidings of attainment break through. These generally are experienced as exhilarating interludes and, more objectively viewed, they are, indeed, marked by the products and processes of intellectual creativity: schools and journals, plays and visual arts, musical compositions and literary compositions, all proliferating in startling profusion and in complementary fashion. The metaphors of 'spring' and 'rebirth' abound, but, even when it is clear that these are merely metaphors and that the circumstances to which they apply are fleeting and exceptional, it remains unclear how they are to be explained as societal processes or as individual experiences. They have an unforgettable impact on those who experience them or who taste of their fruits, these being of the order of those momentous experiences that fashion generations such that they are different than those that have come either before or after. Cause and effect are difficult to disentangle, even more so than in all social process analysis. What remains, once the storm has passed, is a realization that something special occurred and that it is gone and that no one knows where or for how long. The mystery of ethnicity and its link to language is deepened thereby, as is, for some, the conviction that both deserve unending fealty and provide invaluable rewards. Mystery begets mystery, and the charmed circle becomes all the more convinced of its cause, even when it becomes smaller and more engulfed by unsurmountable temptations and obstacles, by the rewards and punishments of re-ethnification and relinguification.

The language and ethnicity link remains an aspect of all human life. The minority counterpart thereof may be more conscious and more poignant and more alterable than the whole, but it is my hope that the part nevertheless helps illuminate the whole, even as social science helps illuminate social life, even though it can neither fully capture it nor fully clarify it. I have devoted many years to the pursuit of this elusive quest. I invite the reader to join me in the future and hope that I may have contributed something to his/her edification and pleasure in doing so.

Index

Flannery, T.O. 113, 279, 300, 310
Folkism 70, 519
Folklorization 394–6, 400
Fournol, Etienne 275
Fox, R.G. 45
Fox, R.G., Aull, C. & Cimino, L. 664
France, language planning 312–15, 380
Franke, C. 282
Franklin, Benjamin 71, 649, 667
French
–as additional language 370, 389
–and nationalism 284–5, 291, 296–7, 373, 573
–in U.S.A. 531, 534–47
Friedland, W.H. 115, 119, 121, 142, 149n., 168n., 173n.
Friedrich, C.J. 136, 145, 275, 286, 322n.
Frisian, policies for 179, 266, 370, 394–5, 660
Functions, language 183–4, 187–8, 191, 199, 219
–breakdown 211
–and continuity 178, 226, 231, 454
–endangered languages 392, 397, 399, 400–1
–international 369–70
–intra-national 370–5, 386
–and modernization 392
–and nationalism 274, 310–11
Furnivall, J.S. 168n.

Gadgil, D.R. 144
Gaj, L. 333n.
Gans, H.J. 682
Gauch, Hermann 18–19
Geertz, C. 25, 30, 55n.
Gellner, E. 122, 150n., 151n., 161n., 167n., 273
German, and early nationalism 277, 284–5, 290–1, 294, 297–8, 300
Glazer, N. & Moynihan, D.P. 49n.
Gobineau, J. 18
Gökalp, Ziya 106, 292, 303, 338n.
Gottsched, J.G. 329n., 332n.
Government, languages of 213, 220

Greek, modern 333n.
Greeley, A. 50n., 56n.
Greene, V.R. 679
Group, ethnic 106–7
Gruffydd, Robert 306
Gumperz, J.J. 520n.
Gurr, T.R. 583–4, 585, 587, 607, 624n.

Ha–'am, Ahad 513, 551
Hall, R.A. 376
Hamann, Johann Georg 324n.
Handlin, O. 679
Hanna, S.A. 283
Hanson, Marcus 557
Harrison, S.S. 326n., 333n.
Hartz, L. 145
Hasidism/Hasidim, language use 79, 183, 192, 206, 513–14, 673
haskole 68–75, 76–80, 521n.
Haugen, E. 48n., 288
Hausheer, R. 685
Hayakawa Amendment 203, 650
Hayde, Father 270
Hayes, C.J.H.
–on national languages 296, 302
–on nationalism 115n., 115–16, 117–18, 134, 151n., 162n., 326n.
–on use of vernaculars 275, 281–2, 291, 321n.
Haym, R. 577n.
Hebrew 69, 71, 182, 214–15, 333n., 377, 380
–and ethnicity 15, 50–1n.
–schools 458
–and Yiddish 82, 500, 513, 516, 518, 520, 551
Hechter, M. 664
Herder, J.G. 172n., 282
–on diversity 3, 11, 15, 277, 412–13, 651–2
–and ethnicity 18, 129
–on French and German languages 277, 285, 332n., 326n.
–and goals of bilingual education 444–6, 447, 633
–on national languages 105, 213, 276–80, 303, 558, 570–4, 578, 630
–on nationalism 111–12, 133–4, 162n., 660